# Photography Is Magic

**aperture**

Essay by Charlotte Cotton

Close-up magic—the kind of intimate, right-in-front-of-you sleight of hand that brings pure wonder and delight—is the inspiration for this book, which gathers the work and words of more than eighty artists operating in the related field of *photographic magic*. The idea that close-up magic has bearing on the critical mass of contemporary photographic art centers on their shared capacity to recalibrate established creative forms in ways that relate to our collective present: to conjure imaginative and open-ended experiences and trains of thought in the viewer.[1] Magic in both realms is a multisensory experience that calls—instantaneously, and without our consciously knowing it—upon our capacity to script our own sense of visual reality.

Let's begin by exploring the literal meaning of *close-up magic*, its characteristics and contexts, and its effects upon the audiences that gather for performances each night across the globe. With their skillful dexterity and the subtle physicality of their work, close-up magicians are different from the charismatic illusionists who perform dazzling visual spectacles to large theater audiences. Close-up magic is a much more intimate affair, often performed for a tightly knit sphere of fellow magicians and small, discerning audiences. As the name of this form of magic suggests, the viewers sit close to the table and the intensity of the magician's rapid prestidigitation. The typical tools of close-up magicians are decks of poker-size playing cards, coins, cups, and balls. The magicians' flourishes and misdirections are played out on and above green baize tabletops. The "card masters" of magic "flip," "slide," "load," and "pocket" their ordinary, mass-produced decks of cards; they focus their audiences' attention upon "force cards" and they "false shuffle." The conception and authorship of sequences used in close-up magic are acknowledged within the fraternity of magicians; each generation in turn reconceives these tricks—respecting their origins, but testing how time-honored maneuvers can be made to work their magic on contemporary viewers.

The art of magic is predicated on a dedication to practice: that is, repeating and repeating each complex sequence of movements until it is embedded seamlessly into the magician's muscle memory. But the ostensible repetition of movements or outcomes in the performance of close-up magic—the gestures the audience sees, or at least perceives—is often realized by a series of different sleights of hand with seemingly identical conclusions.[2] The magician's movements are skilled and fast, but not faster than the eye can see—just quicker than the visual systems of

[1] "What makes a trick work is not the inherent astoundingness of its effect but the magician's ability to suggest any number of possible explanations, none of them conclusive and more of them quite obvious." Adam Gopnik, "The Real Work: Modern Magic and the Meaning of Life," *New Yorker* (March 17, 2008): 56–69.

[2] "The space and time peculiar to the image is none other than the world of MAGIC, a world in which everything is repeated and in which everything participates in a significant context. Such a world is structurally different from that of the linear world of history in which everything has causes and will have consequences." Vilém Flusser, *Towards a Philosophy of Photography* (original German pub. 1983; this citation, London: Reaktion, 2000), 9.

the brain can *understand* given the distractions that the magician puts into play.
Magicians harness our human tendency to believe that we are at liberty to direct
our attention at will, and that we can visually and cognitively unravel a magic trick
and attain a state of clear perception. By our nature, we assume that if a repeated
action *looks* the same each time then it is derived from a repeated process.
Once we enter into the tantalizing psychological frame and physical space
of close-up magic—even while we are consciously suspicious that a trick is being
performed—our attention is deliberately guided by the magician into a realm
where the subterfuge can be camouflaged by carefully scripted dodging.
The audience in the nonsensical arena of close-up magic not only suspends its
disbelief, it plays an active part in the performance. As viewers, then, we feel
in control of our experience, set by the frame that the magician creates;
we automatically comprehend the experience as one that belongs to *us*.

A close-up magic trick can be heightened by magicians incorporating scripted
"mistakes" into their performances—with a master magician, no fumble,
no awkward exchange with audience members is likely to be unintentional.
These purposeful flourishes impart to the audience a perception of spontaneous
happenstance as the trick unfolds in real time. Most important, these "mistakes"
bring the act of magic into the present, and the sense that the progress of a magical
encounter is happening for the very first time. Magicians use language with great
specificity in order to direct and misdirect our attentions.[3] In effect, the magic
begins when its mechanics and linguistic tools are integrated into the evolving
present of the imaginary correlations of a trick's sequence.

It is important to remember that magic is not merely the sum of its technics
and orchestration. What the magician does is use his or her skill and tools to
create an arena *within the viewer's imagination* for the magic to happen.[4] The effect
of magic is in part after the trick, held in the stories we tell ourselves once the
experience is over. The audience turns magic into language and hence into meaning
and narrative, all the while knowing that it is impossible for language to fully
articulate the experience of magic and its playfulness—those things are defined only
temporarily in the presence of the magician. A magic trick, like all performative art
forms played well, creates the conditions for us to explore imaginative possibilities,
while sharing in a slice of the real.[5] It is we who fill the empty cup, envelope,
or playing-card packet with the kaleidoscope of our temporarily collectivized
consciousness in the presence of magic.[6]

[3] "Once a 'natural,' rather than 'supernatural,' basis for theatrical magic is established, its undoubted ability to radically disorder our epistemological assumptions about the world can be understood in terms of the magician's capacity to establish and maintain a frame through which simulated power over natural causality is experienced as real. In this sense, therefore, this form of magic is not only secular, but also simulacral. And it is the intentional presence and infinite malleability of this reifying frame, whether in the form of narrative or other contingent means, that brings simulacral magic alongside its sibling arts, and not least the visual arts with which it now shares more conceptual territory than perhaps at any other time." Jonathan Allen, *Magic Show* (London: Hayward Gallery Publishing, 2009), 21.

[4] "Magic only 'happens' in the spectator's mind, everything else is distraction." Jamy Ian Swiss, quoted in Gopnik, "The Real Work," 58.

The connection of close-up magic to contemporary photography is in the idea that magic is something that happens in the viewers' imaginations. Like magic tricks, the works of art shown in this volume provide visual frames within which we are invited to focus our attention. Photographic magic opens us to multiple possible meanings of our visual world, and calls upon our collective ways of looking at it; it also offers us ideas of what that visual world might imply about our contemporary condition.

Photography is a form of magic—or to put it another way, the photographic provides cerebral experiences for the viewer that are equivalent to magic. Just as sleight of hand facilitates, but does not fully materialize, the magical experience that resides in the dynamic of our own imaginations, so too photography—when liberated from a pedestrian definition as the sum of its mechanics and materials, its chemistry and software—can spark the occurrence of magic in our minds. The artists represented in this book reconsider photographic traditions and implement new skills that have been incorporated into the contemporary photographic repertoire. These photographic tools for "sleight of hand," which derive from the span of photography's rich history, from analog through to its newest imaging technologies, are all set within a framework of the present moment of visual culture.

*Photography Is Magic* privileges the potentials of ideas over the virtuosity of individual authors or the perfection of techniques and mechanisms: as with actual close-up prestidigitation, ideas are what ultimately allow the magic to happen. The works shown here take into account the many ways in which viewers relate to photographic media, materials, and image cultures in our current media environment. They are potent in decidedly new ways, and specifically because of the terms of engagement they propose: calling upon our ability to construct meaning from our collective "muscle memory" of making and consuming photographic imagery.

The artists featured here—like the magicians who masterfully tap into the psychological and neural systems of the spectator—are astutely aware of their viewers' perceptions and trains of thought in ways that are grounded in our shared visual culture. They not only acknowledge, but *stage* viewership at this contemporary moment, in which there is unprecedented compatibility and transparency between viewers and artists, a time unlike any before in history in terms of our ability to comprehend, access, and use photographic tools for capturing, rendering, and disseminating visual ideas.

[5]
"Magicians...engage [our minds] in a permanent maze of possibilities. The trick is to renew the possibilities, to keep them from becoming schematized." Ibid., 67.

[6]
"The pleasure we desire from the representation of the present is due not only to the beauty it can be clothed in, but also to its essential quality of being present." Charles Baudelaire, *The Painter of Modern Life* (original French pub. 1863; this citation, London: Penguin, 2010), 2.

In close-up magic, the stakes are high in that the audience is often made up of fellow magicians and discerning enthusiasts. Similarly, most of the artists here operate in a circle of fellow practitioners with whose work they are in direct and active discourse; they are navigating within the same image environment as their near sphere of viewers.

Photography as magic is a protean idea, situated as it is in the experience of the protean present. It is not a proposal for the future, nor is it a speculation about the psychological or moral destination of new imaging technologies or the social utility of photographic images. By the same token, the artists in *Photography Is Magic* are not approached as the contemporary end to a linear, canonical history of art photography, supplying a fresh vocabulary of stylistic surfaces to existing ideas. Where we do see citations from photography's past, they are likely premeditated camouflages—misdirections, reanimations—essentially, knowingly made flourishes that create these magical photographic experiences.

By considering contemporary photographic practices through the lens of magic, this book has a particular take on the current state of photography's presence—its status as cultural material—within art. This is definitely not the full story of how photography's analog traditions and materials have been interplayed in recent years with phenomena such as the newly acknowledged medium of pixel-based software, the predominance of digital capture, or the possibilities of 3D rendering. In this context, the ways in which photographic materiality can be experienced—what it can represent and prompt—are at play in importantly encompassing and expansive ways.[7] There are nuanced reconsiderations of that materiality—which of course constitutes an important part of the heritage of photography as art—but clearly there are also equally valid and complex inquiries into how to "materialize" contemporary photographic image culture, the scope of which is set well beyond the confines of artistic practice per se. Among the topics under investigation are: the extent to which technologies themselves are "authoring" the images we see, how the movement and behavior of so many of the images currently being generated can be considered forms themselves within art, and how the pervasive automation of photographic rendering has made software the dominant photographic medium.[8]

[7] "Each practice exploring these questions hinges on an implicit definition of what the photograph's material 'is.' These investigations...considering the image's material in terms of a container for manufactured desire (that needs not to be photographic at all but simply 'act like a photograph') is a really inventive solution." Lucas Blalock, in "A Conversation with Kate Steciw," *Lay Flat* magazine blog, March 5, 2012; www.lavalette.com/a-conversation-with-kate-steciw/.

[8] "None of the new media authoring and editing techniques we associate with computers are simply a result of media 'being digital.'" Lev Manovich, *Software Takes Command* (London: Bloomsbury Academic, 2013), 148.

[9] "If we think about photography as a limited mimesis, as a poor copy, instead of a good (or indexical) one, then the photographer is not a cataloguer of fact, nor a purveyor of reportage, but instead is participating in this centuries-old activity of drawing the world closer, attending to its conditions, to the terms of our looking, and, in turn, trying to keep the picture collapsing into image." Lucas Blalock, "Drawing Machine," *Foam*, no. 38 (May 2014): 208.

In this period, when a critical mass of artists is widening rather than attempting to isolate the idea of photography, the discourse is opening up, linking contemporary artistic practice to much older, and deeply human, histories of mark making, envisioning, and modeling new paradigms in ways that take into account cultural changes of the moment.[9] Only time will tell to what extent the works created by the artists represented here will be assimilated into a discrete history of the medium of photography (somehow separate from the rest of art history) that is conventionally thought to begin in the 1830s and is housed in encyclopedic archives. Or, indeed, how photography viewed as a subject in academia or a discipline in art schools will be maintained or reshaped in light of contemporary practices. The photographic works shown here are not in a state of limbo; they are not awaiting the appraisal of the institutional structures of art and a future designation of cultural importance. Part of their significance is in the purposeful precariousness of their making and meaning,[10] and in the rapidly evolving context of viewership in which the artists create and operate. This accumulation of new ideas and experiences of the photographic is generated through artistic practices and motivations, creating imaginative possibilities from the contemporary image environment at large.

Within this exciting recalibration of photographic ideas and materials is the use of explicitly iterative processes: ideas repeat and morph over the course of the artist's practice. Photographic magic is an arena in which the meaning of an individual work of art is invariably both contingent upon and equal to what is made before and after it by its creator. This infinitely additive way of working has created a new conceptual framework for artists working with photographic ideas. The contributions that Photoshop software has made to this new frame are undeniable, especially in the hands and imaginations of younger practitioners who may have little or no psychic baggage of allegiance to photography's analog past.[11] Photoshop brings the practices and lexicon of automation, repetition, and versioning to the fore.

It is no coincidence that this is happening in the context of a networked, commodity-centric culture—where a wholesale movement away from privileging the "source" or "original" is coded into every creative photographic gesture. This opens up new directions for contemporary art photographers, who are helping to define our image world and questioning it from within, and who presume that their works are experienced from the vantage point of this image-making epoch. The conventional strictures of the marketplace have included a preference for

<hr>

[10]

"Precariousness is the centre of the formal universe in which nothing is durable, everything is movement: the trajectory between two places is favoured in relation to the place itself." Nicolas Bourriaud, *Postproduction, Culture as Screenplay: How Art Reprograms the World* (Berlin: Lukas & Sternberg, 2005), 49.

[11]

"Modern creatives who want to work in good faith will have to fully disengage from the older generation's mythos of phantoms, and masterfully grasp the genuine nature of their own creative tools and platforms. Otherwise, they will lack comprehension and command of what they are doing and creating and they will remain reduced to the freak-show position of most twentieth-century tech art." Bruce Sterling, "An Essay on the New Aesthetic," *Wired.com*, April 2, 2012; www.wired.com/2012/04/an-essay-on-the-new-aesthetic/.

unique works of art, "signature styles," and consistent methodologies that allow viewers to distinguish one creator from another. Such conservative expectations have done much to repress iterative photographic practices and discourses concerning the inherent mutability of photography and its capacity for infinite reproduction.[12] It is around these unstable conditions of photographic properties and behaviors—rather than its institutional characterization—that much of the most pertinent contemporary art photography now pivots.[13]

## Constants Become Variables[14]

The great majority of the photographic works represented in this book were made since 2010. Collectively, they provide a timely narrative of art photography's relationship with the technologies of contemporary image culture; they also implicitly show us the critical positions that artists are adopting within media systems. Ours is a cultural chapter in which the actual and symbolic impact of digital hardware and software—the tools that create the preponderance of today's images—begins to shape the story of the small constituency of contemporary art photography.

The previous episodes of this technological narrative of photography—a story that began in the 1990s—were strikingly different from the events that are unfolding today. Now, with the benefit of hindsight, we can see that the end of the twentieth century was dominated by concerns about the supposed impending obsolescence of photography's analog apparatuses and materials. Serious questions were raised about whether the hard-won identity of the medium of photography—as able to transcend its mechanics in the hands of artists—could be sustained in the monolithically (and all too democratically) automated character of "the digital." The governing desire of most established art practitioners was to locate the best ways for the new (at least new to art) algorithmic and pigment-based rendering techniques to *simulate* the beloved heritage of analog photography's history of craftsmanship; many sought some sort of equivalence in aims, skill requirements, and aesthetic ranges from the new tools for photographic capture and postproduction. In the late-twentieth-century image environment, much of the focus was on ways to use digital tools for what was an essentially static idea of how photographic art could be made and read. And this fixed concept extended the shelf life of an equally entrenched idea: that a primary role of the photographic

[12]
"Production thus becomes the lexicon of practice, which is to say, the intermediary material from which new utterances can be articulated, instead of representing the end result of anything. What matters is what we make of the elements at our disposal. We are tenants of culture." Bourriaud, *Postproduction*, 24.

[13]
"The point for me is to propose and develop forms of post-representationalist photography and imaging wherein both the materiality of a work and its 'relations of photography' are intrinsic to what the work is." Trevor Paglen, in Julian Stallabrass, "Negative Dialectics in the Google Era: An Interview with Trevor Paglen," *October*, no. 138 (Fall 2011): 4.

[14]
"Once software enters the picture...constants become variables." Manovich, *Software Takes Command*, 157.

artist was to subvert the common usage of commercially available photographic technologies in a critical, rarefied, and quasi-timeless way to create enduring, "final" object forms. This paradigm, it was thought, would preserve photography's place within art.

The decisions that photographic artists faced in the early 2000s, by contrast, were about how to respond to the increasingly affordable, high-end digital photographic tools, and whether to accept these technologies as the new default for creative image-making. Digital capture, Photoshop, and pigment printing (to name just three digital tools that directly and indelibly impacted artistic practices in the 2000s) were received in a variety of ways by deliberating photographic artists. Digital hardware and materials were rejected outright by some practitioners in favor of the perceived "authenticity" and photographic continuity (albeit now with rather nostalgic, even mournful, undertones) of analog and chemical techniques. Despite a great decrease in the manufacture of photographic film and chemical papers over the past twenty years, the disappearance of analog materials has not become a reality thus far. Other photographic artists embraced the narrative potential of imaging software to construct pictorial alternative realities, often provoking uncanny reactions in viewers, residual belief in photography as a veracious medium was now dismantled. Perhaps most important, digital tools and their outputs became naturalized into analog working practices and thought processes: some artists committed themselves to learning these new ways of working like a second language, while others collaborated with technicians in revamped photo labs to ease the incorporation of digital materials and techniques into their otherwise essentially unchanged processes.

These generalized reactions had particular resonance for students in art-school photography programs in the 2000s (many of the artists represented in this book are among that constituency), when there was still a pervasive pedagogical view that artists operated outside the commercially oriented technological developments and other mainstream possibilities for image-making. In the first decade of the new millennium, many art schools considered their training remit to be part of a trajectory that started in the 1970s, in which artists used photographic tools (such as large-format film cameras) that were as yet technically unsurpassed, and were decidedly separate from the burgeoning industry for digital capture and postproduction tools that were being adopted by the image-making industries. In the realm of art photography, pixel-based software and scanning hardware were likely to be hybridized with photographic film and chemical papers, extending the life but not fundamentally changing the parameters of photographic possibilities in art-school and market models. Furthermore, art students, alongside artists employed as lab technicians, were discovering that Photoshop software could be used in more innovative and meaningful ways than merely simulating analog retouching and wet-darkroom techniques.

Photoshop has a dual heritage. It was born out of software development and shaped into a commercial product against the backdrop of professional image-making culture of the 1980s. The "manual" interface of Photoshop's filters and layers and its step-by-step processes were set up to provide a continuous (although abstracted) connection to the conventions of photographic methods. But Photoshop's lineage of code also features another aspect: algorithmic, strictly rule-bound procedures. Significantly, these automated procedures permit any pixel-based element of an image to be independently altered, with no material consequences to any other image element. While this characteristic can be seen as a related but "hyper" version of photomontage, or of compound-negative printing techniques, Photoshop software's inherent capacity to further liberate the photographic from simulating the perspective of monocular human vision has brought about a profound shift in the use and experience of the photographic in recent years.

Software has, in fact, altered every familiar relationship, every convention that art photographers have developed—notwithstanding the "enduring" qualities and default characteristics that historic photographic materials supposedly afford. Every move made in the process of photographic capture, crafting, and formal resolution is now about *active choices*. By the mid-2000s, Photoshop began to have a genuinely creative impact upon artists' strategies. At the same time, it was the prevalent application being used throughout photographic industries, marking practically all commercial images with its perfecting aesthetic. The distinctions between the tools and material results of professional and artistic working practices were beginning to be undeniably porous.

In the same decade came the technological advent that would so completely alter the baseline of contemporary art: the surge of social media and mobile-technology cameras—and with that, the ubiquity of socially networked photographic images in mass circulation. The resulting changed environment calls so much about the status of artistic photographic practice into question, especially in relation to the networked production and access in the online image world.[15] At this point, the notion that art photography could be separated from the empirical mass of contemporary image production simply by virtue of its craftsmanship, use of particular apparatuses, or the viewing context of gallery walls alone began to seem fundamentally beside the point.

[15]
"Staging different rates of circulation is one type of routine appropriate to art in digital economics—it's a tactic for escaping the 'blind spot' that results from moving along at the same rate as the market." David Joselit, *After Art* (Princeton, NJ: Princeton University Press, 2010), 89.

[16]
"Unlike the previous mode of authorship, where the artist or institution defined context, the divide between artist and viewer becomes negligible when users of social media are able to more powerfully define the context (and thus the meaning) of an artwork." Brad Troemel, "Art after Social Media," in Omar Kholeif, ed., *You Are Here: Art After the Internet* (Manchester, UK: Cornerhouse, 2014), 39.

These twenty-first-century factors mark the profound changes in the broad terrain of image culture and, concomitantly, in the values ascribed to and the readings of artistic photographic practices. The conventional distinctions between *artists* and *amateurs, producers* and *consumers* of photographic images and objects have become unclear in interesting ways; indeed, these terms themselves are now increasingly mutable and capable of being converged. Many of the artists coming through art-school programs in the past decade have chosen to face head-on the deeper meanings and implications of this paradigm shift as it affects creative practices and the circulation of their ideas.[16] We begin to see the tangible implications of operating in this utterly new media environment, where the origins, behavior, and reading of the photographic have all been culturally upended.[17]

Purposefully destabilized photographic practices are coming into play, and photographic objects no longer necessarily constitute the formal conclusion—the end result—of artistic inquiries.[18] This artist-led approach has been largely at odds with the prevailing characterization of art photography in art institutions and marketplaces. Not surprisingly, these established centers prefer a more stable idea of photography's cultural possibilities; certainly they have a vested interest in the supposition that photographic art objects themselves can be somehow understood in a different way to the lived experience of making and viewing photographic imagery.

*Photography Is Magic* highlights artistic approaches that may be seen as belonging to the same system of image versioning and flux as any other authored photographic idea circulating in the current image environment. The force of the global developments that affect our image/media landscape are such that the ubiquitous apparatuses and automated systems have now become constants. Increasingly, contemporary art photographers are working with the possibilities of creating variance within this visual system.[19] They deploy destabilized practices and explicitly iterative dynamics to create photographic objects and gestures that are intended to be experienced in this moment of a decidedly flattened—even horizontal—image hierarchy. The systematized "rules" of contemporary image-making have become the terrain that artists are using as a site of play, proving how far they can go in creating contemporary experiences of photographic magic that—in the vein of real magic—are orchestrated very precisely for the present moment and contingent on activating viewers' experiences and assumptions of the contemporary visual world.

17
"Culture and language are fundamentally changed by the ability for anyone to gain free access to the same image-creation tools used by mass-media workers, utilize the same or better structures to disseminate those images, and gain free access to the majority of canonical writings and concepts offered by institutions of higher learning." Artie Vierkant, "The Image Object Post-Internet," 2010; http://jstchillin.org/artie/vierkant.html.

18
"The artwork functions as the temporary terminal of a network of interconnected elements, like a narrative that extends and reinterprets preceding narratives....The artwork is no longer an end point but a simple moment in an infinite chain of contributions." Bourriaud, *Postproduction*, 19–20.

19
"Previously the tool was the variable and the human being was the constant, subsequently the human being became the variable and the machine the constant." Flusser, *Towards a Philosophy of Photography*, 24.

The artists represented in *Photography Is Magic* are firmly embedded in our image-making and image-disseminating culture. That position is important to acknowledge for what it is: a vantage point from which close attention can be paid to the incipient nature of our visual processes. To different degrees, all the artists represented here make it clear that they subjectify the photographic systems in which they operate.[20] The modes of subjectivity vary, from the visual signs that perfecting imaging software is being "incorrectly" deployed to tactics of layering and juxtaposing visual materials; from intentionally confusing the boundaries between images and ostensible subjects, processes, and media to the emphatic use of repetition and versioning in the development of an artistic idea. What all these practices have in common is an immeasurable quantity of active choices being made—in a subjective and nonlinear fashion—by their creators. These subjective choices share the same nonhierarchical characteristics that derive from the patterns and processes that systematize contemporary visual culture. We can now recognize individual artists' signatures through their repeated navigation and articulation of the dynamic behavior of photographic culture at large.[21]

CAMOUFLAGE

One of the areas that most obviously shows the difference between these artists and their forebears is their interaction with photography's analog past. Analog photographic notions—both materials and mindset—staccato through the image sequence of this book. But this presence of analog does not imply that photography's history provides an enduring gold standard to which contemporary practitioners are held. The use of analog is much more agnostic and strategic than any attempt to nostalgically recall the past as a legible contemporary mode. To draw a connection to stage magic: a century ago, a magician's top hat and coattails constituted the adopted signs of genteel respectability in the fashion of a gentleman's evening attire. When a magician wears this costume now, it is a reenactment of the uniform (or camouflage) for creating an illusion, a culturally loaded ideogram of the past. Just so, the artists represented here are using historic analog tools in the image environment of the present, making intentional choices to confound the default idea of what constitutes contemporary photographic technology by reactivating the medium's heritage in the present.

Today's climate—with its acquisitive drive, stimulated partly by the built-in obsolescence of so many manufactured products—privileges the idea of technology at the center of a forward-gazing tale of invention and innovation. The use of analog photography in contemporary photographic practices is like the specter at

<hr>

20

"In our day-to-day lives, omission, repetition, and juxtaposition become the primarily creative gestures or points of agency over an otherwise highly prescribed matrix of use." Steciw to Blalock, "A Conversation."

21

"We identify emotionally, subjectively—and yet at one and the same time we evaluate politically objectively in relation to society." Peter Brook, *The Empty Space* (New York: Penguin Modern Classics, 2008), 35.

the commodity feast, prompting us to think about technology not in terms of what is commercially new, but in terms of what is still useful and meaningful.[22] The contemporary presence of analog tools and mindsets contradicts the idea of technological invention and also the expected relationships between apparatus and image. We see, for example, artists using classic "in-camera" techniques— the alchemy that can happen at the moment of image capture within the machine, not immediately seen by the photographer—with digital tools, outwitting default settings to create the improbable.[23] In a double-back, there are also contemporary artists using classic SLR cameras and precise lenses to create intensely information-laden and layered images of details from the real world that mimic the filter settings of Photoshop, revealing just how much our visual antennae have been shifted by the aesthetics of software. In both of these examples, digital thinking and image aesthetics are being retro-fitted to the idiosyncratic tools of analog and its spirit of experimentation. Such approaches breathe new life into the instruments of photography's history and of its present, and remind us that the creative desire to push the possibilities of image techniques is nothing new.

Black-and-white photography is present, too, in *Photography Is Magic*, rendered by algorithmically switching almost entirely chromatic digital capture to monochrome printing methods, or by seemingly ingenuous uses of traditional analog roll-film and gelatin-silver papers. The character of black-and-white photography has always been one of abstracting and distilling frames from real time; now it is being consciously repurposed in the context of the twenty-first century.[24] The experience of contemporary black-and-white photography is beautifully slippery, coded as it is with both the past and the present of photographic ideas.[25] In today's context, in which the systems of software take on the role of medium, black-and-white becomes an ideogram of photographic practice: an almost symbolic "material." The presence of black-and-white photography—like the top hat and tails worn by an illusionist—directs the viewer toward thinking about the *persona* and motivations of the maker as a recognizable entity, shaped by and adhering to the historic conventions of a creative discipline. The use of such classic analog techniques implies that this creator is a "photographer": an embodiment of craftsmanship and devotion to a defined set of materials and techniques.

22

"By thinking about the history of technology-in-use a radically different picture of technology and indeed of invention and innovation, becomes possible." David Edgerton, *Shock of the Old: Technology and Global History since 1900* (London: Profile, 2008), xi.

23

"[Tools] can perform complex work only because we have, as adults, learned to play with their possibilities rather than treat each tool as fit-for-purpose." Richard Sennett, *The Craftsman* (New York: Penguin, 2009), 273.

24

"Old media are not being displaced. Rather, their functions and status are shifted by the introduction of new technologies." Henry Jenkins, *Convergence Culture: Where New and Old Media Collide* (New York: New York University Press, 2008), 14.

25

"Analogue photography can be something else...it doesn't have to be intrinsically bound to the visible world...it is full of possibility." Jessica Eaton, quoted in Diane Smyth, "The Perfect Playground," *British Journal of Photography* (March 2012): 45.

The donning of an old-time magician's costume, or the co-option of the photographer's historic means, is only one form of readily available camouflage. Artists in *Photography Is Magic* adopt other classical guises—borrowed from other media: painting and sculpture—reconfigured into characterizations, liberated from the bounds of time, within the flattened hierarchy of contemporary creative roles and identities. The notion of contemporary artists being sculptors, painters, and photographers in a traditional sense is an impossibility—because the very idea of separate disciplines of art is now defunct. *Photographer, painter, sculptor*: all three of these terms are highly abstracted and unfixed; they are forms of camouflage that provide artists with temporary positions and relationships within the history of art, but pointedly staged in the context of the present.

The momentum of the artists under discussion here offers a shift from *photography, painting,* and *sculpture* as stable nouns to dynamic adjectives, concerned with the possibilities of our mercurial contemporary image environment. Thus, in what we might now call this postdisciplinary age of art, we can begin to consider how the history of art is animated in the present in consciously deployed gestures of the *photographic, painterly,* and *sculptural.* The lexicons of these creative fields become agents of creative originality—ways of selecting, combining, and subverting visual language.

There are many examples in this book of Photoshop's painterly filters—its "manual" settings—being used with such creative originality.[26] These painterly approaches use software as their material, placing computational devices at the aesthetic center of the works and allowing them to function as contemporary marks of artistic creativity.[27] Viewers engage with this when Photoshop's filters and layers are visible and pronounced: manifest in formal alterations, combinations, and contradictions[28] that are rendered out of the algorithmic settings of "paint" and "ink brushes" and photographic "fades." Such options bring the material possibilities of software into focus, essentially calling out Photoshop as a medium in its own right, with inherent possibilities for creative subjectivity. The repetitive use of generic forms of Photoshop's simulation of "airbrush strokes" or "dodging" and "burning" both constitute and transgress the traditional idea of painterly and photographic authorship. Its practitioners consciously participate in this realm of out-of-whack manifestations of automated imaging systems.[29]

---

[26]
"In the same way that all cultural images and objects become general…so too does the authorial stance of the artist become general." Vierkant, "The Image Object Post-Internet," 6.

[27]
"One must use not simply the delivery mechanisms of popular culture, but also its generic forms." Seth Price, "Dispersion," 2002, 5; www.distributedhistory.com/Dispersion2008.pdf.

[28]
"Object and image systems are entirely reliant on context and composition and are fatally disrupted by even minor intervention." Steciw to Blalock, "A Conversation."

[29]
"The commodity is the form in which things come to be in the world. Beyond any concept of alienation in relation to labor, we can see that our very social relations constitute the commodity's material. This composition gives the commodity a subjectivity that is not particular to any one of us, but is rather one in which we all participate in forming." Joshua Simon, *Neomaterialism* (Berlin: Sternberg, 2013), 104–5.

The notion of the "sculptural" in *Photography Is Magic* bears clarifying; it should be distinguished from the trend in much art photography toward emphasizing the simple physicality of photographic materials. It is of course true that the tangible form of the photographic print has become much more charged in this moment of screen-based image circulation. We have seen a resurgence of "sculptural" installations of photography: undoubtedly responses—very literal ones—to the renewed appreciation of photography as a material form. There are numerous references to photography's historic past in the broad spectrum of contemporary art photography; these references range from a recharged use of early nineteenth-century "proto-photographic," lens-free processes to the revisiting of photography-sculpture combinations that were popular in the 1970s and 1980s. But the deployment of photography's chemical roots and the structural possibilities of three-dimensionality alone do not fulfill the fluid, imaginative potentials of contemporary declarations of the sculptural and photographic. In the context of *Photography Is Magic*, the characterization of the sculptor is as a *renderer of objects*[30]—exerting control over images as materials and cultural artifacts. We see this in *Photography Is Magic* in the preponderance of objects and forms made out of images, at times seeming to encase empty volumes that are structured by photographic materials. Similarly, the sense of the photographic as a dimensional concept is brought to the fore by the increasing use of 3D-printing technologies, and by photographic forms constructed not with a camera, but instead with image-rendering software. Photography's analog heritage and image-making's digital present are being conflated and used in ways that remove the once-essential idea of the medium as a process of "capturing" a subject.

Thus our encounters with the photographic in artistic culture are undergoing a profound shift. The binding together of image and object (or image as object) is a fundamental cultural phenomenon that the artists represented here are consciously designating and navigating.[31] This is a field in which distinctions between original and copy do not dominate and where images act as objects and vice versa, comprehended through their ongoing state of circulation and versioning.[32]

CHANNELING HISTORIES

Many of the artists represented in *Photography Is Magic* are starting to be subject to serious critical appraisal, much of it concerned with aligning their energies

---

[30] "In this process they change the form of the objects. They imprint a new, intentional form onto them. They 'inform' them: the object acquires an unnatural, improbable form: it becomes cultural." Flusser, *Towards a Philosophy of Photography*, 23.

[31] "In a social system in which so much culturally relevant information is transmitted via images, it is in the form of images that we most often encounter the objects of our desire...due to the object's origins in mechanical reproduction, it too behaves as an image unto itself—an image both of its representational intention but also its ideological function. Images and objects function as delivery systems for commerce-driven ideologies." Steciw to Blalock, "A Conversation."

[32] "Even if an image or object is able to be traced back to a source, the substance (substance in the sense of both its materiality and its importance) of the source object can no longer be regarded as inherently greater than any of its copies." Vierkant, "The Image Object Post-Internet," 3.

and discourses with previous movements of art history. Spurred in part by new terms in art and media criticism, including "post-Internet" art[33] and the "New Aesthetic,"[34] the story of modern and contemporary art is framed as one in close conversation with the image environment of its time. Unquestionably, there have been other points in history since the conception of photography where rapid "image explosions" have occurred (consider, for example, advances in printing and broadcasting technologies), and with them the experience of the visual world has been altered in the course of single lifetimes. Artists have absorbed these cultural shifts into the momentum of their practices, thus determining the dialogues and interactions between imaging technology and modern and contemporary art.[35] This is a manifestation of a profoundly human tendency, which is embedded in the workings of our neural system: each time we call forth a memory, we neurologically and psychologically remake and reposition it, and create new paths of accessibility to that memory or idea out of the new relations that we have conjured.

Artists tend to interpret culture at large and the art of the past in a nonhierarchical and expansive way, creating constellations of interconnected references. The theoretical metaphor for this generative and constantly evolving idea of knowledge is the *rhizome*—the model being the node-based plant that sends out underground roots and shoots in all directions.[36] In the field of creative media especially, the rhizome has been a pervasive concept and is a useful metaphor for thinking about dynamic ways to map seemingly disparate forms of ideas, their meanings held in the constantly changing connections we make between them.[37] The history of art circulates in this network of contemporary creative practices, released from a fixed or traditional meaning, chronology, or status. When previous art movements are "channeled" into contemporary practices, they are being tapped to operate within the subjective maps of contemporary artists' ideas.[38]

One of the most radical concepts of modern art that has been recently revived in light of our image world is the *readymade*. Proposed by the artist Marcel Duchamp in the early twentieth century, this incendiary idea defined artistic authorship as the act of conferring or electing artistic status to ready-made

---

[33]
"Artist, curator and writer Marisa Olson's use of the phrases 'after the internet' and 'post-internet' [began] in 2006... Olson's use of the term 'post-internet,' which implies an ability to stand outside the internet to some extent, contrasts with more recent practices that have been associated with the same term, in which the artist, even art itself, is assumed to be fully immersed in network culture and is no longer quite able to assume the position of the observer....Even the term 'post-internet' itself has been redefined and changed; it has come to stand less for a clear demarcation of 'before' and 'after' than to represent a continuously evolving critical dialogue." Michael Connor, "Post-Internet: What It Is and What It Was," in Kholeif, ed., *You Are Here*, 57.

[34]
"The New Aesthetic is inherently modish because it is ferociously attached to modish passing objects and services that have short shelf-lives. There is no steampunk New Aesthetic and no remote-future New Aesthetic. The New Aesthetic has no hyphen-post, hyphen-neo or hyphen-retro." Sterling, "New Aesthetic."

[35]
"This is one of those moments when the art world slides over toward a visual technology and tries to get all metaphysical. This is the attempted imposition on the public of a new way of perceiving reality. These things occur. They often take a while to blossom. Sometimes they're as big and loud as Cubism, sometimes they perish like desert roses mostly unseen. But they always happen for good and sufficient reasons. Our own day has those good and sufficient reasons." Ibid.

objects, recontextualized to the physical and intellectual spaces of art.[39] The use of the readymade mode drew a dramatic distinction between the conventional characterization of the artist as an embodiment of exceptional talent, creating unique works of excellent and timely craftsmanship, and the notion of art making as a conceptual practice that might involve only slight or even imperceptible physical gestures (or none at all). The readymade is a resonant concept for today, in the sense that many artists are co-opting existing object-commodities (including photographic images) into their work—intact and unmanipulated. The historic idea of the readymade would, indeed, seem to be a perfect fit with the approaches of many contemporary artists—understood as the appropriation of commodity-objects into the structure of art—if it were not for the manifestly dispersed and dynamic nature of artistic practice in our contemporary image landscape.[40] In an important sense, *every* discrete act of rendering an object or image (whether industrial or artistic) is now a manifestation of the endless circulation of the already made, commodified, and systematized.

Another defining art moment that is often cited in relation to today's seismic shifts is the early-twentieth-century avant-garde movement of Cubism. A main tenet of the perceived relationship between Cubism and contemporary artistic practices is that both have been fueled by the phenomenon of mass-distribution media of their day. The Cubist works that have perhaps the most enduring resonance are the collages, in which newspaper headlines and printed advertisements were pasted, layered, and visually suspended into single picture frames, creating a radical and immediate experience of their present day as chaotic and multilayered. The utter confidence with which early-twentieth-century artists conflated the "high" and "low" of visual culture by collaging readymade materials remains a force to be reckoned with. Again, of course, there are marked differences between artists working in today's media landscape and the Cubists, drawing upon their popular-image environment for new materials to make art. The Cubists adopted the momentum of the image culture at large from the vantage point of the avant-garde;

36

"The rhizome is an acentered, nonhierarchical, nonsignifying system without a General and without an organizing memory or central automation, defined solely by a circulation of states." Gilles Deleuze and Félix Guattari, *A Thousand Plateaus* (original French pub. 1980; this citation, London: Bloomsbury Academic, 2013), 21.

37

"A rhizome ceaselessly establishes connections between semiotic chains, organizations of power, and circumstances relative to the arts, sciences, and social struggles." Ibid., 6.

38

"We find ourselves at a similarly challenging aesthetic junction but also because new technologies again have created new spatial and perceptual potentials that must be considered from the vantage point of the current artistic paradigm." Steciw to Blalock, "A Conversation."

39

"To give a new idea to an object is already production. Duchamp thereby completes the definition of the term creation: To *create* is to insert an object into a new scenario, to consider it a character in a narrative." Bourriaud, *Postproduction*, 25.

40

"Nothing is in a fixed state, i.e. everything is anything else, whether because any object is capable of becoming another type of object or because an object already exists in flux between multiple instantiations." Vierkant, "The Image Object Post-Internet," 2.

this is a position that artists do not fully share in our era, which lacks the same boundaries between art and the empirical mass of images in common circulation.[41] On the other hand, the Cubist artists have been credited with a collective aim to create work that had the power to recalibrate cultural perception by embodying the frenetic visual tempo of the time; today's artists might be considered as constructing equivalent entry points with their work, interpreting existing viewing behaviors into the dynamic of their practice.[42]

The avant-garde of the early twentieth century is a frequent point of comparison with contemporary art photography also because of the plethora of experiments with photographic apparatuses and materials that were happening internationally, tapping into the essentialist and formally abstracting character of the medium. On a general level, it is easy to think of current practitioners as experimenting with the contemporary photographic toolkit—forming subjective and close relationships with their materials that seem to mirror the practices of their avant-garde antecedents.[43] But abstractions of today's experience are no longer the preserve of artists alone. In our networked culture, creative play takes place on an open field, and is not the preserve of an artistic vanguard, and subversion through experimentation is integrated into the contemporary image system at large.

While the avant-garde of the early 1900s provides some material models for contemporary art photography's relationship with image culture, the theoretically driven approaches of the late twentieth century offer others. We see something of the spirit of postmodernism, for example, in the current simulation of the daily language of image signs—the repetition of Photoshop color fades, online graphics and ideograms, and the hollow forms of 3D-rendered objects. The often intentionally ironic assessment of image-commodity culture that reverberated through postmodernist art crops up in a different form today, in contemporary photographic strategies of simulation.[44]

[41]
"Today, online, there is no home base: no building or context that contains and describes art in a way that uniformly attributes meaning for all." Troemel, "Art After Social Media," in Kholeif, ed., *You Are Here*, 40.

[42]
"Artistic creation is more explicitly embedded in overlapping systems of circulating brands, images, and objects, together forming an internet-enabled neoliberal ether....Not an airy declaration of independence, but a reckoning of one's immersion." Connor, "Post-Internet," in Kholeif, ed., *You Are Here*, 63.

[43]
"The discussions the producer holds may be mentally with materials rather than with other people....Another more balanced view is that thinking and feeling are contained within the process of making." Sennett, *The Craftsman*, 7.

[44]
"By crossing into a space whose curvature is no longer that of the real, nor that of truth, the era of simulation is inaugurated by a liquidation of all referentials—worse: with their artificial resurrection in the systems of signs, a material more malleable than meaning, in that it lends itself to all systems of equivalences, to all binary oppositions, to all combinatory algebra. It is no longer a question of imitation, nor duplication, nor even parody. It is a question of substituting the signs of the real for the real, that is to say of an operation of deterring every real process via its operational double, a programmatic, metastable, perfectly descriptive machine that offers all the signs of the real and short-circuits all its vicissitudes. Never again will the real have the chance to produce itself—such is the vital function of the model in a system of death, or rather of anticipated resurrection, that no longer even gives the event of death a chance. A hyperreal henceforth sheltered from the imaginary, and from any distinction between the real and the imaginary, leaving room only for the orbital recurrence of models and for the simulated generation of differences." Jean Baudrillard, *Simulacra and Simulation* (original French pub., 1981; this citation, Ann Arbor: University of Michigan Press, 1994), 2.

The infinite feedback loop between image and commodity was epitomized in the mid-1980s by the loose grouping of artists known as the Simulationists.[45] Their practices—which hovered ambiguously between critique of and desire for commodity image culture—have resonance today, in substantial part because of their adoption of a range of artistic positions within the increasingly market-driven arena of contemporary art. As with all the historical movements cited in this text, the parallels go only so far, but as artist-led strategies for engaging the complexity and transience of artistic practice, these approaches continue to resonate and be reenacted within the terrain of contemporary art.

The term that most clearly encapsulates the spirit of contemporary art practices— their shared motivations and dynamics—is *post-Internet*. Its most common use today is as a broad description of artistic practices that take for granted the networked and integrated nature of the Internet.[46] Post-Internet is of course not a specific form of work—the loose definition applies as much to artists working with traditional materials (such as photographic prints) as to artists using the vernacular language of online culture; the term encapsulates both actual and symbolic channeling of the pervasive impact that the Web, social media, and mobile imaging technologies have had on the ways we make, consume, and understand visual culture.[47] *Post-Internet* is increasingly used to describe work by artists who embed their practices in fluid versioning and scrolling information streams in our commodified systems of communication, using the same iterative processes and dynamic structuring of relations between works to the point that they become inseparable from the systems themselves.[48] Some of the artists represented in *Photography Is Magic* are directly aligned with critical and curatorial projects that are exploring the scope of this post-Internet environment. But in a more pervasive sense, the term gives us dialogical permission to know that we experience these artists' practices by invitation: we have been asked to be present in the immanence of the networked image dynamics of our time.

[45] "The artists who lay claim to Simulationism considered the work of art to be an 'absolute commodity' and creation a mere substitute for the act of consuming....The object was shown from the angle of the compulsion to buy, from the angle of desire, midway between the inaccessible and the available." Bourriaud, *Postproduction*, 27.

[46] "The term 'post-internet' suggests that the focus of a good deal of artistic and critical discourse has shifted from 'internet culture' as a discrete entity to an awareness that all culture has been reconfigured by the internet, or by internet-enabled neoliberal capitalism." Connor, "Post-Internet," in Kholeif, ed., *You Are Here*, 61.

[47] "Art after social media is paradoxically the rejection and reflection of the market. In practice and theory these two seemingly divergent developments are reconcilable because each contains parts of the other. For all that is communal about a decentralized network of artistic peers sharing and recreating each other's work, the dispersion of this work takes the shape of free market populism; of free exchange of information sorting itself out amongst those willing to produce and consume it....This setup is not unlike that of the secondary art auction market, where art critics' opinions of the works for sale mean little to nothing and the bidding power of a room of collectors takes precedence." Troemel, "Art After Social Media," in Kholeif, ed., *You Are Here*, 42.

[48] "The removal of the physical constraints on effective information production has made human creativity and the economics of information itself the core structuring facts in the new networked information economy." Yochai Benkler, *The Wealth of Networks: How Social Production Transforms Markets and Freedom* (New Haven, CT: Yale University Press, 2007), 4.

Photography can be magic when it is perfectly timed for its close-up audience, taking into account our ordinary interactions with image culture, even as that culture continues to manifest and change.[49] Contemporary art photography, as attested by the artists represented here, derives its magical charge from its capacity both to articulate *and* to participate in our collective image environment.

Much has been made in this essay of the mechanics of these acts of photographic creativity. Again, this is not to suggest that the magic of these practices is the sum of their parts—far from it. This level of detail is important in order for us to know and appreciate these works as being part of our shared visual context.[50] The reason for highlighting historic artistic precedents is not to suggest that we have been here before, but to encourage us to remember the present of artistic practice for its parallel openness of spirit and imaginative innovation.[51]

The magical possibilities that are created in our imaginations by these artistic gestures may be taken as our entry points into deeper thinking about the image world around us, and may inspire meaningful ideas and dialogues about photography in circulation at this moment. They are ideas that are on the move, disseminating through visual culture and the states of mind of their viewers. They are prompts for the future of photographic practice, activated by their special form of magic.

[49] "Ordinary affects are public feelings that begin and end in broad circulation, but they're also the stuff that seemingly intimate lives are made of. They give circuits and flows the forms of a life." Kathleen Stewart, *Ordinary Affects* (Durham, NC: Duke University Press, 2007), 2.

[50] "The question [ordinary affects] beg is not what they might mean in an order of representations, or whether they are good or bad in an overarching scheme of things, but where they might go and what potential modes of knowing, relating and attending to things are already somehow present in them in a state of potentiality and resonance." Ibid., 3.

[51] "Nearly all our originality comes from the stamp that time impresses upon our sensibility." Baudelaire, *The Painter of Modern Life*, 18.

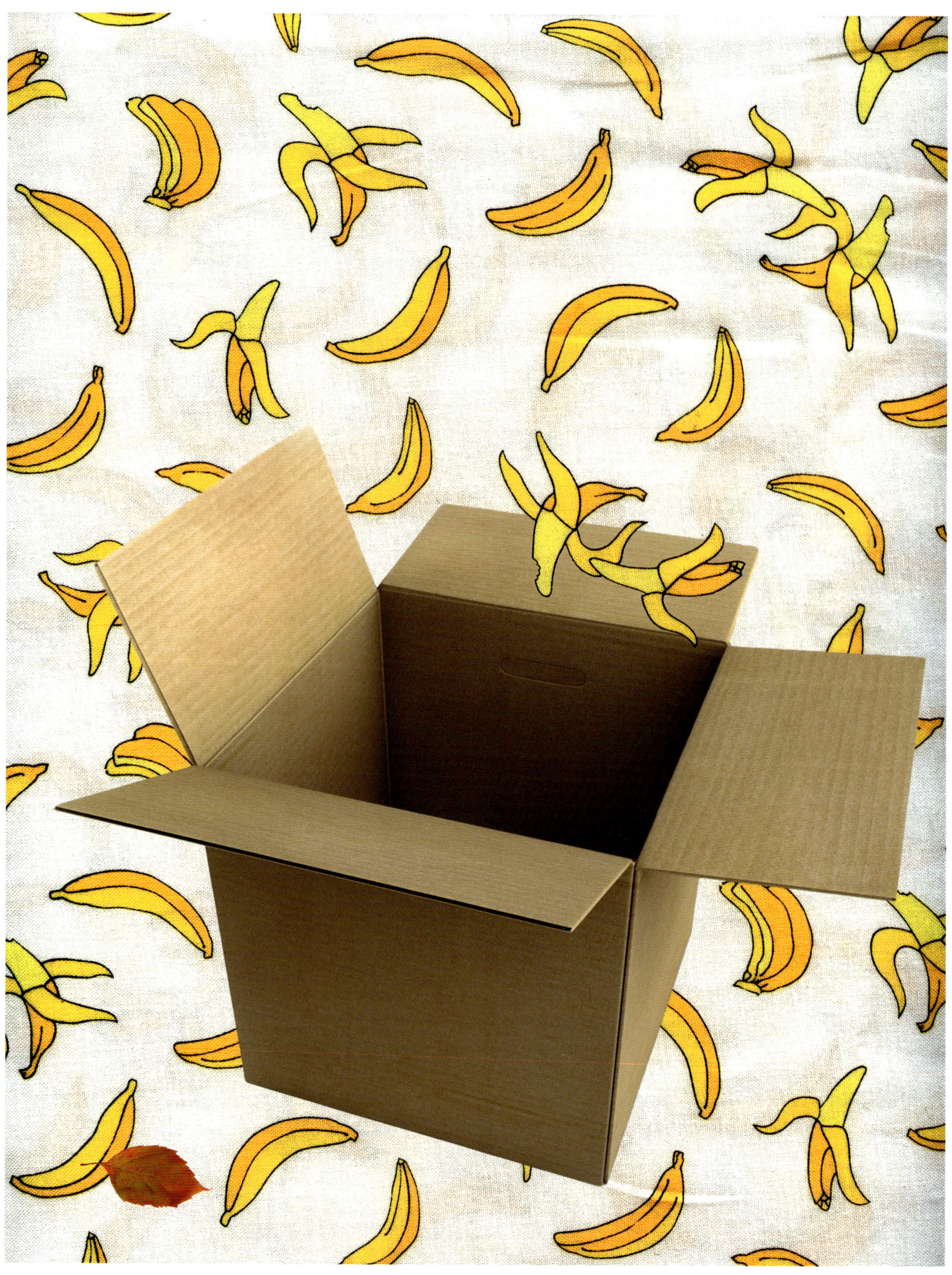

   Asha Schechter, *Picture 049 (Cardboard Box, Autumn Leaf Red, Funky Monkeys)*, 2013. C-print

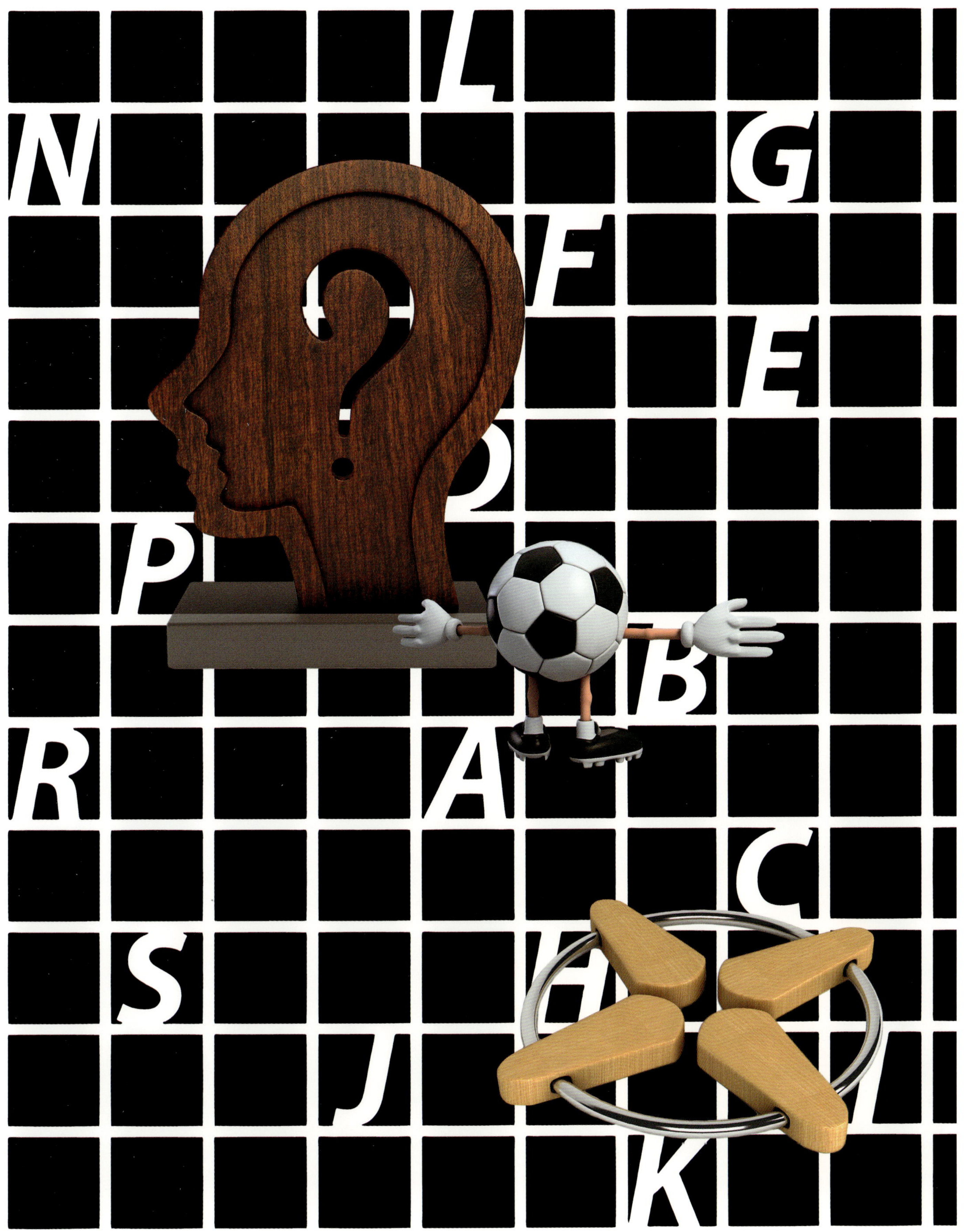


21    Asha Schechter, *Picture 050 (Artistic Sculpture of Thought, Trivet 03, Character Cartoon Football, Alphabet Pattern)*, 2013. C-print

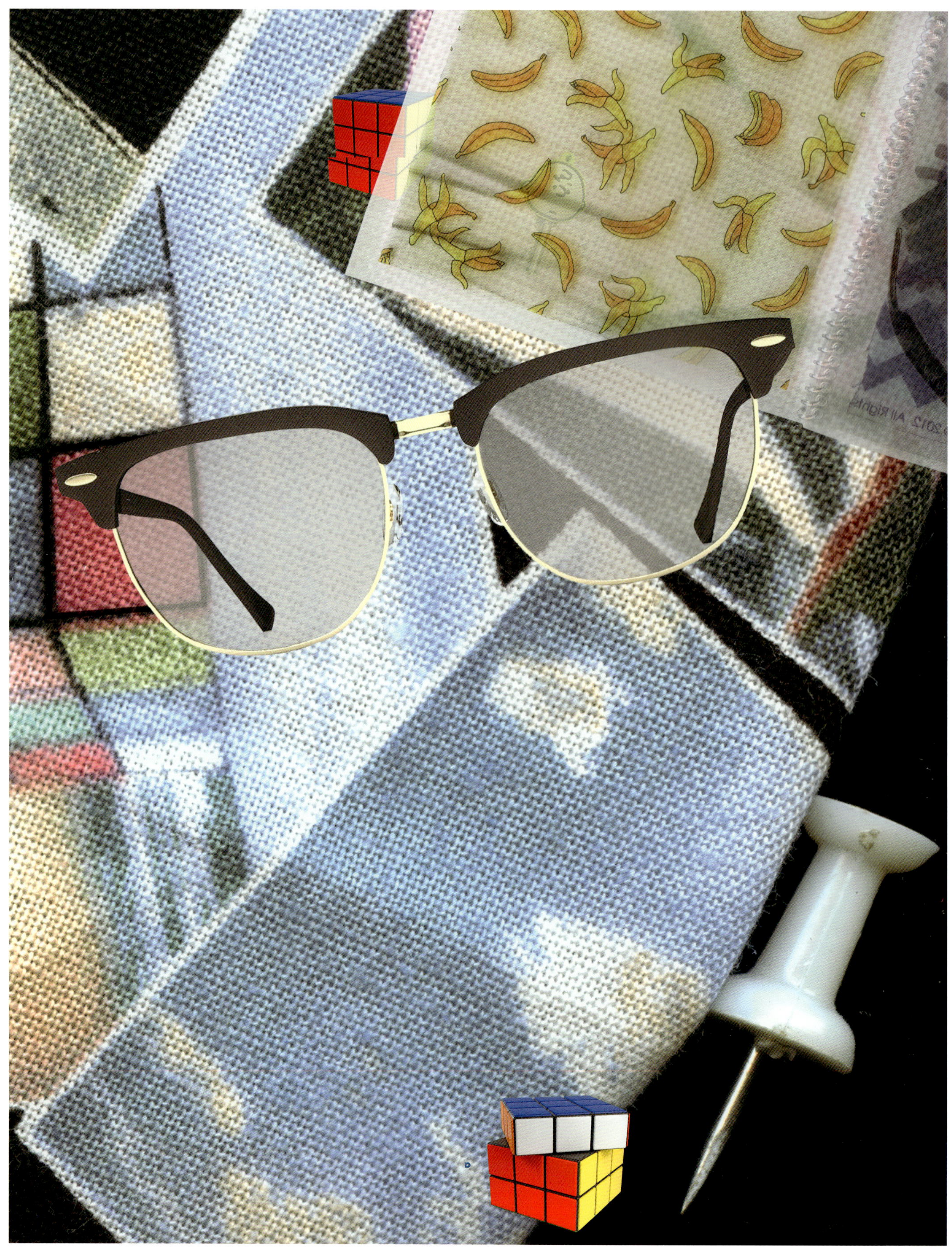

  Asha Schechter, *Picture 066b (Rubik's Cube, Clear Book, Clubmasters, Rubik's Cube, Vintage Pictures Retro Photos Cotton Fabric, Thumbtack)*, 2013. C-print

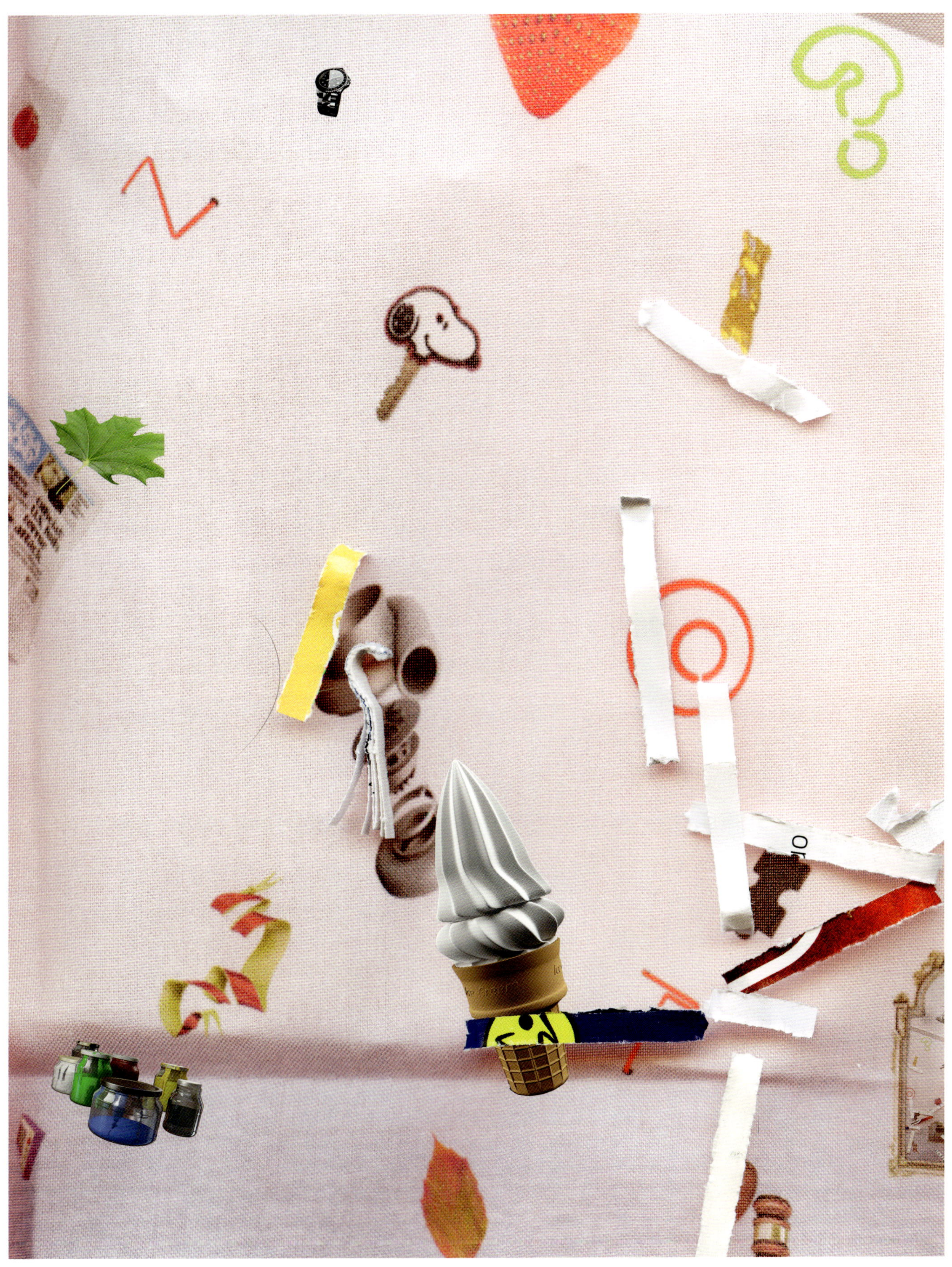

   Asha Schechter, *Picture 092b (Rolex GMT-Master II Steel, Autumn Leaf Red, Paint in Jars, Ice Cream V1, Shredded Paper, Spoonflower Fabric)*, 2013. C-print

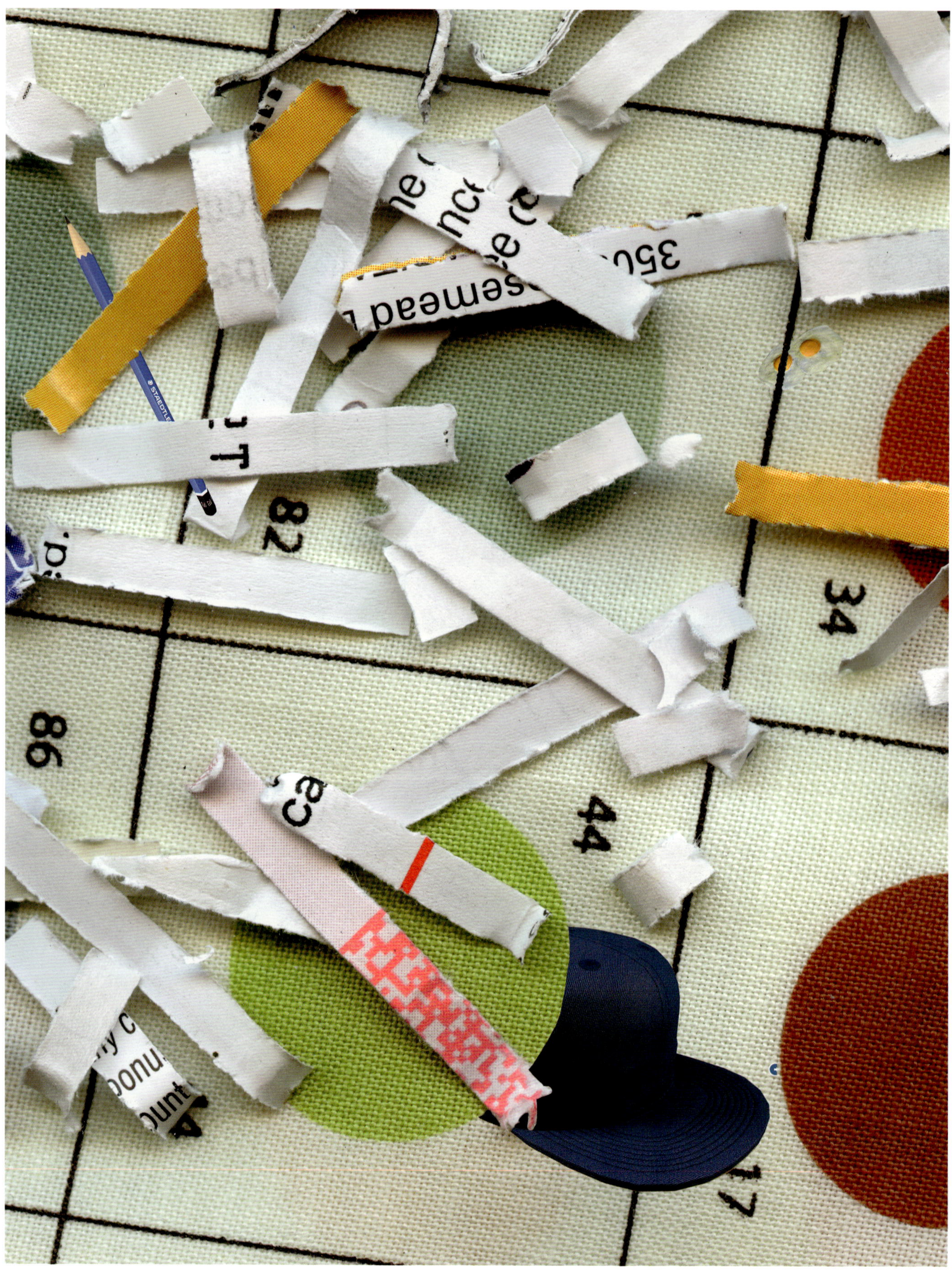

24    Asha Schechter, *Picture 097 (Pencil, Shredded Paper, Baseball Hat V2, Fried Eggs, Lush Uptown Paint-by-Number Paint Palette Dot by Erin Michael)*, 2014. C-print

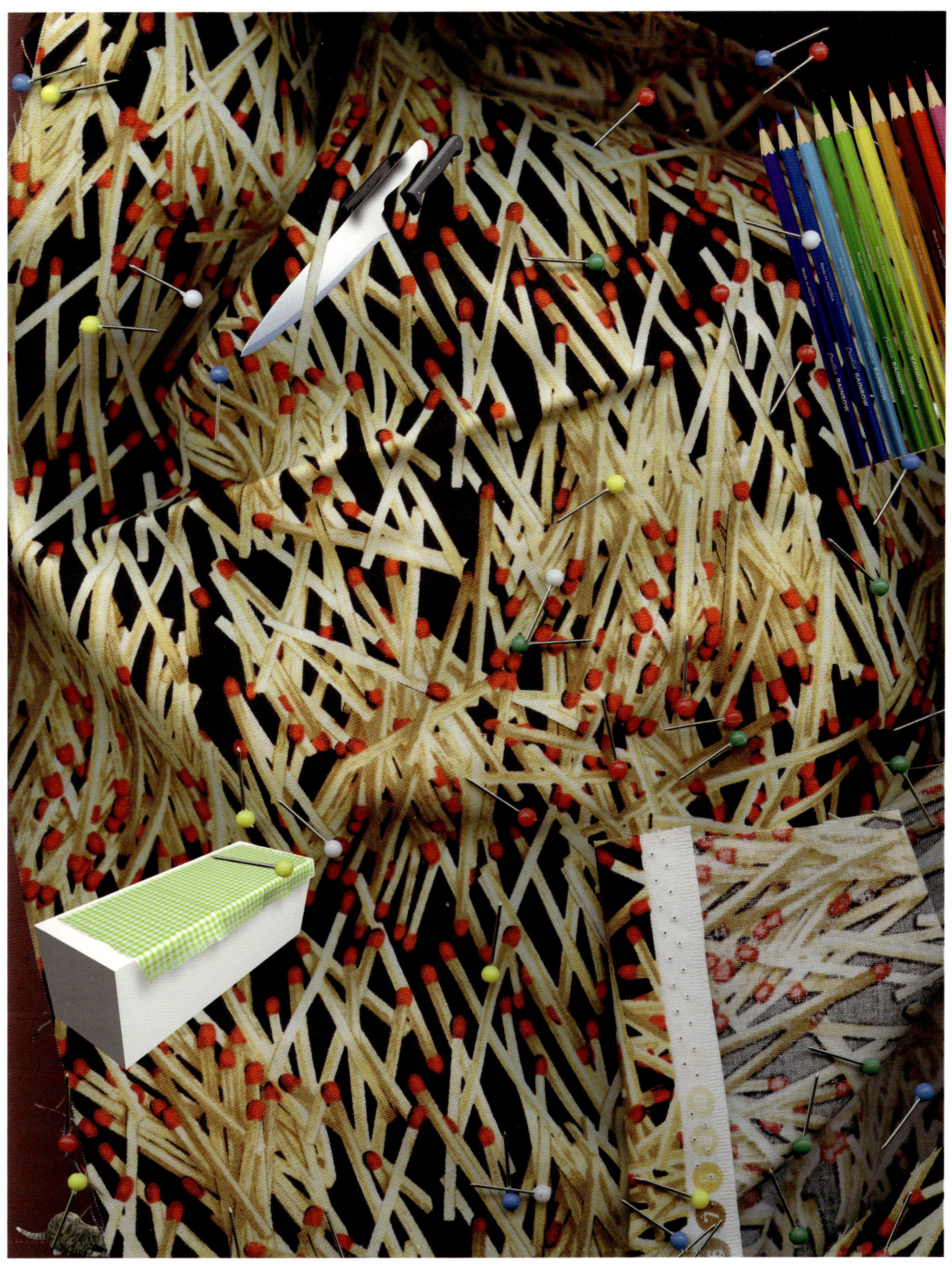

25 Asha Schechter, *Picture 075 (Cook's Knife, Colored Pencils, Old Gingham Cloth, Cat [Mackerel] [FUR] [ANIMATED], Multicolored Push Pins, Match Black by Benartex)*, 2013. C-print

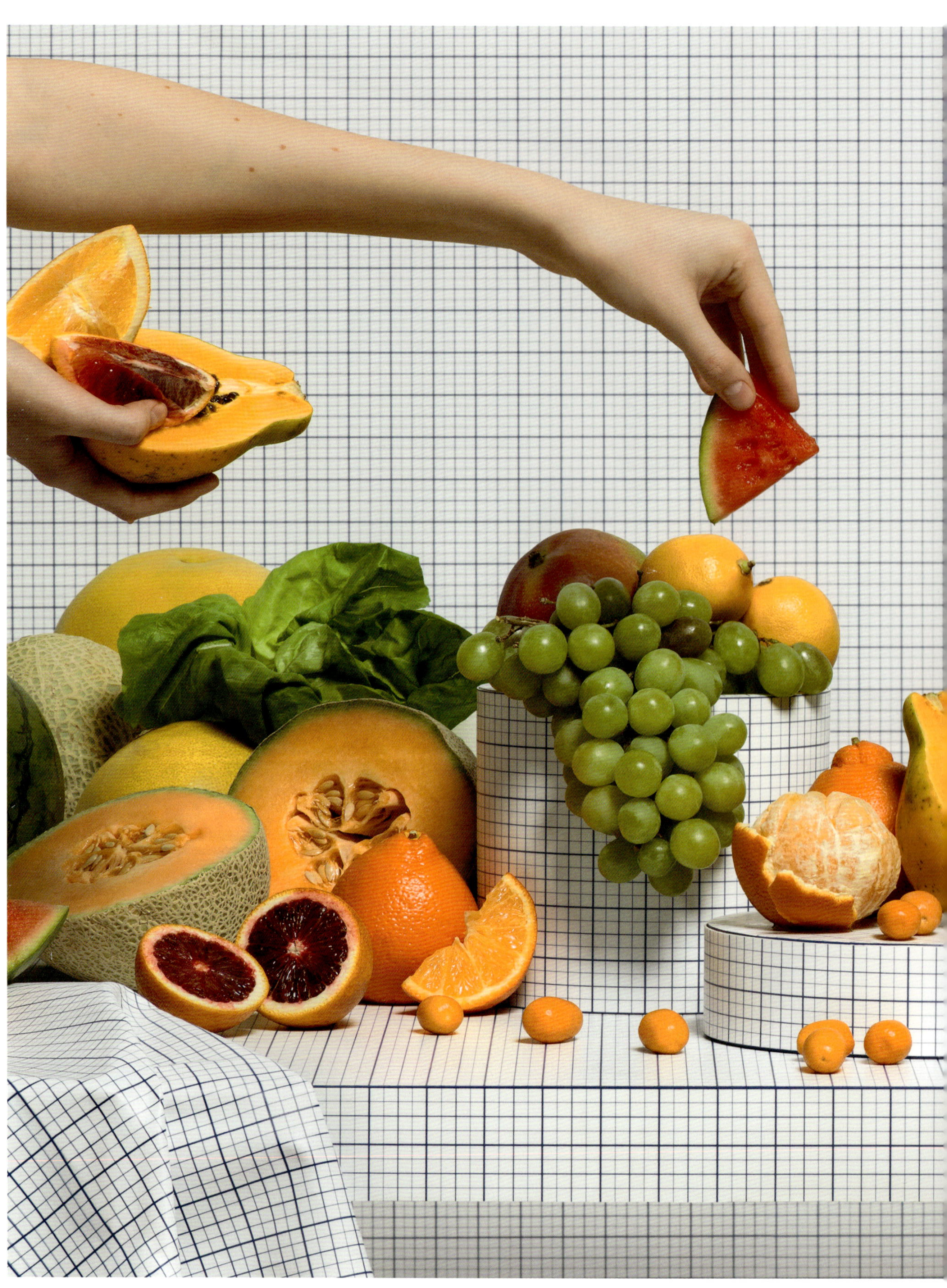

    Charlie White, *Still Life of Fruits with Taker*, 2014. C-print

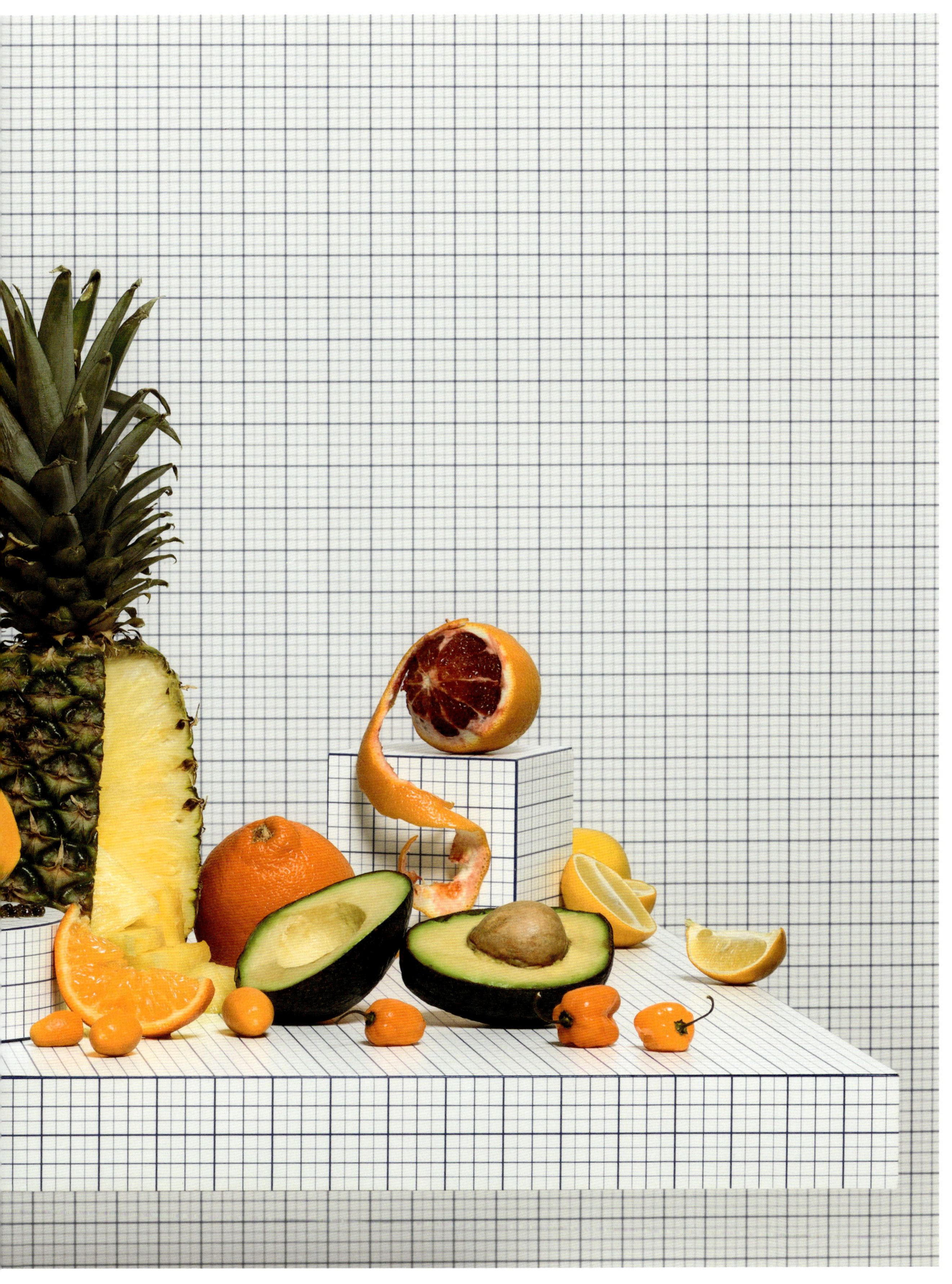

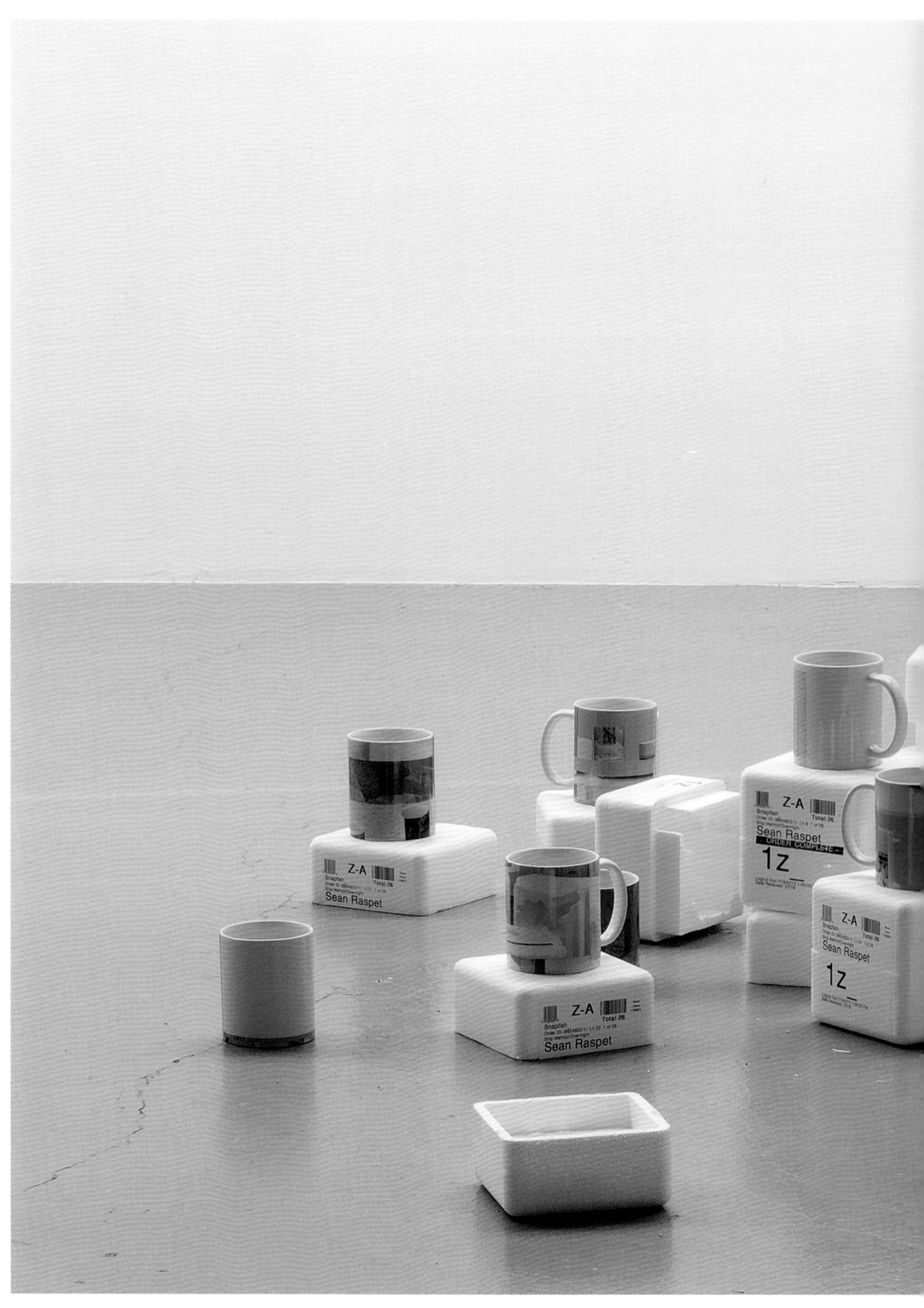

    Sean Raspet, *[2Registration::(ÒUntz\'tled (Police Incident (8[d])) 9)], ((((2007-2012) 2007-2011, Ó) Ó) 2012) 2012–2013) 2014)*, 2010–14.
Commercially printed ceramic mugs and Styrofoam shipping containers

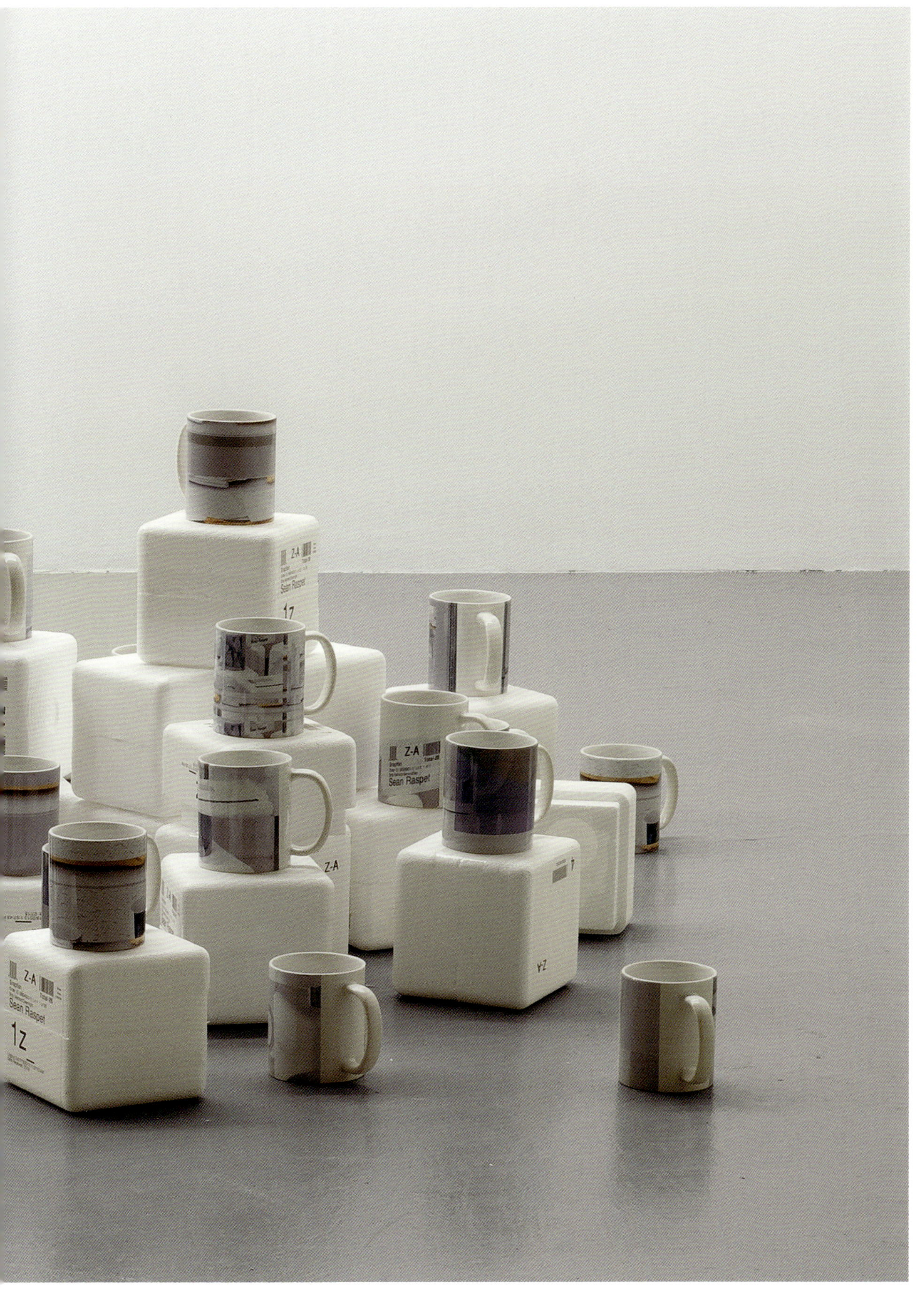

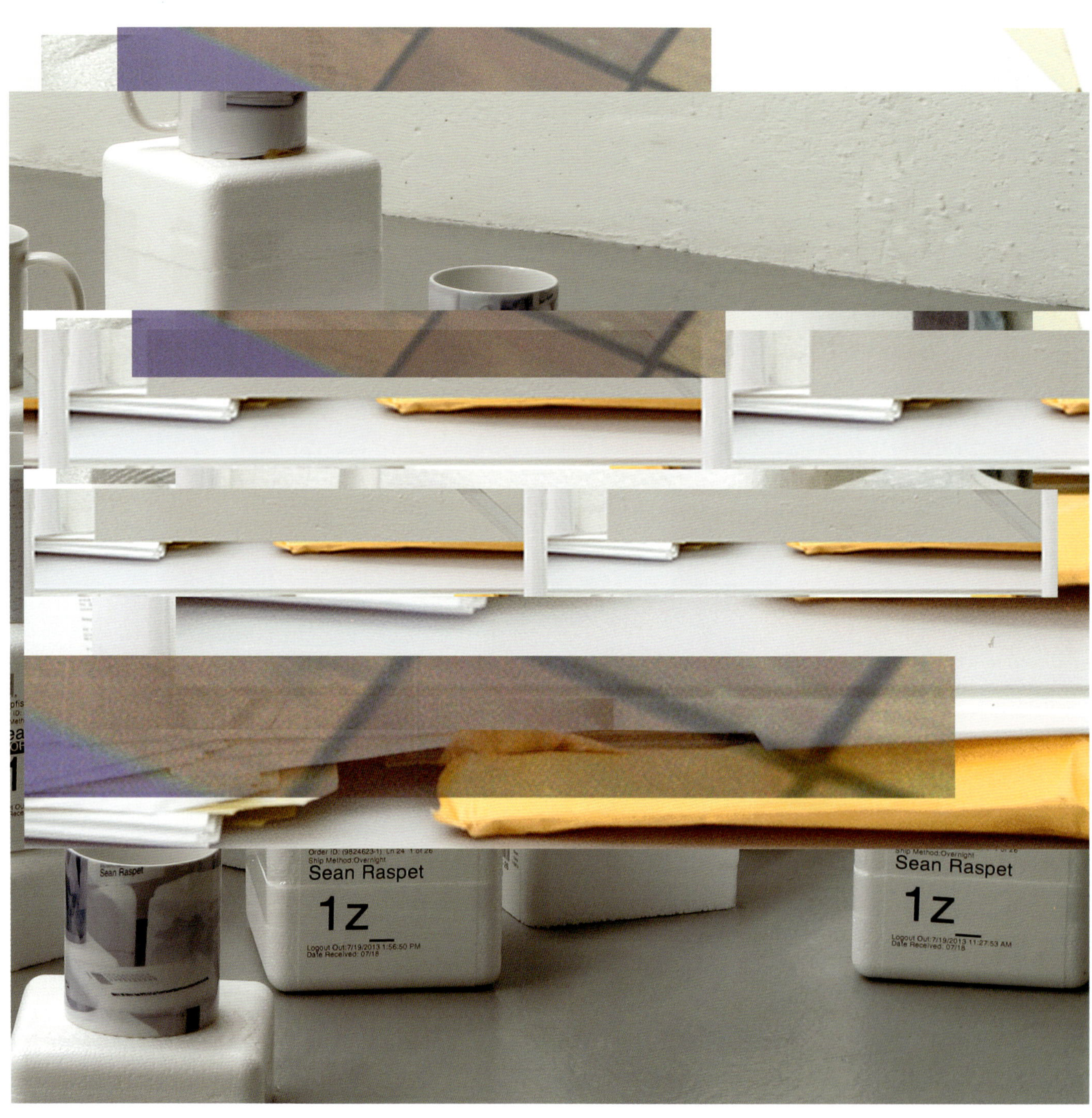


    Sean Raspet, *[2Registration::(ÒUntz'tled (Police Incident (7[c])) 6, (((2007-2012) 2007-2011, Ó) Ó) 2012) 2012–2013)*, 2013, 2010–13.
Commercially printed ceramic mugs and Styrofoam shipping containers

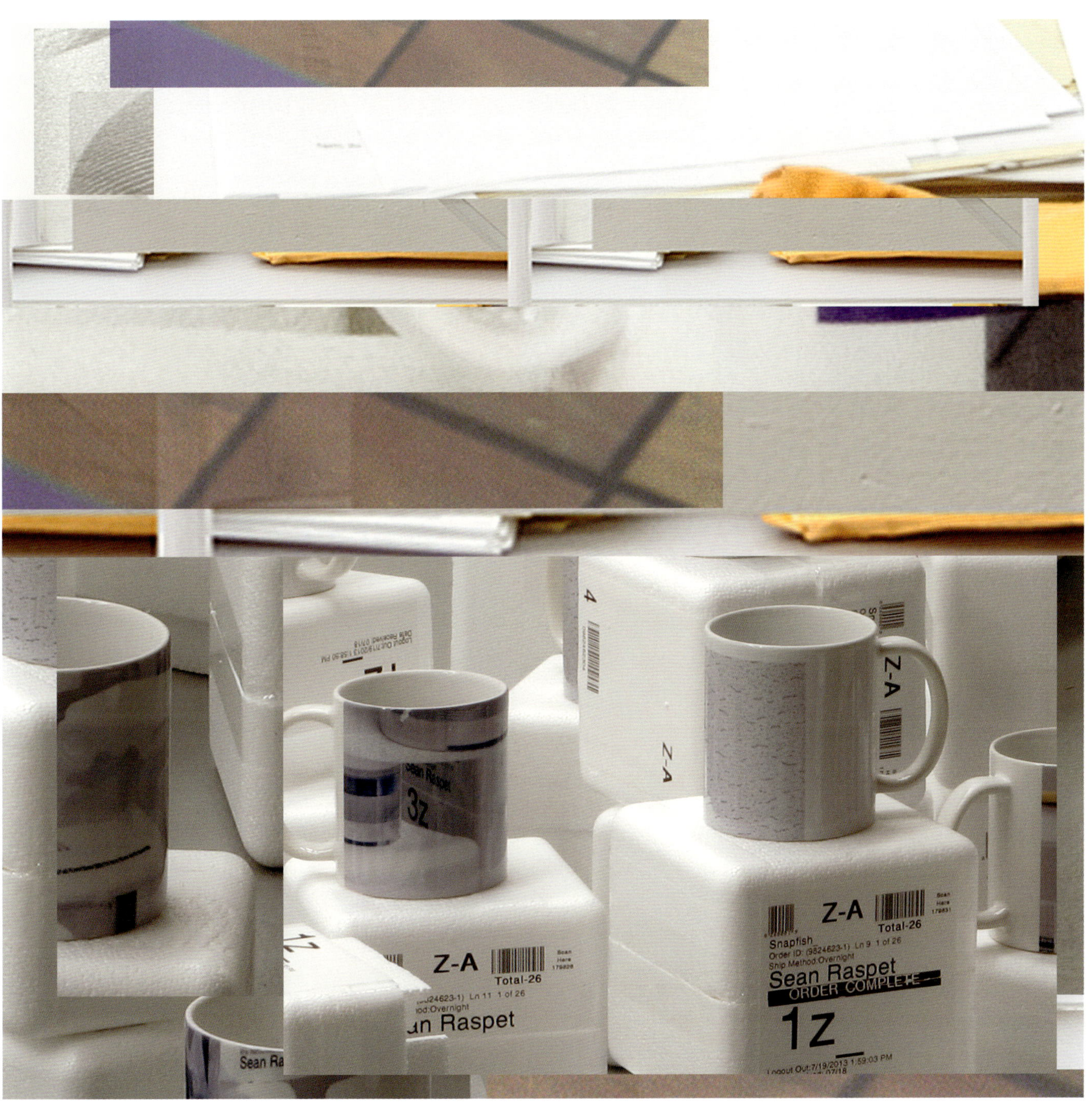


31    Sean Raspet, *[2Registration::(ÒUntz\'tled (Police Incident (8[d])) 9)], (((((2007-2012) 2007-2011, Ó) Ó) 2012) 2012–2013) 2014)*, 2010–14.
Commercially printed ceramic mugs and Styrofoam shipping containers

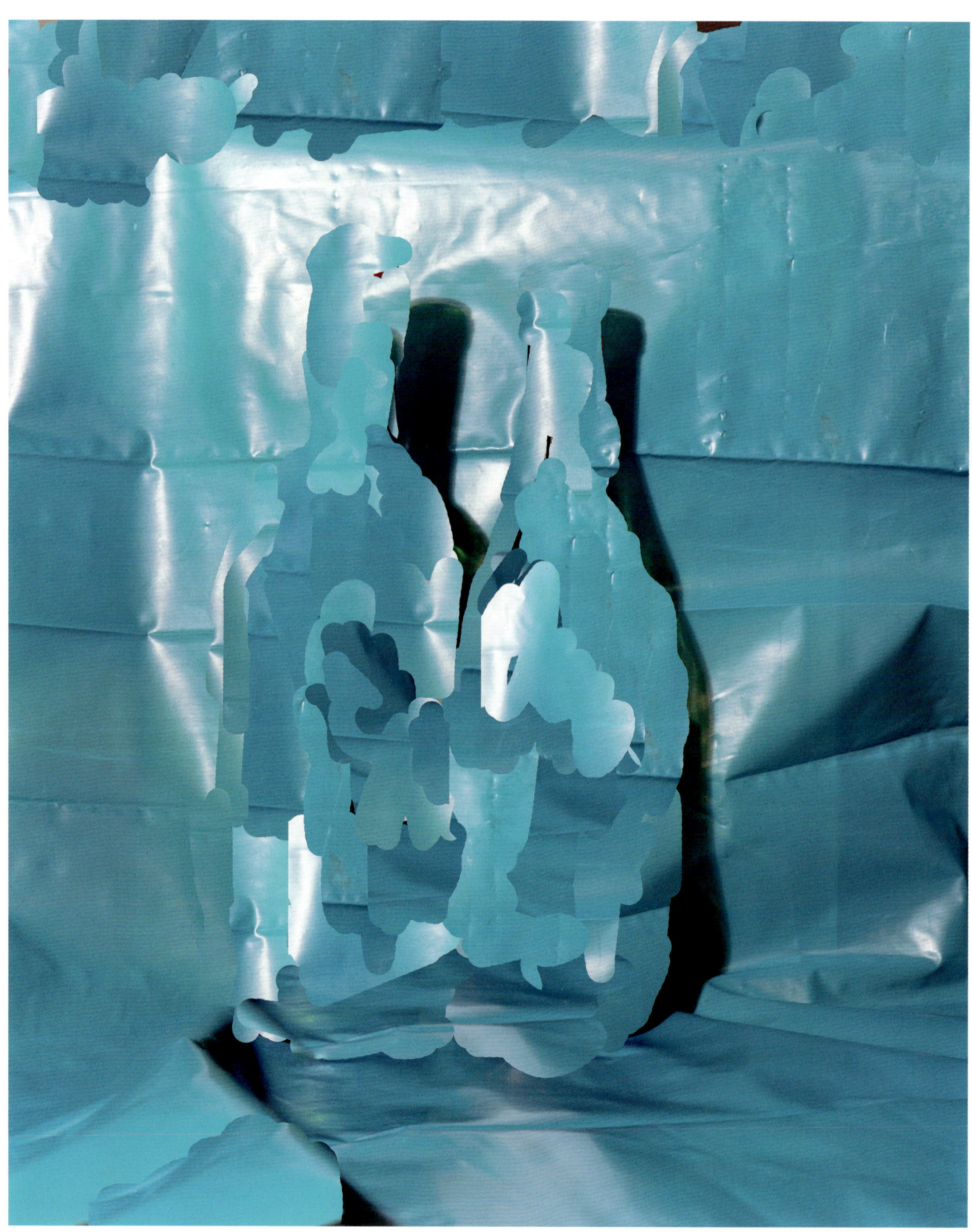

32  Lucas Blalock, *Blue Bottles*, 2013. Archival inkjet print

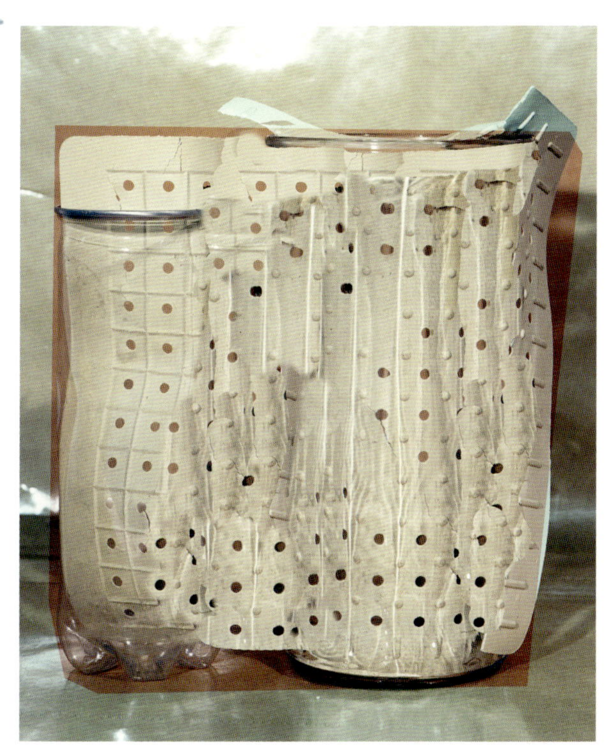

33    Lucas Blalock, *Untitled with Containers*, 2013. Archival inkjet print

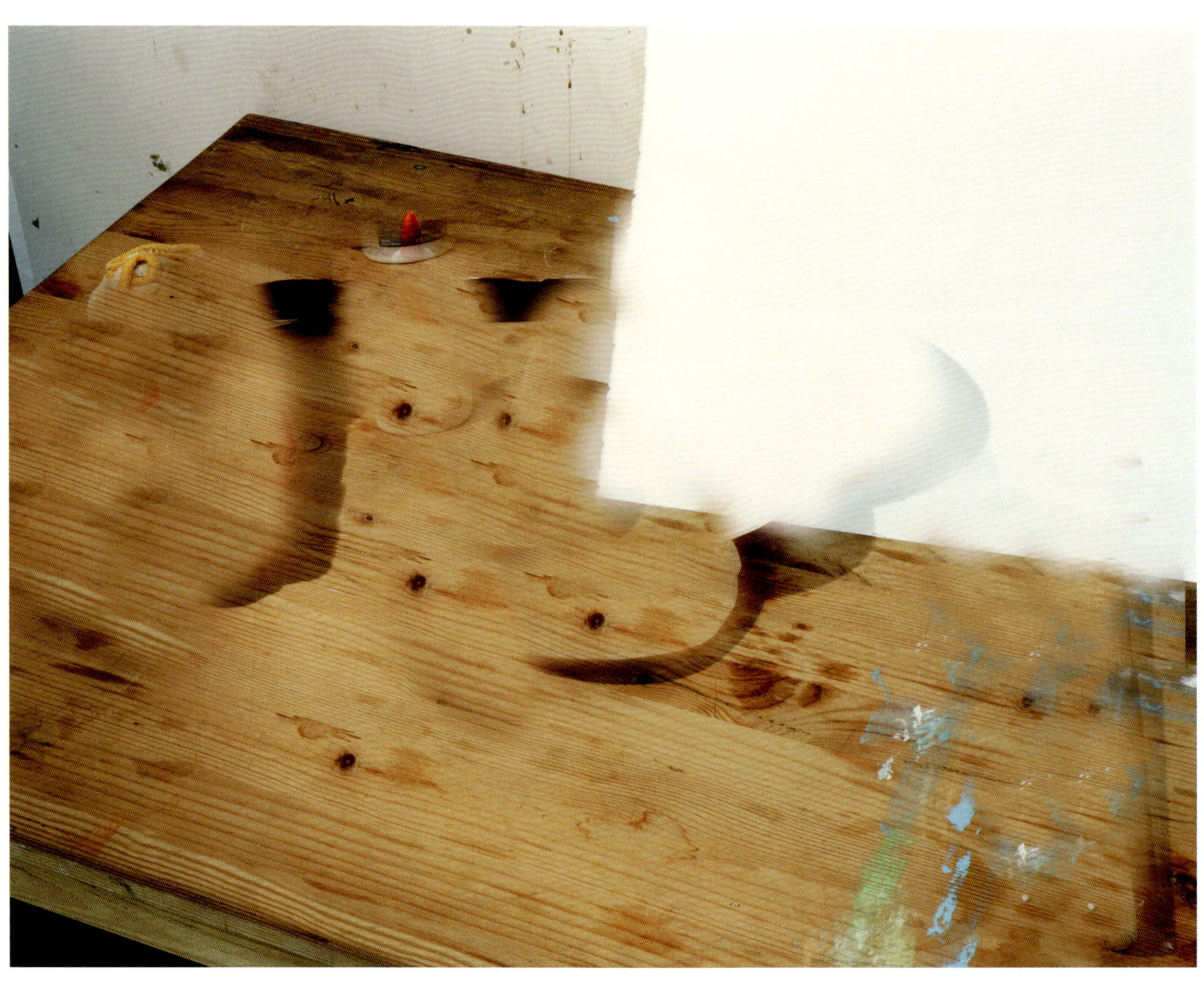

34    Lucas Blalock, *III*, 2013. Archival inkjet print

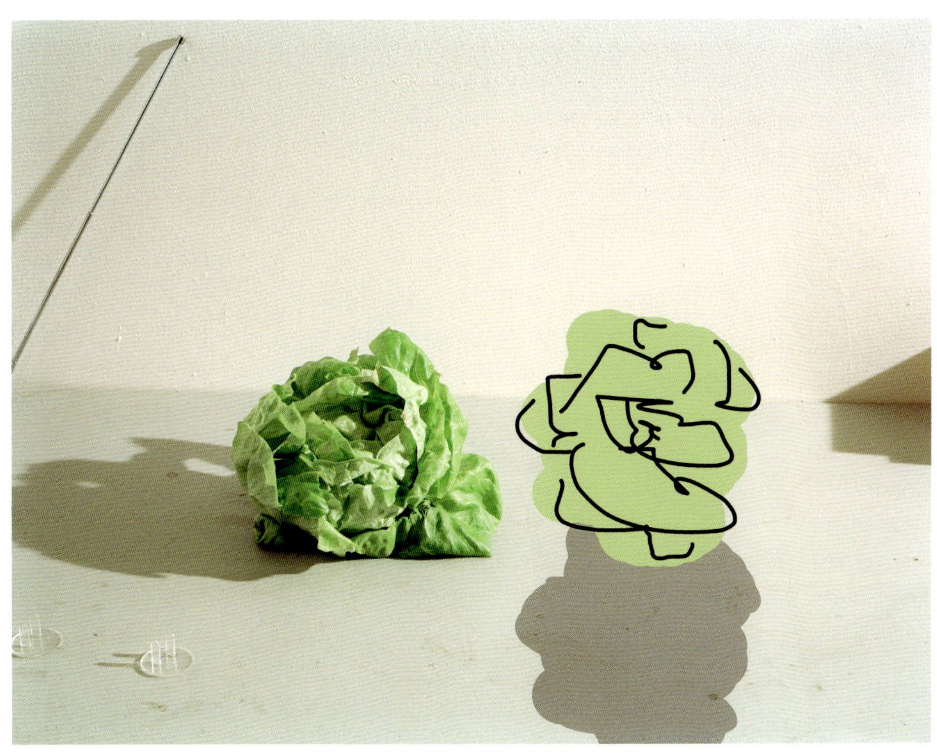

35    Lucas Blalock, *Two Lettuces*, 2013. Archival inkjet print

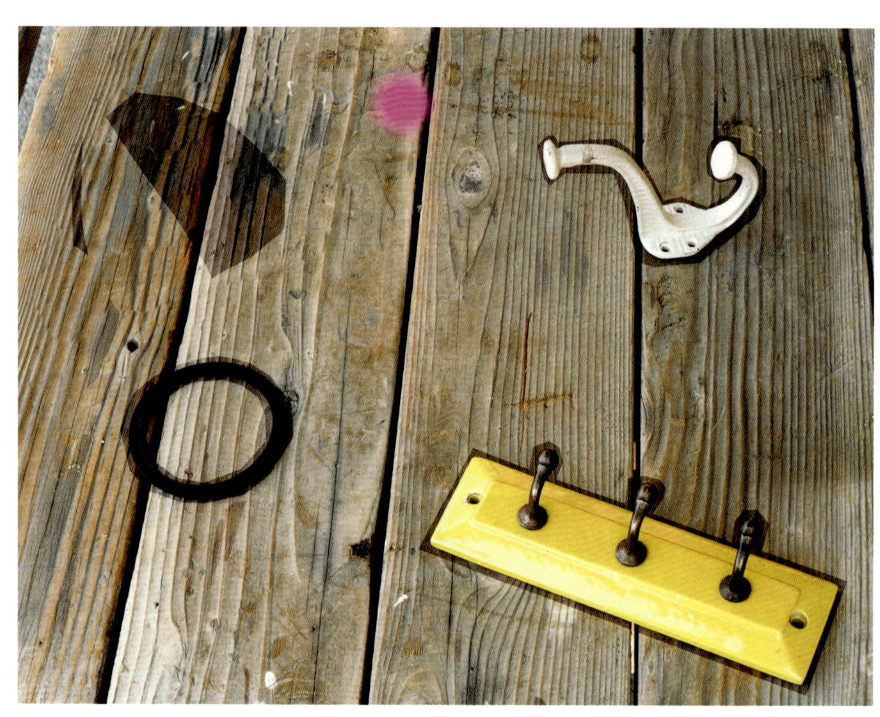

36    Lucas Blalock, *Five Positions*, 2012. Archival inkjet print

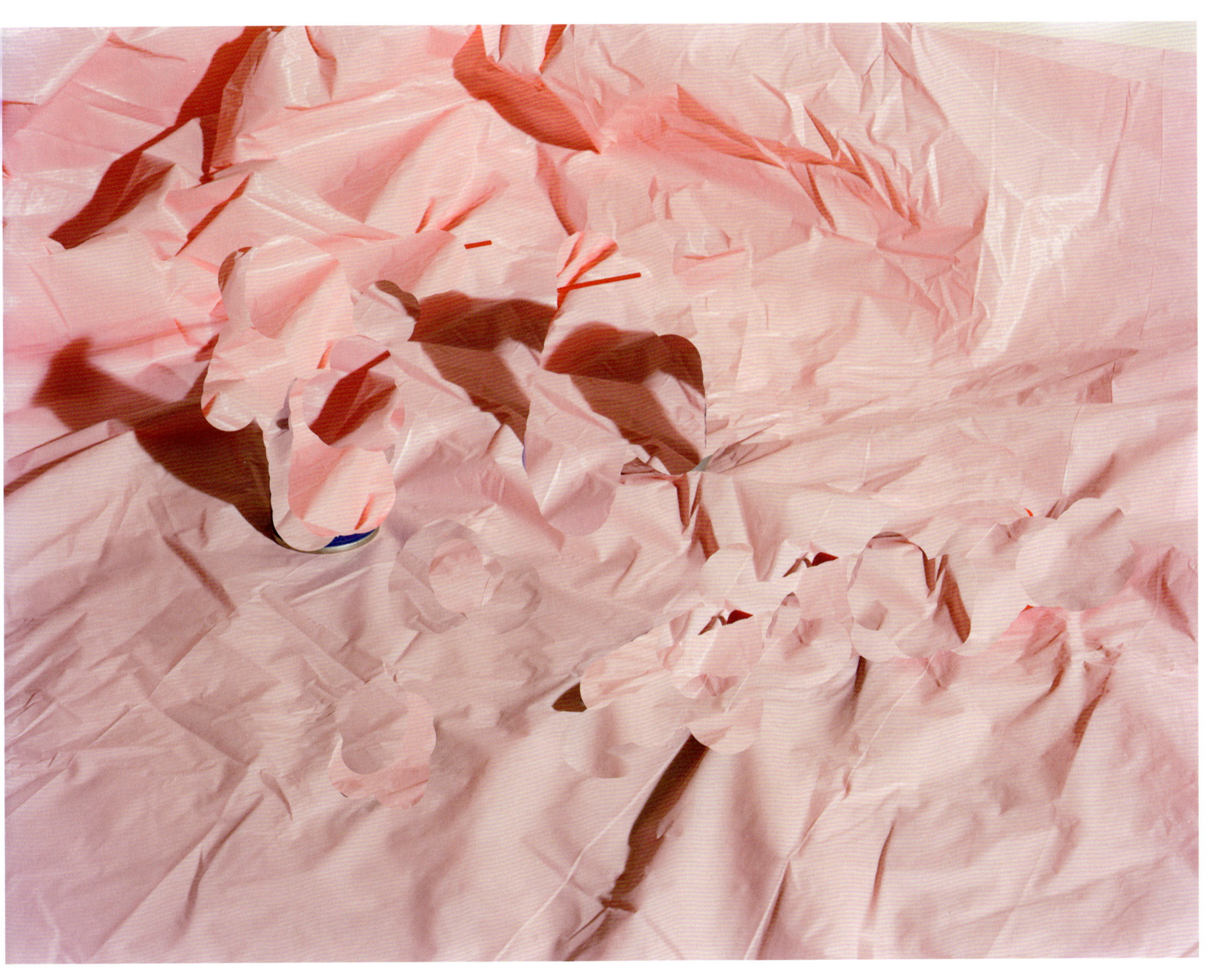

  Lucas Blalock, *Night Decisions I*, 2012. Archival inkjet print

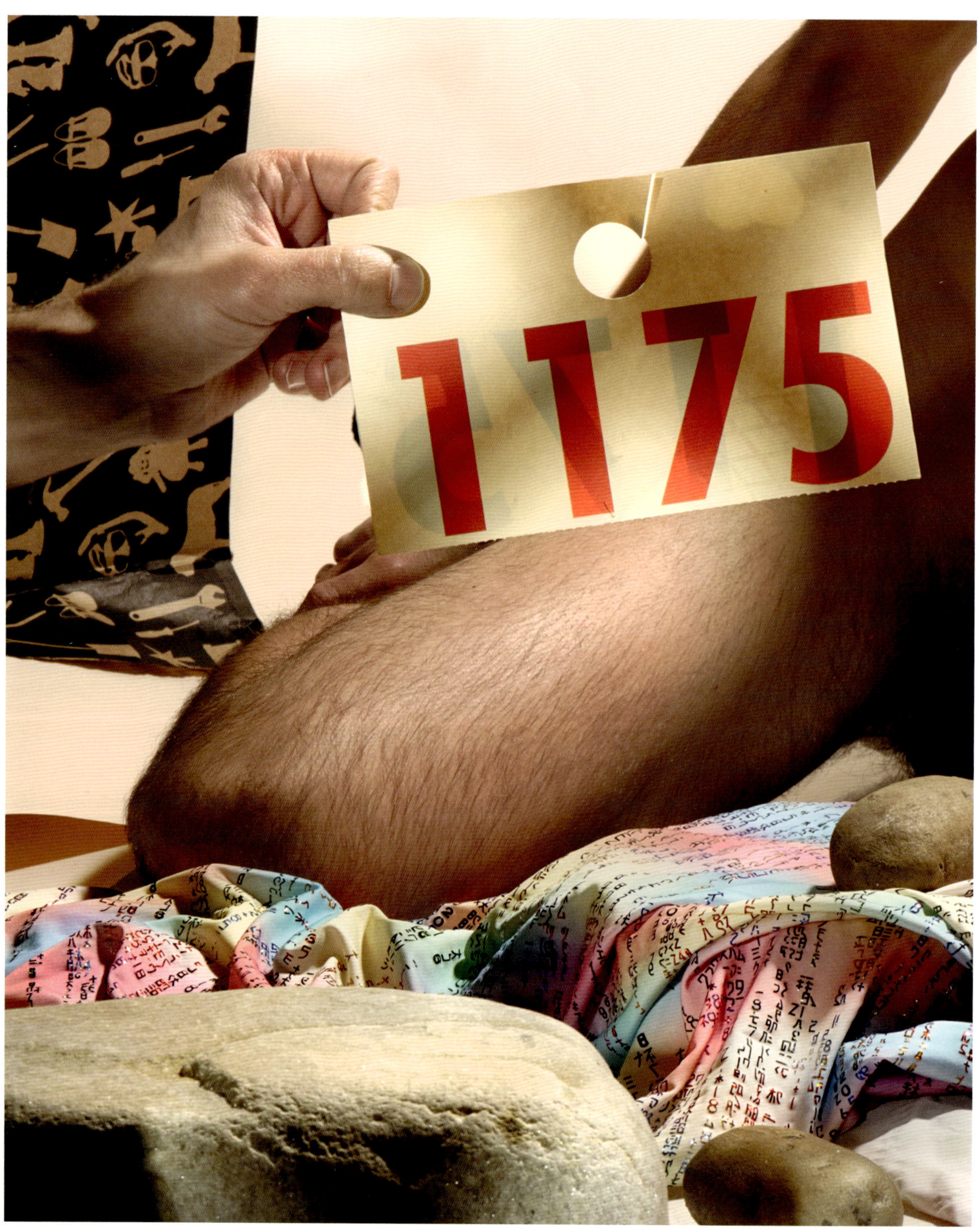

  Michele Abeles, *Number, Lycra, Man, Hand, Rock, M, L, Cardboard*, 2009, from the series *Re:Re:Re:Re:Re:*. Archival pigment print

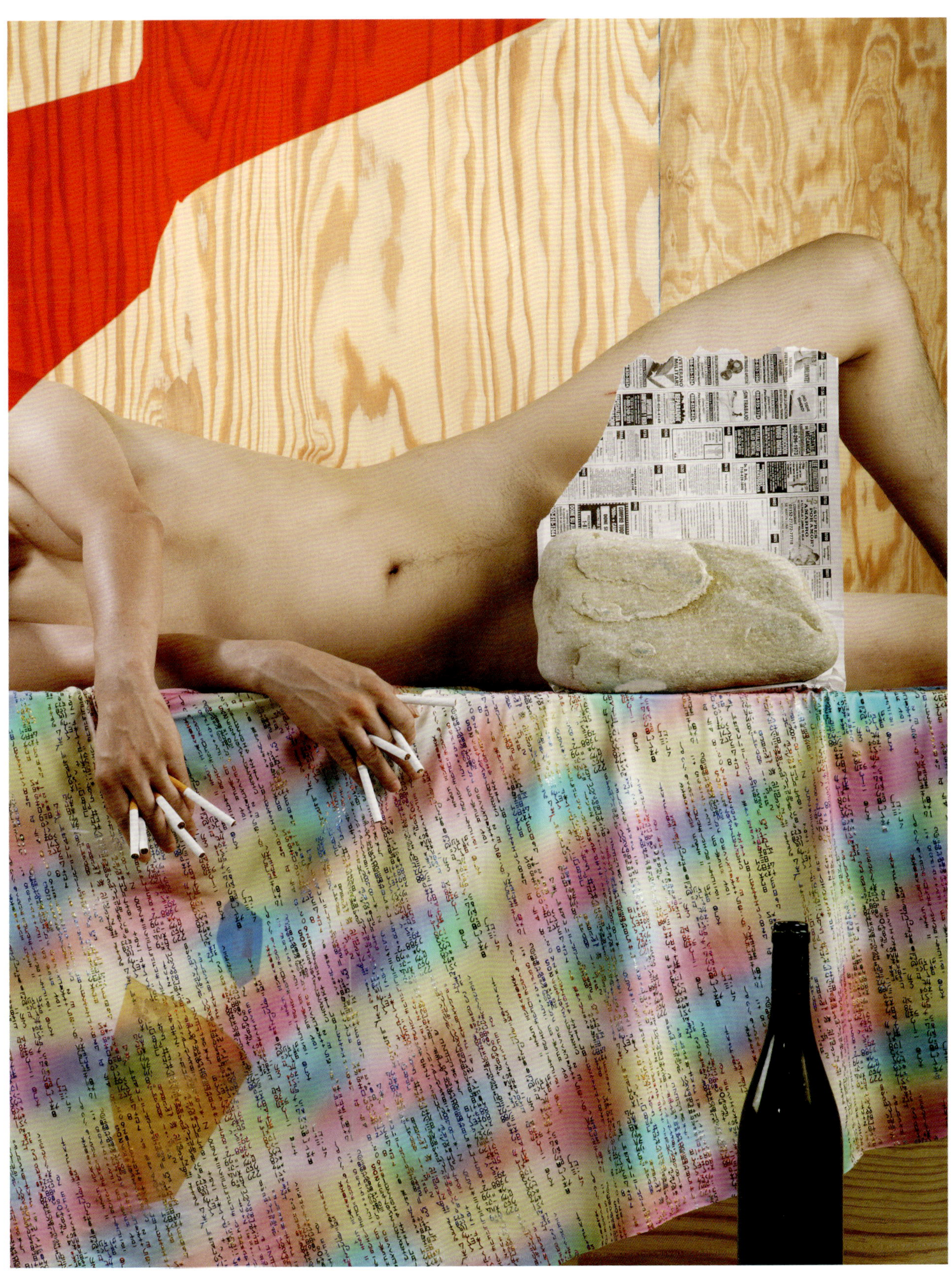

39    Michele Abeles, *Red, Rock, Cigarettes, Newspaper, Body, Wood, Lycra, Bottle*, 2011, from the series *Re:Re:Re:Re:Re:*. Archival pigment print

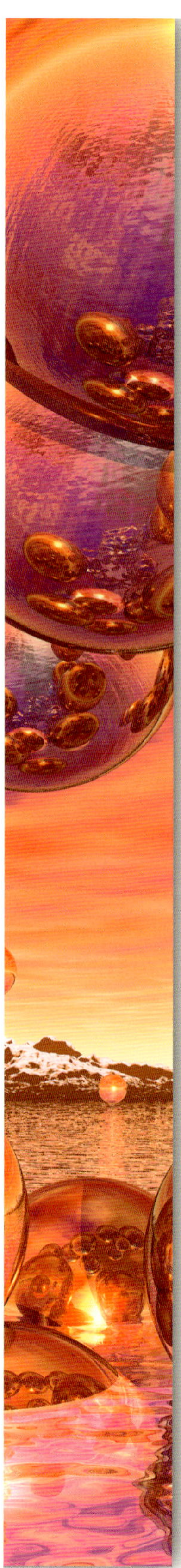

    Michele Abeles, *#4*, 2012. Archival pigment print

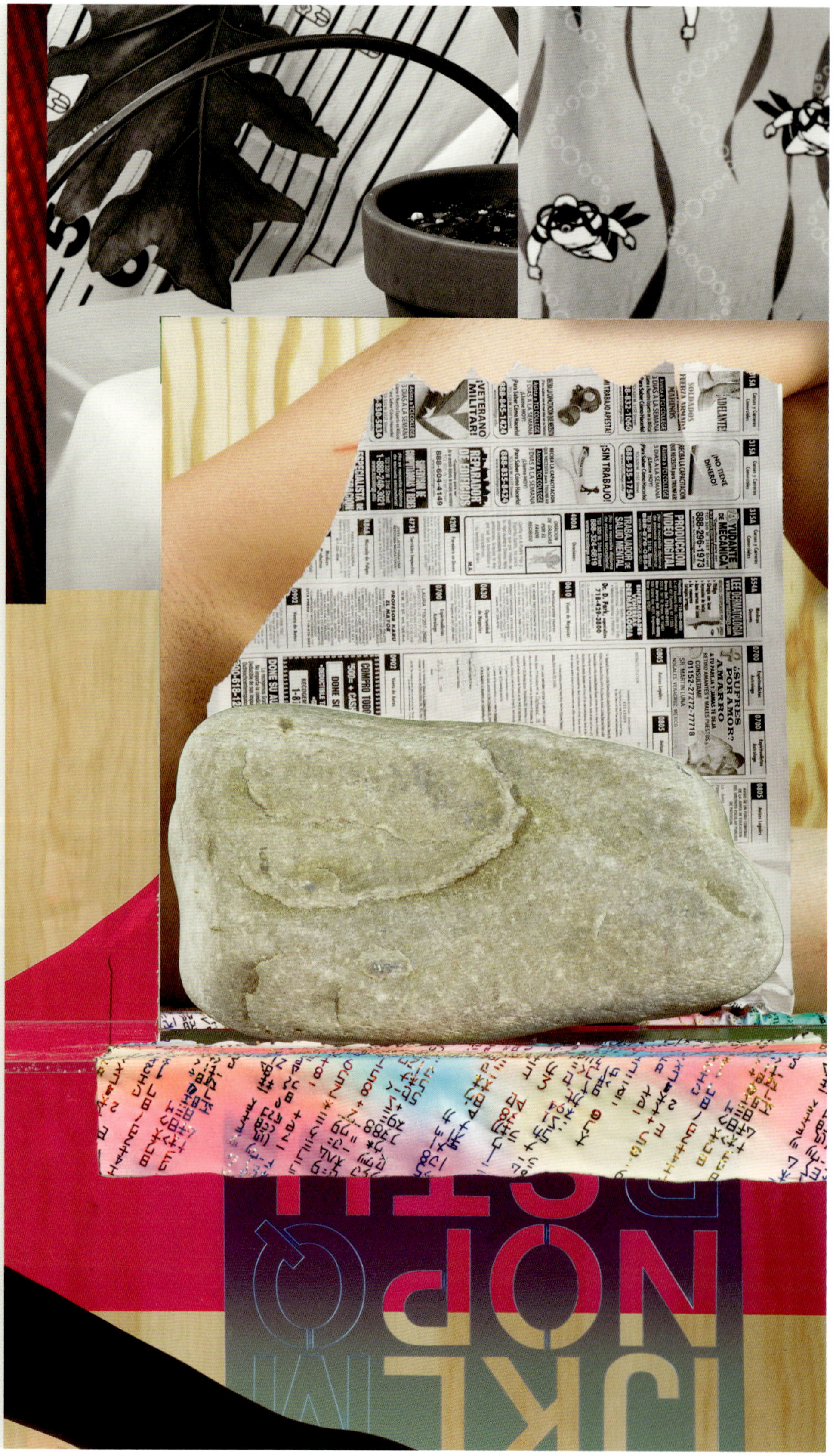

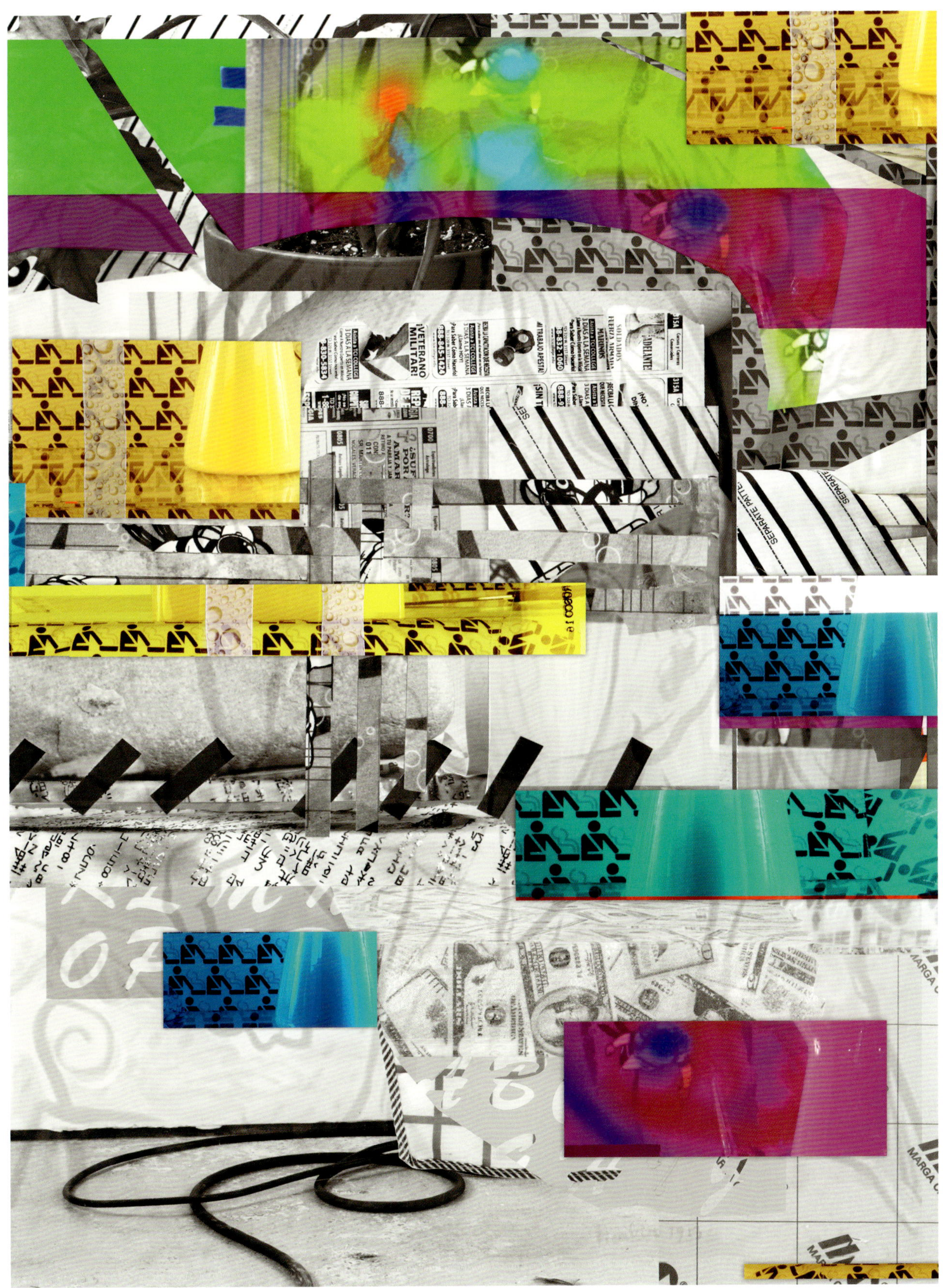

    Michele Abeles, *Where is the closest Italian restaurant?*, 2013. Archival pigment print

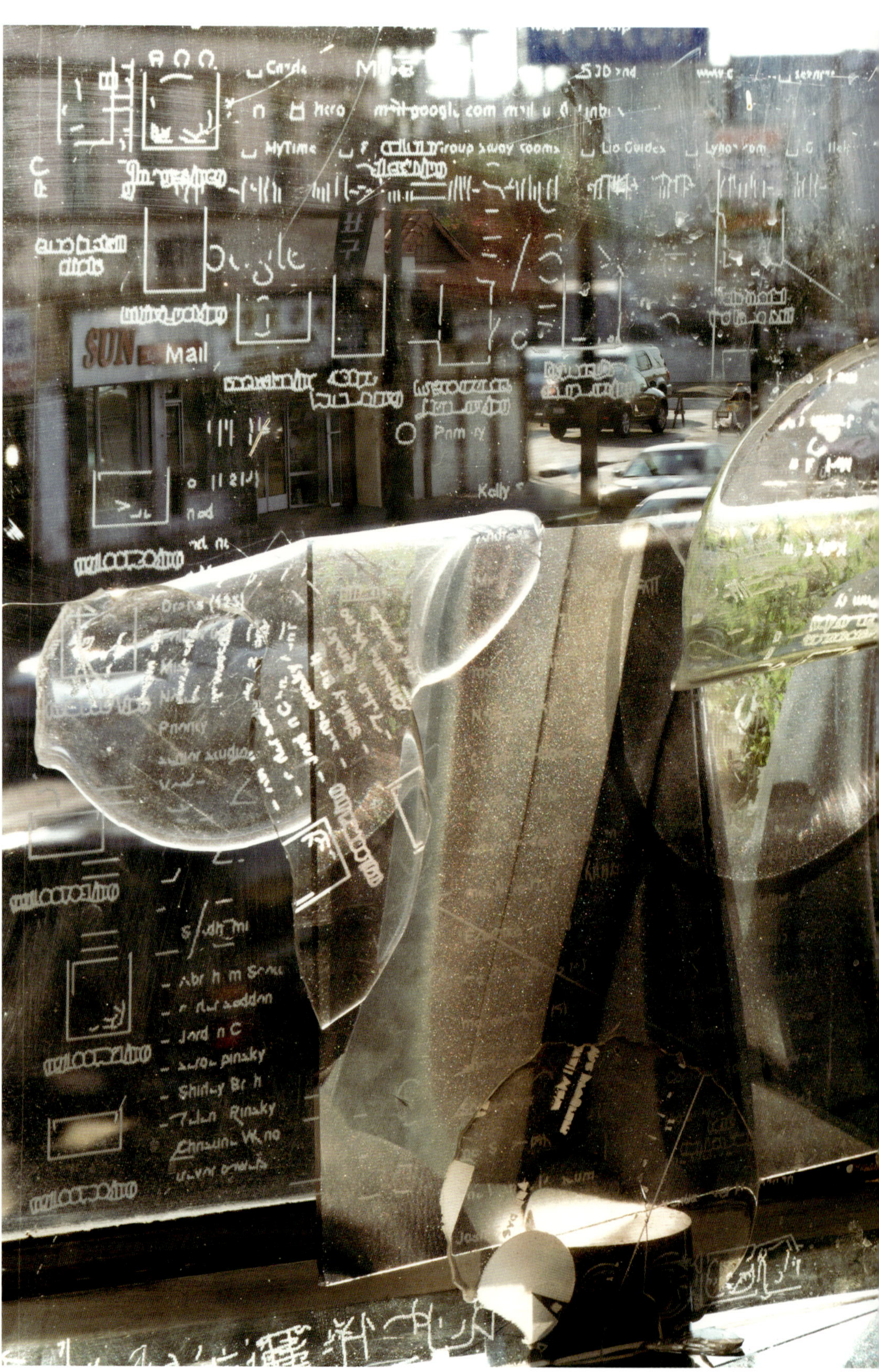

42    Marina Pinsky, *Untitled*, 2013. Archival inkjet print

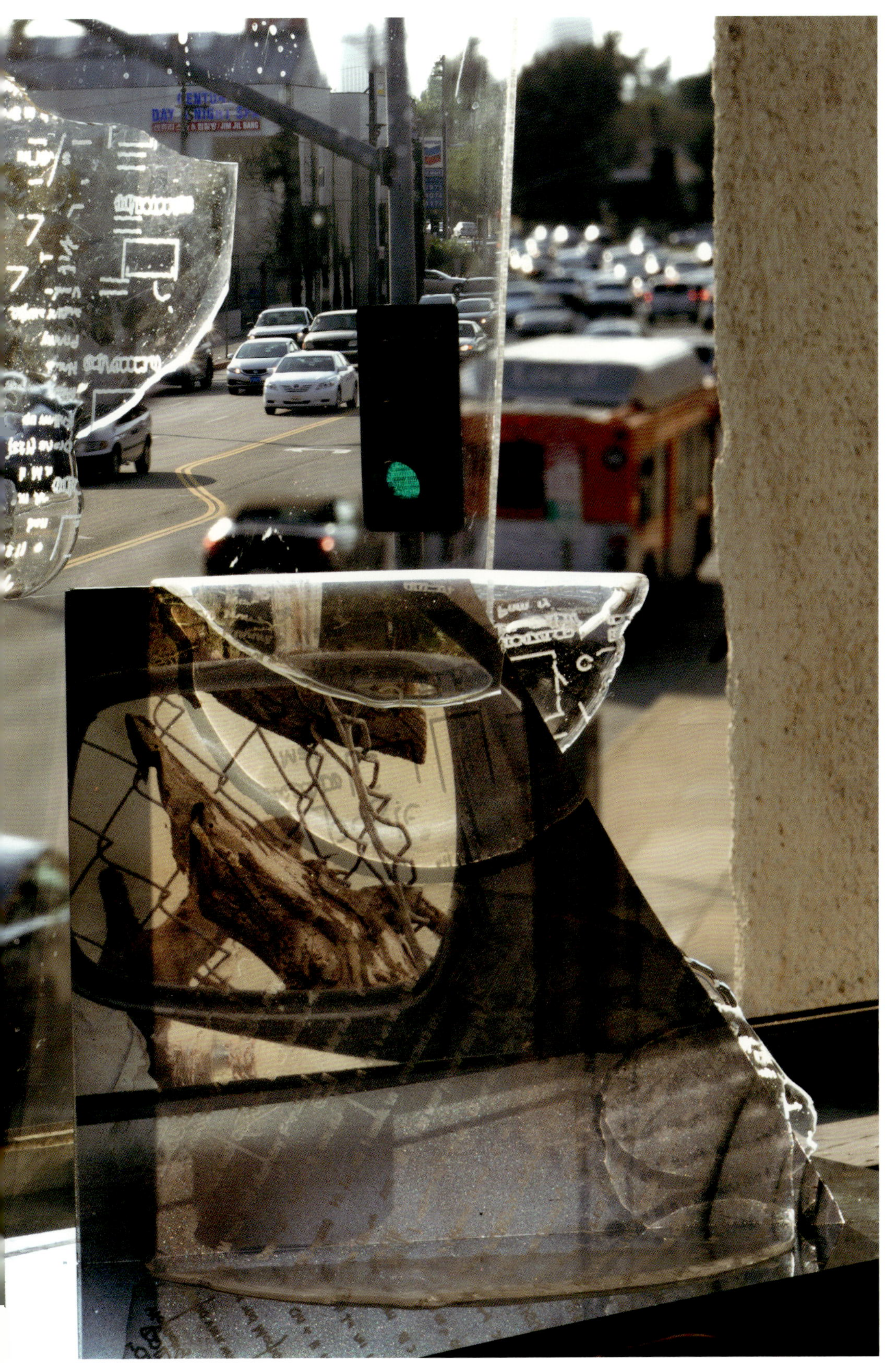

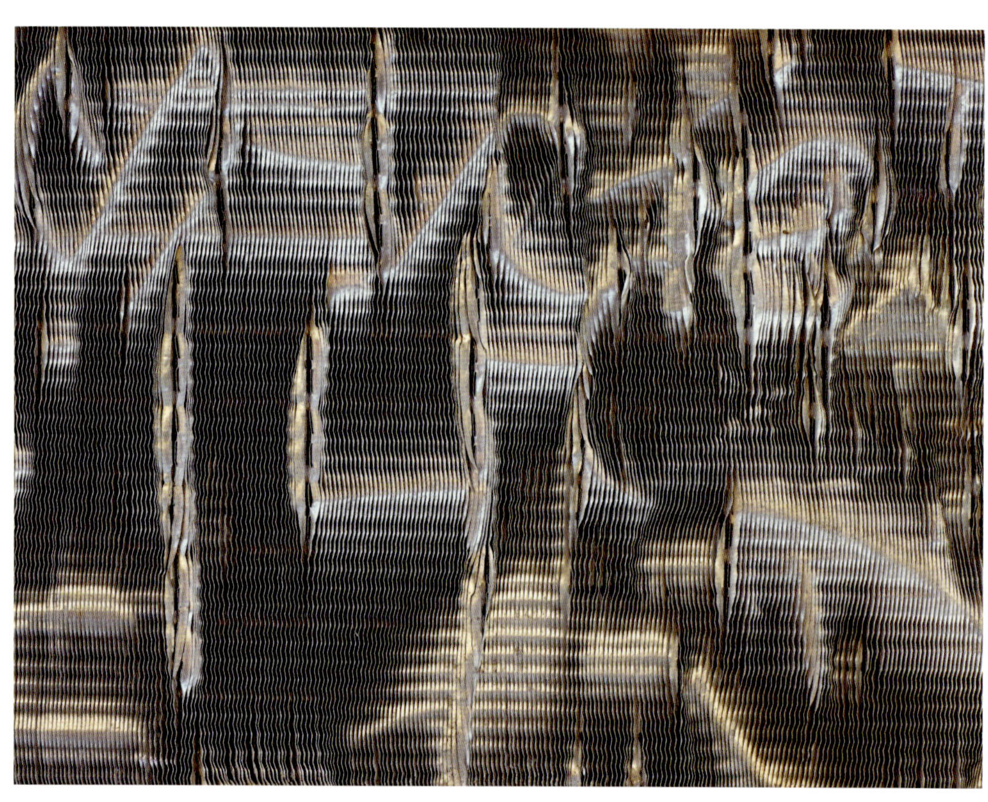

44     John Lehr, *Grate*, 2012, from the series *Low Relief*. Pigmented inkjet print

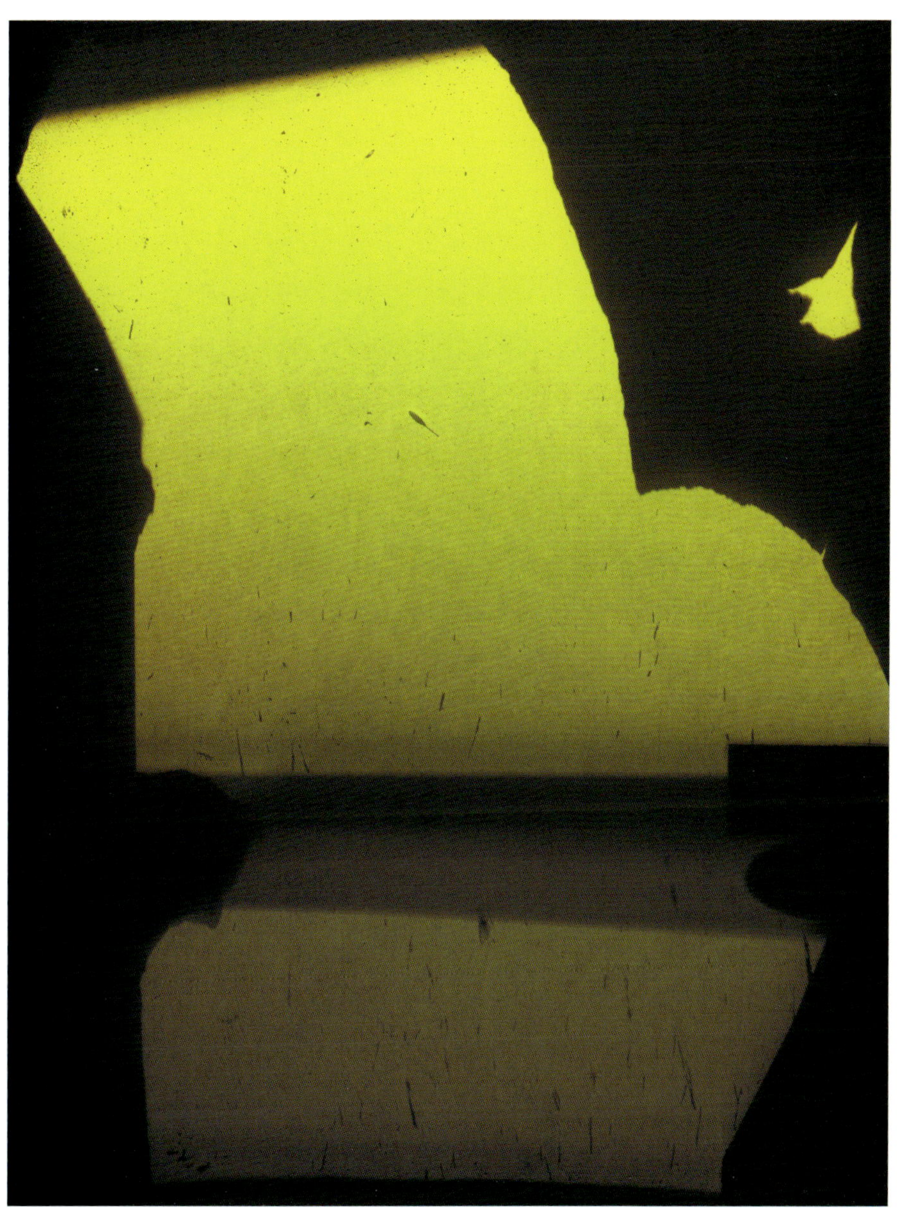

45      John Lehr, *Vacancy Film*, 2014, from the series *Low Relief*. Pigmented inkjet print

46   John Lehr, *Untitled*, 2012, from the series *Low Relief*. Pigmented inkjet print

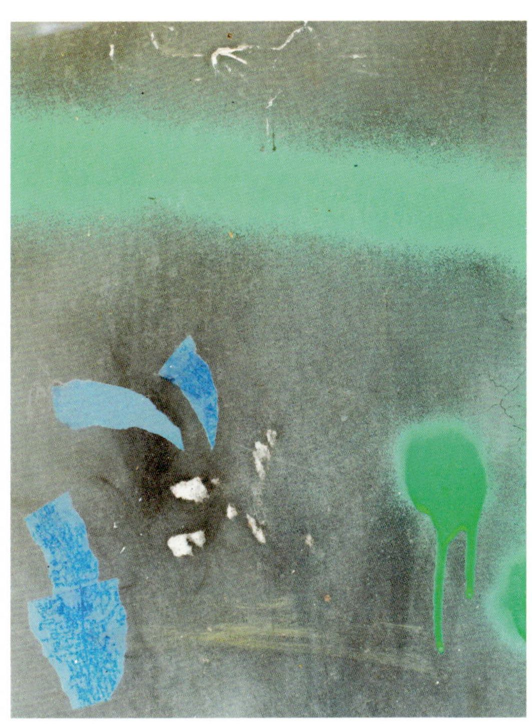

47    John Lehr, *Office Door*, 2012, from the series *Low Relief*. Pigmented inkjet print

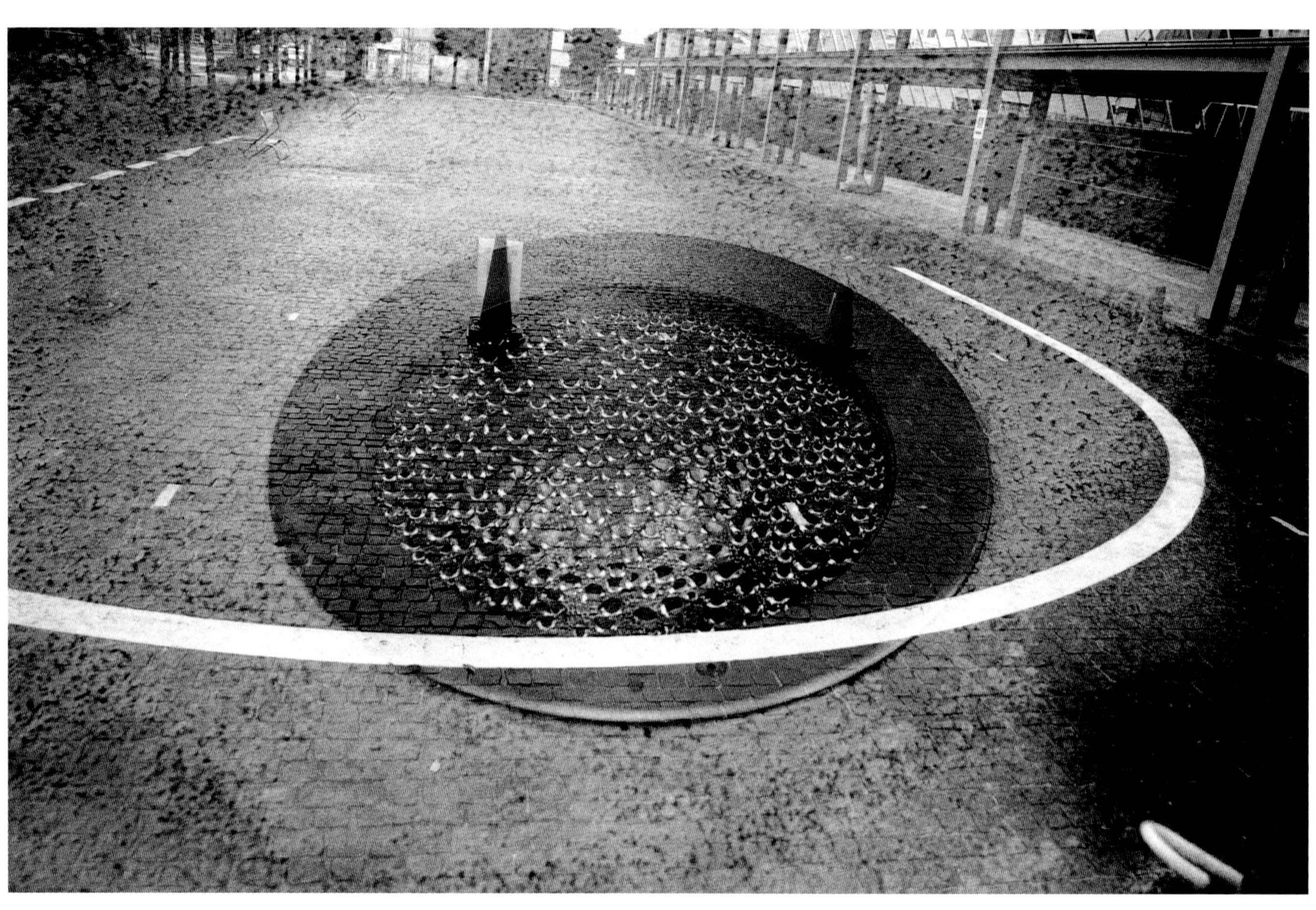

48    Jason Evans, *Untitled*, from the series *NYLPT*, 2005–12. Various formats

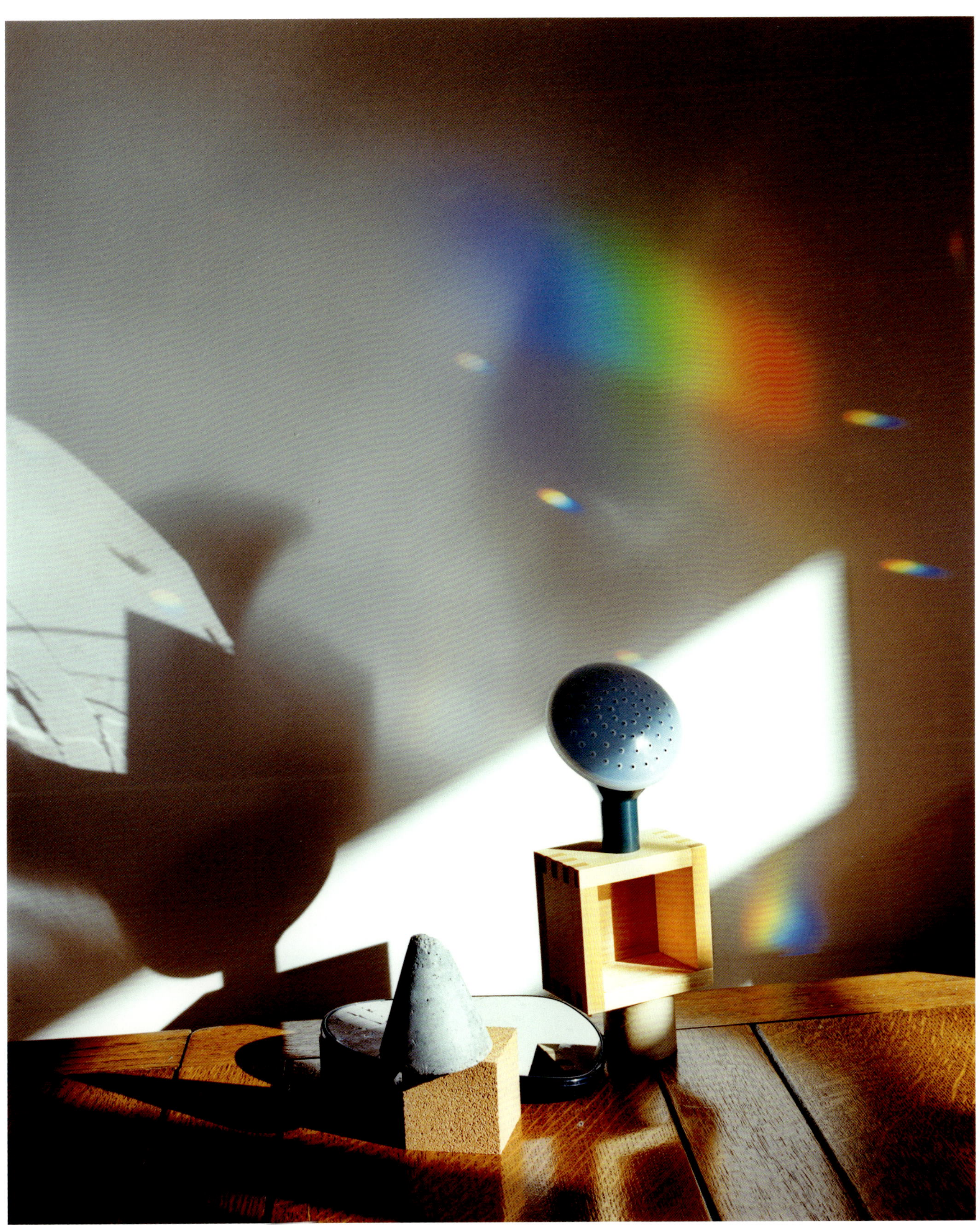

49    Jason Evans, *Untitled*, from the series *Pictures for Looking At*, 2007–12. Various formats

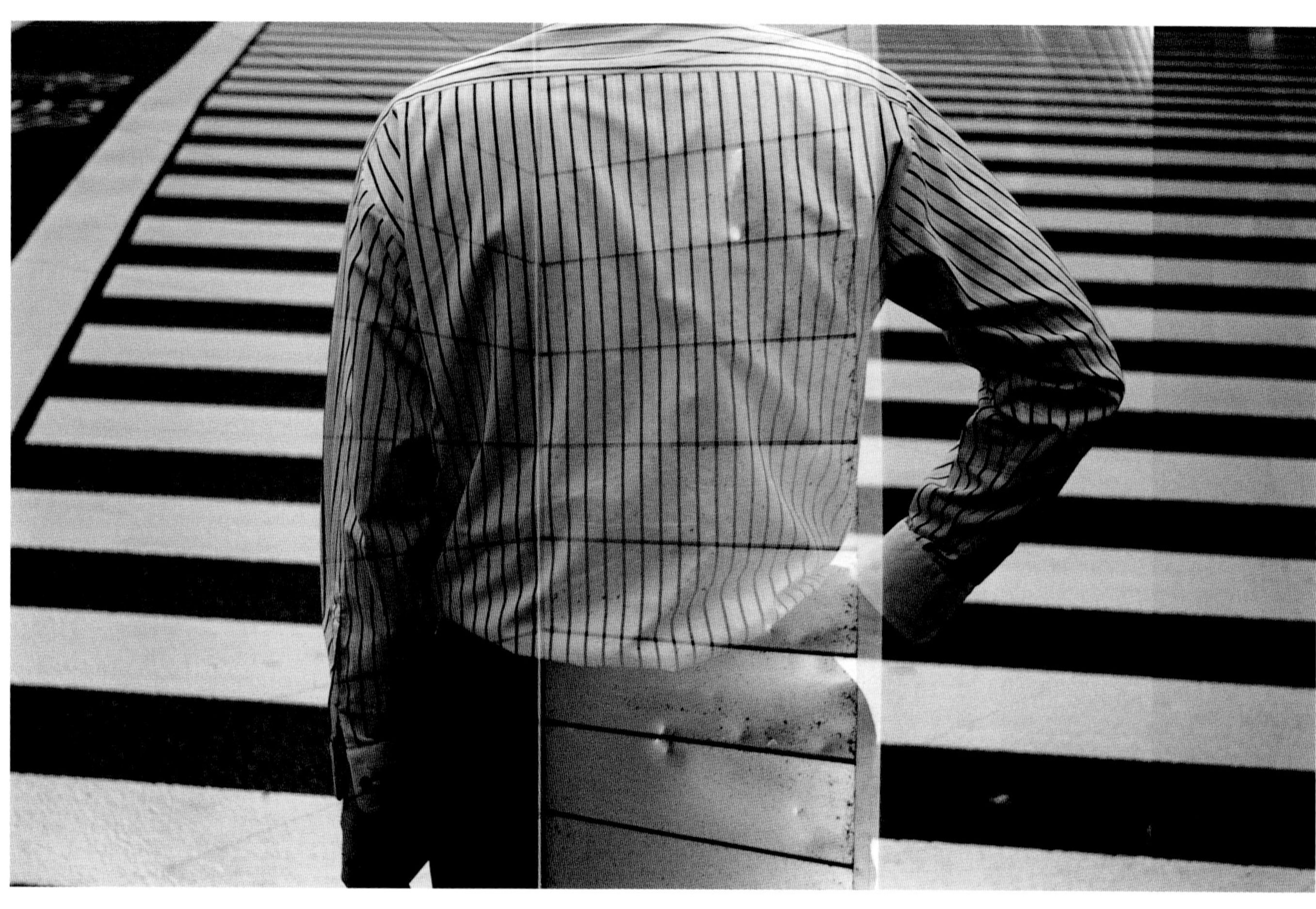

50    Jason Evans, *Untitled*, from the series *NYLPT*, 2005–12. Various formats

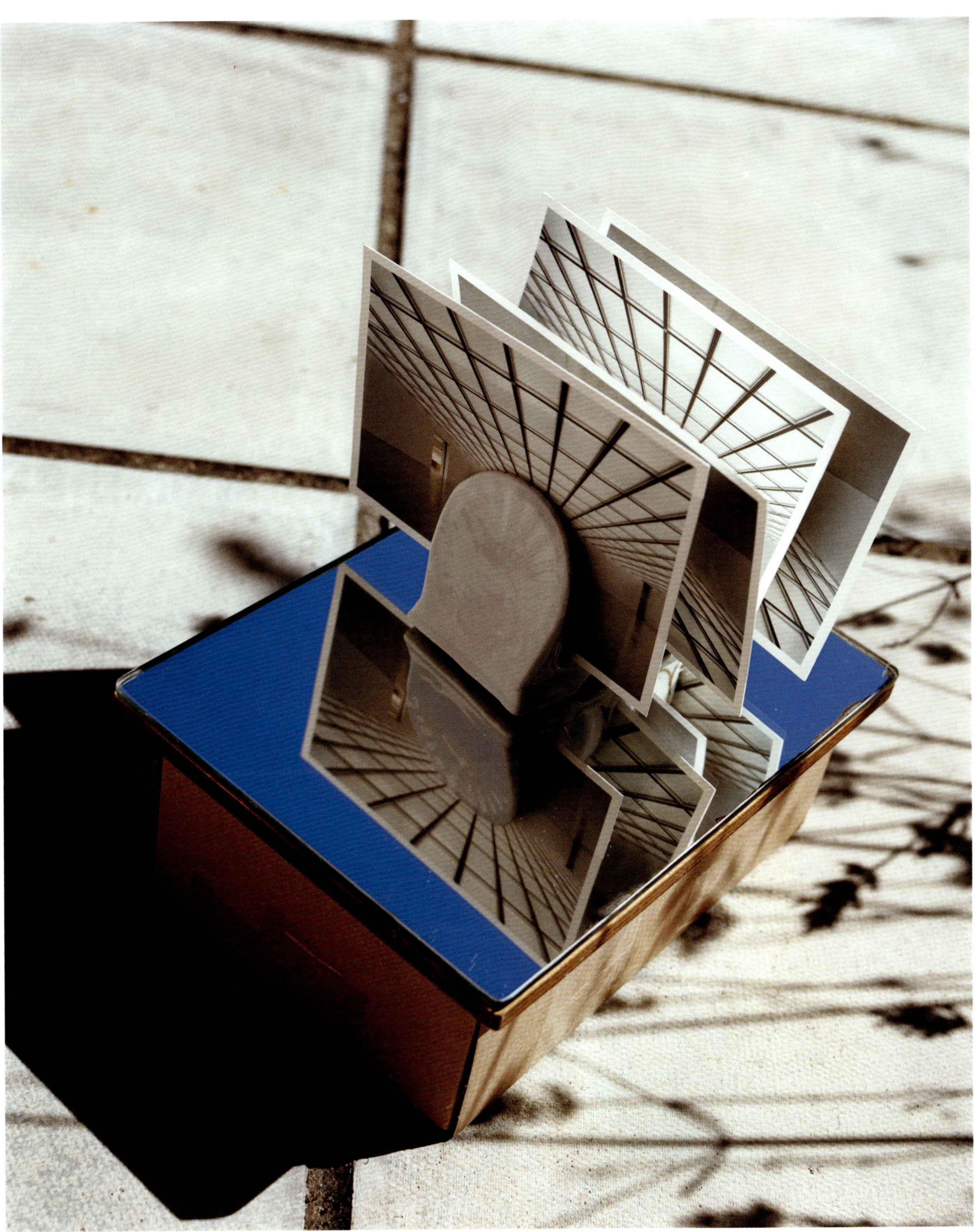

51    Jason Evans, *Untitled*, from the series *Pictures for Looking At*, 2007–12. Various formats

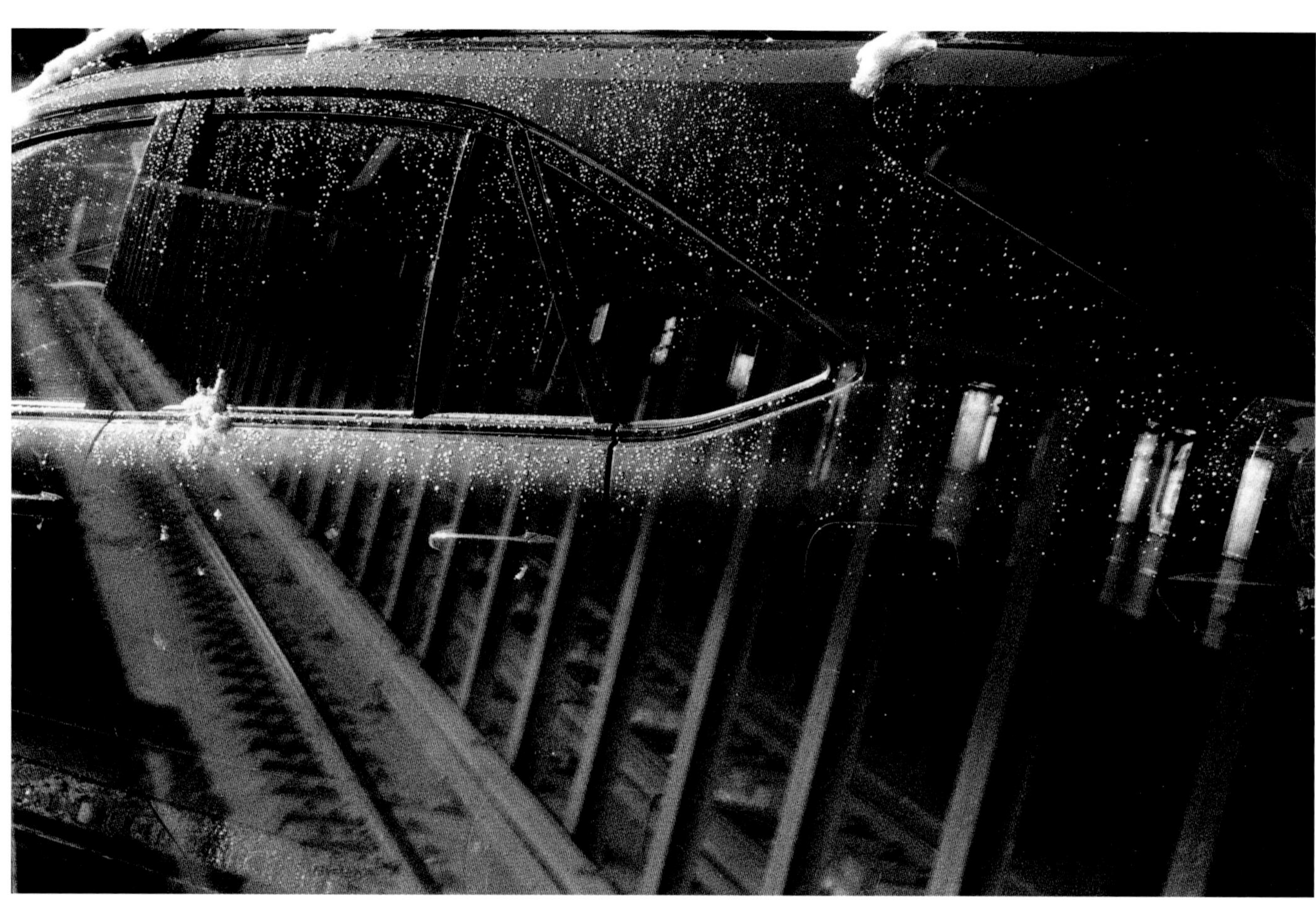

52    Jason Evans, *Untitled*, from the series *NYLPT*, 2005–12. Various formats

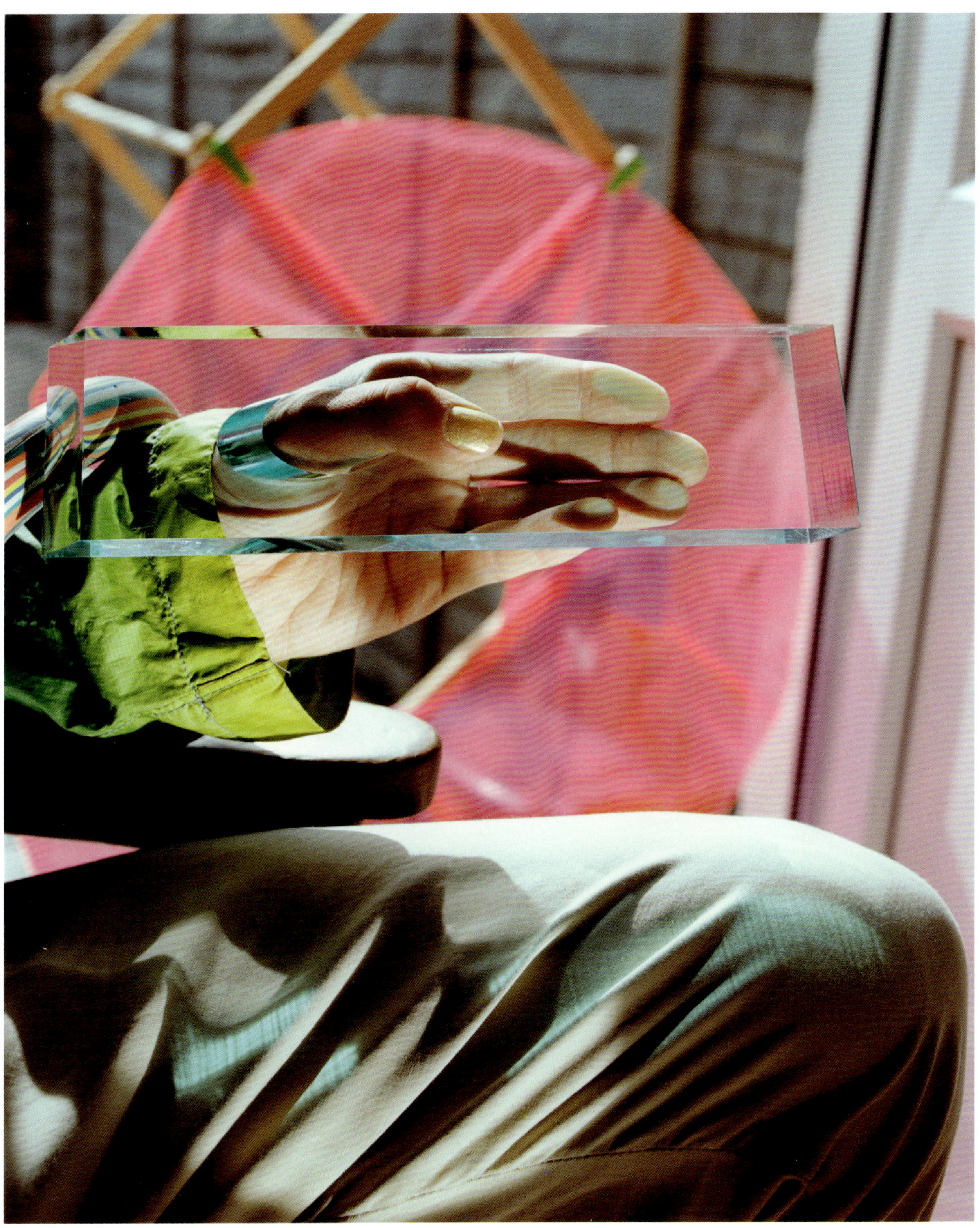

53    Jason Evans, *Untitled*, from the series *Pictures for Looking At*, 2007–12. Various formats

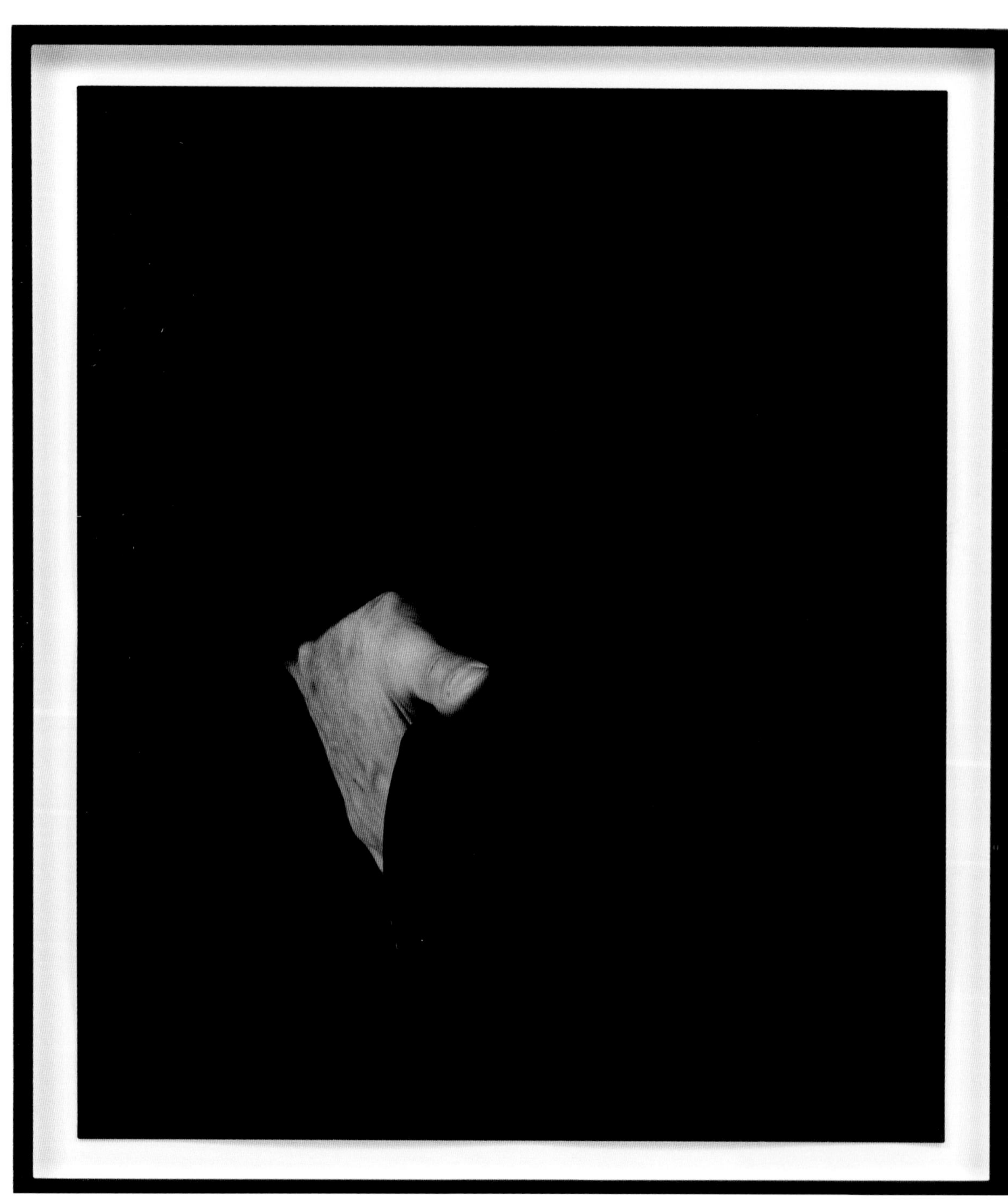

54    Talia Chetrit, *Hand on Body (Crotch #1)*, 2012. Gelatin-silver print

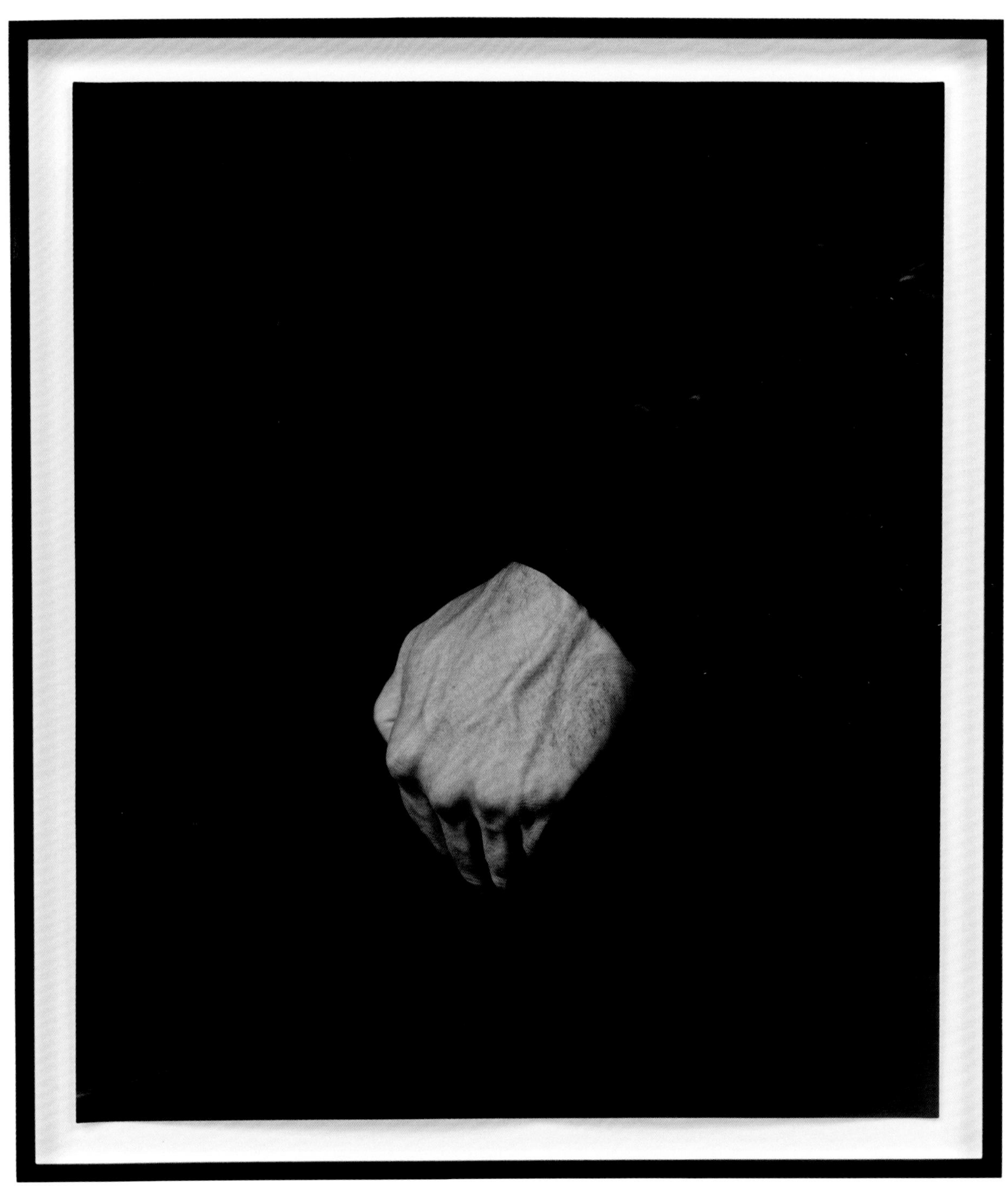

55    Talia Chetrit, *Hand on Body (Ass)*, 2012. Gelatin-silver print

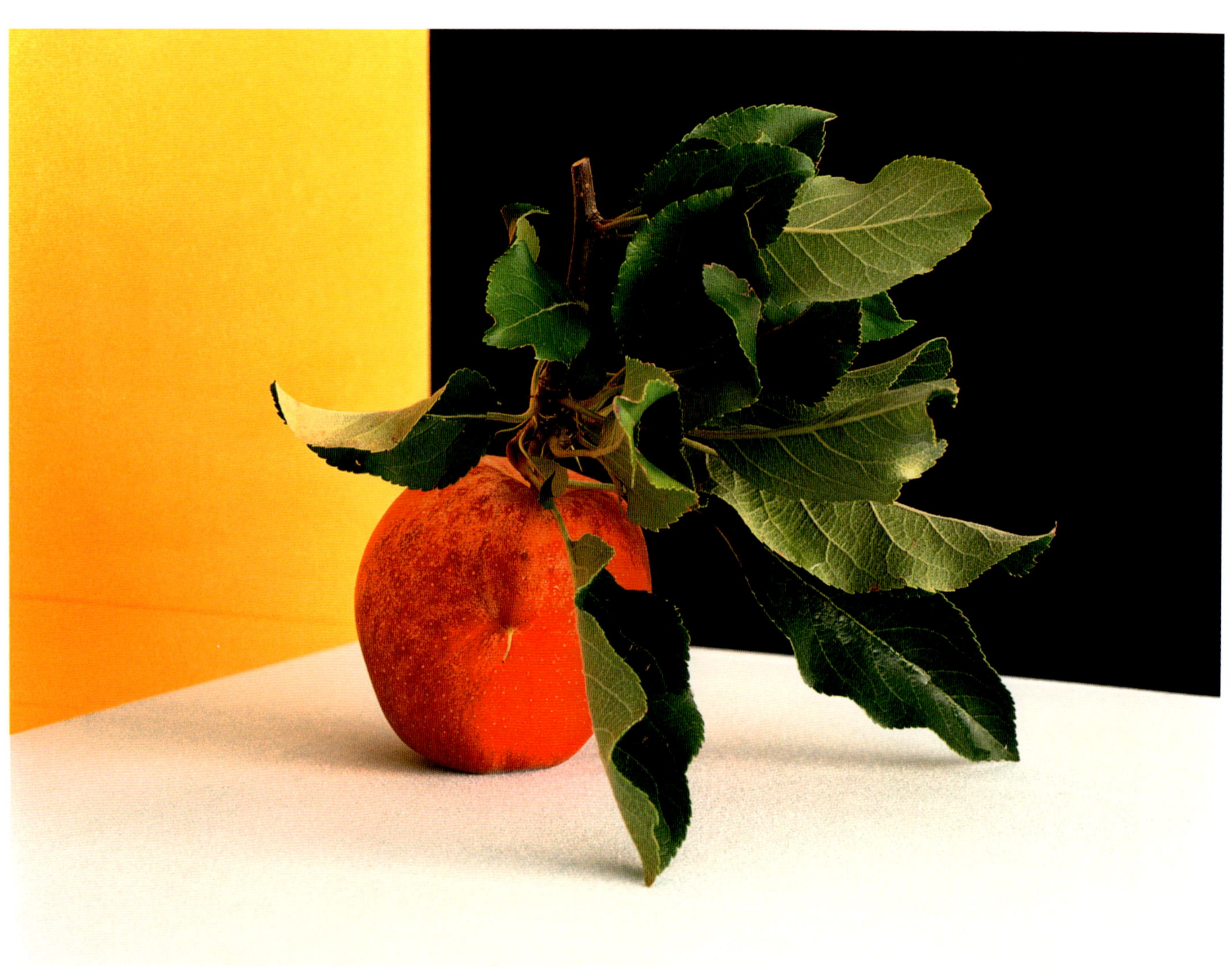

56    Shirana Shahbazi, *Frucht* 07-2009 (Fruit 07-2009), 2009. C-print on aluminum

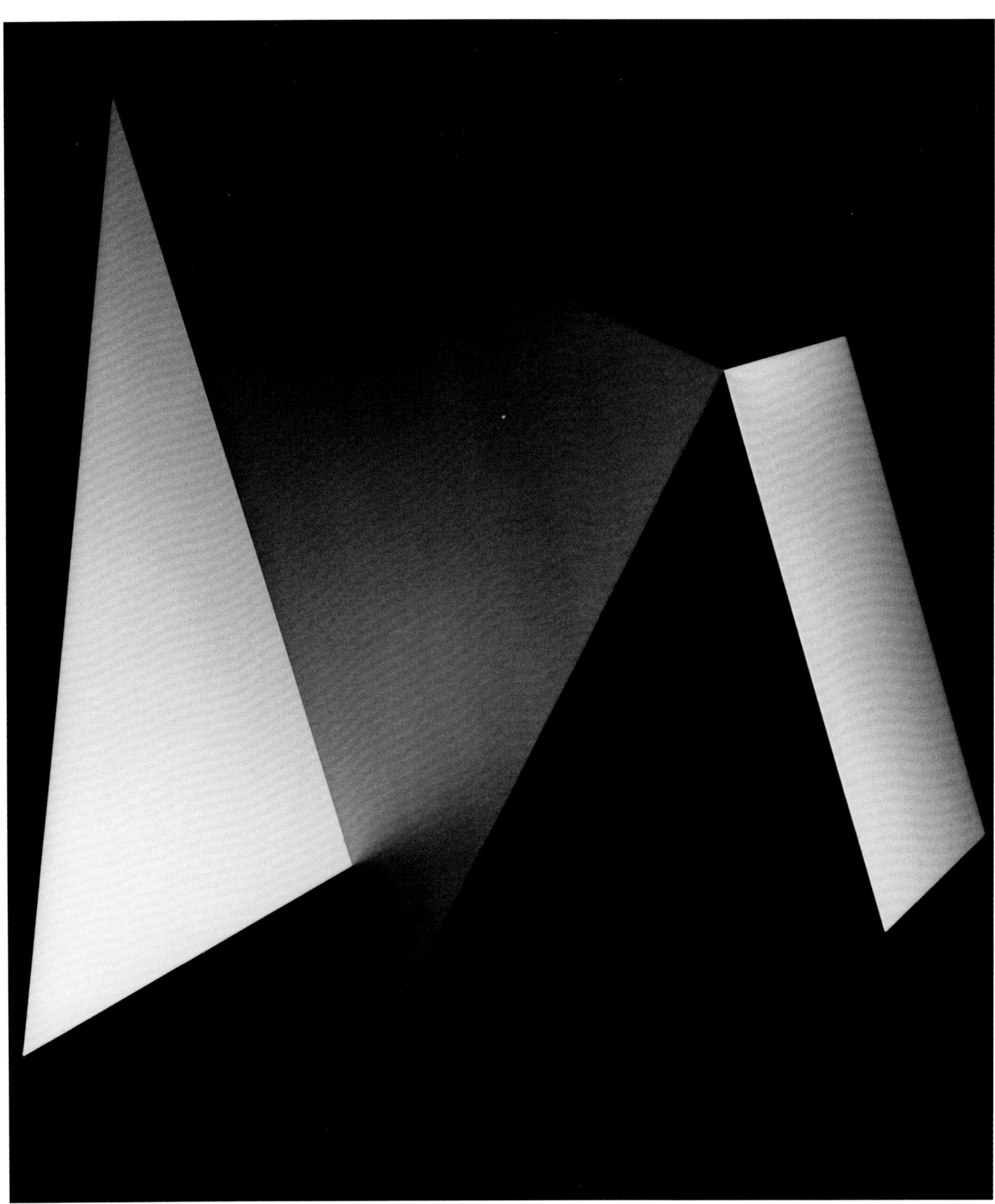

  Shirana Shahbazi, *Objekt 27-2013* (Object 27-2013), 2013. Gelatin-silver print on aluminum

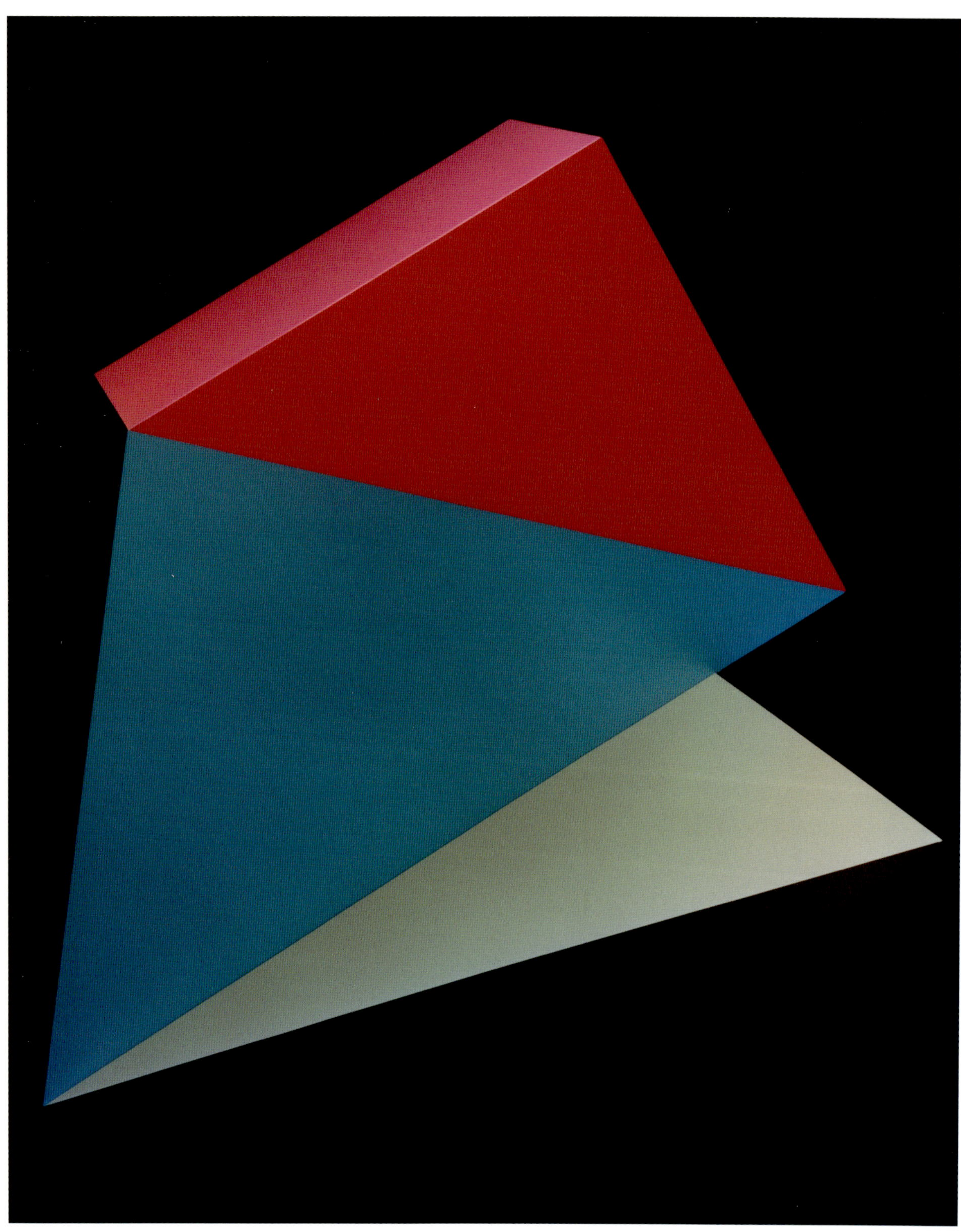

58    Shirana Shahbazi, *Objekt 24-2013* (Object 24-2013), 2013. C-print on aluminum

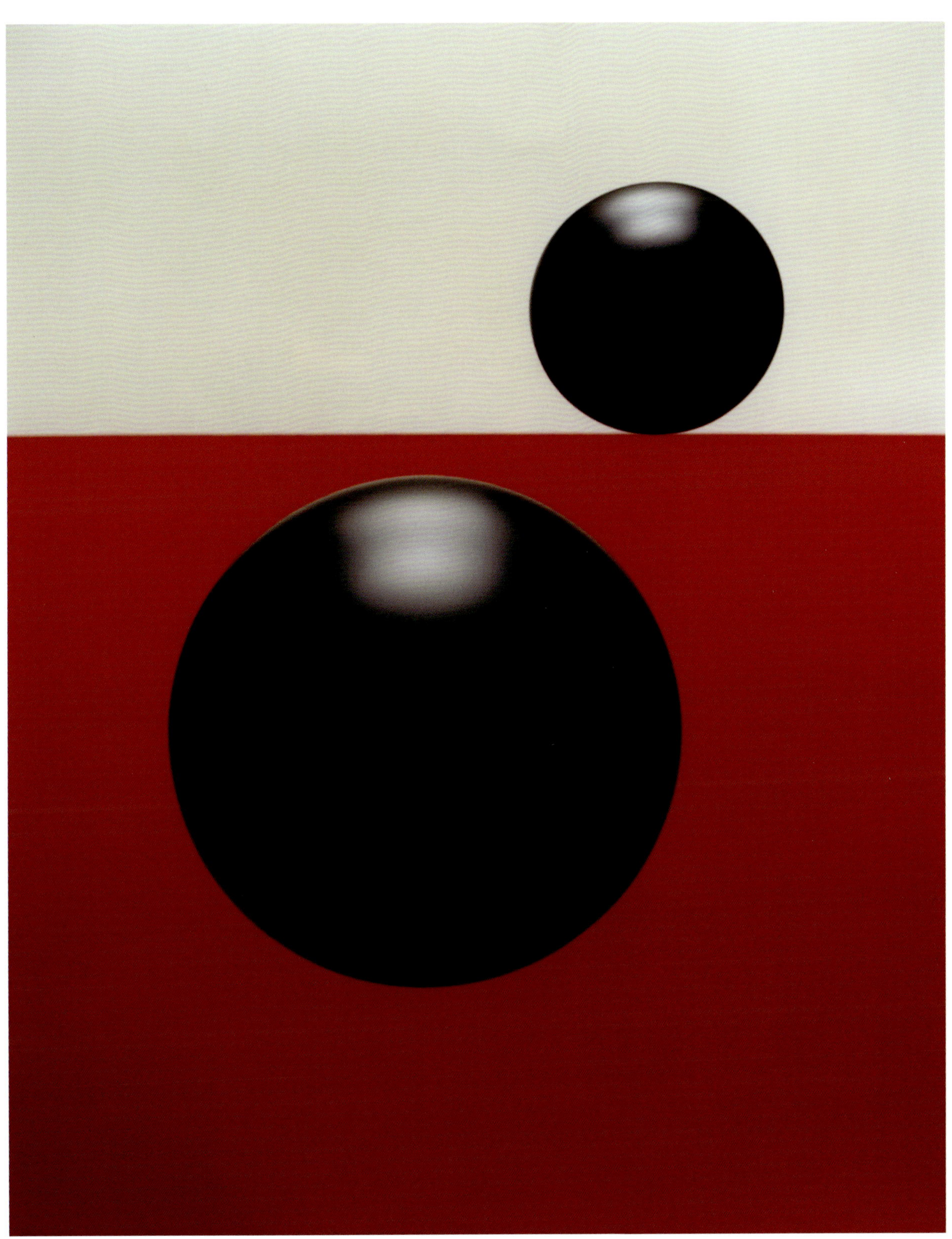

59    Shirana Shahbazi, *Kugel 02-2013* (Ball 02-2013), 2013. C-print on aluminum

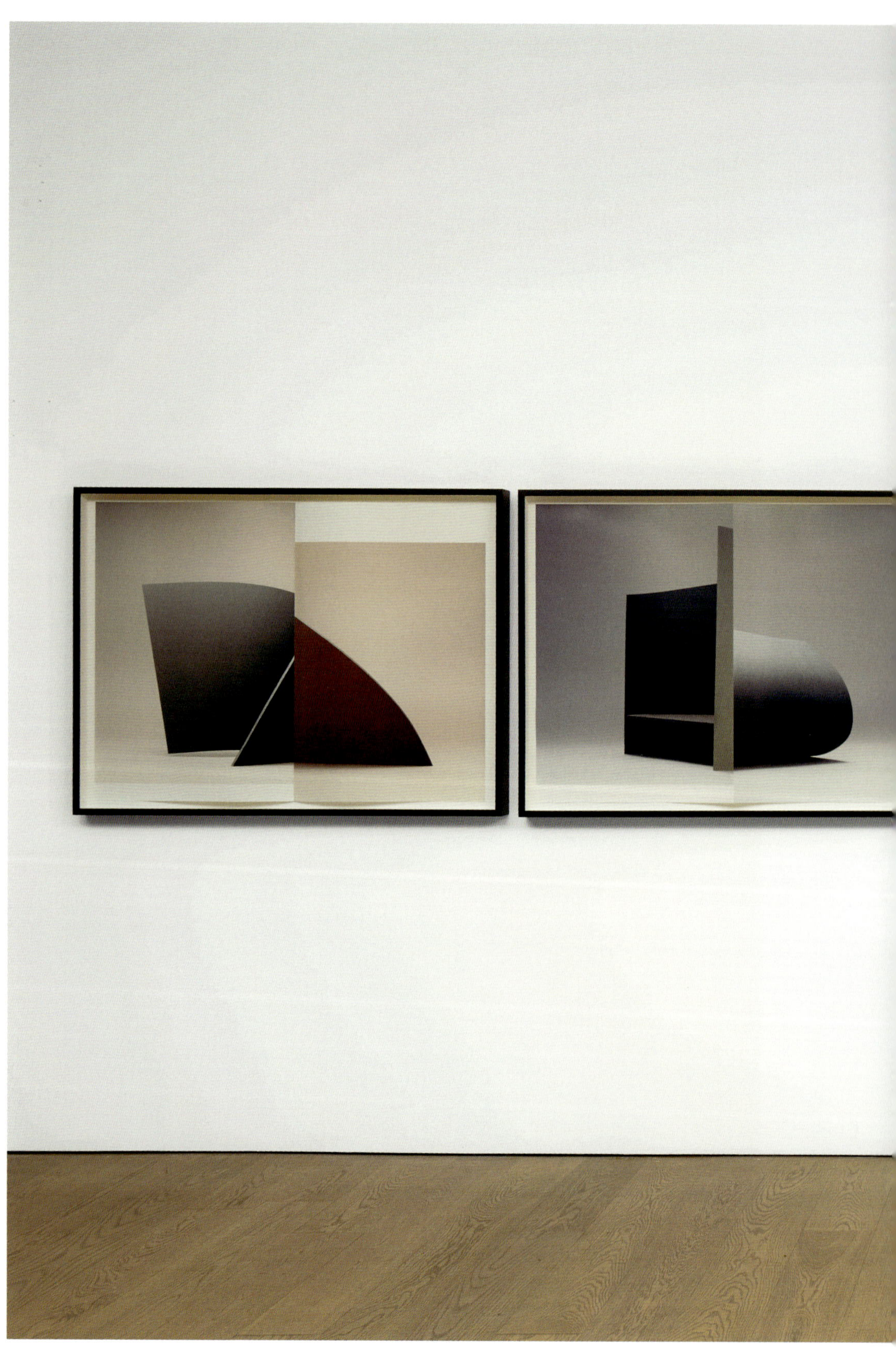

    Erin Shirreff, *Monograph (no. 4)*, 2014. Five archival pigment prints

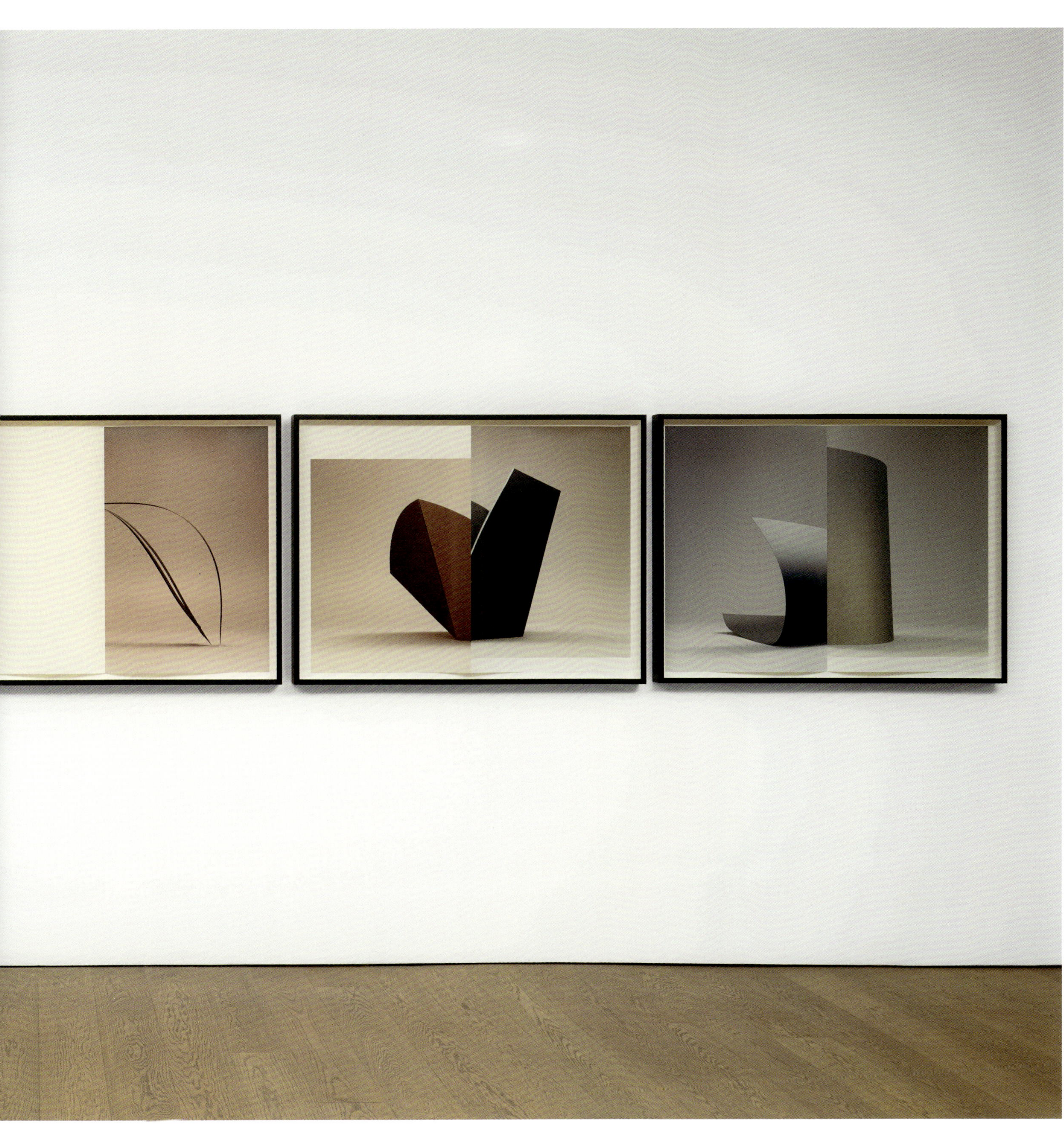

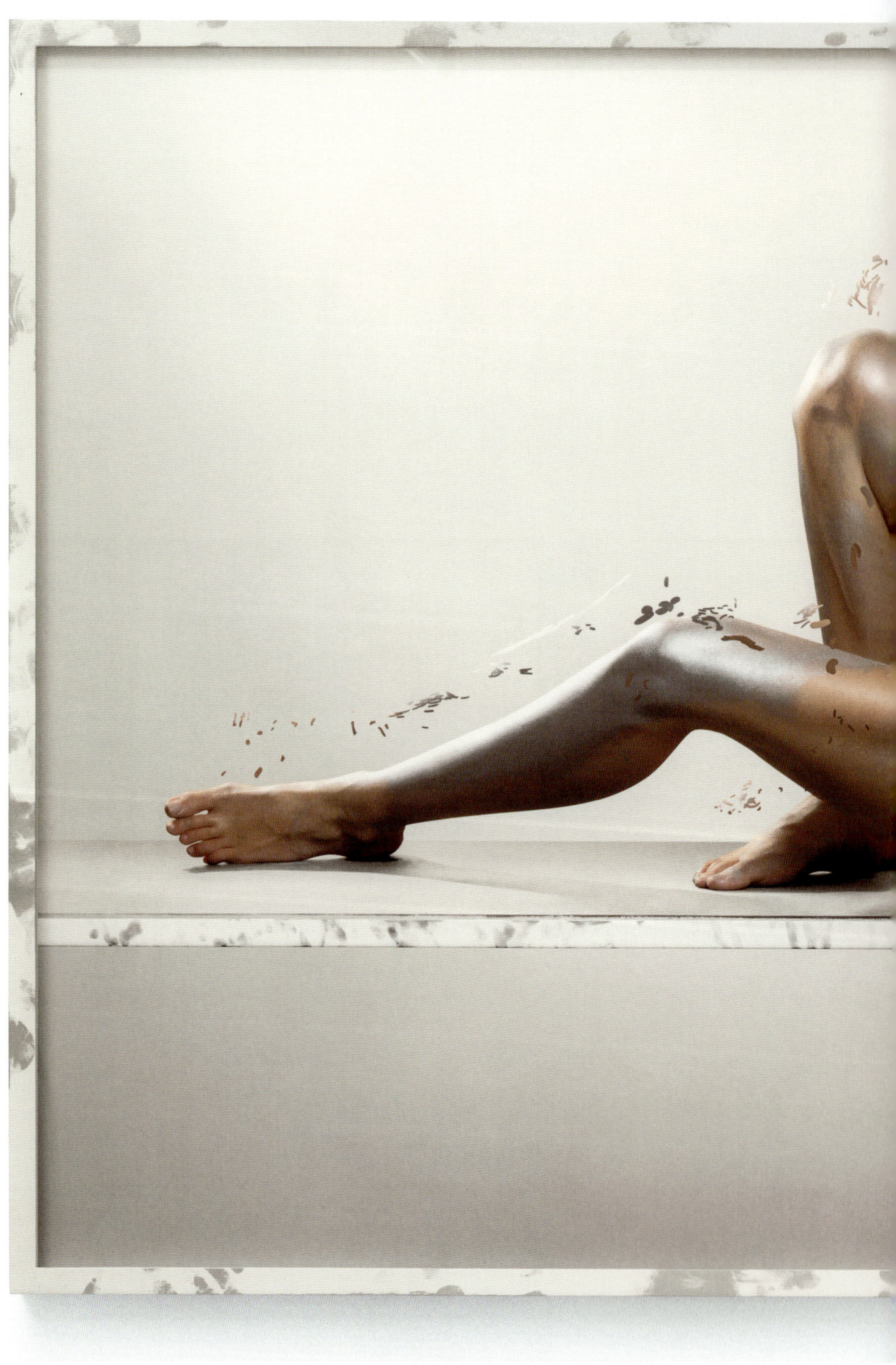

62    Joshua Citarella, *Body Anointed with Nitroglycerin Awaits Transfiguration*, 2013. C-print, frame, nitroglycerin

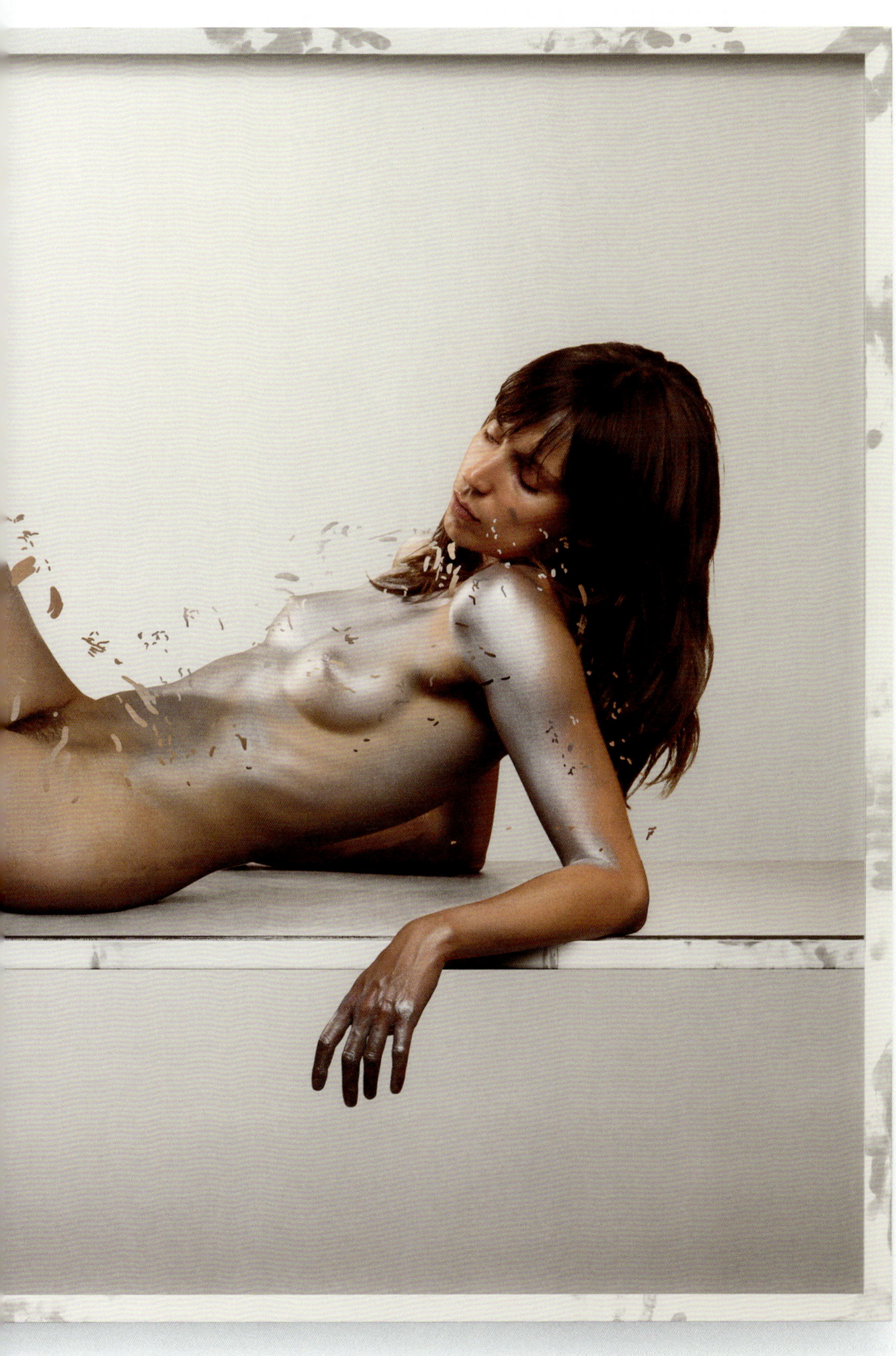

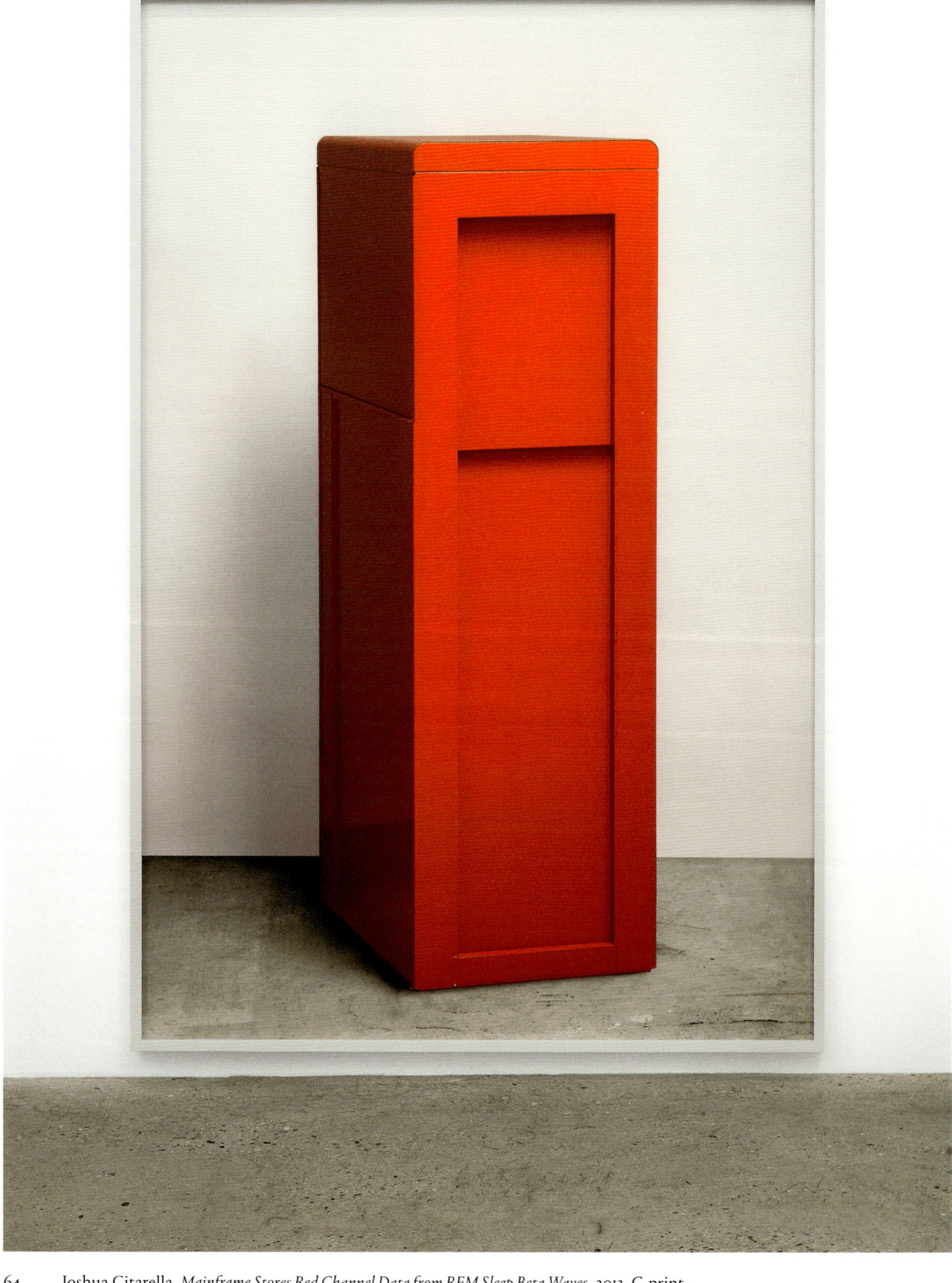

64    Joshua Citarella, *Mainframe Stores Red Channel Data from REM Sleep Beta Waves*, 2013. C-print

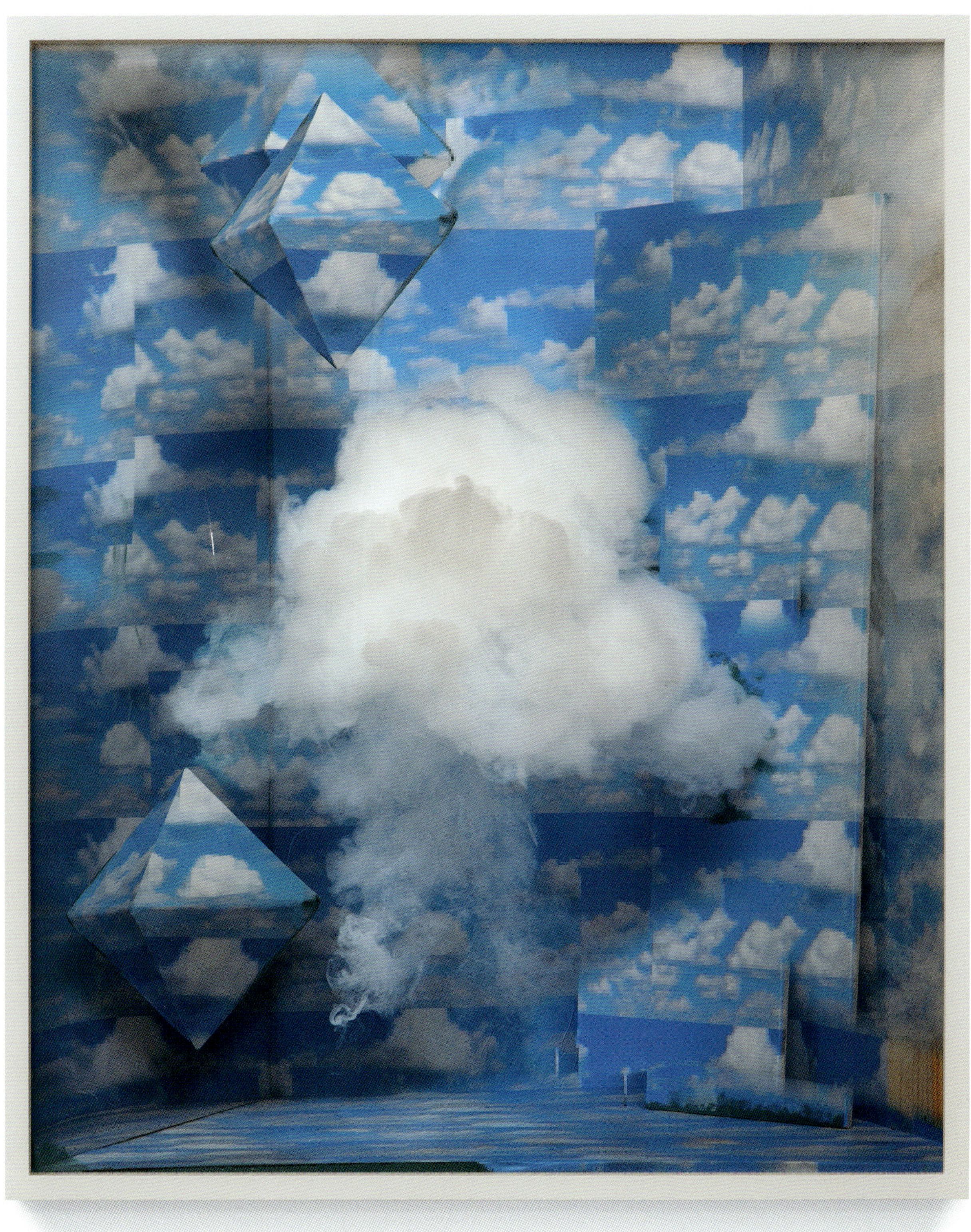

65    Joshua Citarella, *Render and Difference*, 2013. C-print

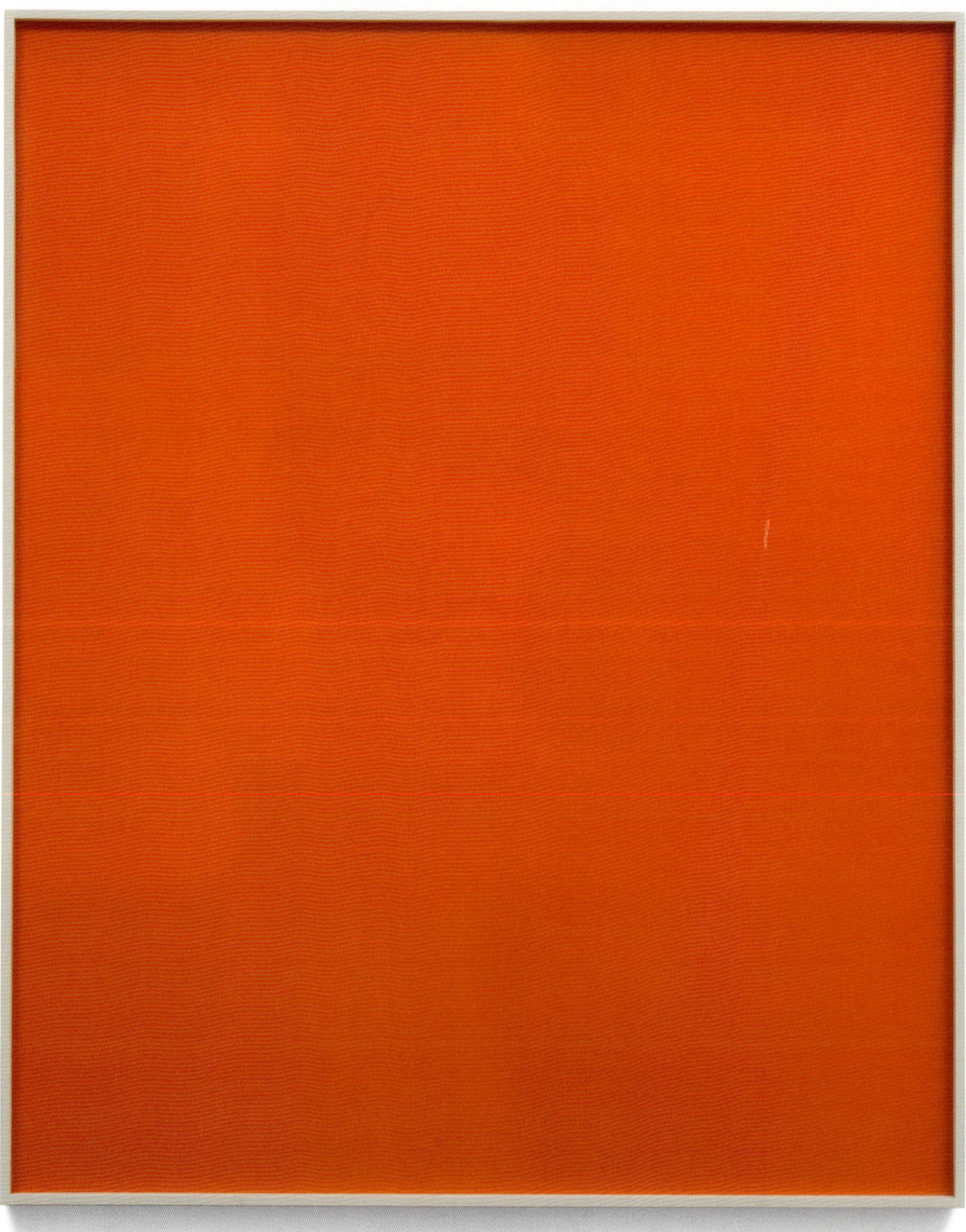

66 Phil Chang, *Untitled (Orange Monochrome)*, 2014. Unique C-print

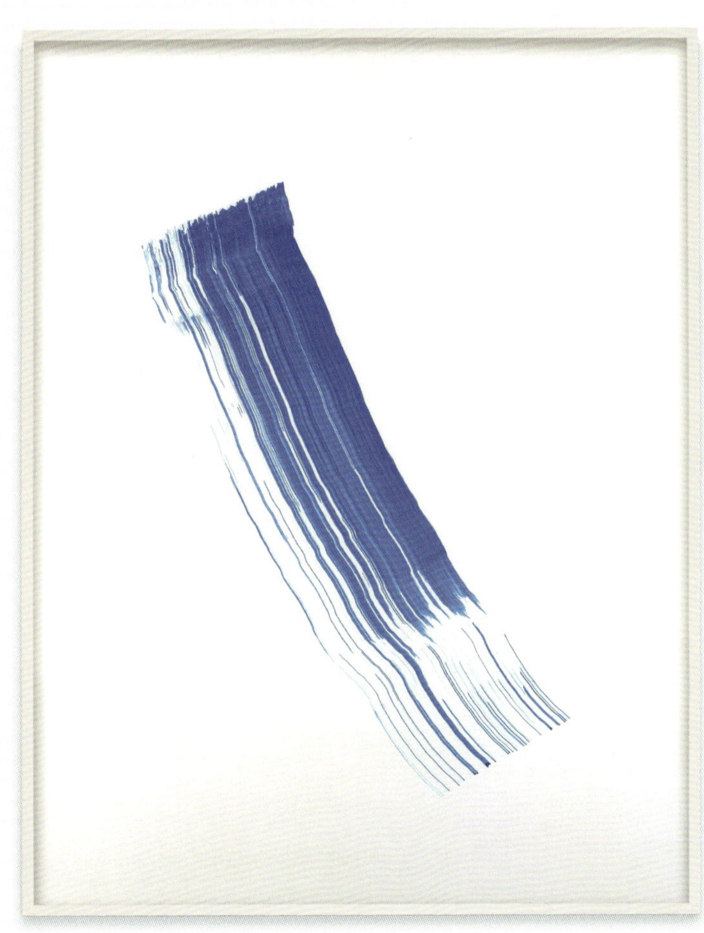

 Phil Chang, *Replacement Ink for Epson Printers (Cyan 131901) on Museo Silver Rag Paper*, 2013. Unique archival pigment print

    Phil Chang, *Untitled (50% Gray Monochrome)*, 2014. Unique C-print

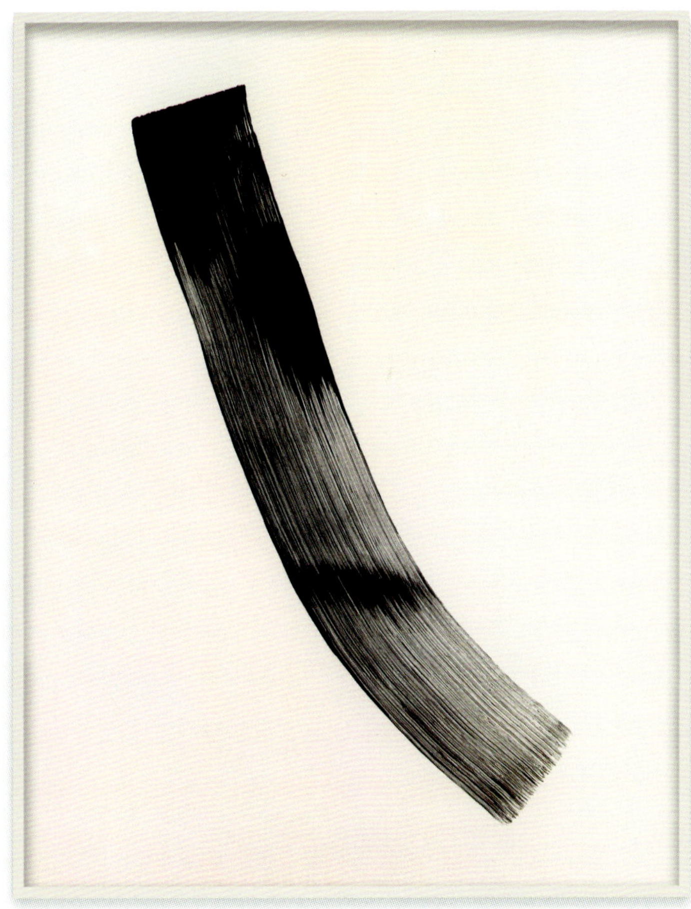

69    Phil Chang, *Replacement Ink for Epson Printers (Black 172203) on Epson Premium Luster Paper*, 2014. Unique archival pigment print

70    Phil Chang, *Untitled (Yellow Monochrome)*, 2014. Unique C-print

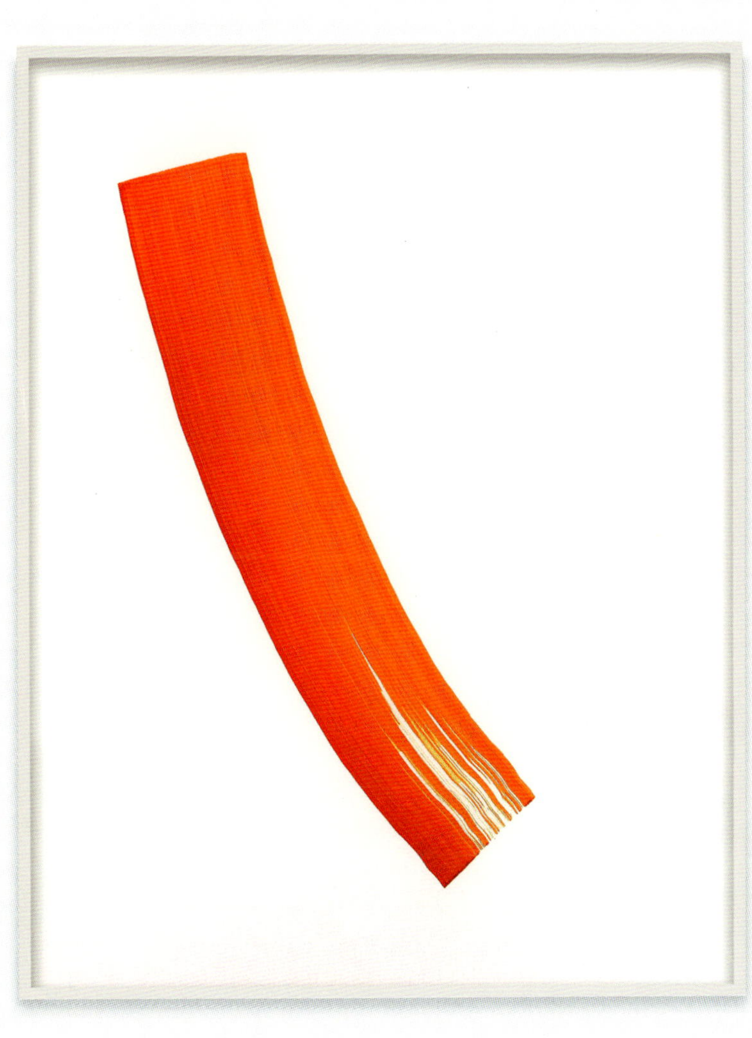

 Phil Chang, *Replacement Ink for Epson Printers (Red and Yellow 172201) on Canson PhotoSatin Premium RC Paper*, 2014.
Unique archival pigment print

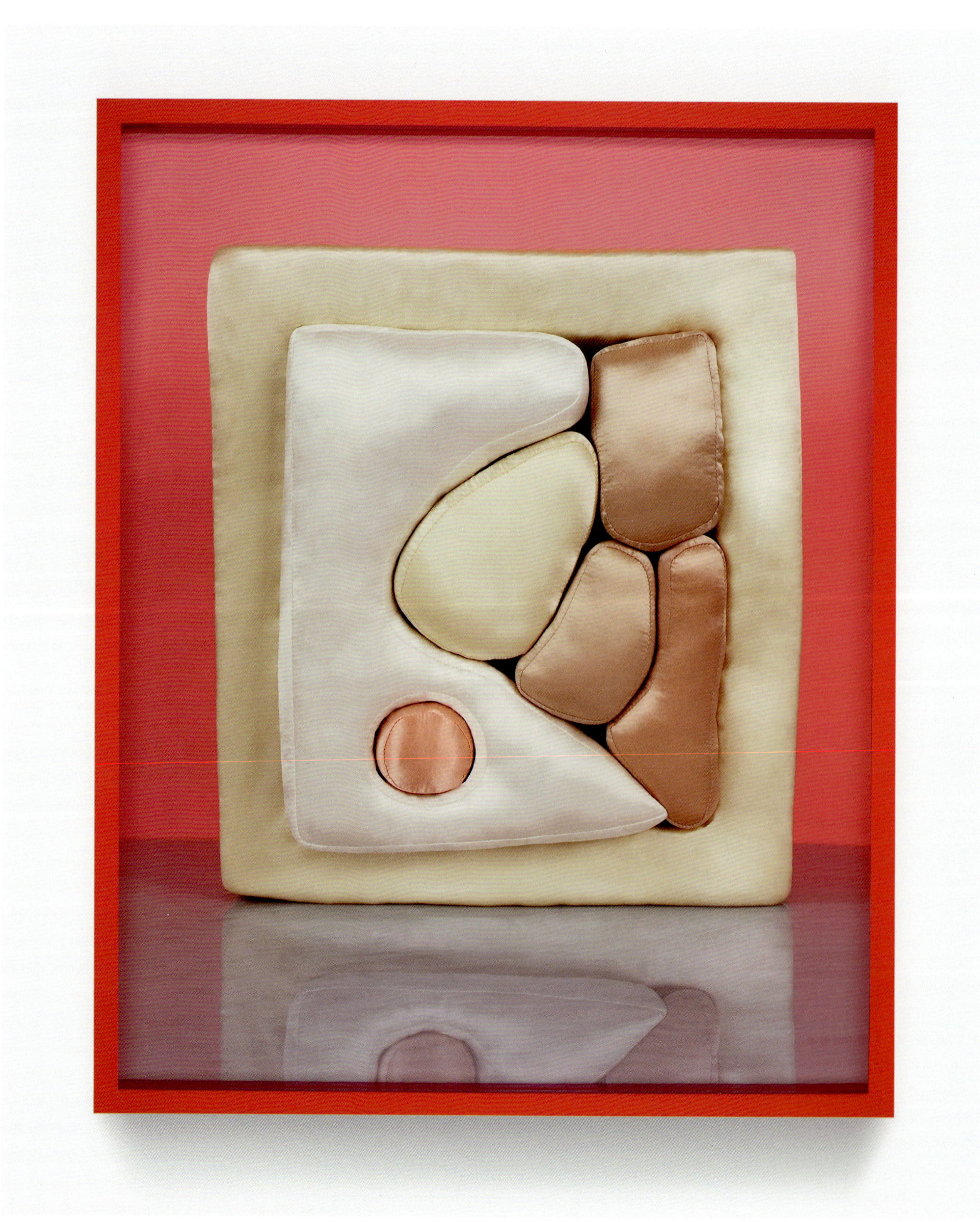

    Elad Lassry, *Pillow*, 2010. C-print, painted frame

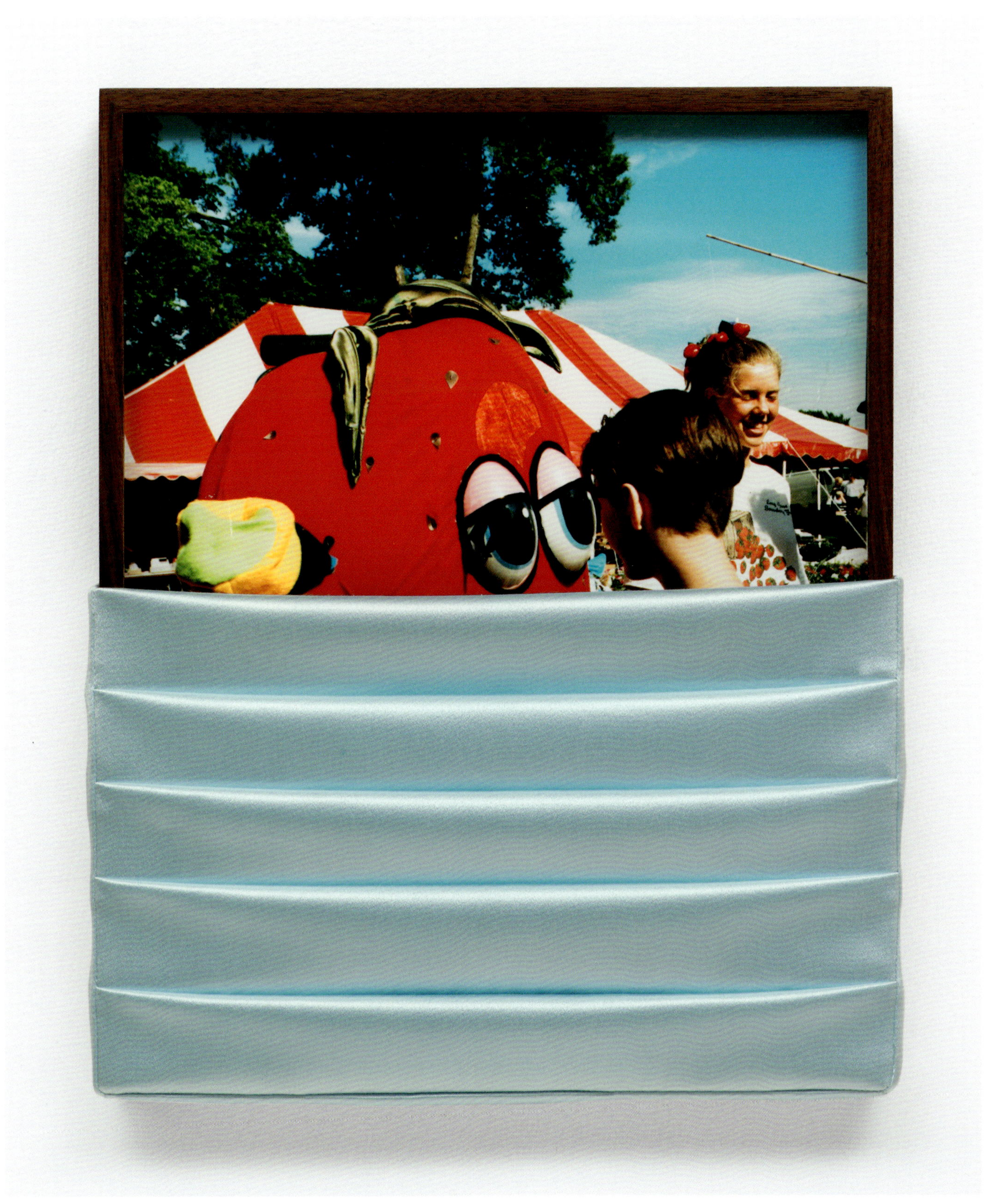

73    Elad Lassry, *Untitled (Strawberry, Kids)*, 2013. C-print, walnut frame, four-ply silk

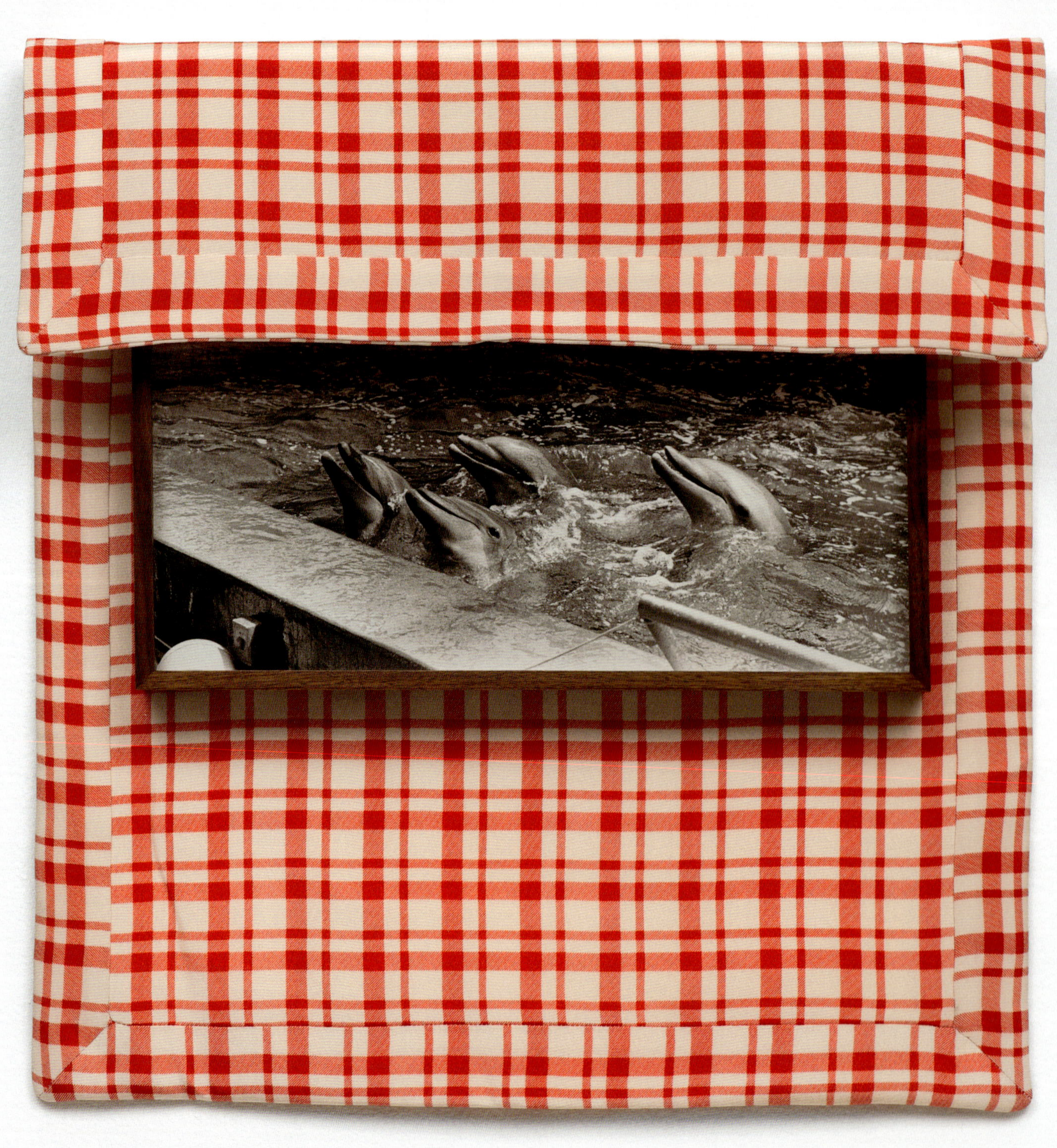

74    Elad Lassry, *Untitled (Dolphins)*, 2013. Gelatin-silver print, walnut frame, four-ply silk

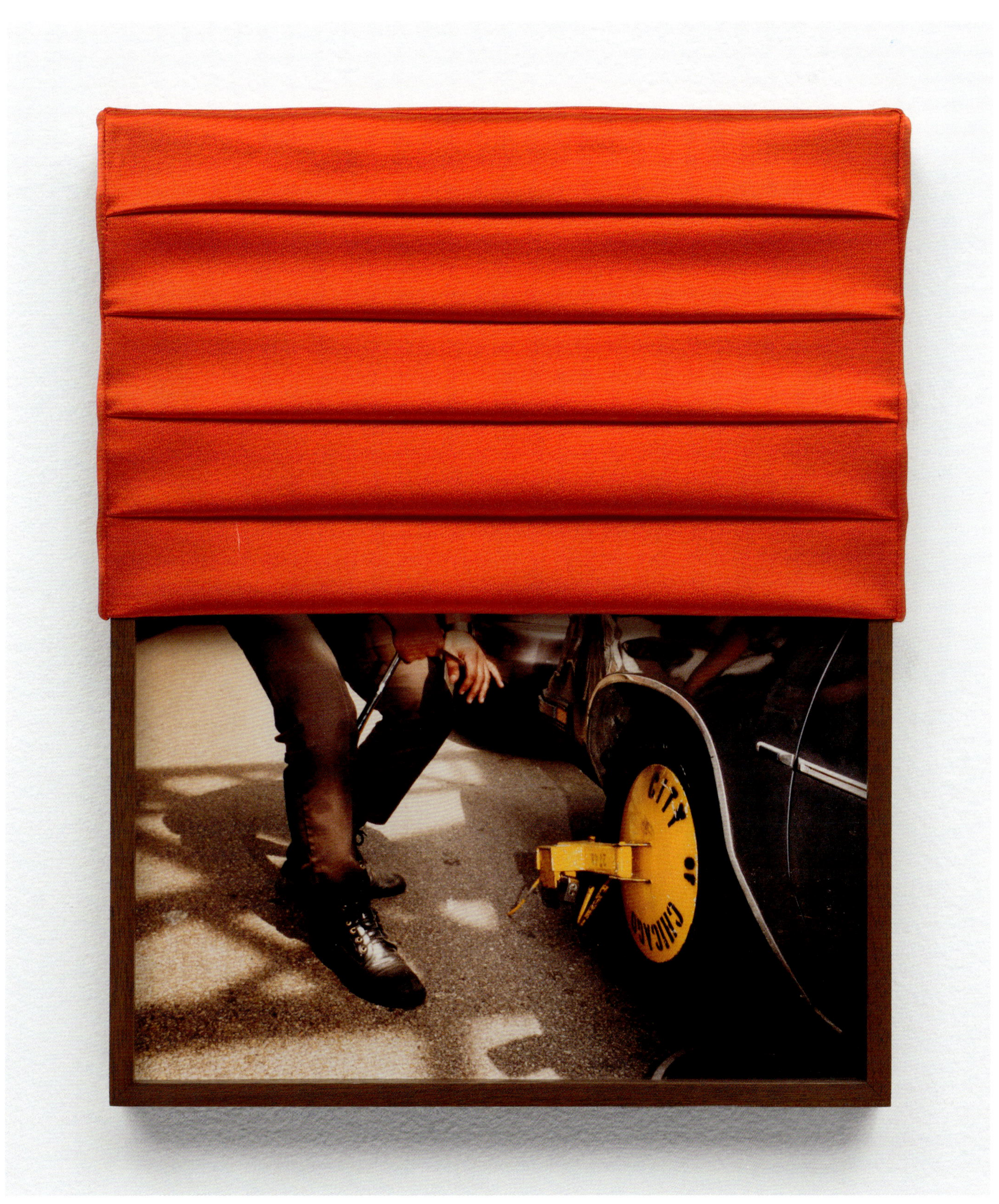



75    Elad Lassry, *Untitled (Boot)*, 2013. C-print, walnut frame, four-ply silk

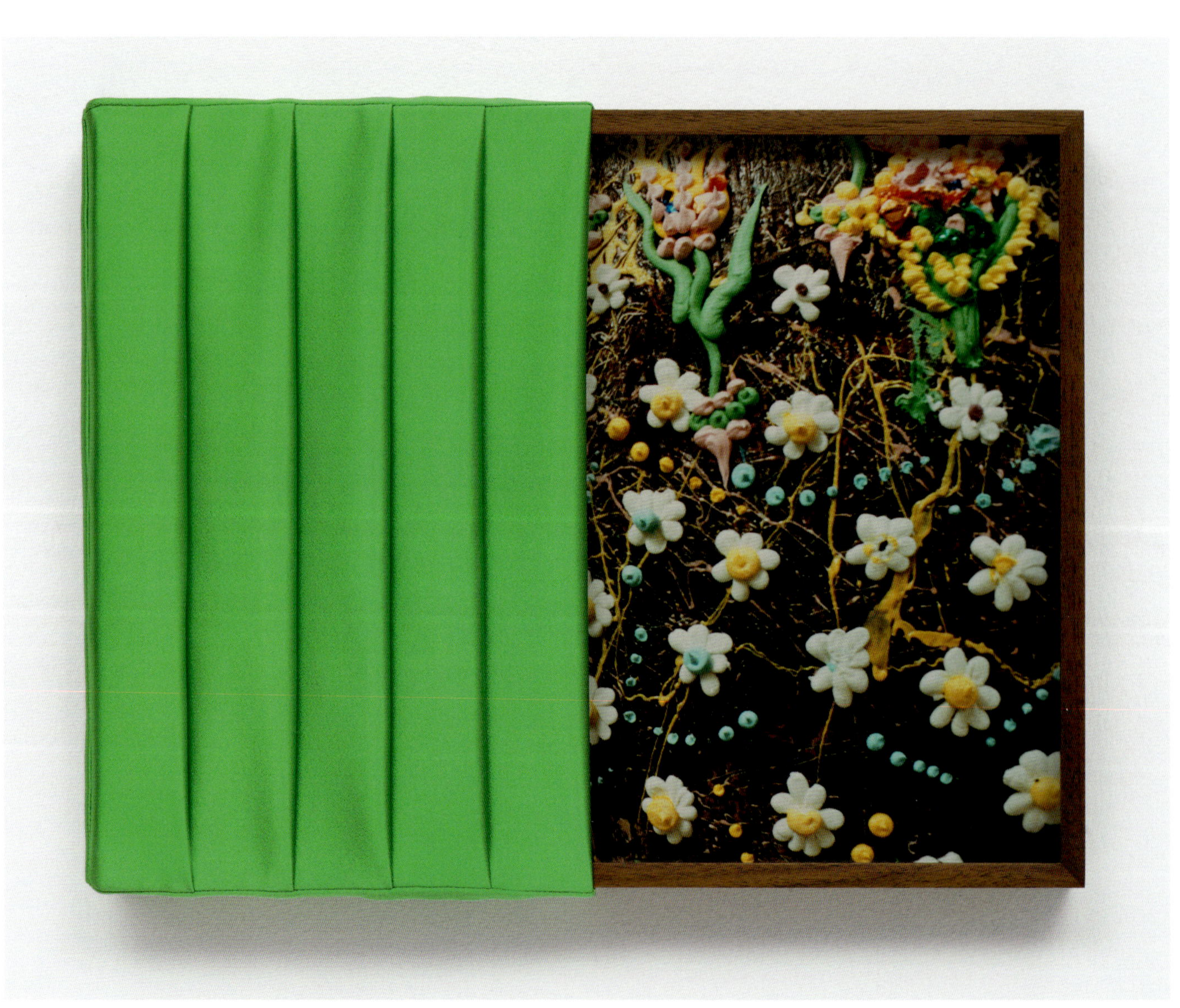

76    Elad Lassry, *Untitled (Yellow, Blue)*, 2013. C-print, walnut frame, four-ply silk

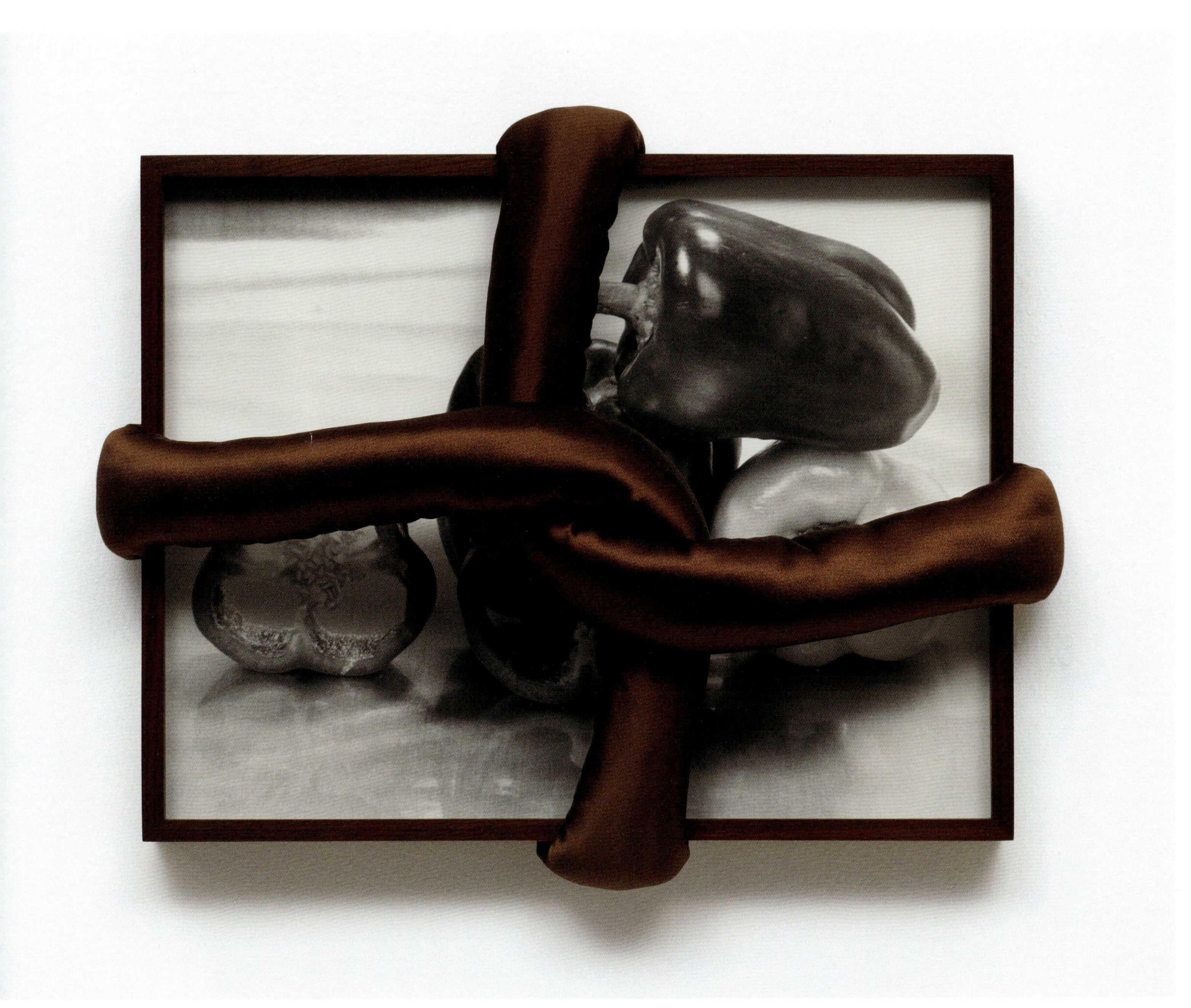

    Elad Lassry, *Untitled (Bell Peppers)*, 2013. Gelatin-silver print, walnut frame, four-ply silk

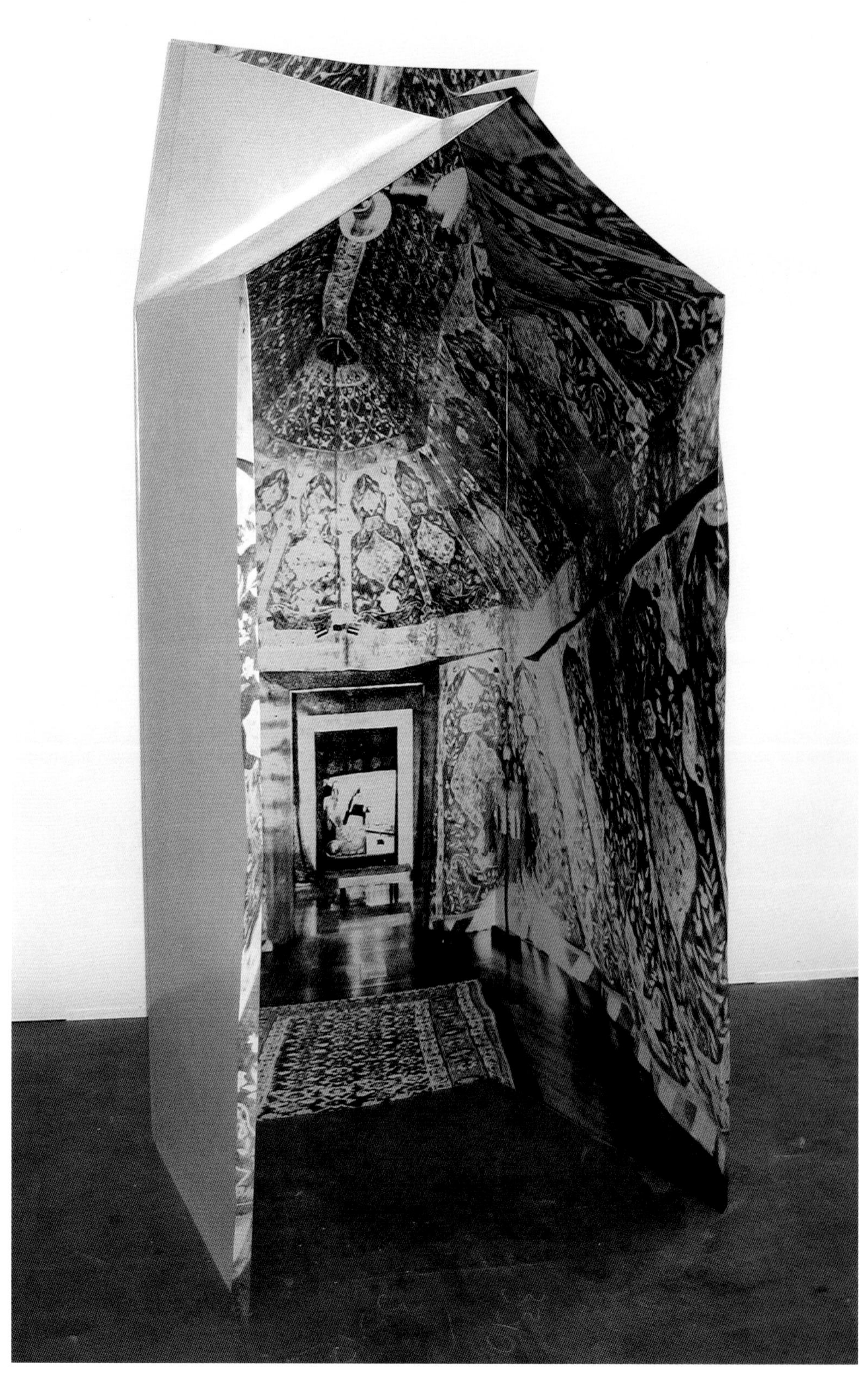

78    Alexandra Leykauf, *Tent*, 2012. Screen-print on aluminum

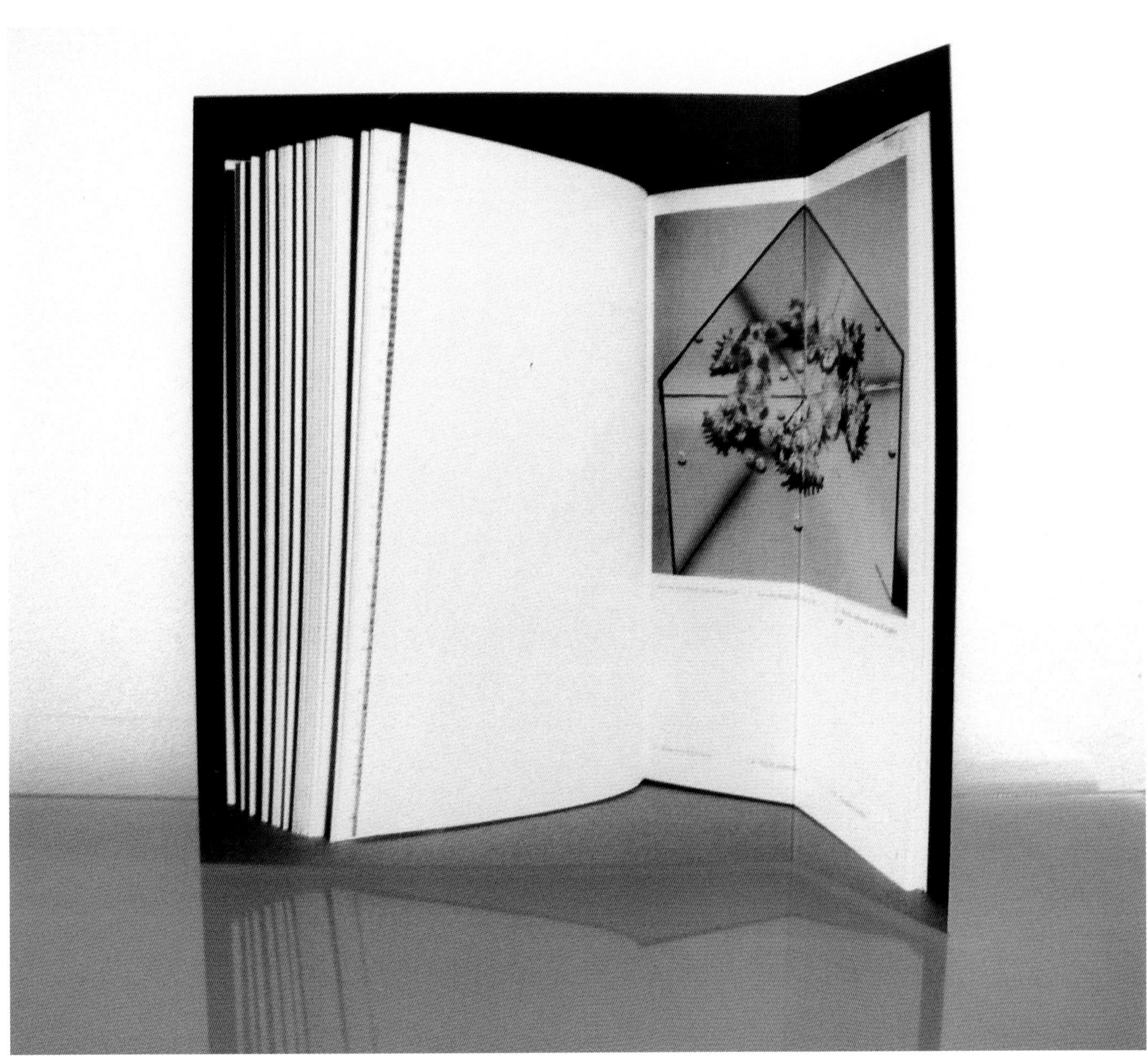

79    Alexandra Leykauf, *Katoptrische Experimente* (Light-reflection experiment), 2013. Folded offset print

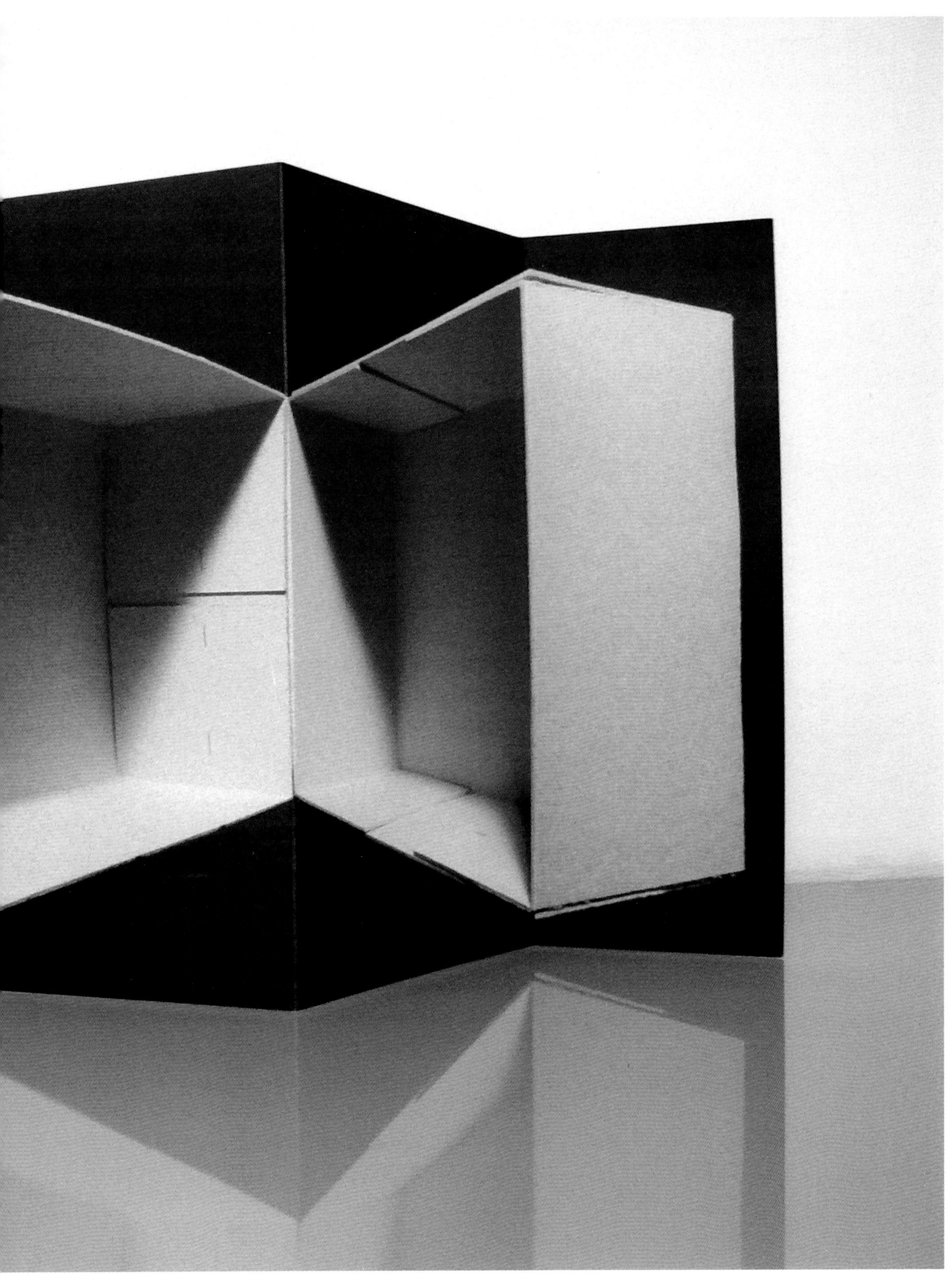

81    Alexandra Leykauf, *Spanische Wand* (Spanish wall), 2013. Folded offset print

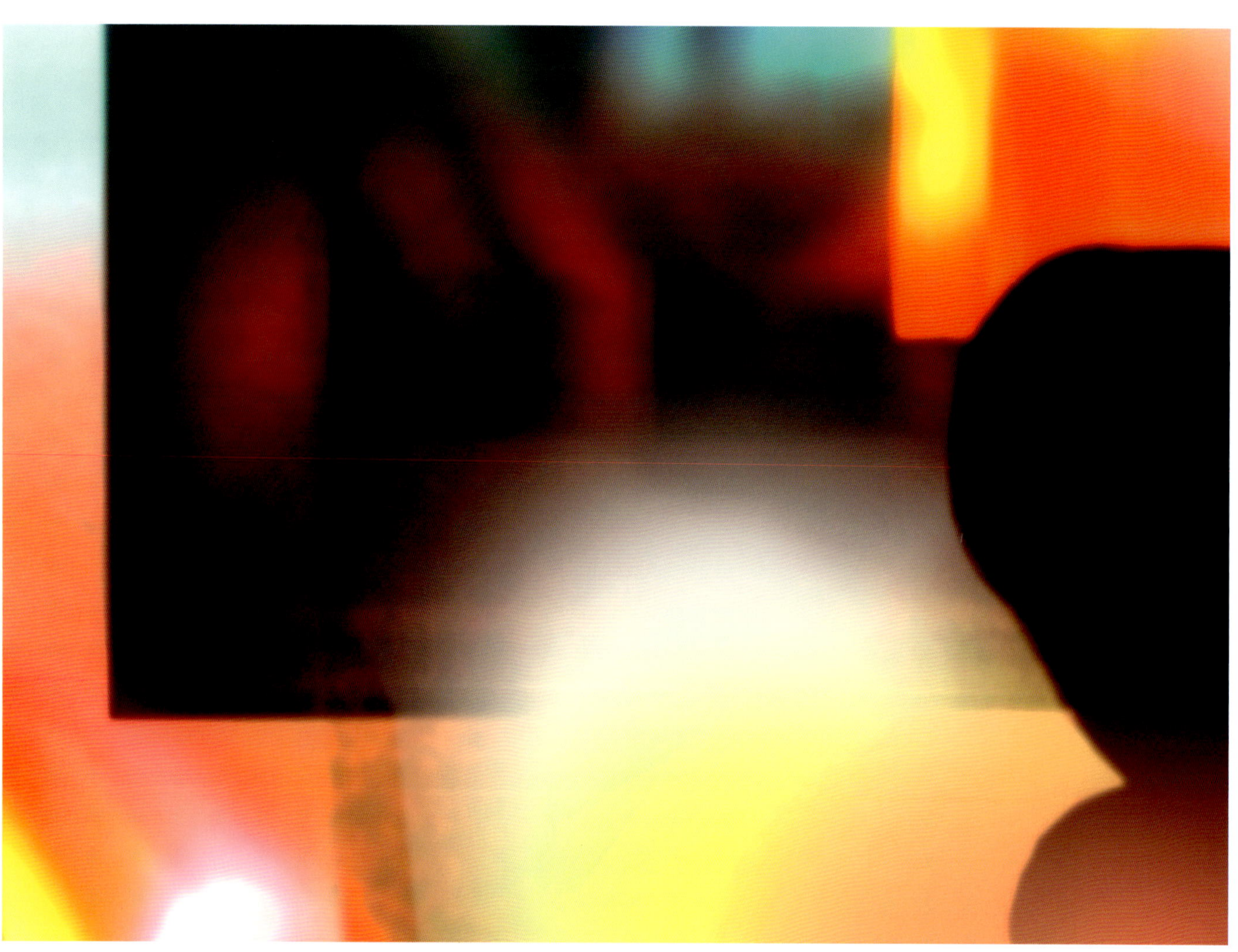

82    Victoria Fu, *Untitled (shadow)*, 2013. Inkjet print

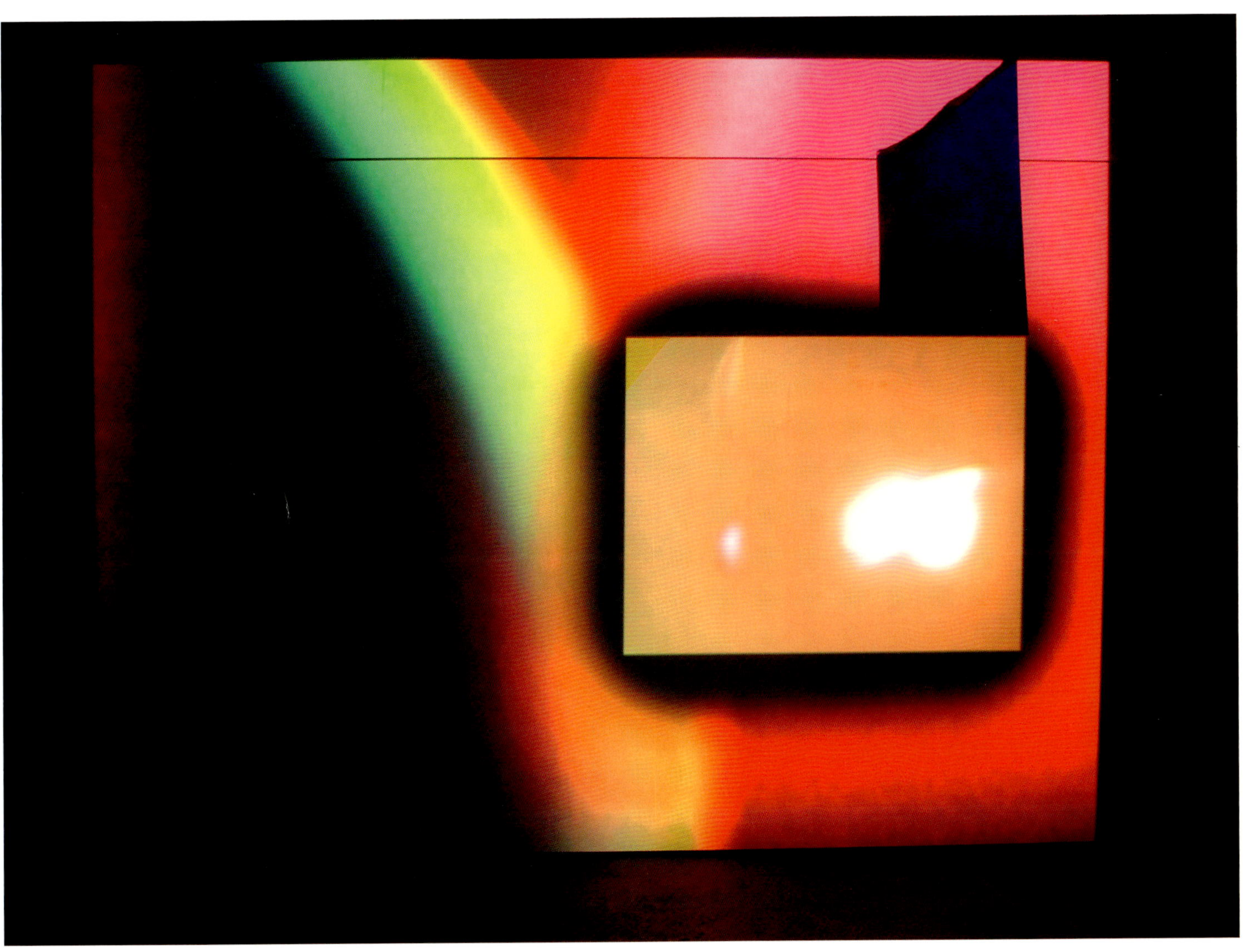

83   Victoria Fu, *Untitled (pink)*, 2013. Inkjet print

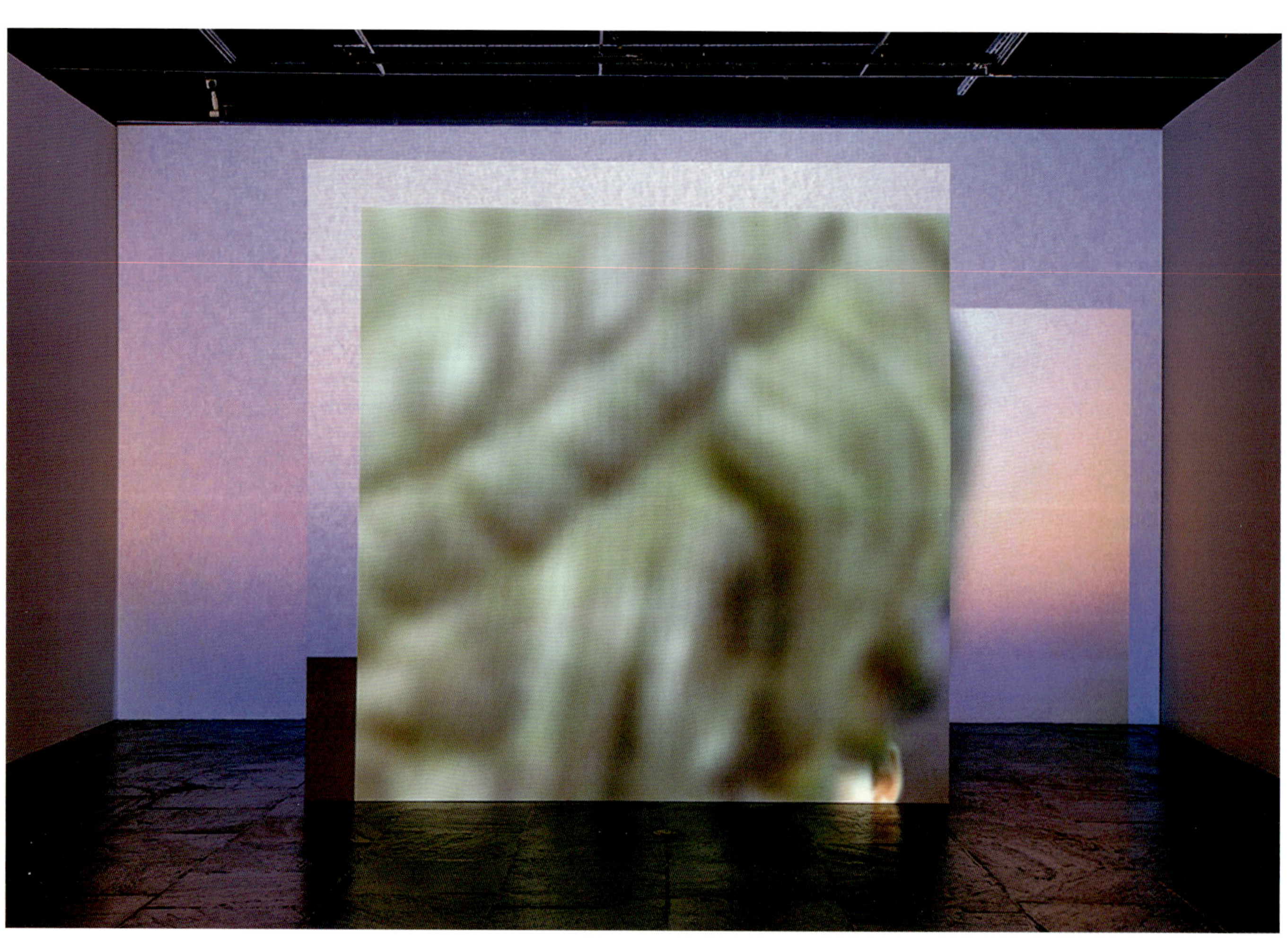

84    Victoria Fu, *Belle Captive I*, 2013. Video installation with sound

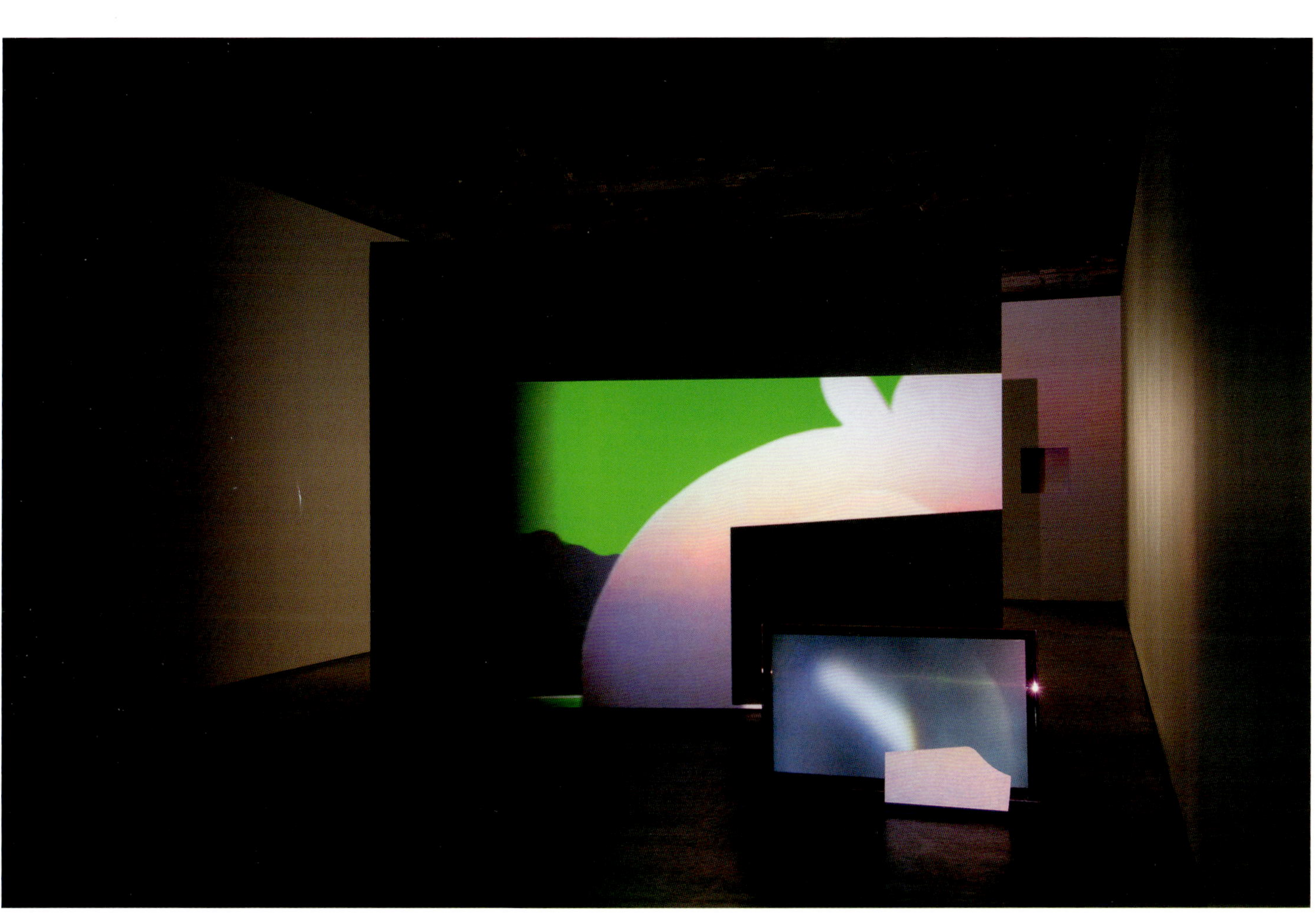

85   Victoria Fu, *Belle Captive 3*, 2013. Video installation with sound

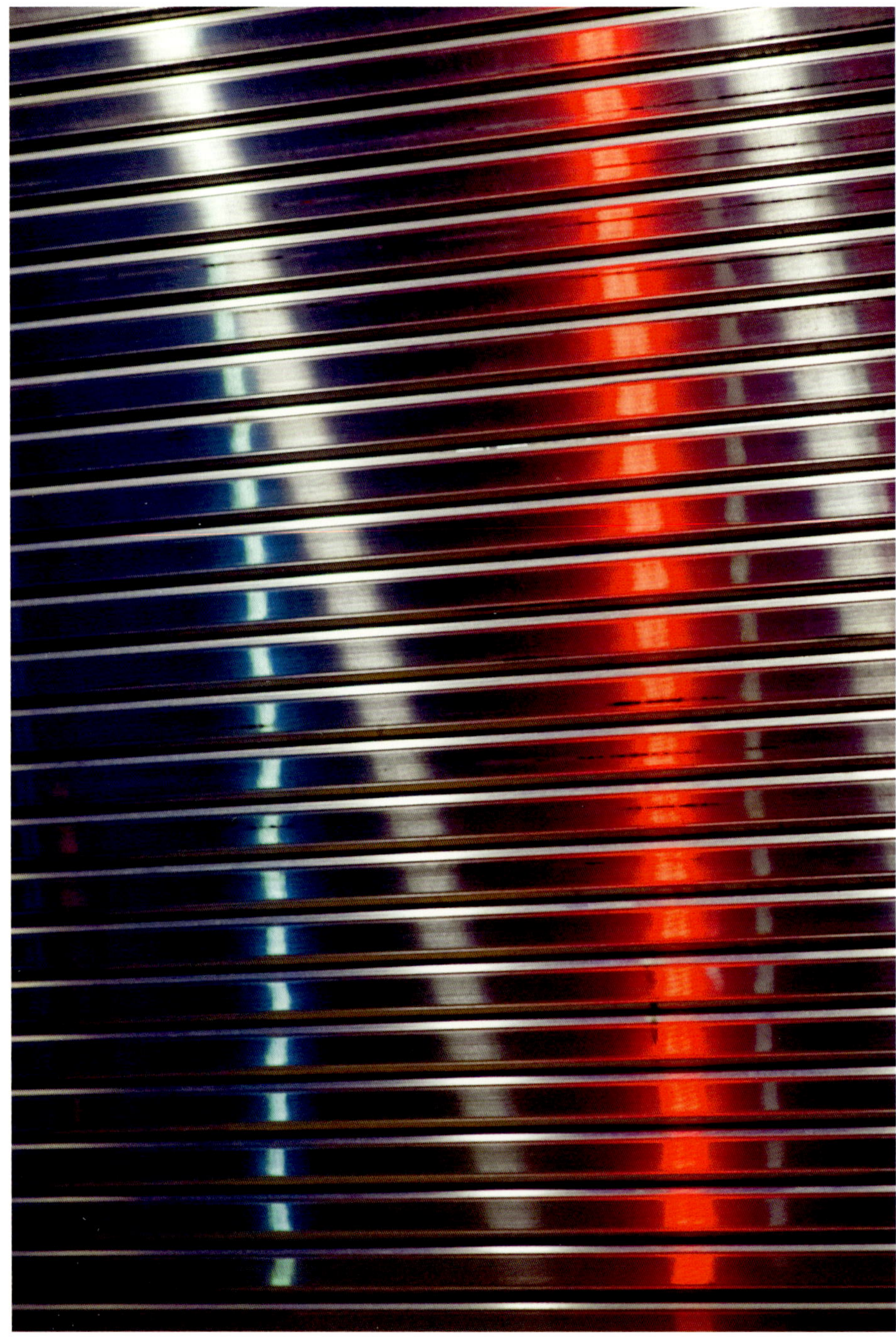

86    Yosuke Takeda, *220357*, 2010. LightJet print

87    Yosuke Takeda, *050020*, 2010. LightJet print

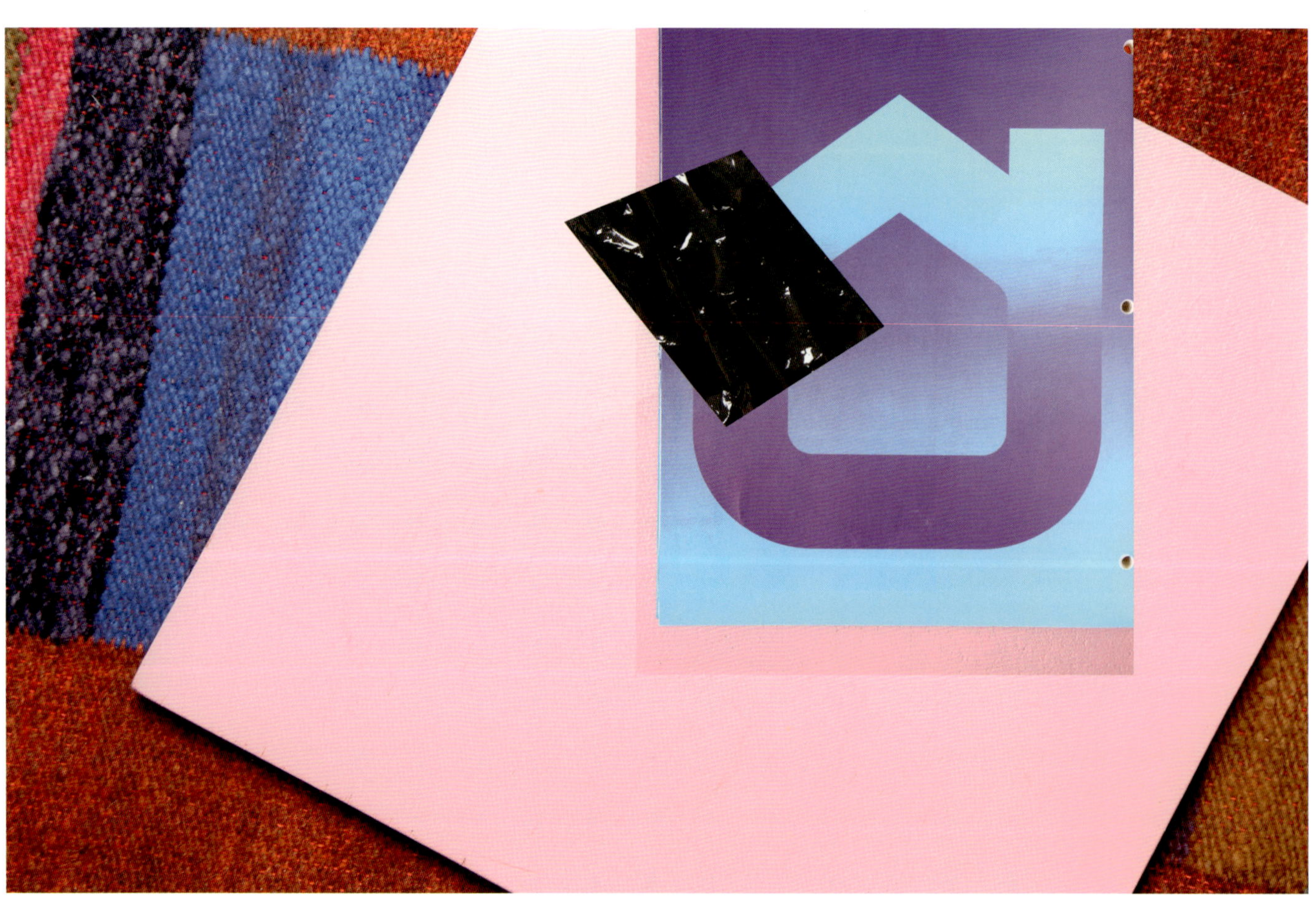

 Emmeline de Mooij, *Inviting the Stranger*, from the series *Oxytocin*, 2013. Archival inkjet print

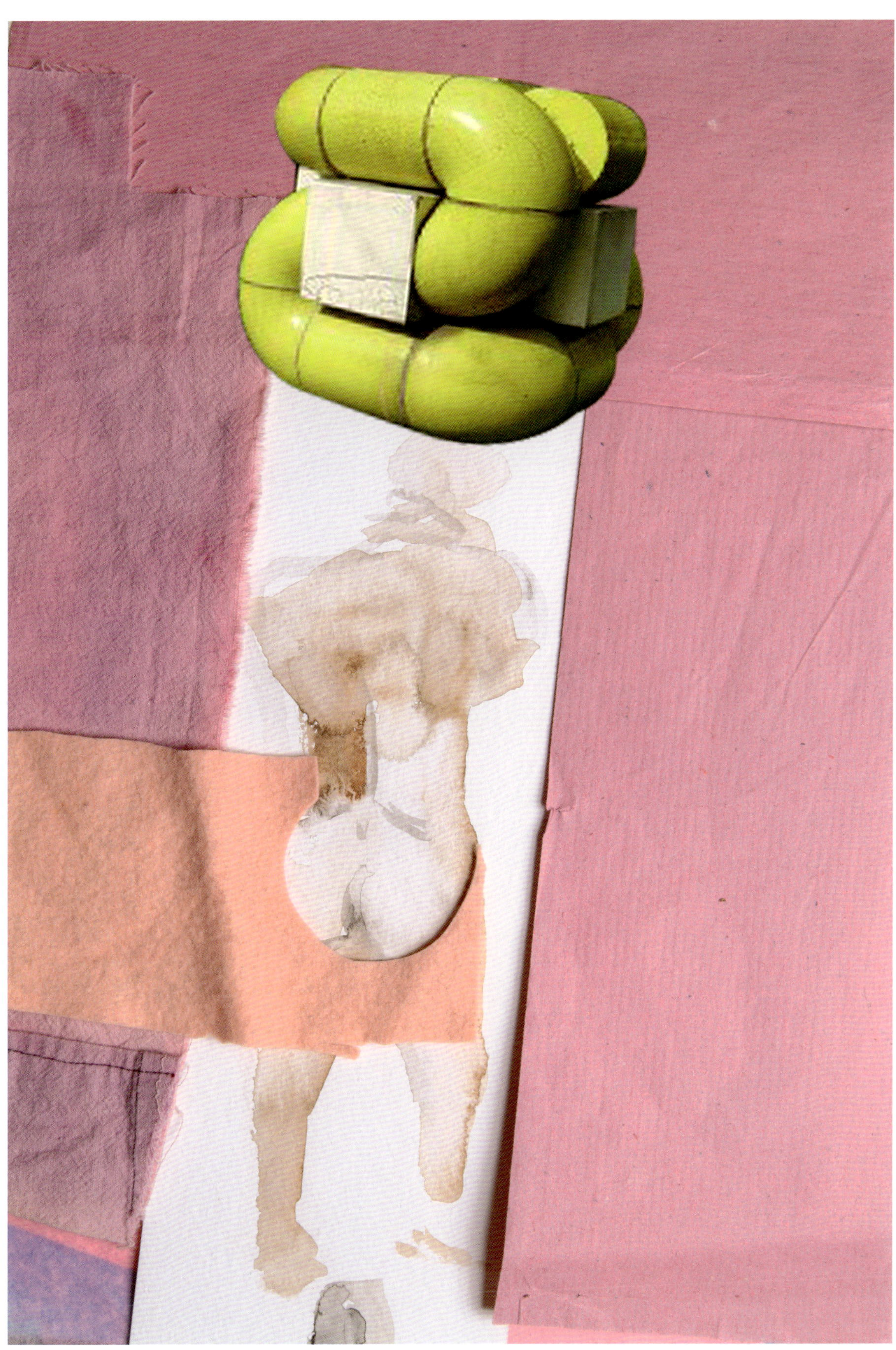

89　　Emmeline de Mooij, *Untitled*, from the series *Oxytocin*, 2013. Archival inkjet print

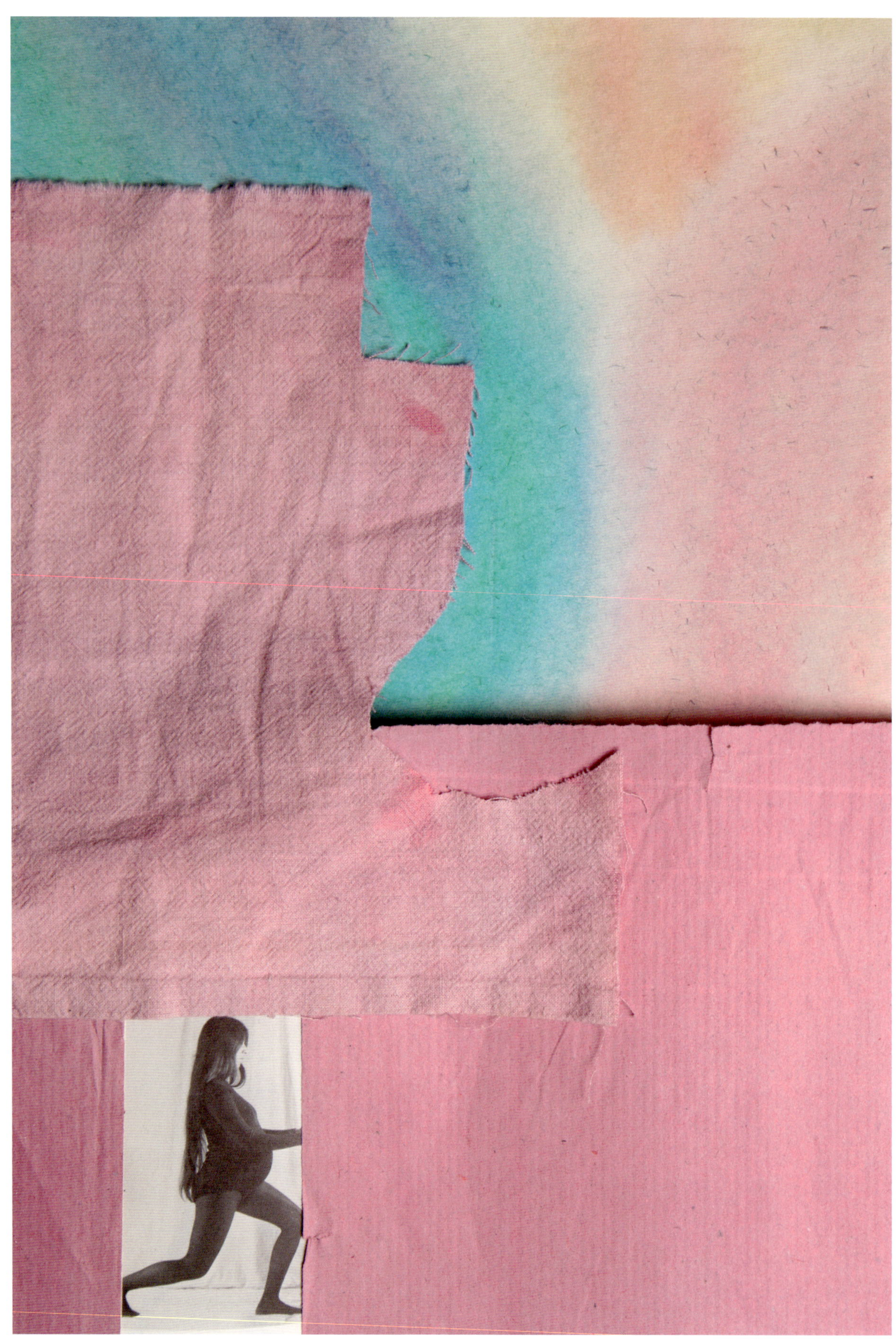

90    Emmeline de Mooij, *Untitled*, from the series *Oxytocin*, 2013. Archival inkjet print

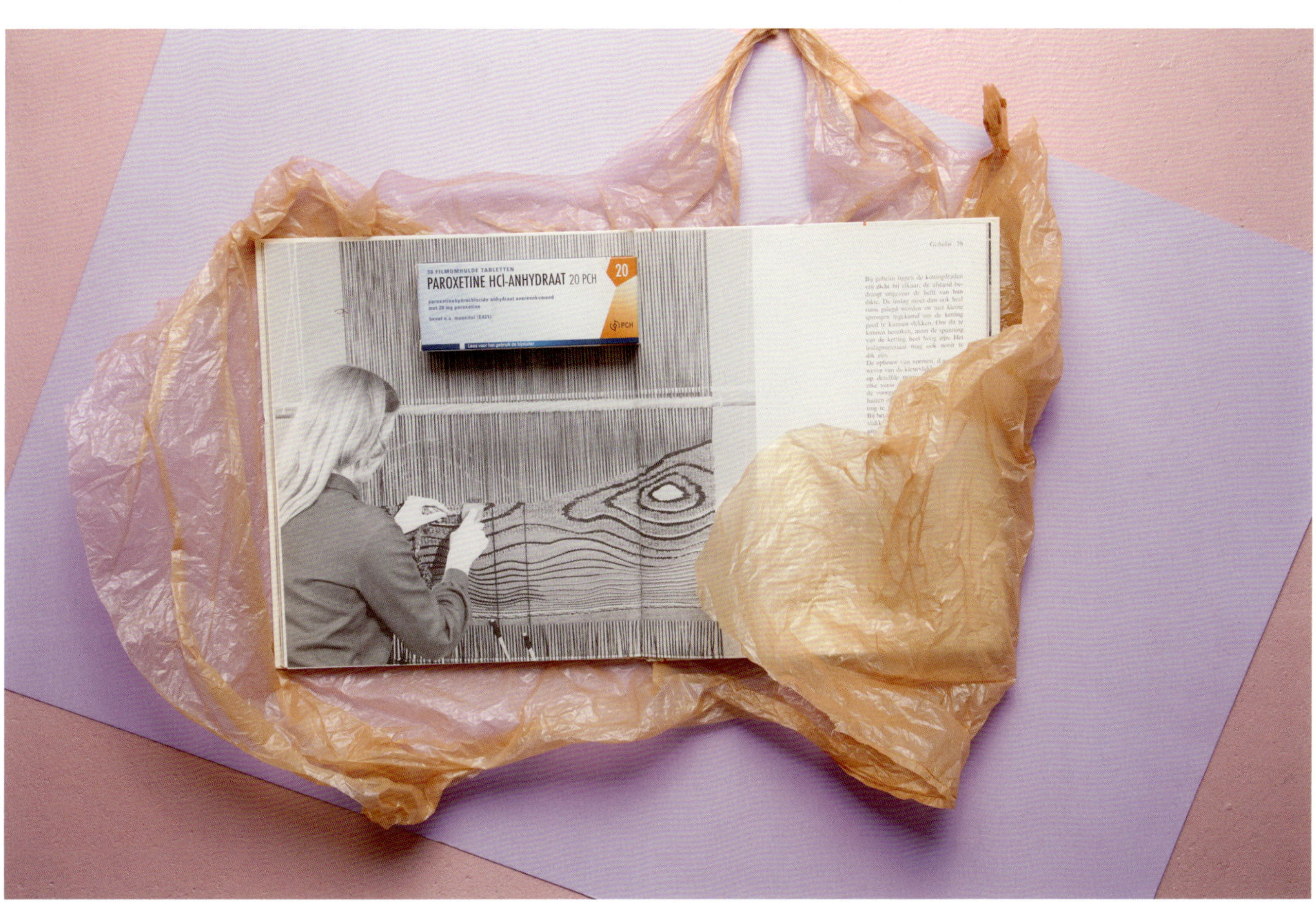

   Emmeline de Mooij, *Attempt to Overcome Polarity*, from the series *Oxytocin*, 2013. Archival inkjet print

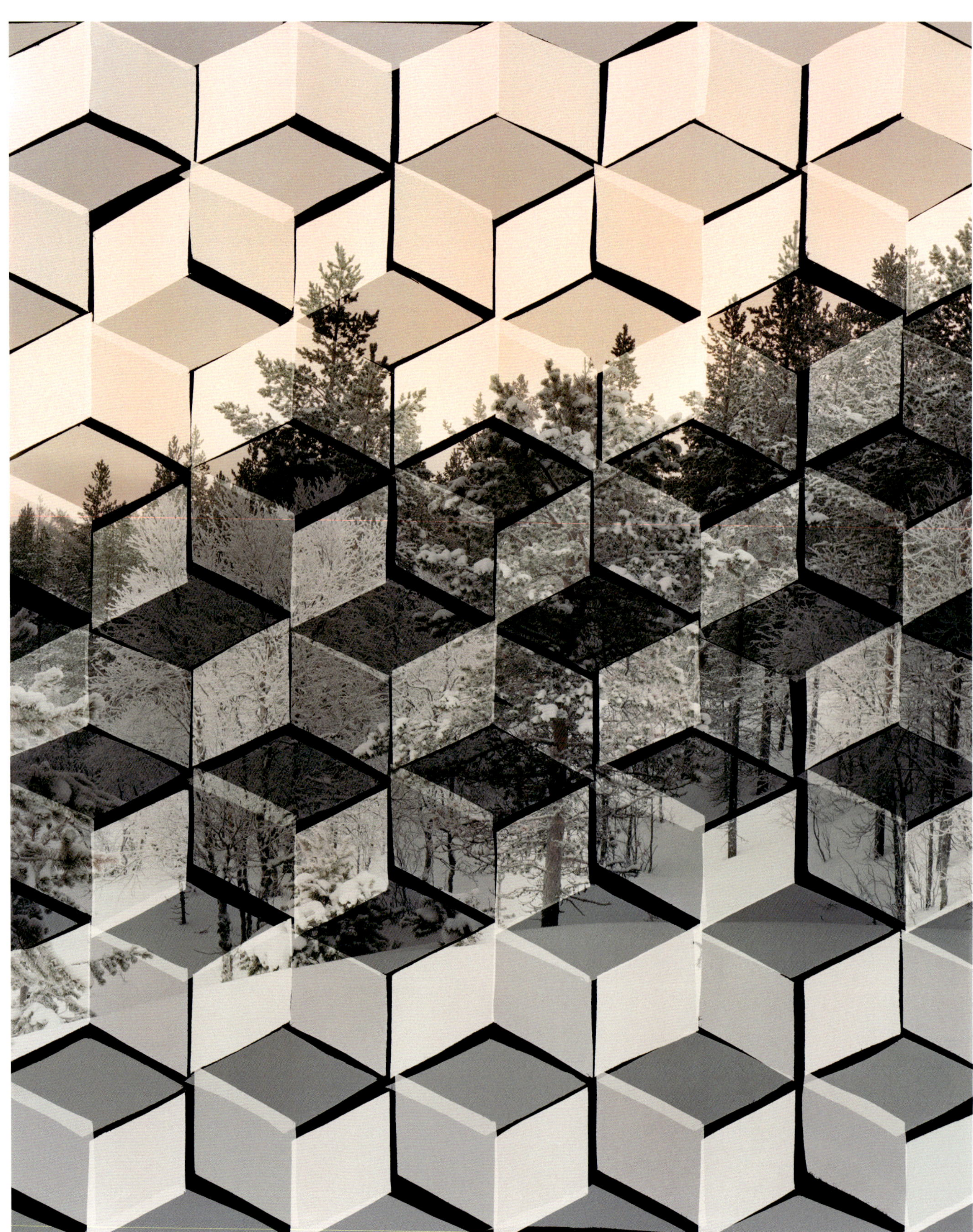

    Hannah Whitaker, *Arctic Landscape (Pink Sky)*, 2014. Archival pigment print

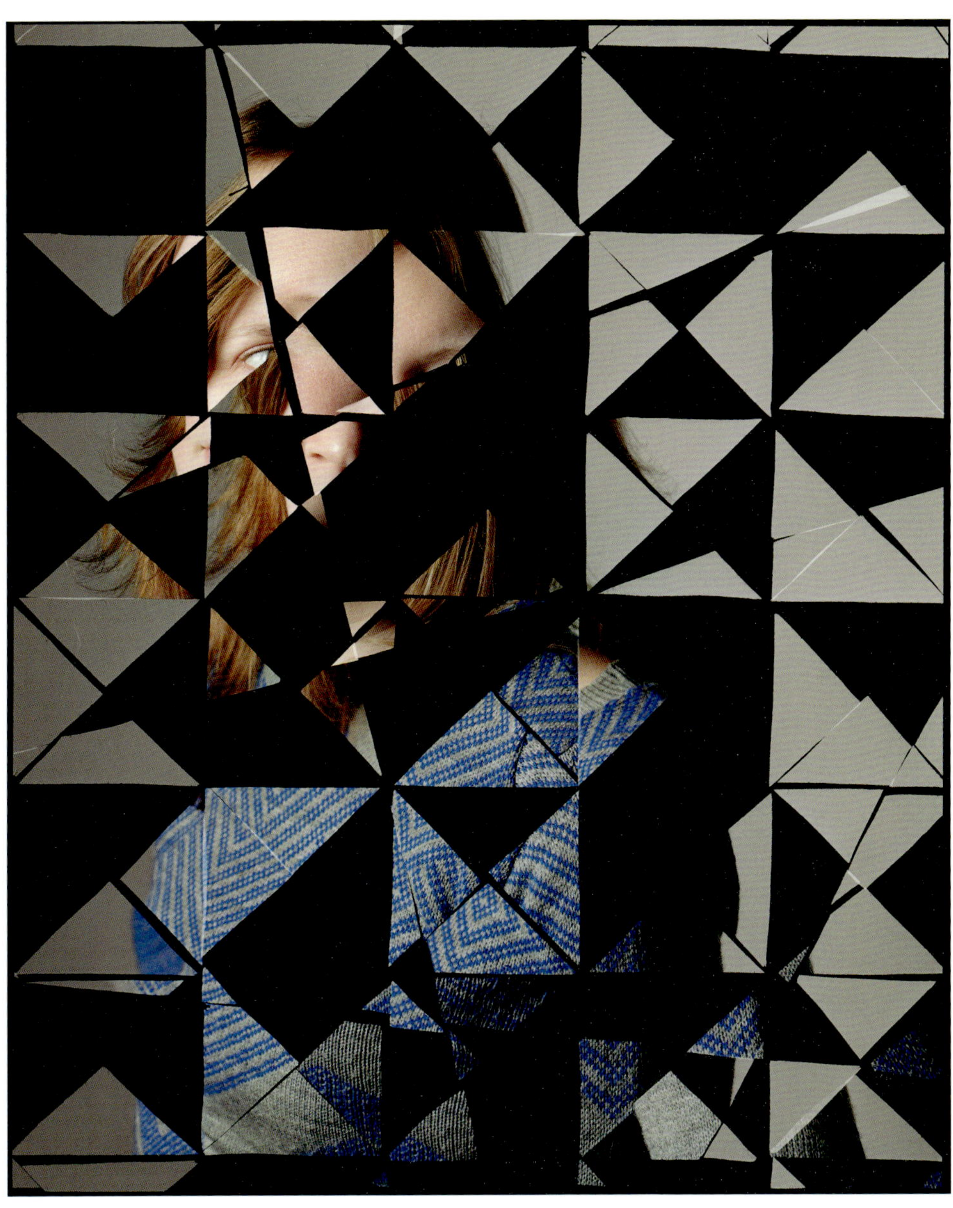

93    Hannah Whitaker, *Nose (Bomberg)*, 2014. Archival pigment print

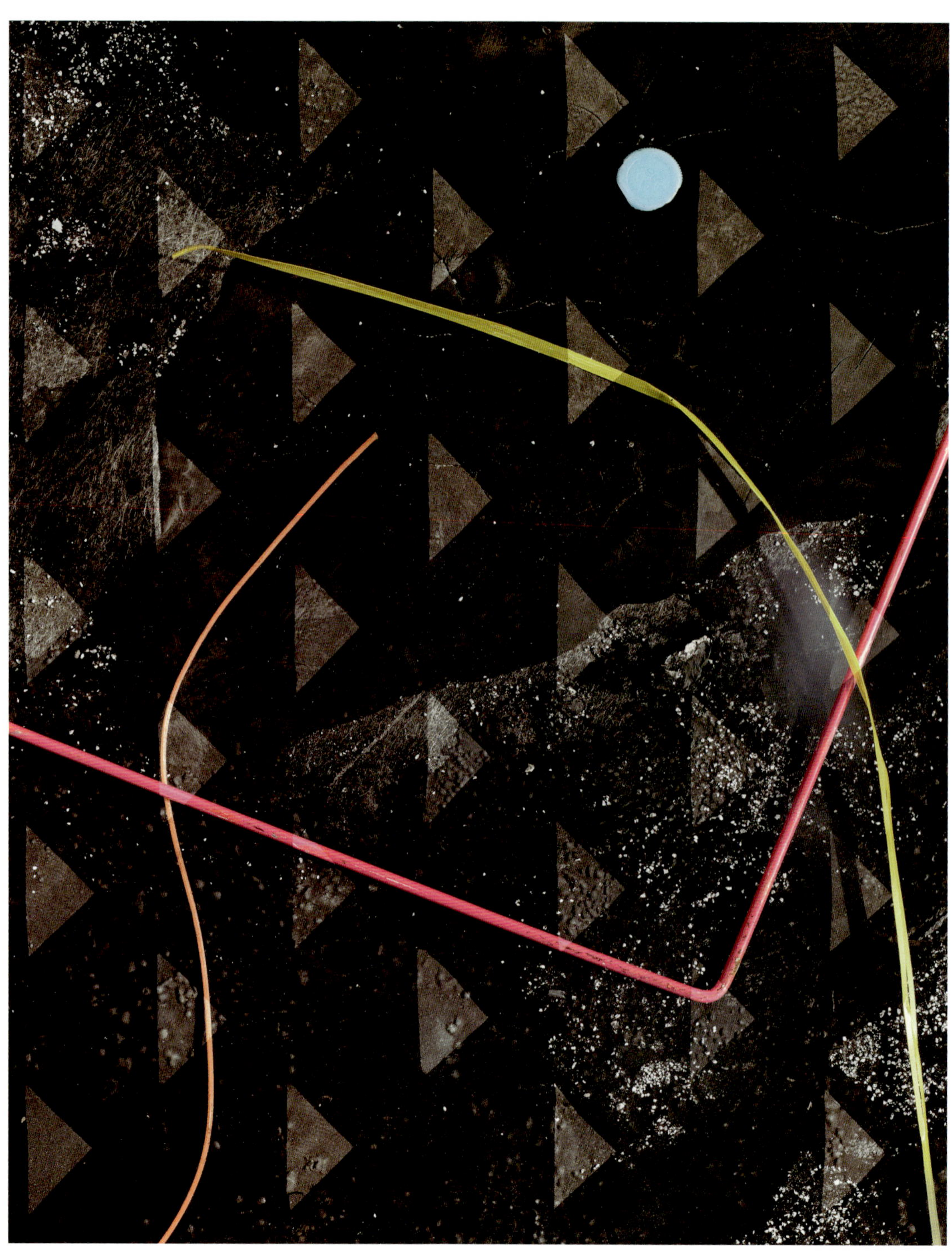

    Hannah Whitaker, *Limonene 15*, 2014. Archival pigment print

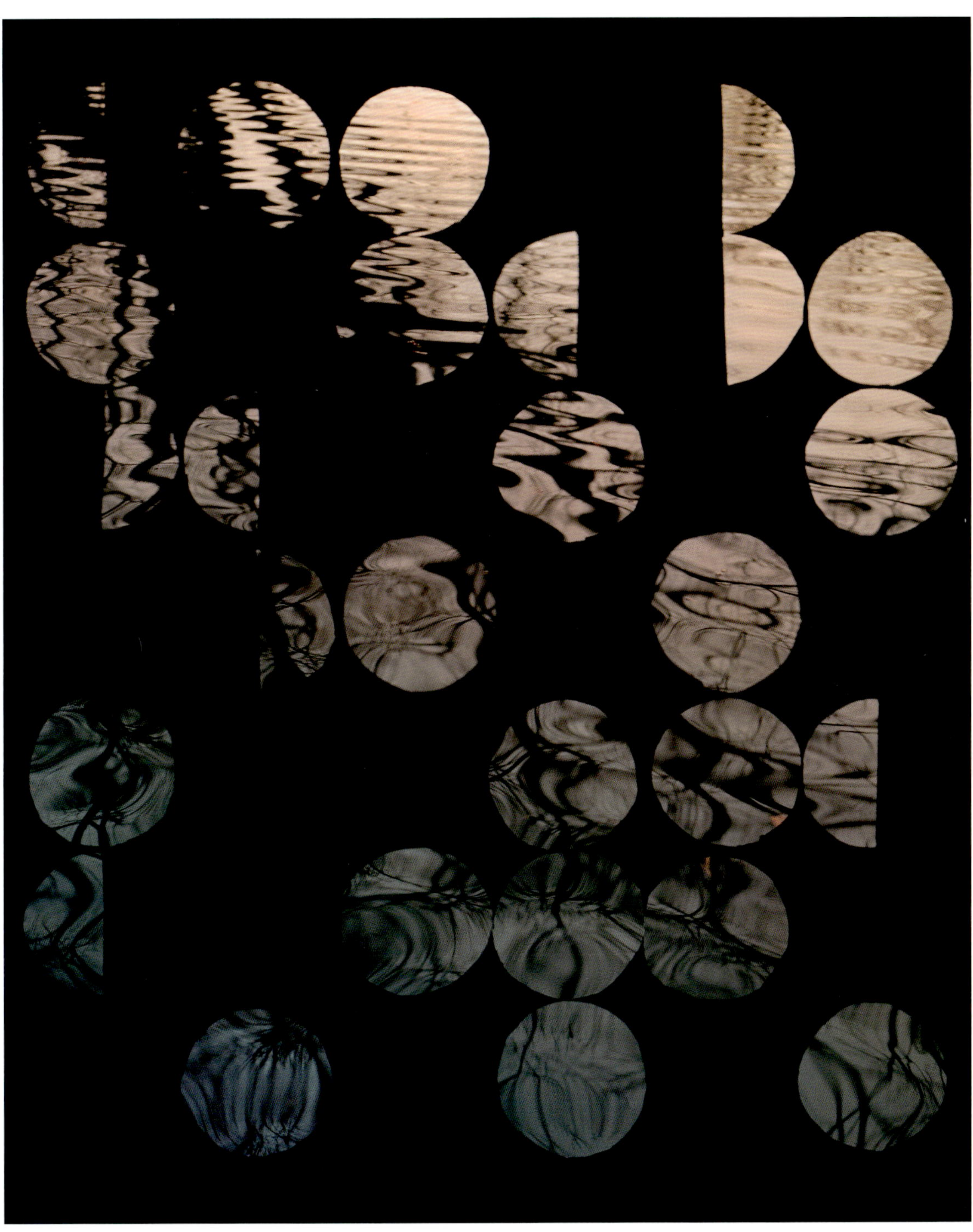

    Hannah Whitaker, *Barcroft (Taeuber-Arp)*, 2014. Archival pigment print

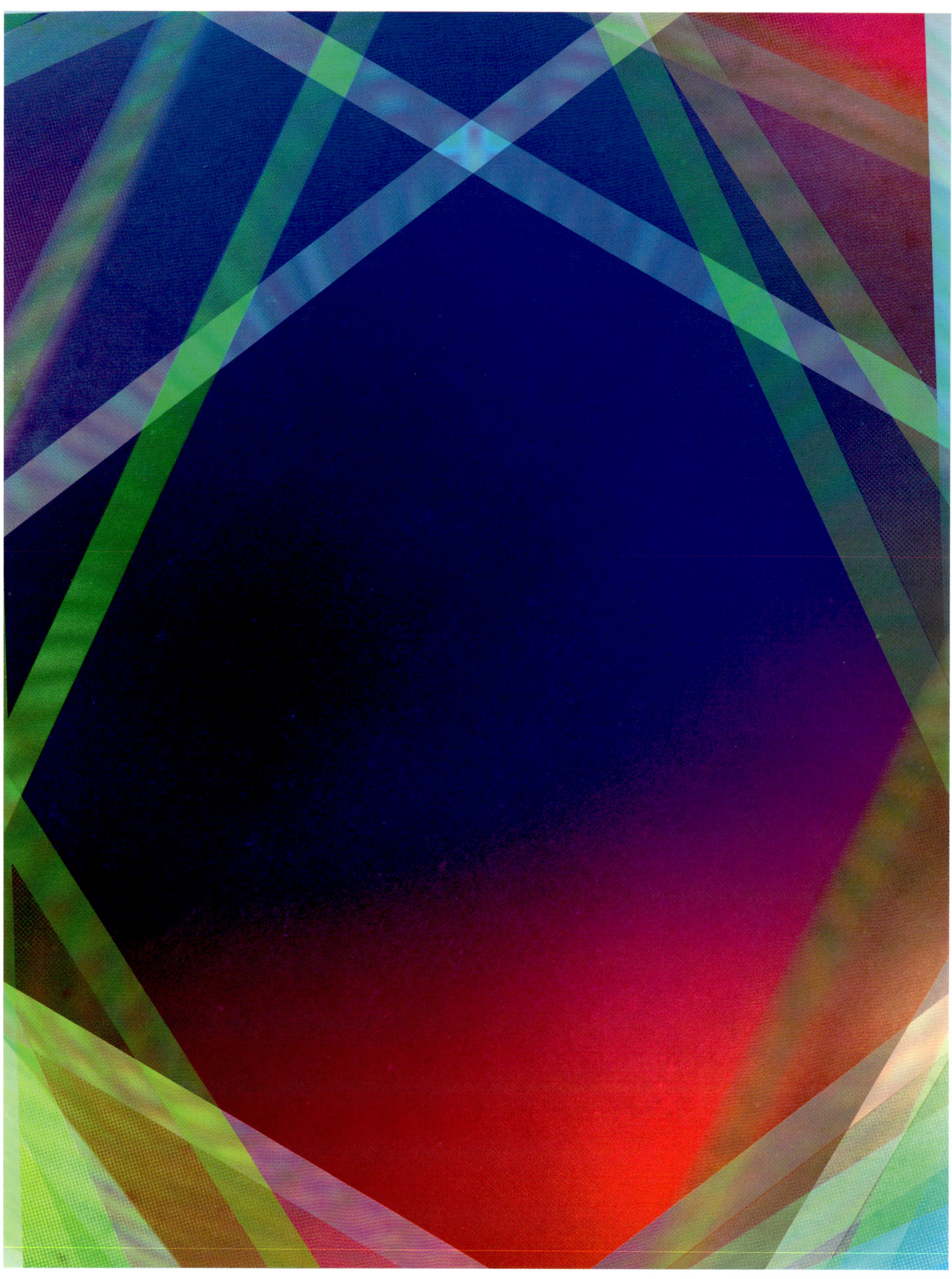

96    Taisuke Koyama, *Untitled (Seventh Depth 035)*, 2014. Archival pigment print

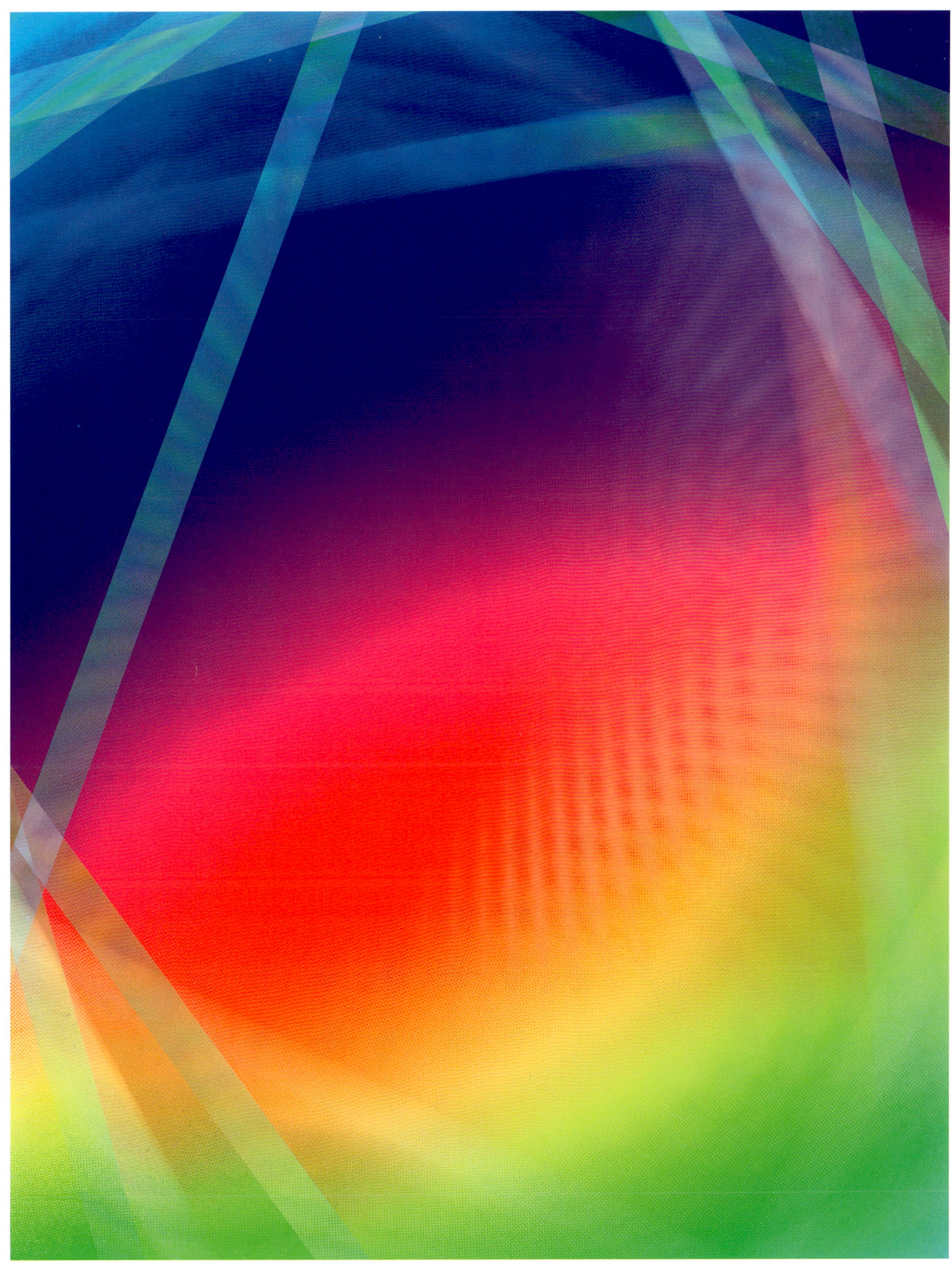

97    Taisuke Koyama, *Untitled (Seventh Depth 009)*, 2014. Archival pigment print

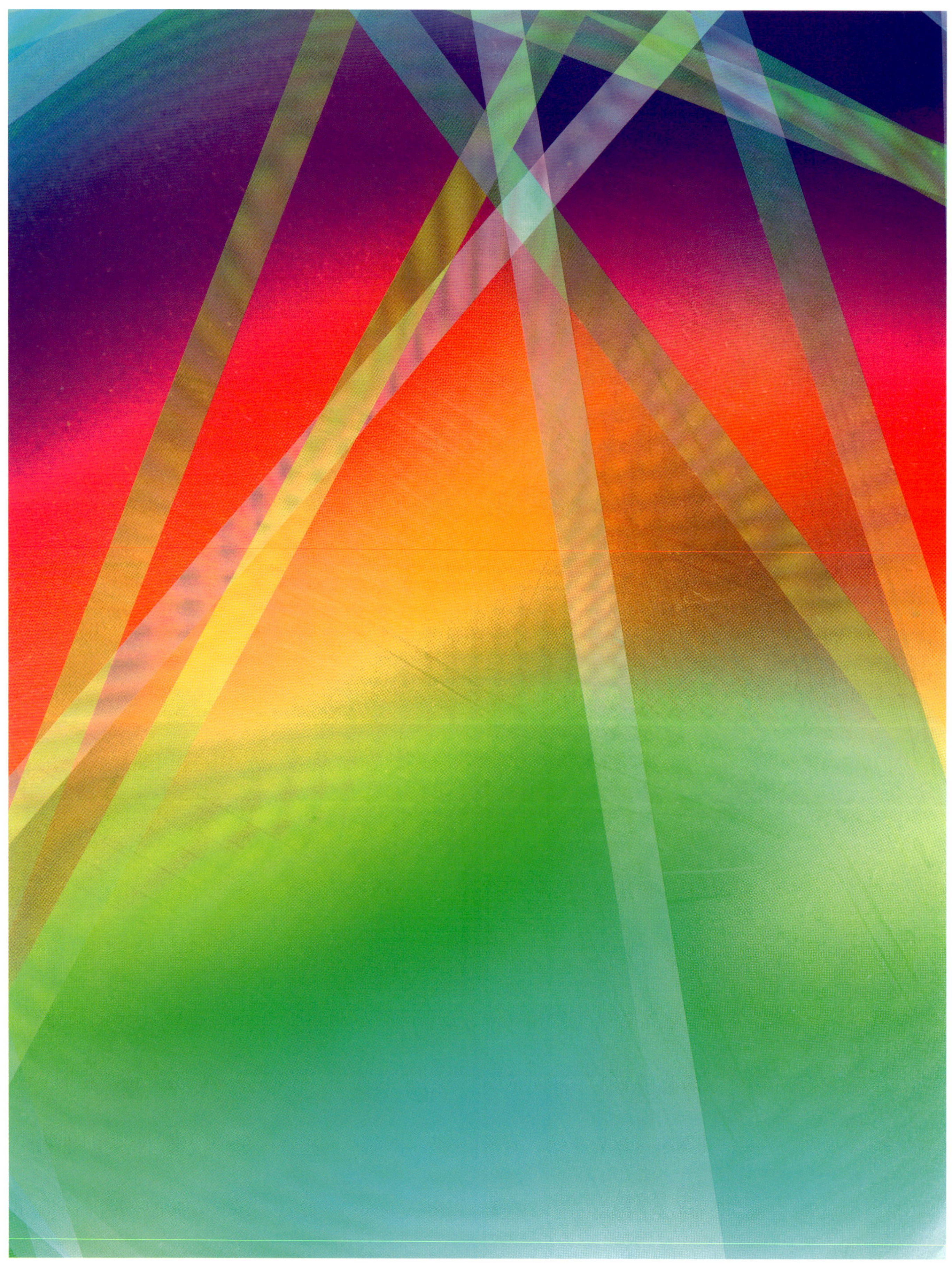

98    Taisuke Koyama, *Untitled (Seventh Depth 013)*, 2014. Archival pigment print

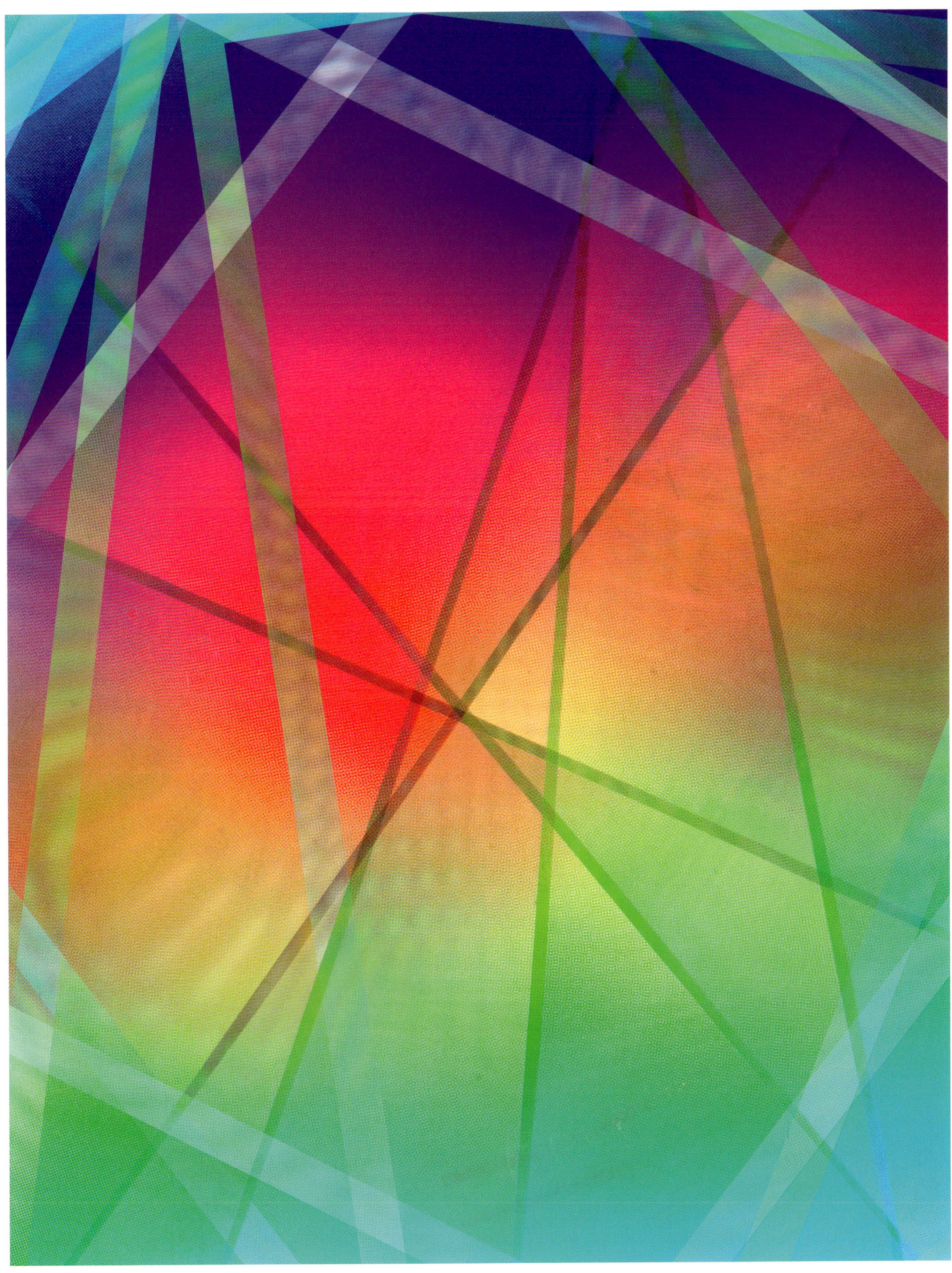

   Taisuke Koyama, *Untitled (Seventh Depth 079)*, 2014. Archival pigment print

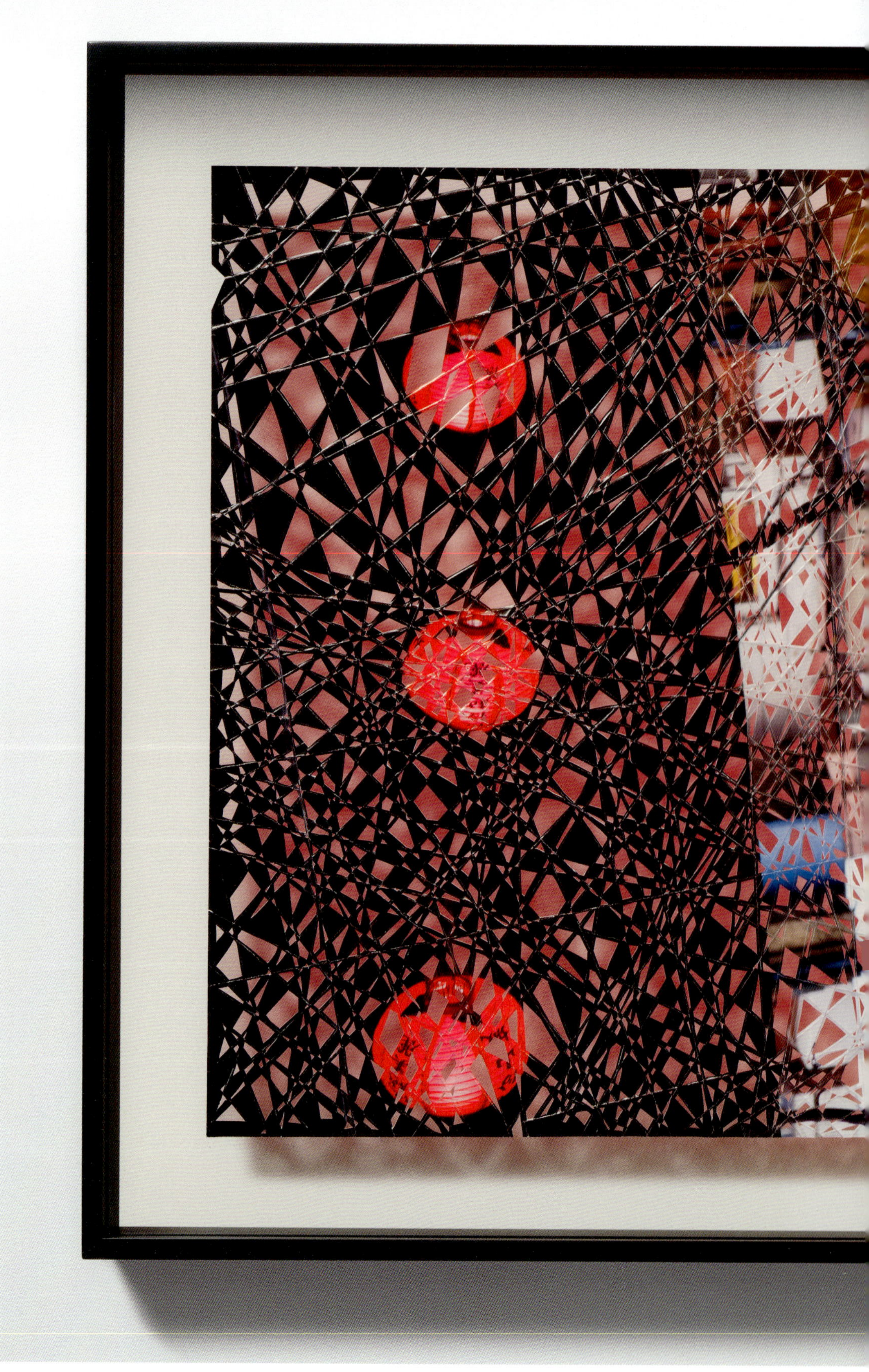

100    Soo Kim, *Approaches him—quieter*, 2014. Hand-scored and -cut inkjet print, acrylic lacquer

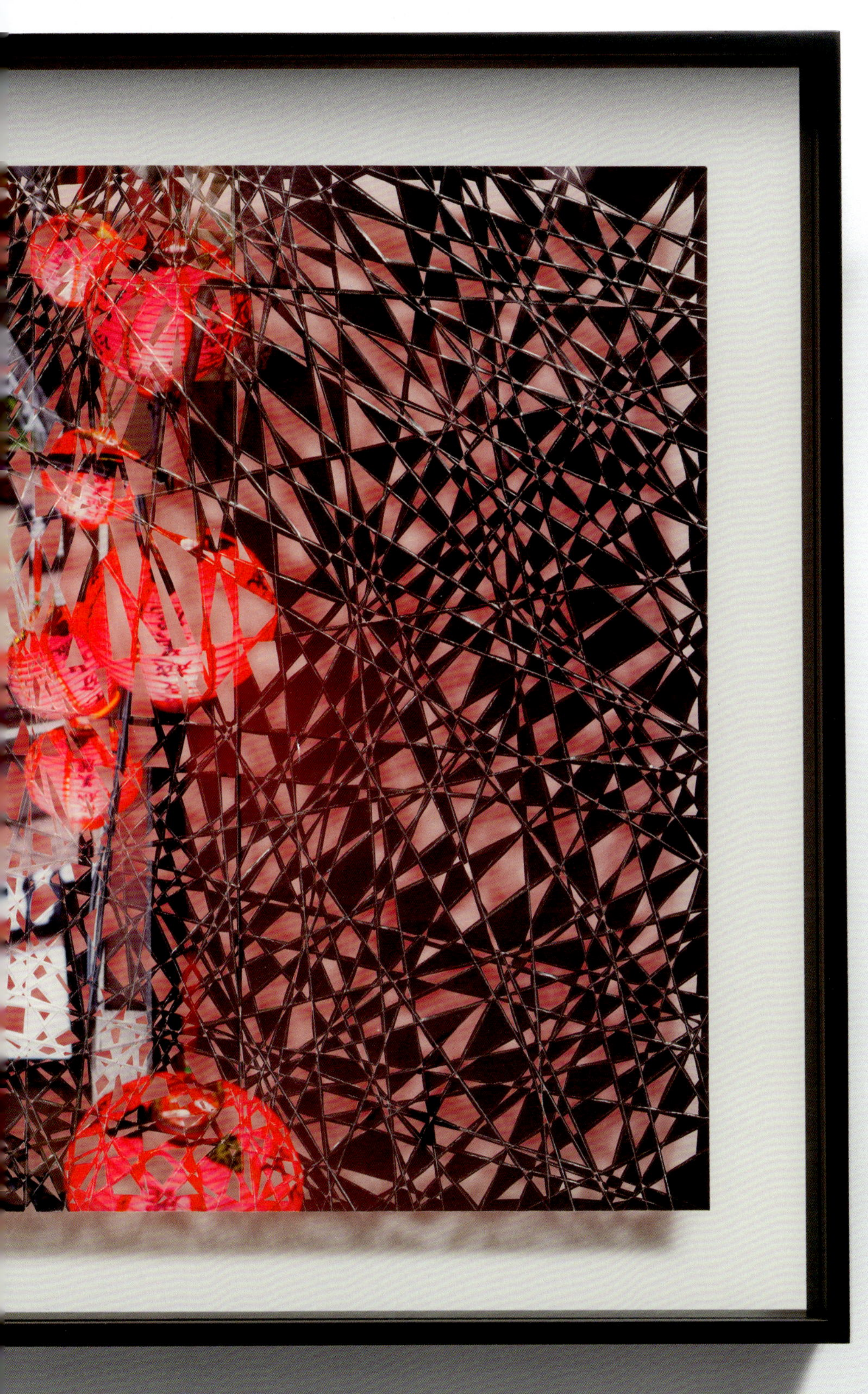

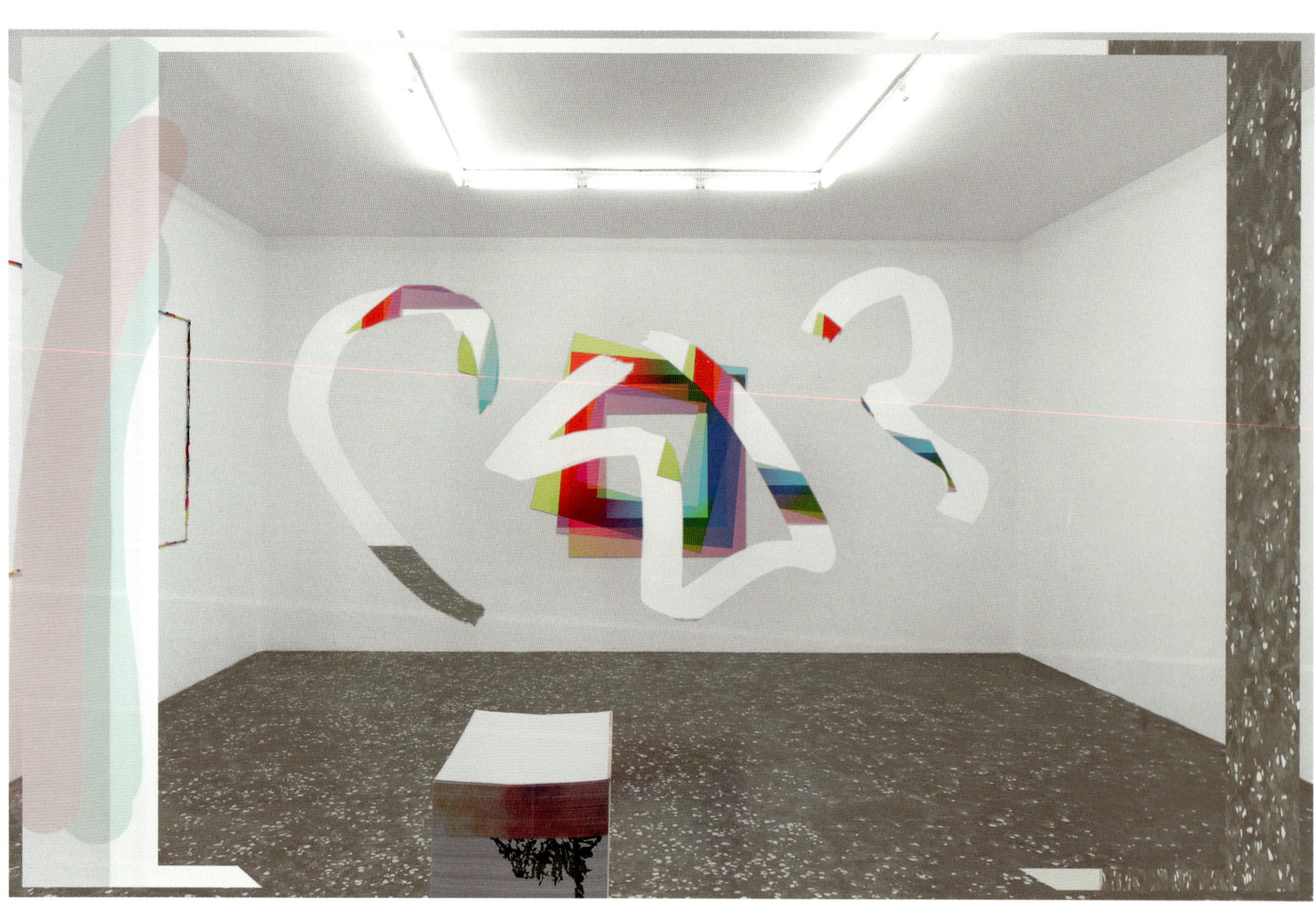

102    Artie Vierkant, *Image Objects (installation view, Fonds M-ARCO, Marseille)*, 2013. UV print on Dibond, altered documentation images

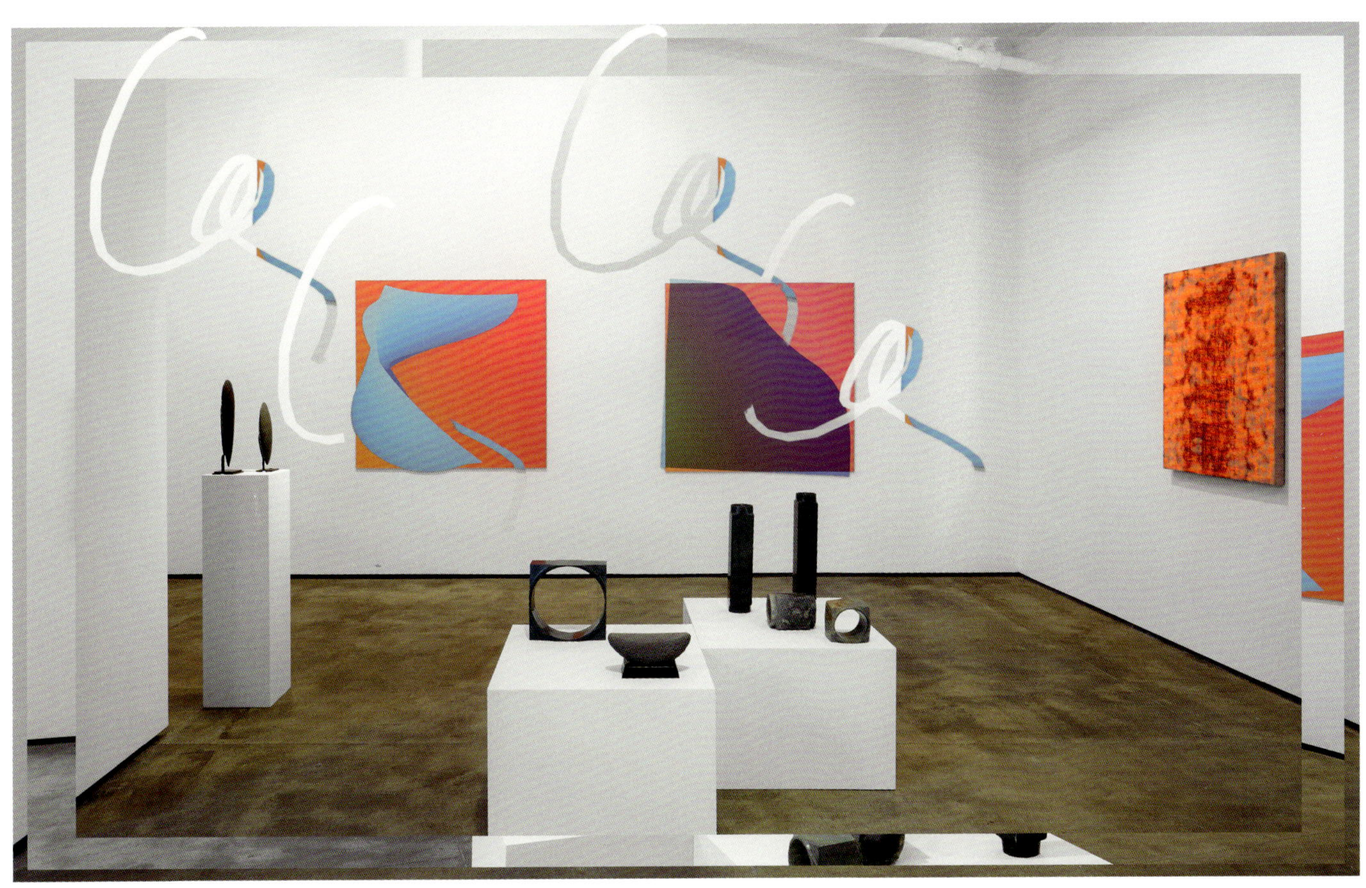

103    Artie Vierkant, *Image Objects (installation view, group show at Sean Kelly, New York)*, 2014. UV print on Dibond, altered documentation images

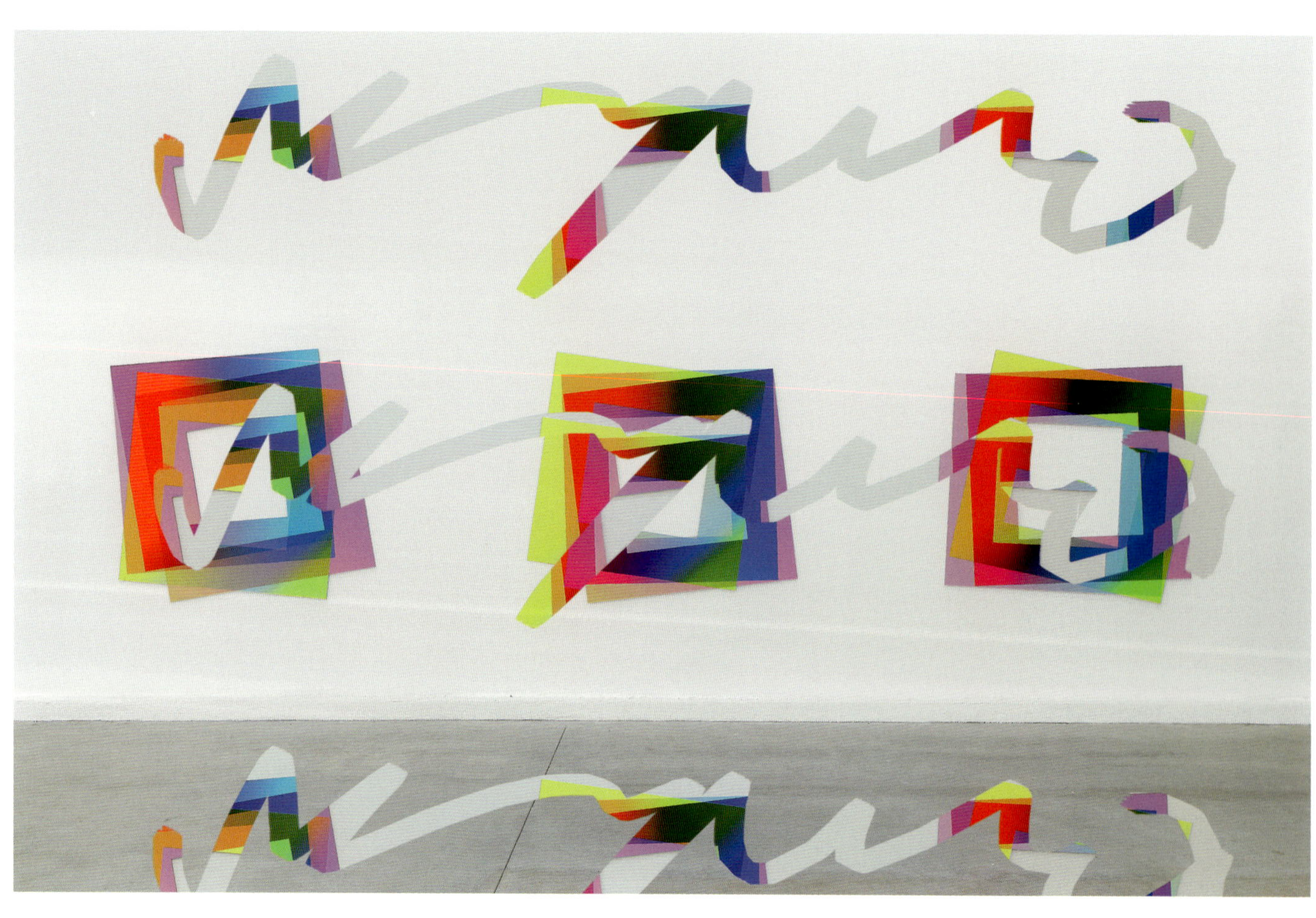

    Artie Vierkant, *Image Object, Monday 11 March 2013*, 2013. UV print on Dibond, altered documentation images

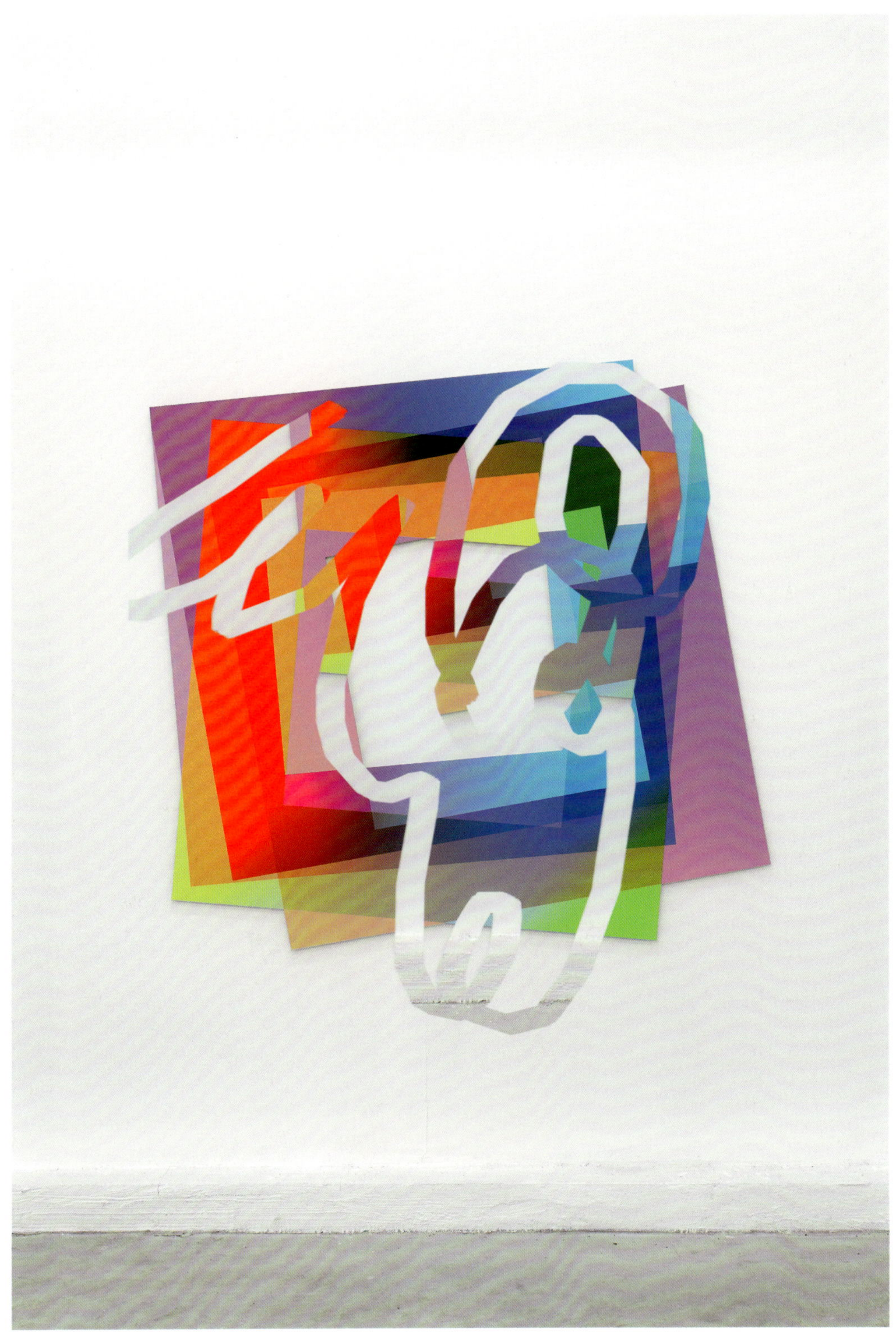

105    Artie Vierkant, *Image Object, Monday 11 March 2013*, 2013. UV print on Dibond, altered documentation images

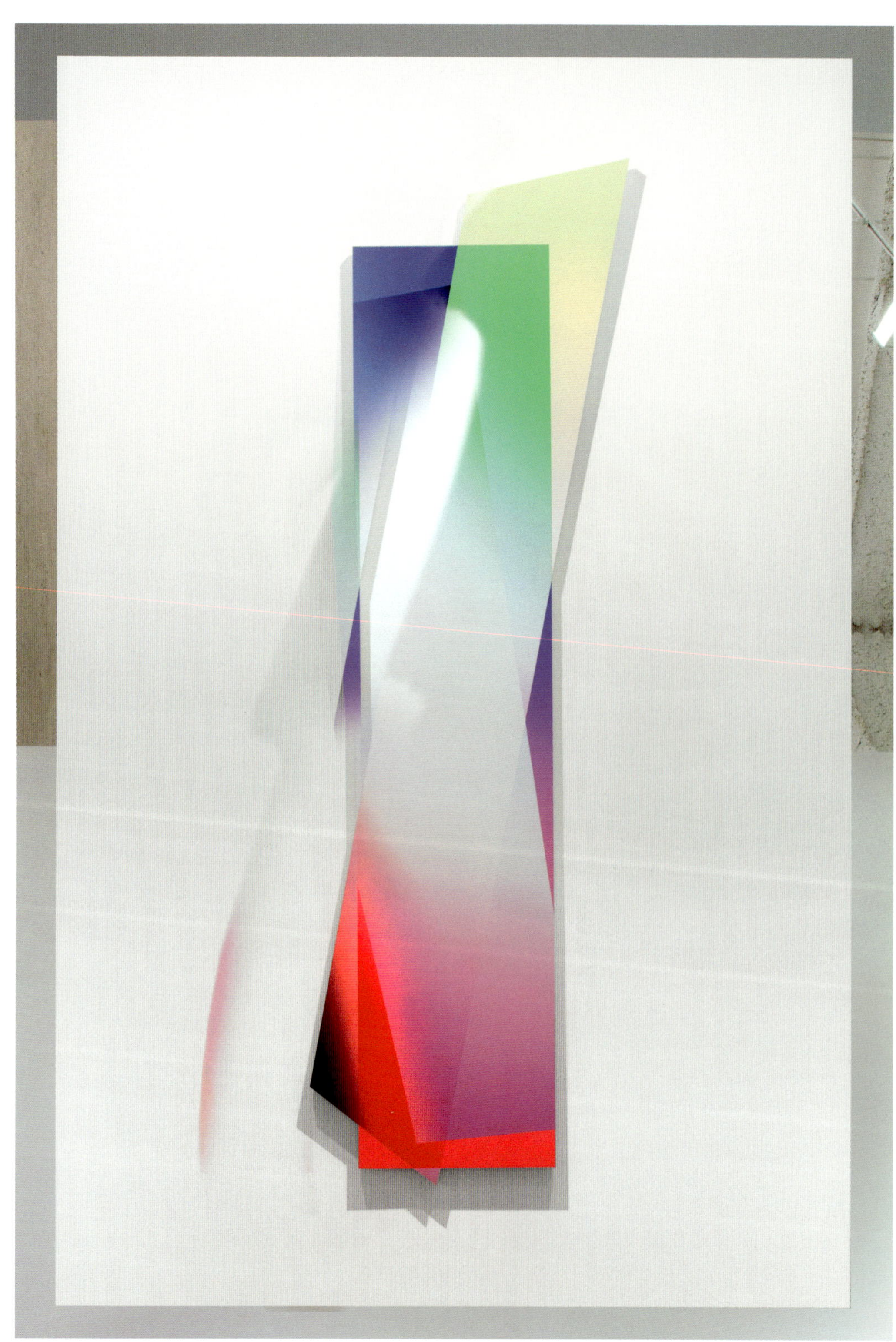

106    Artie Vierkant, *Image Object, Monday 11 March 2013*, 2013. UV print on Dibond, altered documentation images

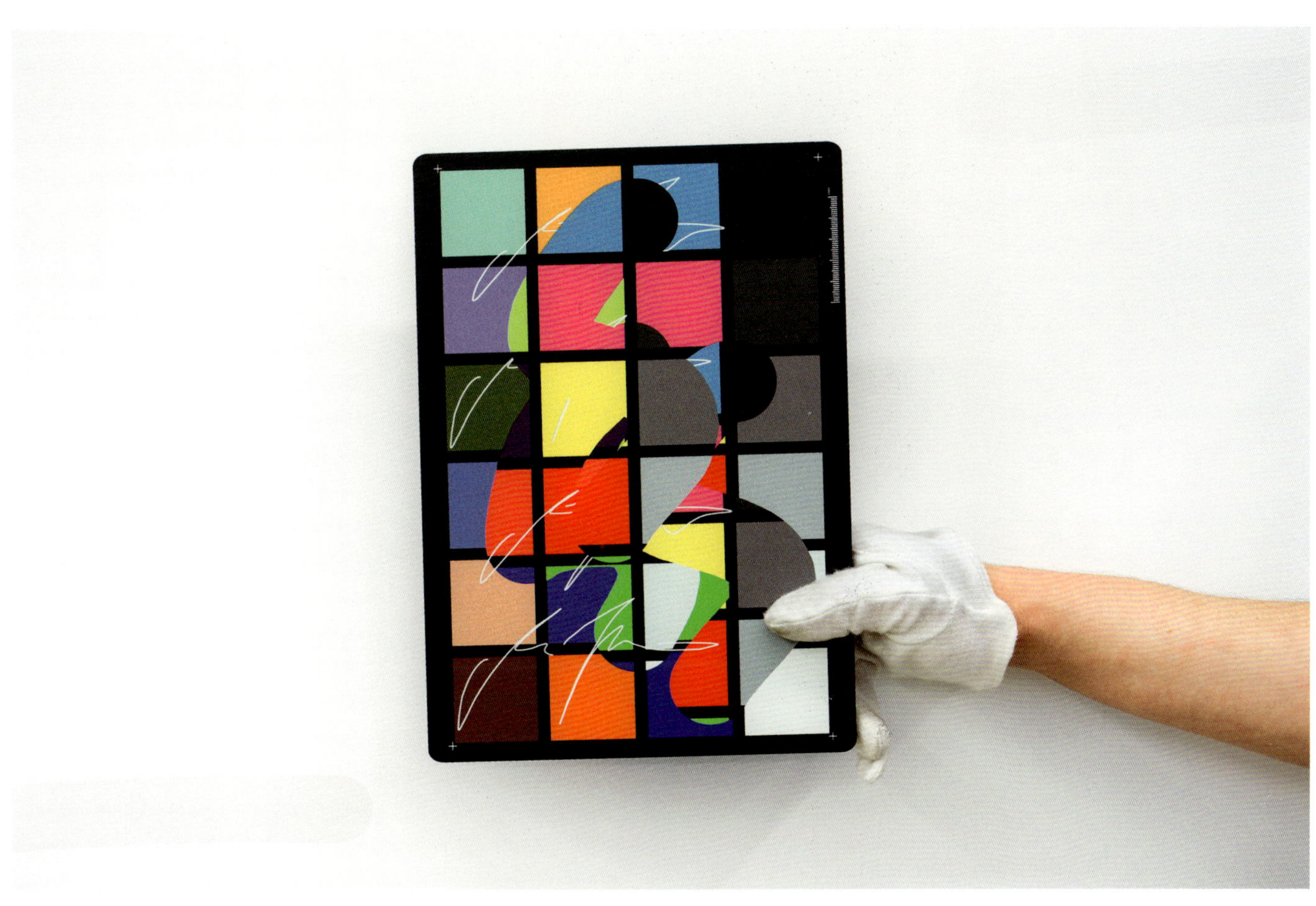

107     Artie Vierkant, *Color Rendition Chart, Thursday 28 March 2013 2:47 PM*, 2013. UV print on Sintra

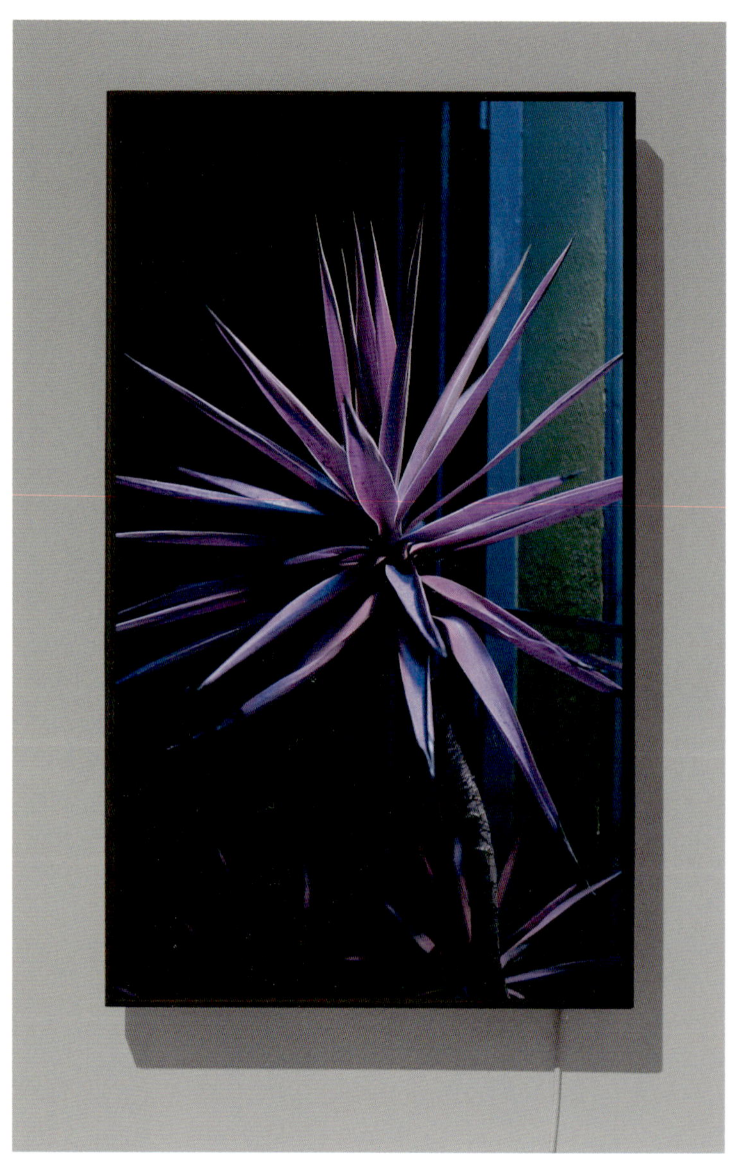

108    Owen Kydd, *Yucca Color Shift*, 2012. Video on 24-inch display

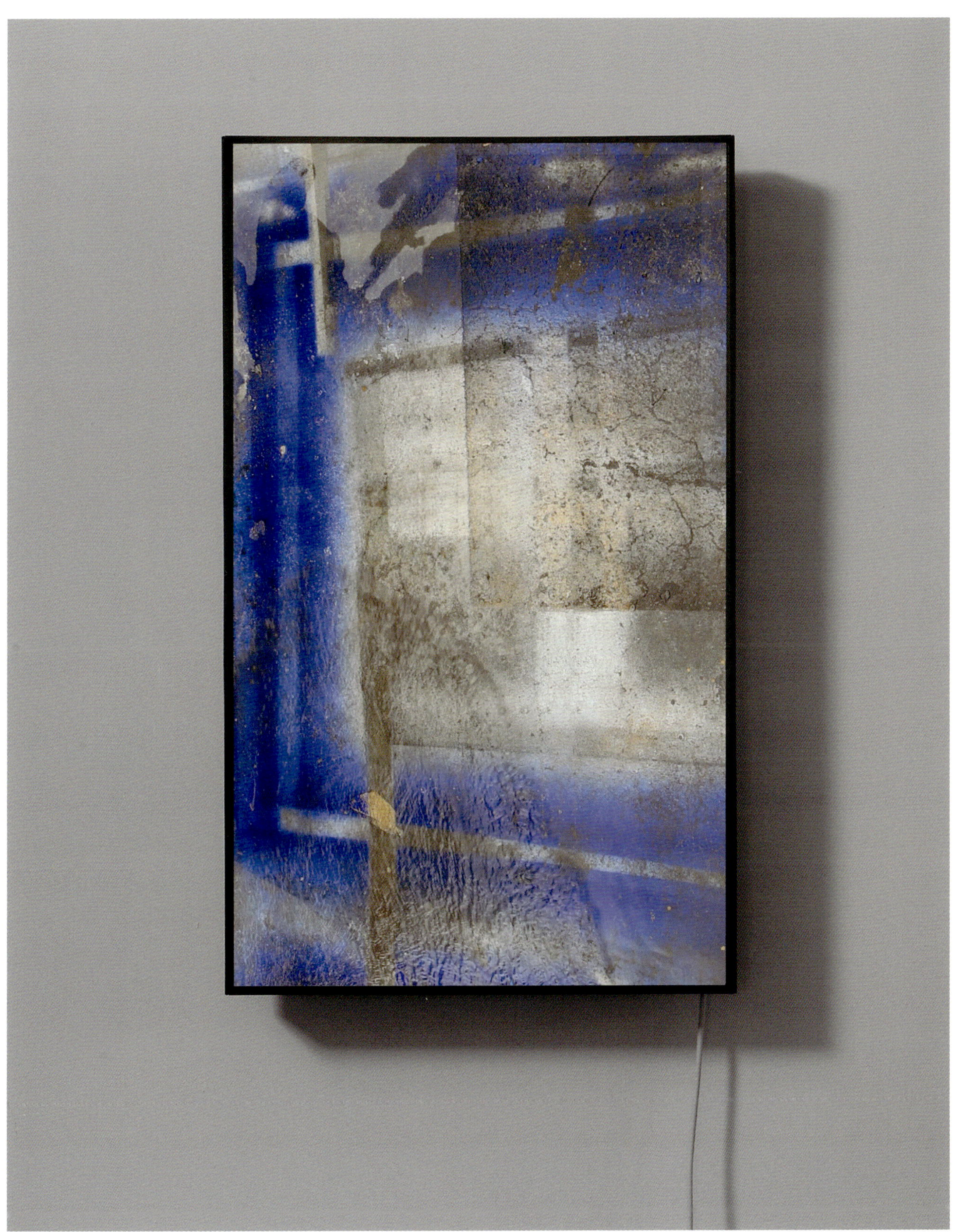

109    Owen Kydd, *Warner Studio Framing Floor*, 2012. Video on 40-inch display

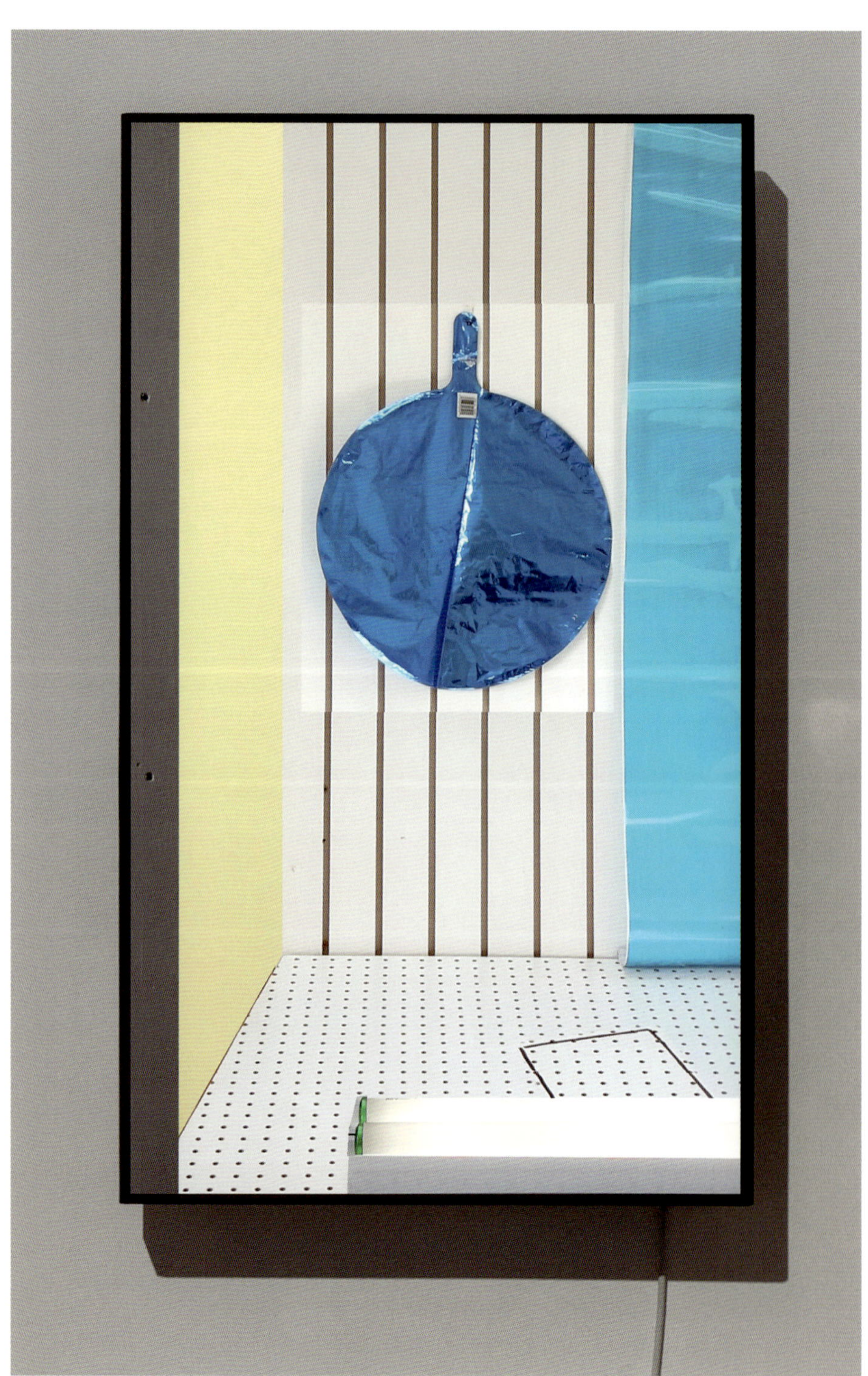

    Owen Kydd, *Window Study*, 2014. Video on two 40-inch displays

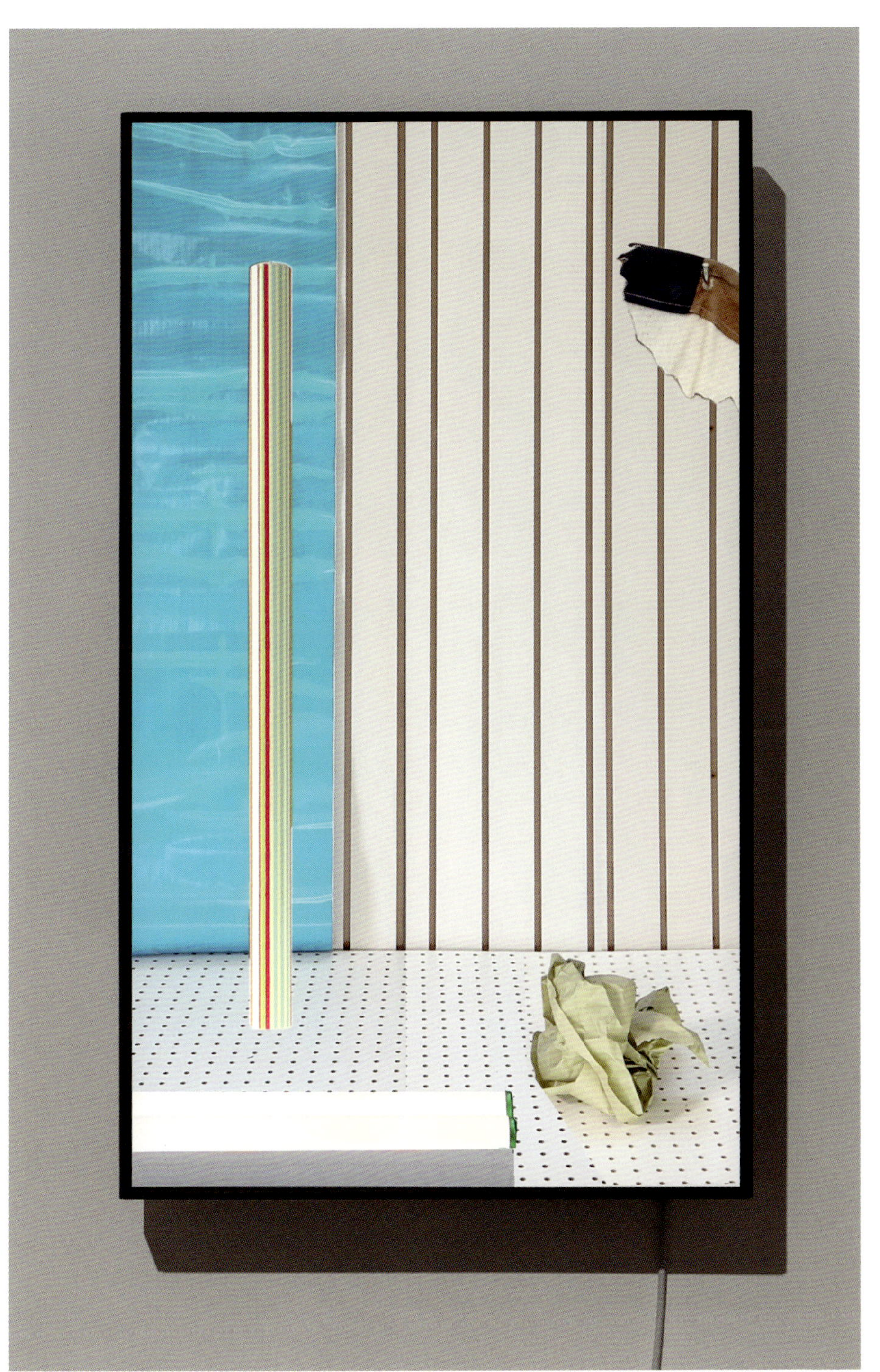

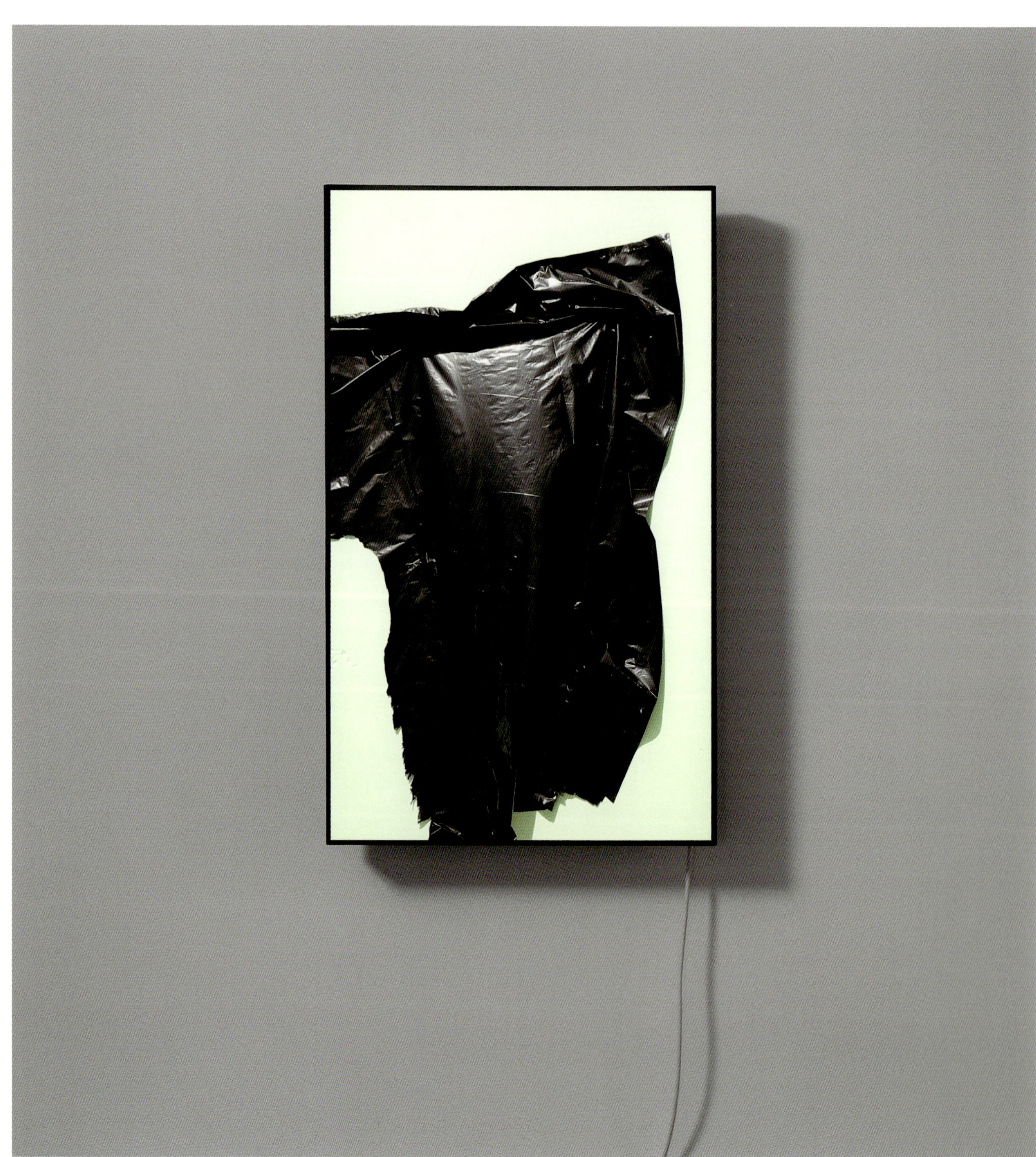

112   Owen Kydd, *Composition Warner Studio (on green)*, 2012. Video on 40-inch display

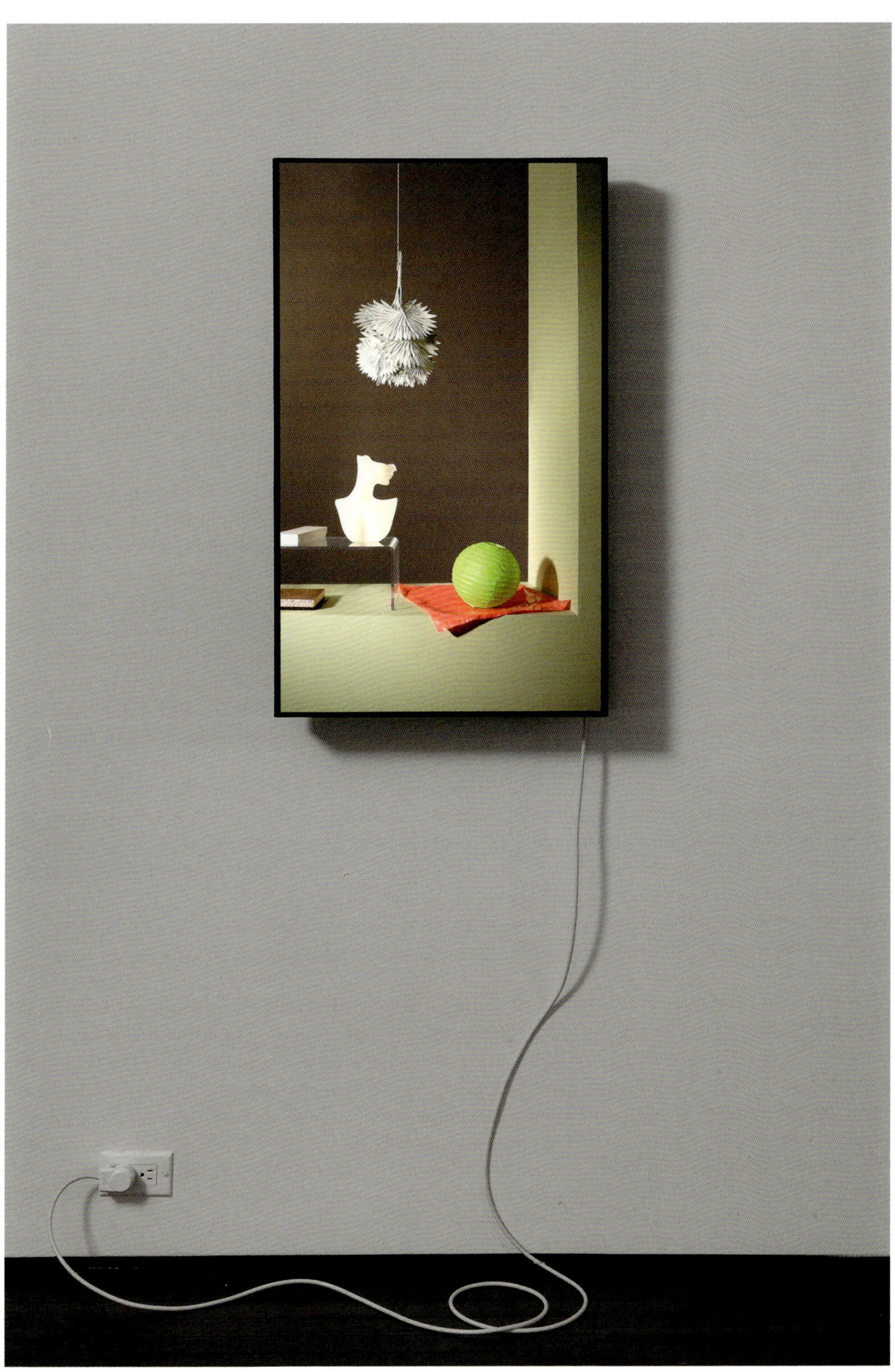

     Owen Kydd, *Canvas Leaves, Torso, and Lantern*, 2012. Video on 40-inch display

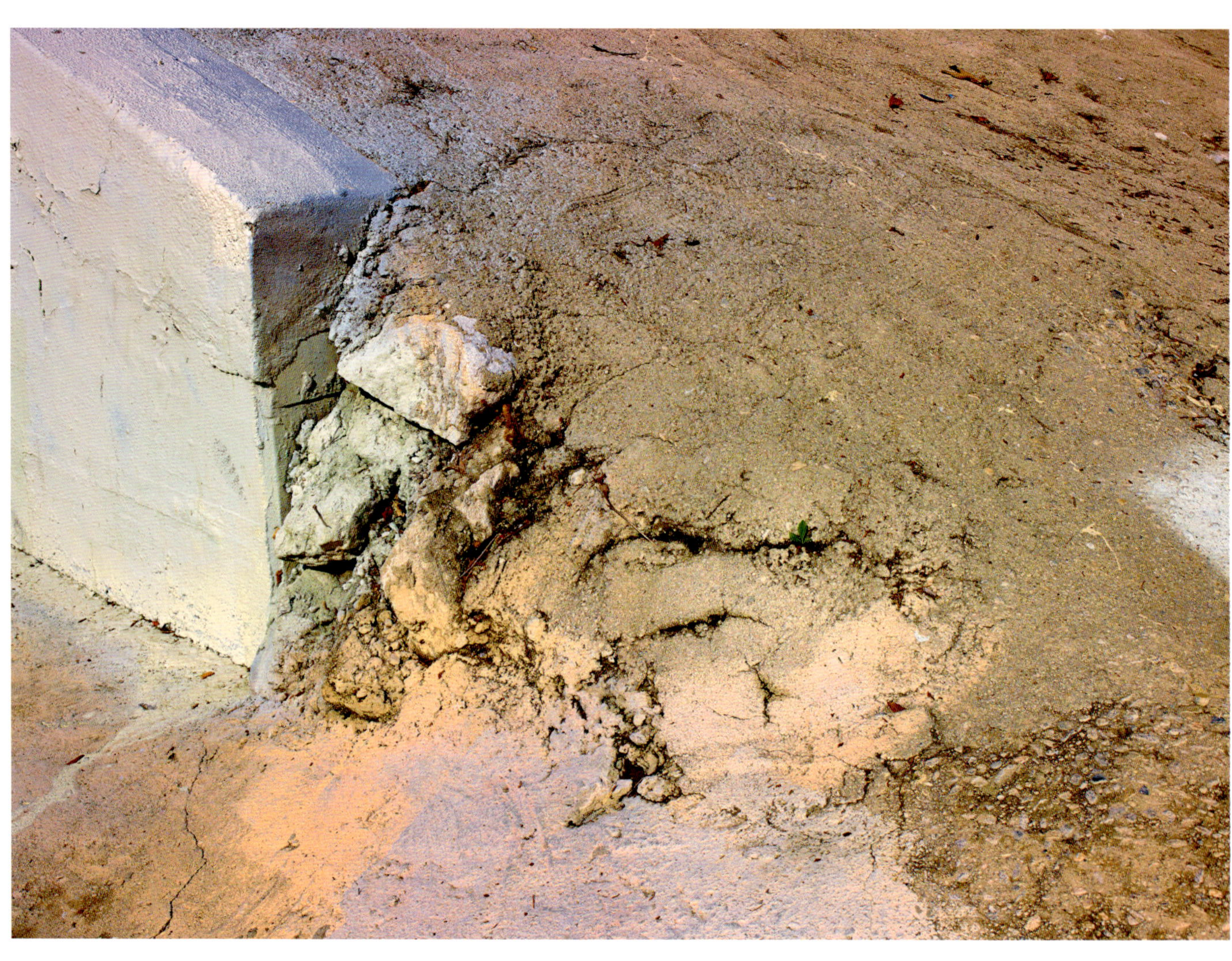

114     Marten Elder, *noc 6*, 2013. Archival pigment print on fiber-based paper

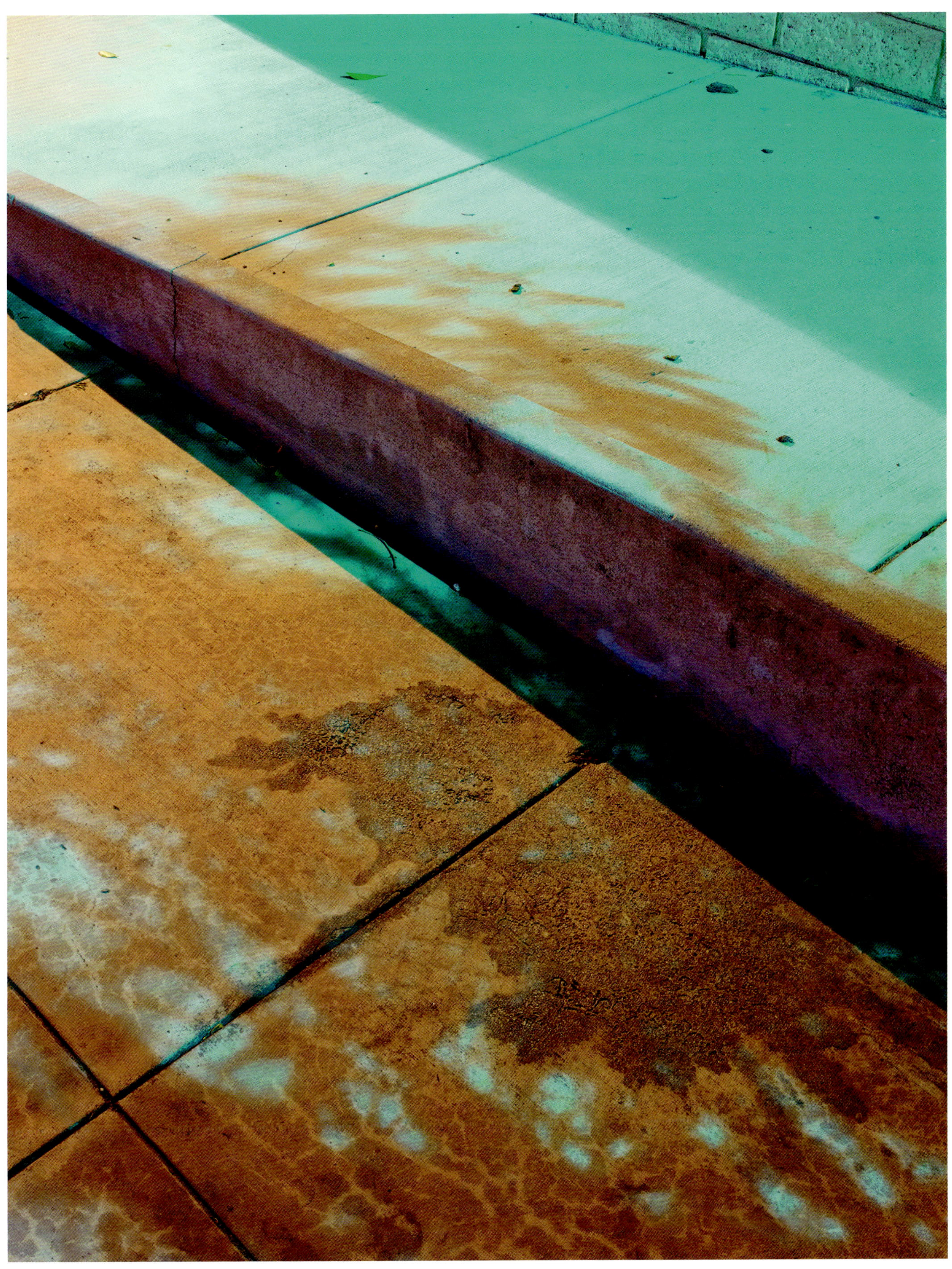

115    Marten Elder, *noc* 7, 2013. Archival pigment print on fiber-based paper

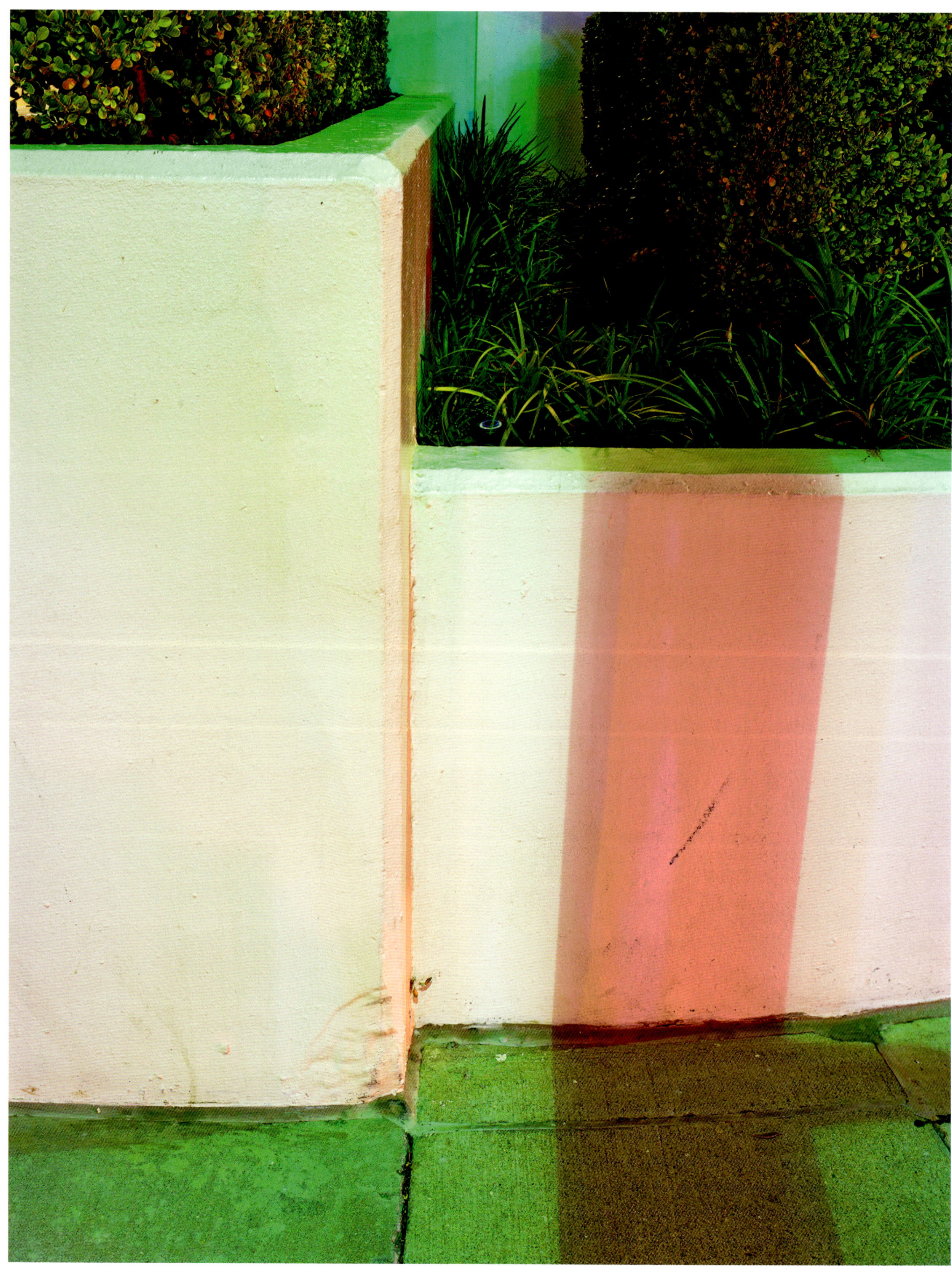

116　Marten Elder, *noc 9*, 2013. Archival pigment print on fiber-based paper

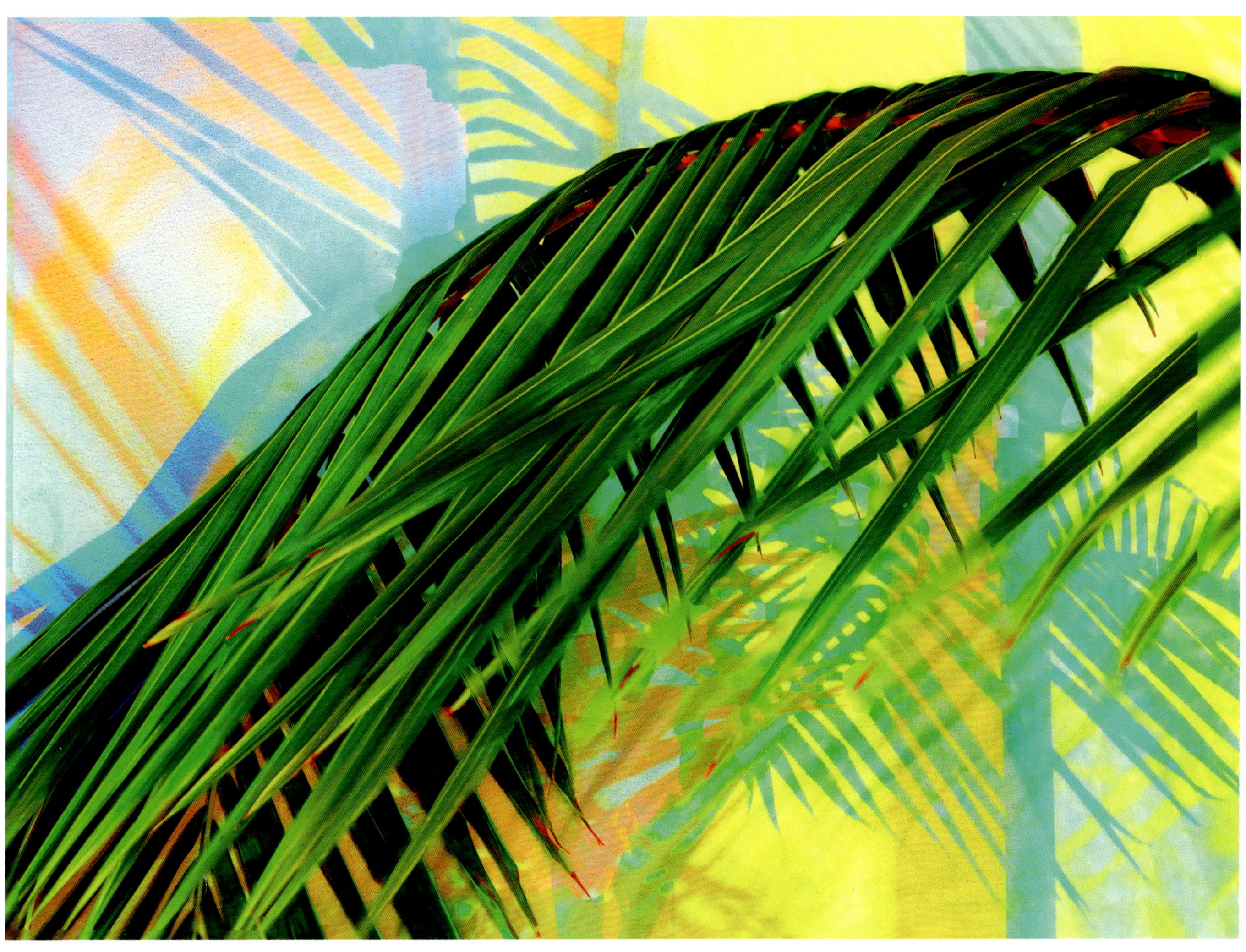

117    Marten Elder, *pr 14*, 2014. Archival pigment print on fiber-based paper

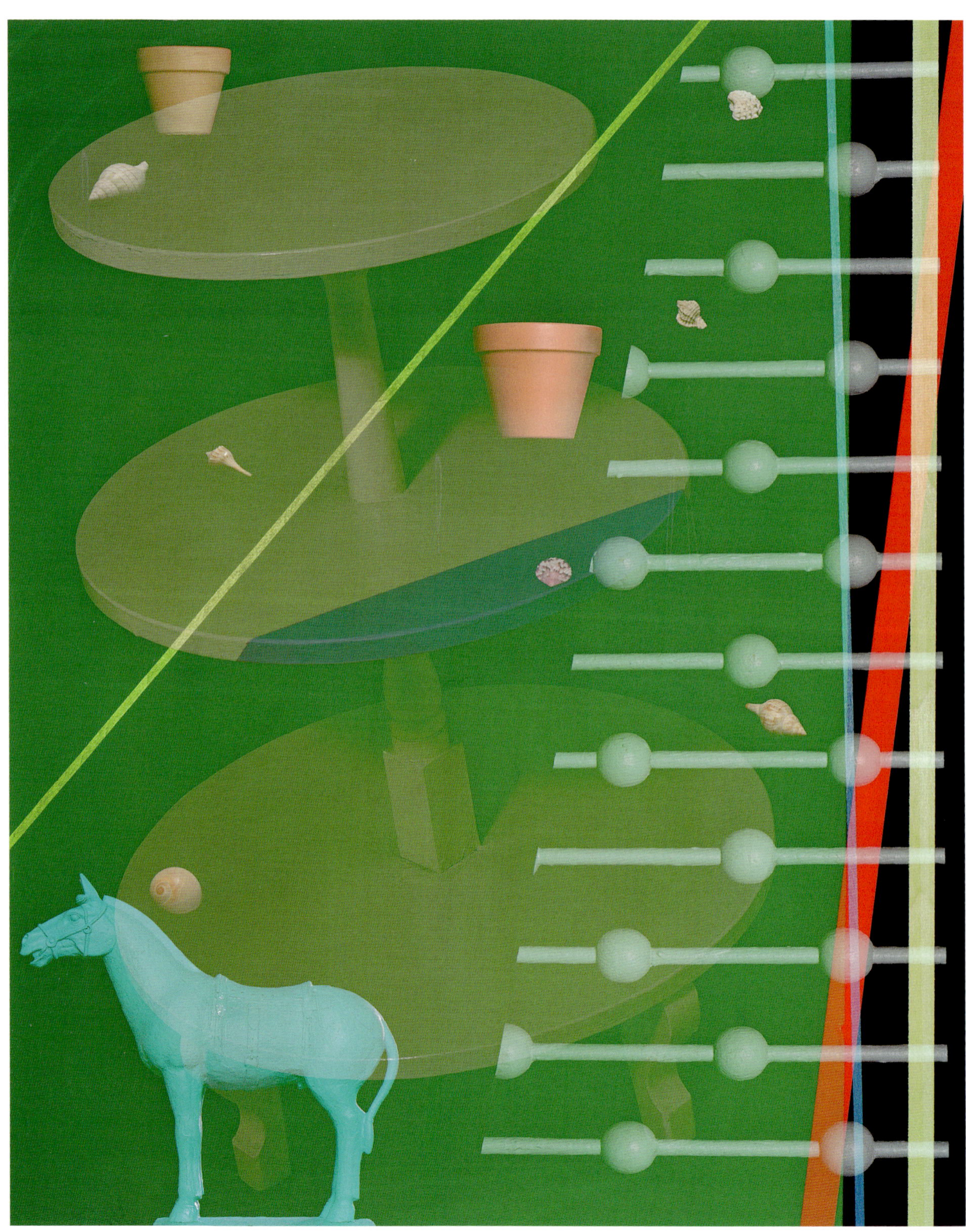

    Matthew Porter, *Garden*, 2014. Inkjet print

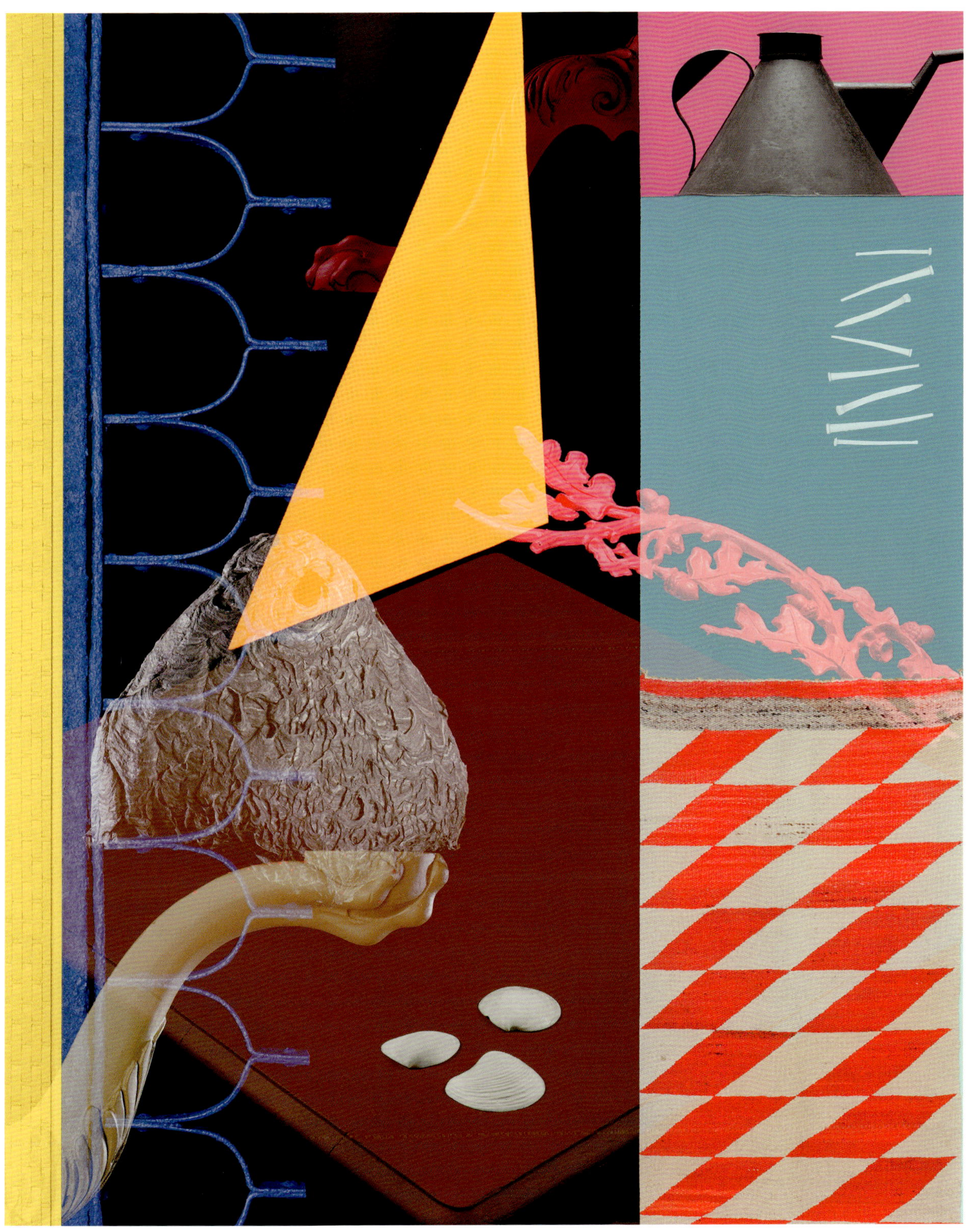

119    Matthew Porter, *This Is Tomorrow*, 2013. Inkjet print

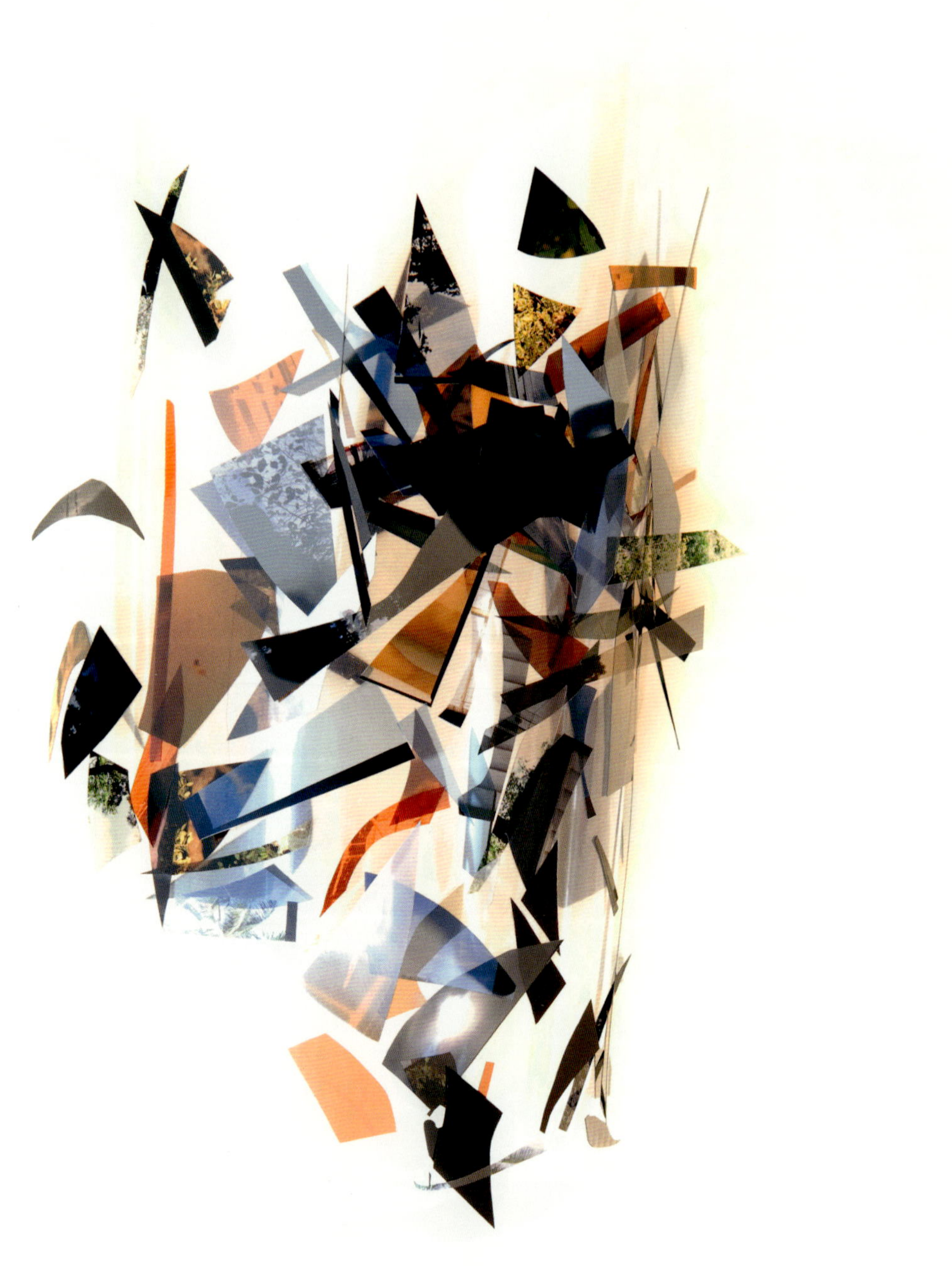

120    Brea Souders, *Film Electric #9*, 2013. Archival pigment print

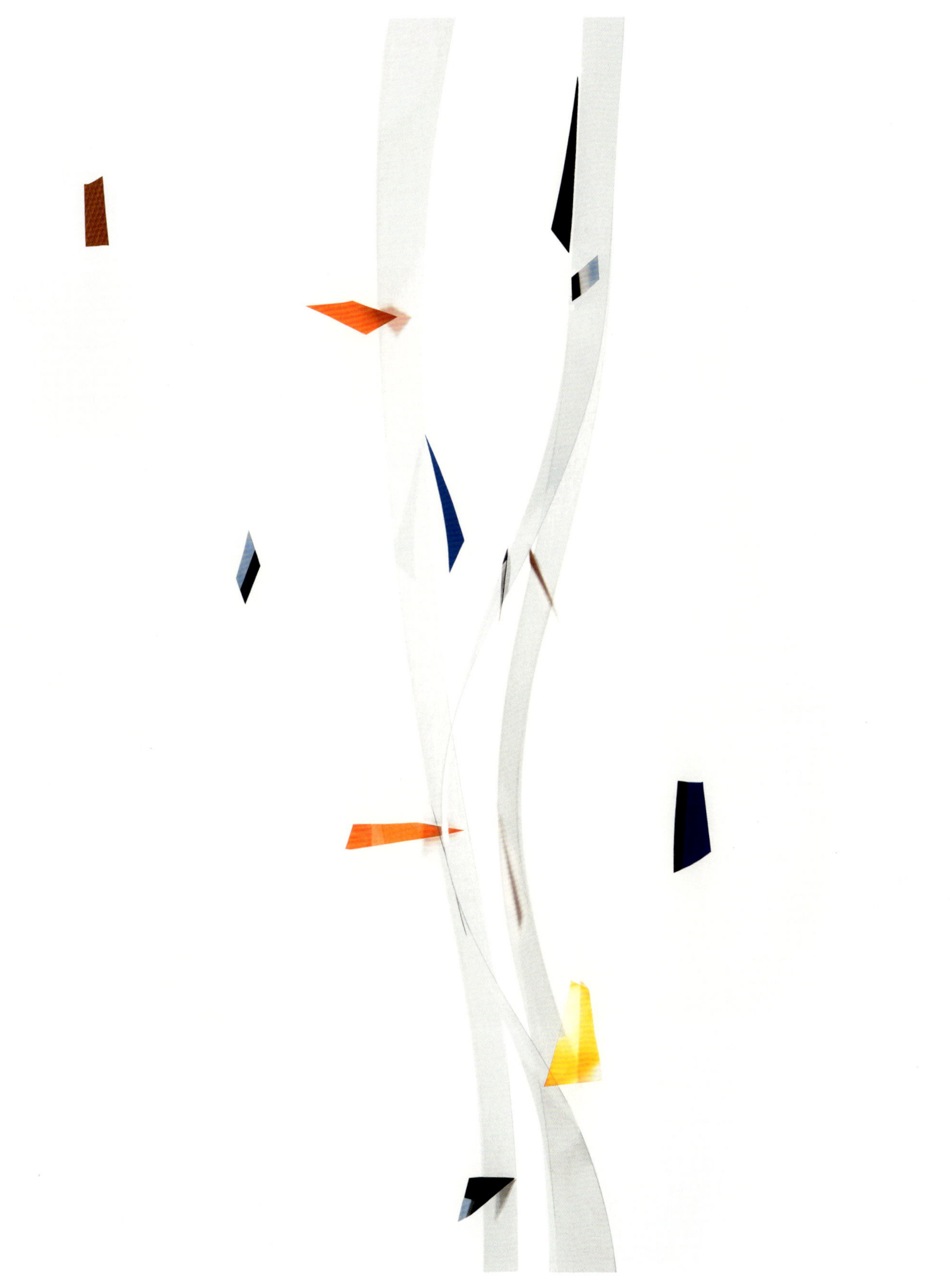

121 Brea Souders, *Film Electric #21*, 2013. Archival pigment print

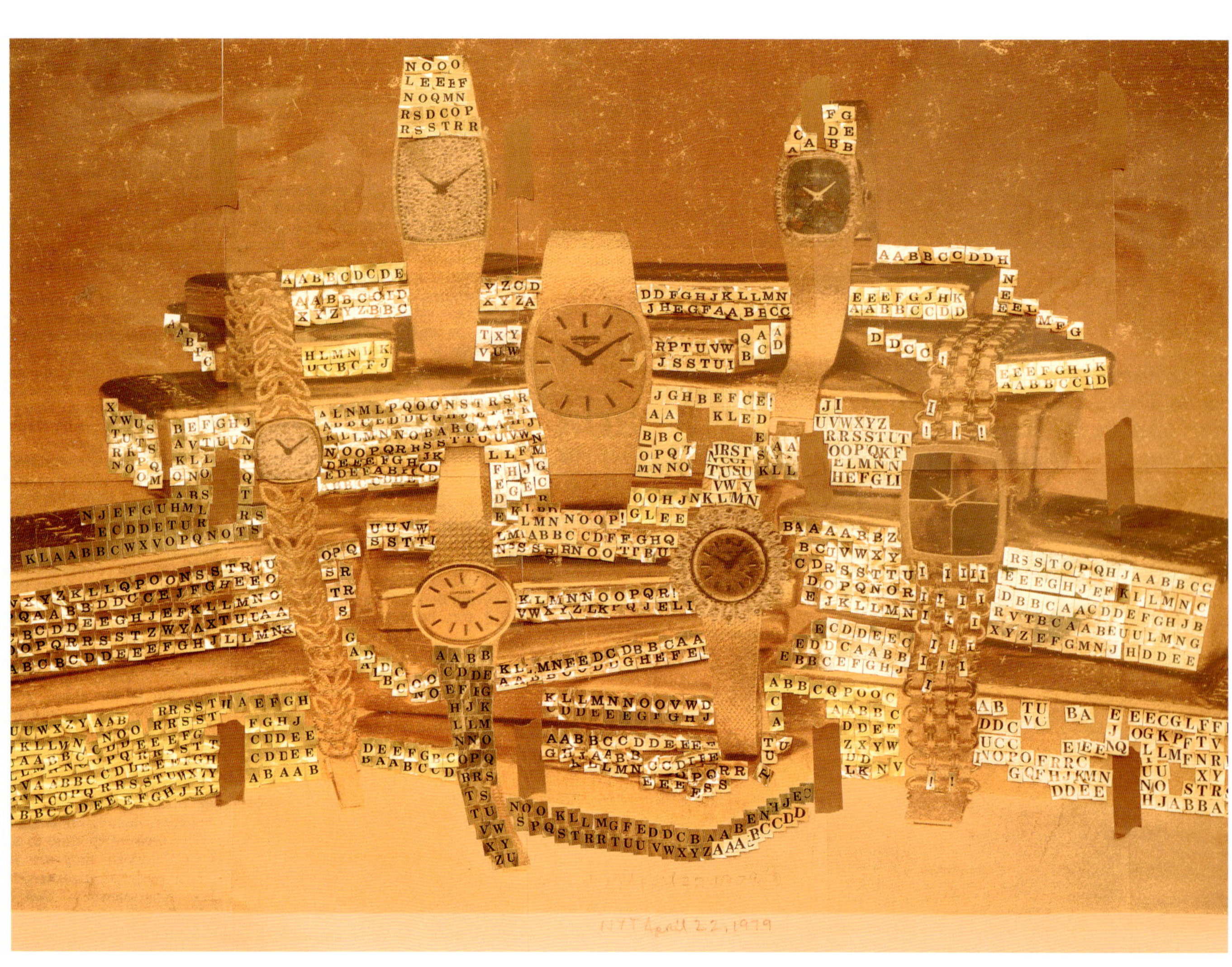

122    Sara Cwynar, *Gold-NYT April 22, 1979 (Alphabet Stickers)*, 2013. C-print

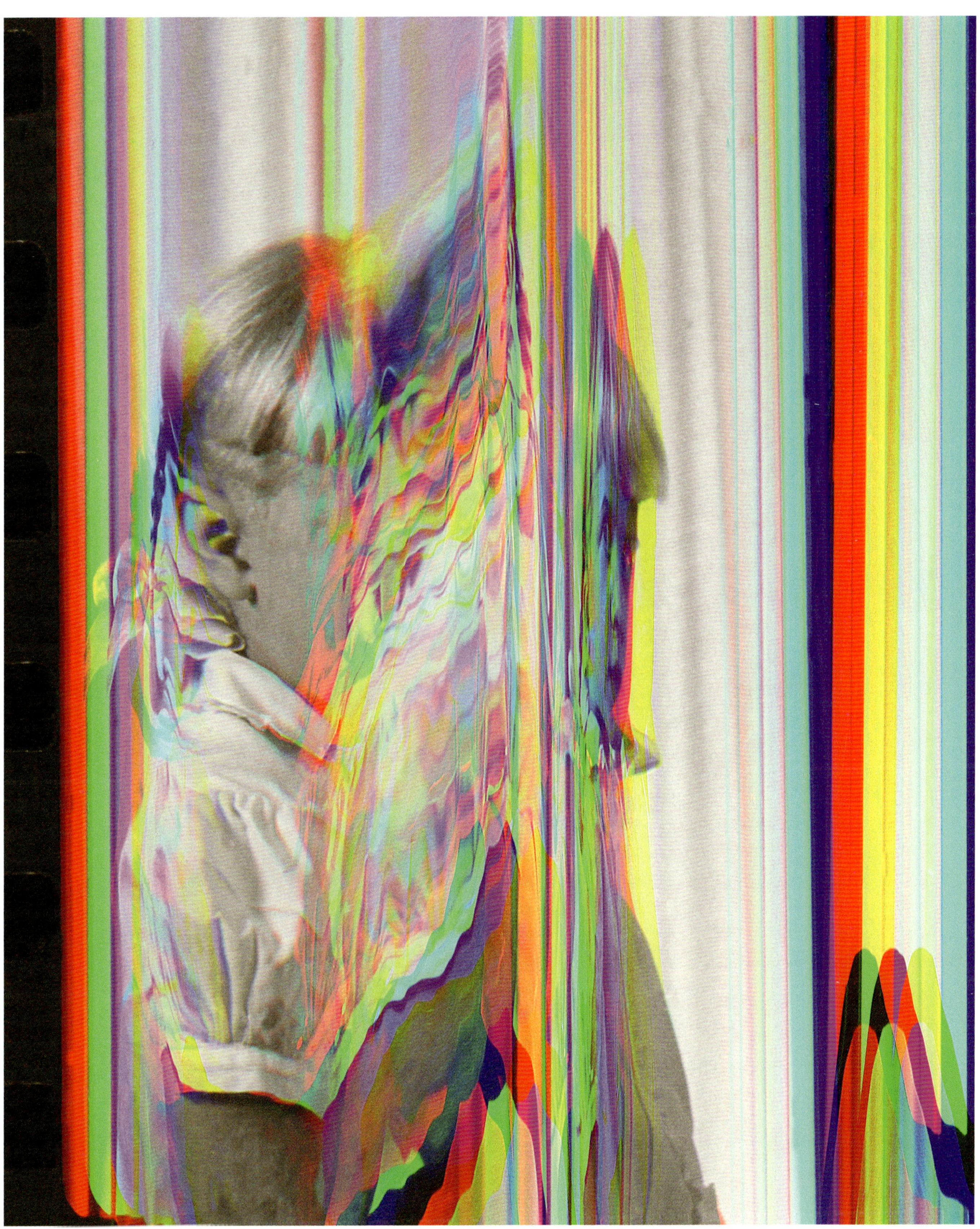

123    Sara Cwynar, *Girl from Contact Sheet 2 (Darkroom Manual)*, 2014. C-print

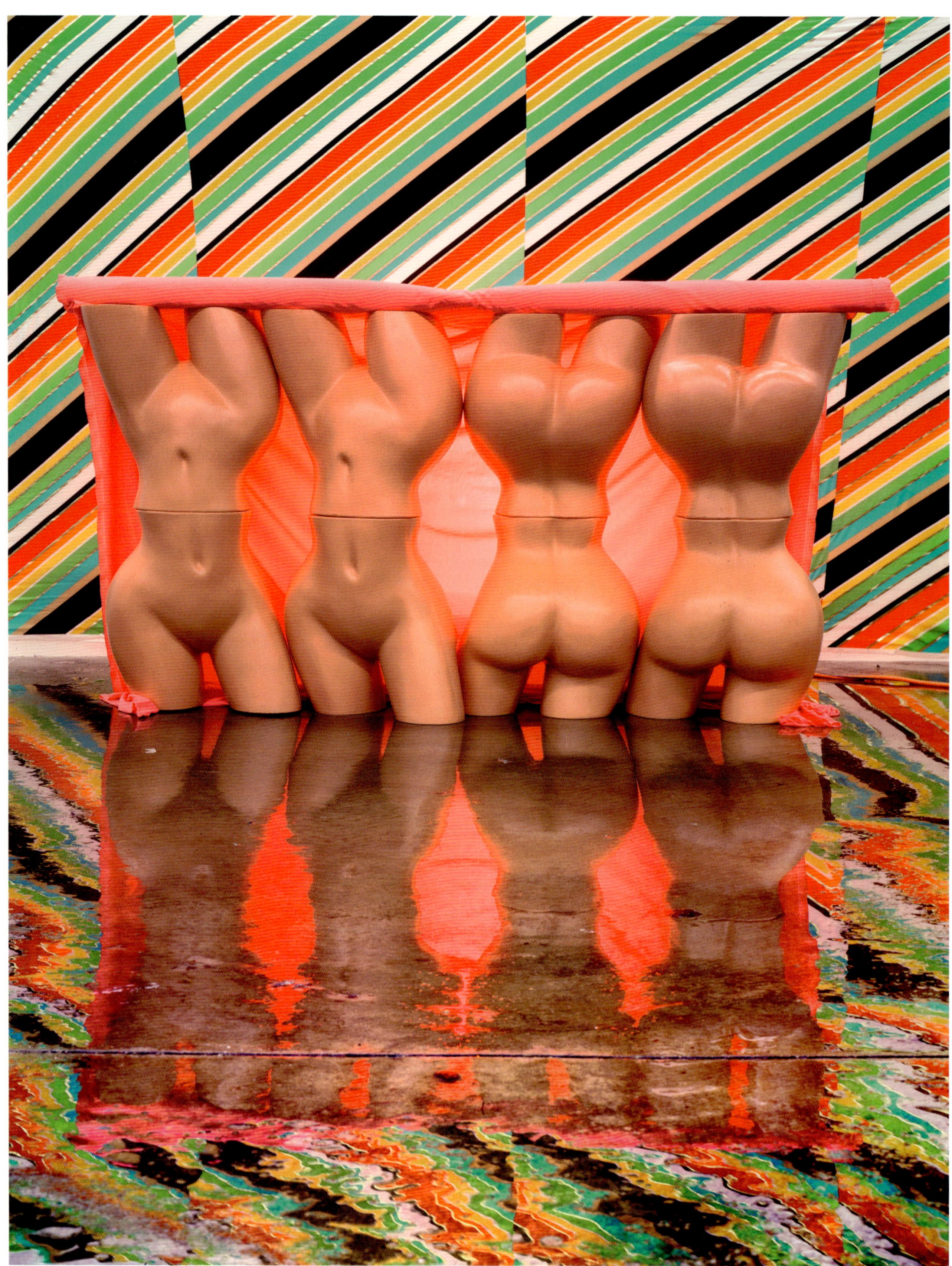

124    Anthony Lepore, *Mirage*, 2014. Archival pigment print

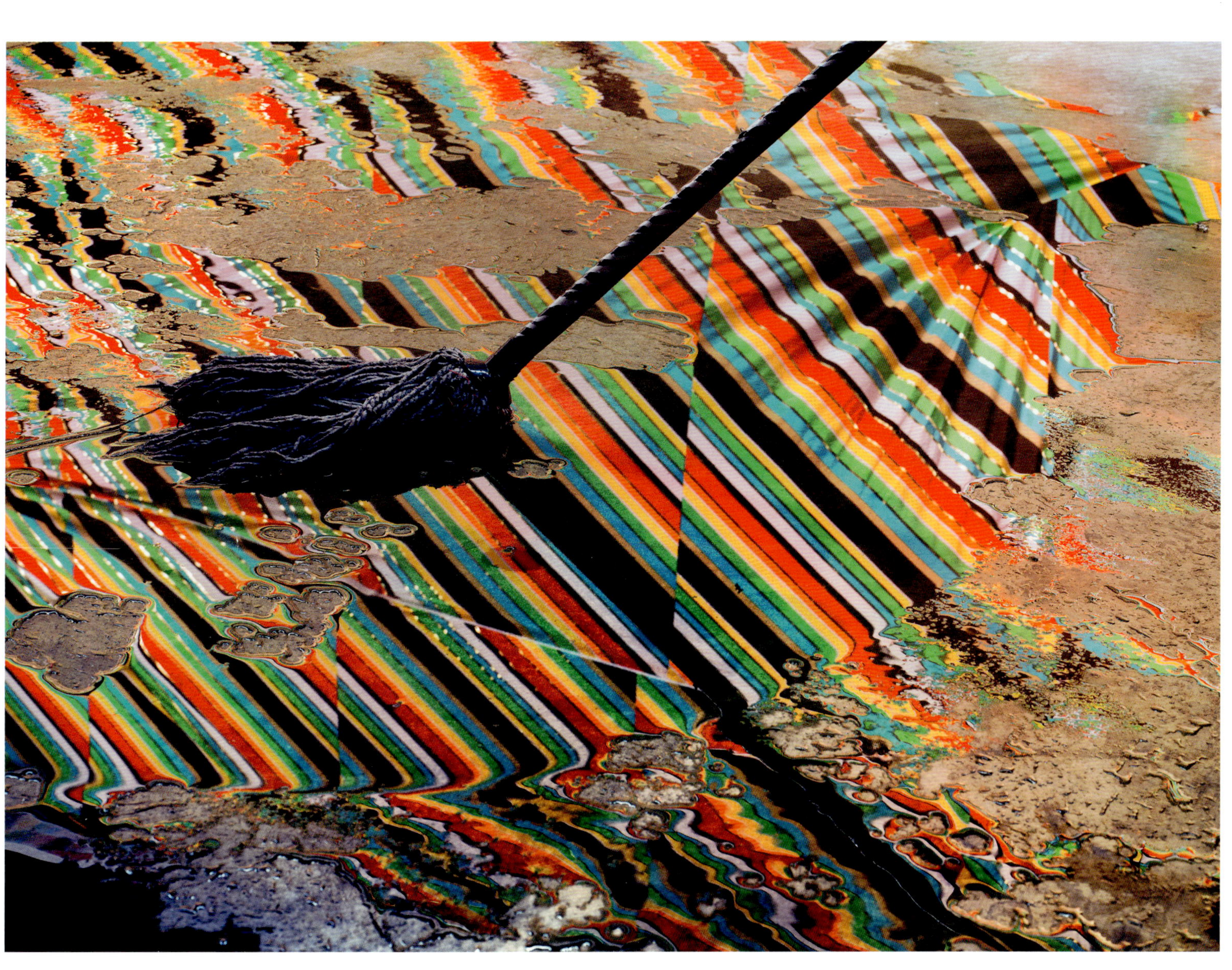

125    Anthony Lepore, *Floor Show*, 2014. Archival pigment print

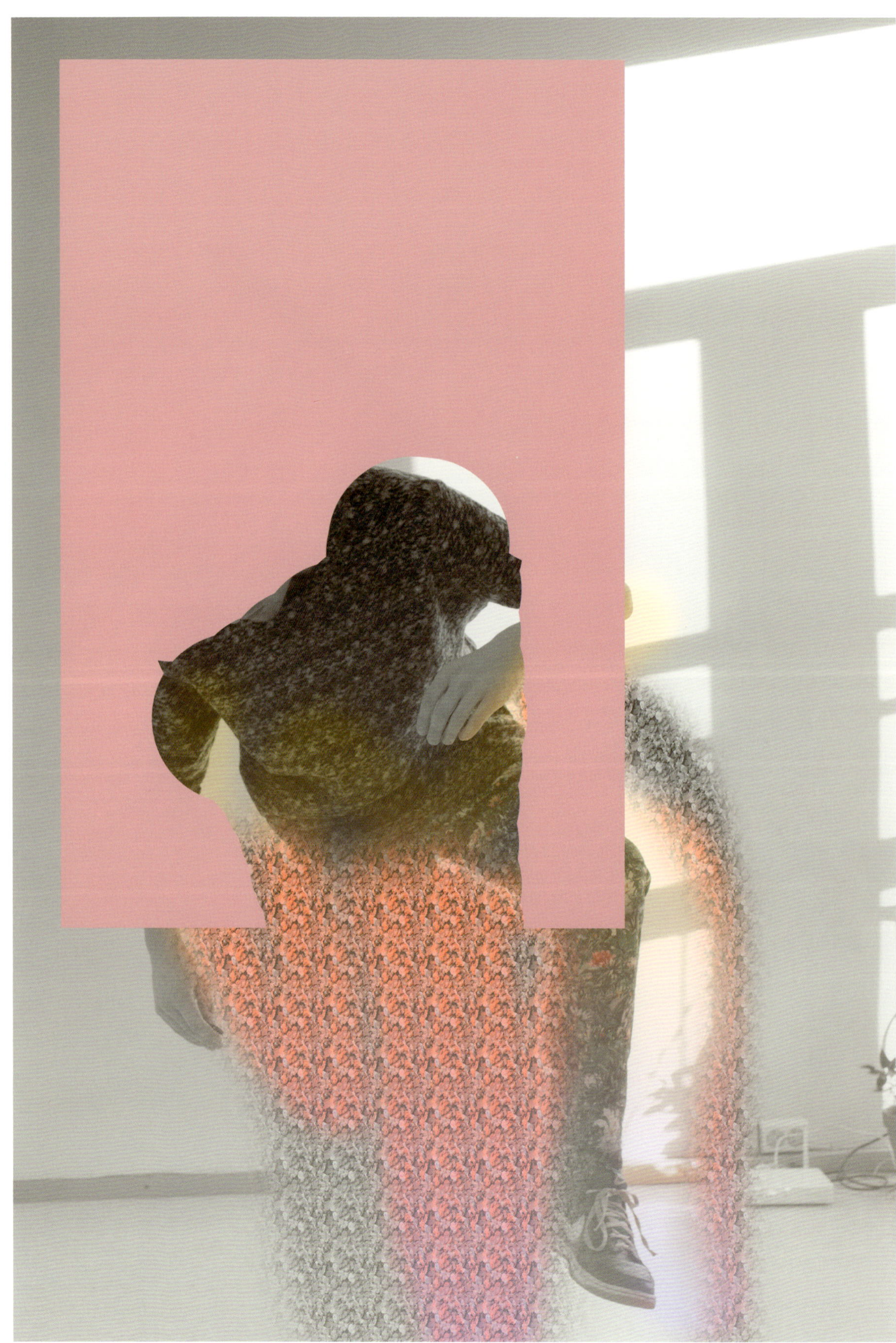

126    Andrey Bogush, *20140122_0620.jpg*, from the project *Proposals*, 2014. Inkjet print

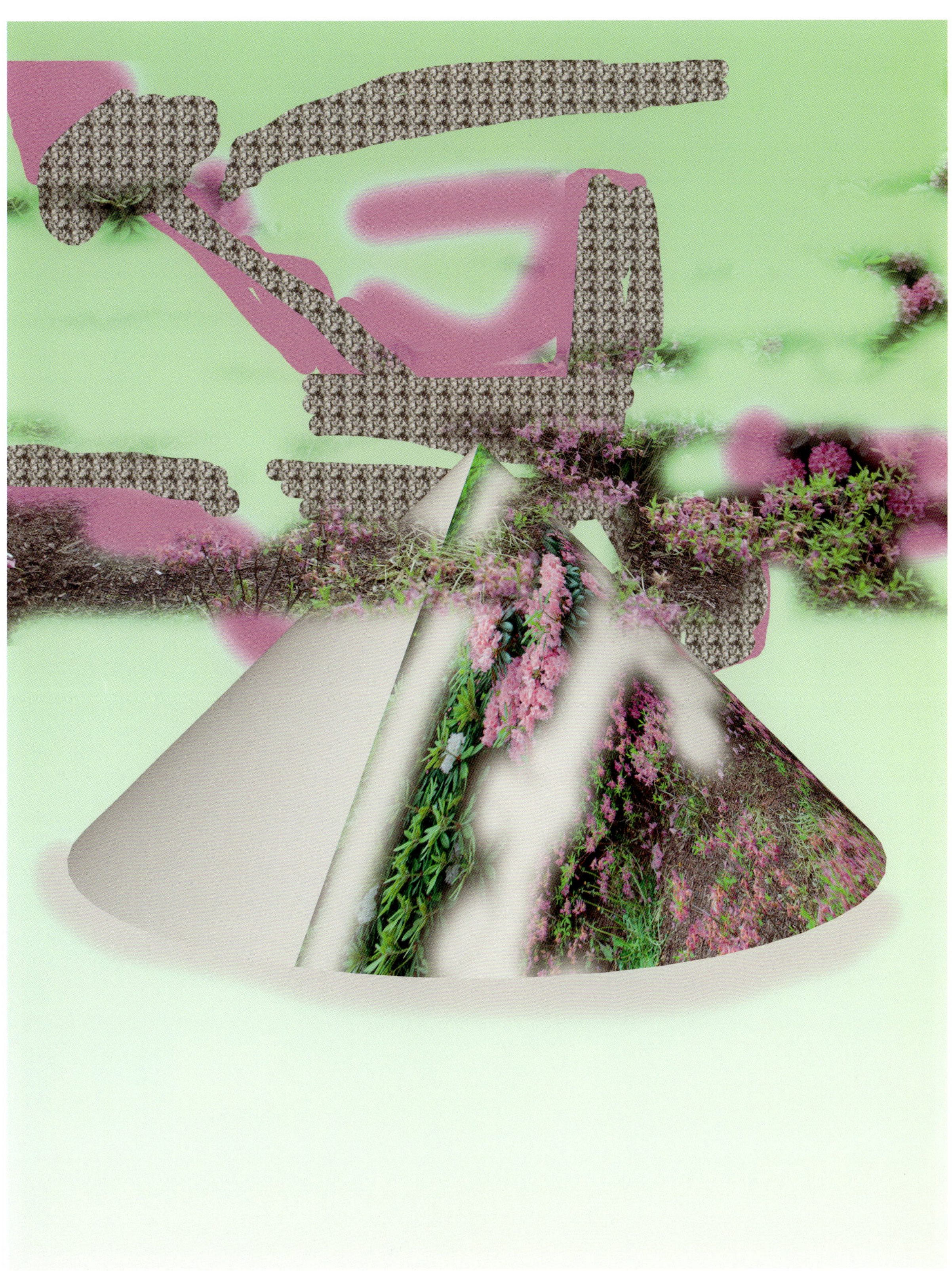

127 Andrey Bogush, *Proposal for Rhododendron Cone, Pattern and Gradient Green*, 2014. Inkjet print

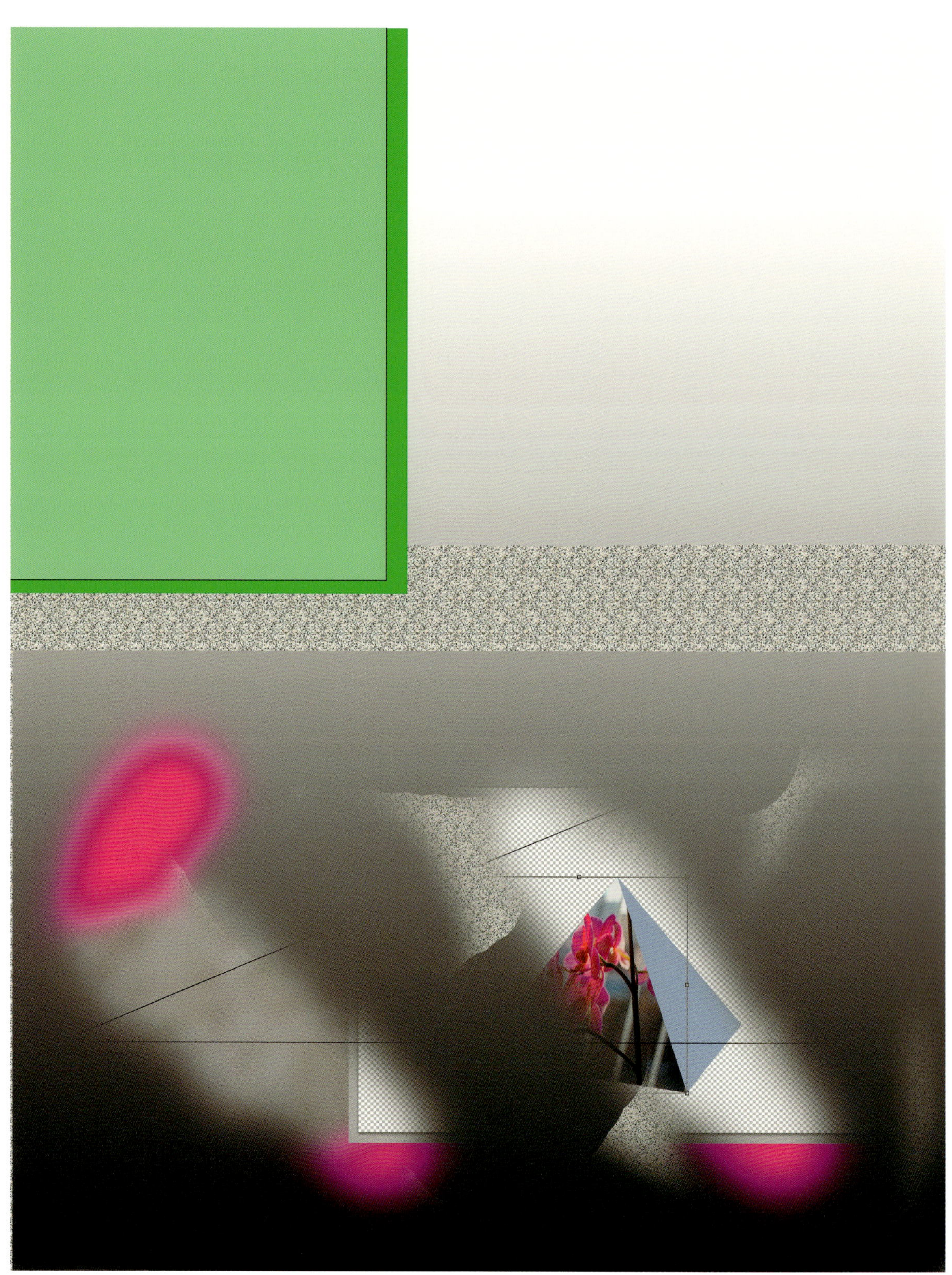

 Andrey Bogush, *Orchid Pyramid and Two Lines*, 2013. Inkjet print

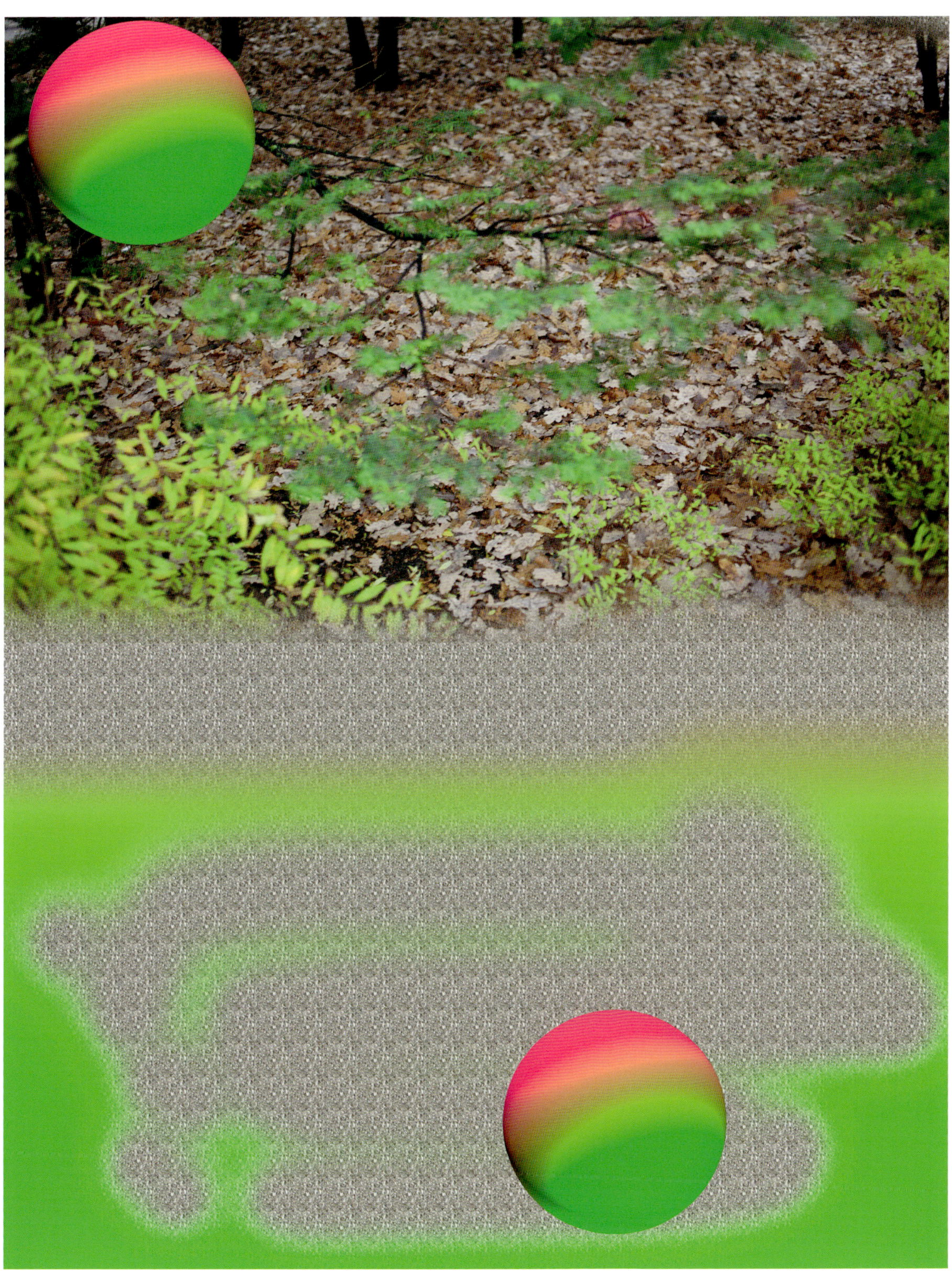

    Andrey Bogush, *Proposal for Landscape (Garden)*, 2013. Inkjet print

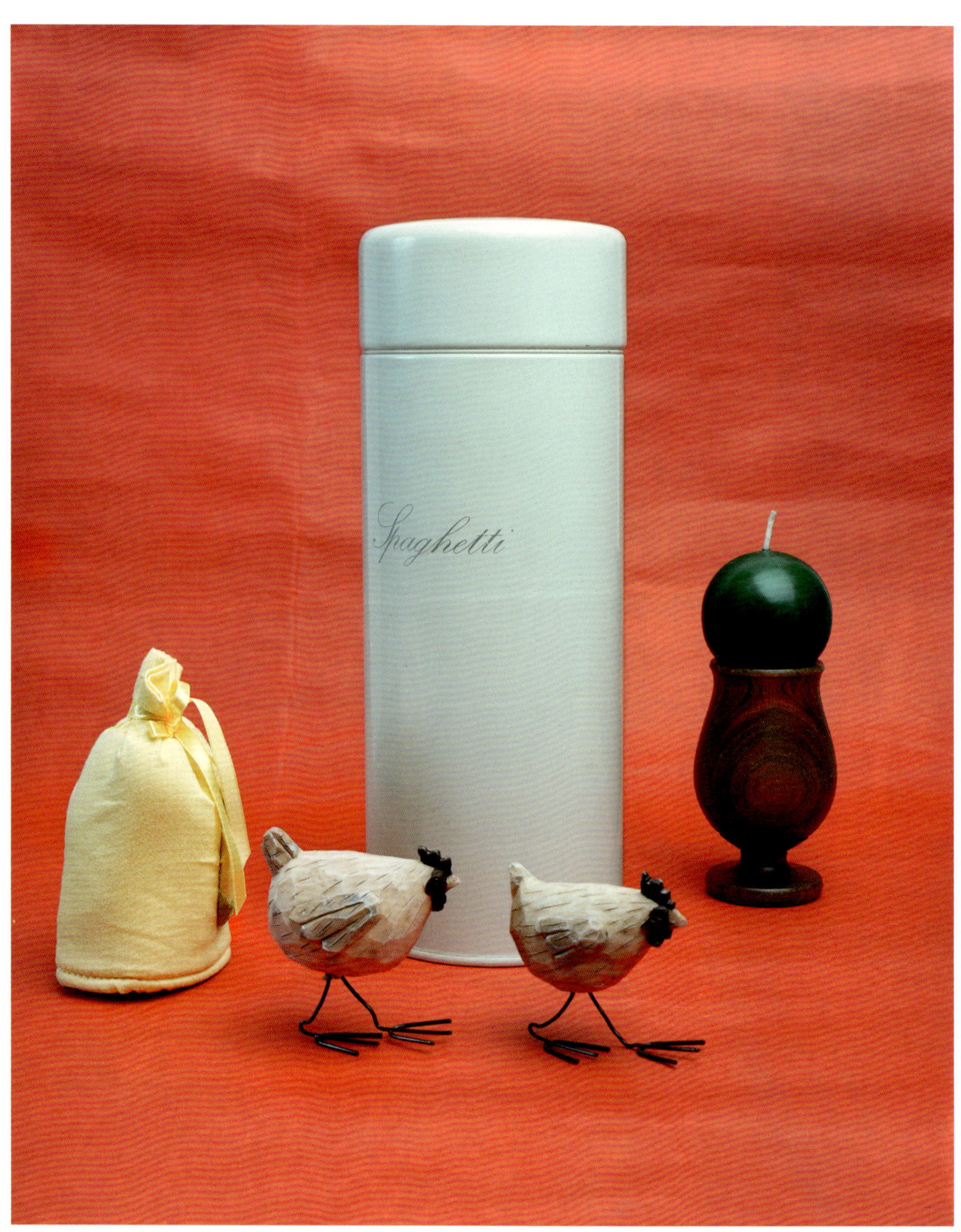


    Stefan Burger, from the artist's book *The Pommel Horse Popo* (Kodoji Press, 2013)

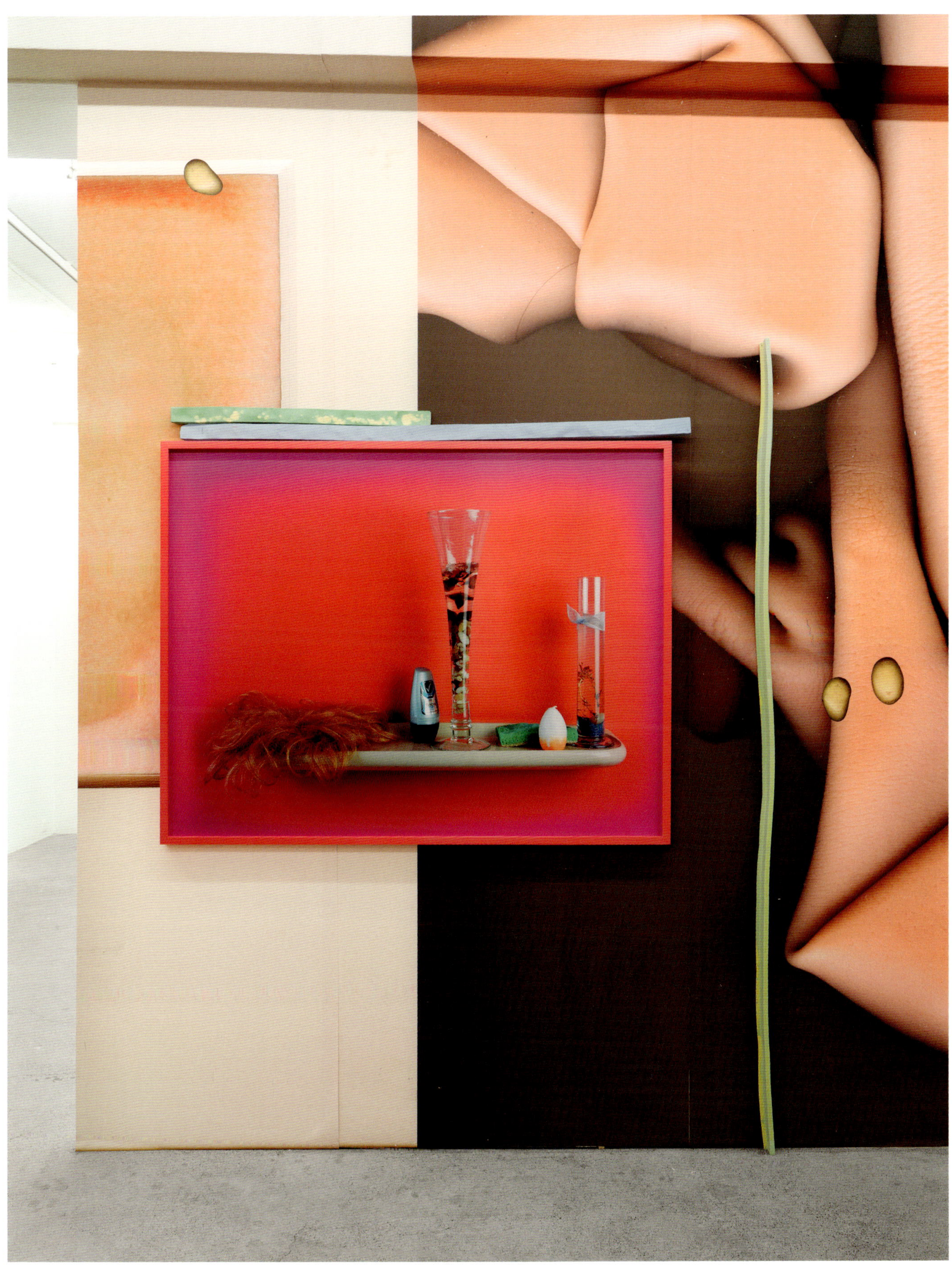

131    Stefan Burger, *Still untitled*, 2013. LightJet print on aluminum, frame (installation view)

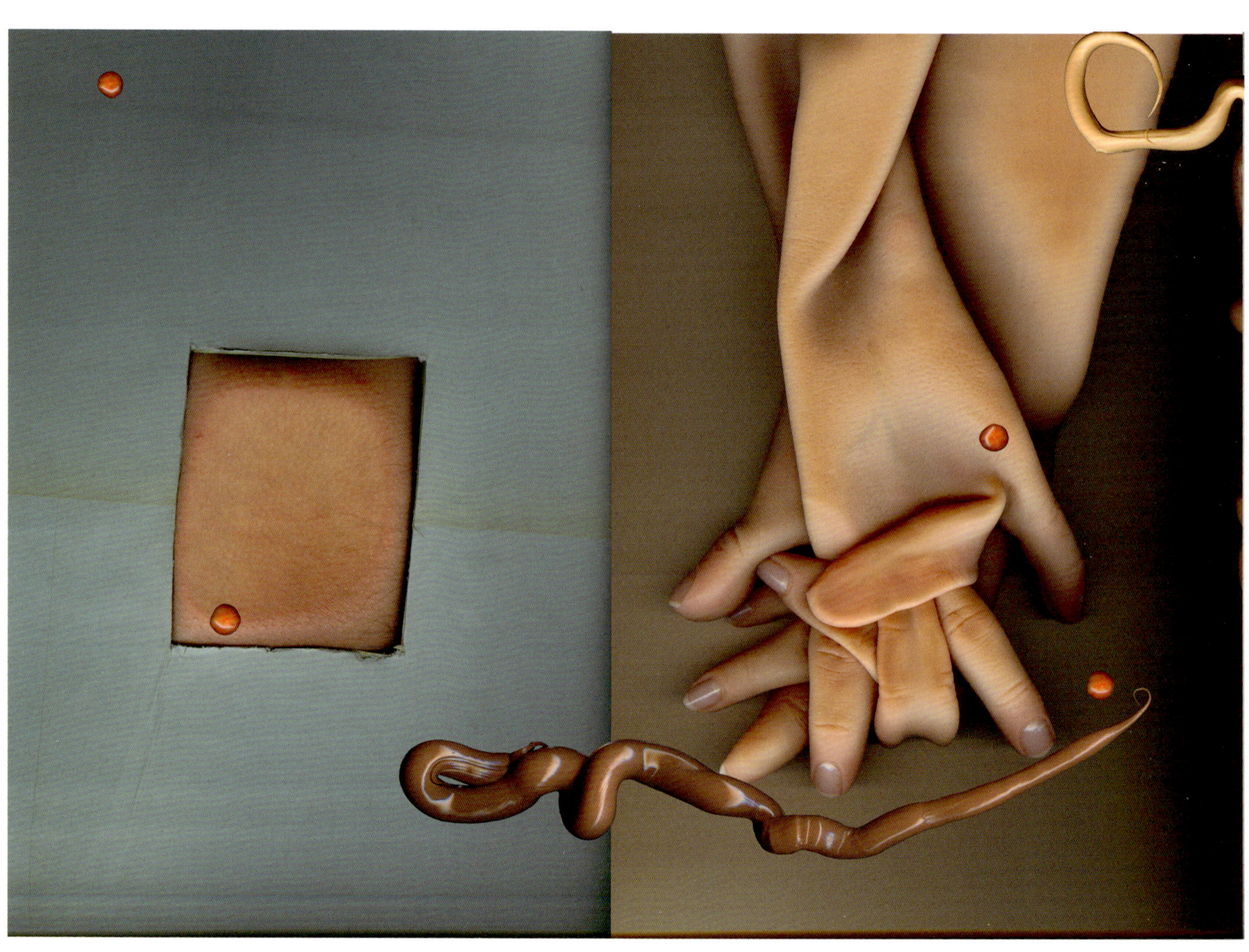

   Stefan Burger, *Not yet titled*, 2013. Inkjet print on wall, LightJet print on aluminum

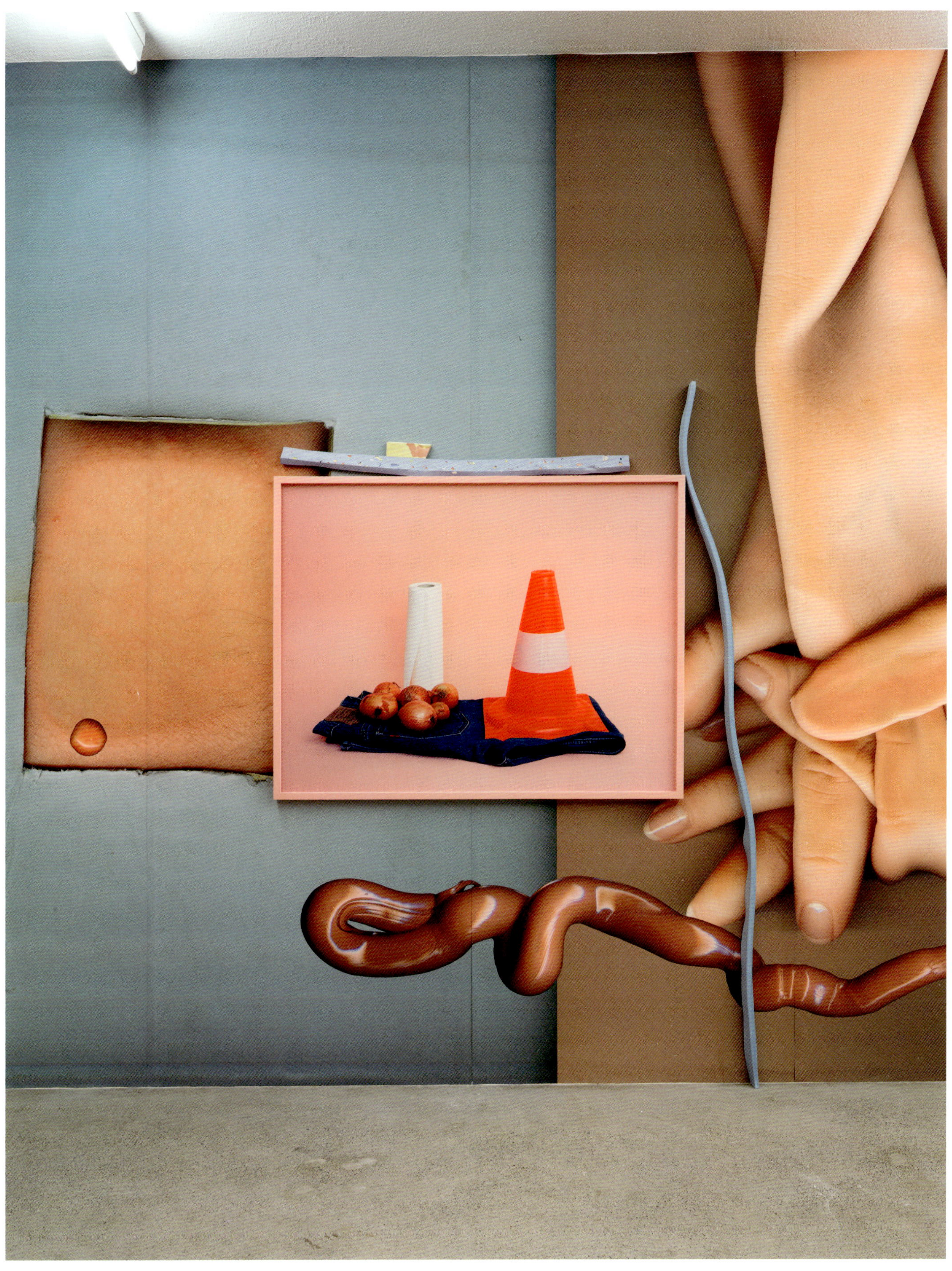

133    Stefan Burger, *Not yet titled*, 2013. Inkjet print on wall, LightJet print on aluminum, frame (installation view)

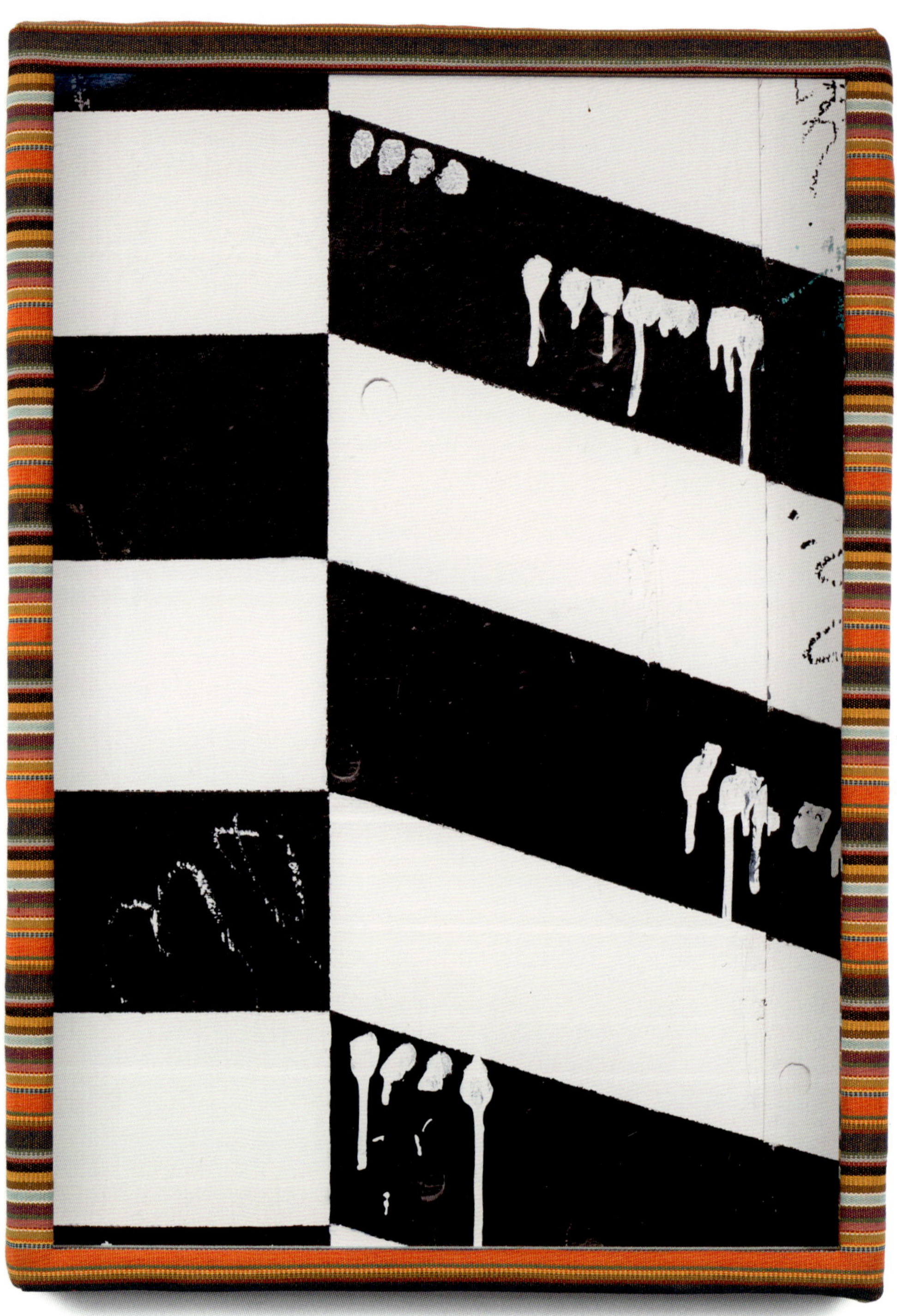

134     Chris Wiley, *Dingbat (10)*, 2014. Archival inkjet print on aluminum, artist's frame with fabric

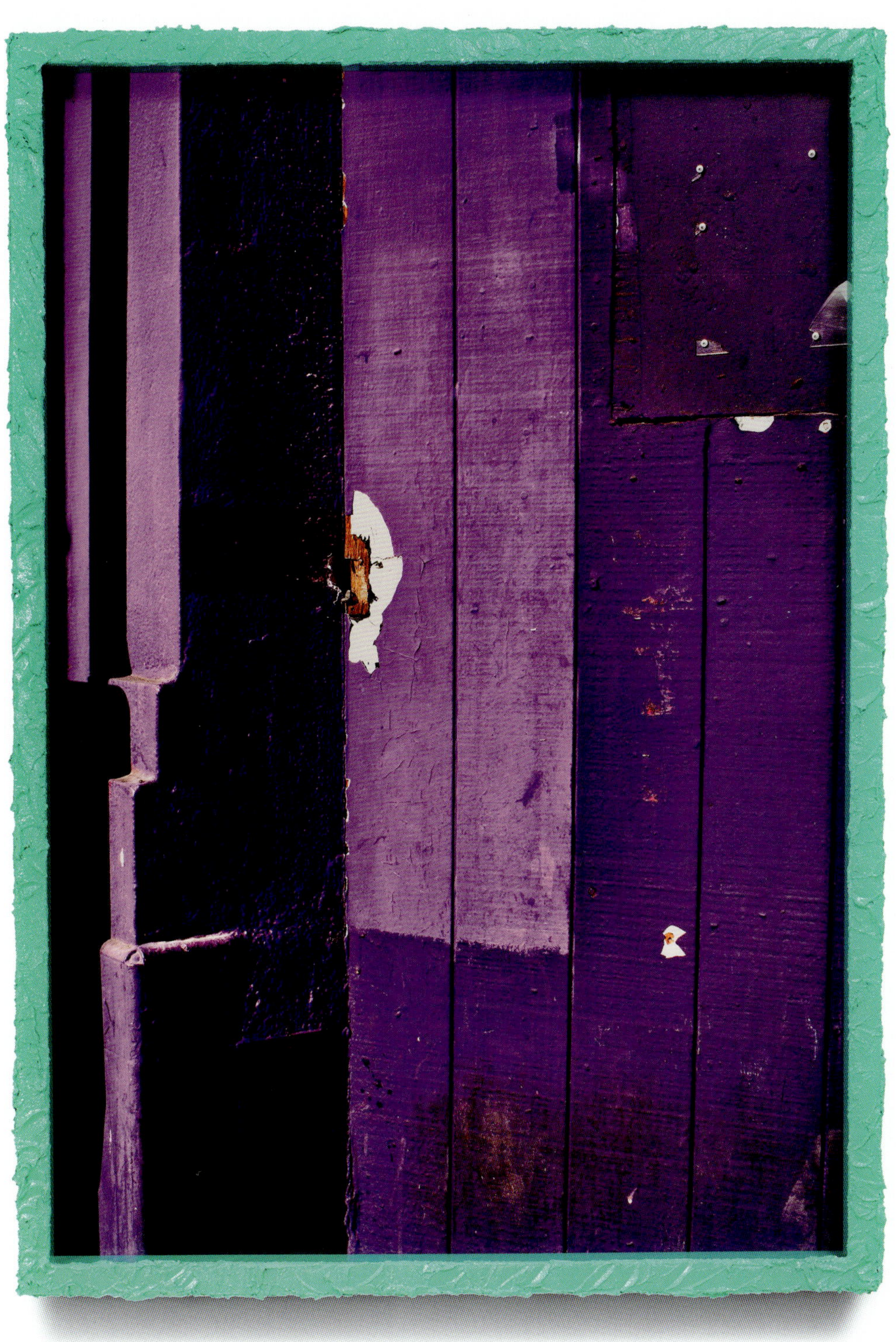

135  Chris Wiley, *Dingbat (9)*, 2014. Archival inkjet print on aluminum, artist's frame with stucco and sprayed acrylic

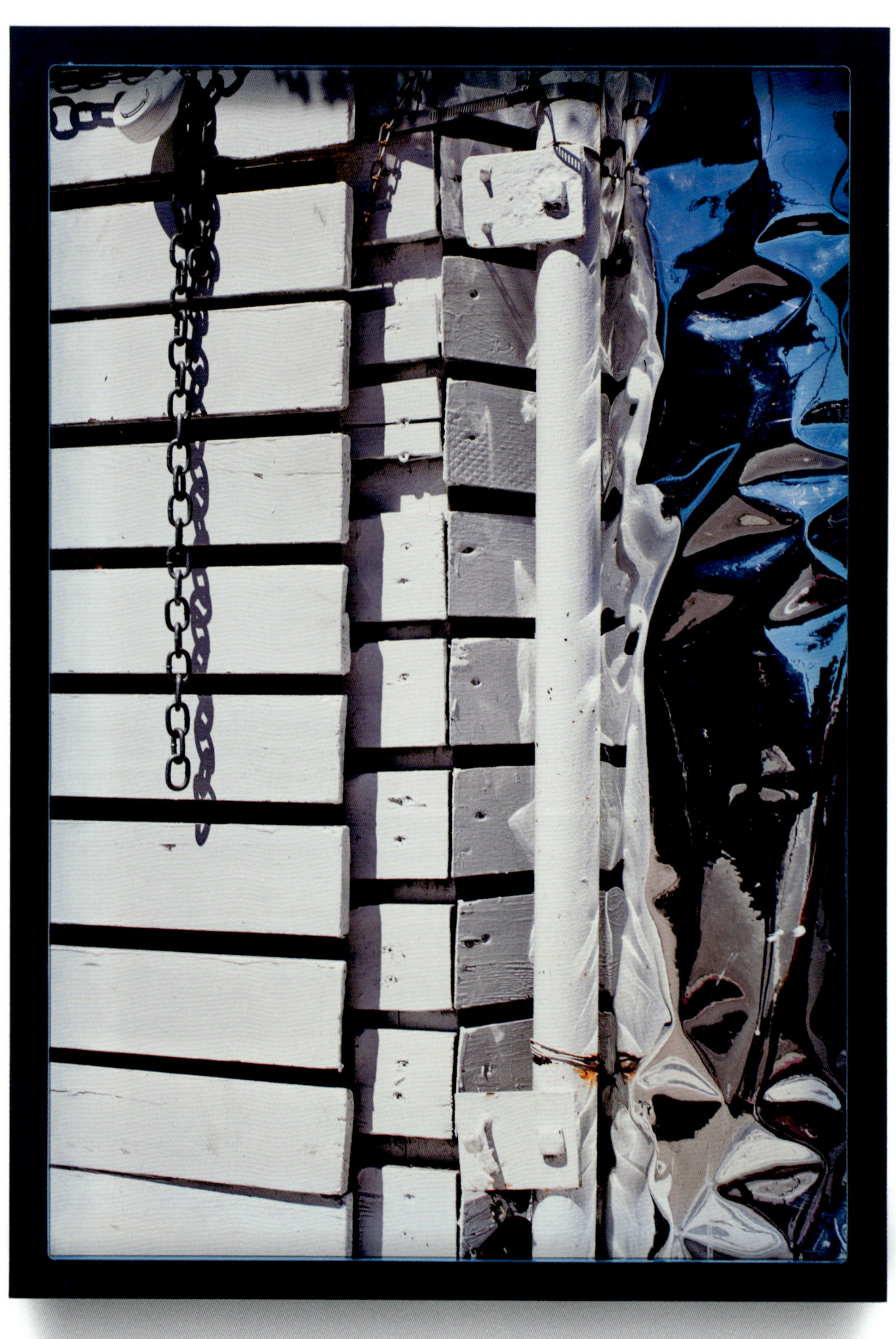

136    Chris Wiley, *Dingbat (23)*, 2014. Archival inkjet print on aluminum, artist's frame with mirrored Plexiglas

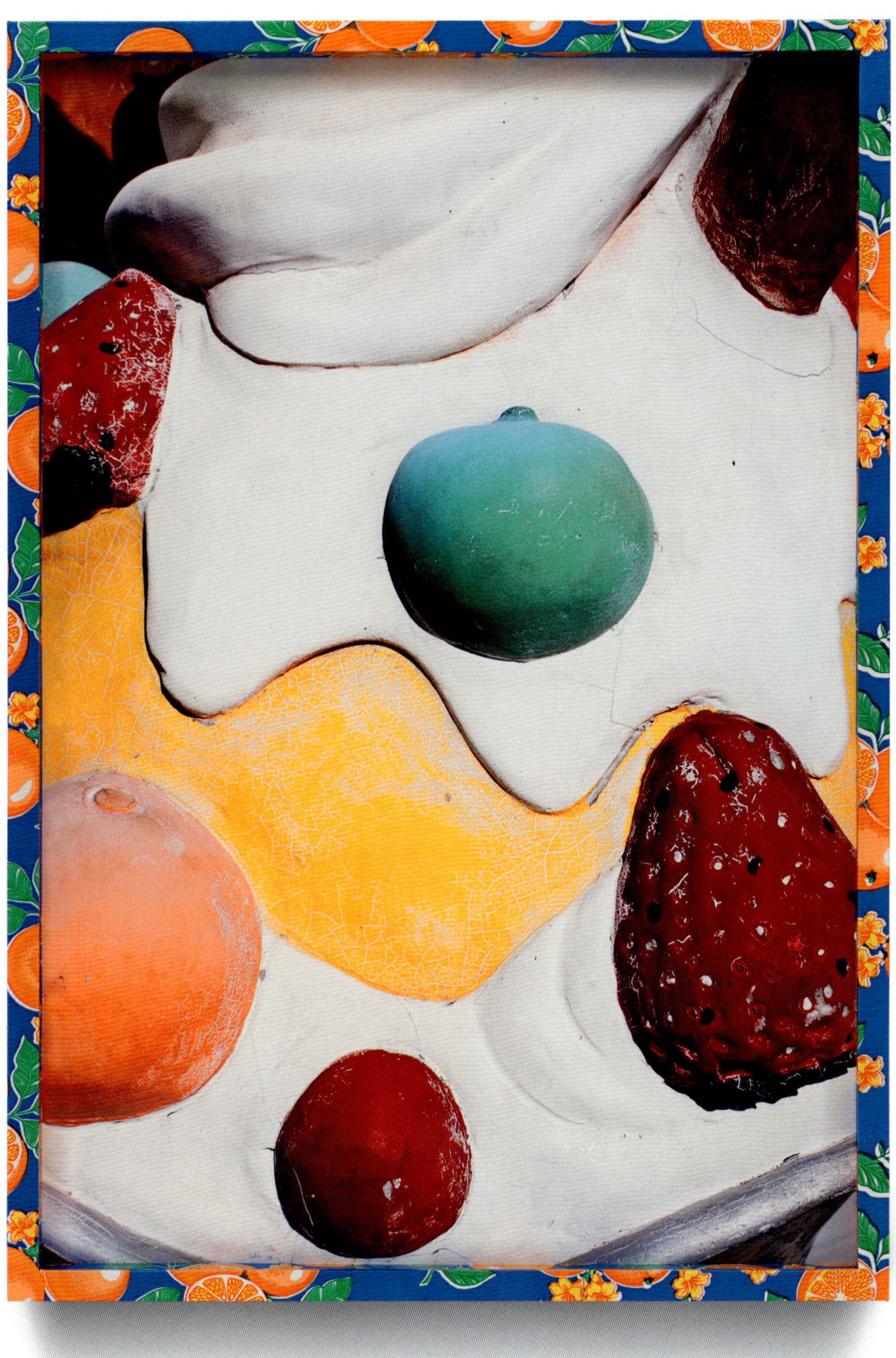

137    Chris Wiley, *Dingbat (24)*, 2014. Archival inkjet print on aluminum, artist's frame with vinyl fabric

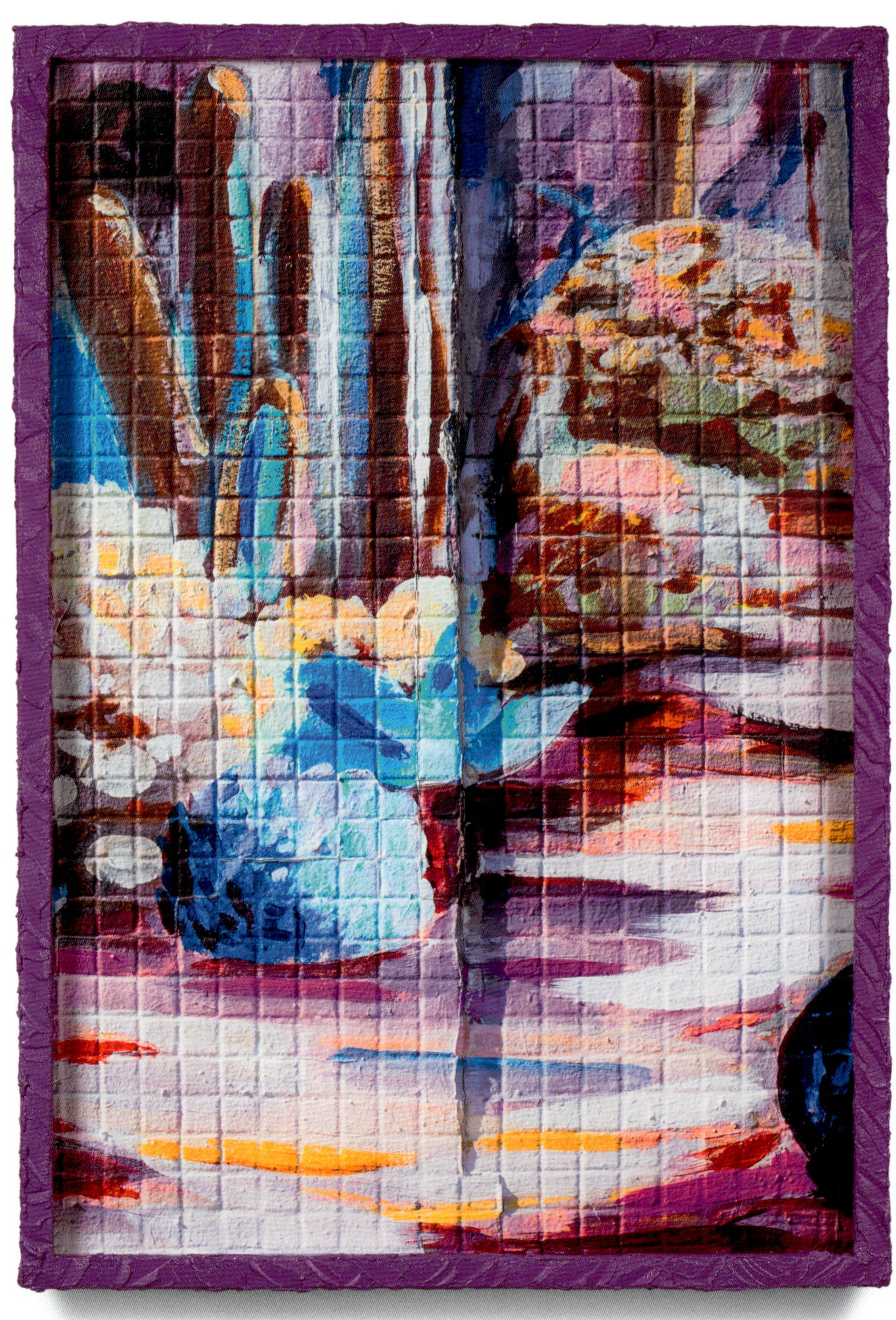

138     Chris Wiley, *Dingbat (21)*, 2014. Archival inkjet print on aluminum, artist's frame with stucco and sprayed acrylic

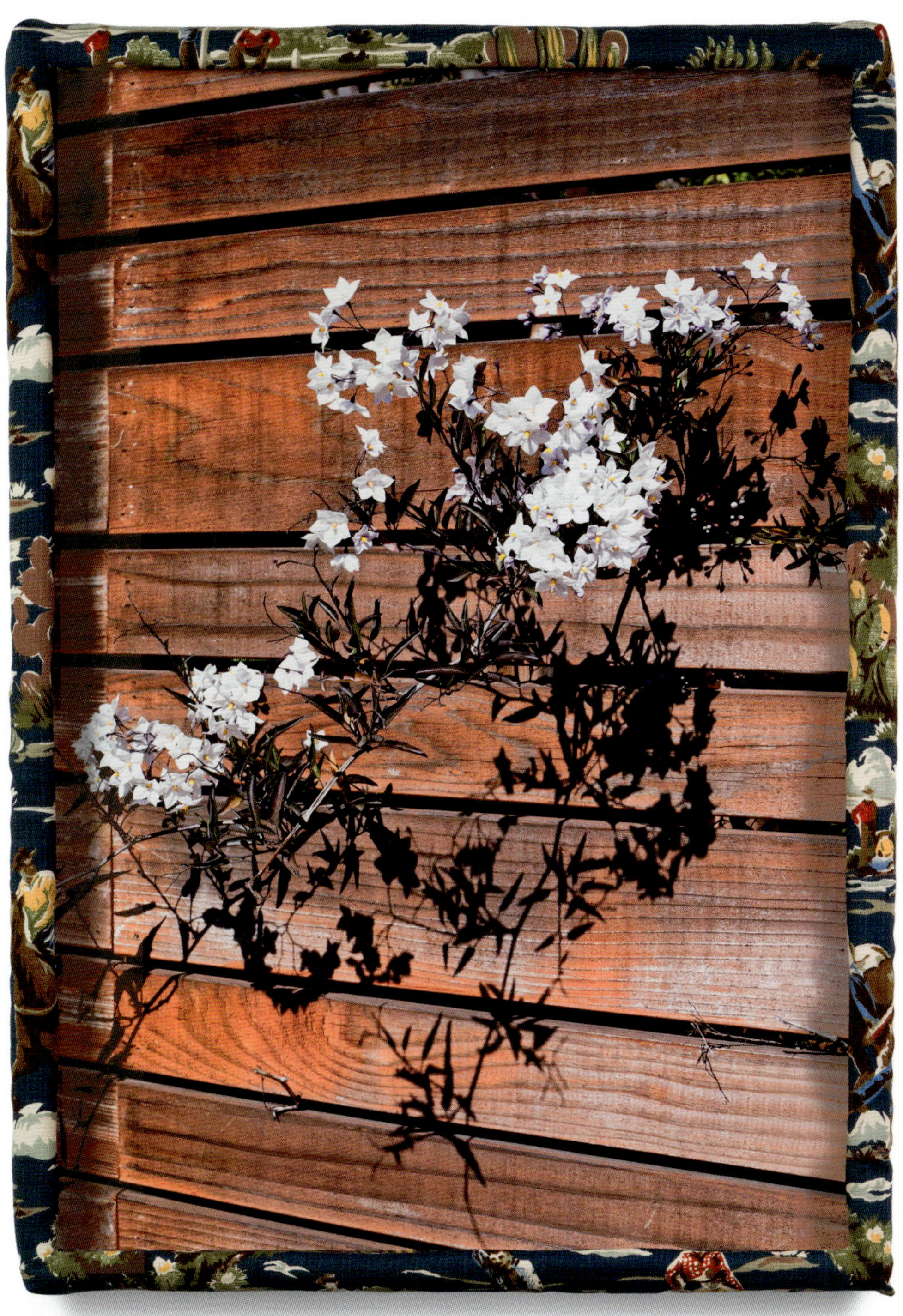

139      Chris Wiley, *Dingbat (20)*, 2014. Archival inkjet print on aluminum, artist's frame with fabric

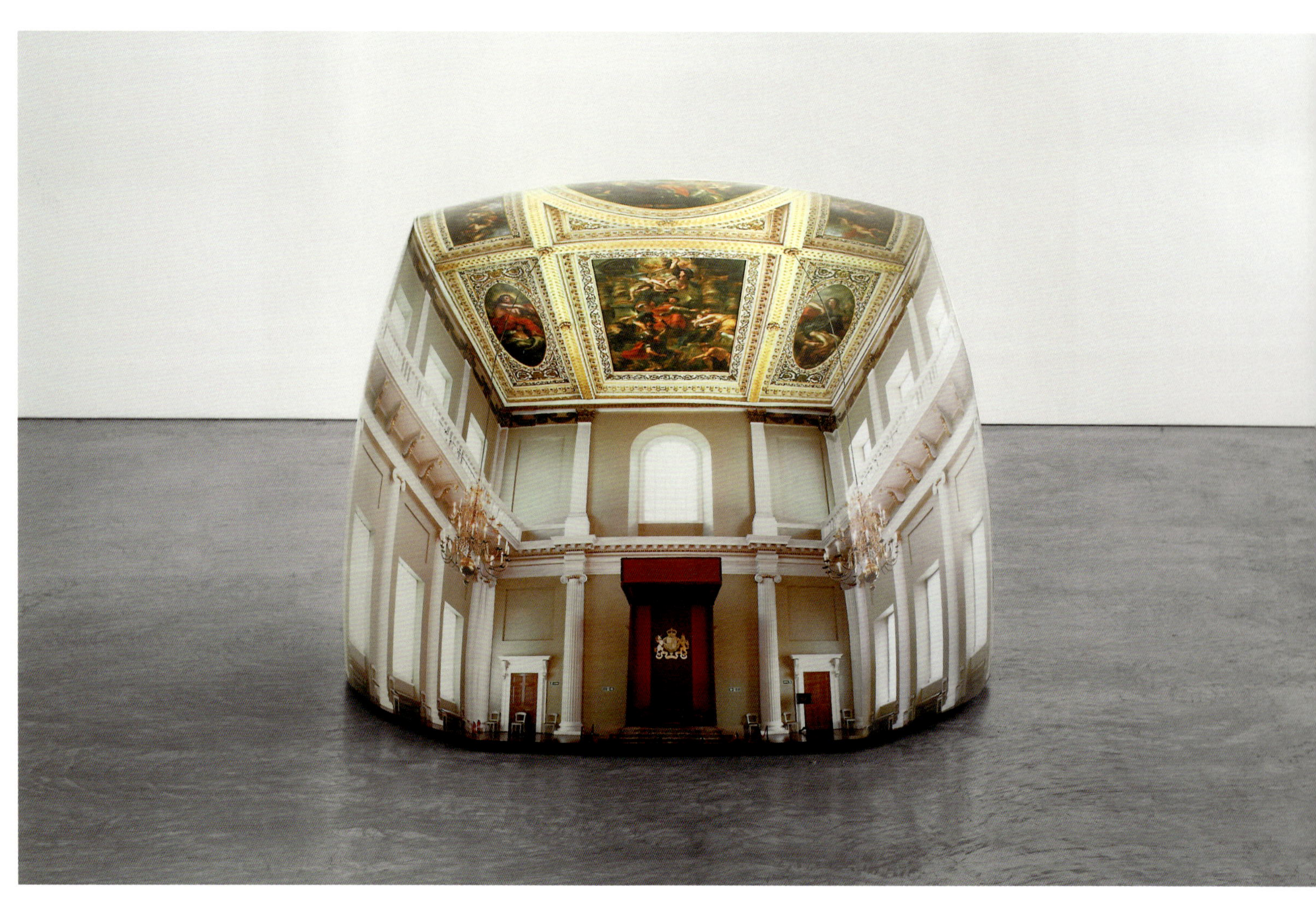

140    Brandon Lattu, *Banqueting House*, 2007. Inkjet print on vinyl, fiberglass, urethane foam

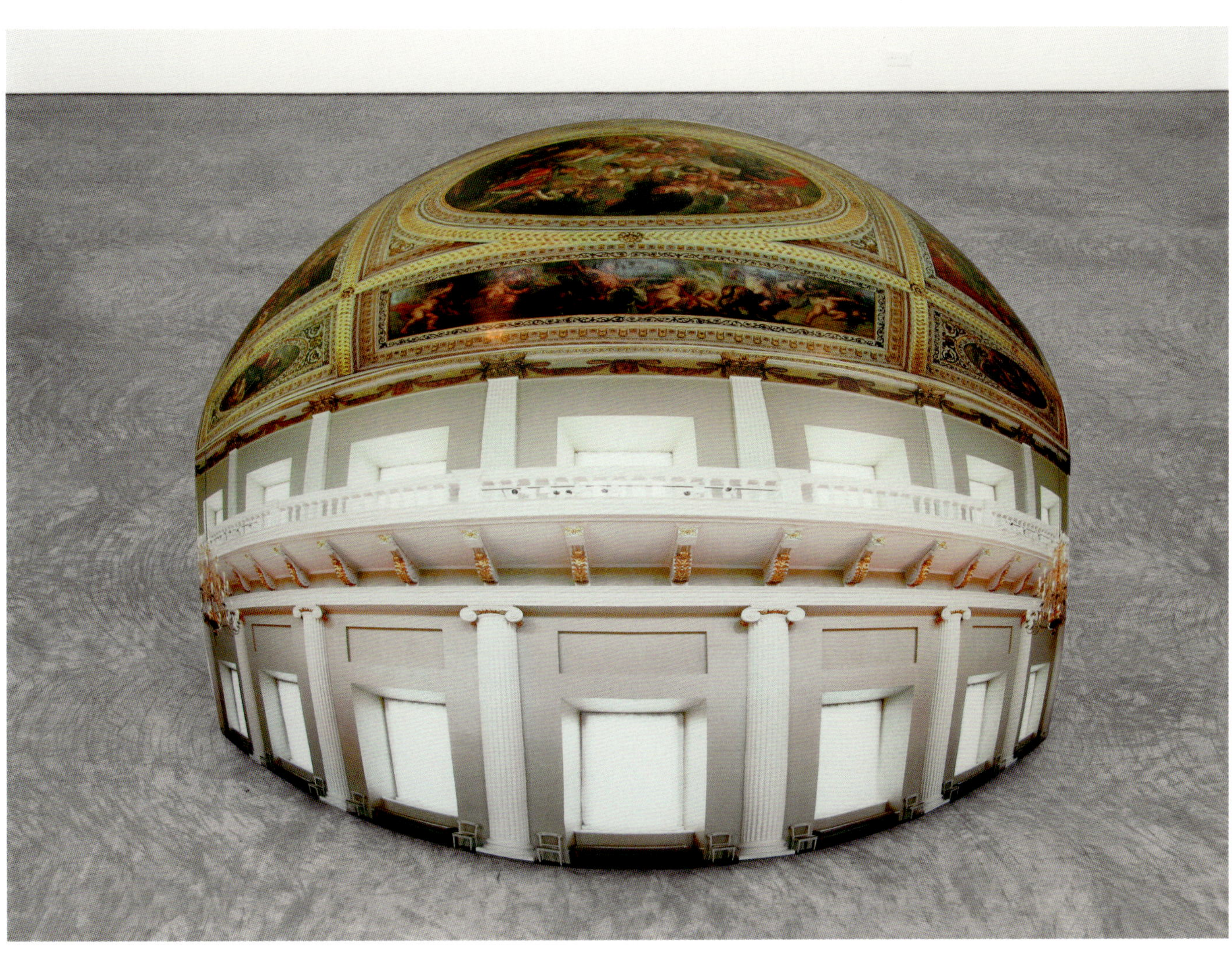

141 Brandon Lattu, *Banqueting House*, 2007. Inkjet print on vinyl, fiberglass, urethane foam

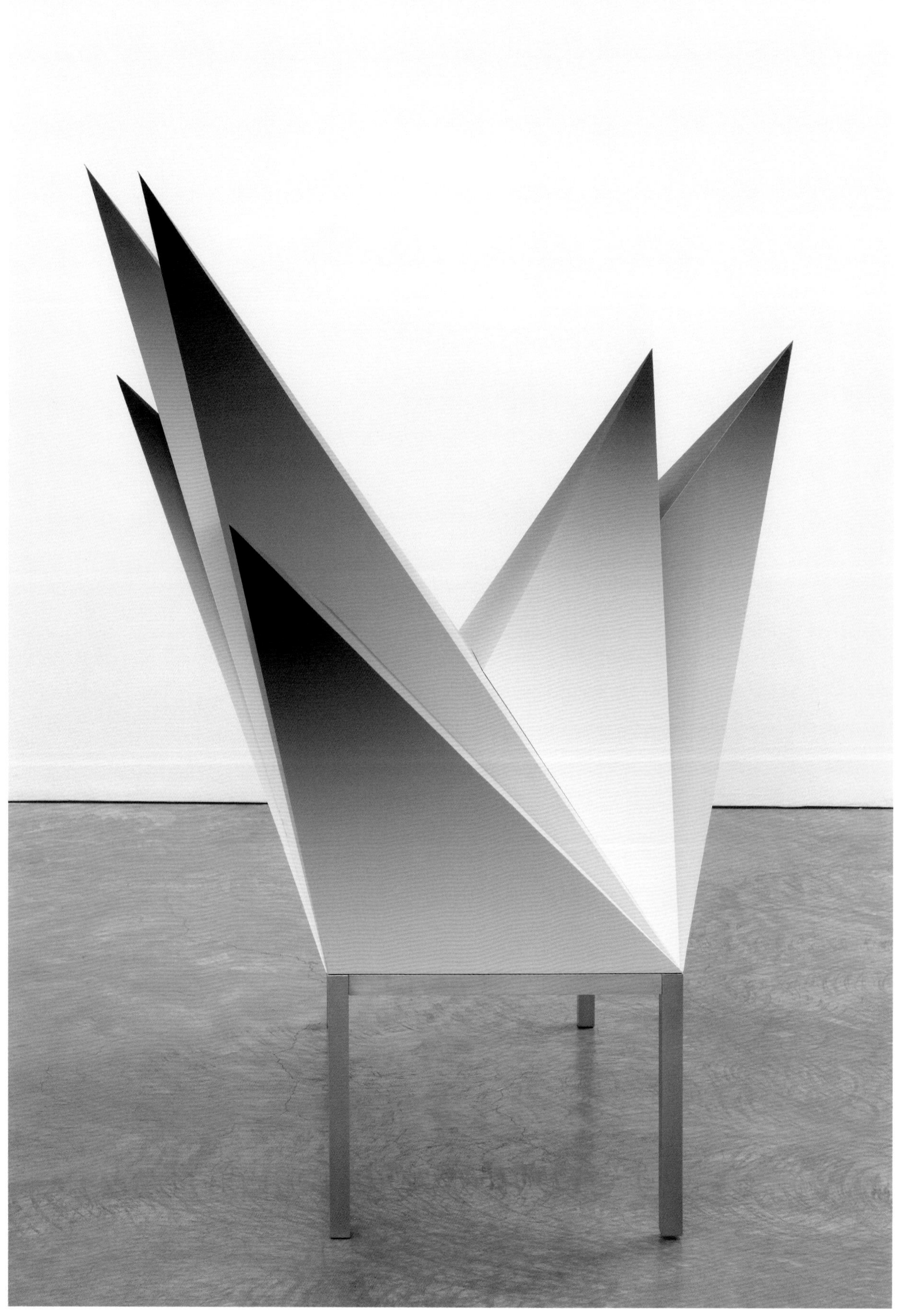

142     Brandon Lattu, *Seven Projections*, 2010. Pigment print on polypropylene, plywood, aluminum base

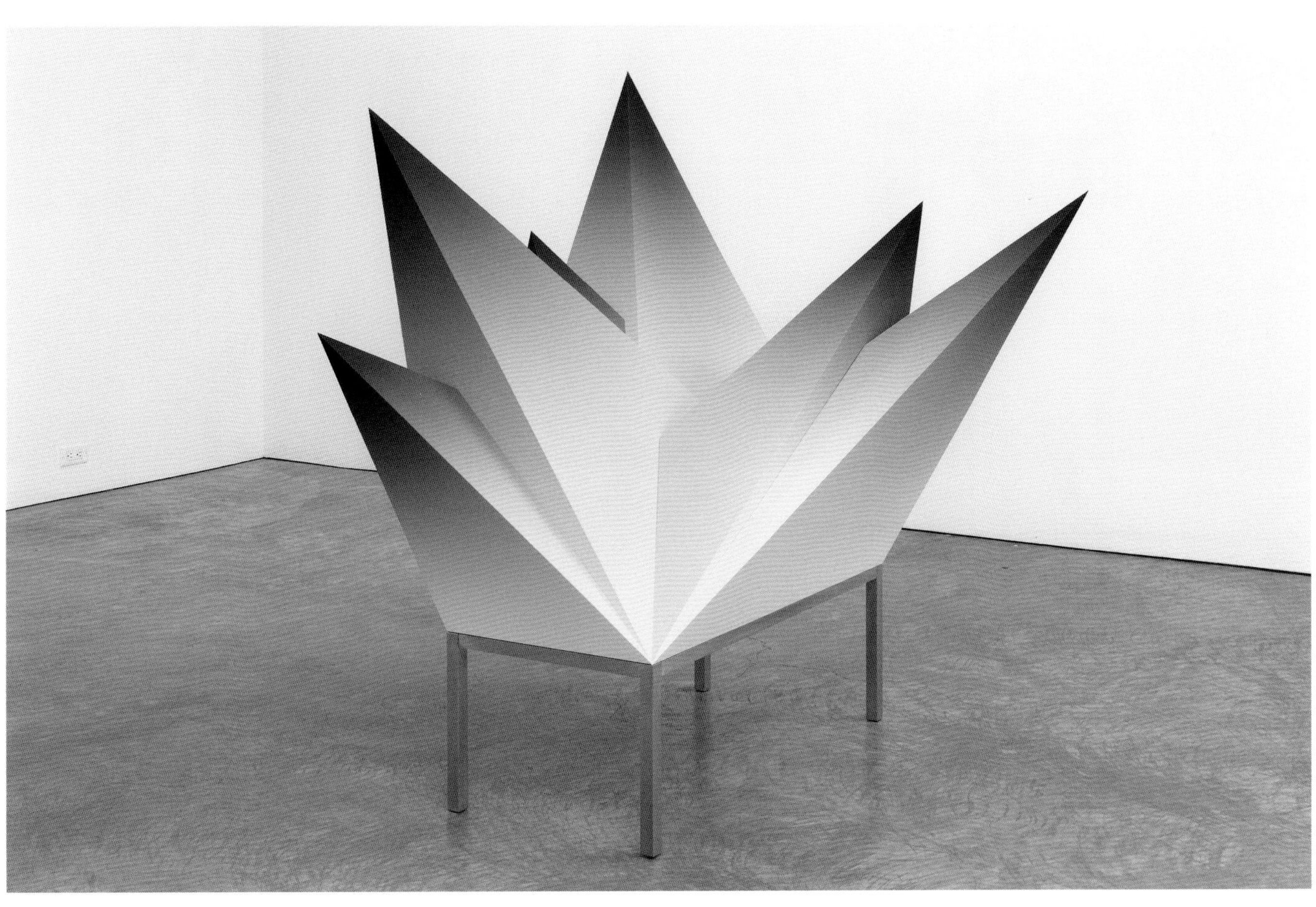

143　Brandon Lattu, *Seven Projections*, 2010. Pigment print on polypropylene, plywood, aluminum base

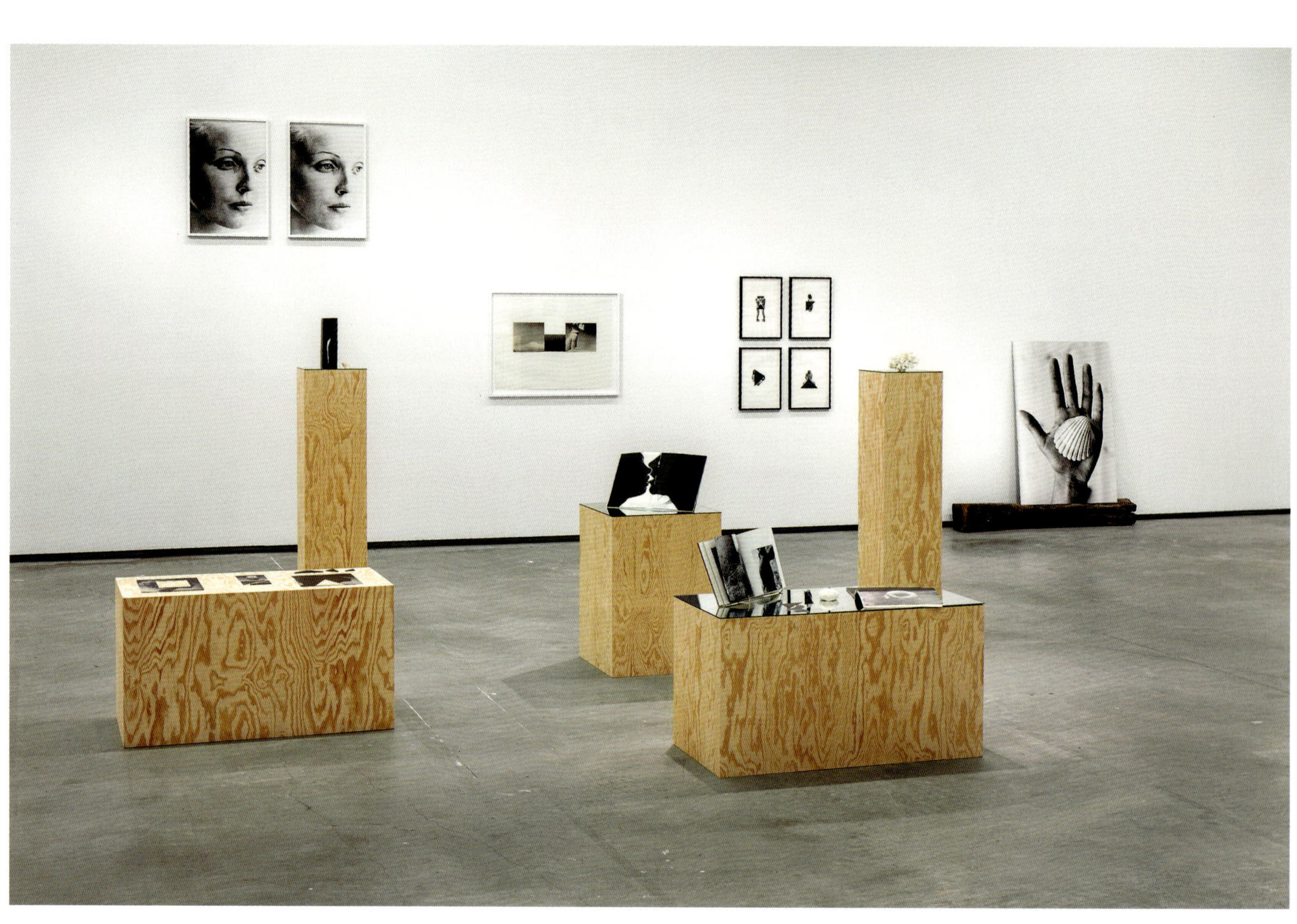

144    Lotta Antonsson, *Arrangements I–VI*, 2012. Gelatin-silver prints, mirror, coral shells, wood, printed matter, collage, Plexiglas

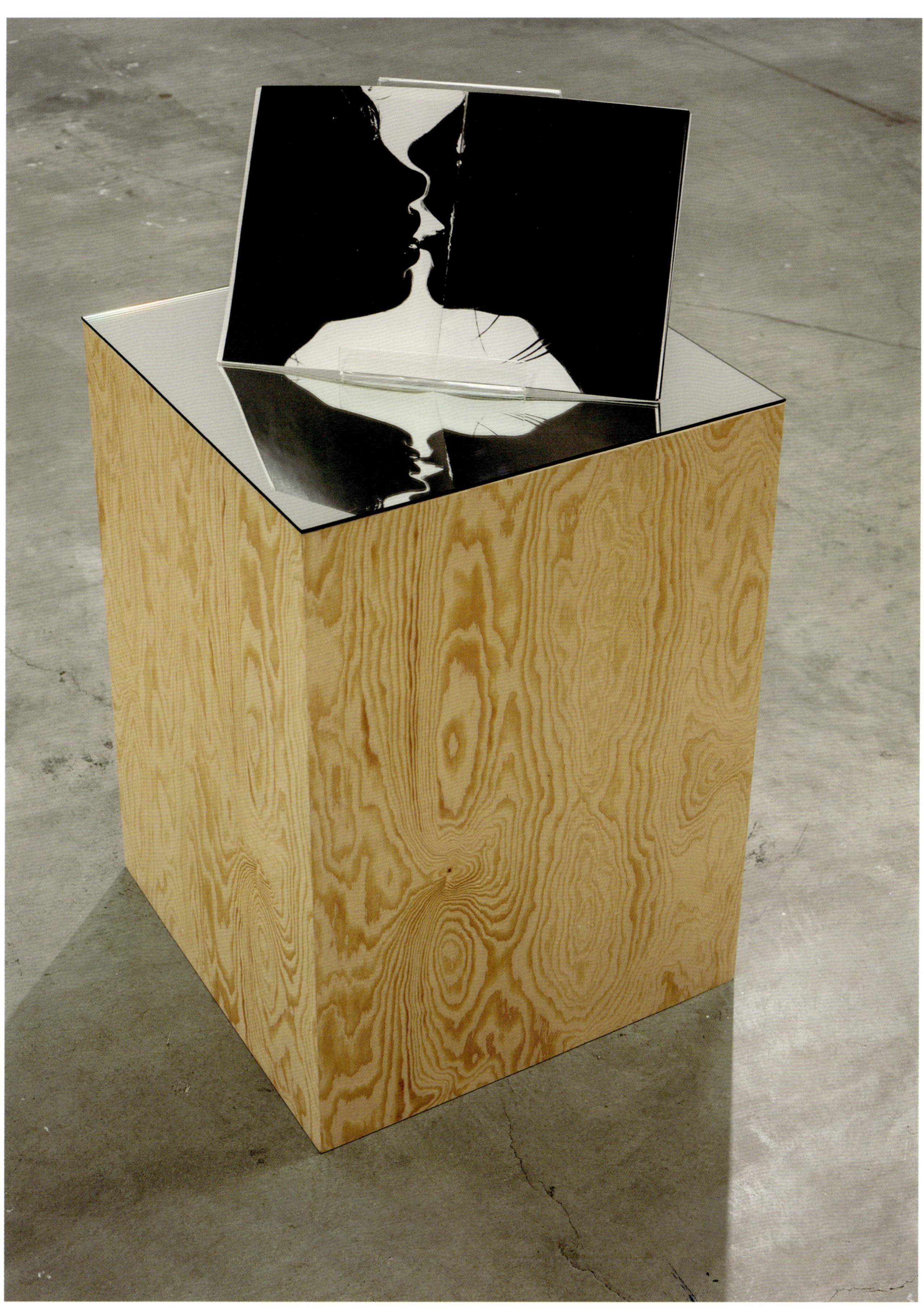

145    Lotta Antonsson, *Kiss (Hommage à K.S.)*, 2012. Printed matter, wood, Plexiglas

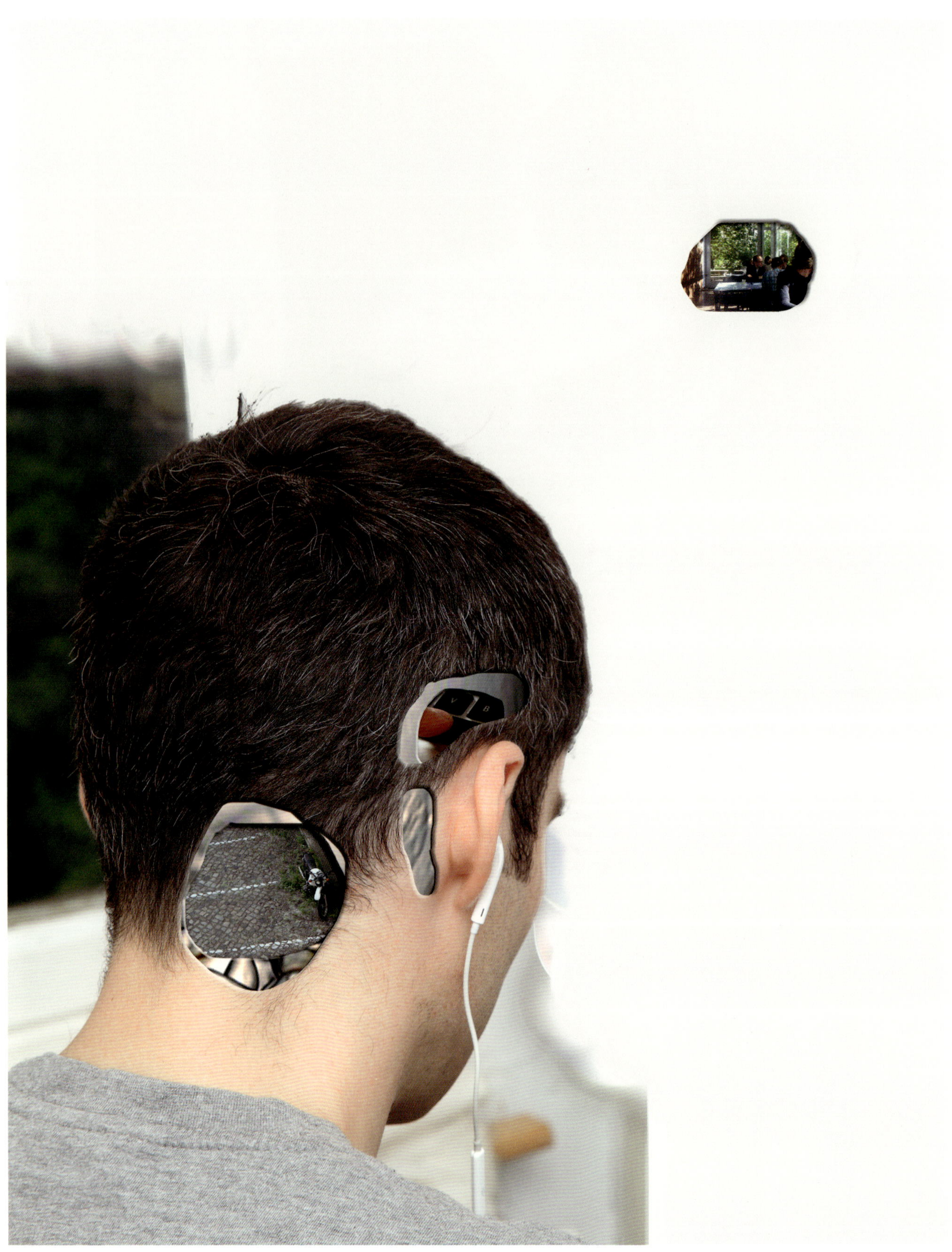



146    Anne de Vries, *At Work*, from the series *Interface*, 2014. Two digital prints on two sheets of Forex, with digital cut-outs

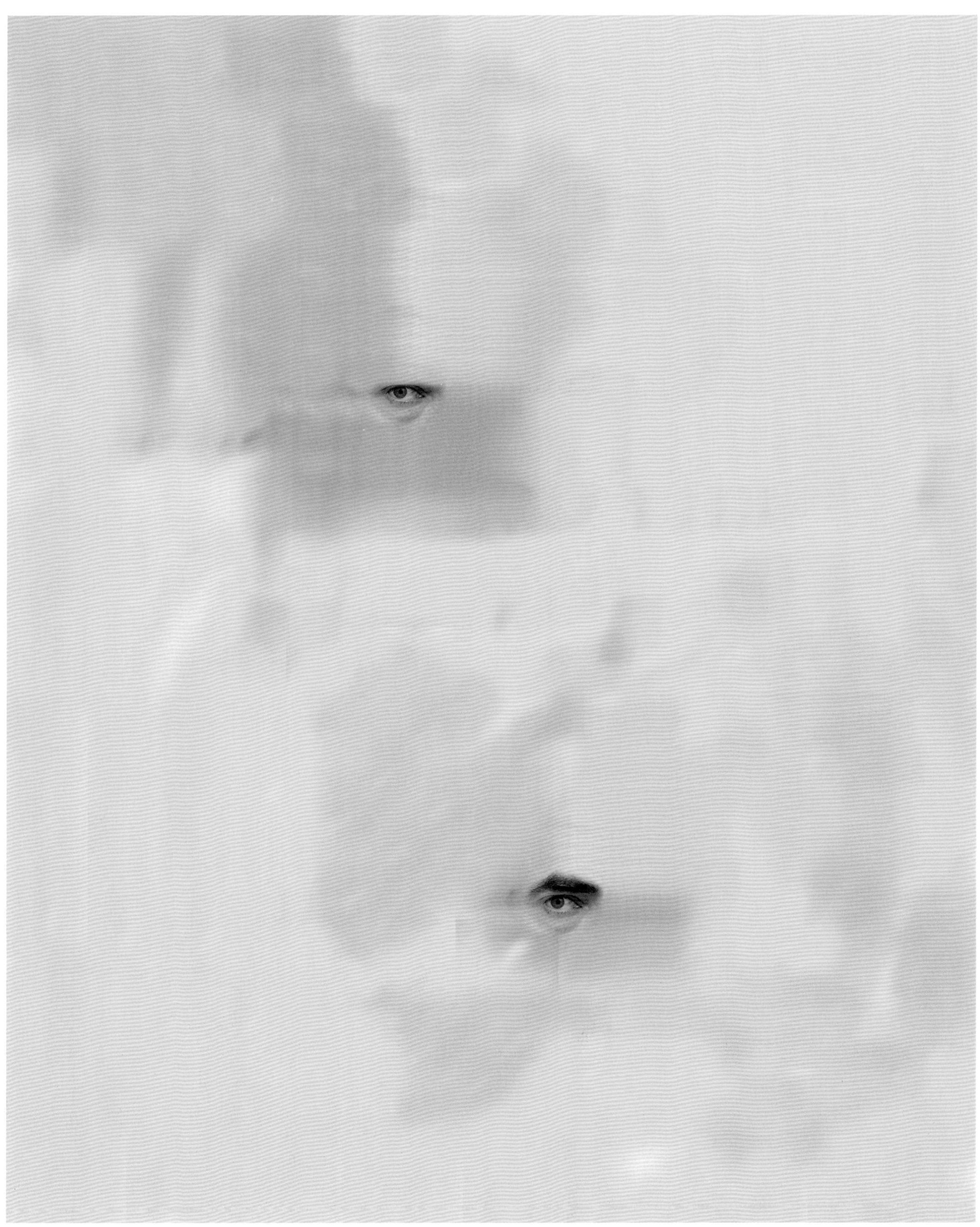

147    Anne de Vries, *Untitled*, from the series *Around the Eye*, 2014. Digital print on extruded polystyrene XPS, Plexiglas

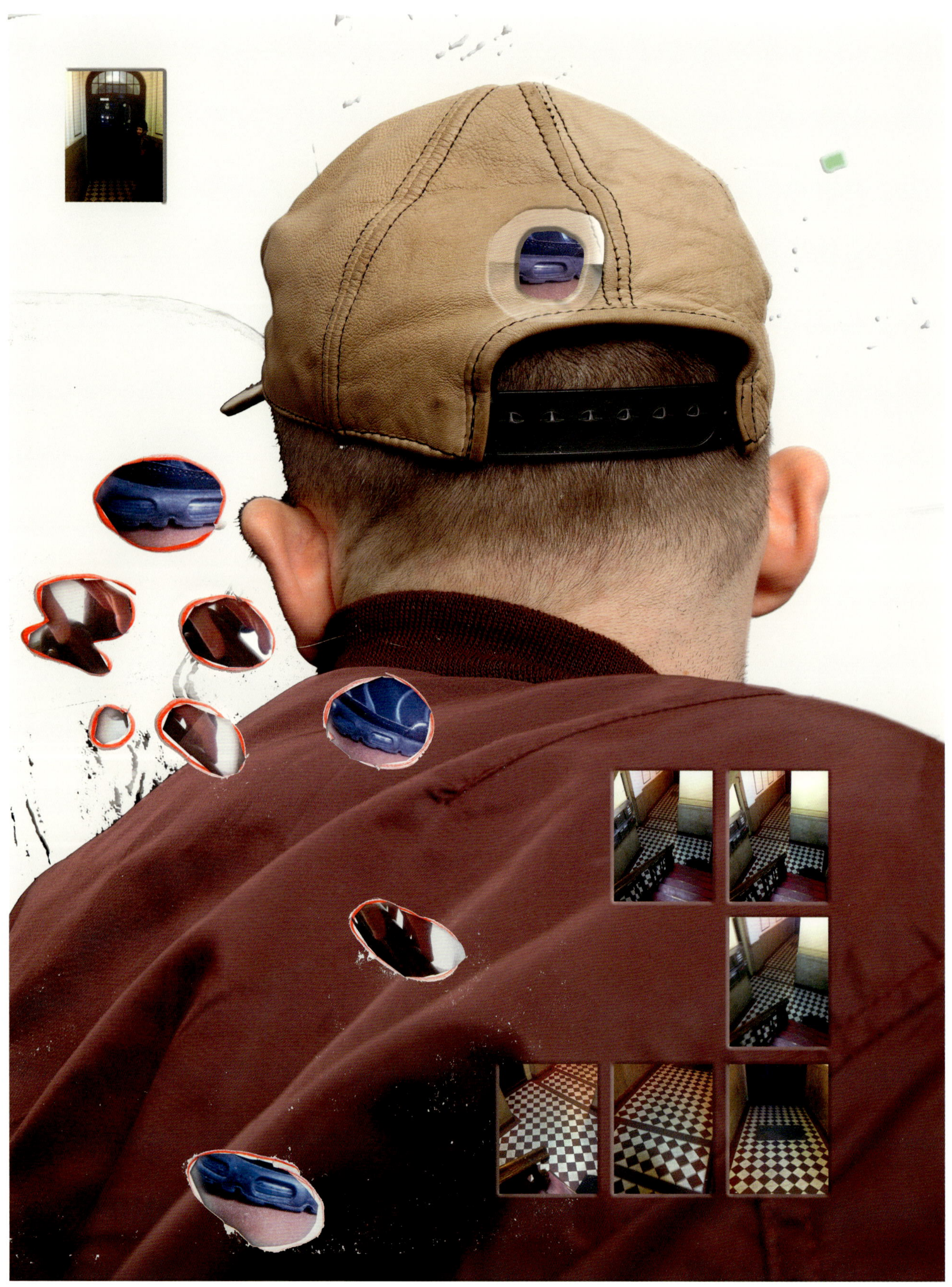

     Anne de Vries, *Downstairs*, from the series *Interface*, 2014. Two digital prints on two sheets of Forex, with digital cut-outs

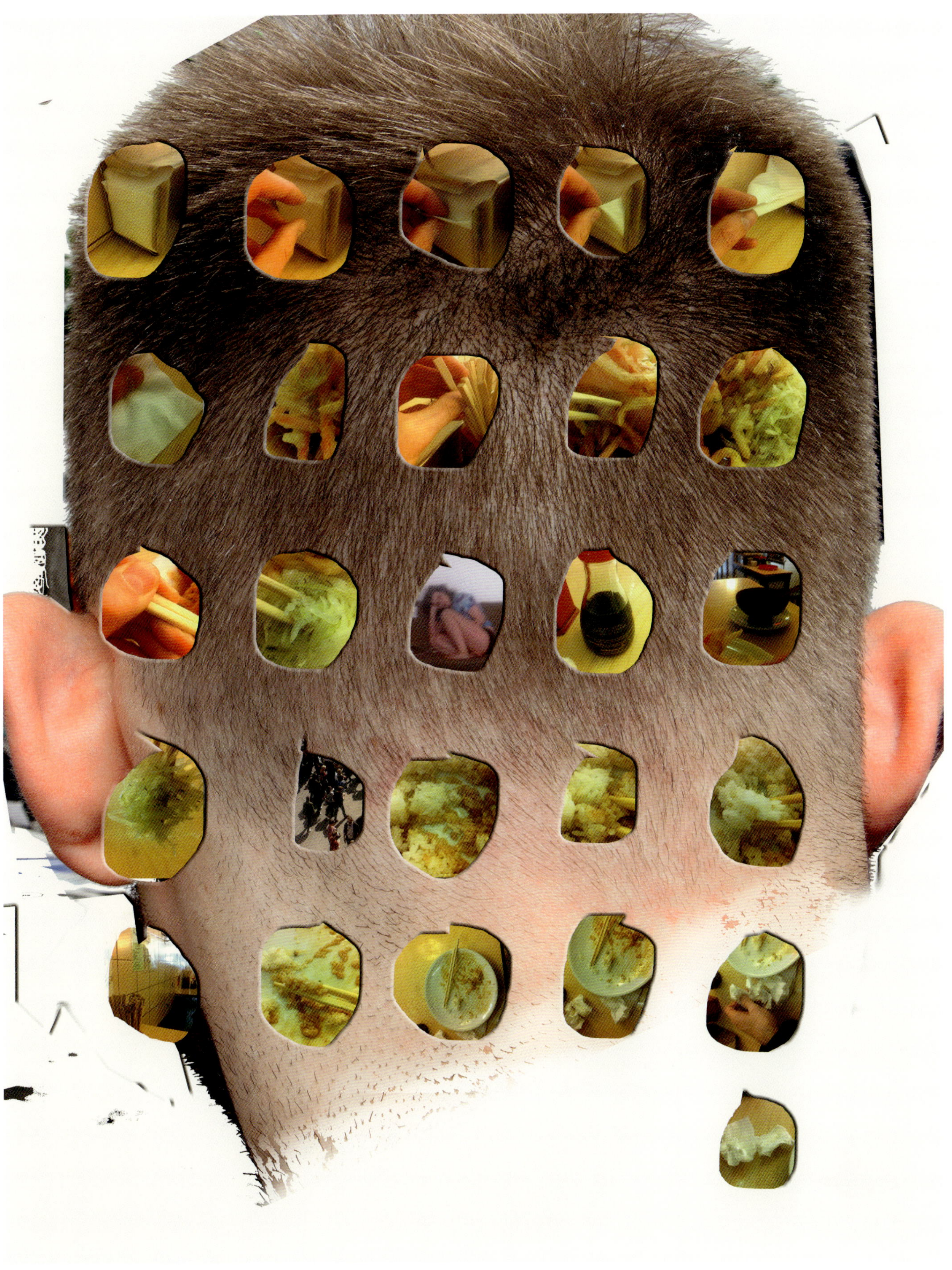

149    Anne de Vries, *Musashi*, from the series *Interface*, 2014. Two digital prints on two sheets of Forex, with digital cut-outs

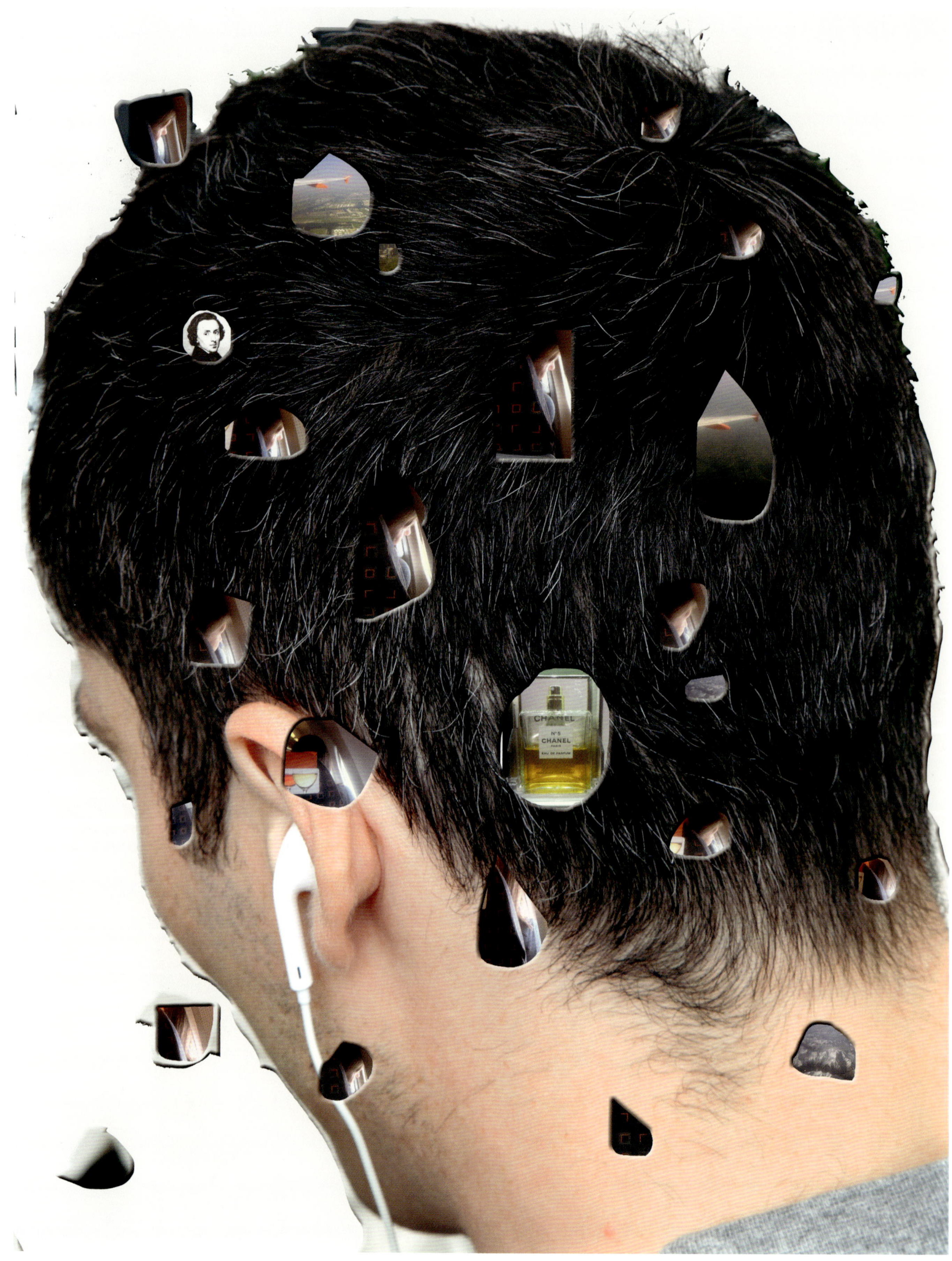



150     Anne de Vries, *Gate 48*, from the series *Interface*, 2014. Two digital prints on two sheets of Forex, with digital cut-outs

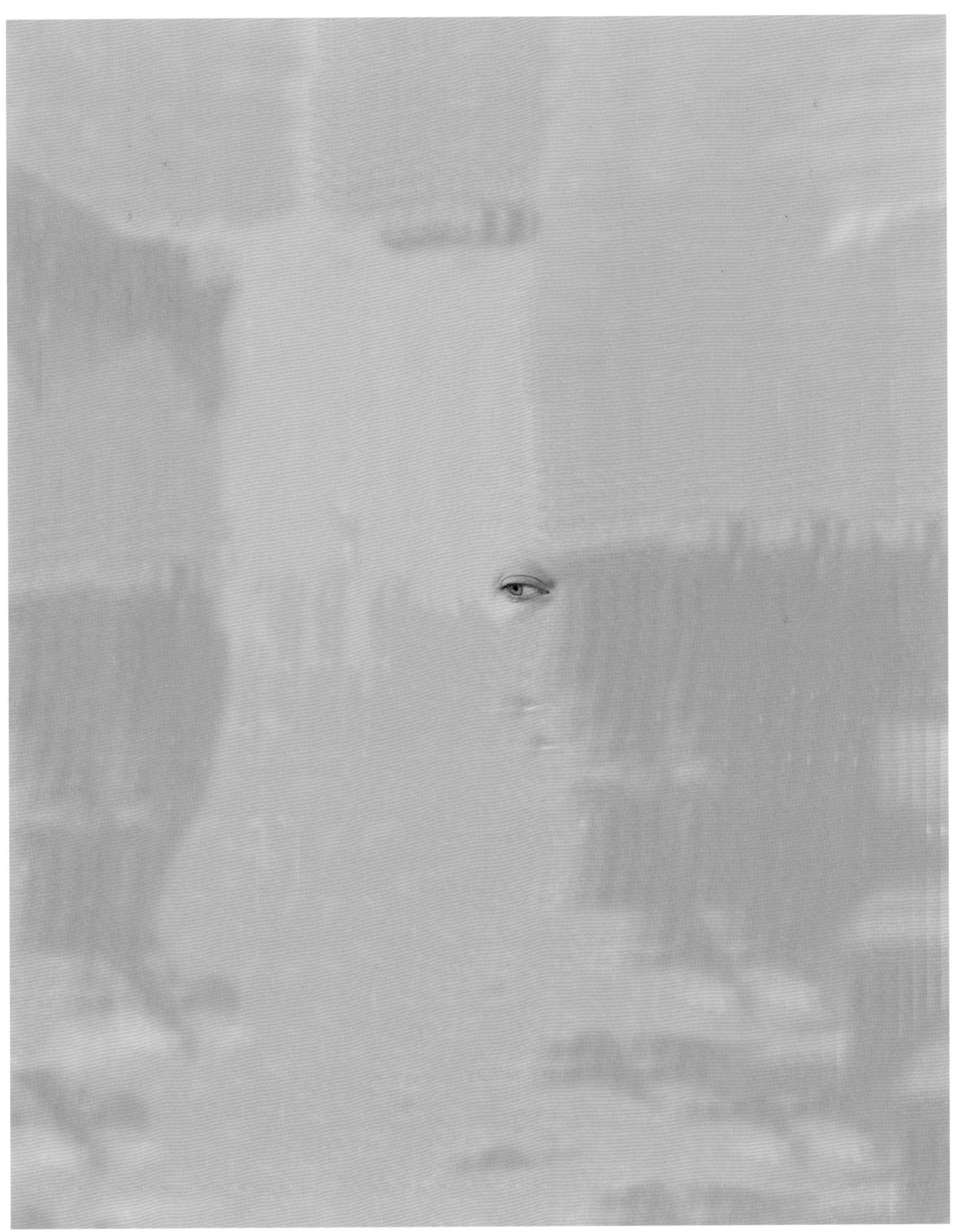

 Anne de Vries, *Untitled*, from the series *Around the Eye*, 2014. Digital print on extruded polystyrene XPS, Plexiglas

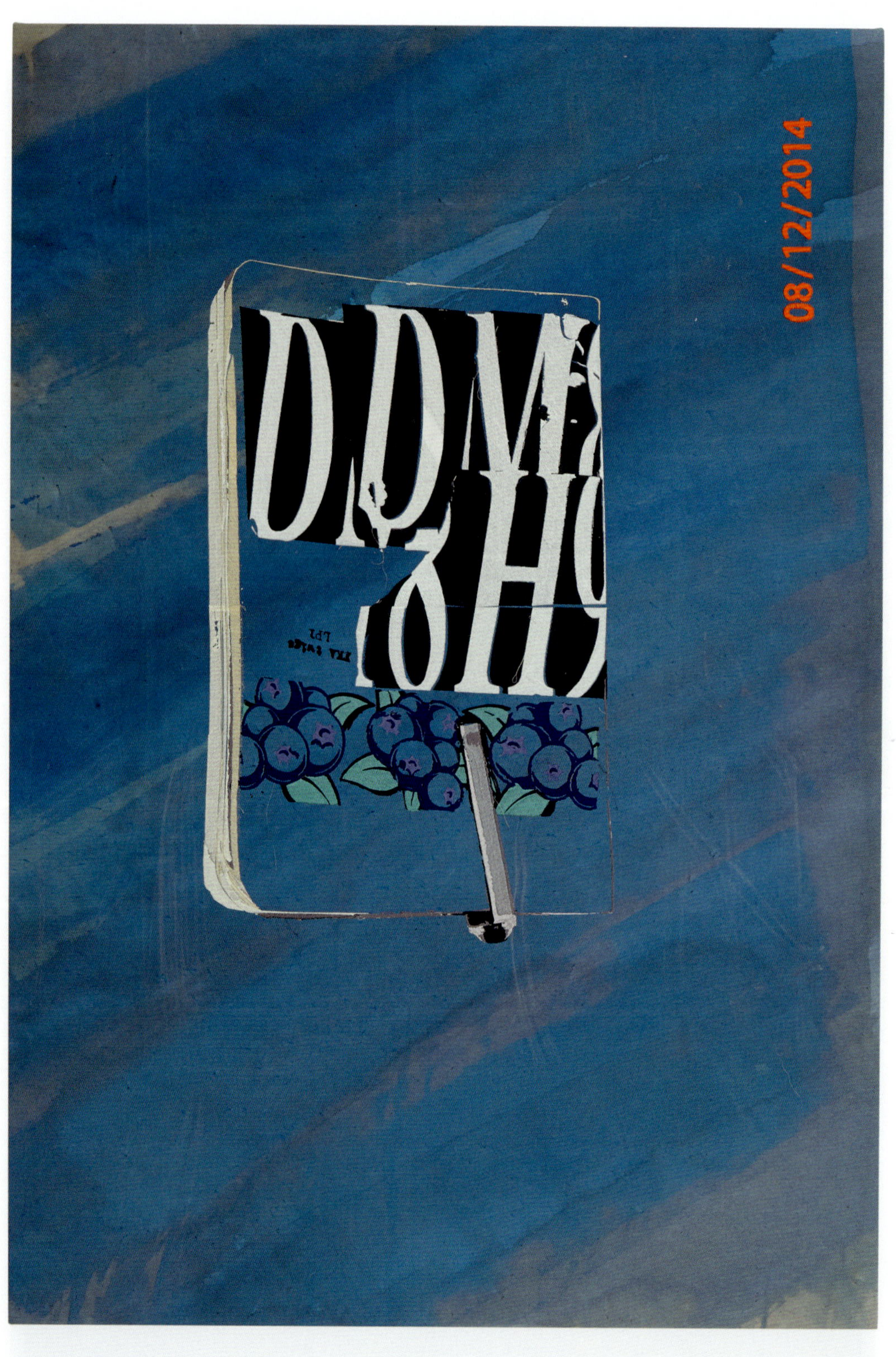



152     Brendan Fowler, *Notebook*, 2014, from the series *New Camera*. Polyester, rayon, and acrylic on canvas with aluminum stretchers

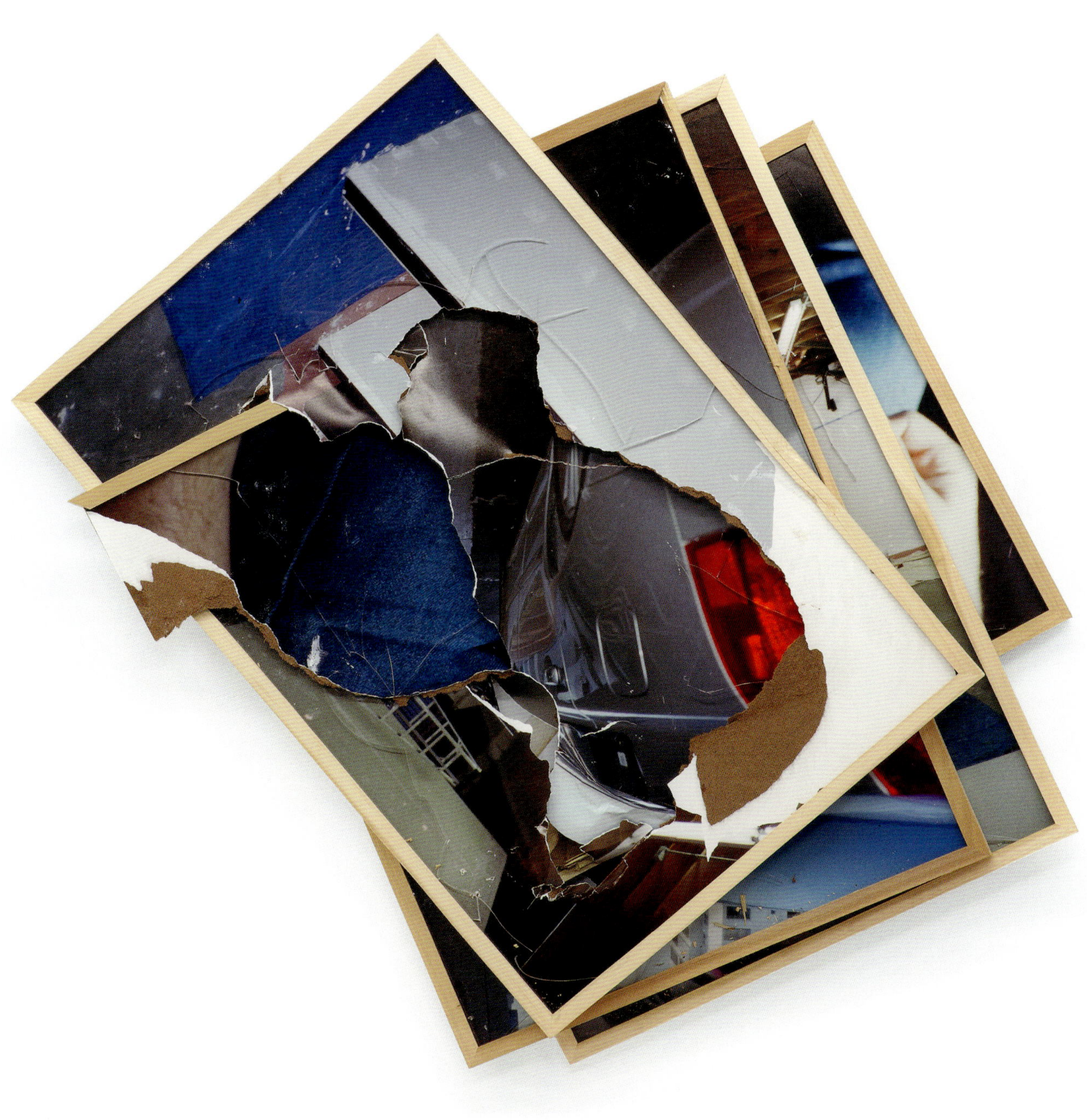

153 Brendan Fowler, *Fall 2011, Spring 2012 (White Flats Drying 2, Car Waiting at Convention Center, White Flats Drying 1, Max in the Car on His Birthday)*, 2012, from the series *New Camera*. Archival inkjet prints, frames, Plexiglas

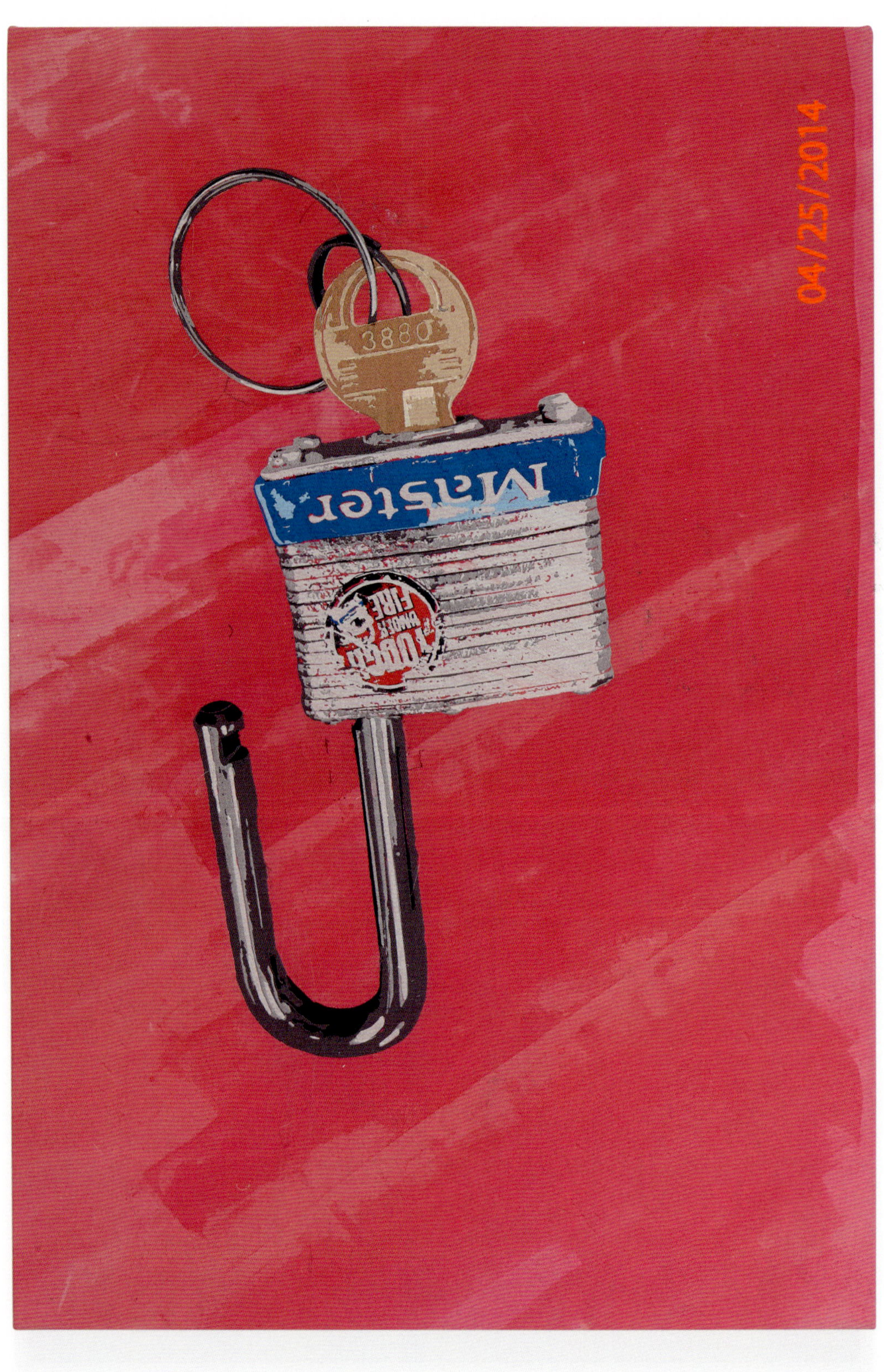


154    Brendan Fowler, *Open Lock*, 2014, from the series *New Camera*. Polyester, rayon, and acrylic on canvas with aluminum stretchers

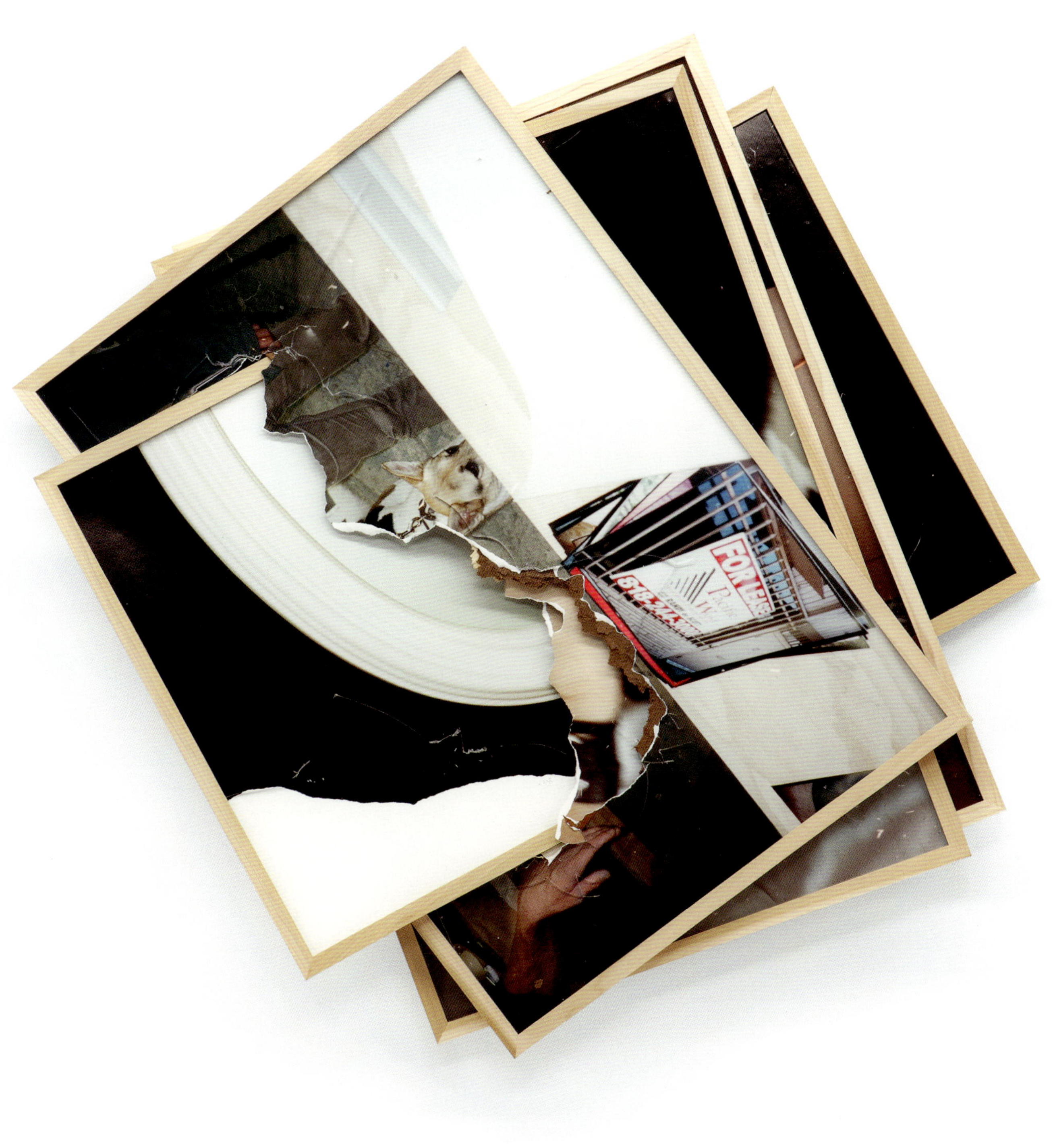

155    Brendan Fowler, *Spring 2011–Spring 2012 (Colin/Angelo/Dane, Andrea's Hand on Hat Head in Coronado Ter. House, Graham in Truck, Mirror Reflecting White Flat 1)*, 2012, from the series *New Camera*. Archival inkjet prints, frames, Plexiglas

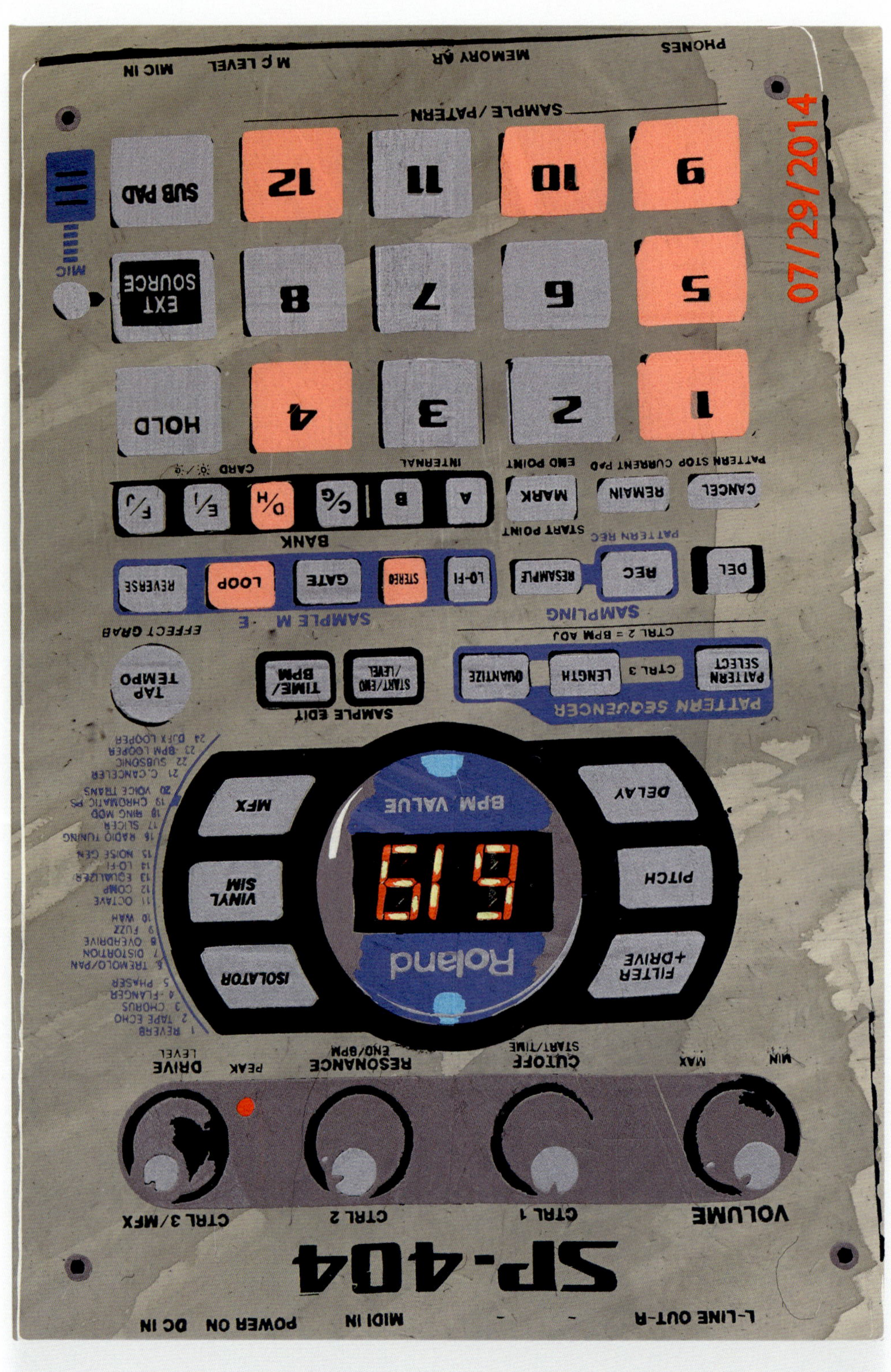

156 Brendan Fowler, *Roland SP-404 Playing Bank D, Pads 1, 4, 5, 9, 12*, 2014, from the series *New Camera*. Polyester, rayon, and acrylic on canvas with aluminum stretchers

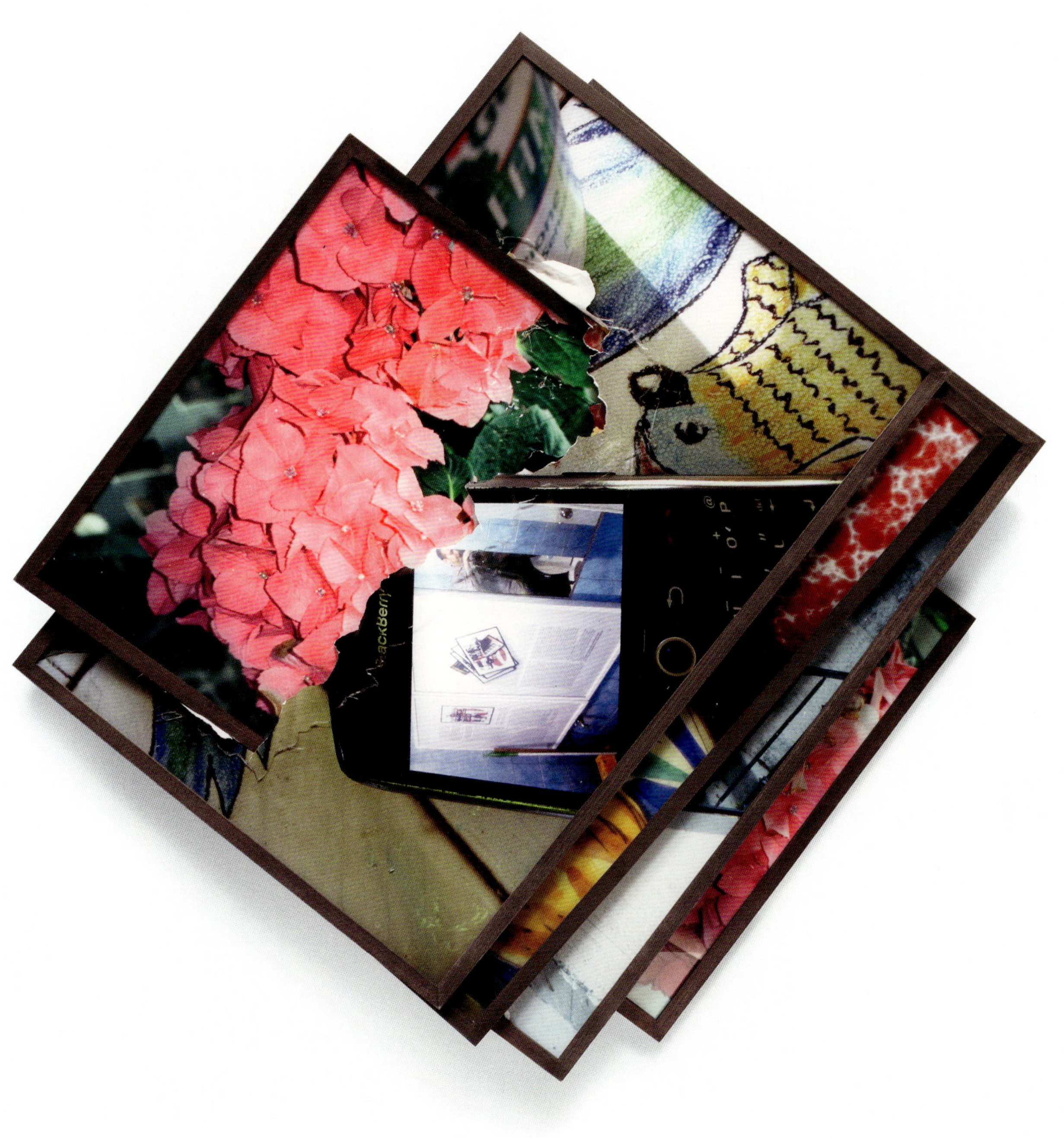

157    Brendan Fowler, *Fall 2010 (Joel's Phone on Lauro Table 1, Debbie's Chair at Rick's House 4, Lucile Ave Apt Steps 1, Flowers in Patty's Gazebo 2)*, 2010, from the series *New Camera*. Archival inkjet prints, frames, Plexiglas

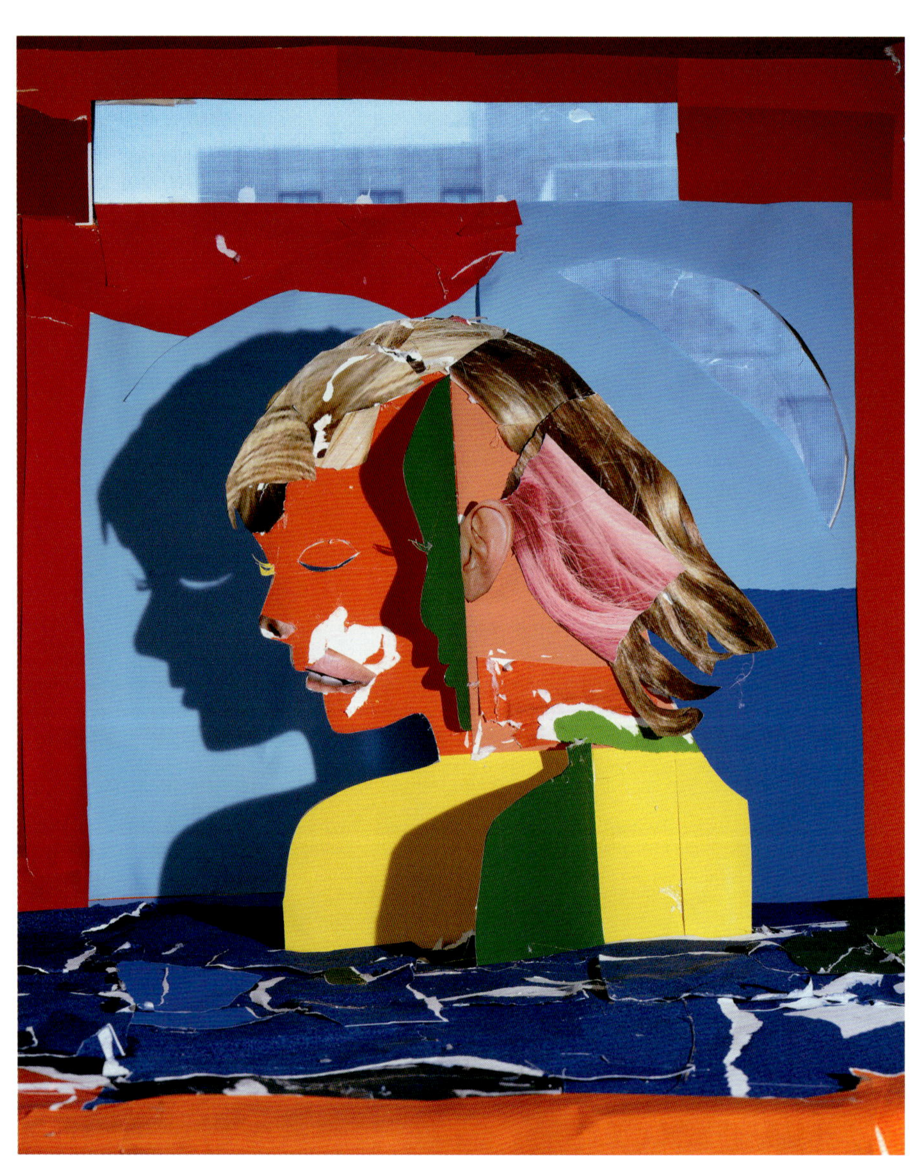

  Daniel Gordon, *Crescent-Eyed Portrait*, 2012. C-print

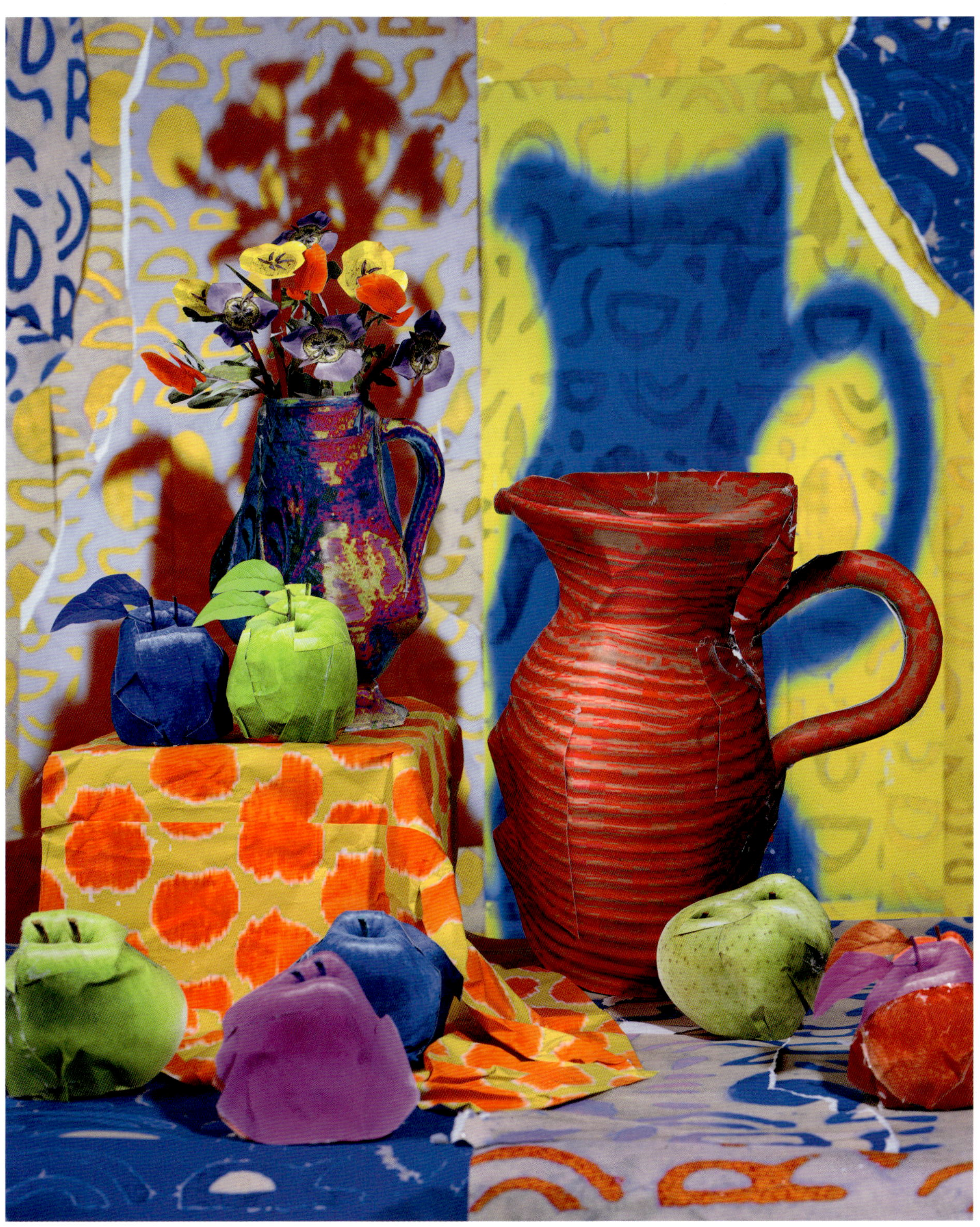

159     Daniel Gordon, *Still Life with Pitcher and Apples*, 2013. C-print

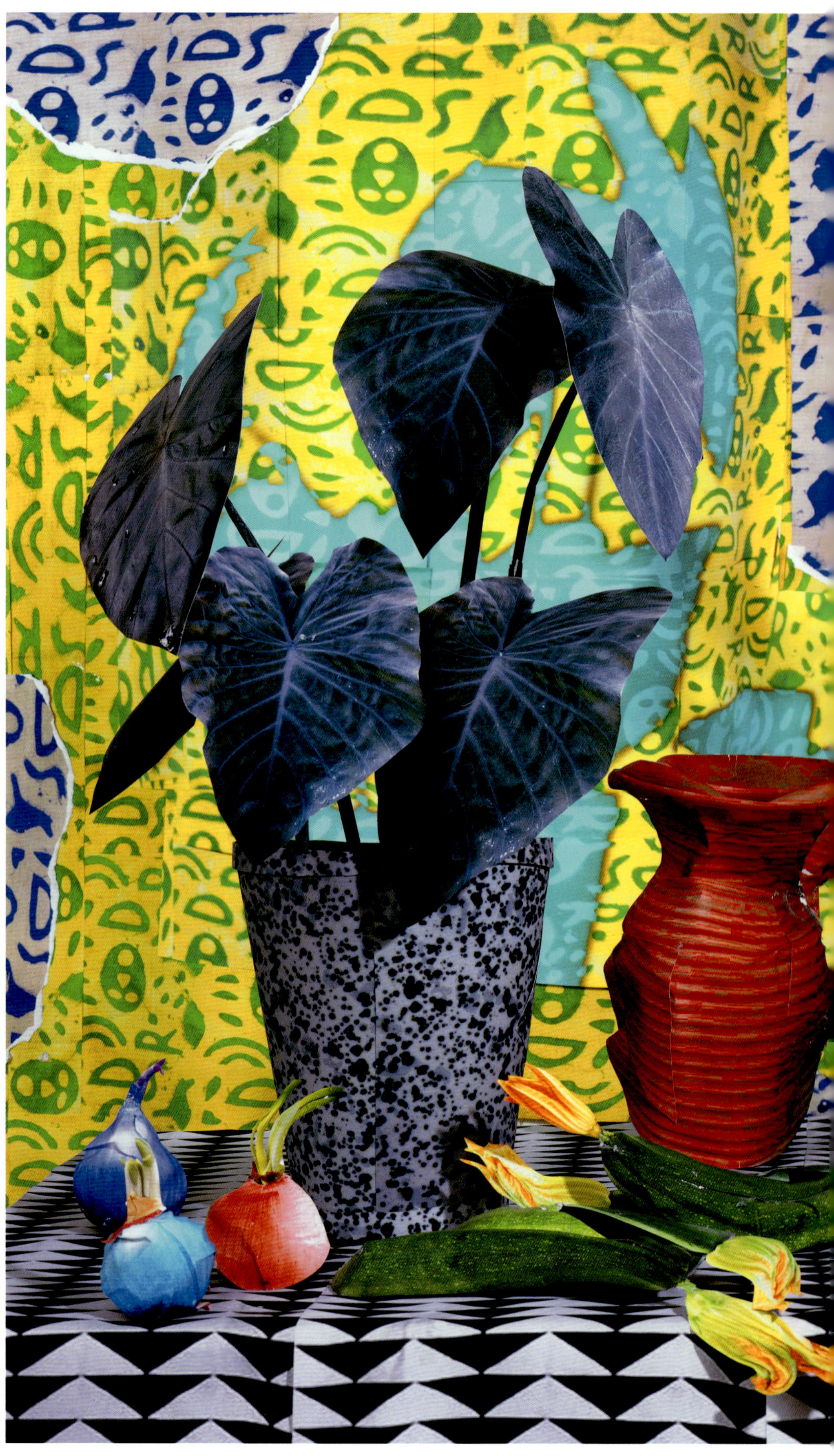

160    Daniel Gordon, *Still Life with Cherry Blossoms and Zucchini*, 2013. C-print

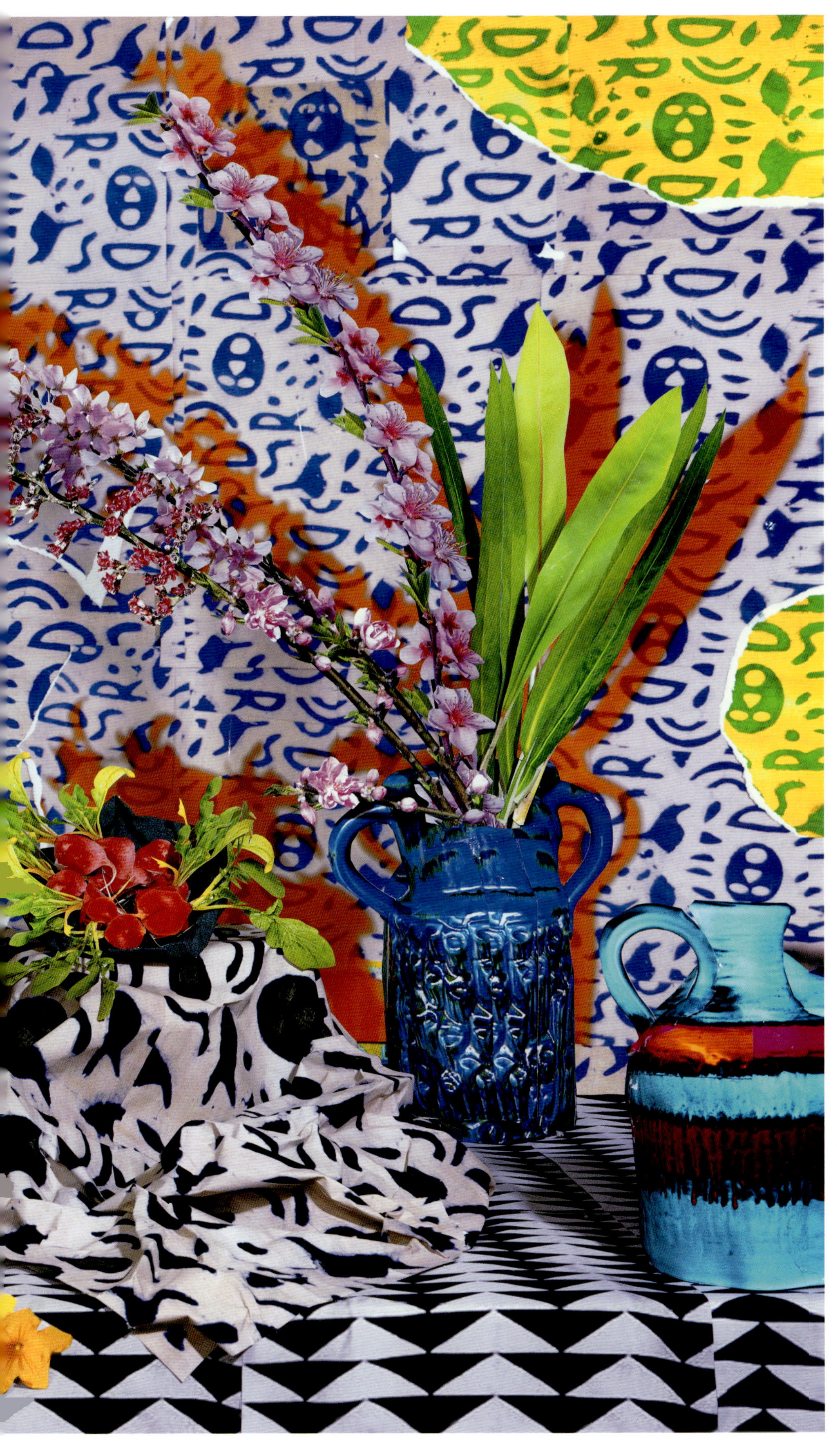

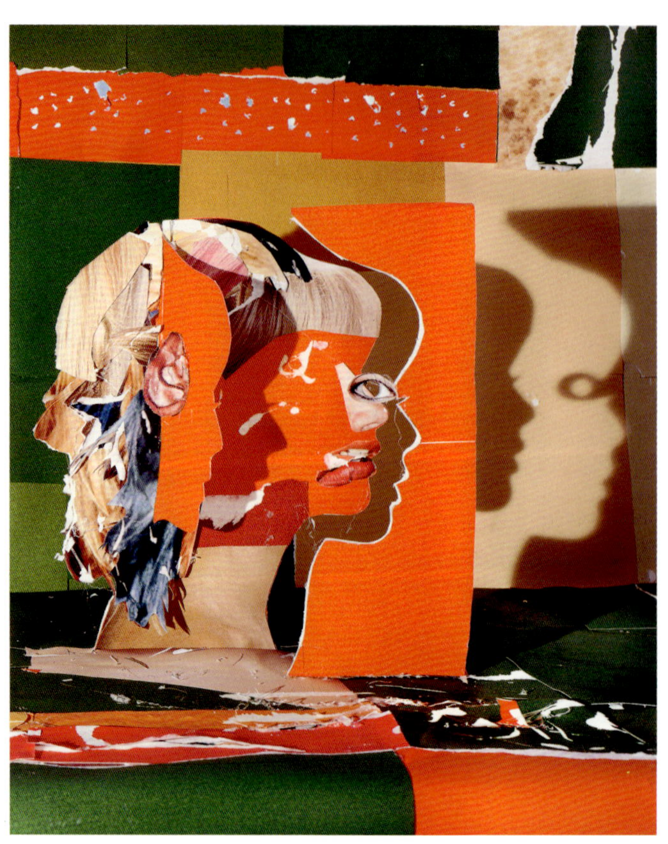

162    Daniel Gordon, *Portrait in Orange and Green*, 2012. C-print

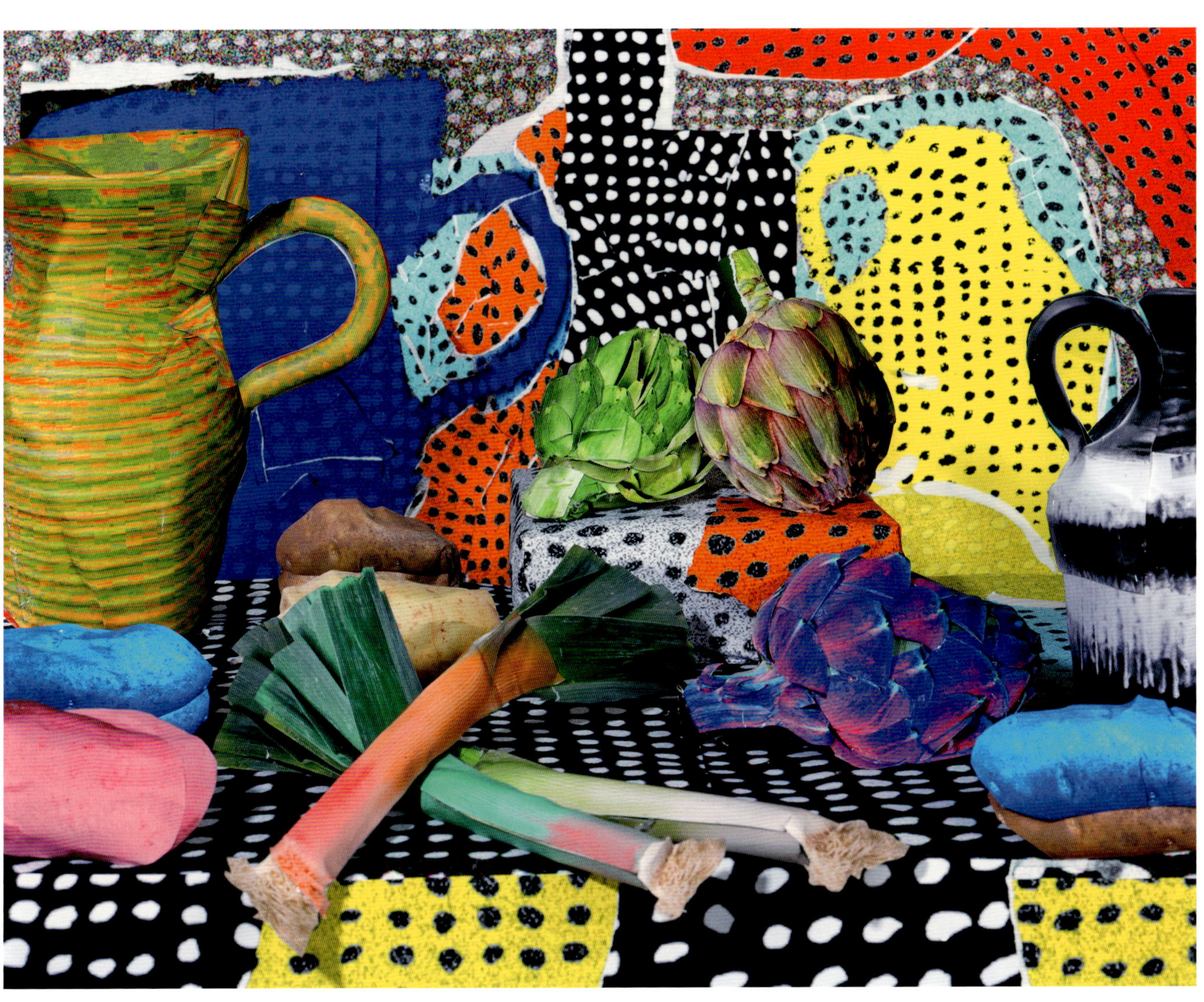

163    Daniel Gordon, *Artichokes and Leeks*, 2014. C-print

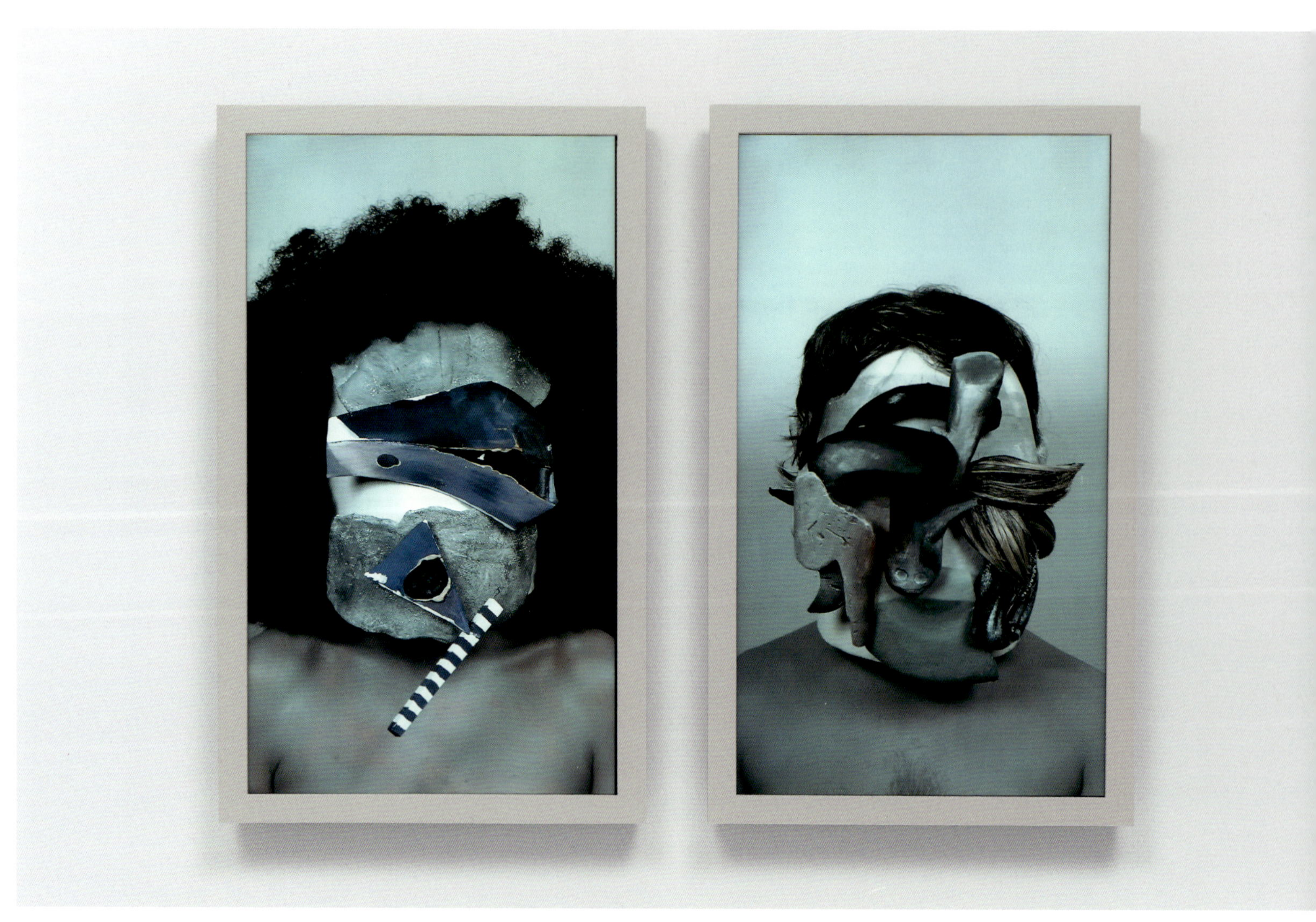

164  Brian Bress, *Pair (Justin, Cara)*, 2012. High-definition dual-channel video (color), high-definition monitors and players, wall mounts, frames

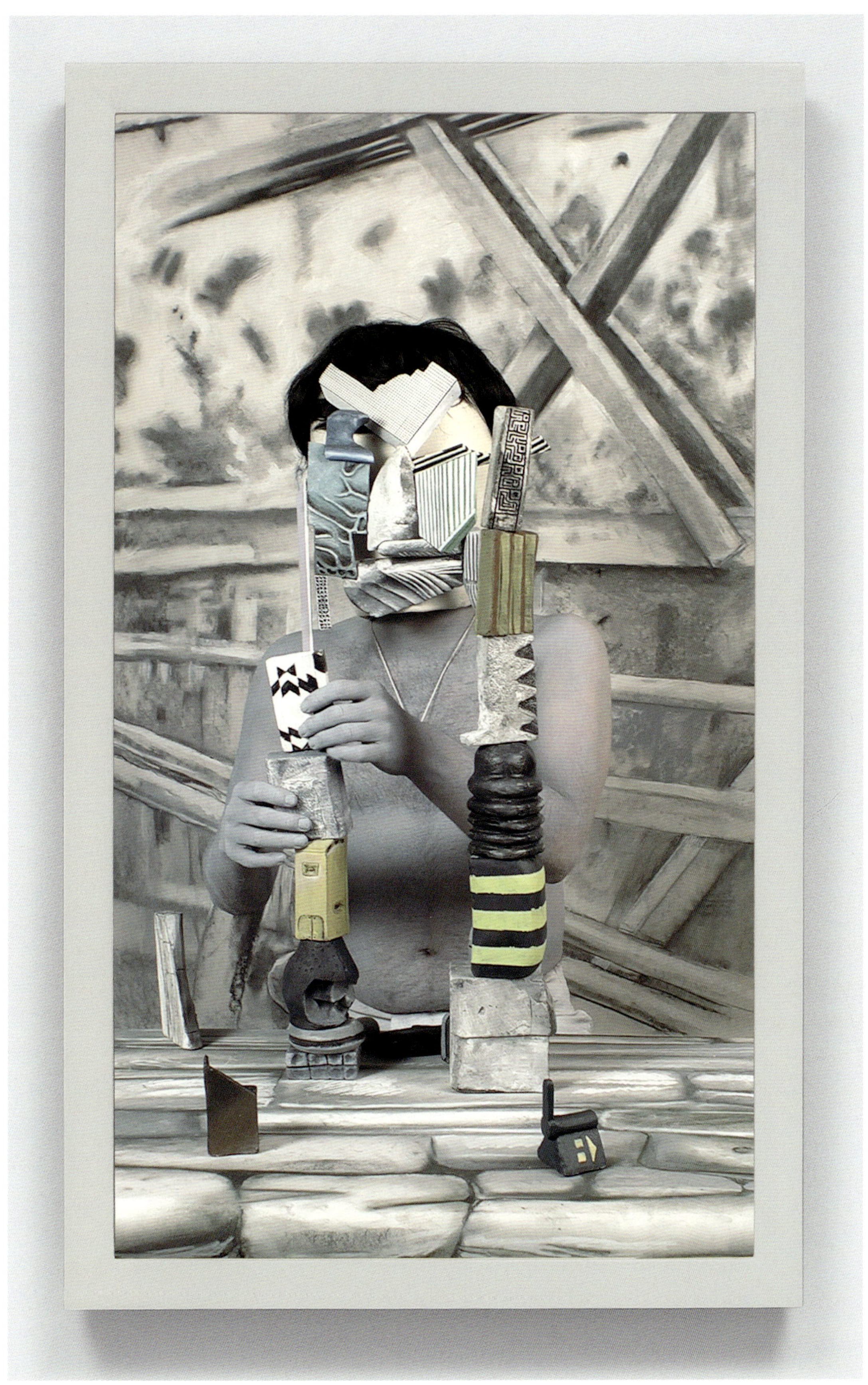

165     Brian Bress, *The Architect (Nick)*, 2012. High-definition single-channel video (color), high-definition monitor and player, wall mount, frame

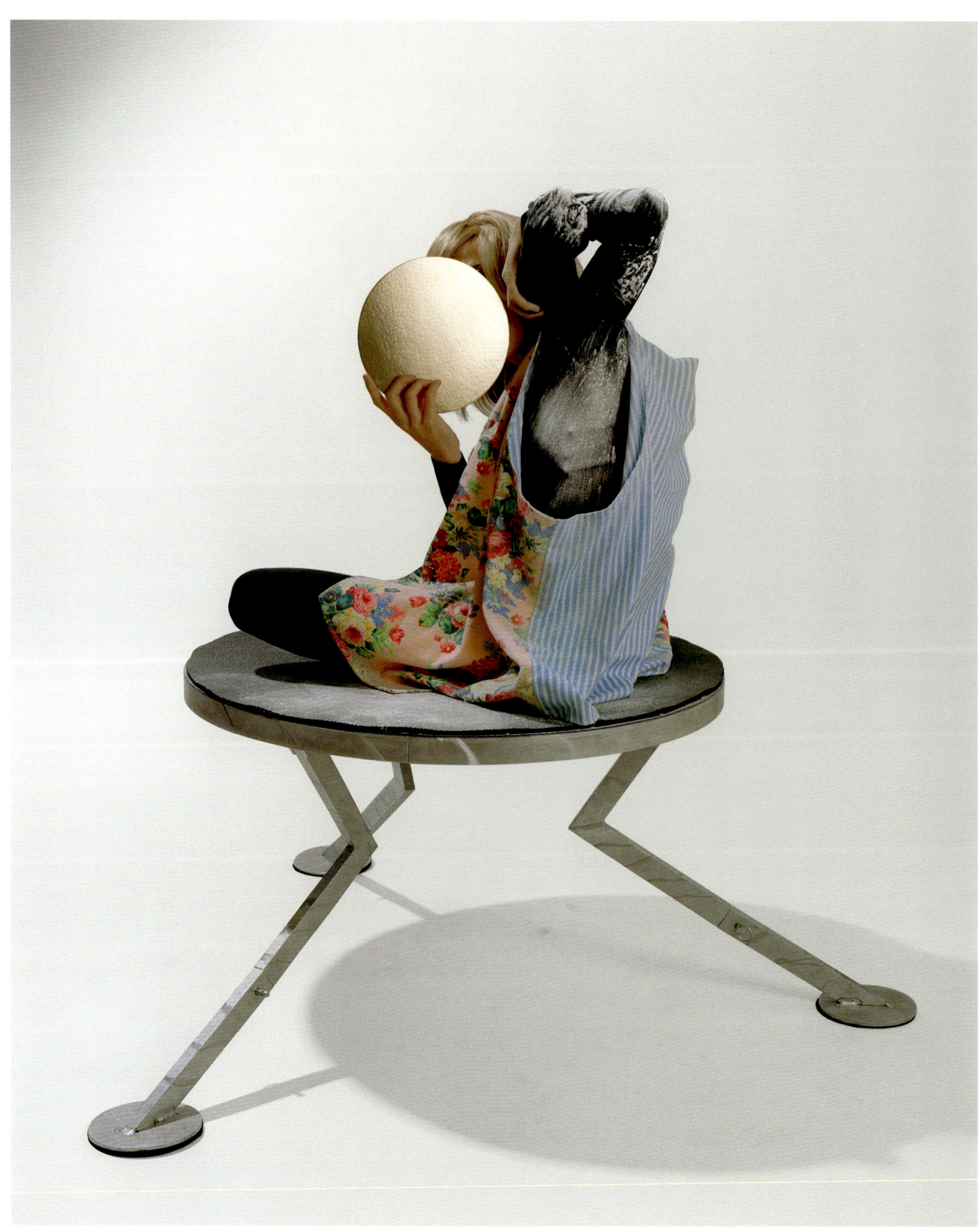

166    Nancy de Holl, *A Crossbreed*, 2007. Digital C-print

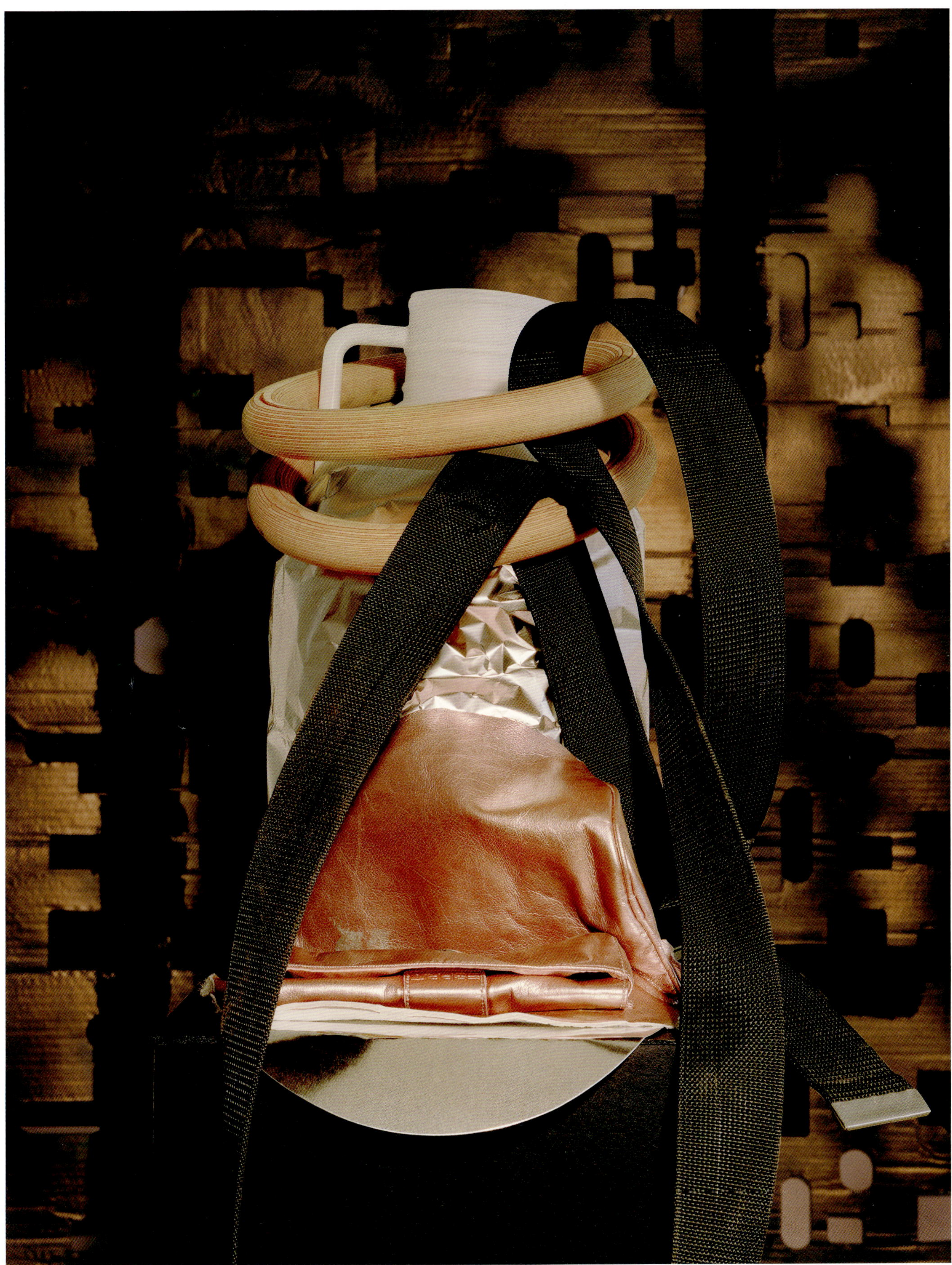

167    Nancy de Holl, *Skid Rogue*, 2007. Digital C-print

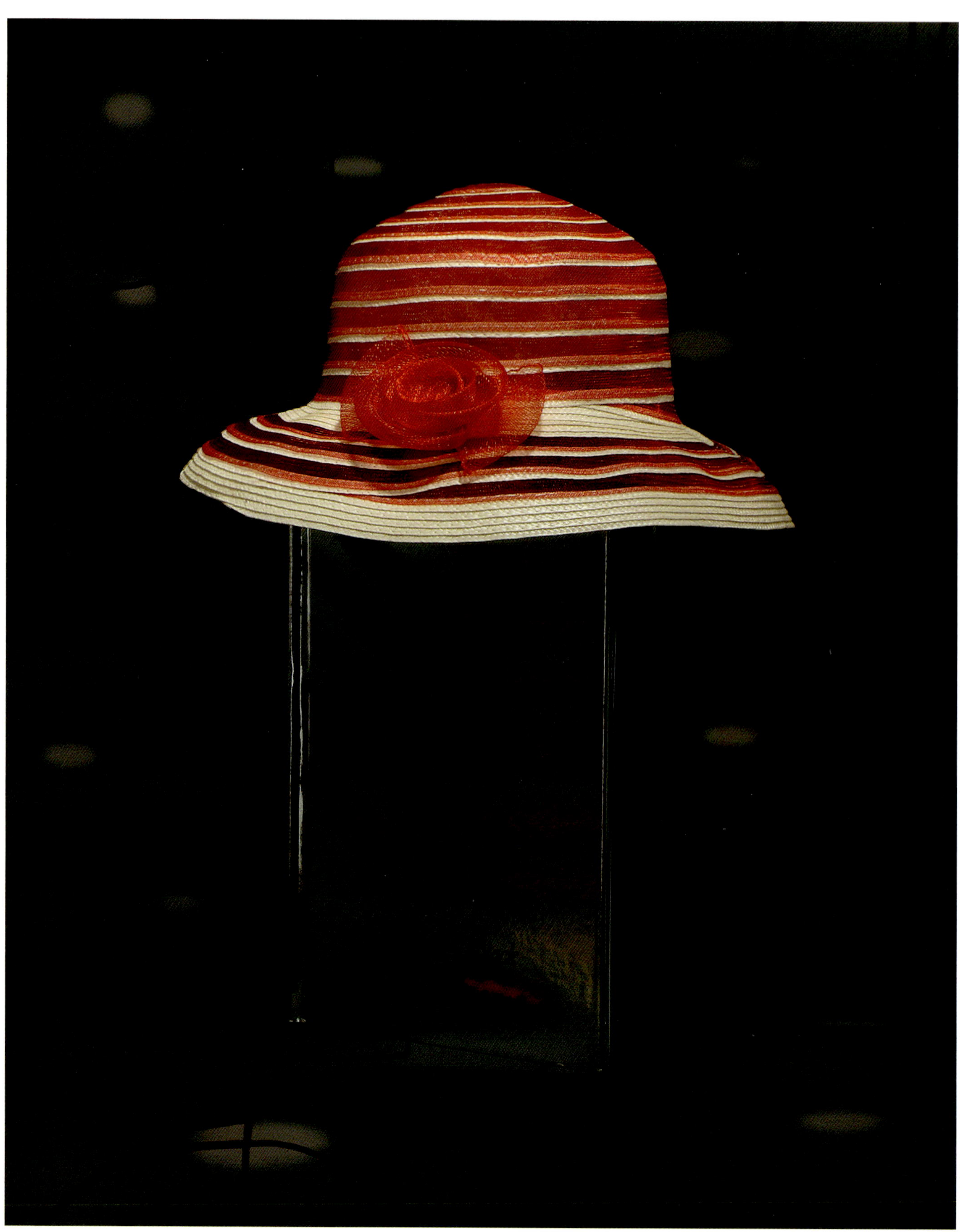

168    Nancy de Holl, *Private Stock*, 2012. Pigment print

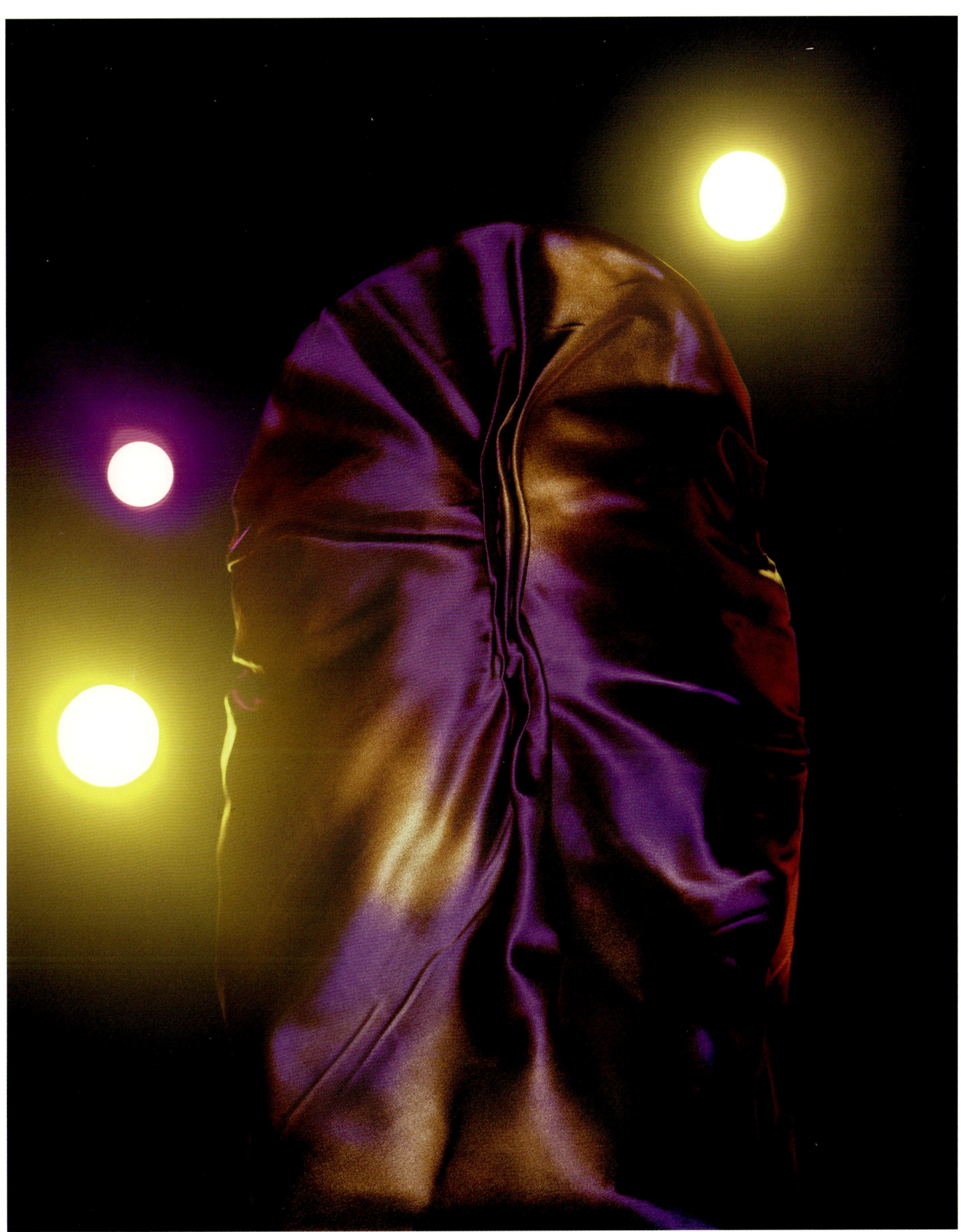

169    Nancy de Holl, *Monologue*, 2007. Digital C-print

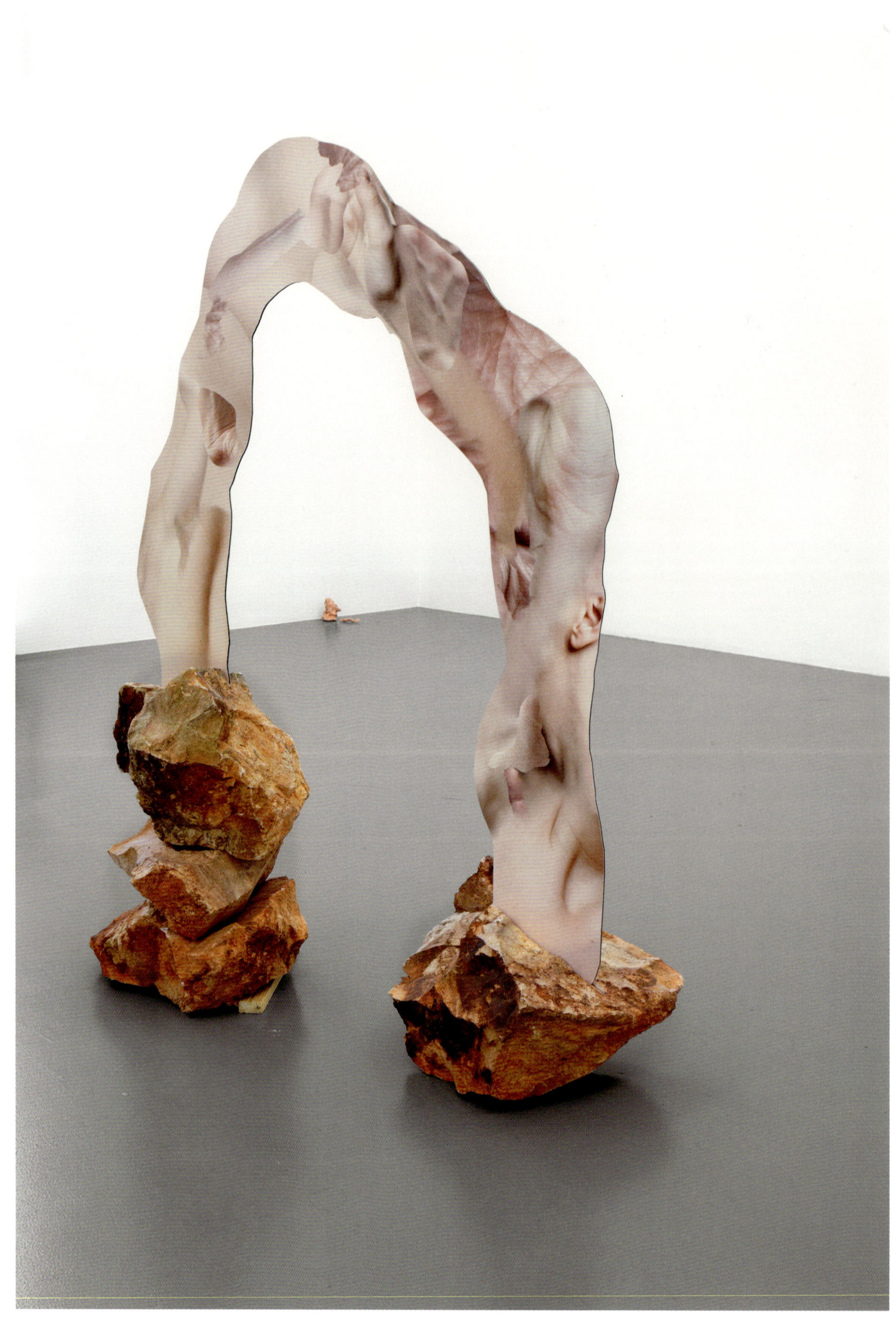

    Rachel de Joode, *Sculpted Human Skin in Rock I*, 2014. Digital C-print mounted on aluminum Dibond, installed in red and gray marble

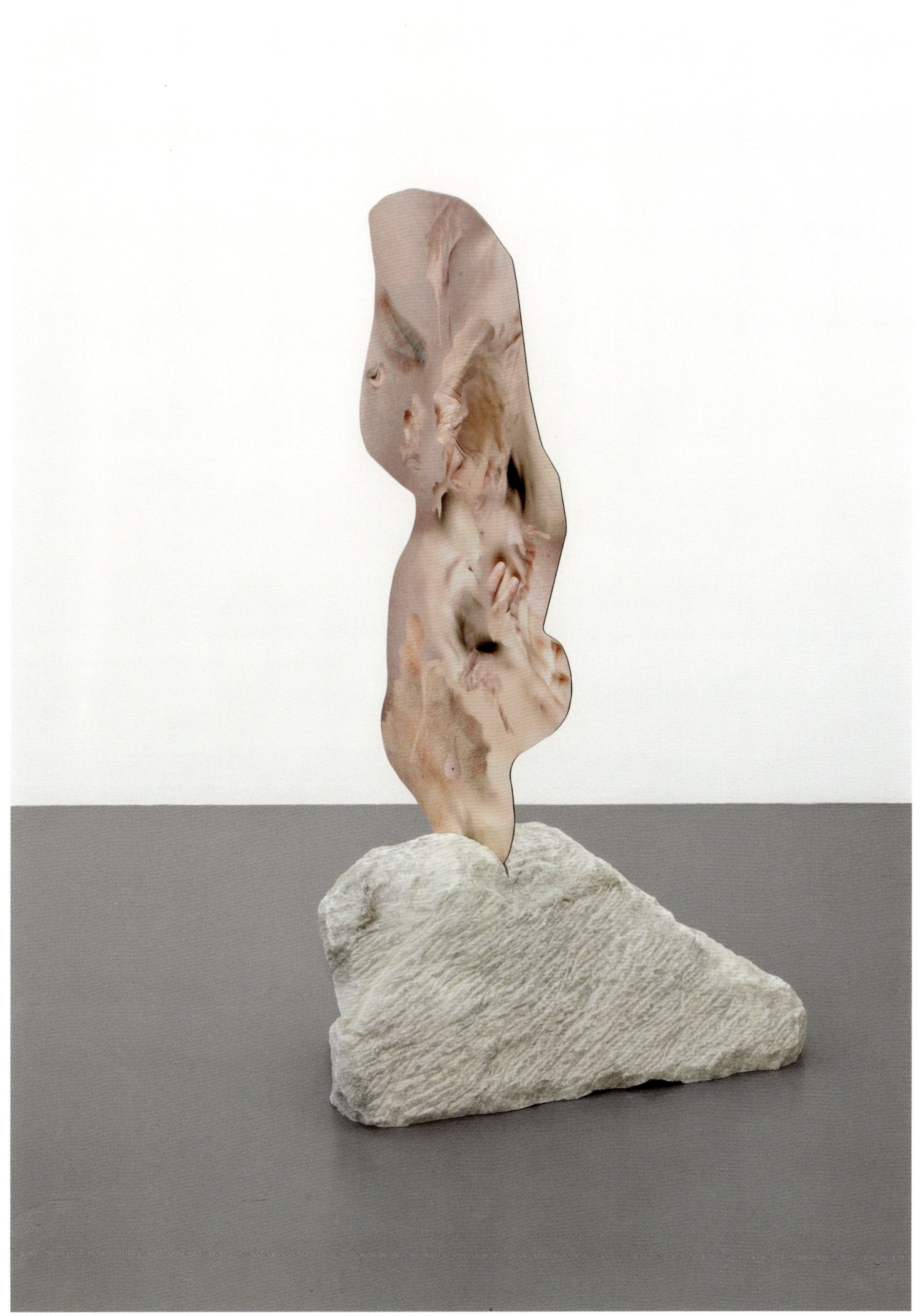

171    Rachel de Joode, *Sculpted Human Skin in Rock II*, 2014. Digital C-print mounted on aluminum Dibond, installed in red and gray marble

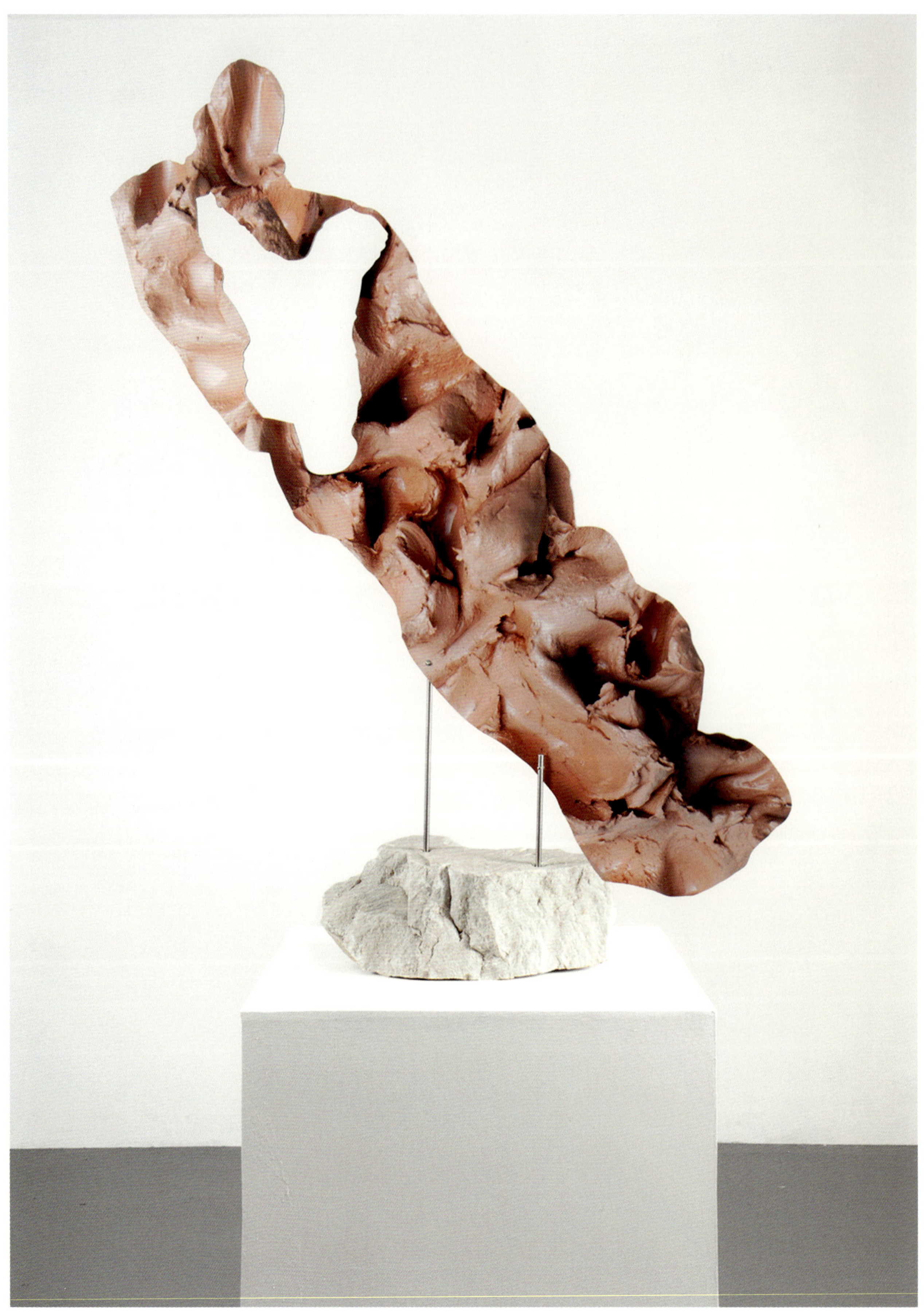

172    Rachel de Joode, *Reclining Wet Clay on Greek Marble*, 2014. Laser-cut photograph mounted on aluminum Dibond, marble, stainless steel, brass

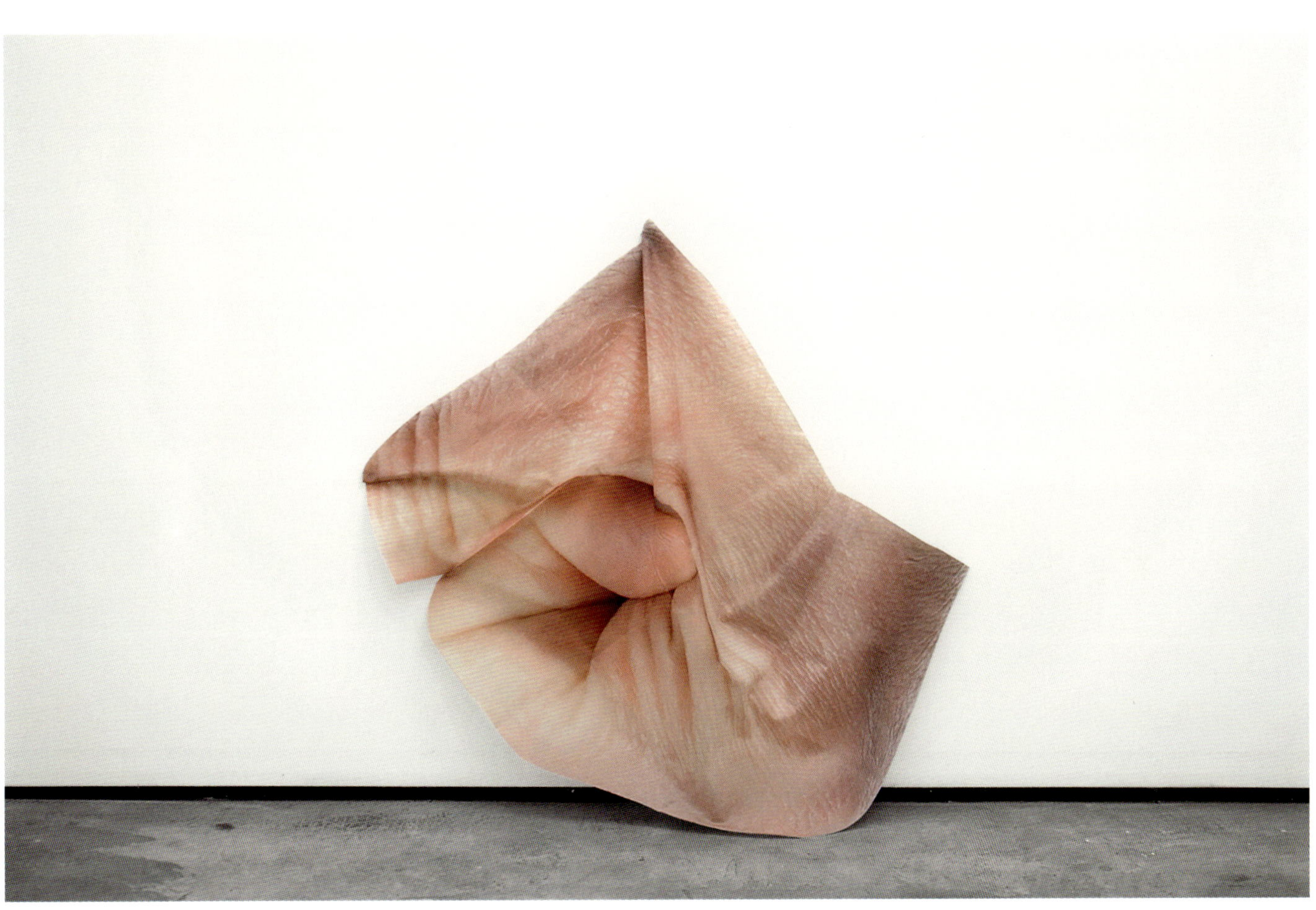

    Rachel de Joode, *SKIN*, 2013. Print on fabric

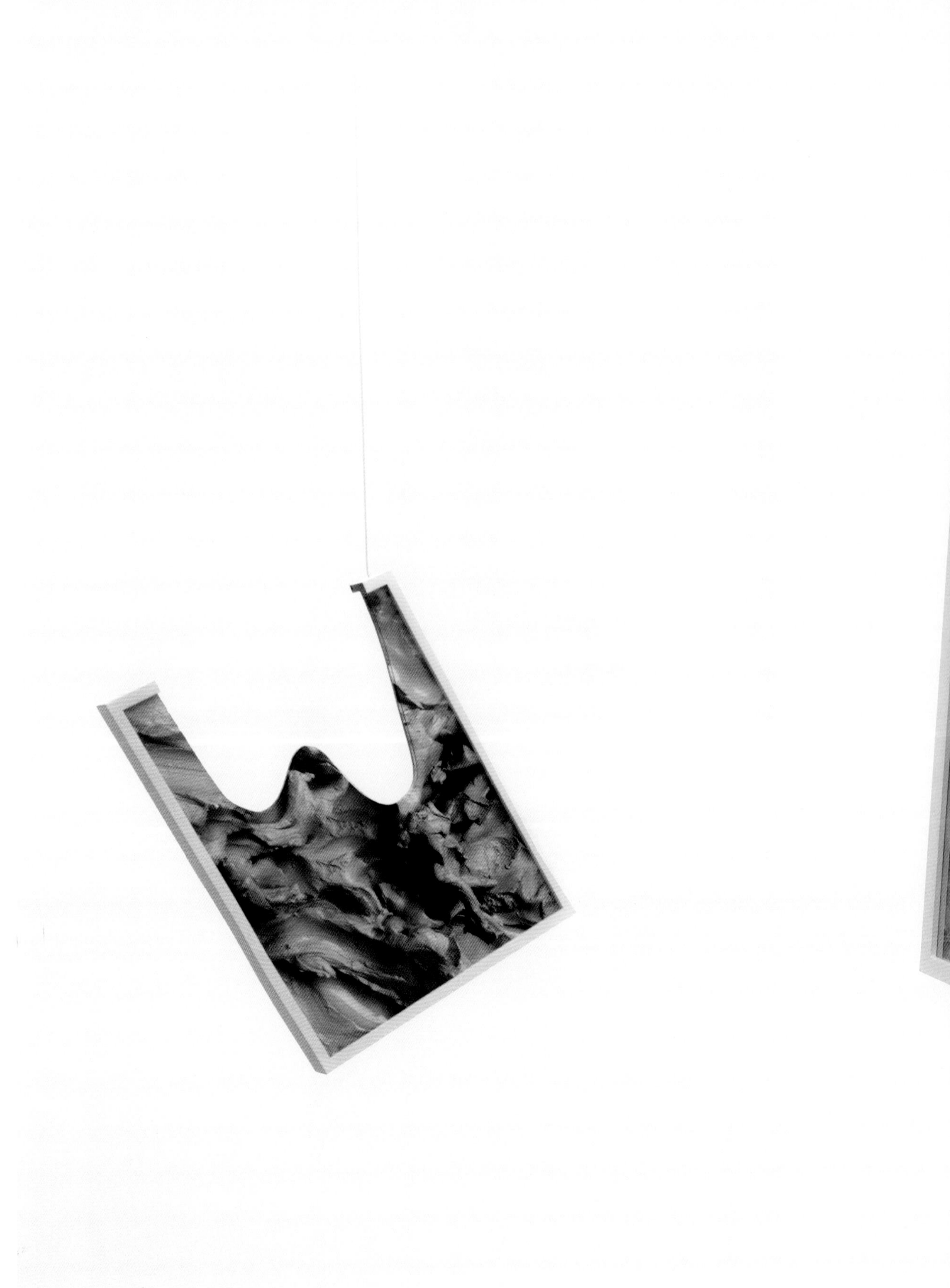

    Rachel de Joode, *A Ruin, I, II, & III*, 2014. Digital fine-art print on Hanemühle Photo Rag paper in partially cut custom frames

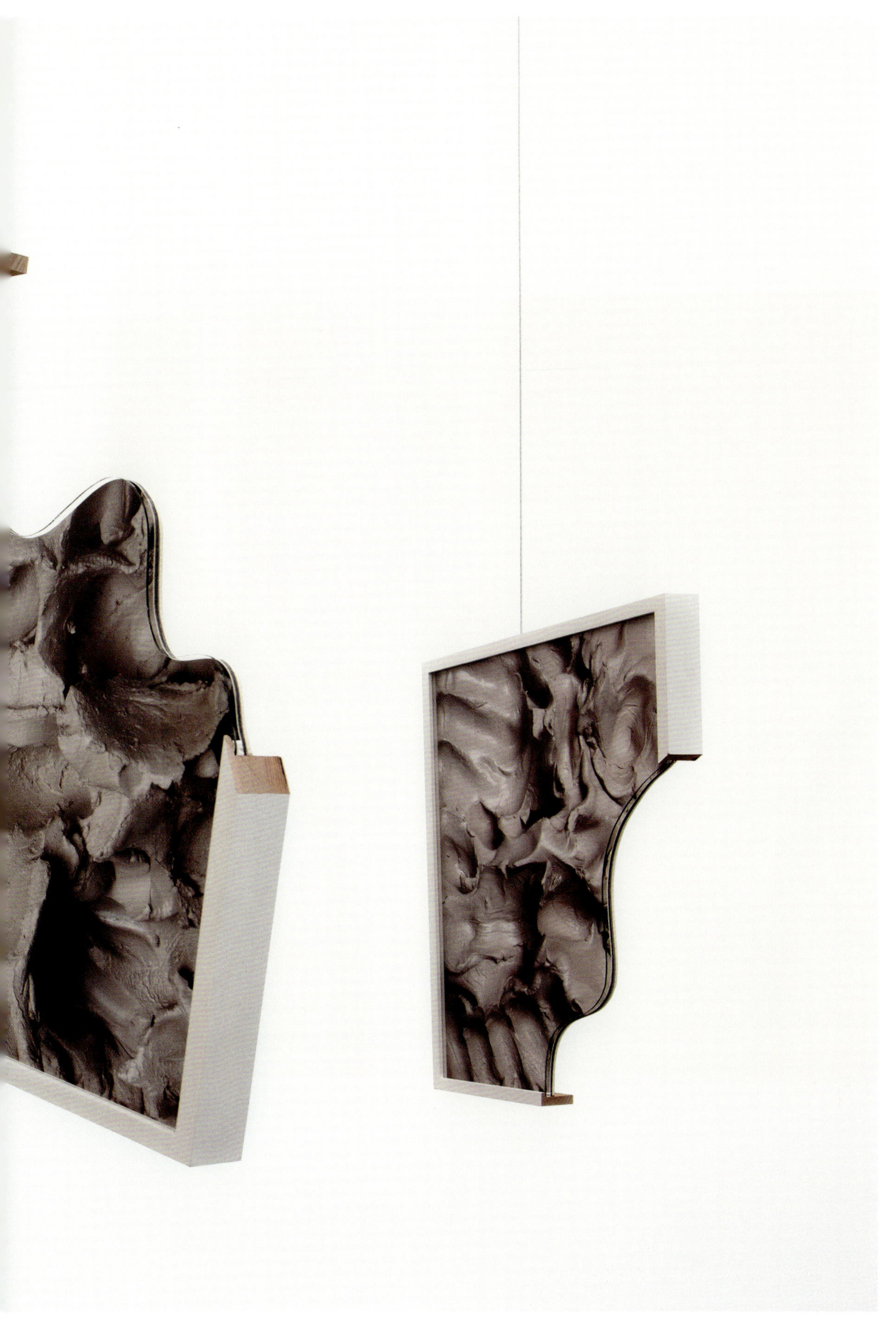

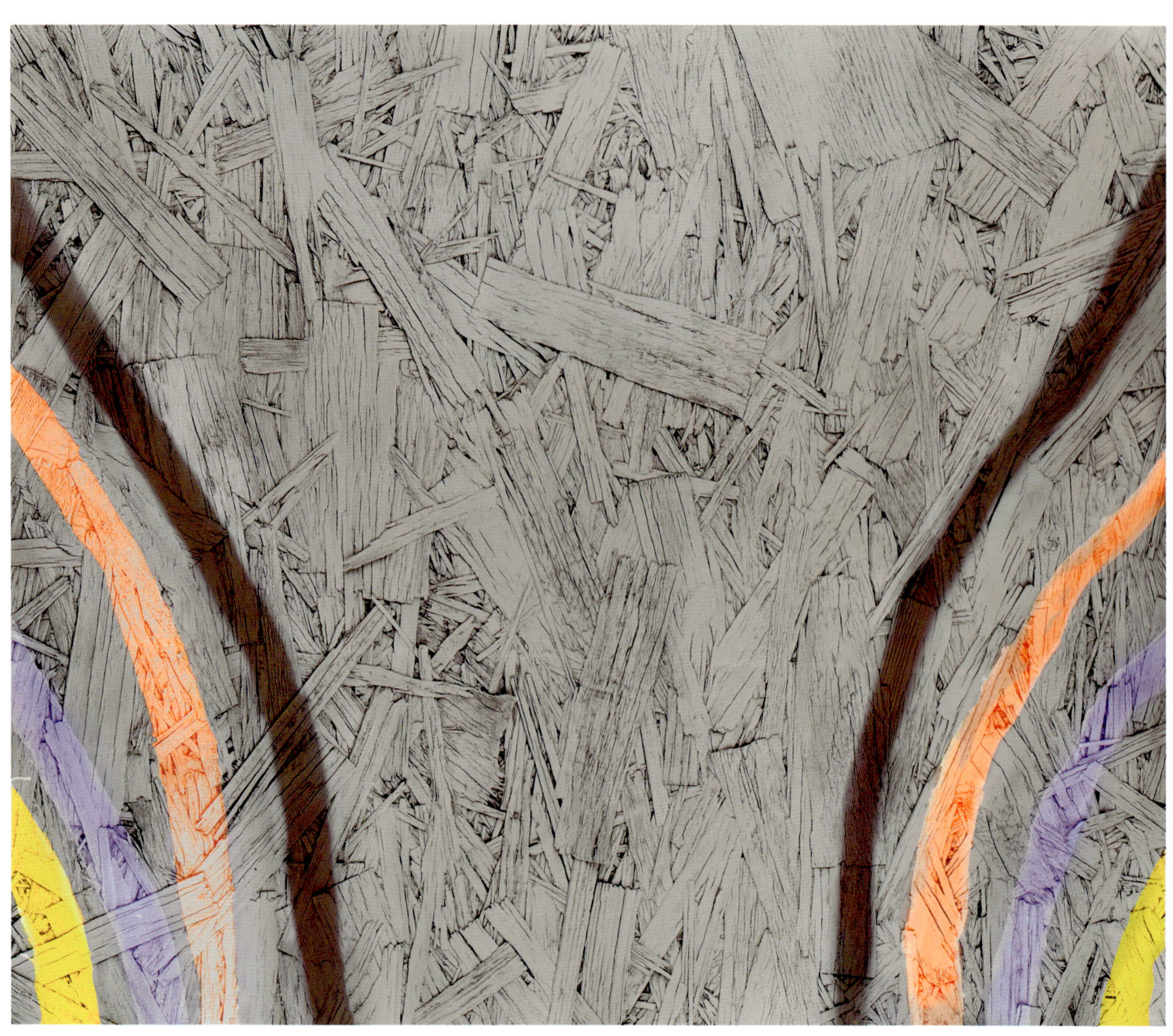

176    Arthur Ou, *Untitled (Gamma Pi)*, 2013. Archival pigment print on rag paper

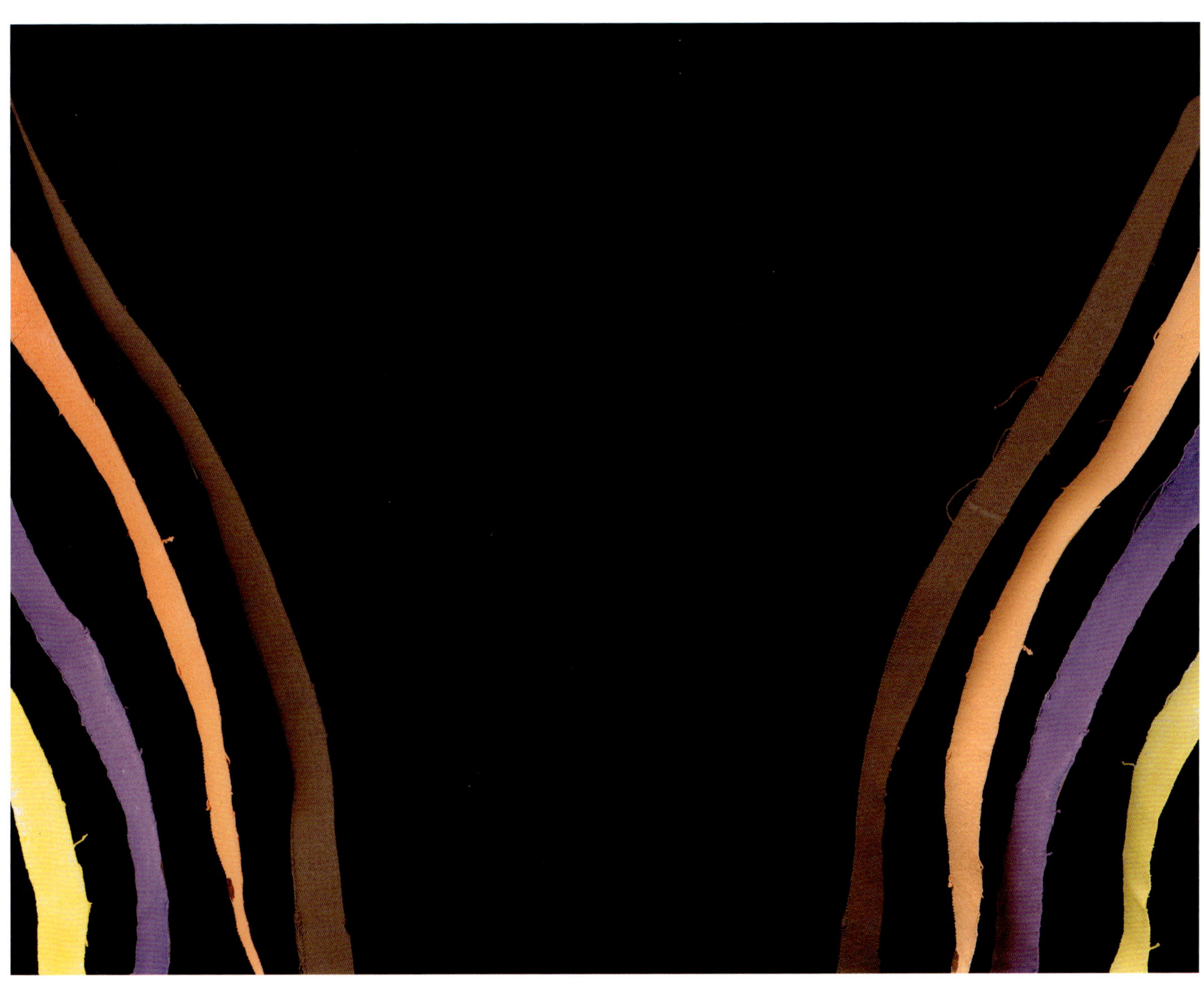

177  Arthur Ou, *Untitled*, 2013. Archival pigment print on rag paper

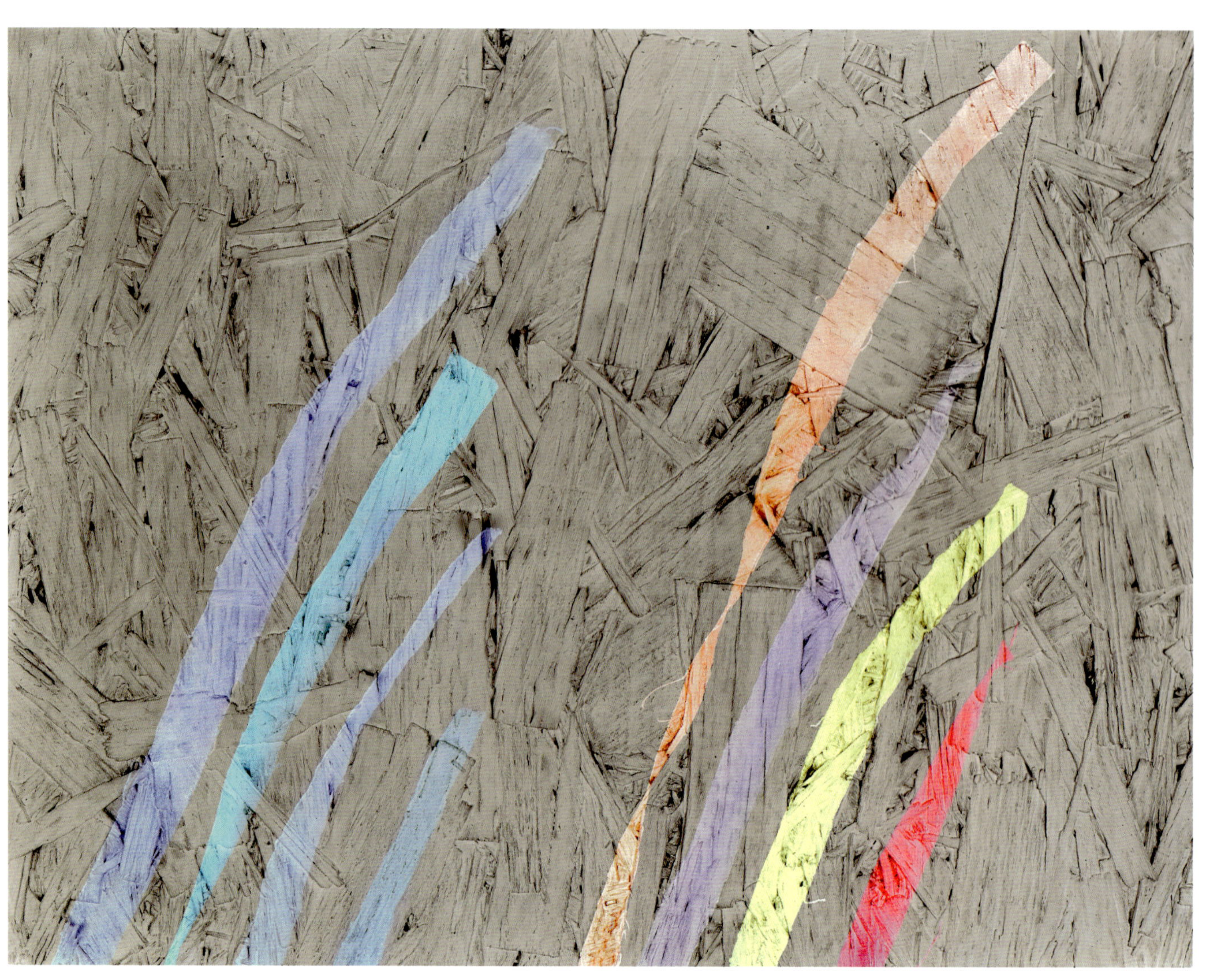

178    Arthur Ou, *Untitled (Delta Sigma)*, 2013. Archival pigment print on rag paper

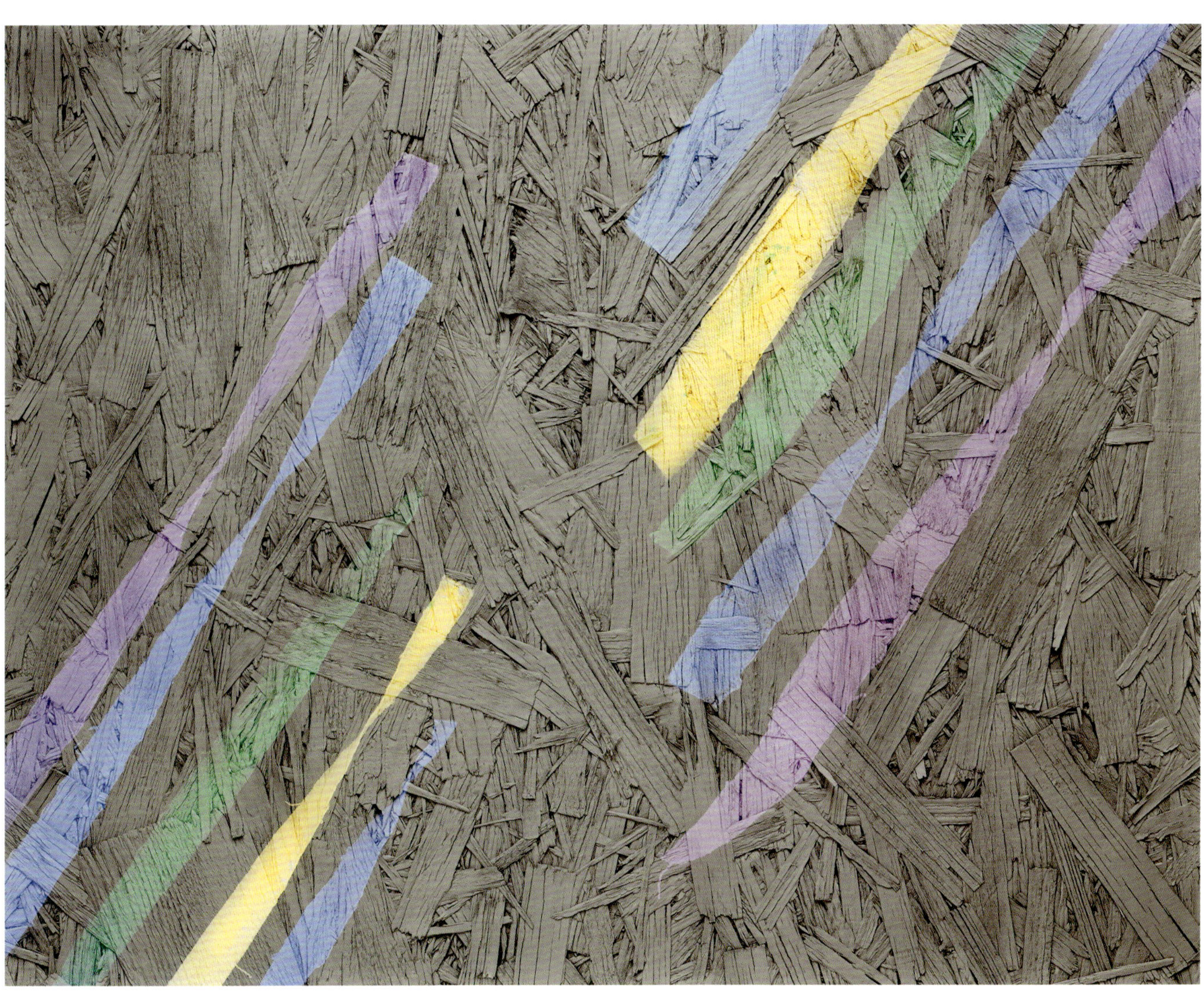

179    Arthur Ou, *Untitled (Phi)*, 2013. Archival pigment print on rag paper

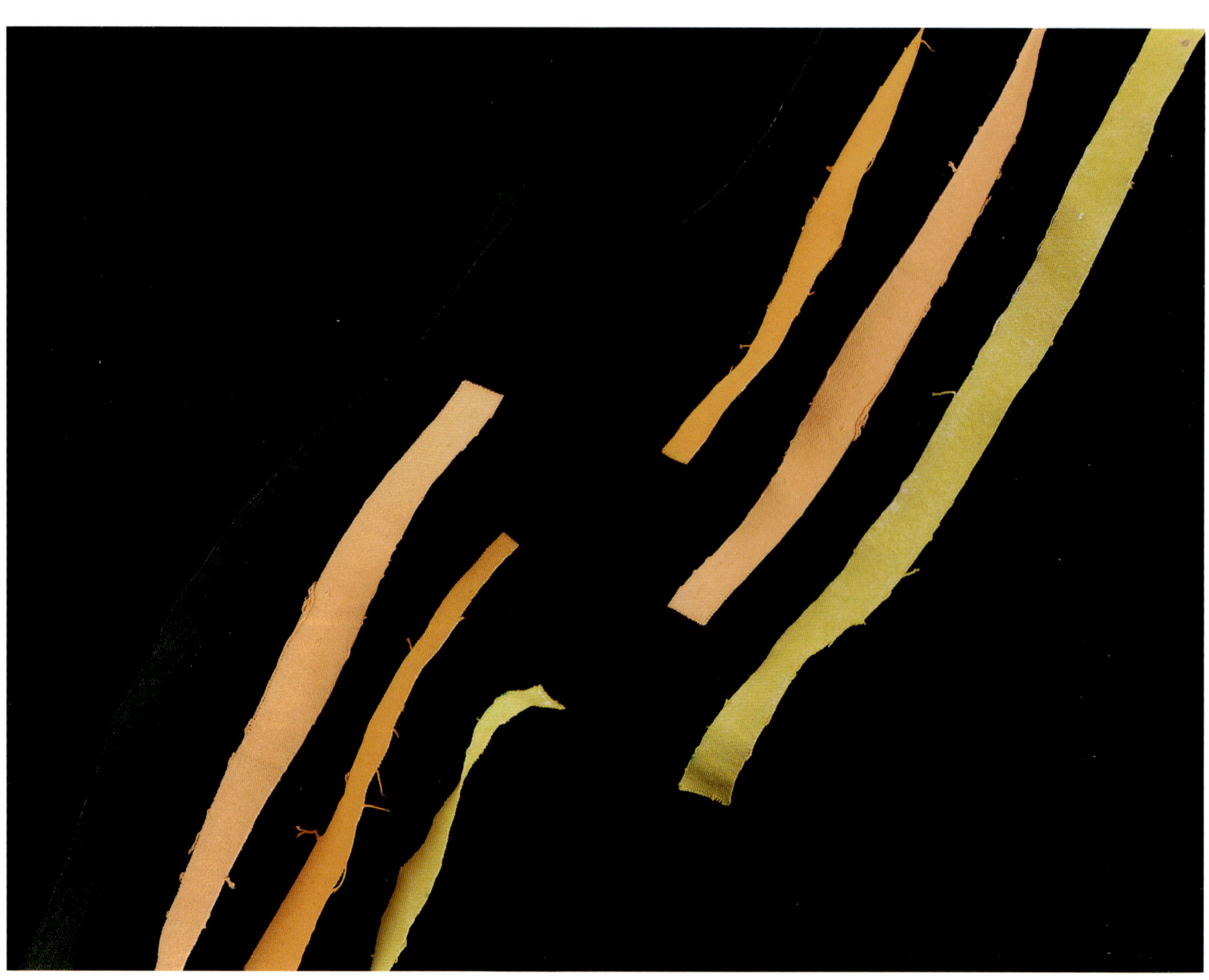

180    Arthur Ou, *Untitled (Theta Alpha 1)*, 2013. Archival pigment print on rag paper

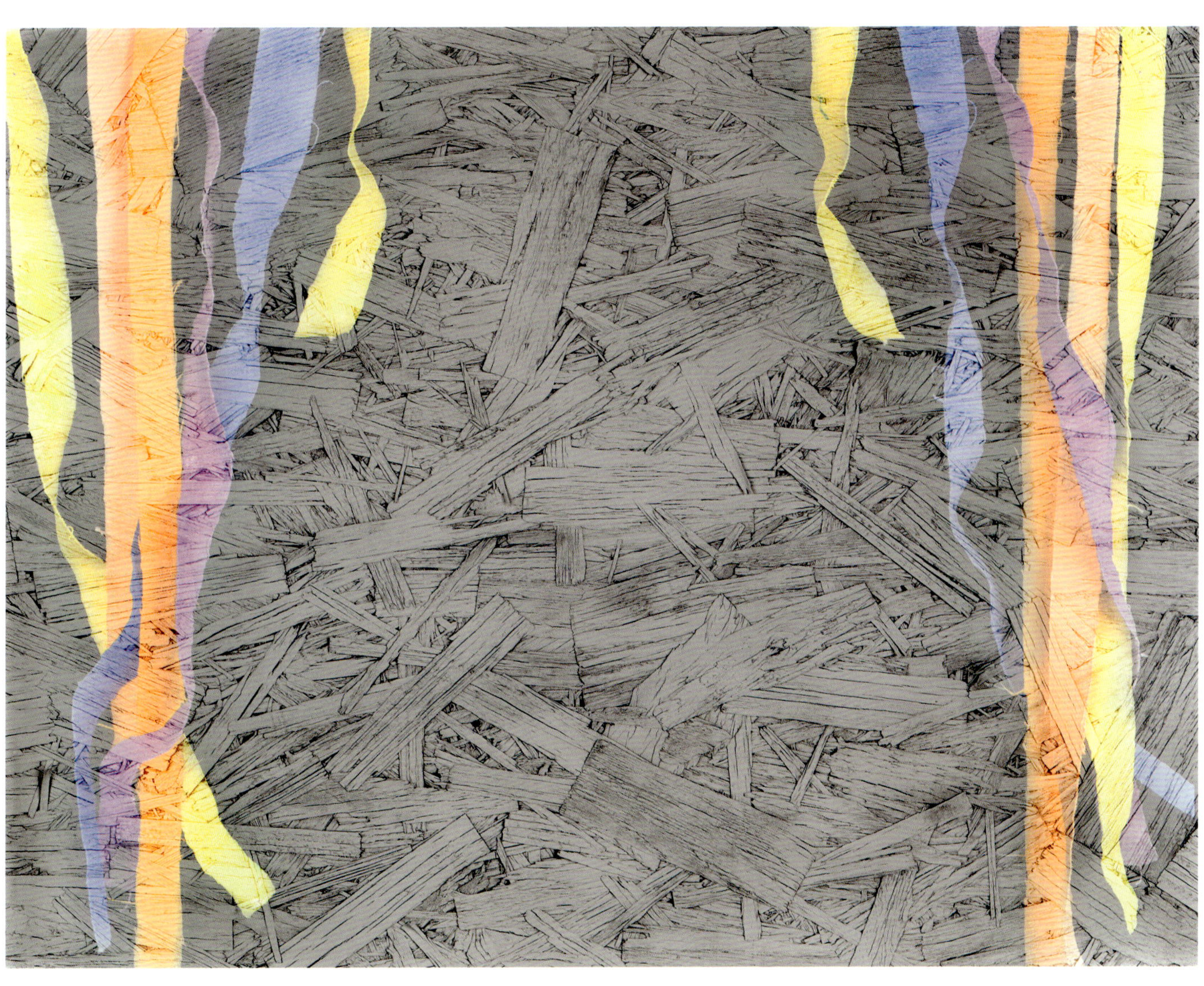

181     Arthur Ou, *Untitled (Delta Zeta)*, 2013. Archival pigment print on rag paper

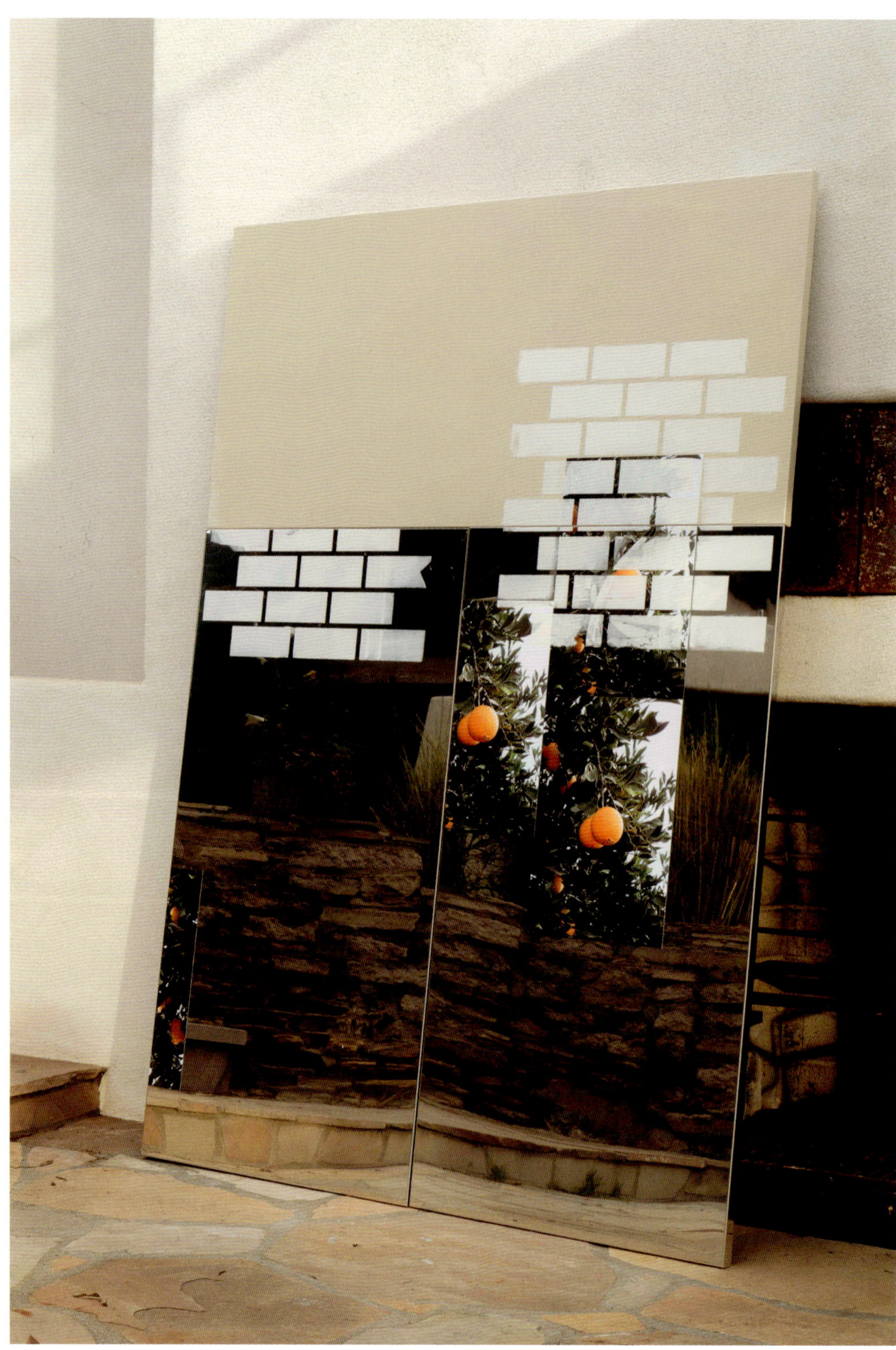

182    Bryan Dooley, *Three Rivers Orange Tree #1*, 2014. Powder-coated steel, mirror-polished steel, screen-print, digital print

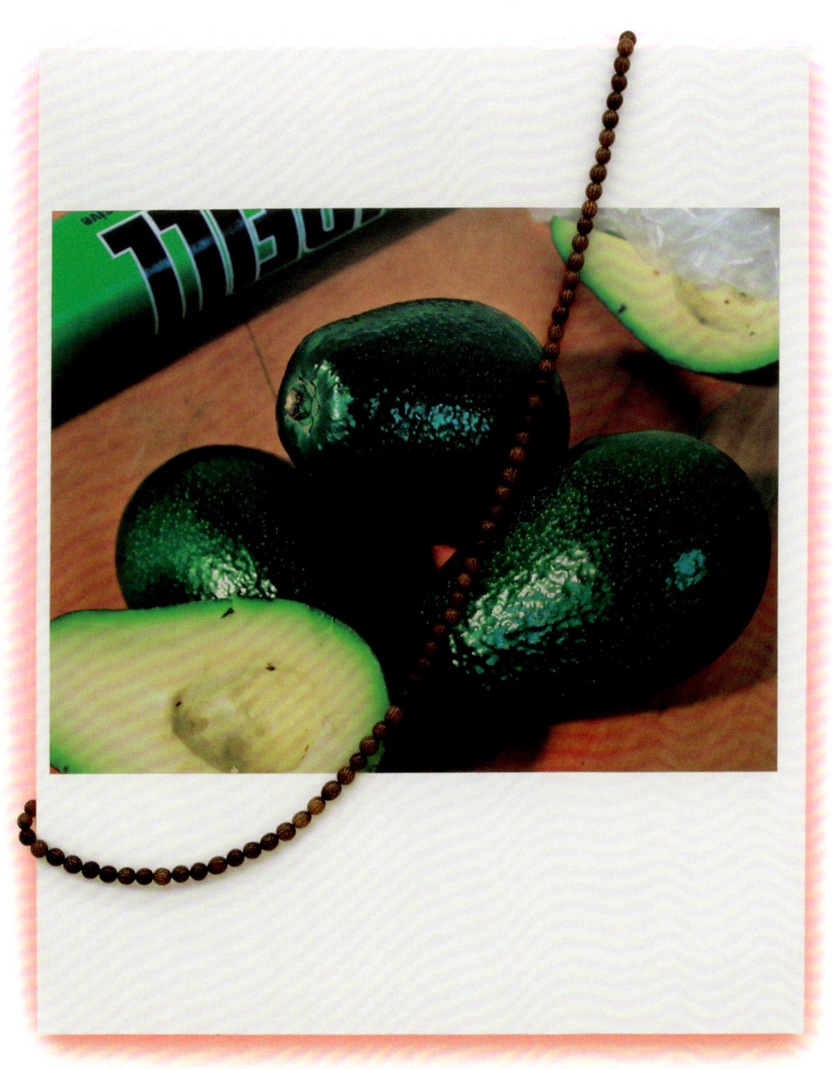

183    Bryan Dooley, *Mount Judge (Avocado + Grip Fill)*, 2013. Sprayed aluminum panel, camouflage tape, PVC, adhesive print, beads

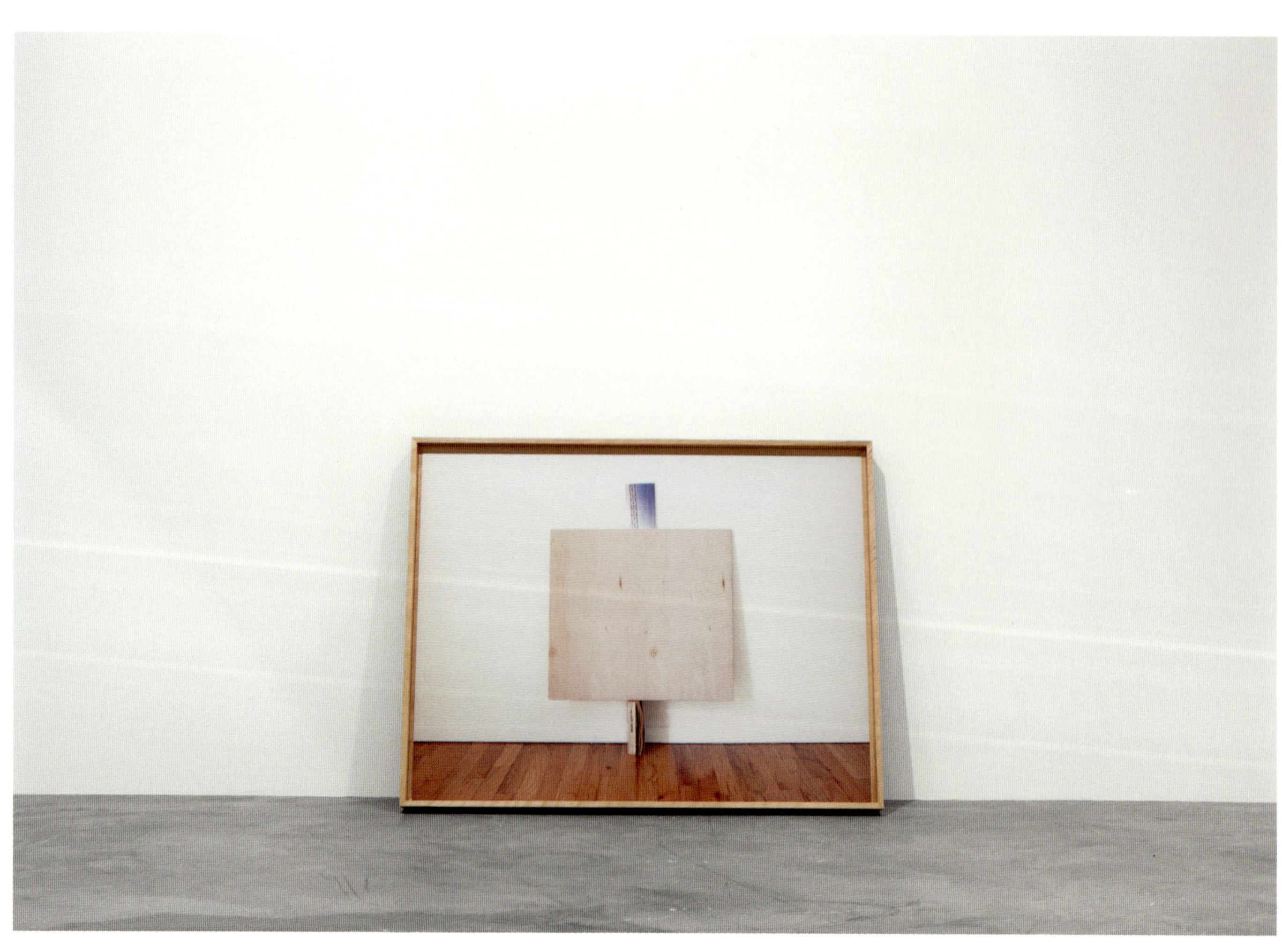

184    Leslie Hewitt, *Untitled (Arc)*, 2011. Digital C-print, custom birch frame

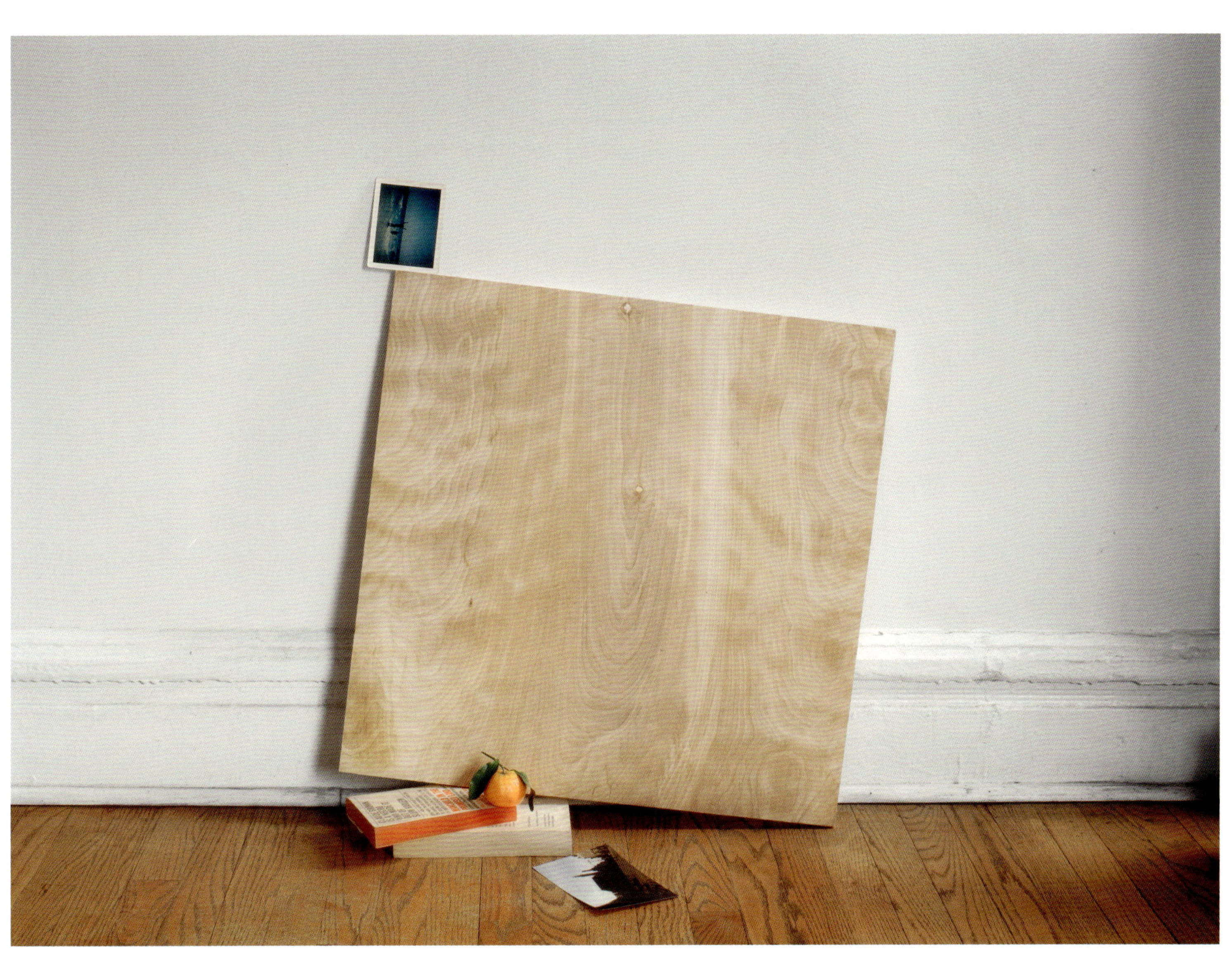

185  Leslie Hewitt, *Untitled (Mirage)*, 2010. Digital C-print

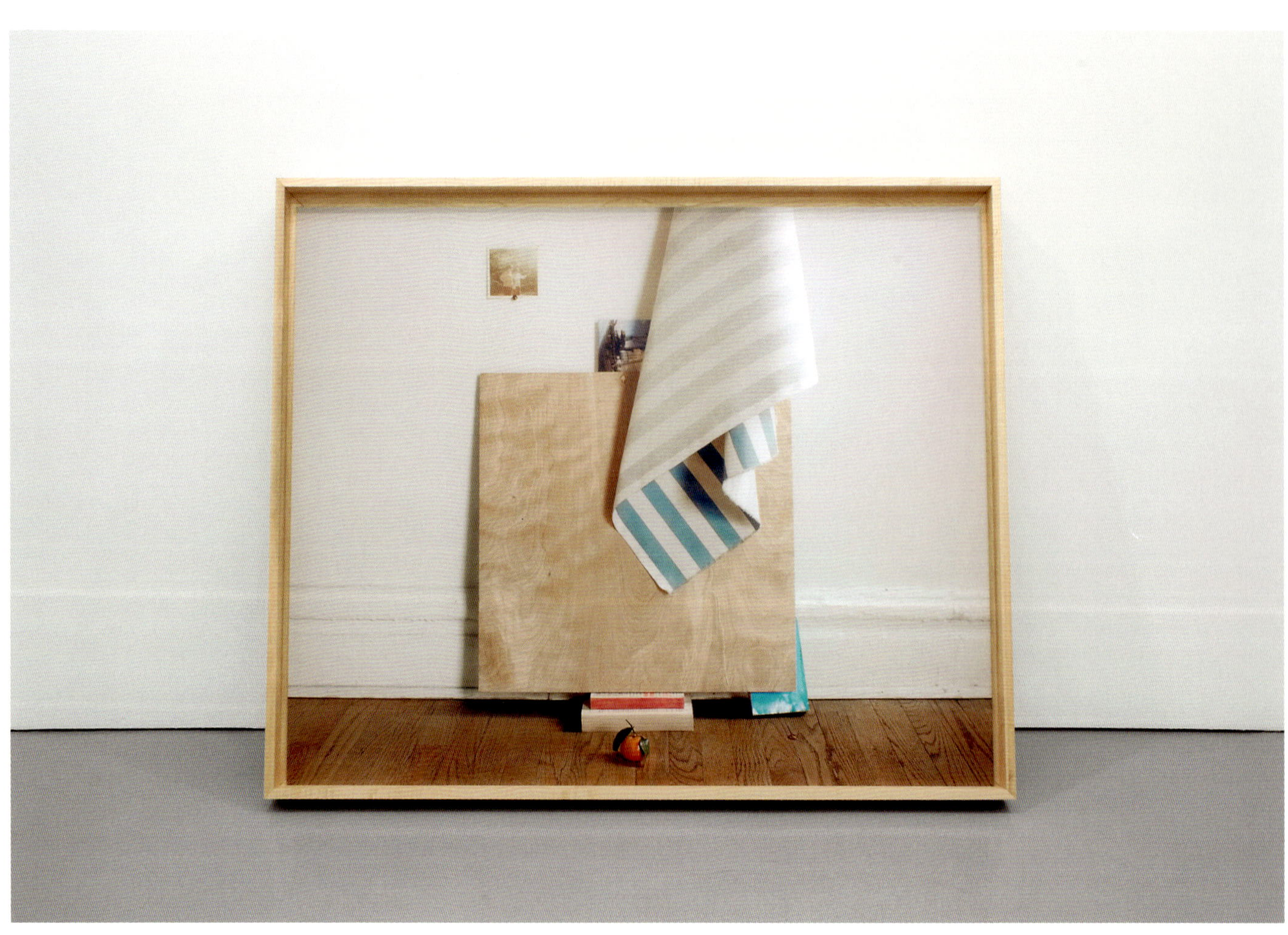

186    Leslie Hewitt, *Untitled (Seems to Be Necessary)*, 2009. Digital C-print, custom maple frame

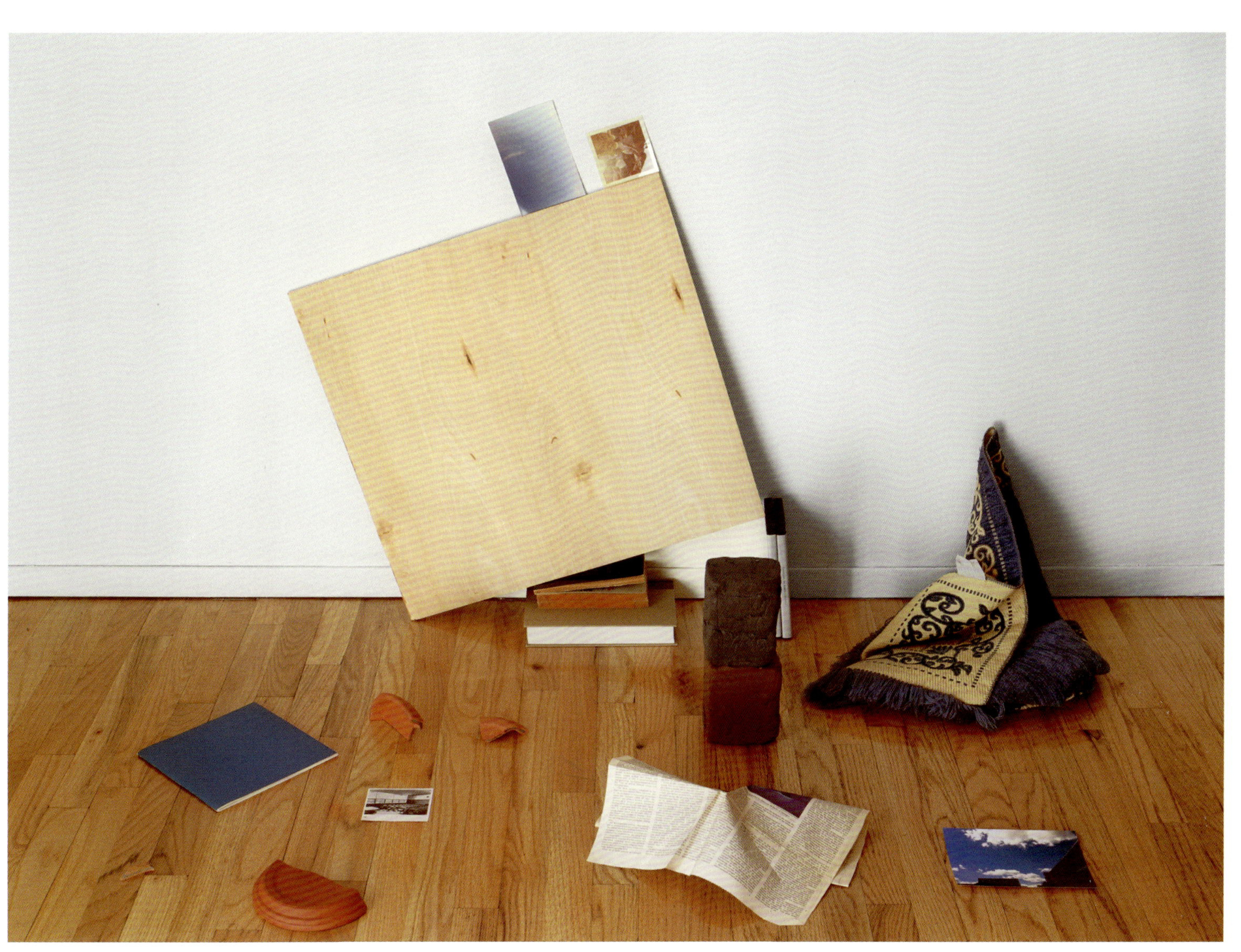

187    Leslie Hewitt, *Untitled (Abloom)*, 2012. Digital C-print

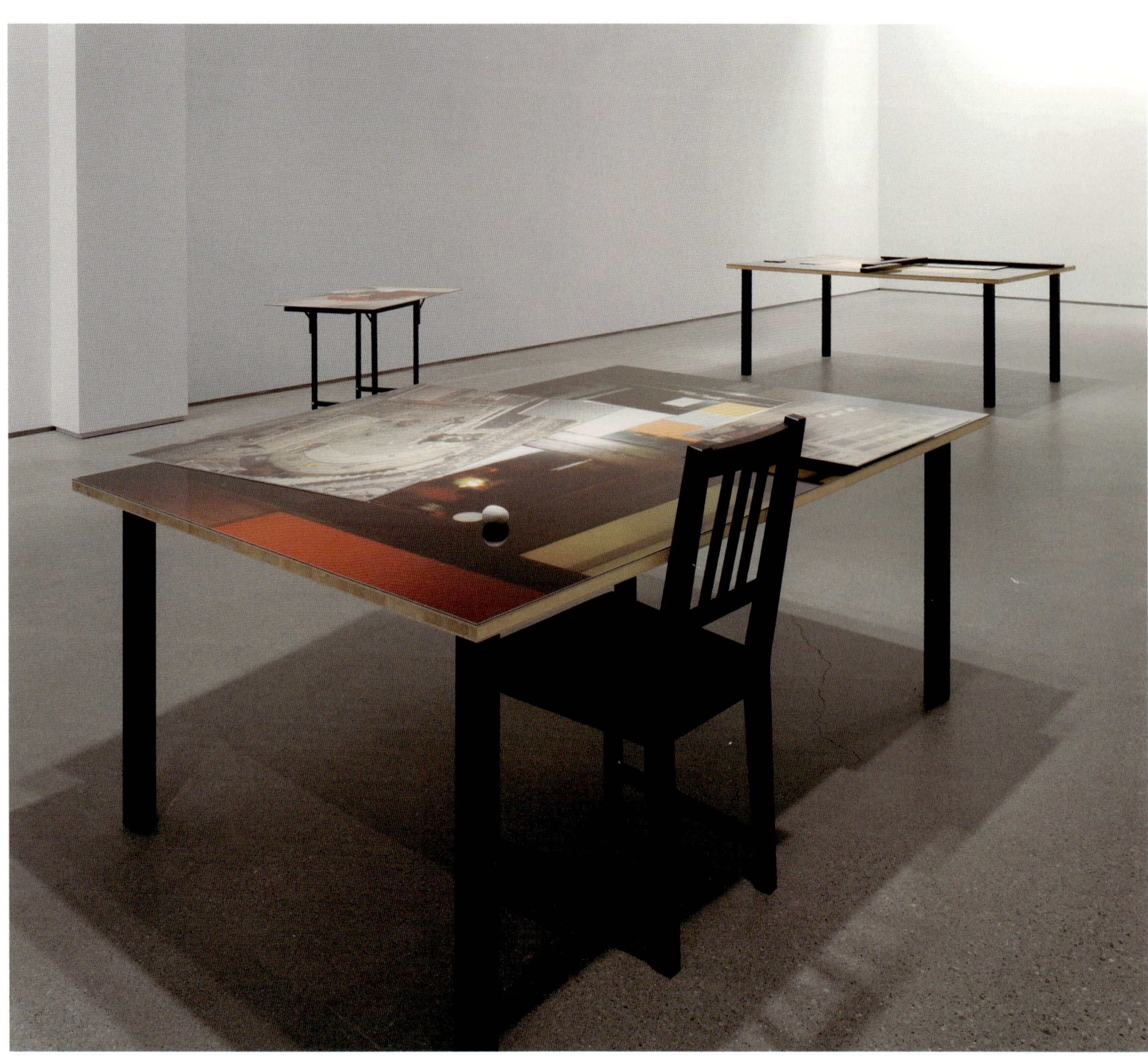

188    Yuki Kimura, *Untitled*, 2010. Three Lambda prints on Alpolic, wood, iron, lacquer, chair, stone

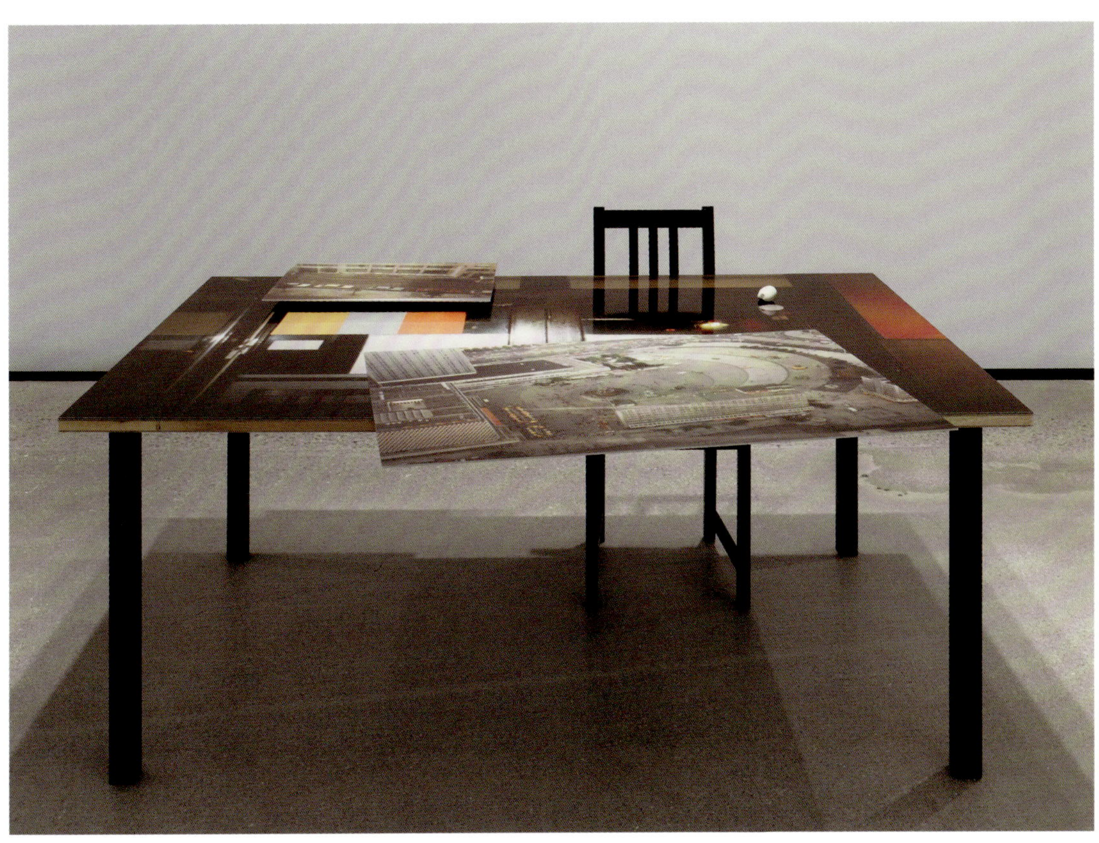

189    Yuki Kimura, *Untitled*, 2010. Three Lambda prints on Alpolic, wood, iron, lacquer, chair, stone

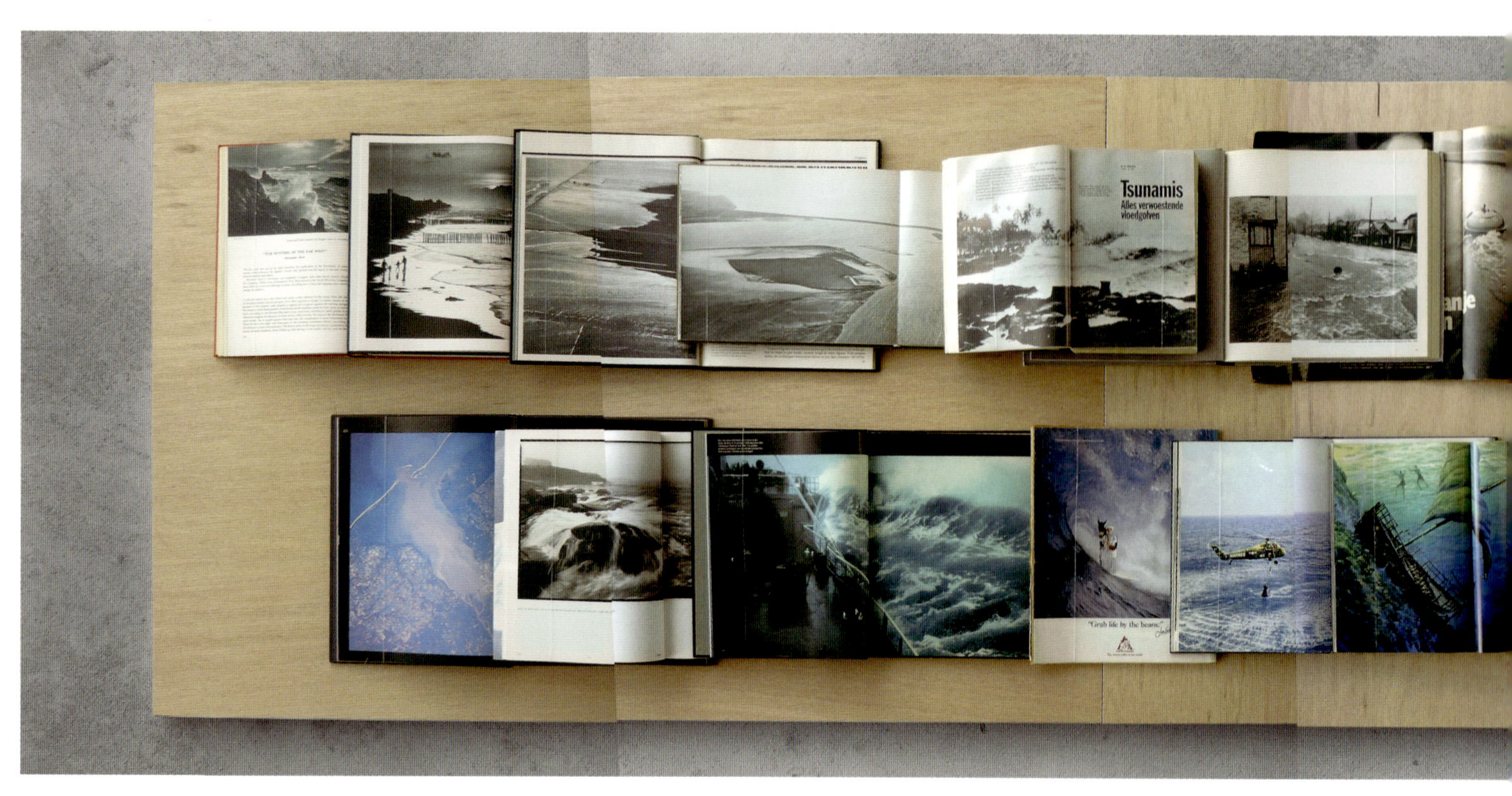

    Batia Suter, *Wave, Floor Version #1*, 2012. Seventeen books

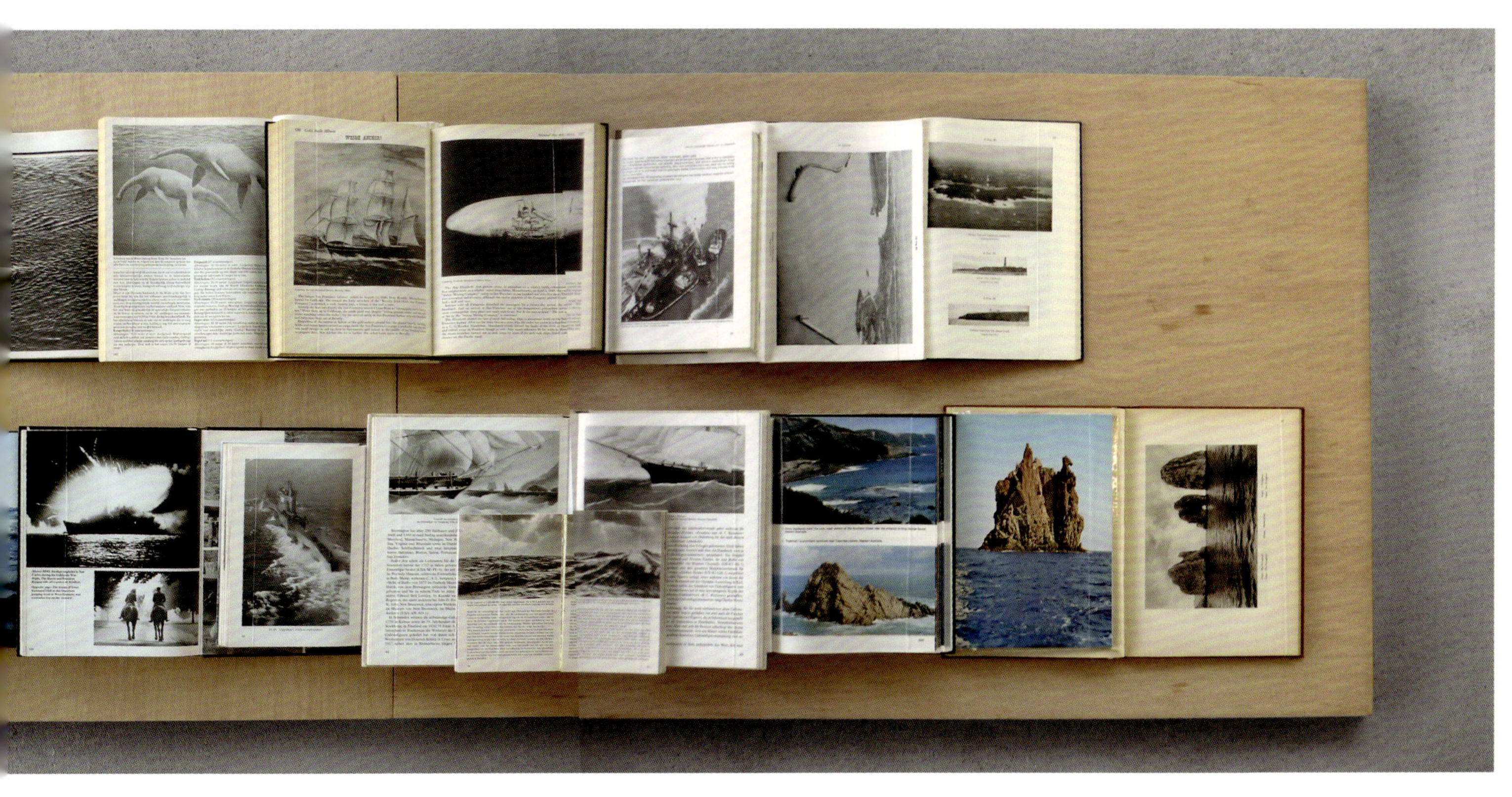

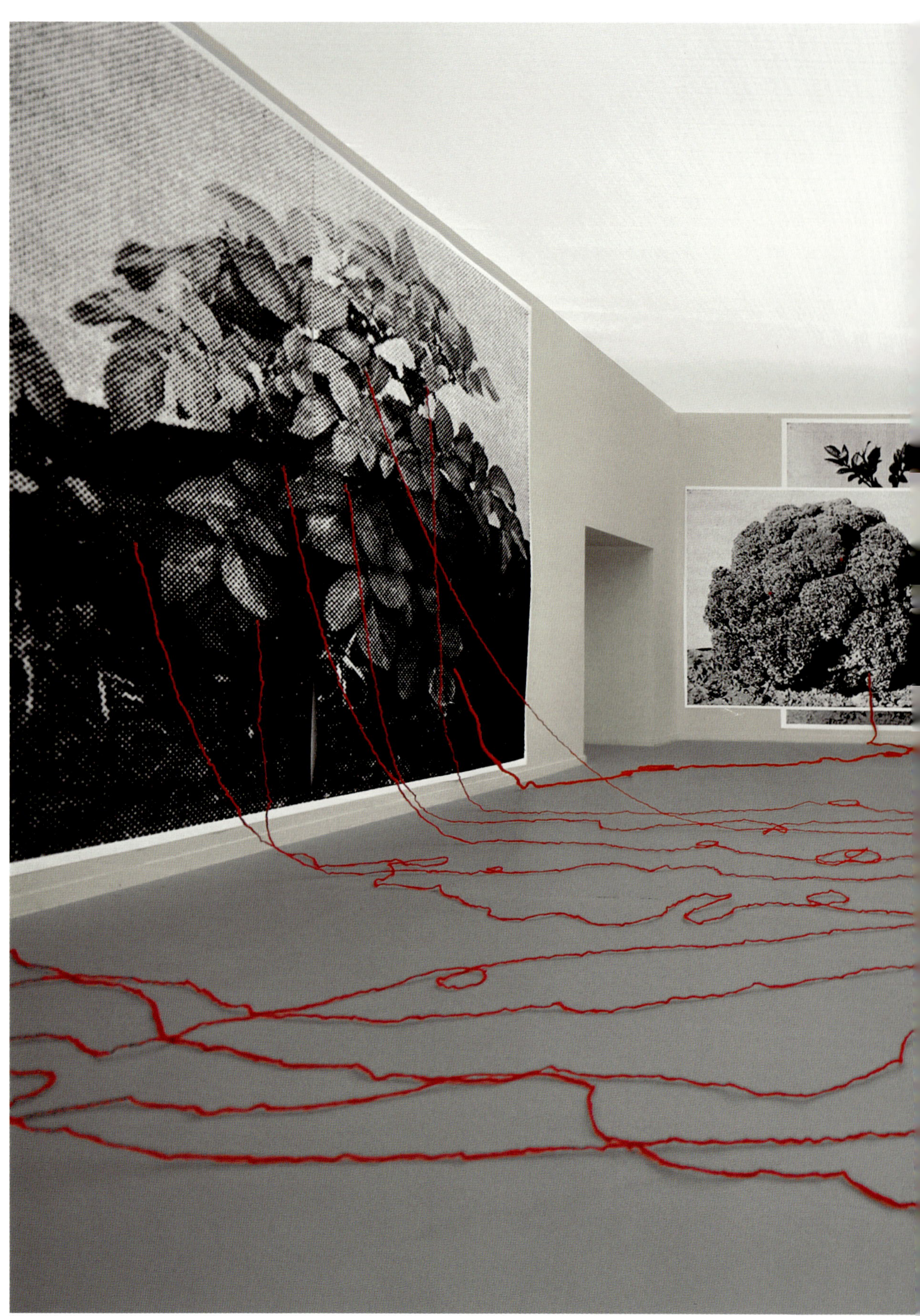

192    Batia Suter, *Lecture*, 2012. Installation with posters and rope, for Probe exhibition space (Arnhem, the Netherlands)

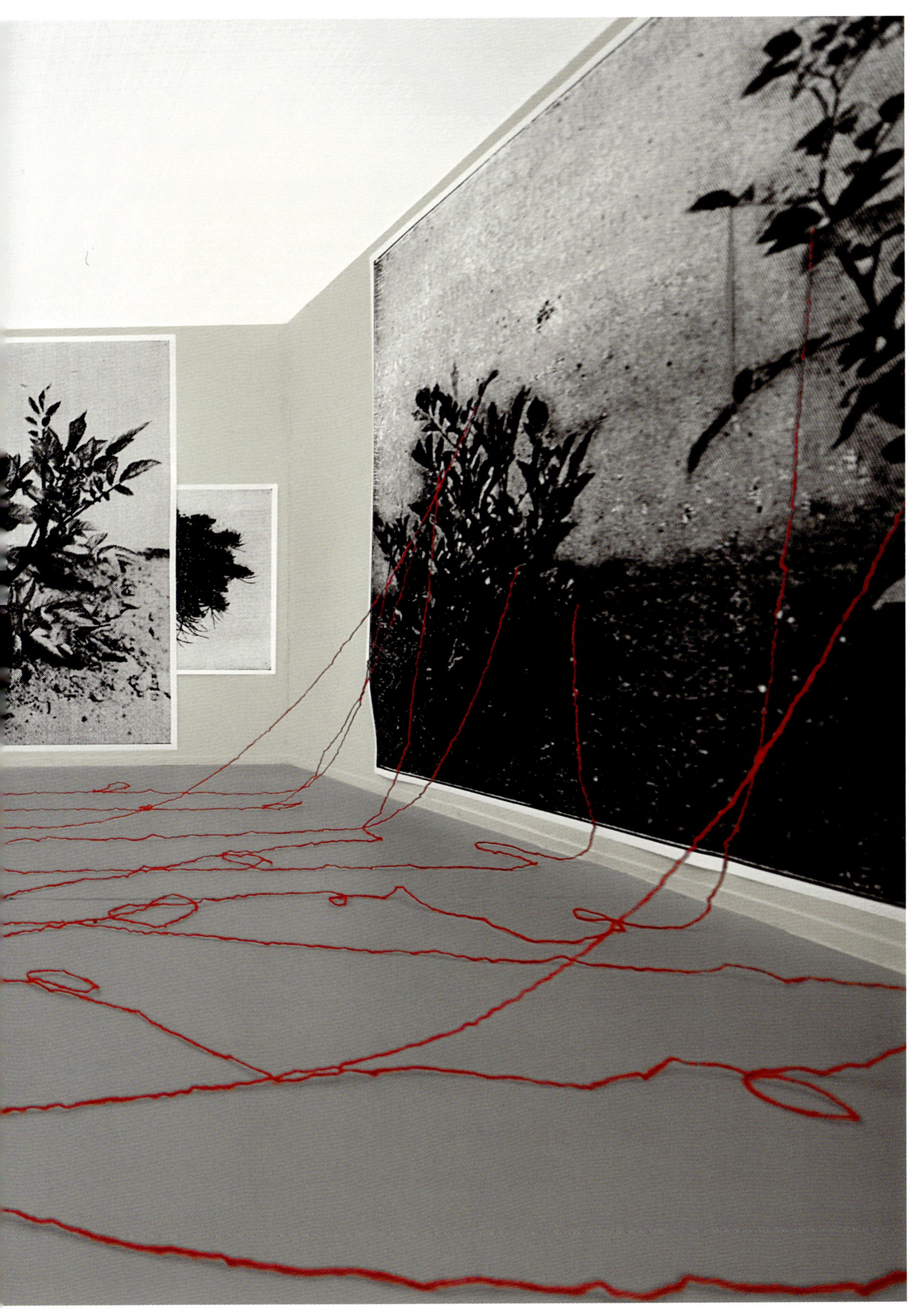

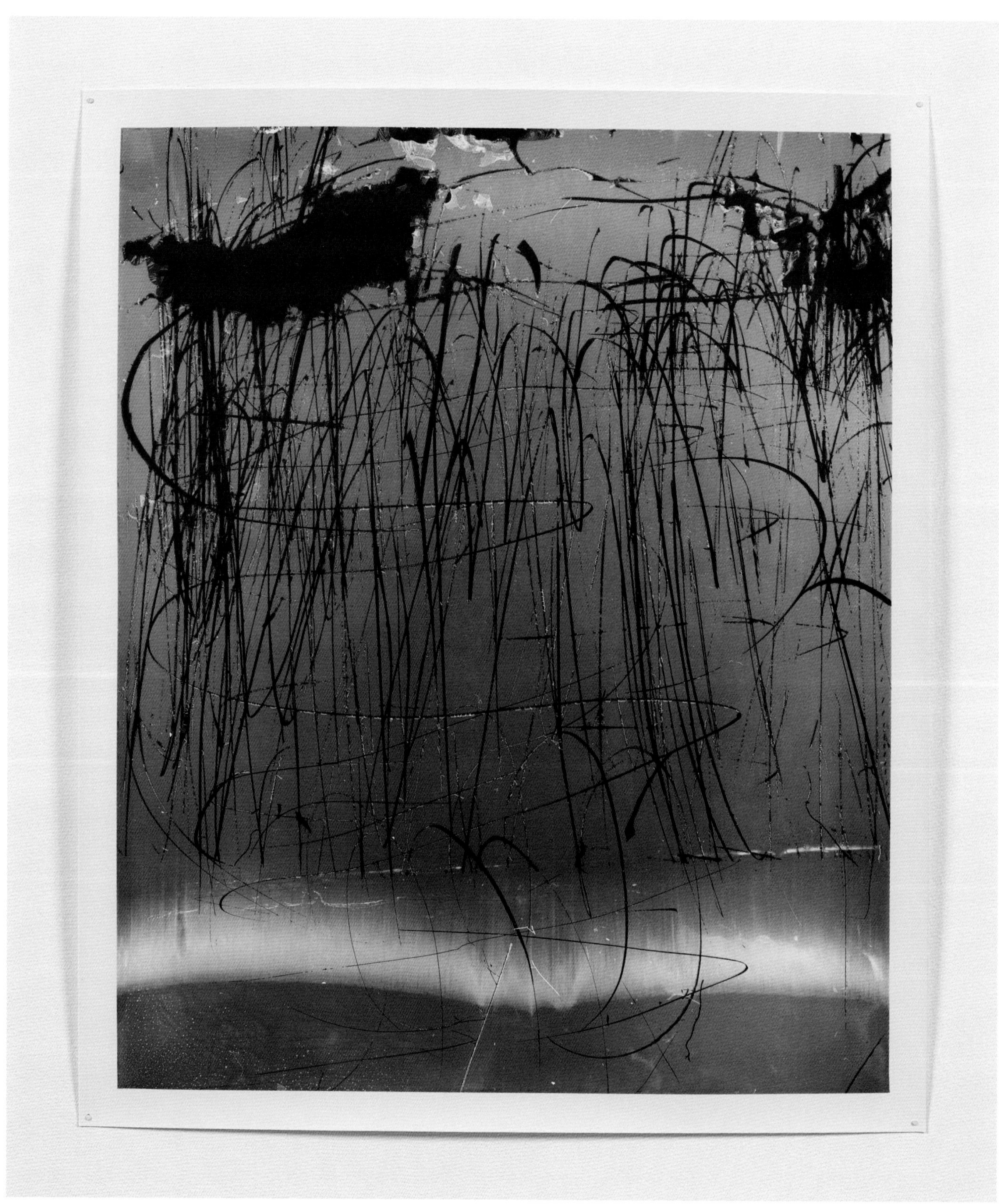

194    Eileen Quinlan, *A Record*, 2013. Gelatin-silver print

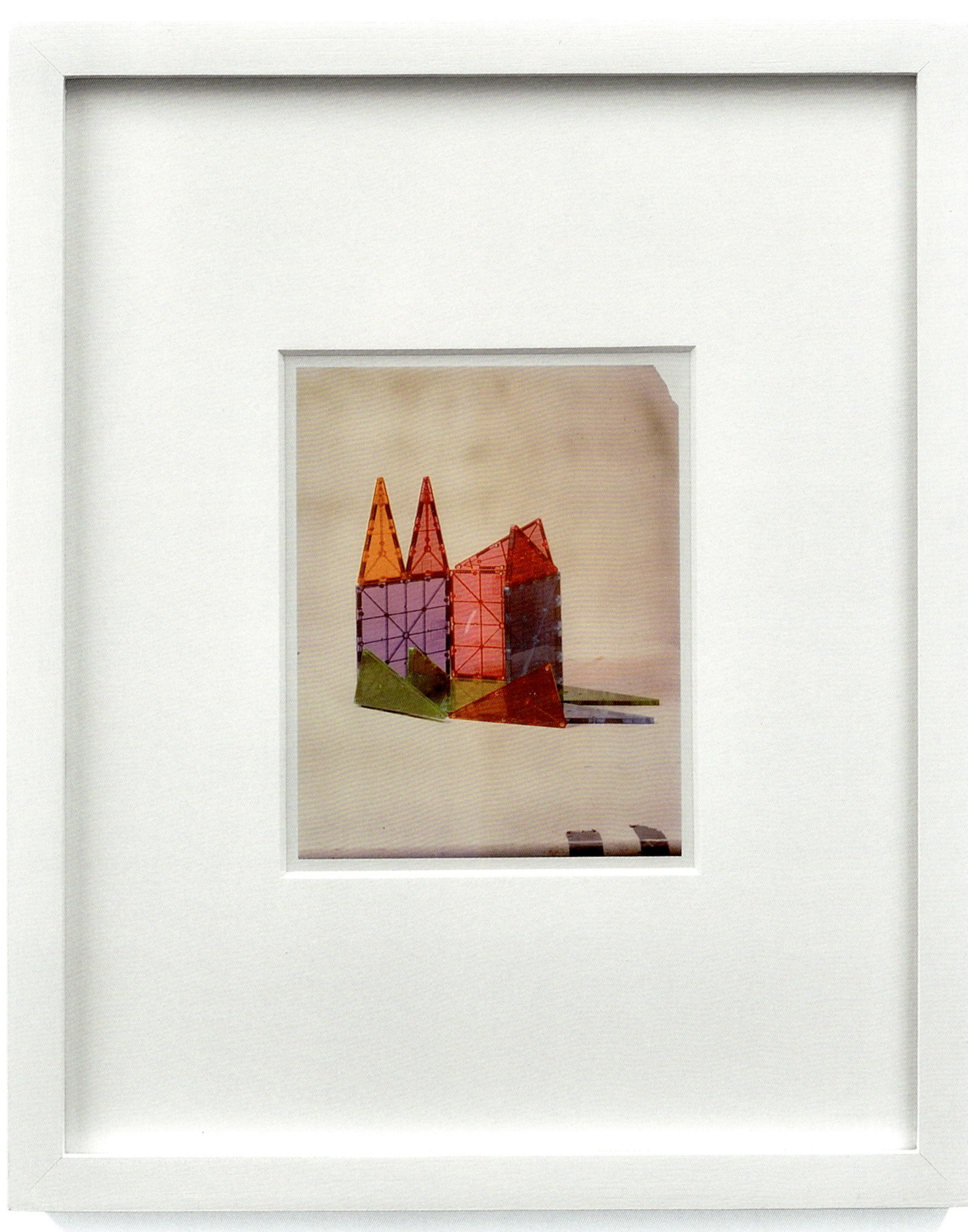

195   Eileen Quinlan, *Fine Motor Skills*, 2014. Polaroid

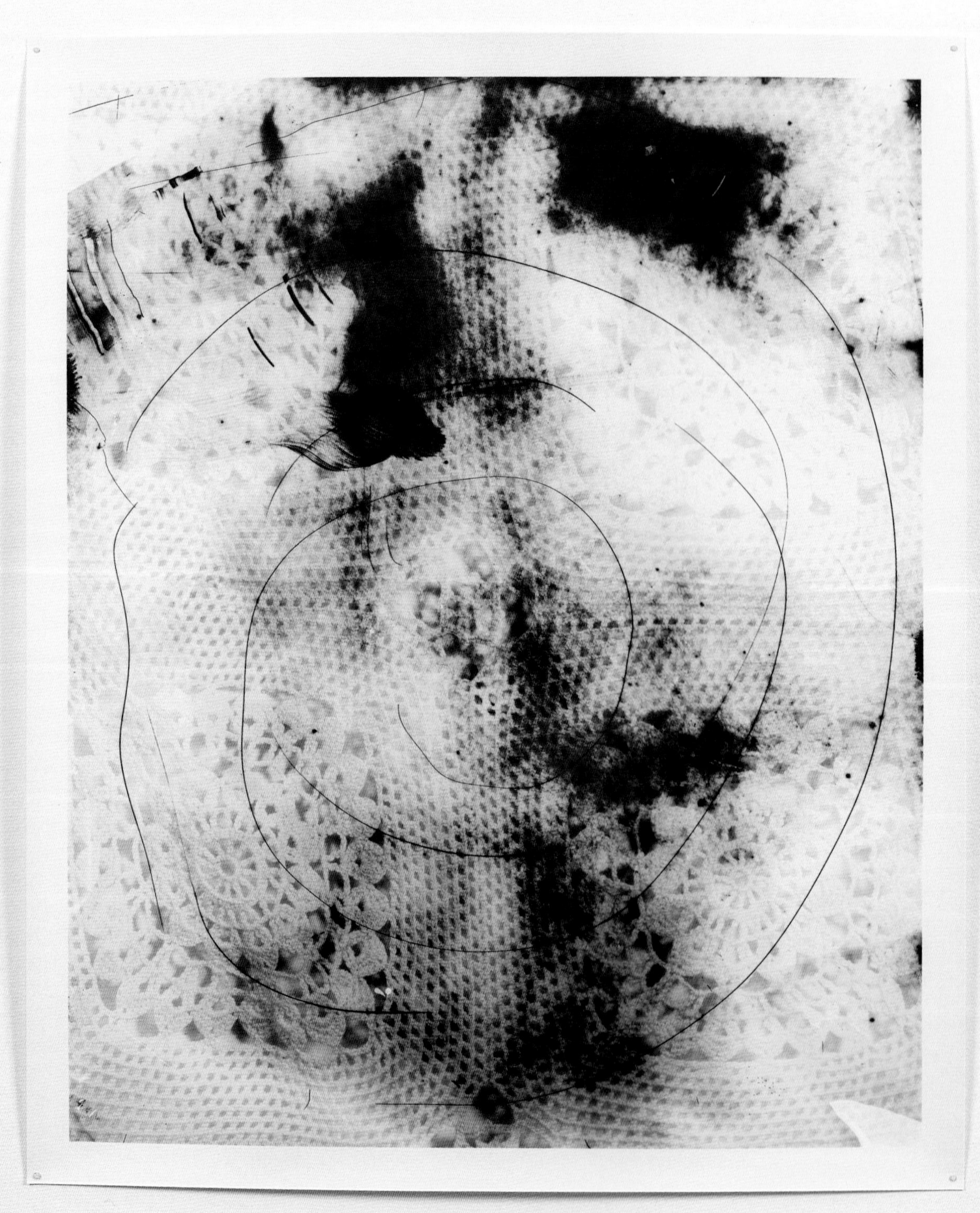

196    Eileen Quinlan, *The Voidist*, 2013. Gelatin-silver print

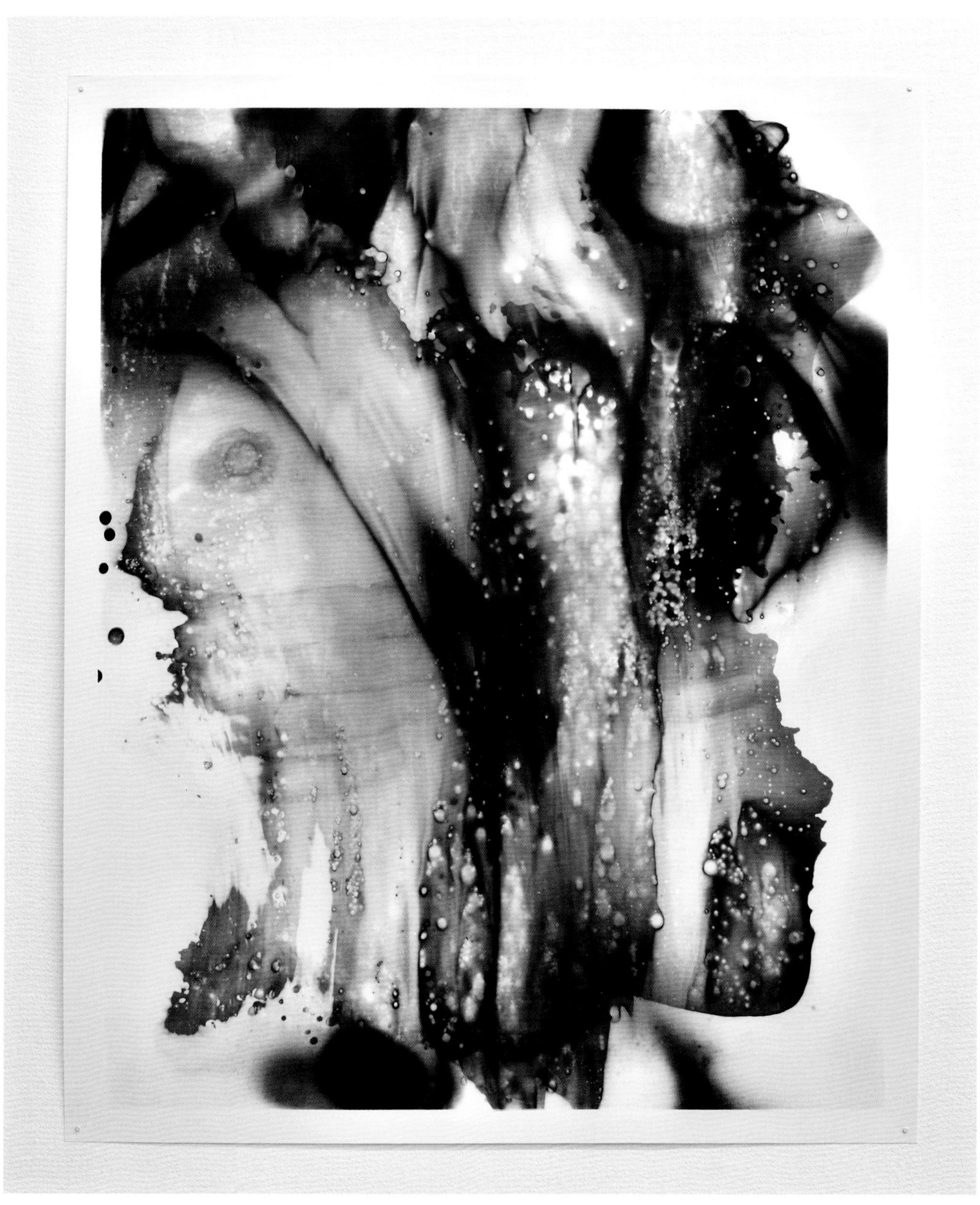

197    Eileen Quinlan, *No One Sleeps*, 2014. Gelatin-silver print

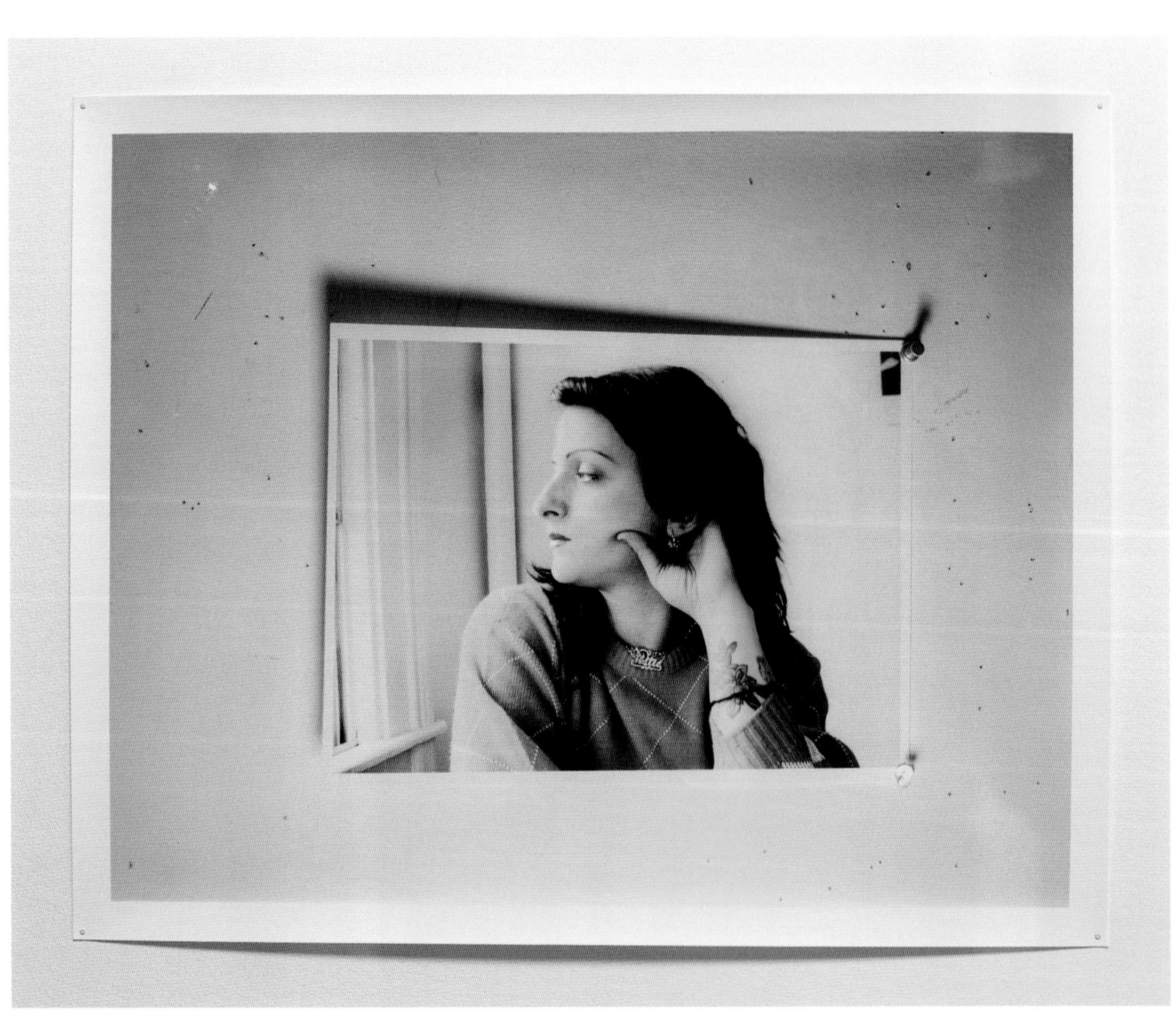

198    Eileen Quinlan, *Lady*, 2013. Gelatin-silver print

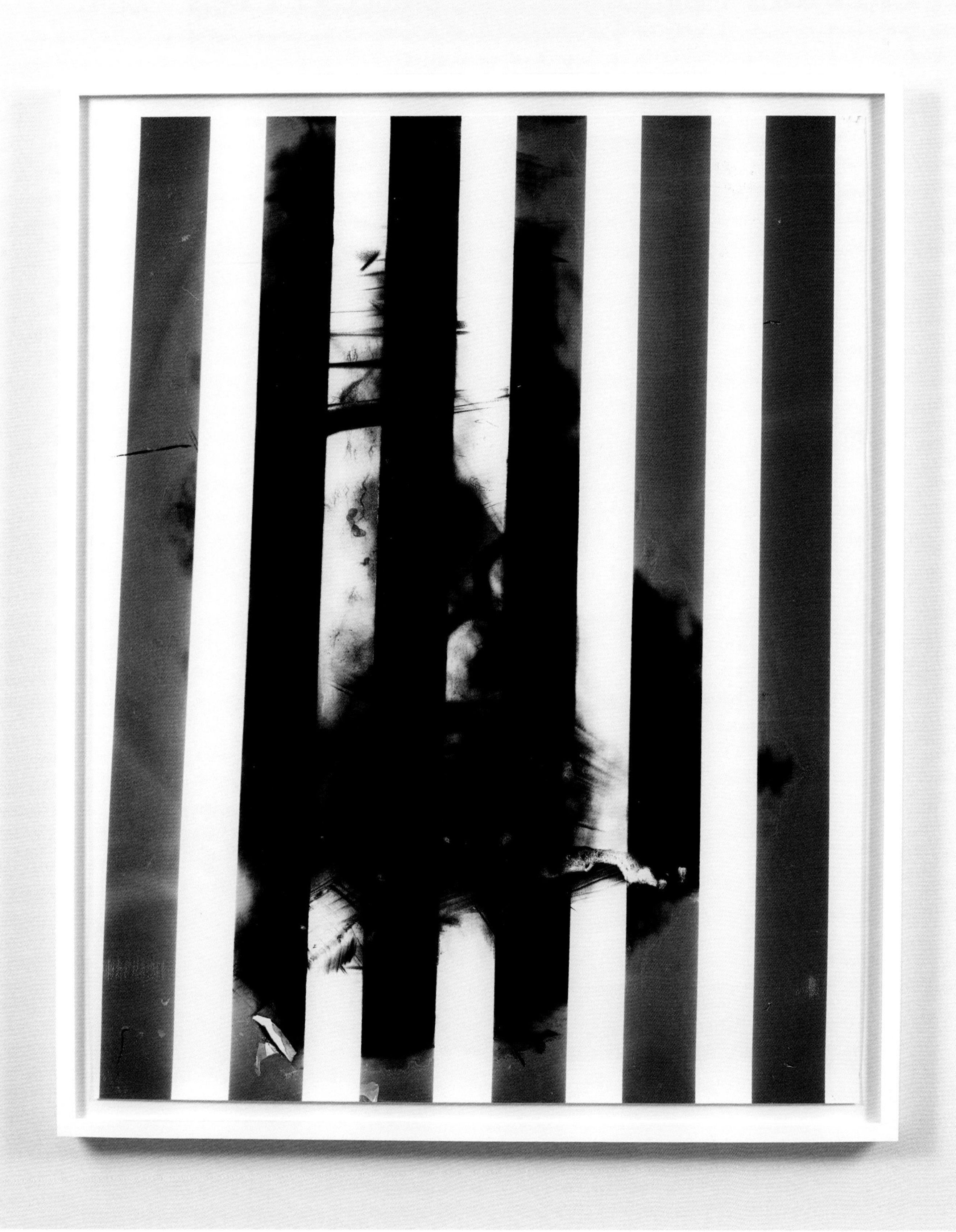

199    Eileen Quinlan, *The Nothing*, 2013. Gelatin-silver print

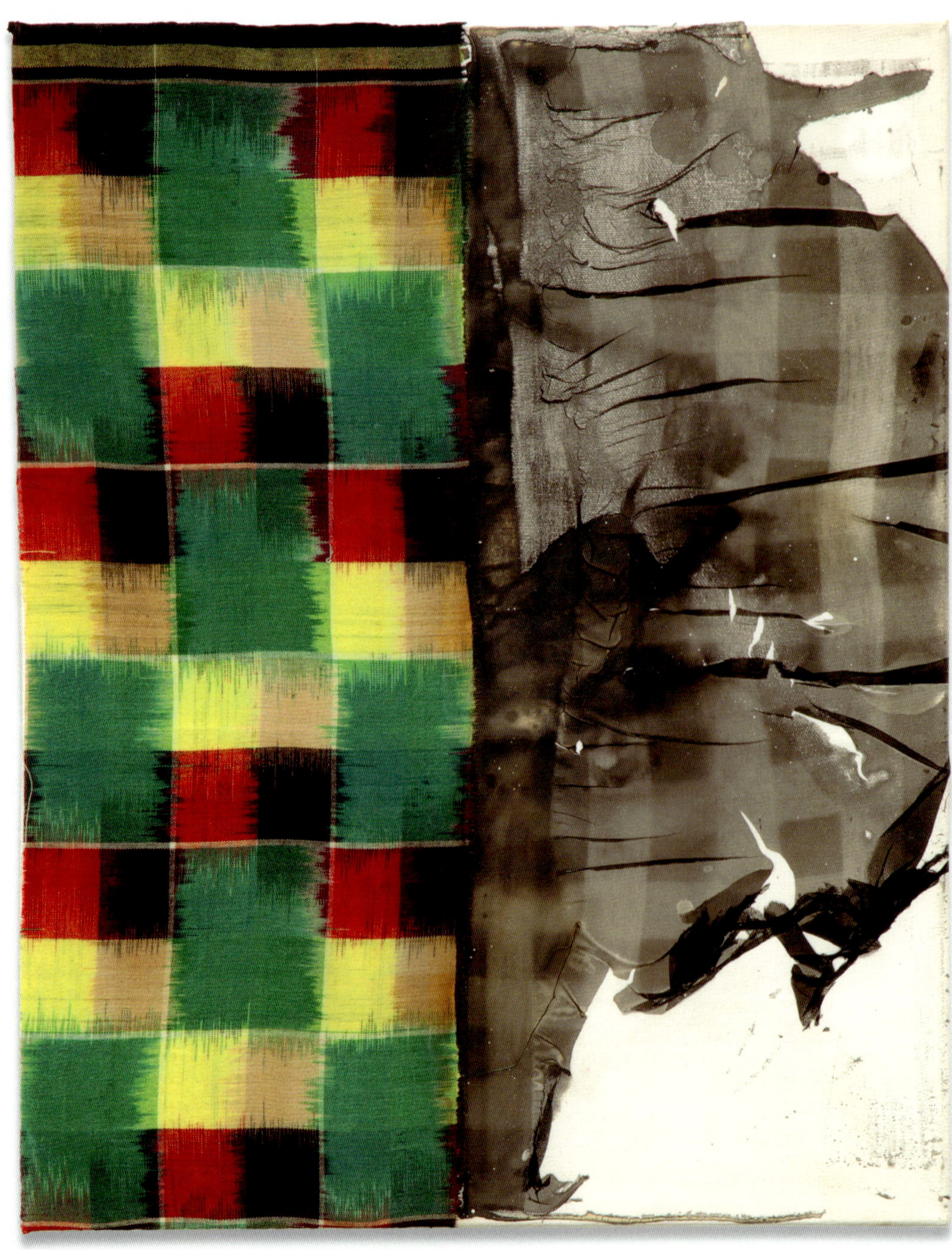

    Lucas Knipscher, *Untitled*, 2013. Ikat fabric and photographic emulsion on canvas

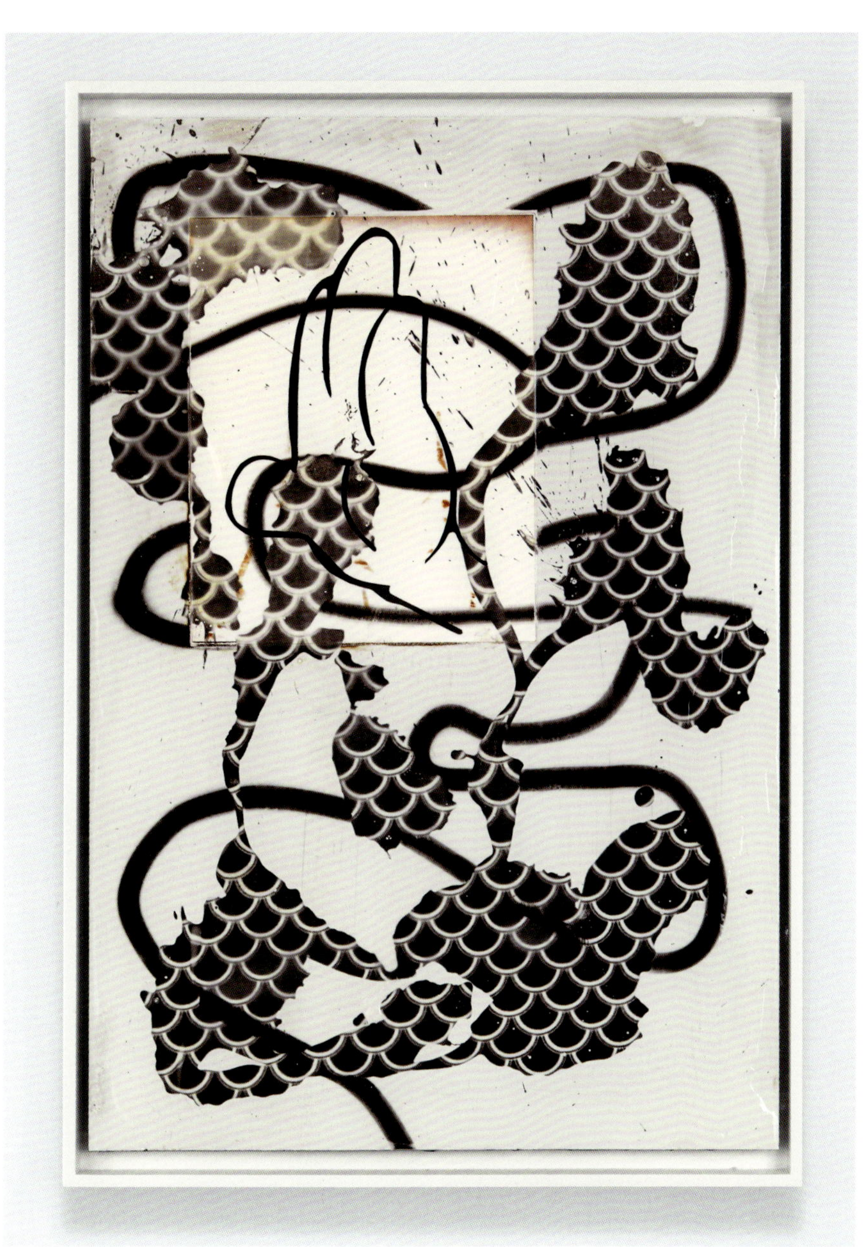

201    Lucas Knipscher, *Spirits Lend Strength*, 2014. Ikat fabric and photographic emulsion on canvas

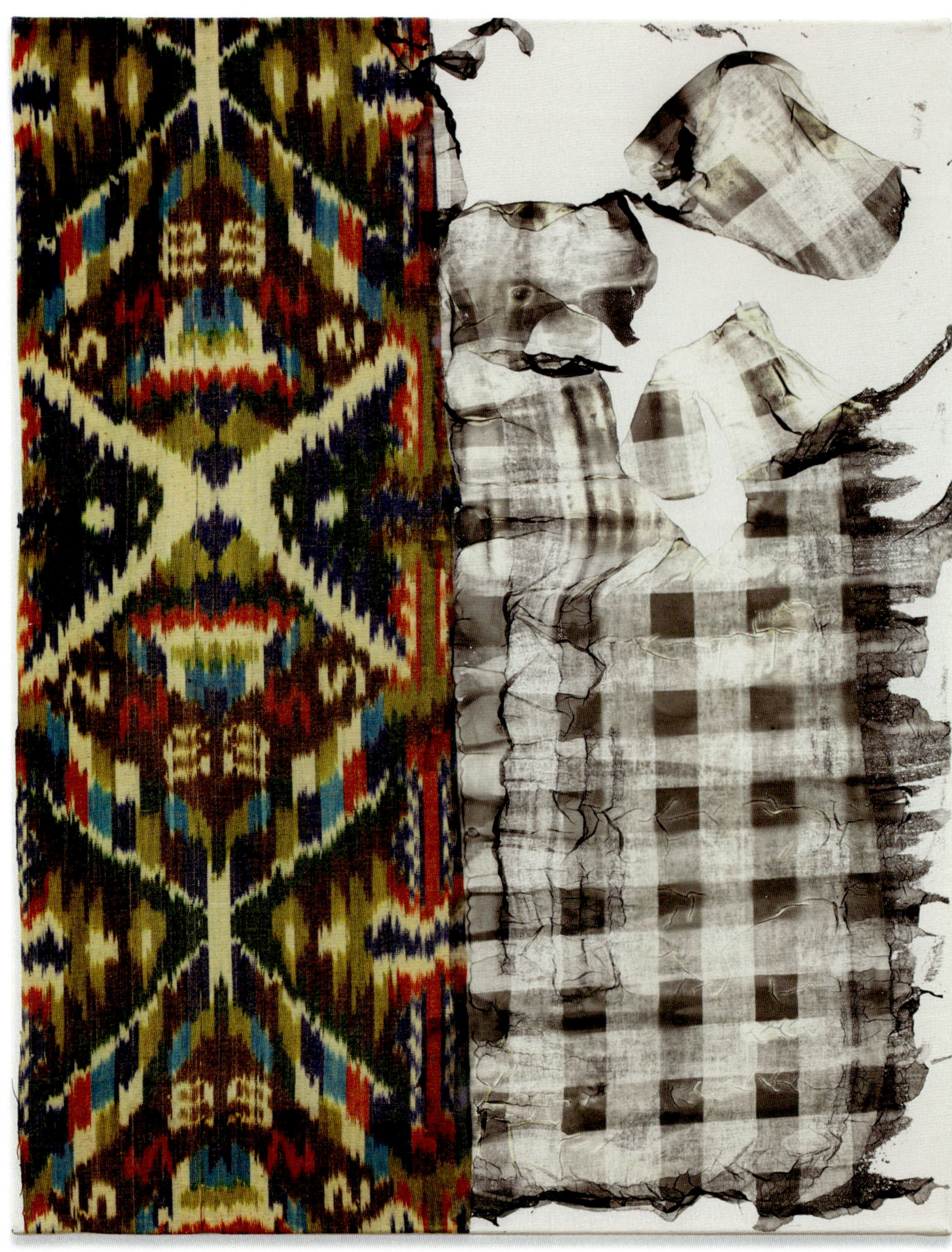

202    Lucas Knipscher, *Untitled*, 2013. Ikat fabric and photographic emulsion on canvas

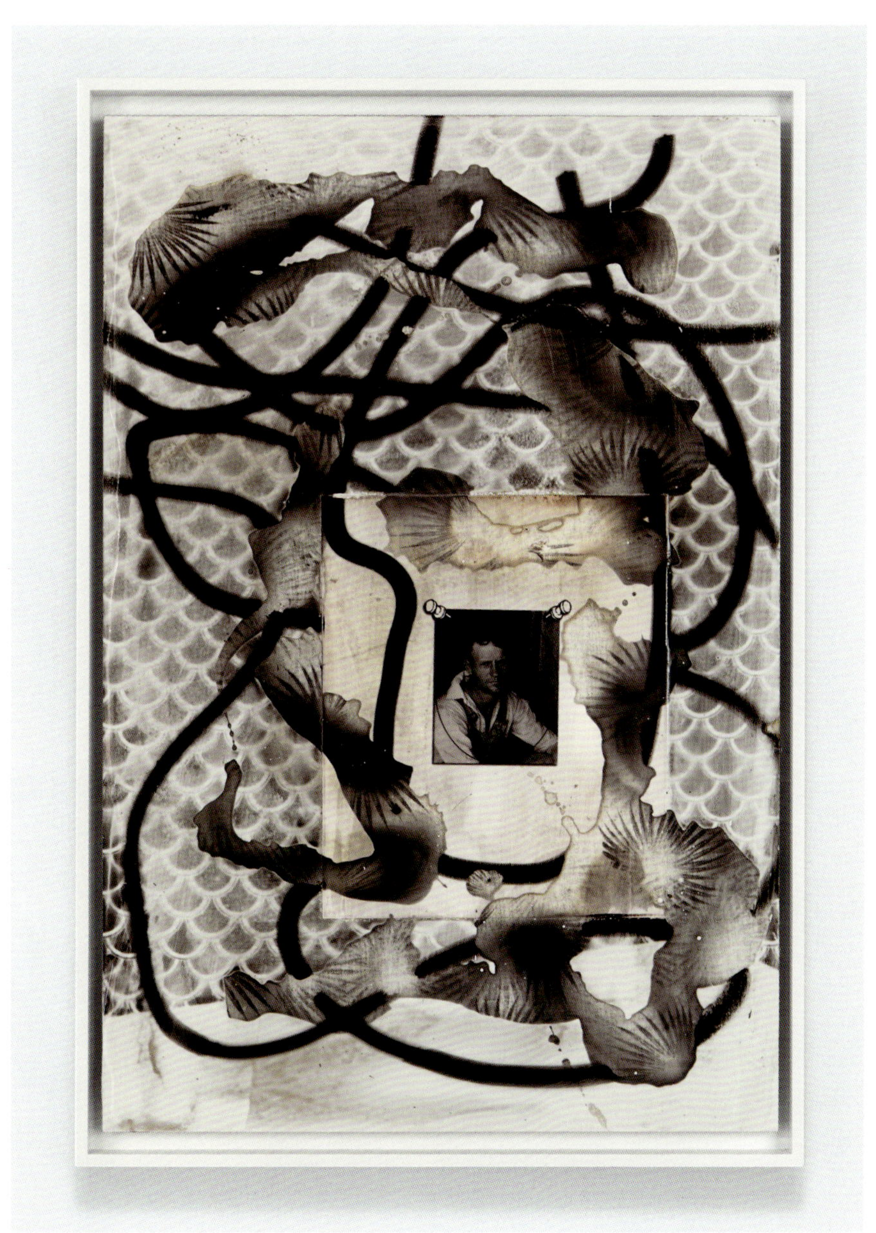

203    Lucas Knipscher, *Spirits Lend Strength*, 2014. Ikat fabric and photographic emulsion on canvas

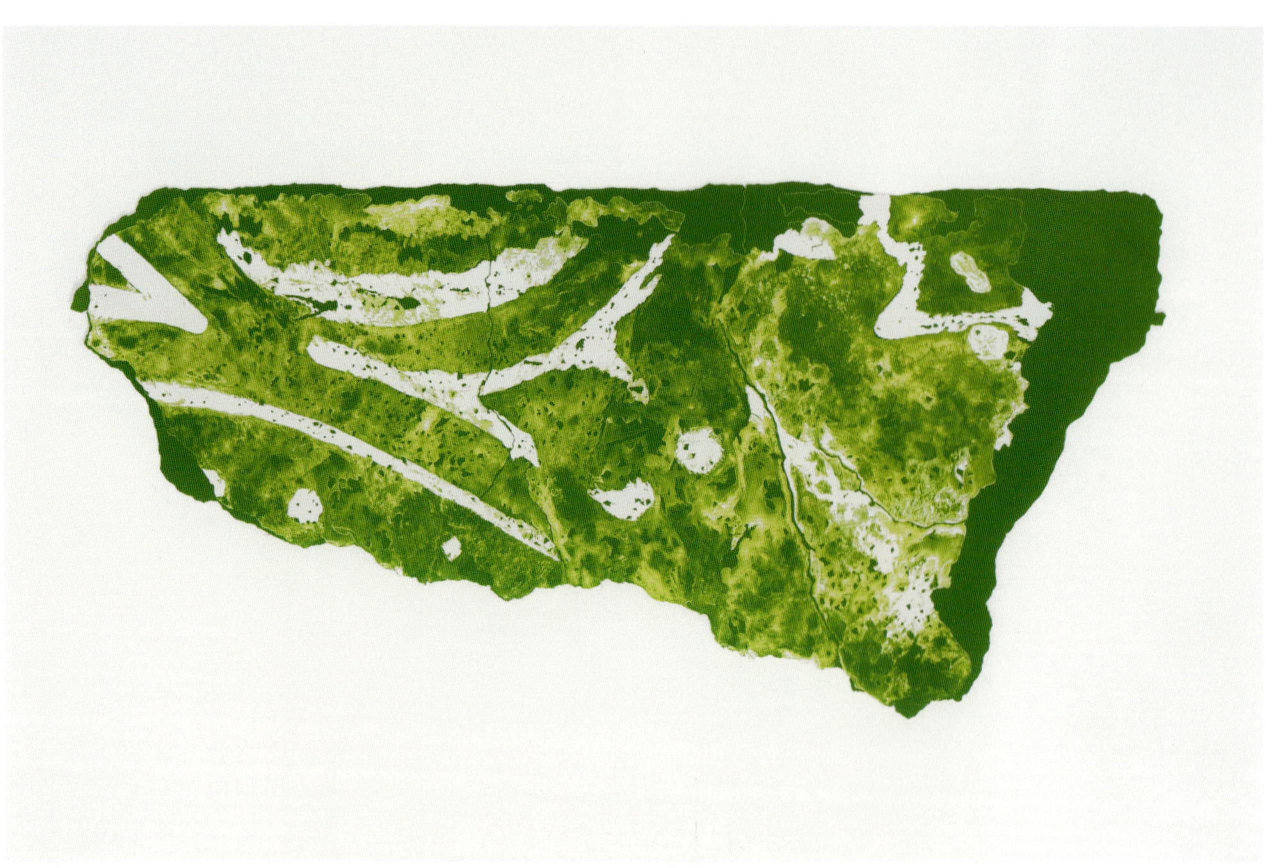

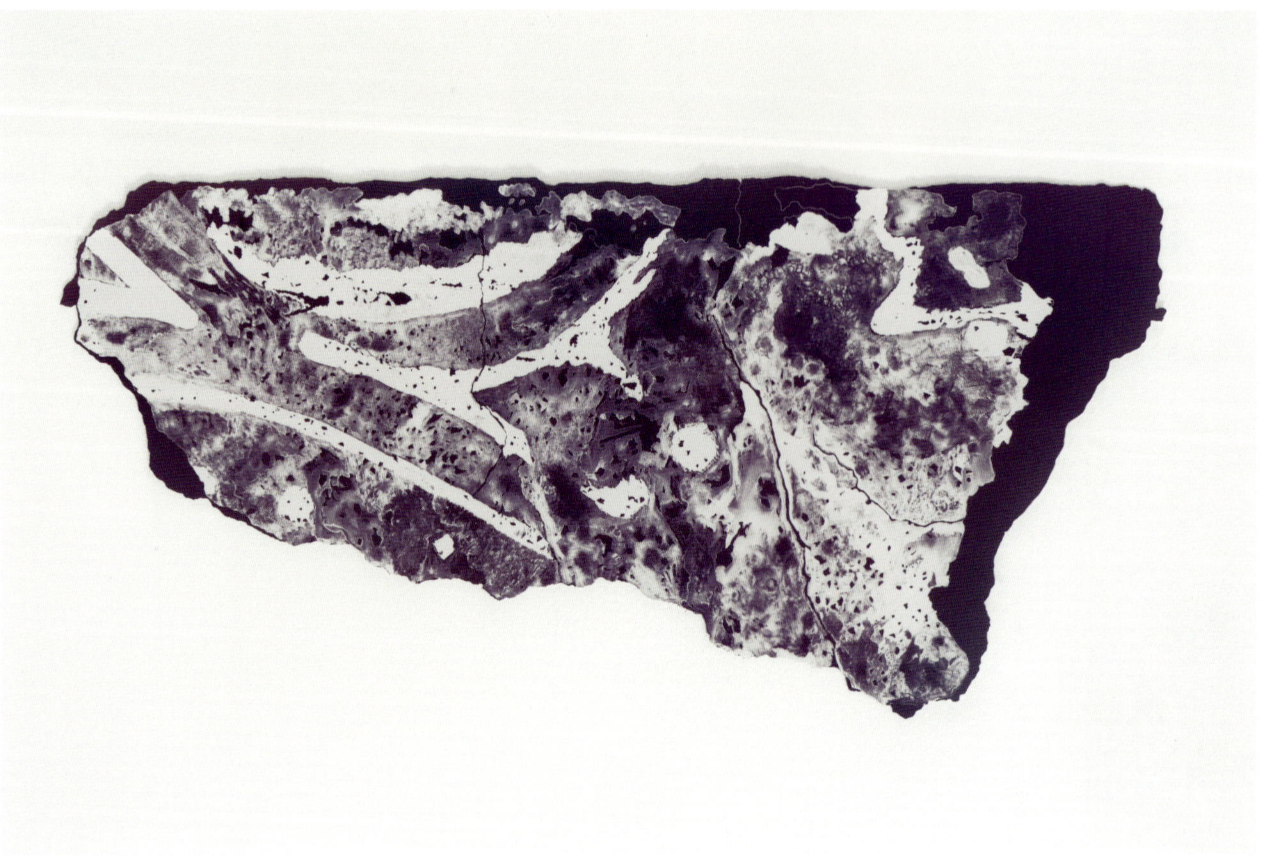

204    Farrah Karapetian, top: *Souvenir (Light Green)*, 2009. Chromogenic photogram from constructed negative, silhouetted
bottom: *Souvenir (Lavender)*, 2009. Chromogenic photogram from constructed negative, silhouetted

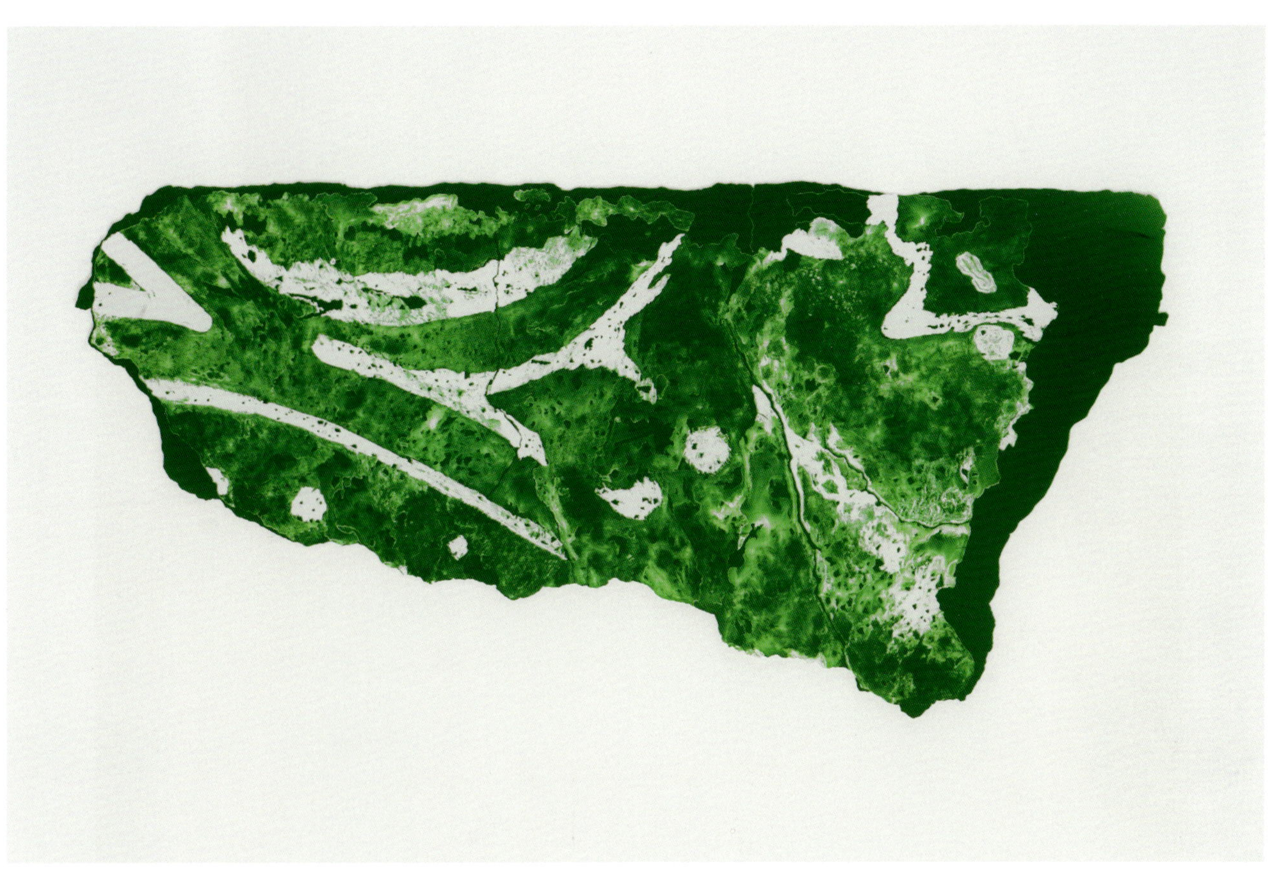

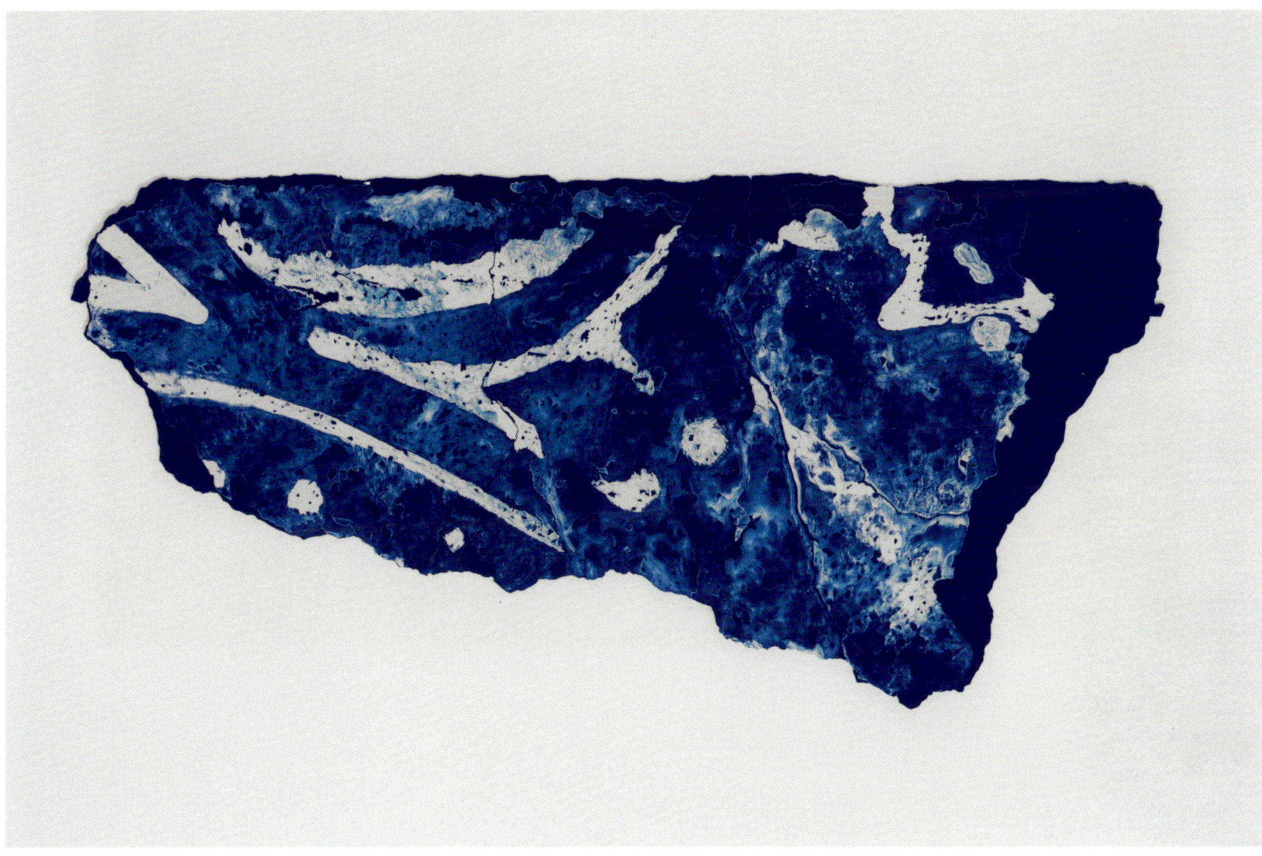

205    Farrah Karapetian, top: *Souvenir (Kelly Green)*, 2009. Chromogenic photogram from constructed negative, silhouetted
bottom: *Souvenir (Blue)*, 2009. Chromogenic photogram from constructed negative, silhouetted

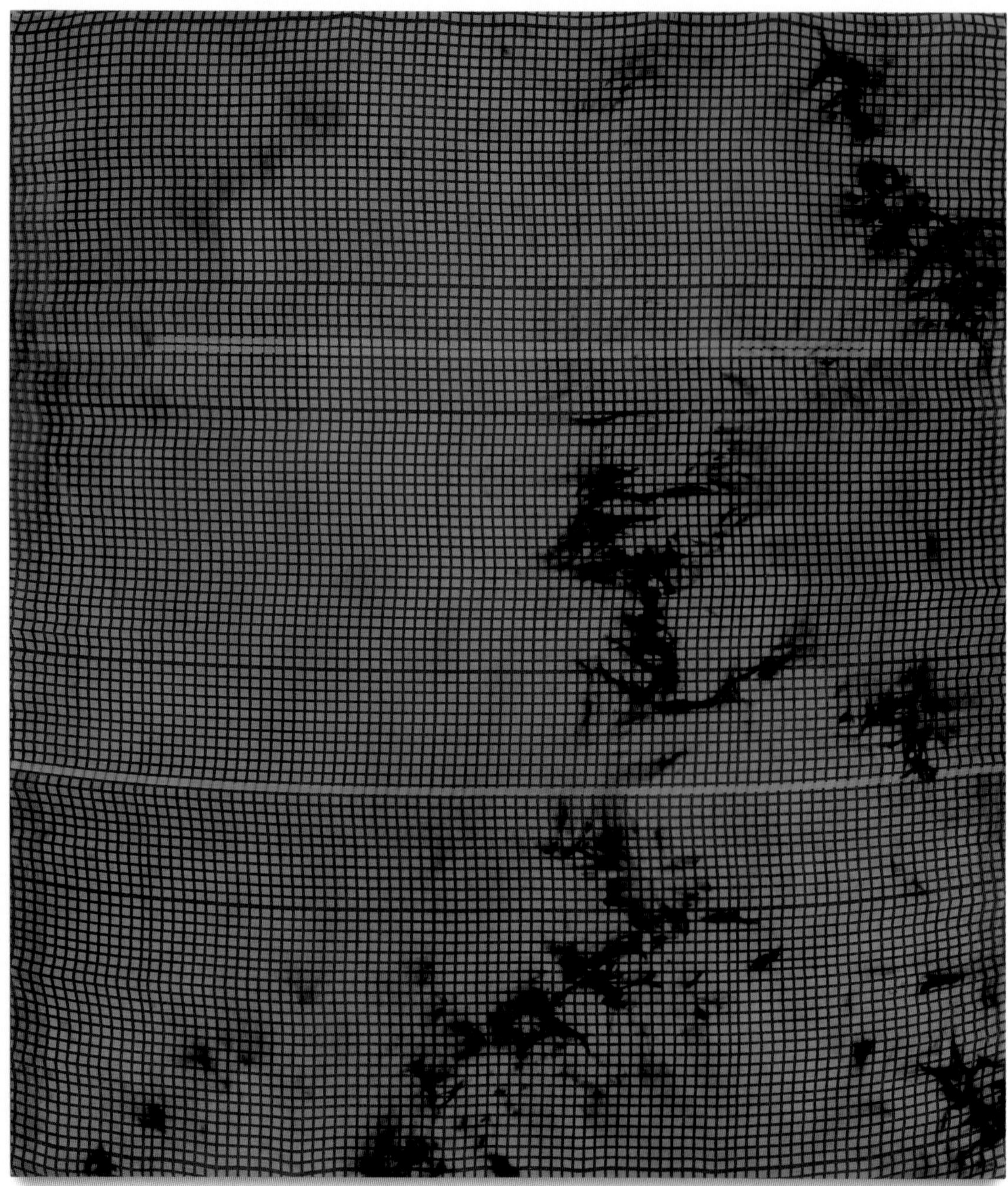

    Hugh Scott-Douglas, *Untitled*, 2013. Cyanotype

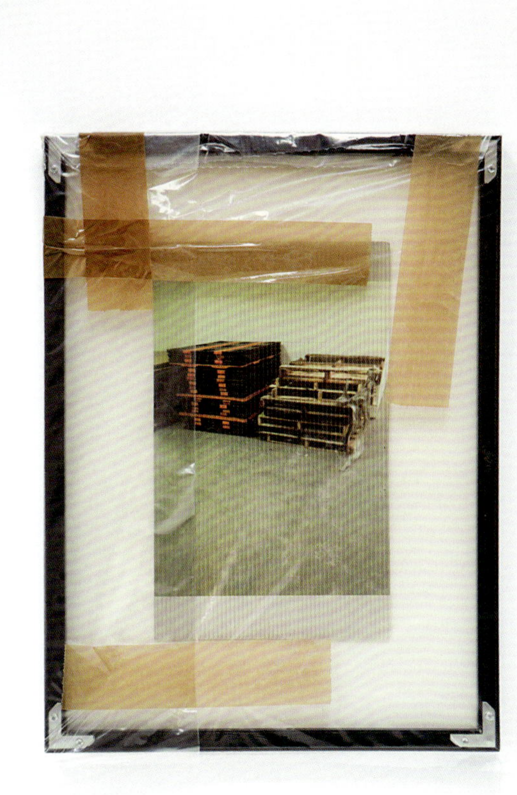

207     Hugh Scott-Douglas, *Untitled*, 2014. UV-curable ink on styrene in frame, wrapped in polyester with tape

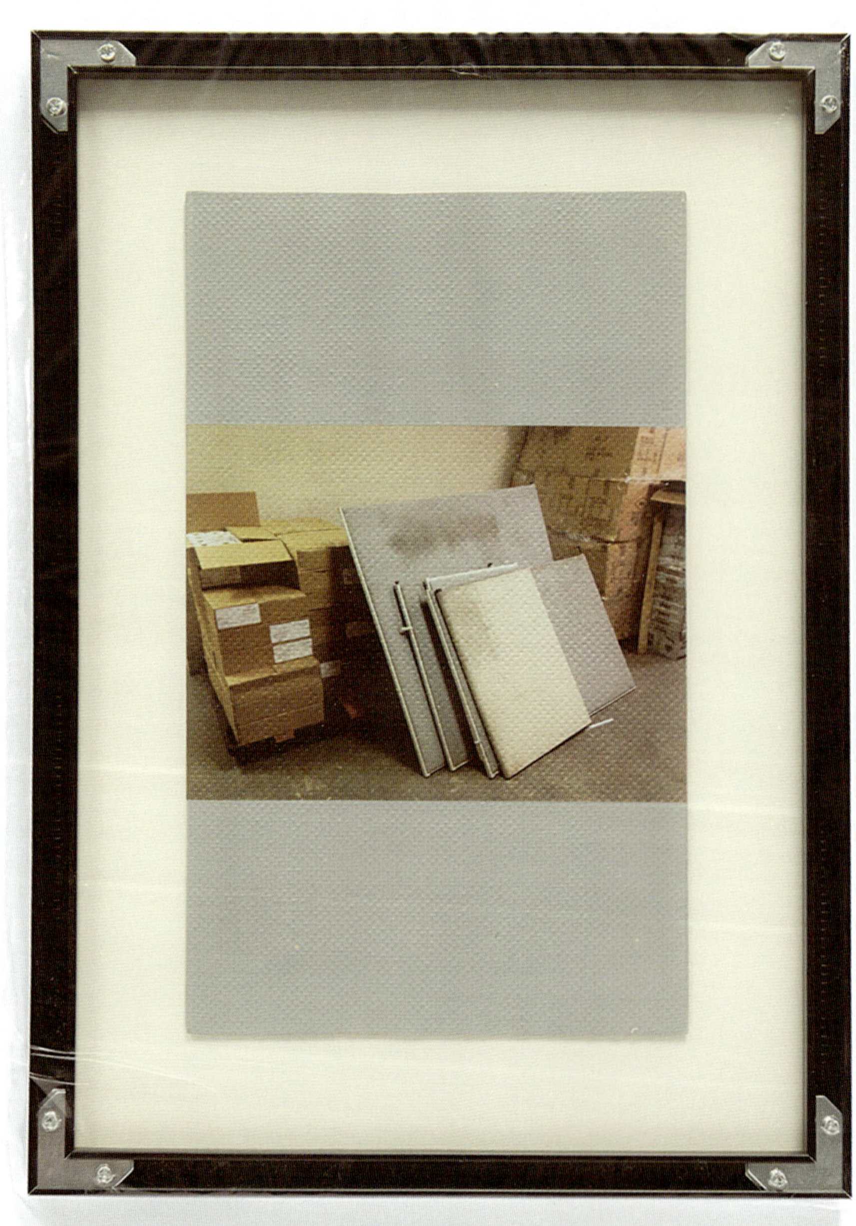

208    Hugh Scott-Douglas, *Untitled*, 2014. UV-curable ink on styrene in frame, wrapped in polyester with tape

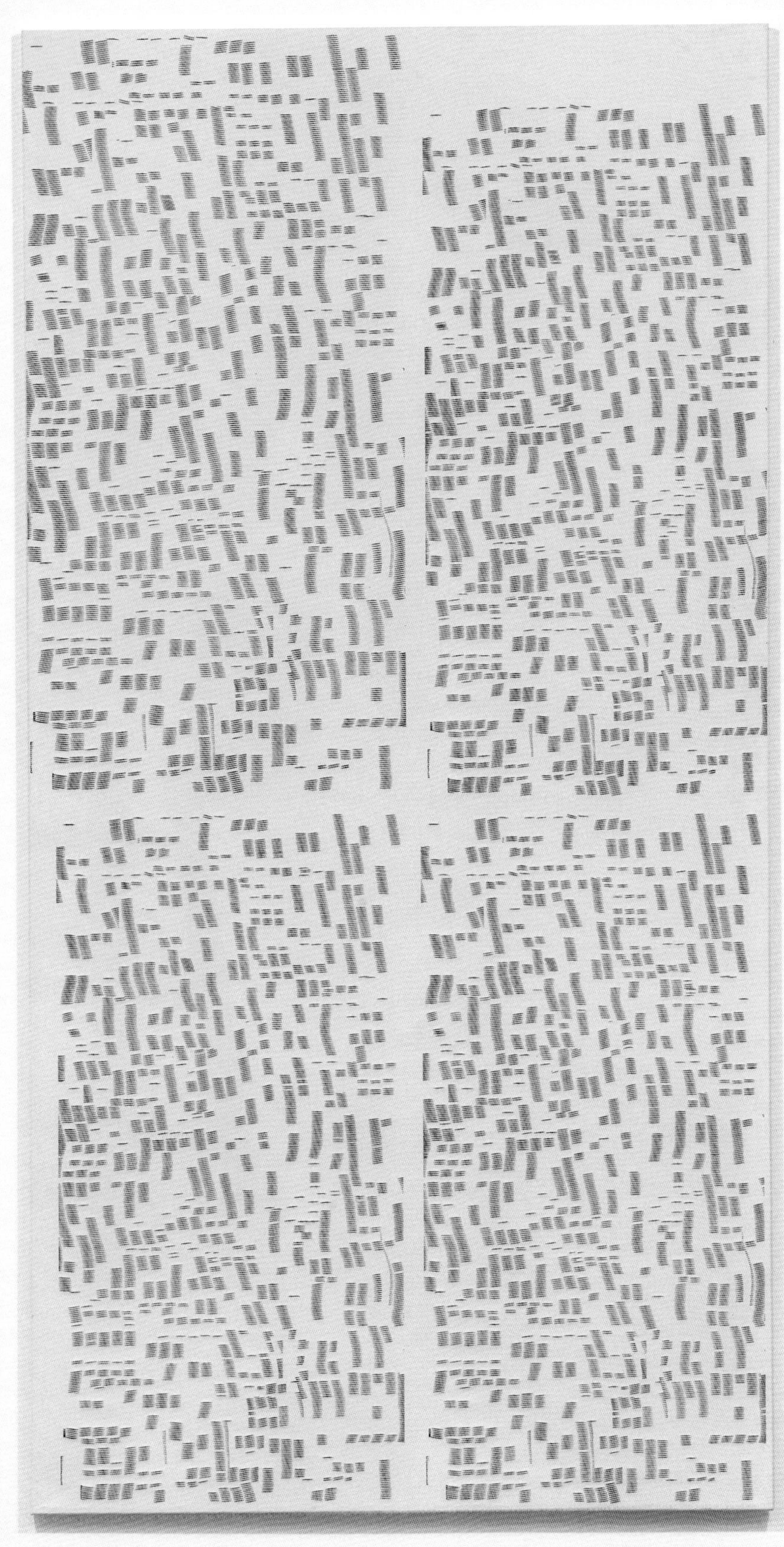

209     Hugh Scott-Douglas, *Untitled*, 2014. Laser cut on gessoed linen

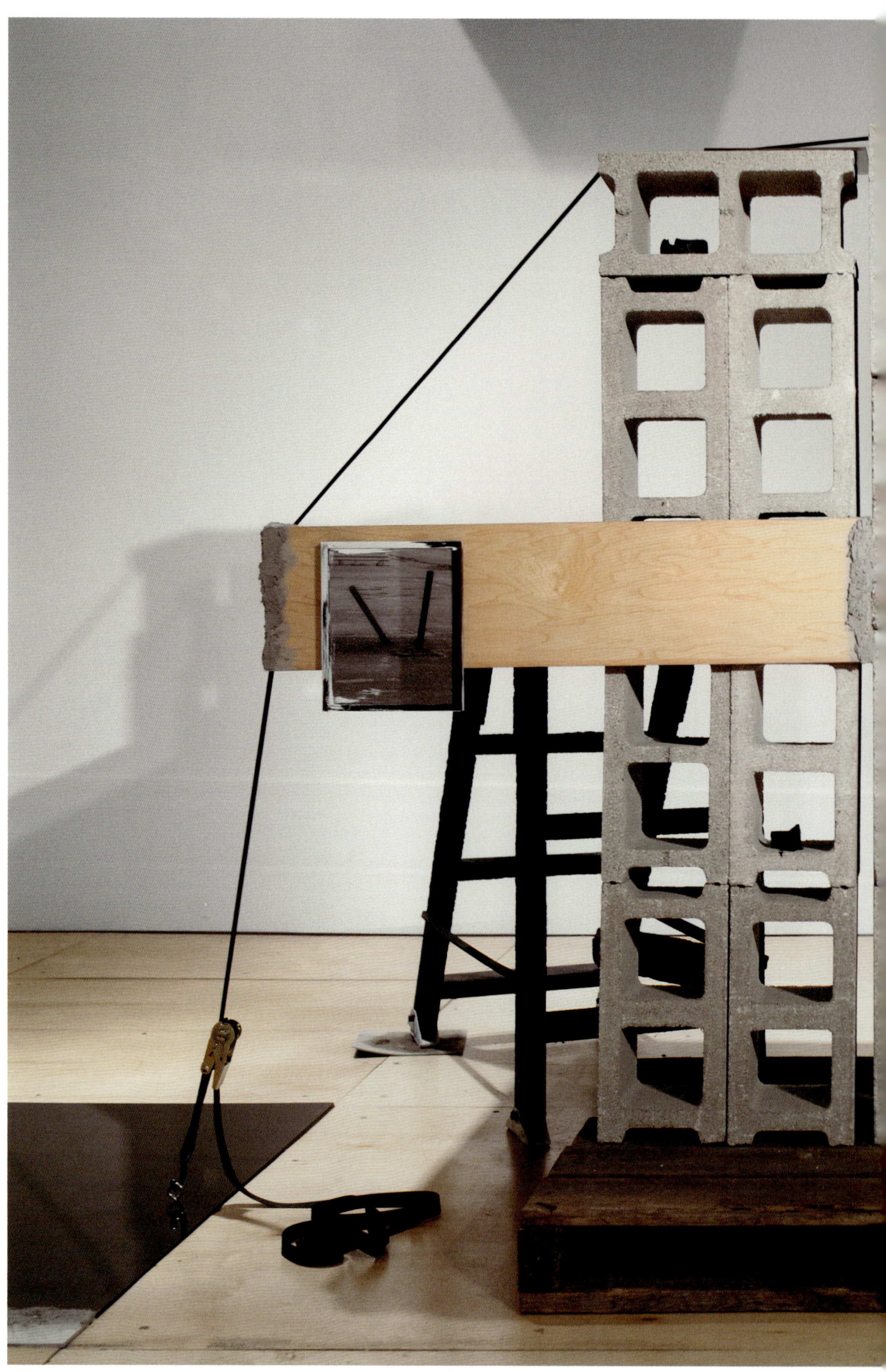

    Daniel Shea, *Blue Island, IL IV*, 2013. Found and fabricated mixed media

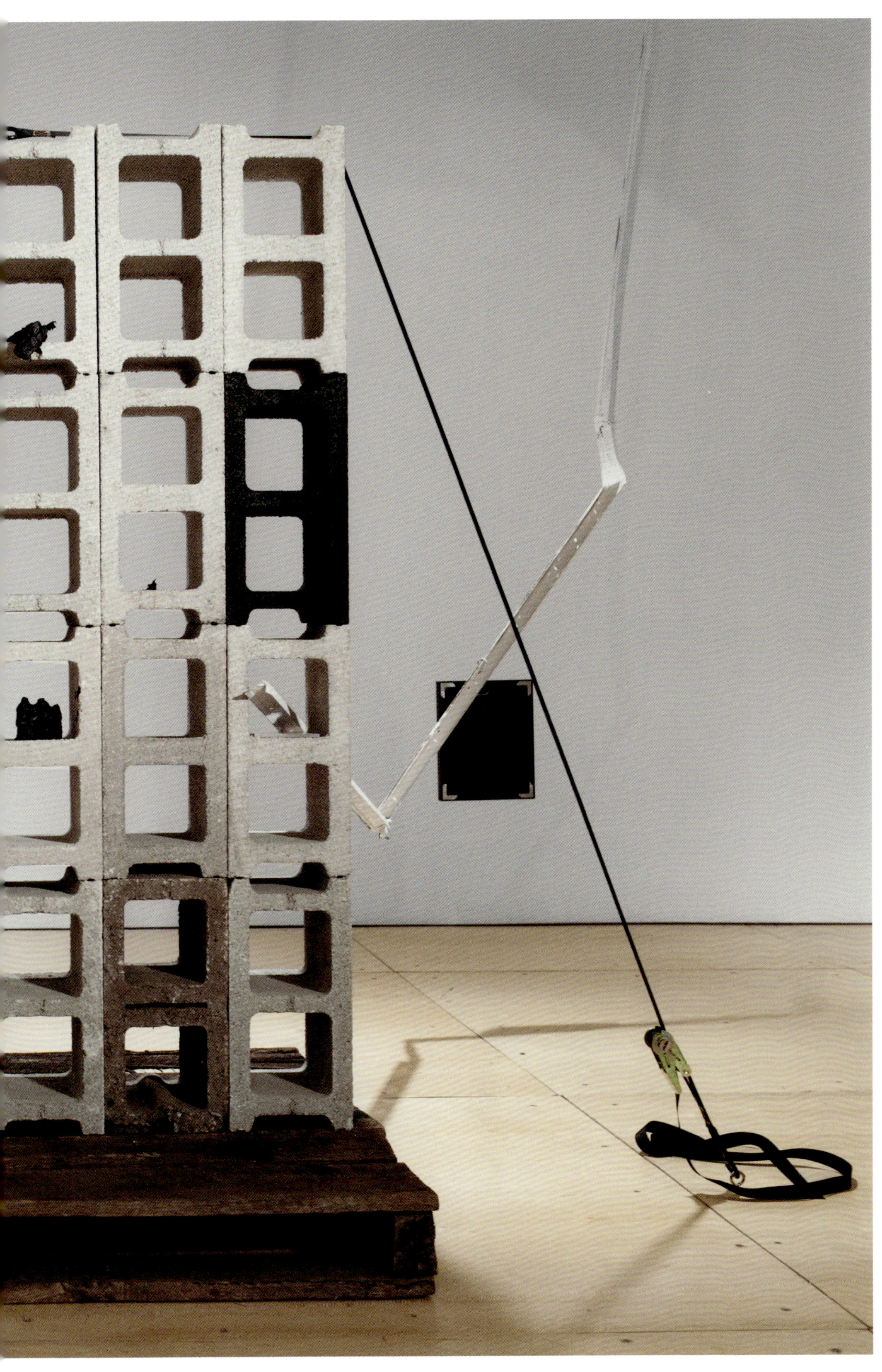

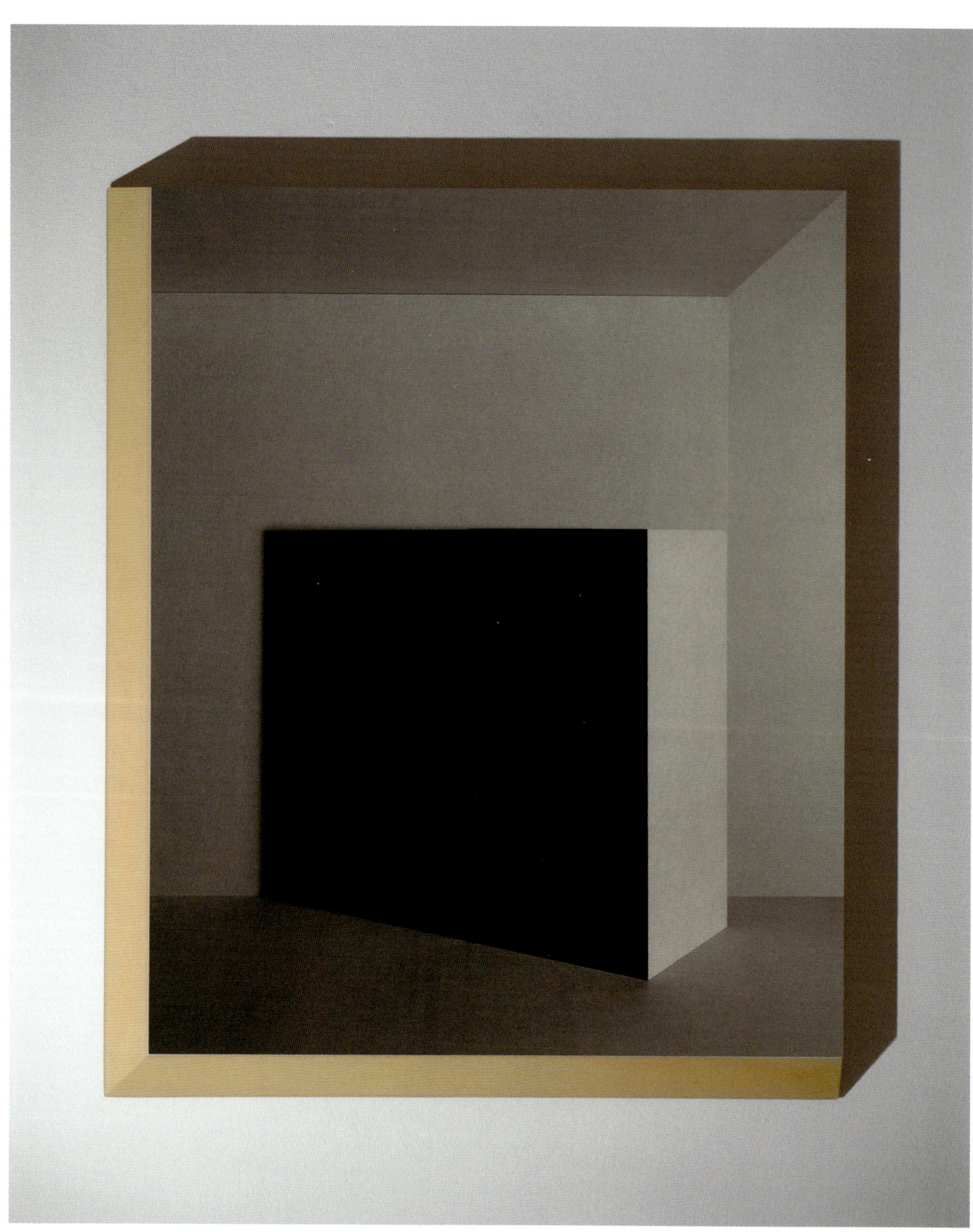

212    Darren Harvey-Regan, *When Is an Image Not an Image?*, 2013. Fiber-based handprint on medium-density fiberboard

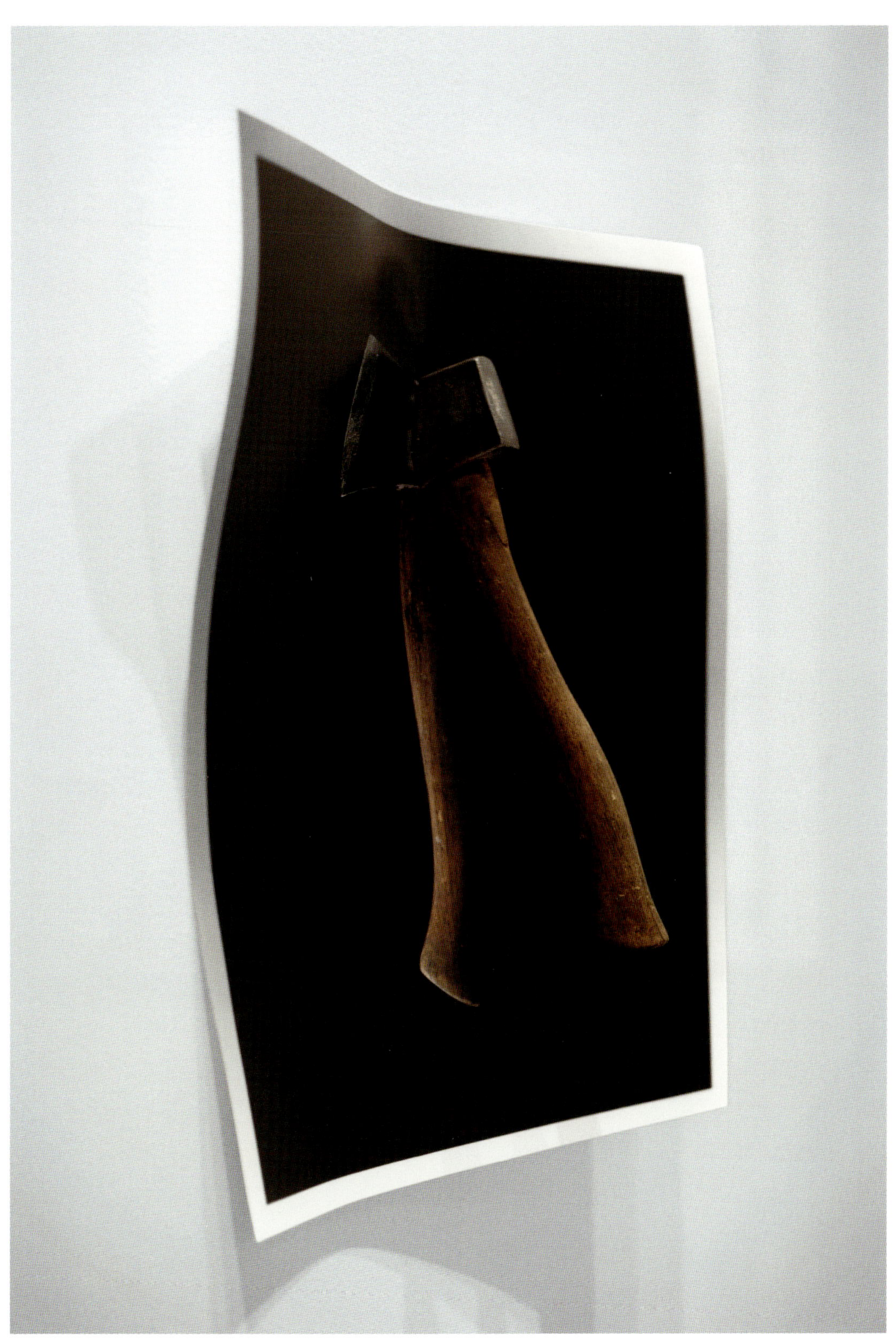

213    Darren Harvey-Regan, *The Halt*, 2011. C-print with axe

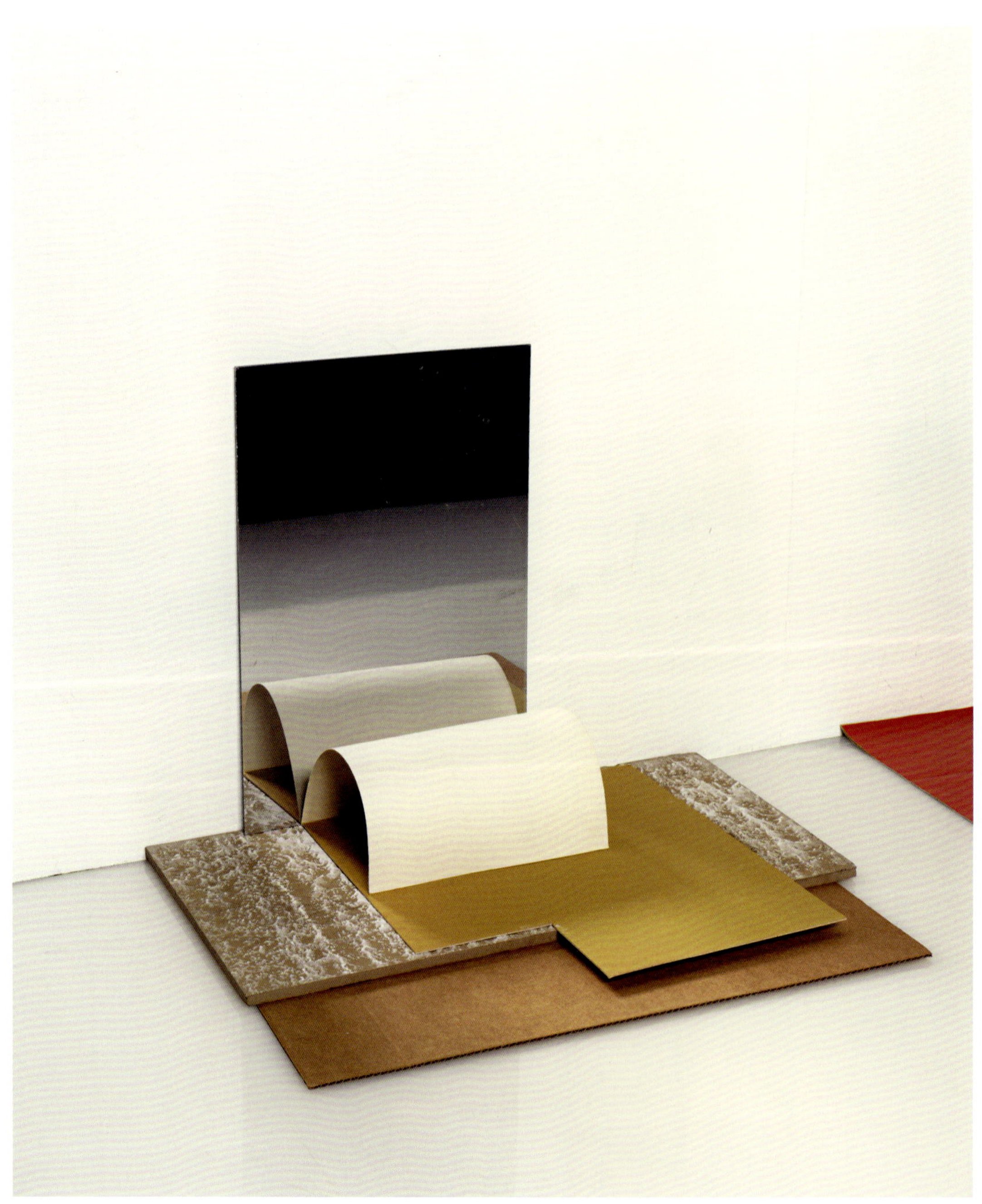

214    Phil Maisel, *Stack V (6629)*, 2014. Archival pigment print

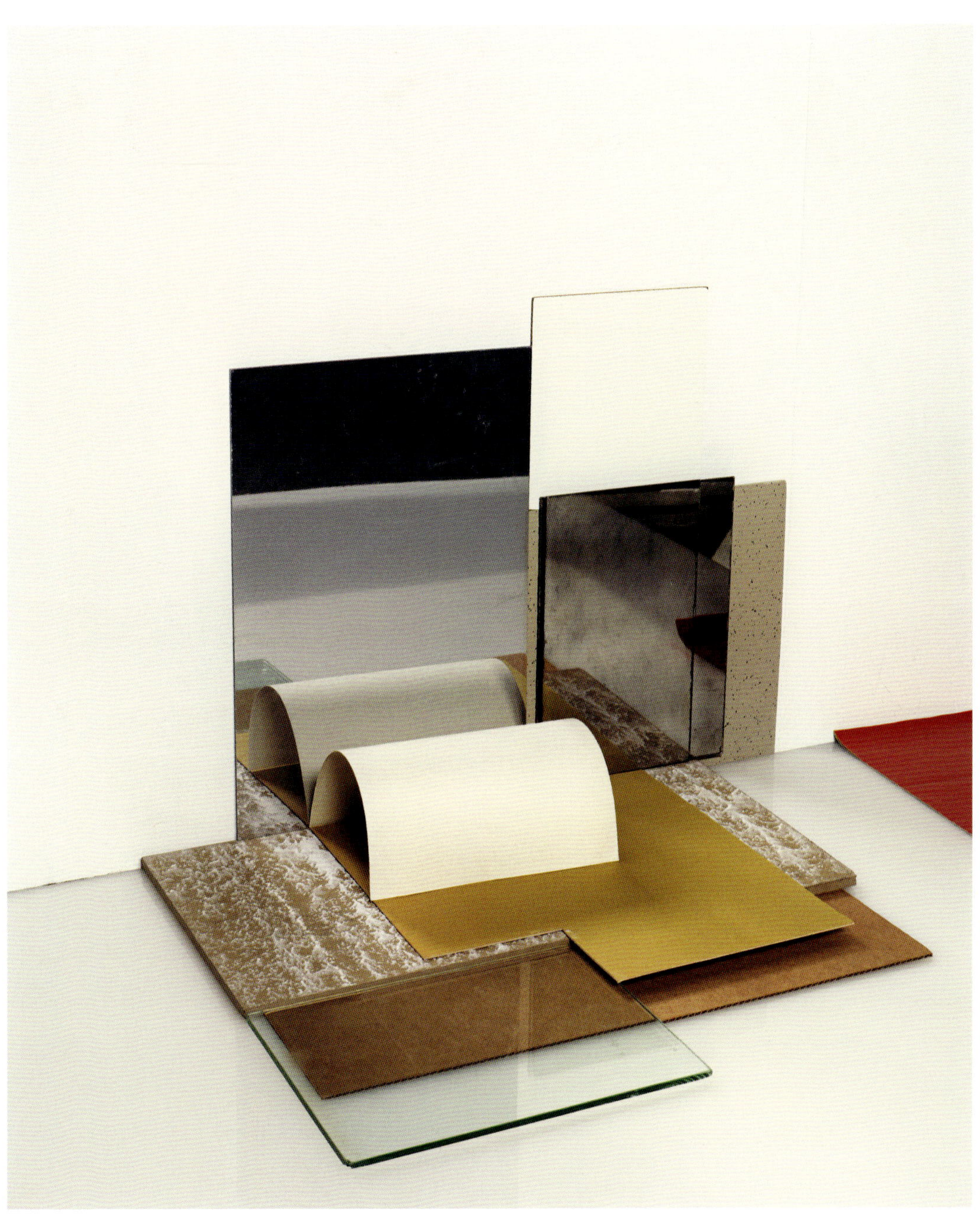

215  Phil Maisel, *Stack V (6636)*, 2014. Archival pigment print

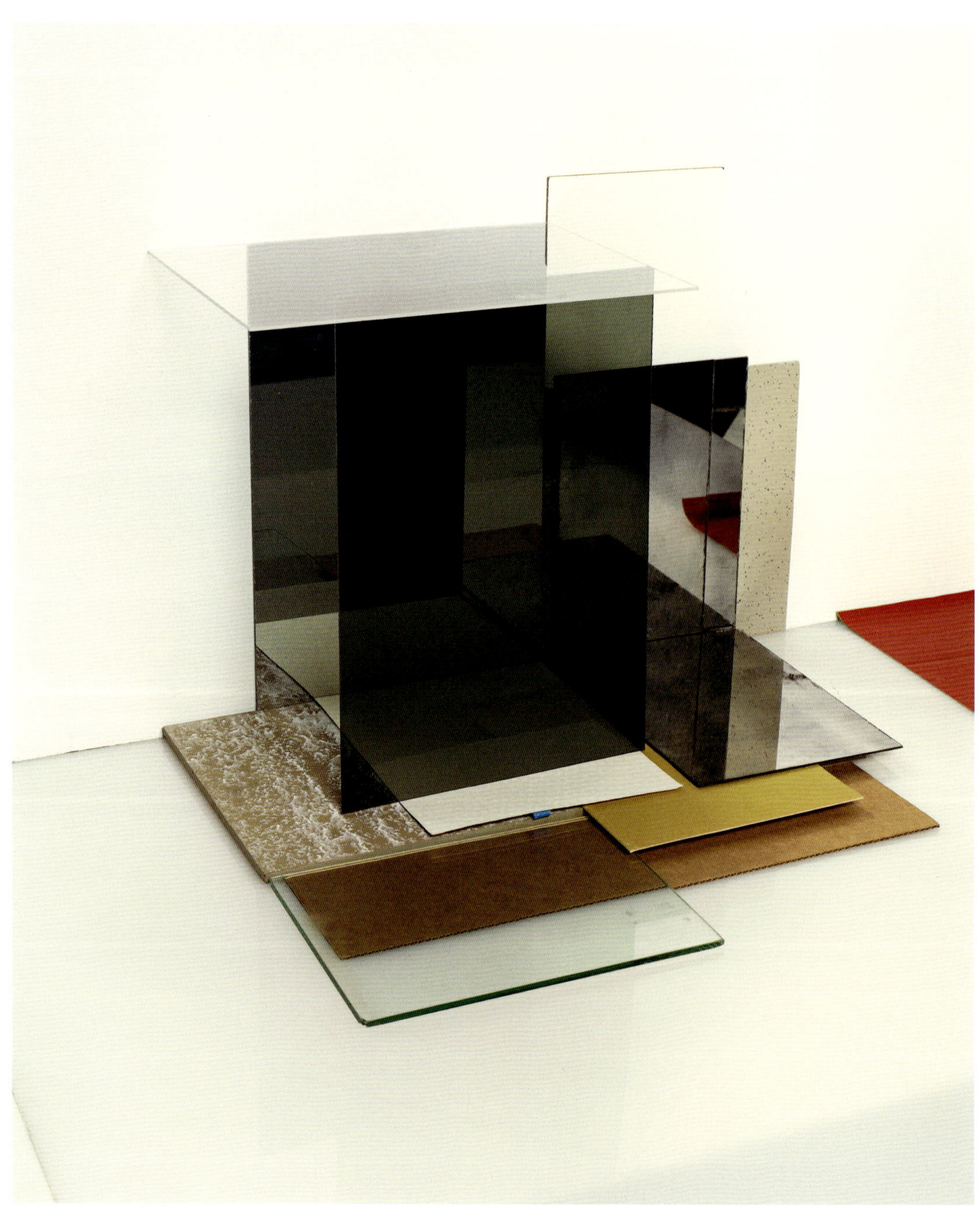

216    Phil Maisel, *Stack V (6643)*, 2014. Archival pigment print

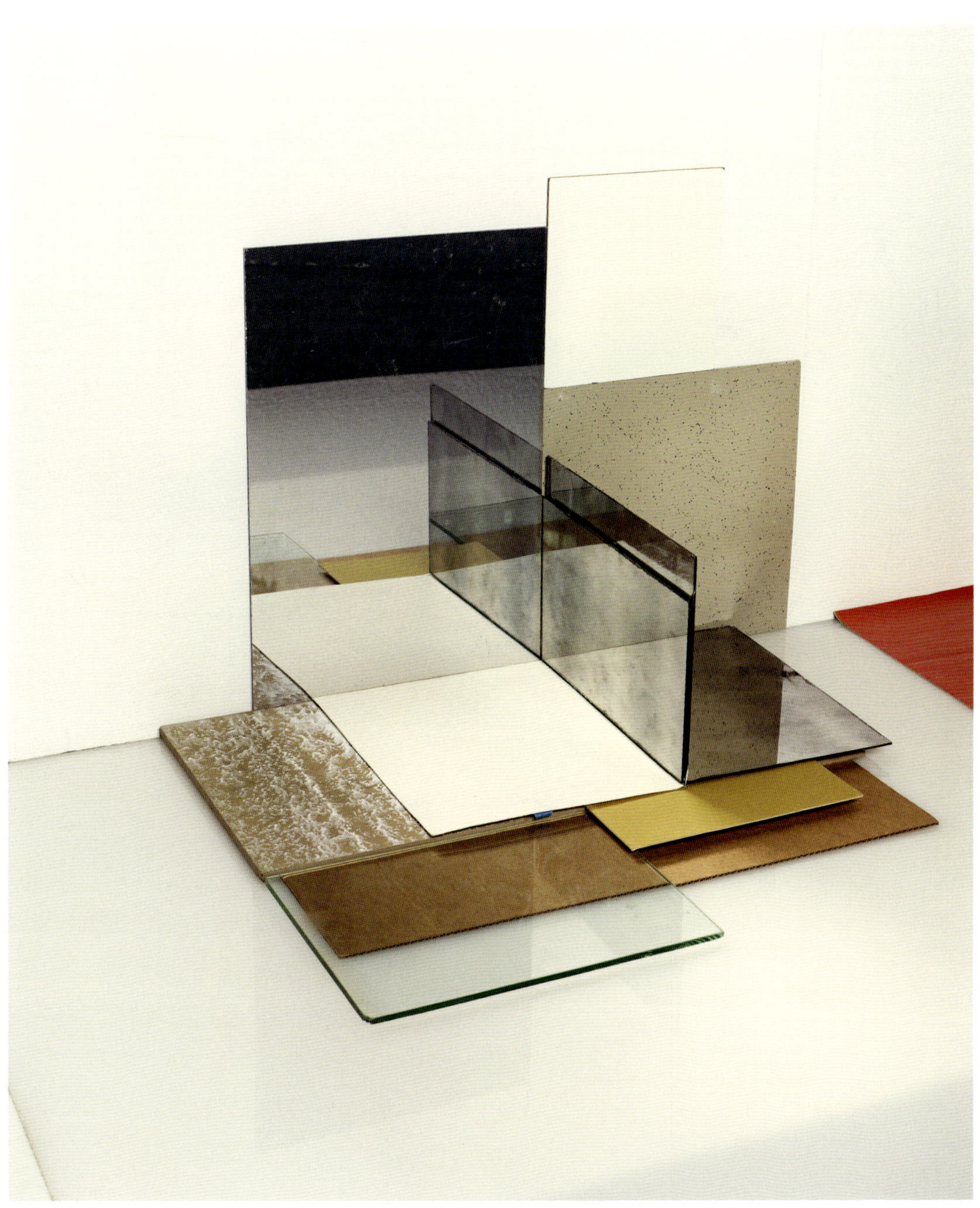

217   Phil Maisel, *Stack V (6649-1)*, 2014. Archival pigment print

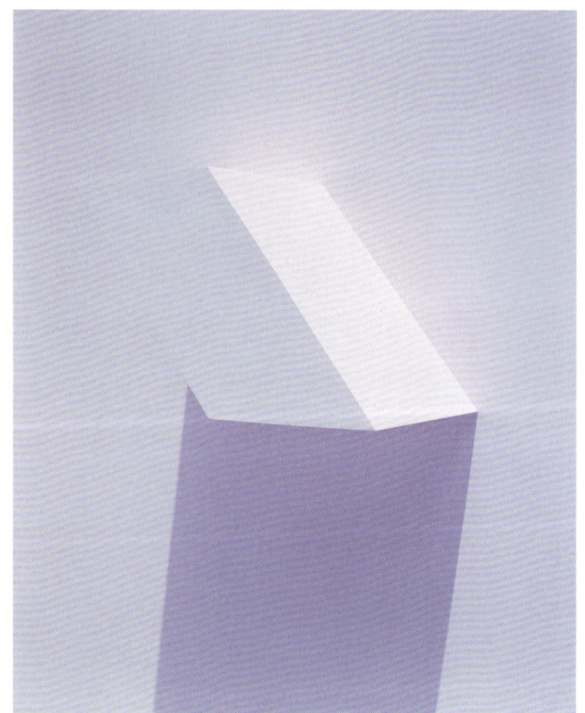

218    Sara VanDerBeek, *Synthetic Geometry*, 2014. Two digital C-prints

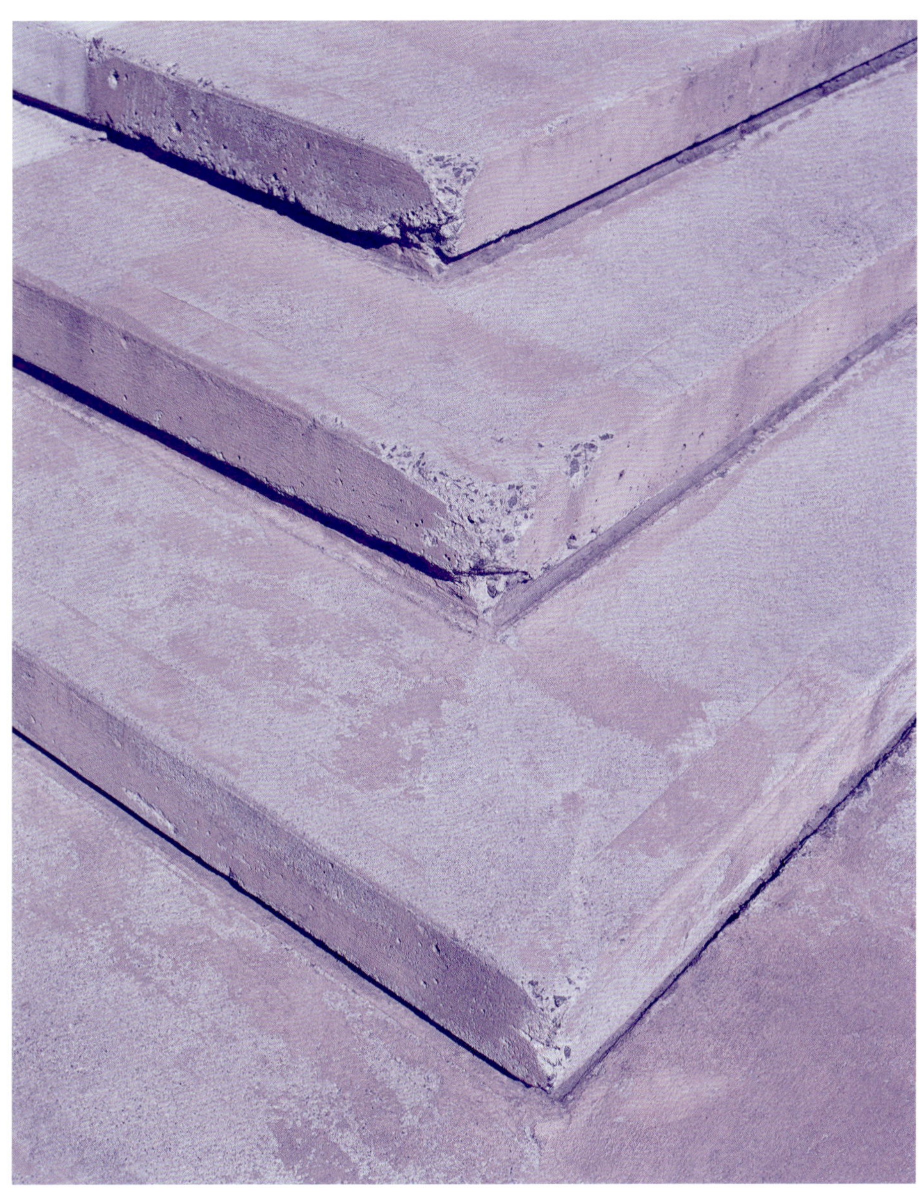

219    Sara VanDerBeek, *Pyramid Steps, Day*, 2014. Digital C-print

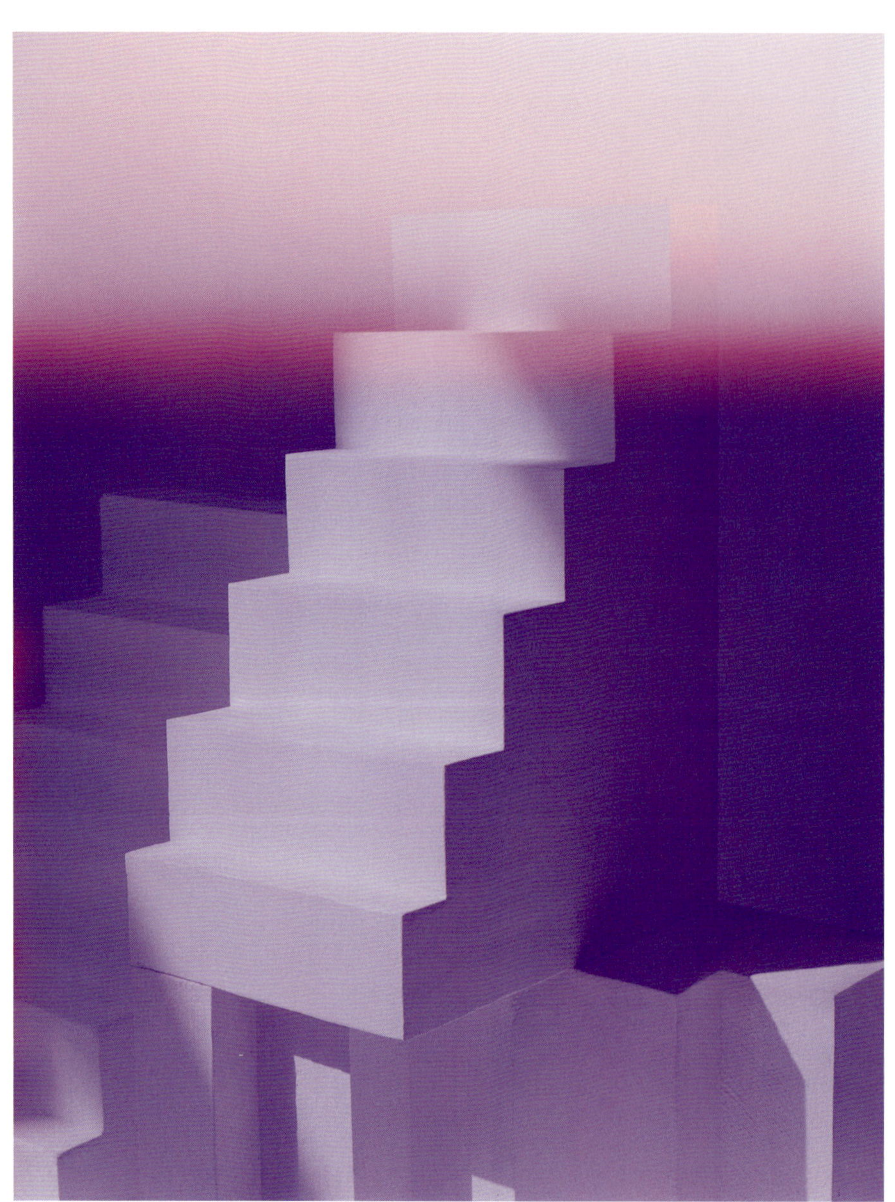

220    Sara VanDerBeek, *Ancient Solstice*, 2014. Digital C-print

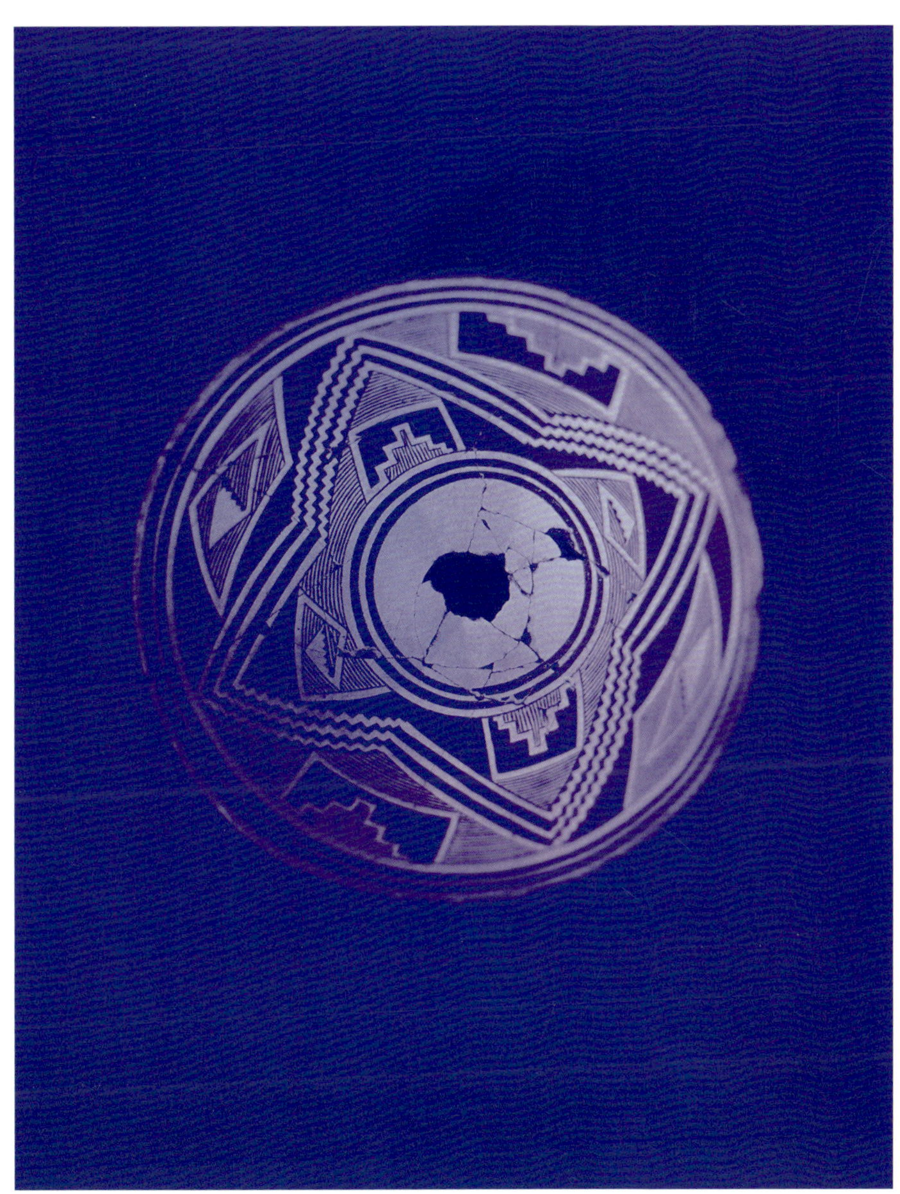

221    Sara VanDerBeek, *Mimbre*, 2014. Digital C-print

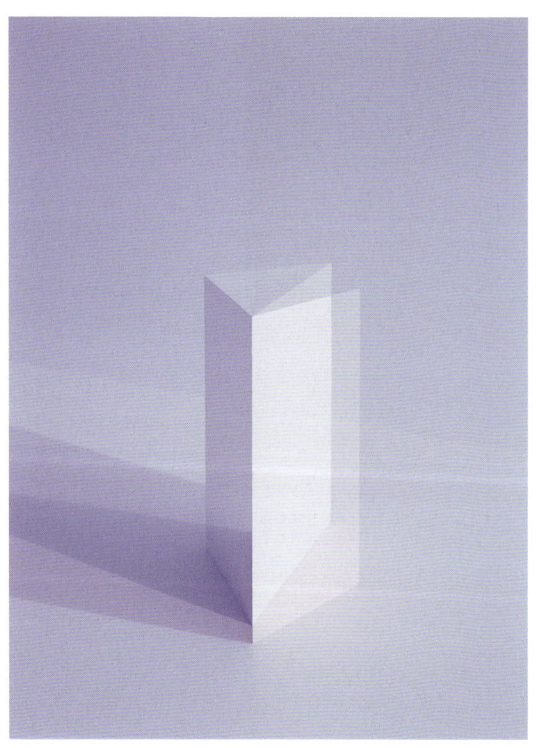

   Sara VanDerBeek, *Incidence*, 2014. Two digital C-prints

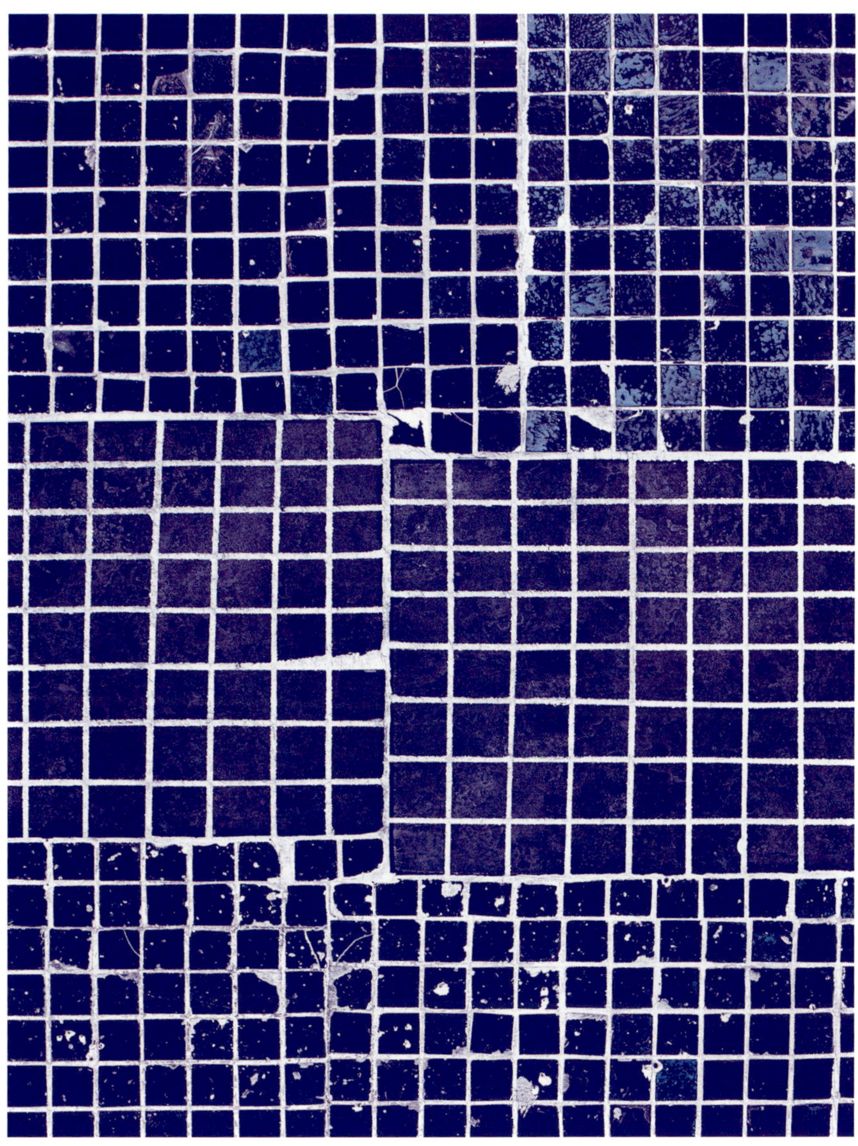

223    Sara VanDerBeek, *Axis Mundi*, 2014. Digital C-print

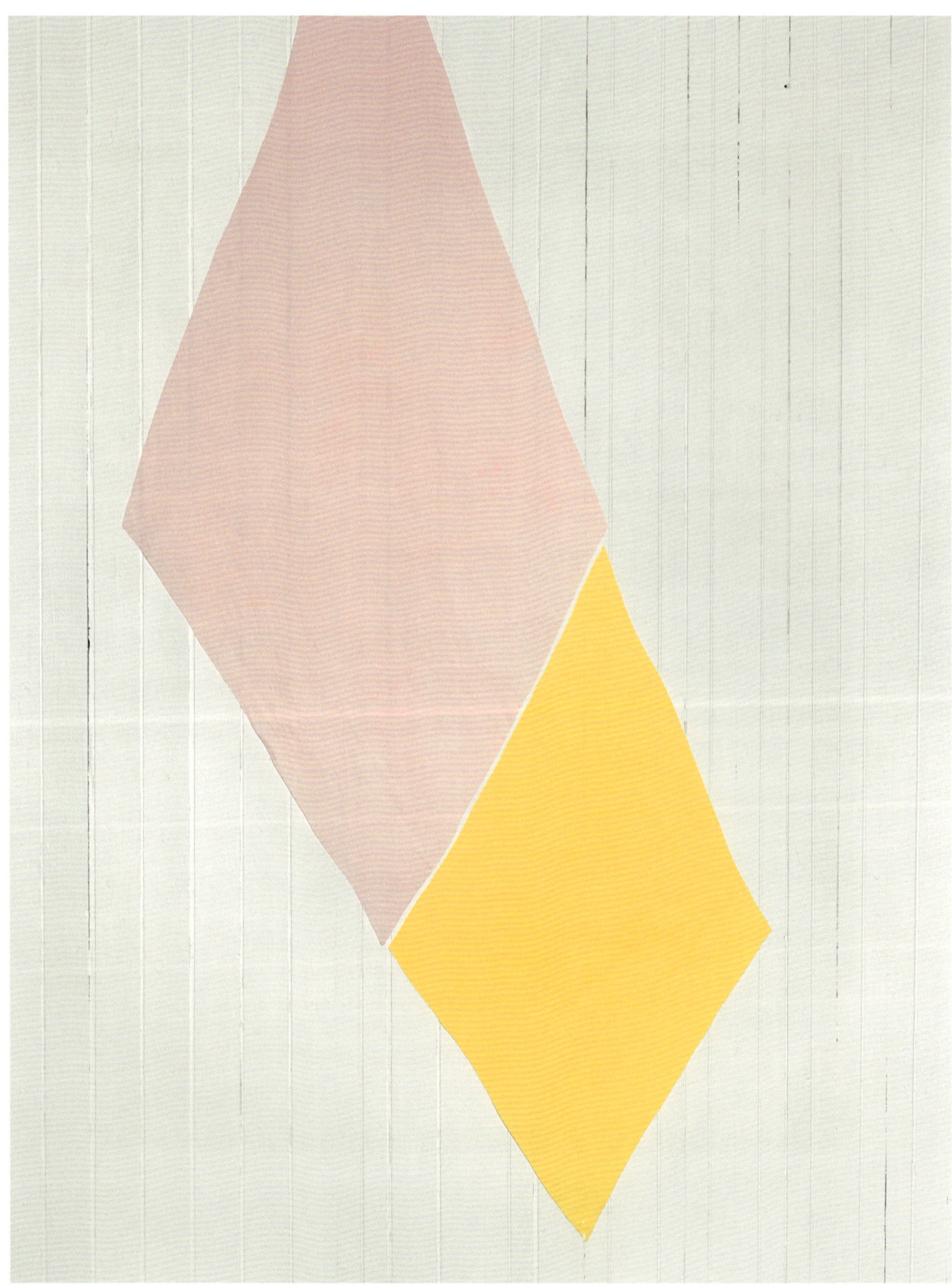

224    Bianca Brunner, *Harlequin (3)*, 2014. C-print

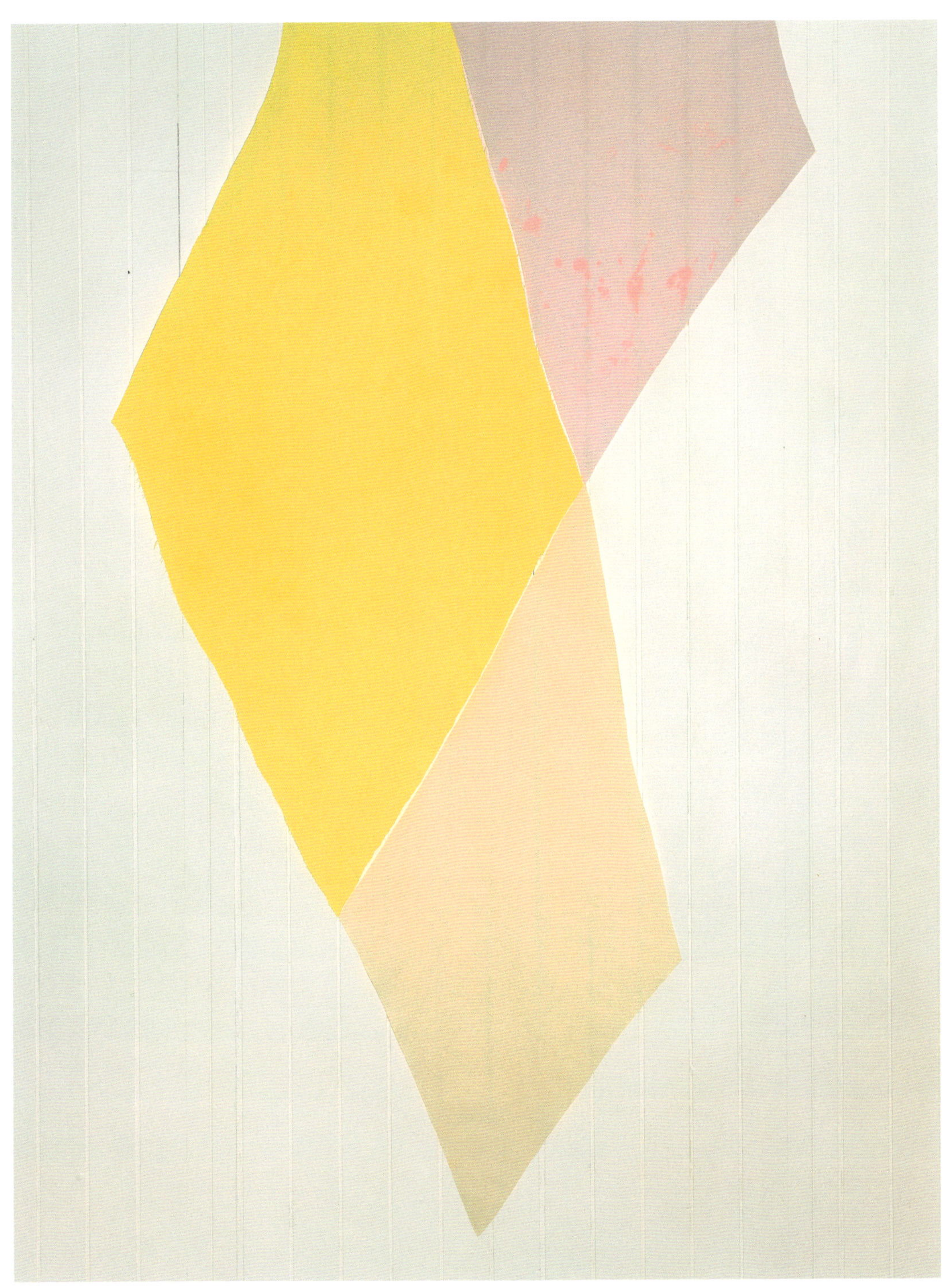

225  Bianca Brunner, *Harlequin (1)*, 2014. C-print

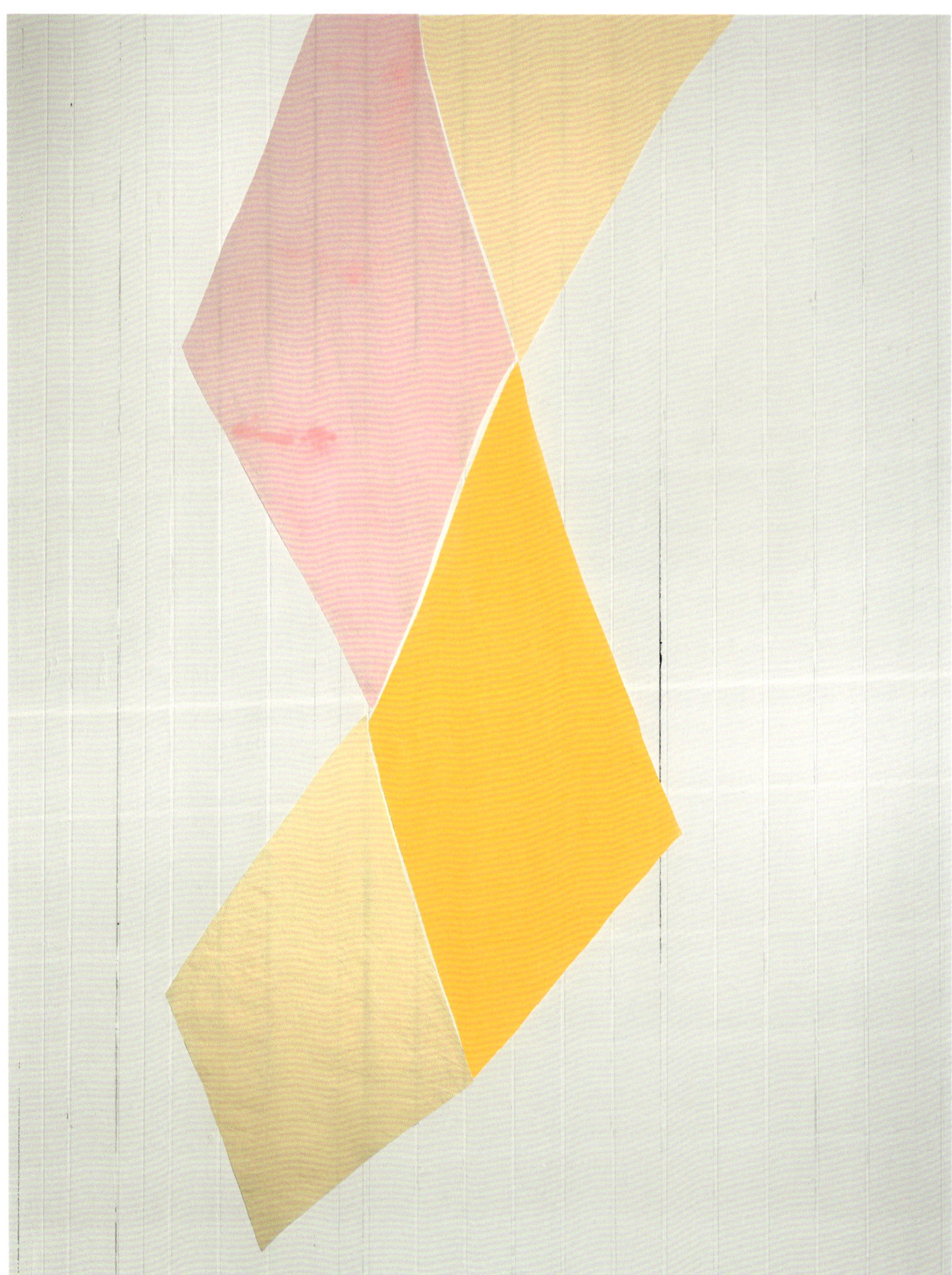

226    Bianca Brunner, *Harlequin (4)*, 2014. C-print

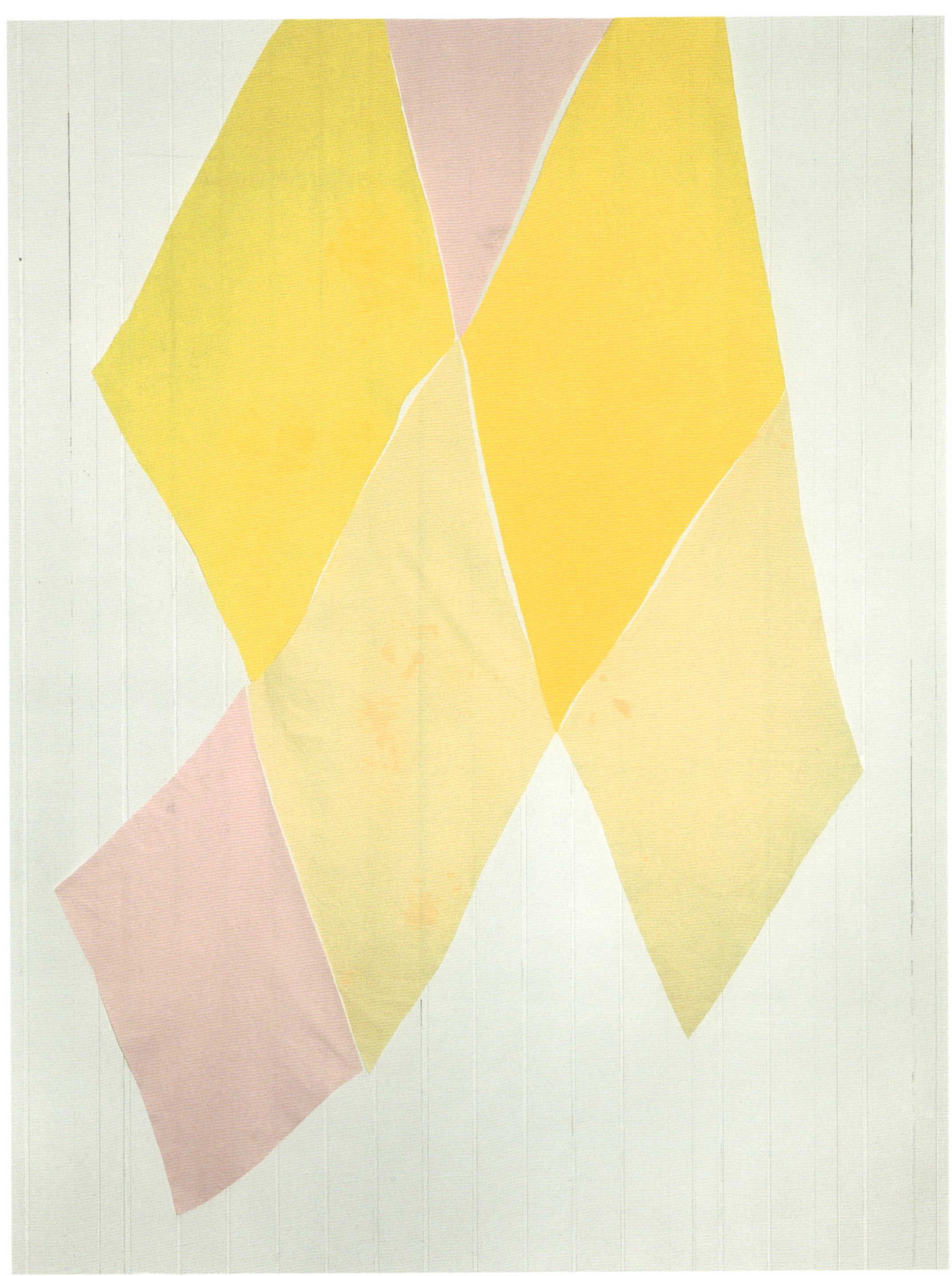

227    Bianca Brunner, *Harlequin (2)*, 2014. C-print

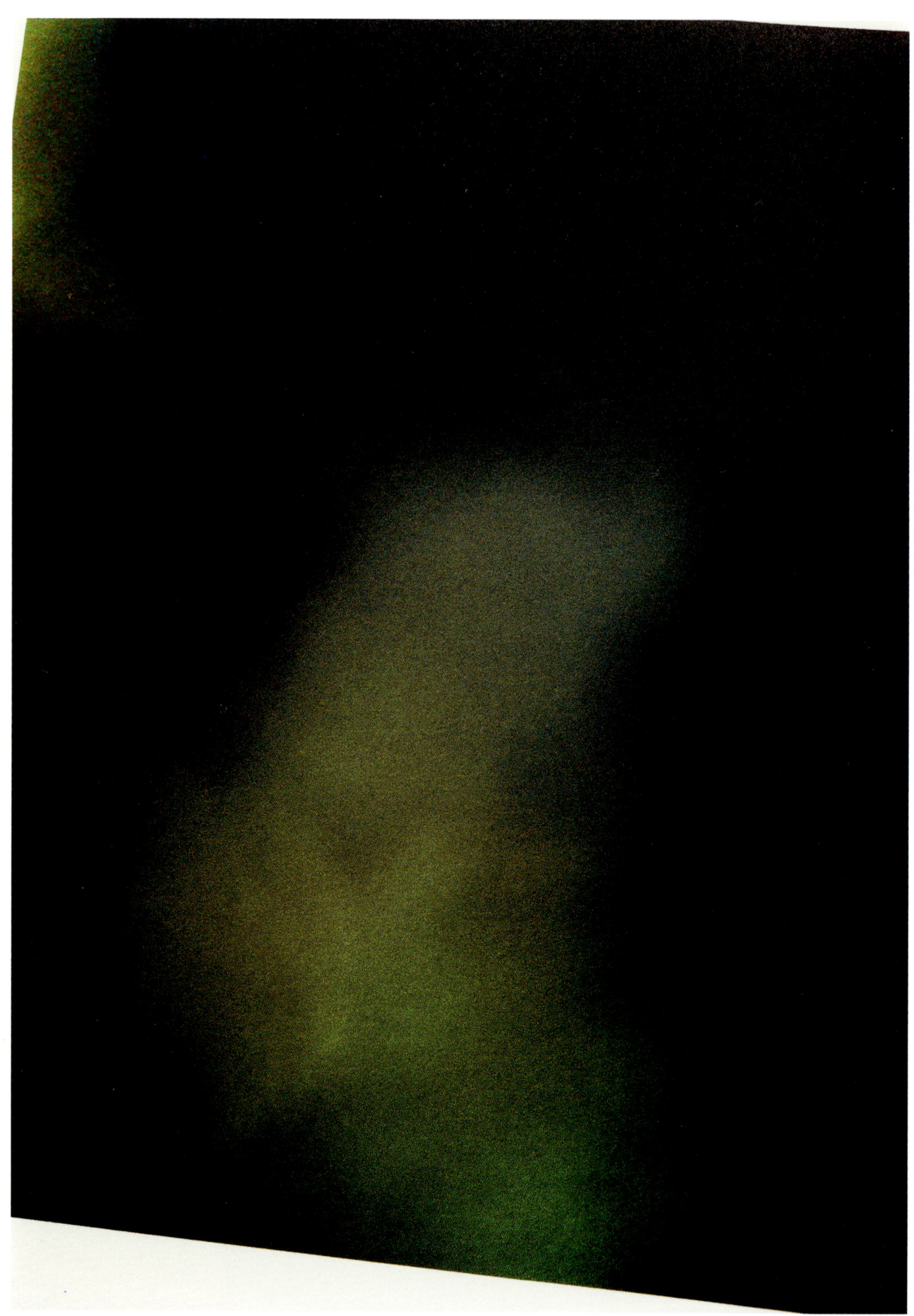

228    Go Itami, *Untitled*, 2014. Pigment print

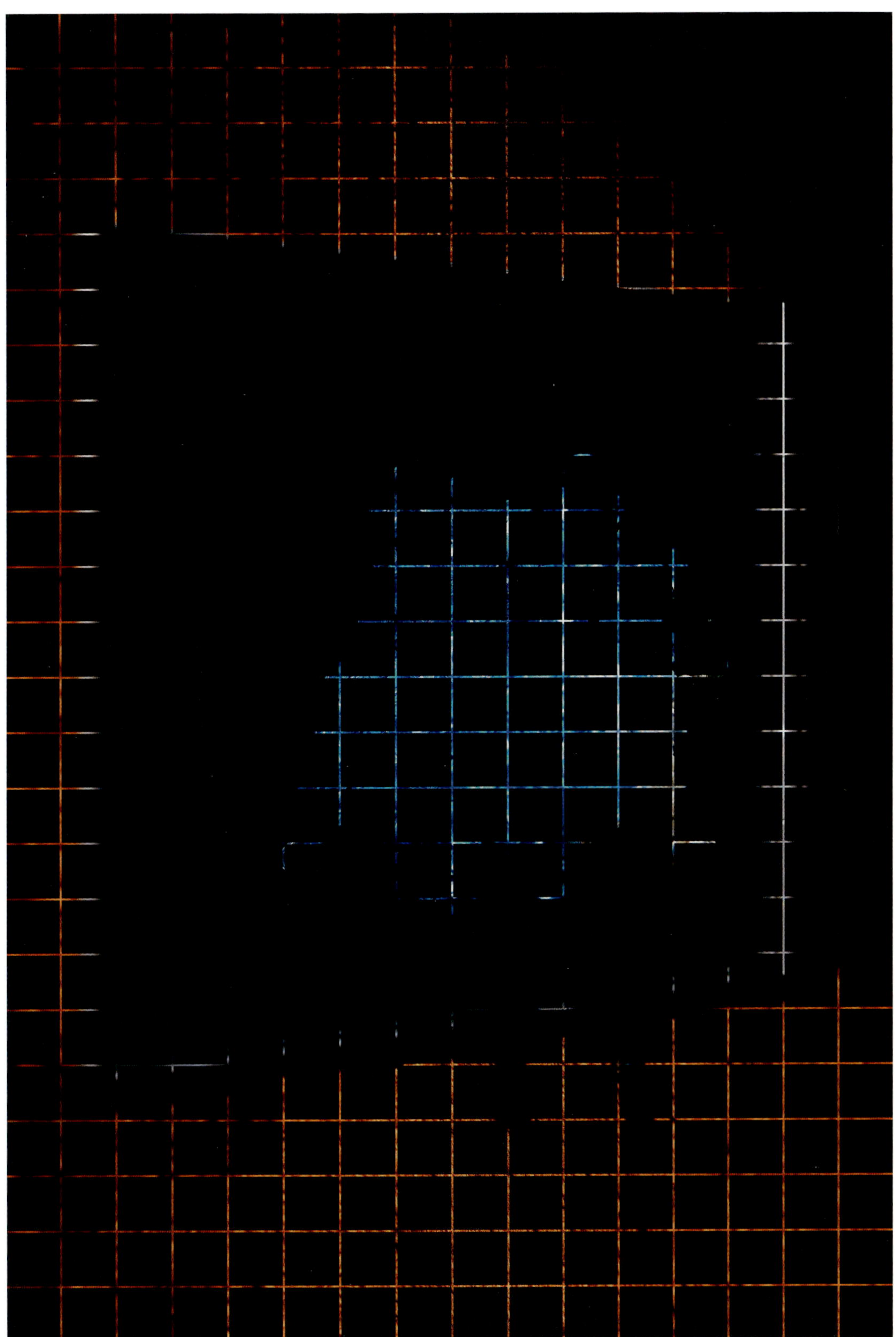

229    Go Itami, *Untitled*, 2014. Pigment print

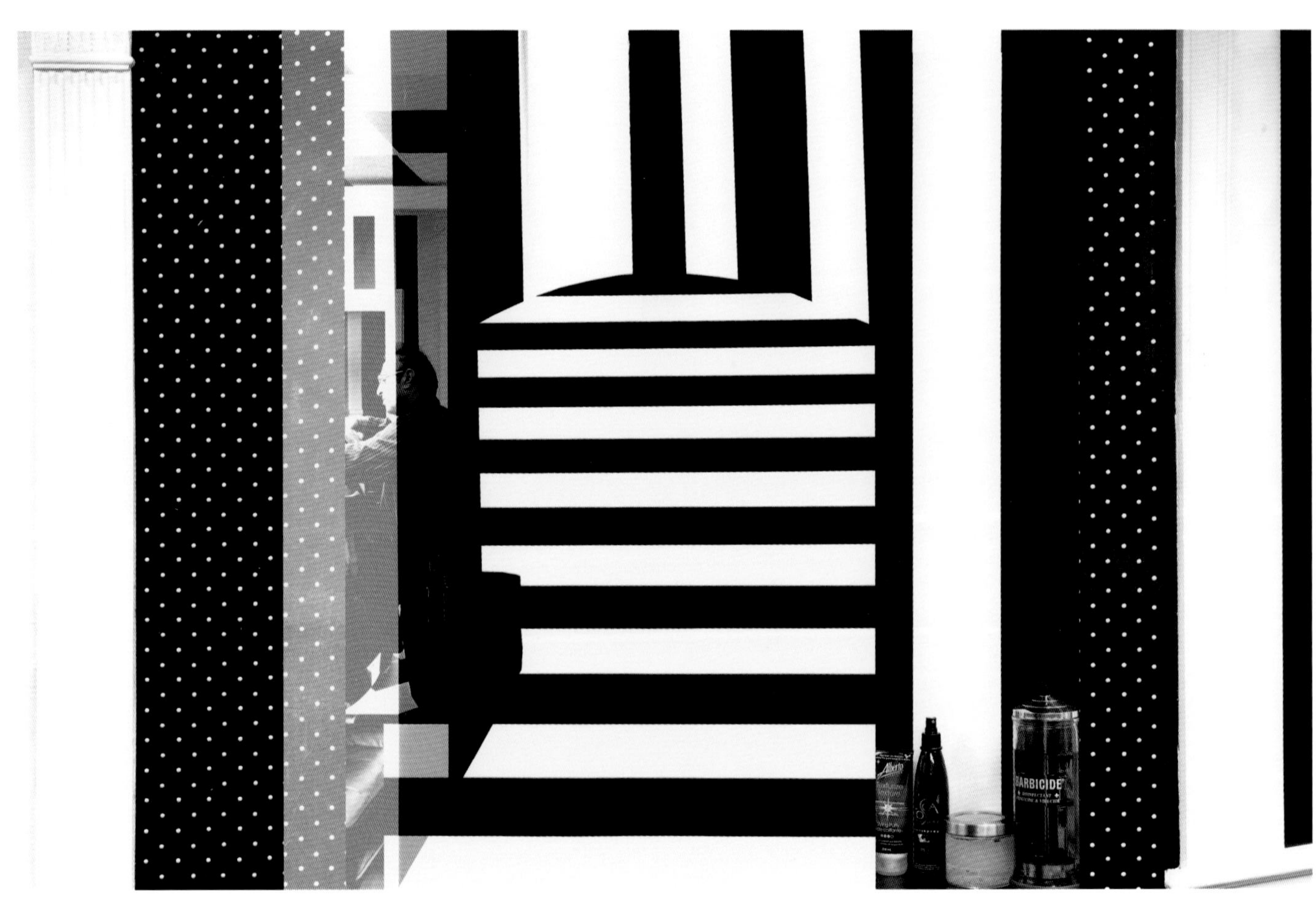

230    Annie MacDonell, *Untitled*, from the series *Flatness, Light, Black & White*, 2013. Inkjet print

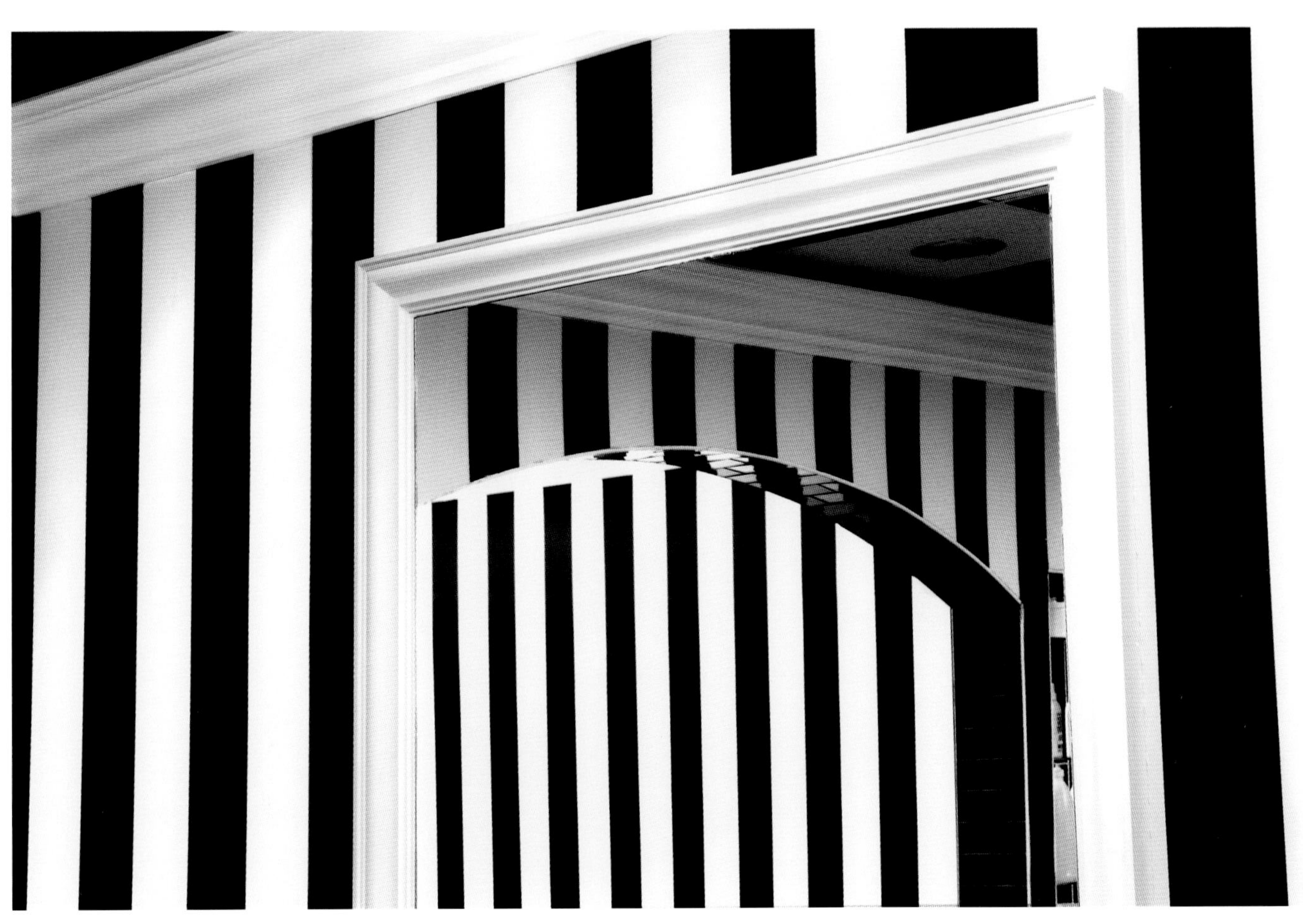

231  Annie MacDonell, *Untitled*, from the series *Flatness, Light, Black & White*, 2013. Inkjet print

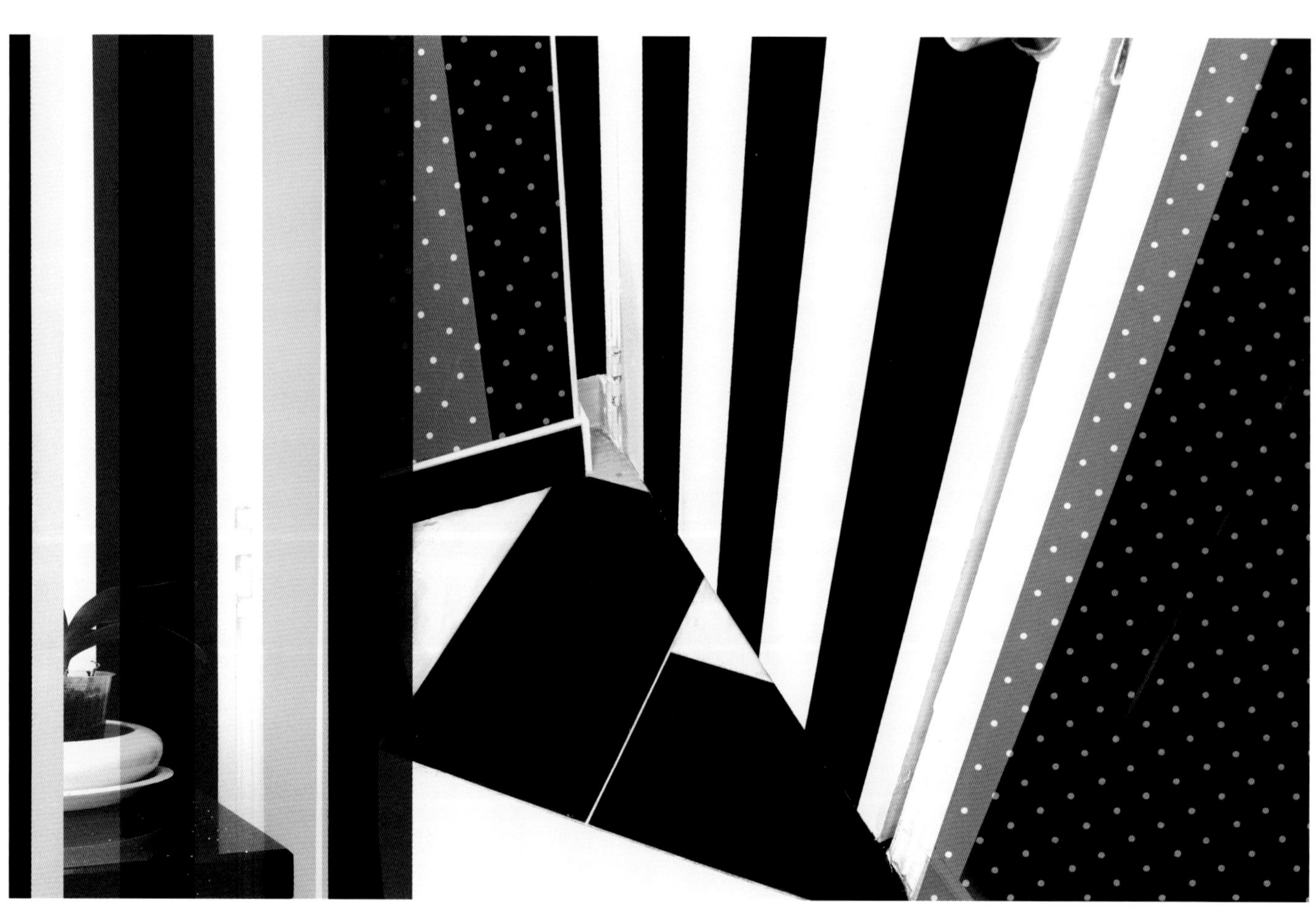

232    Annie MacDonell, *Untitled*, from the series *Flatness, Light, Black & White*, 2013. Inkjet print

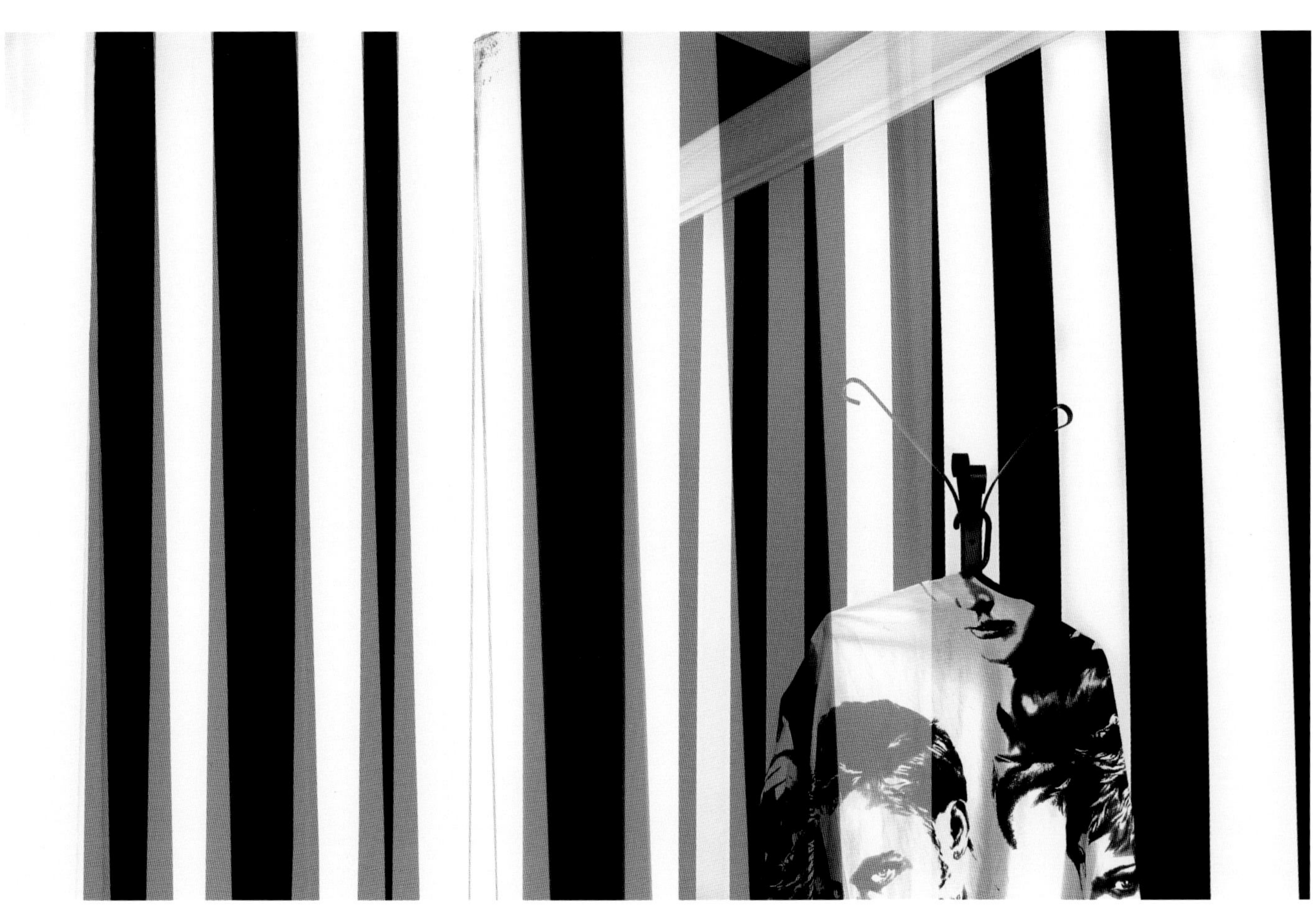

233    Annie MacDonell, *Untitled*, from the series *Flatness, Light, Black & White*, 2013. Inkjet print

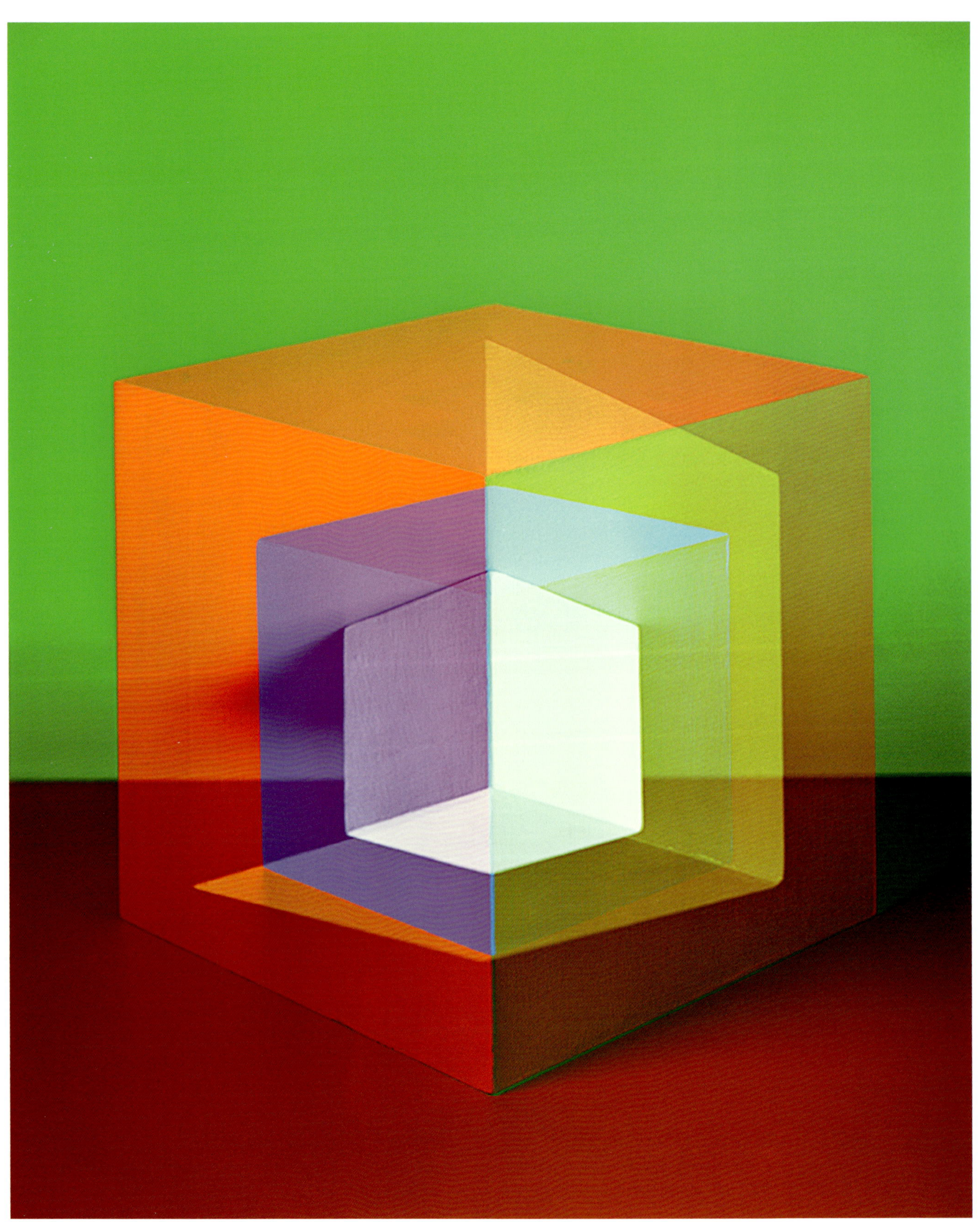

234    Jessica Eaton, *cfaal 340*, 2013. Archival pigment print

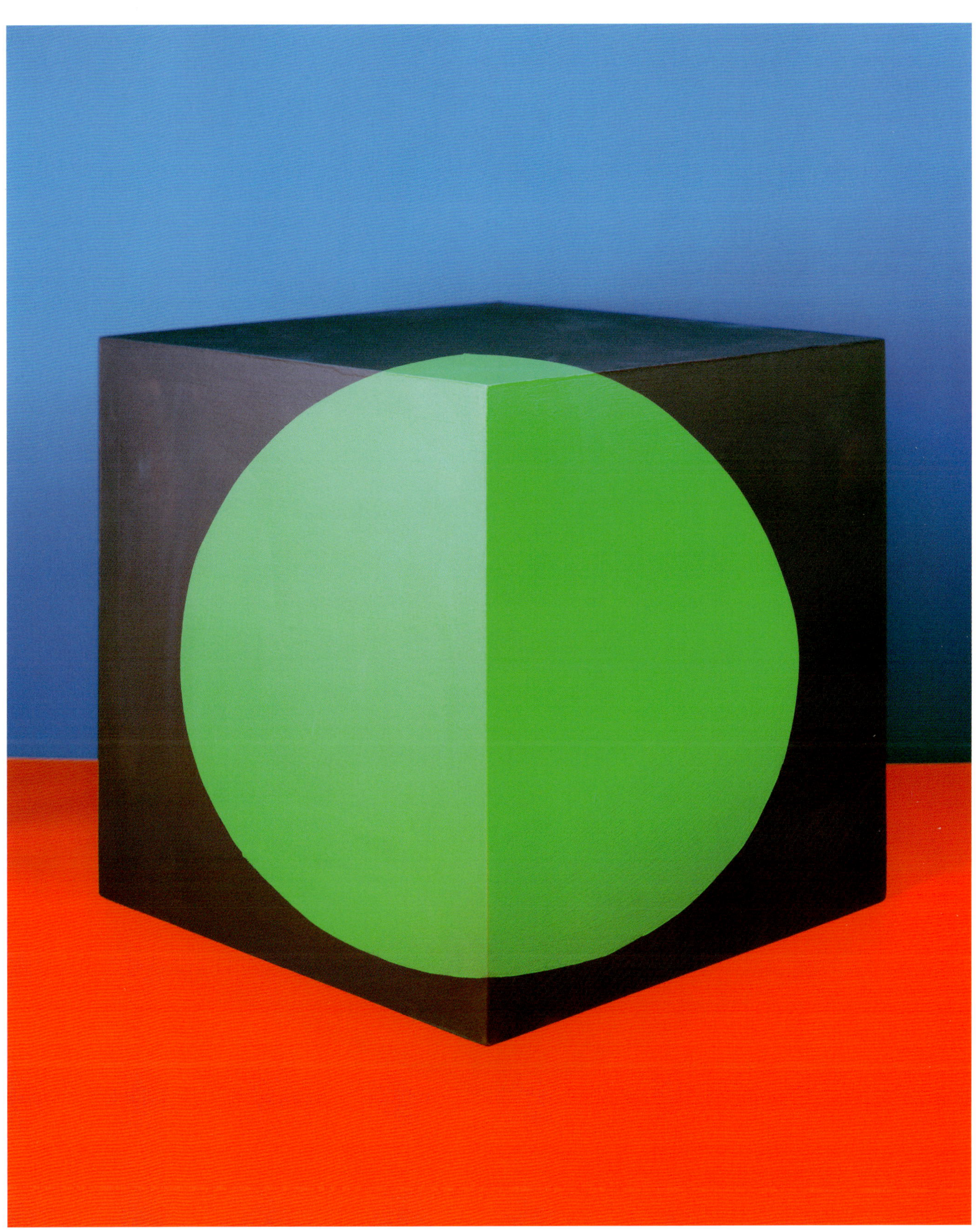

   Jessica Eaton, *cfaal 380*, 2013. Archival pigment print

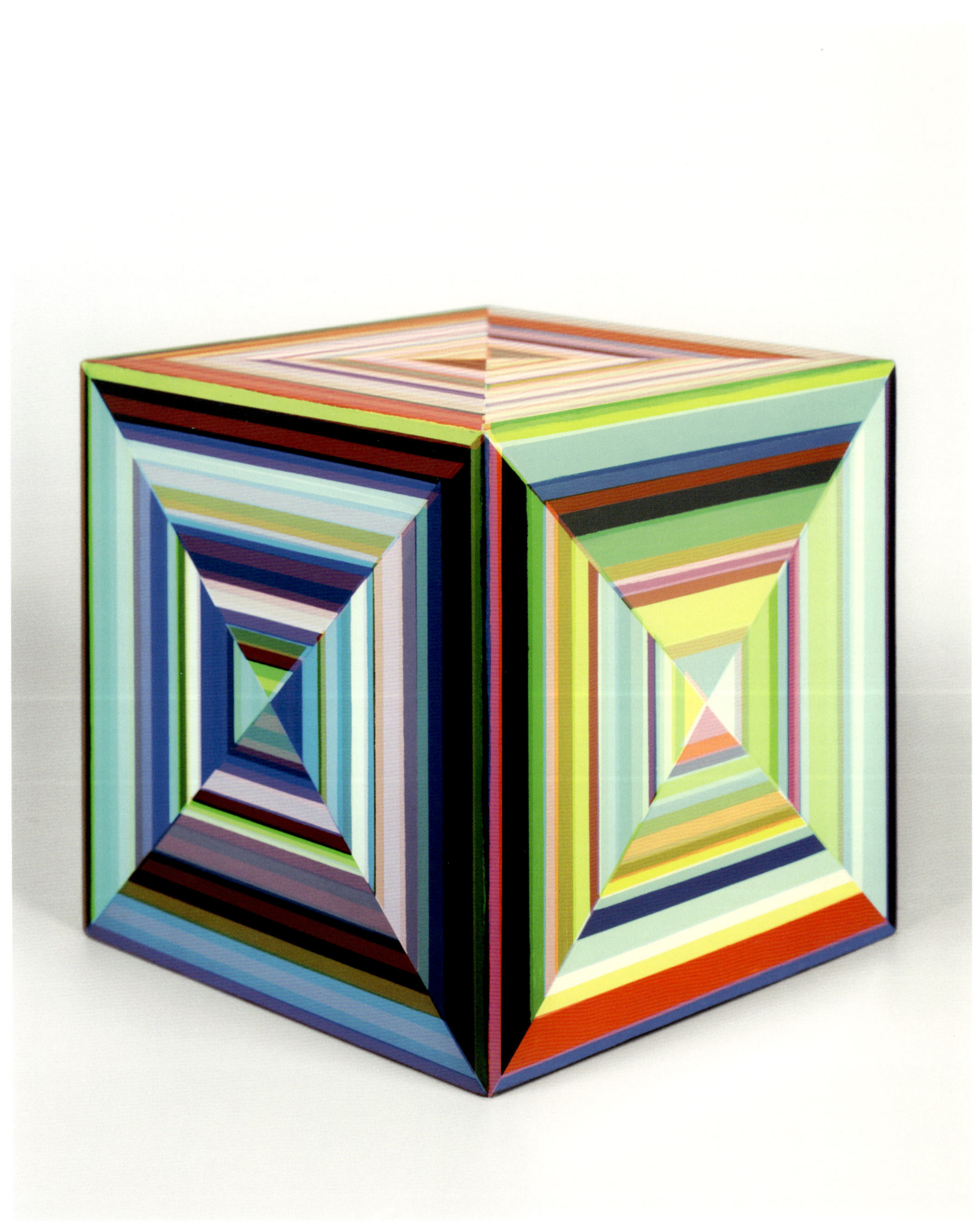

236    Jessica Eaton, *cfaal 352*, 2013. Archival pigment print

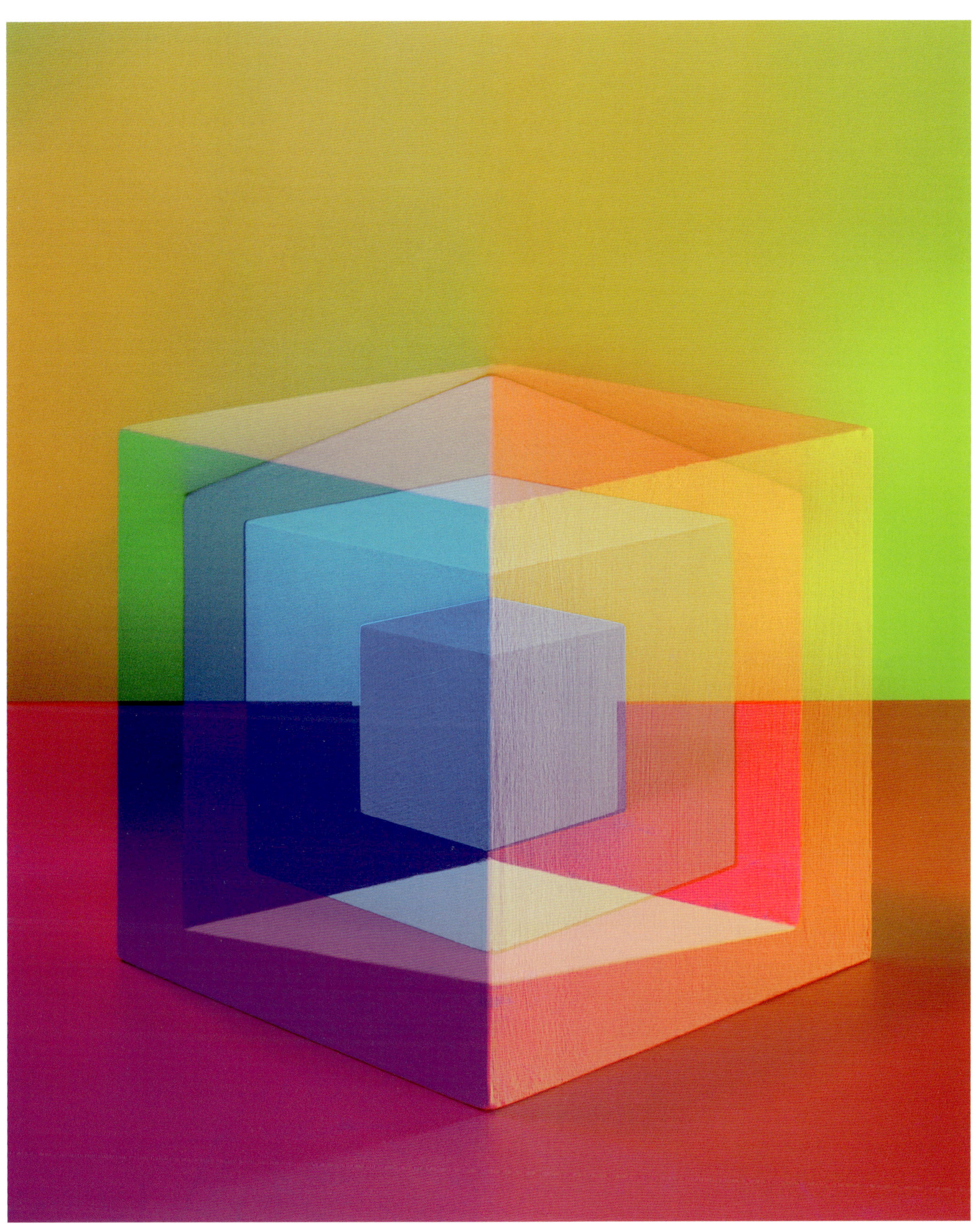

237    Jessica Eaton, *cfaal 346*, 2013. Archival pigment print

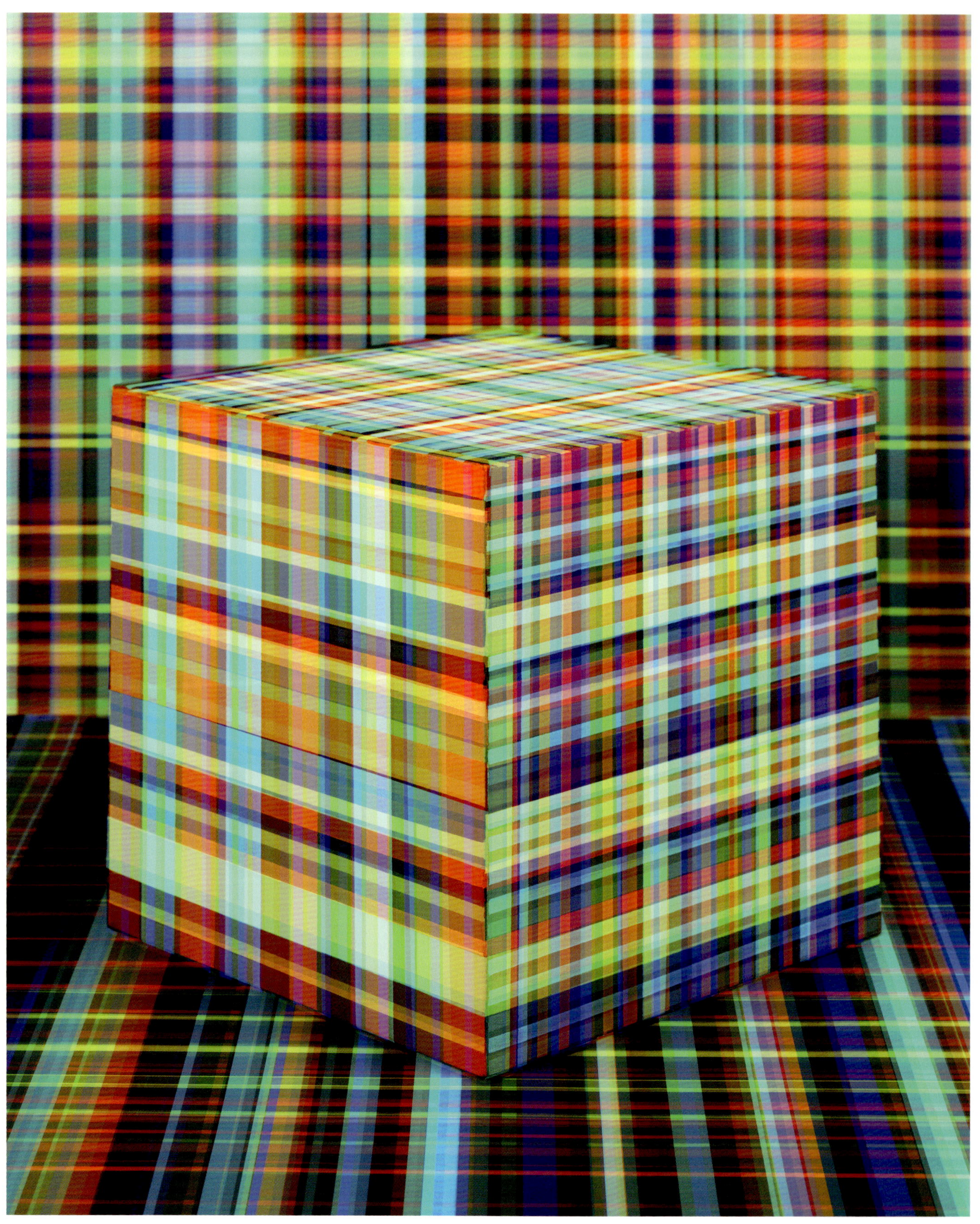

238    Jessica Eaton, *cfaal 397*, 2013. Archival pigment print

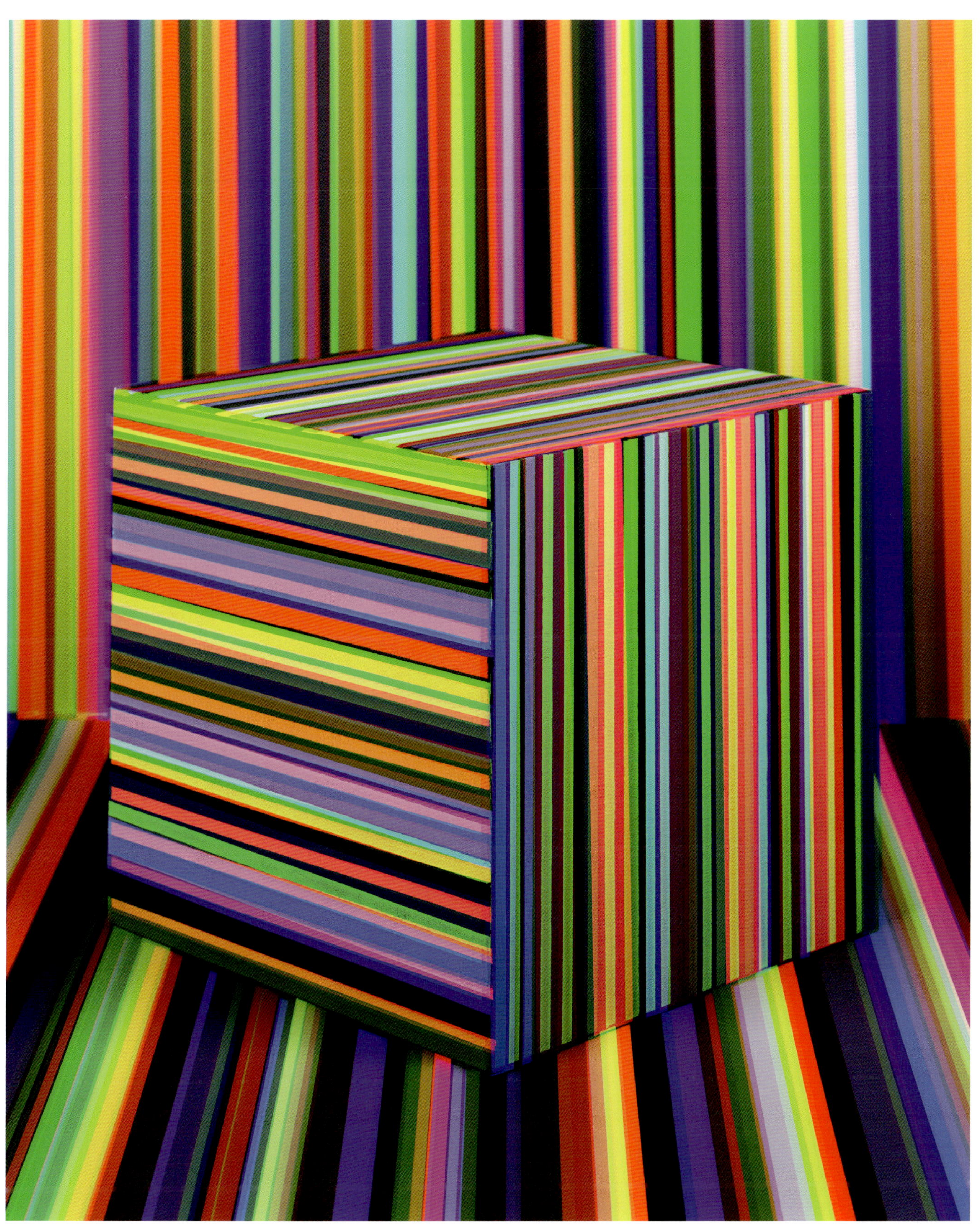

239    Jessica Eaton, *cfaal 393*, 2013. Archival pigment print

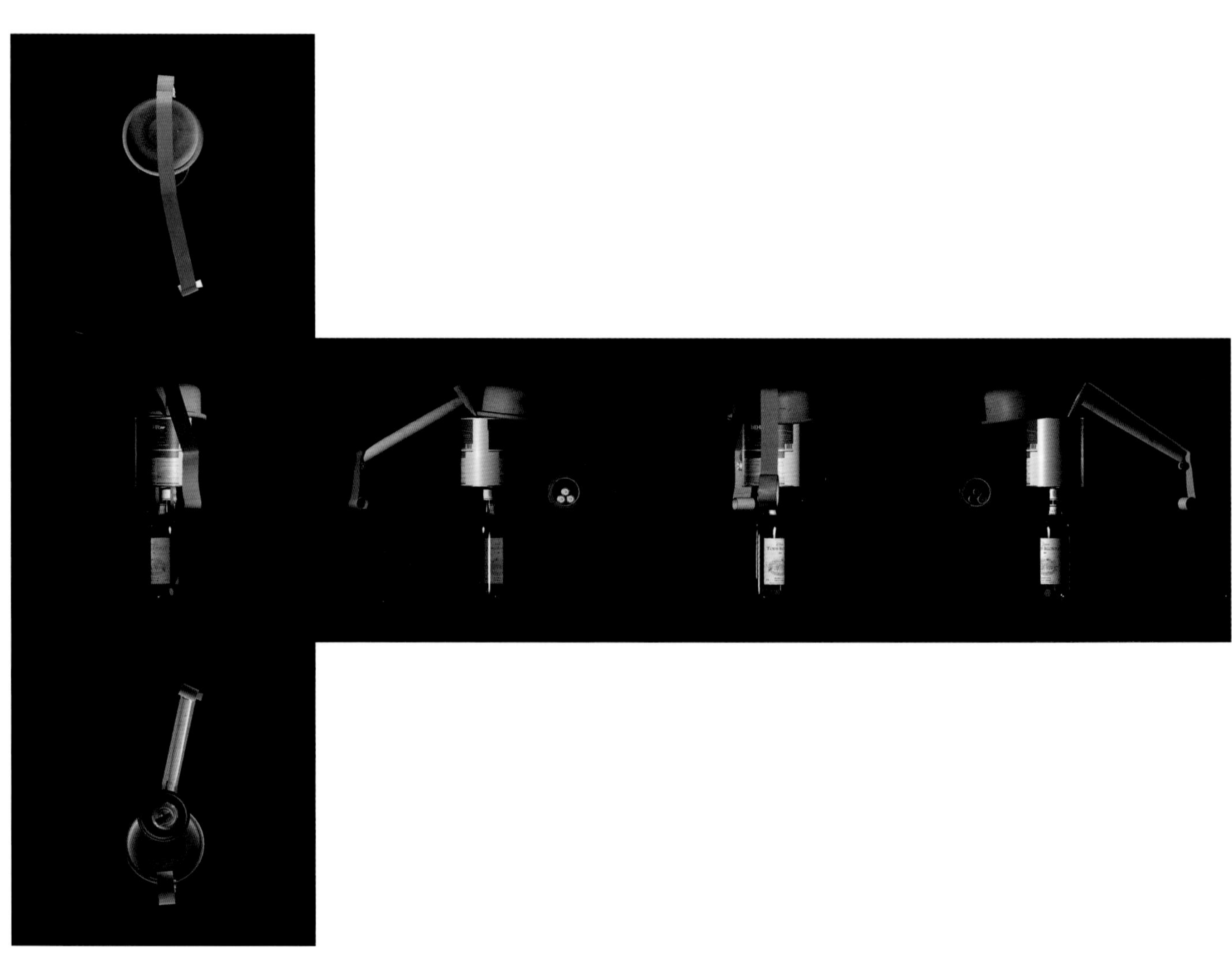

    Amir Zaki, *Plate 5*, from the project *Eleven Minus One*, 2010. Limited-edition foldout book

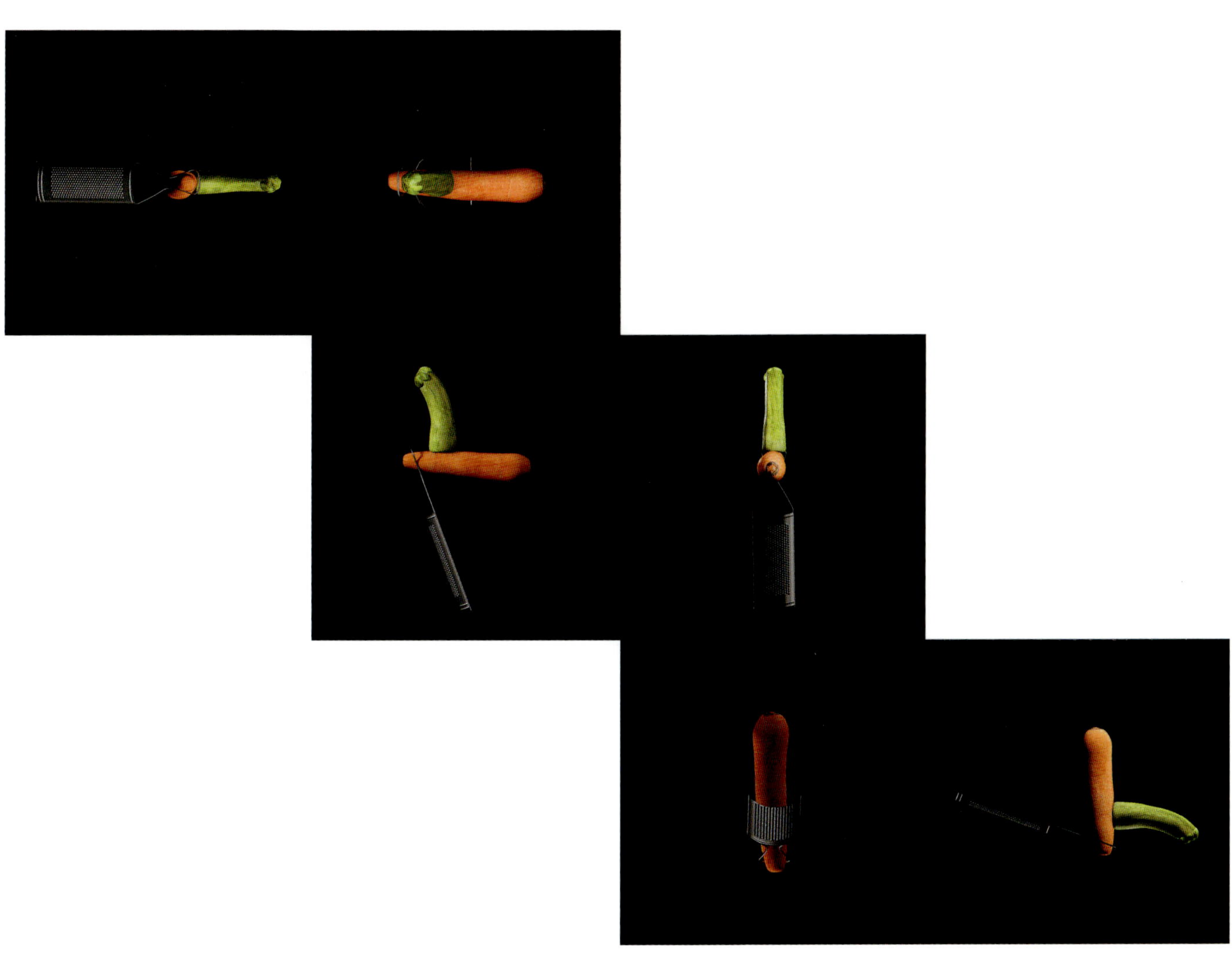

    Amir Zaki, *Plate 8*, from the project *Eleven Minus One*, 2010. Limited-edition foldout book

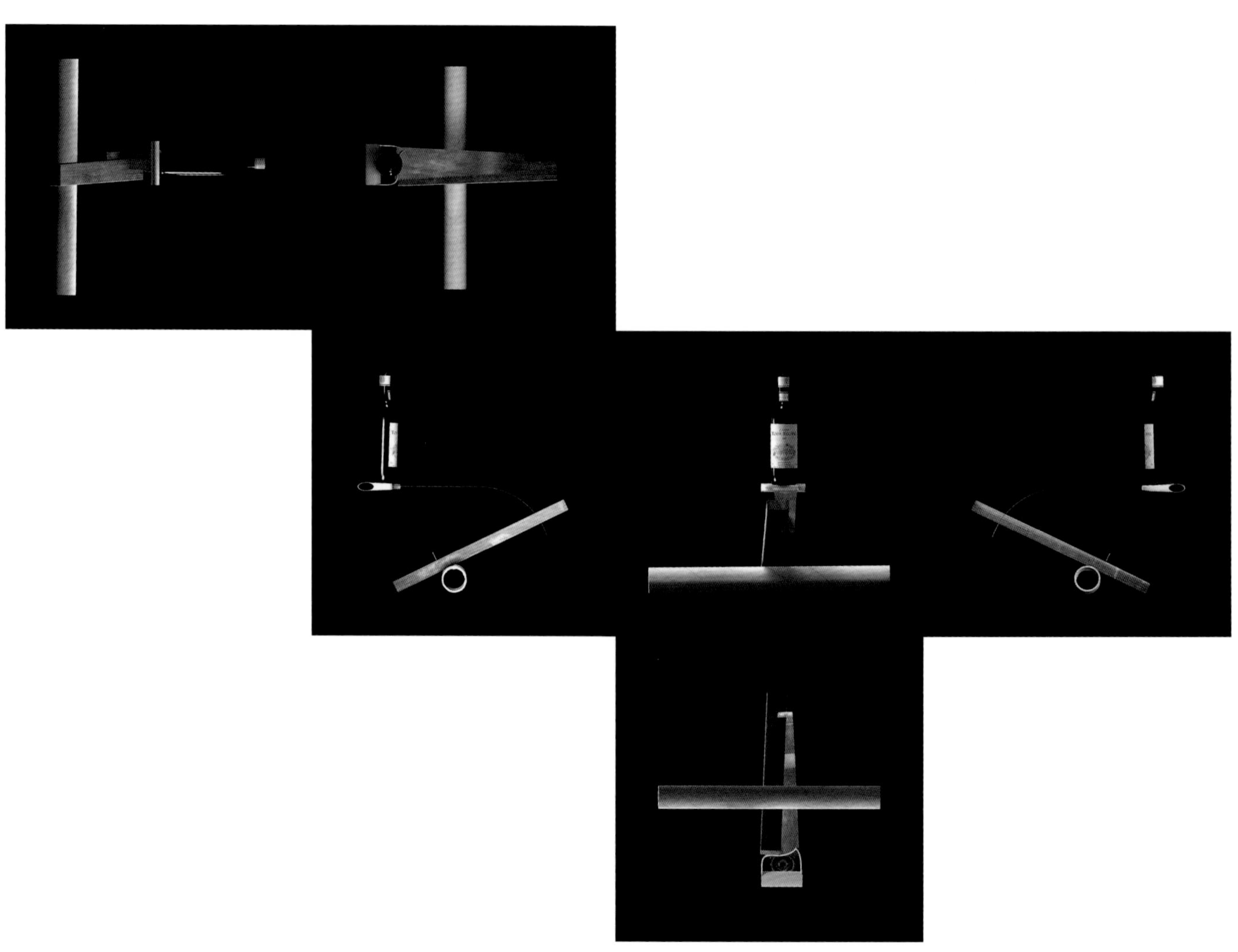

242    Amir Zaki, *Plate 1*, from the project *Eleven Minus One*, 2010. Limited-edition foldout book

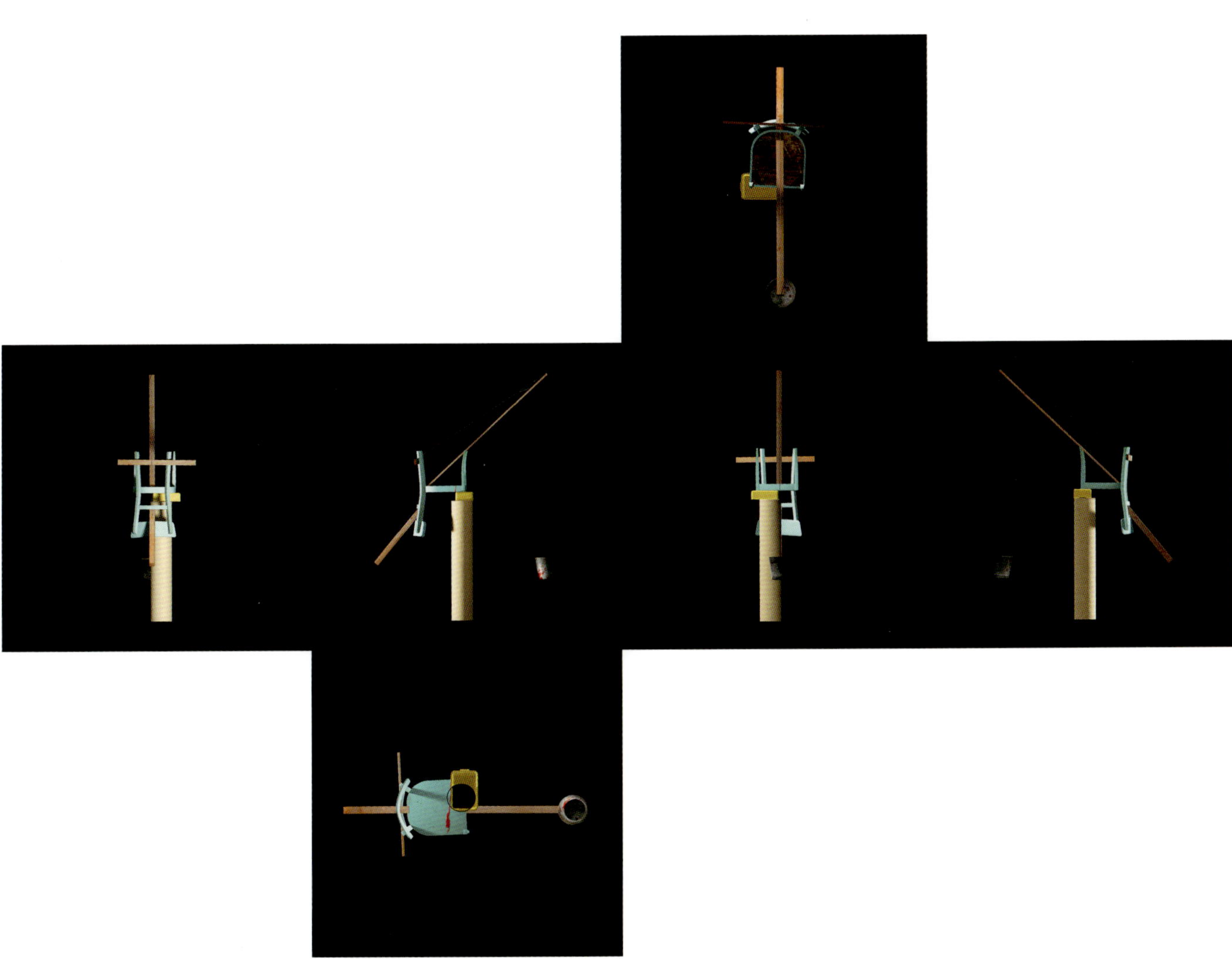

243    Amir Zaki, *Plate 4*, from the project *Eleven Minus One*, 2010. Limited-edition foldout book

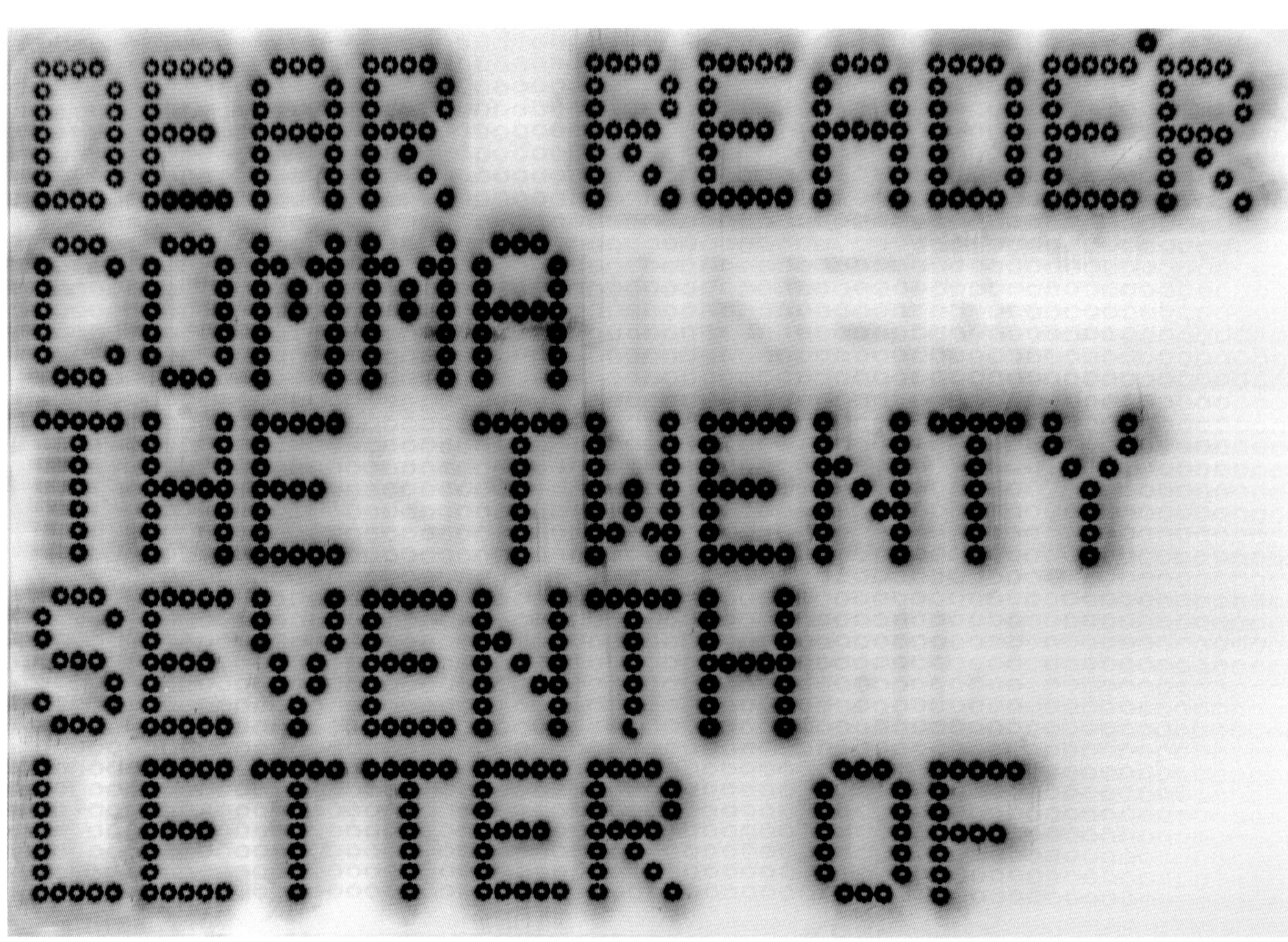


    Shannon Ebner, *One*, from the series *The Electric Comma*, 2011–13. Epson print

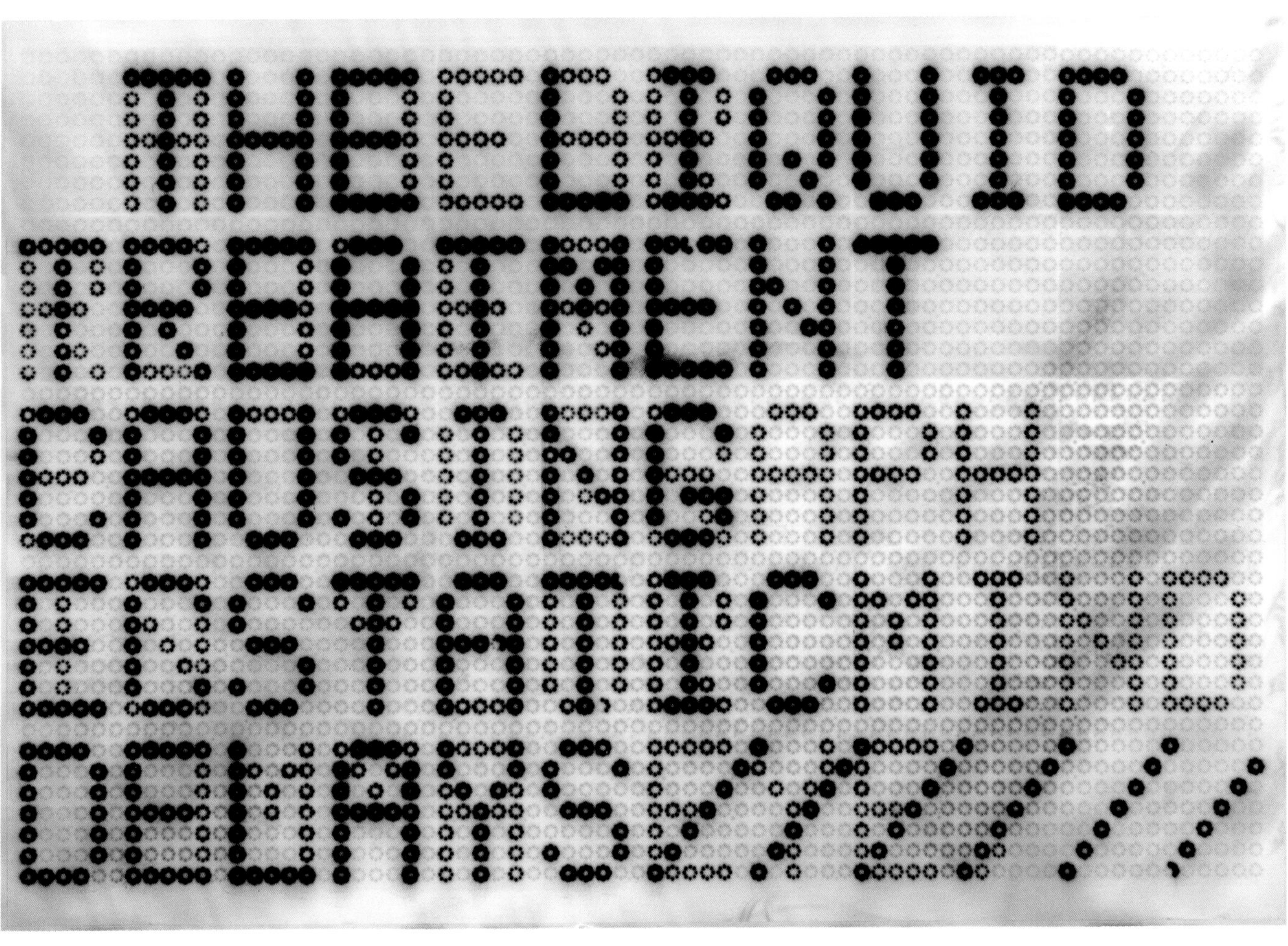


245 Shannon Ebner, *Two*, from the series *The Electric Comma*, 2011–13. Epson print

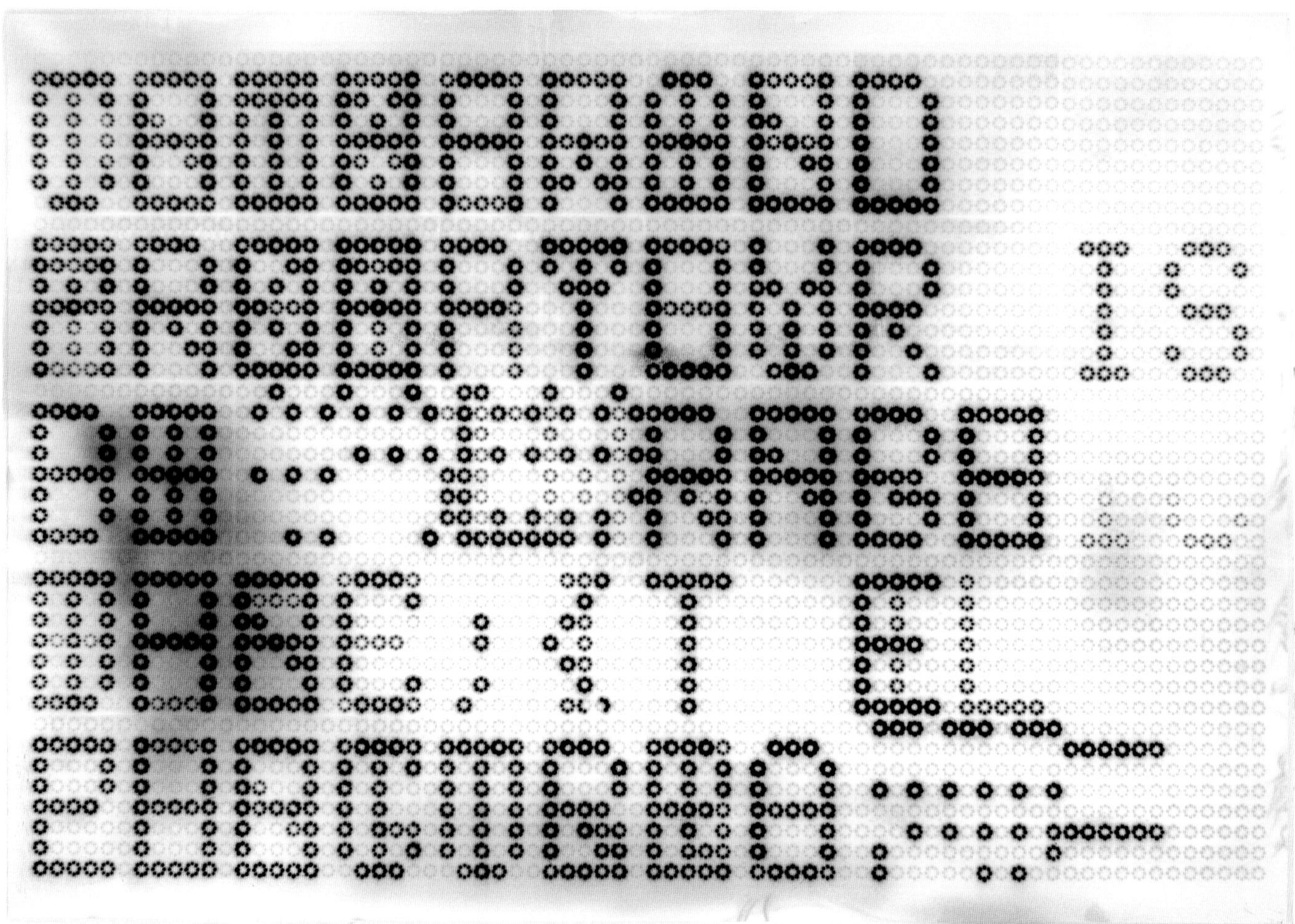

246    Shannon Ebner, *Three*, from the series *The Electric Comma*, 2011–13. Epson print

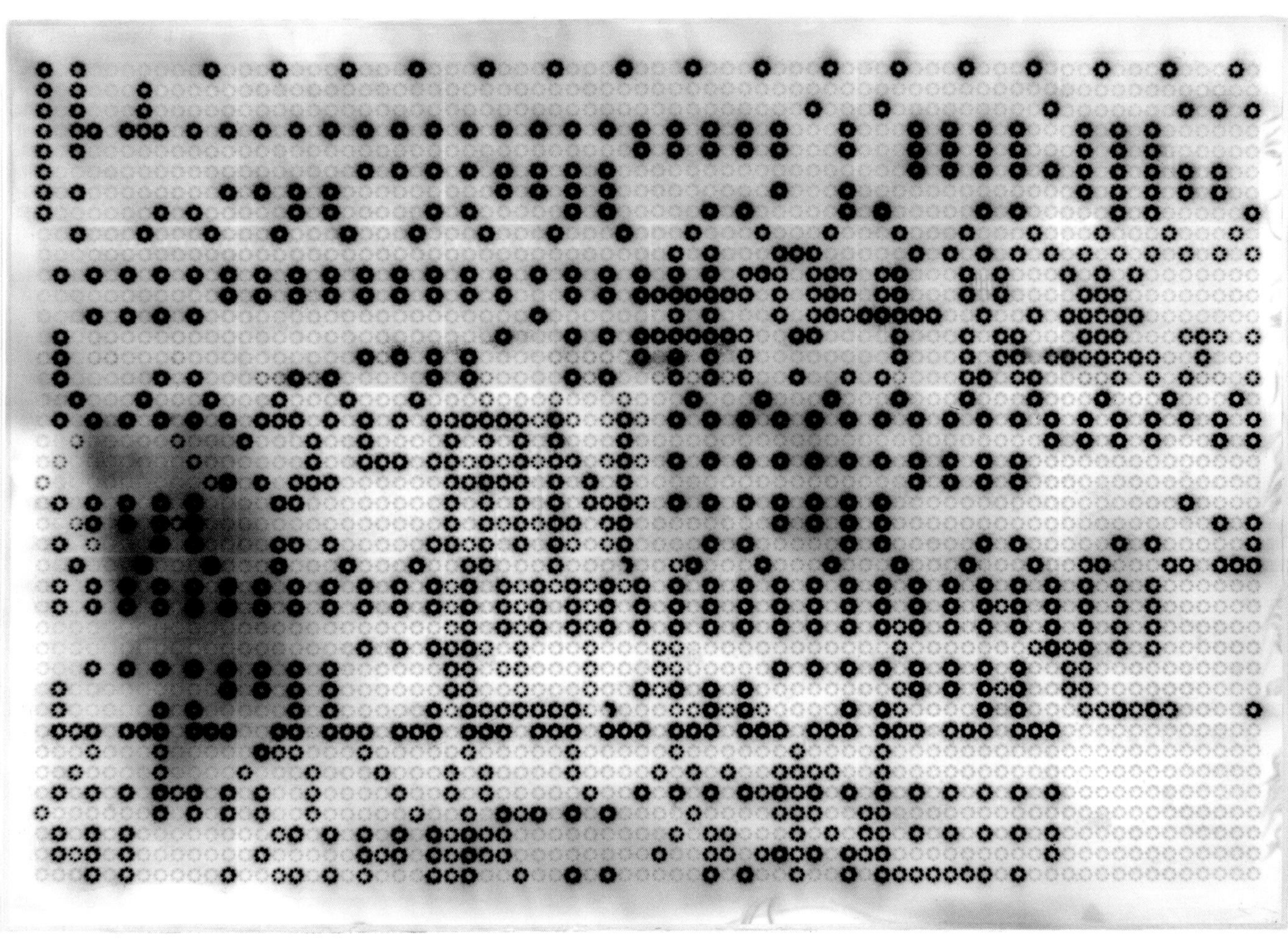

247    Shannon Ebner, *Five*, from the series *The Electric Comma*, 2011–13. Epson print

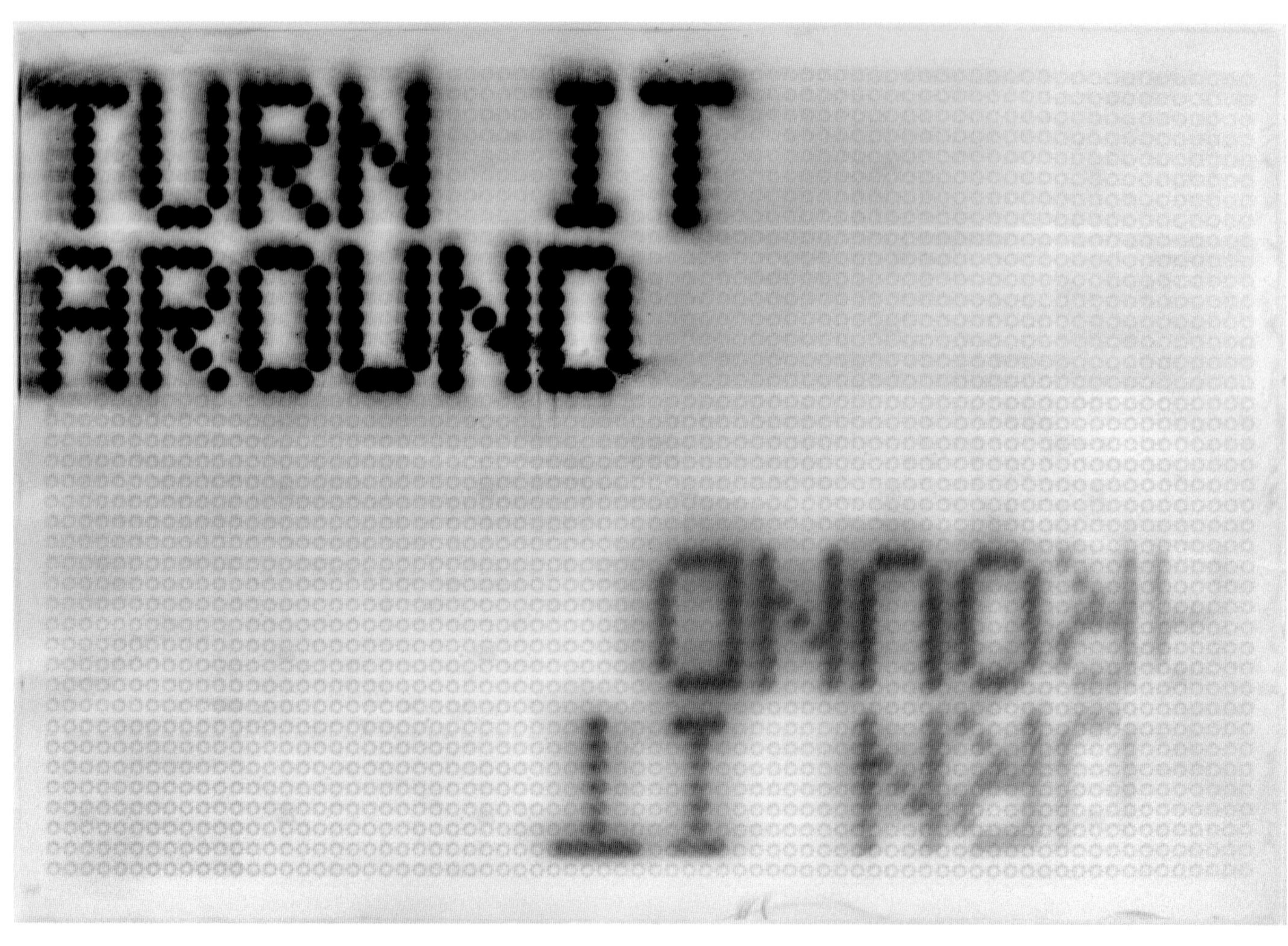



 Shannon Ebner, *Six*, from the series *The Electric Comma*, 2011–13. Epson print

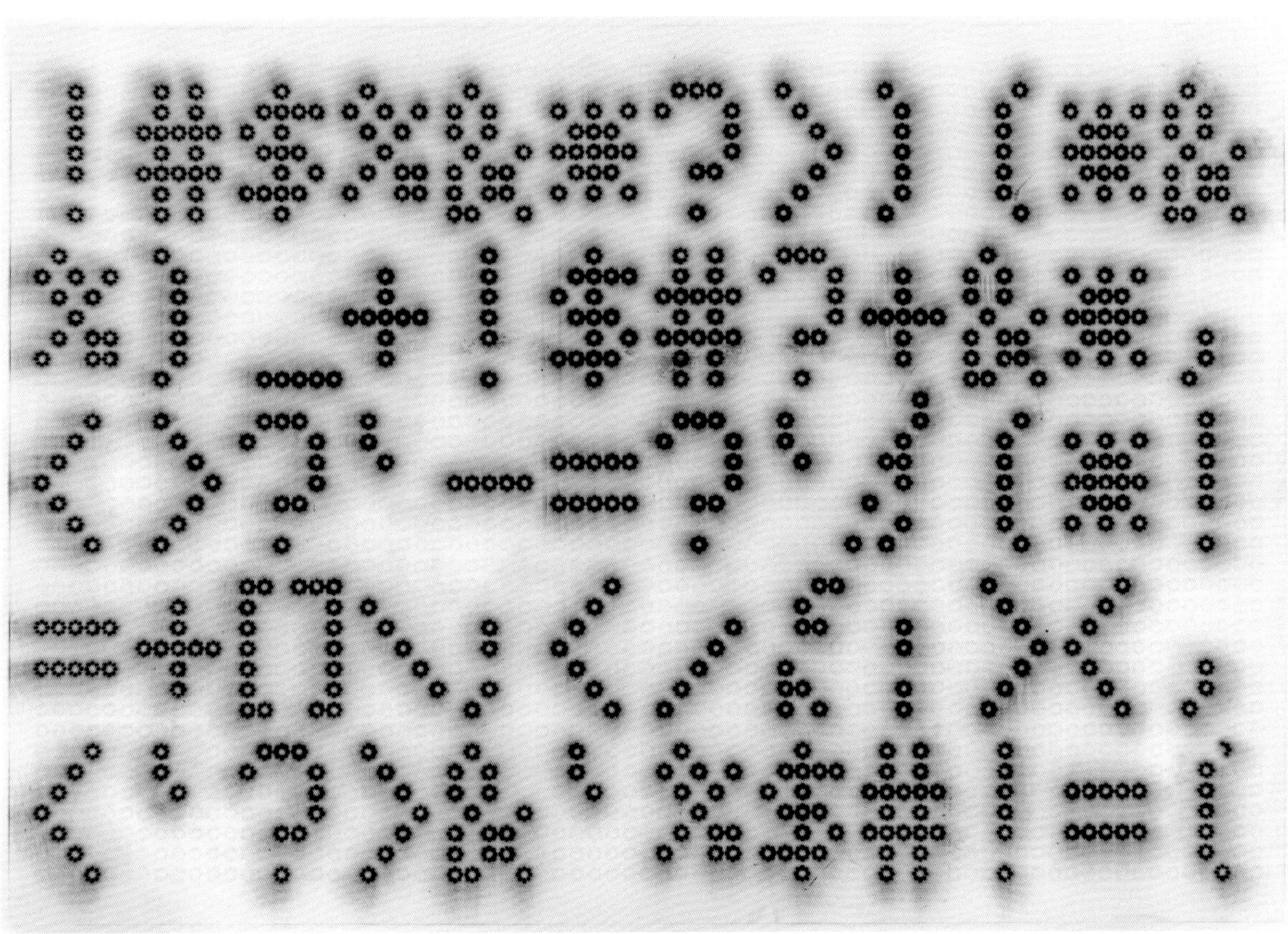

 Shannon Ebner, *Four*, from the series *The Electric Comma*, 2011–13. Epson print

250     Shannon Ebner, *The Electric Comma Poster*, 2013

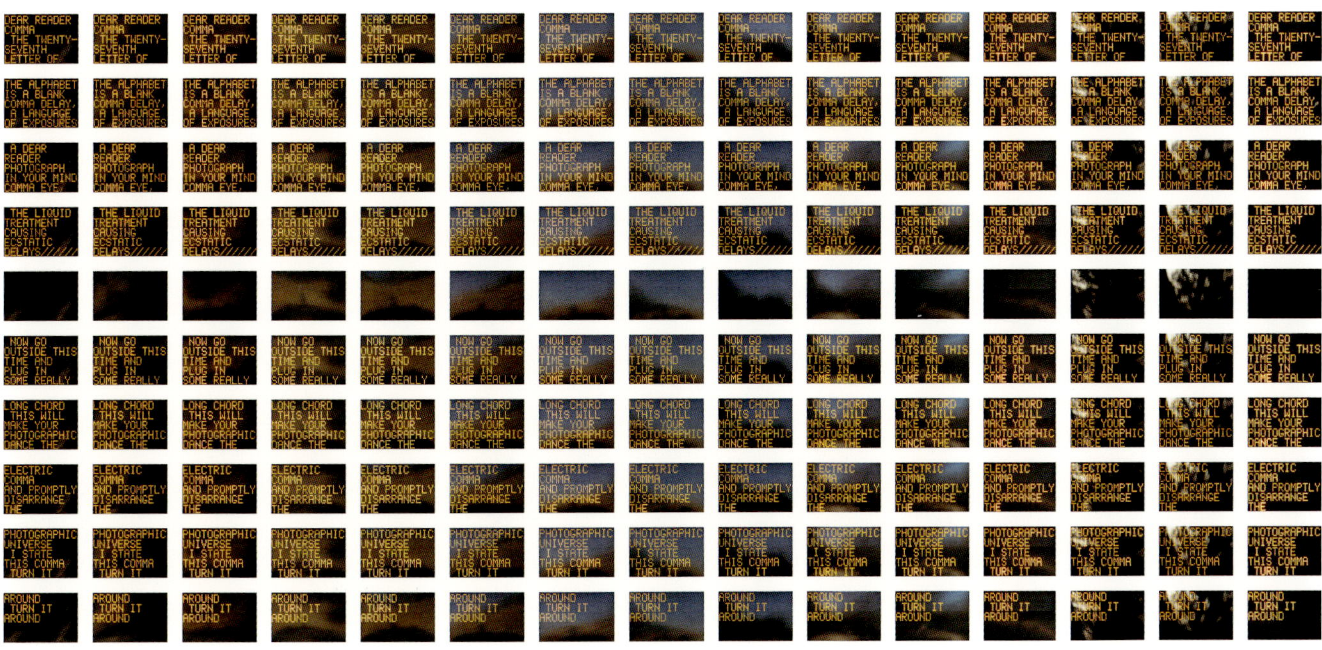

251    Shannon Ebner, stills from photographic animation for *Dear Reader,* from the series *The Electric Comma,* 2011–13

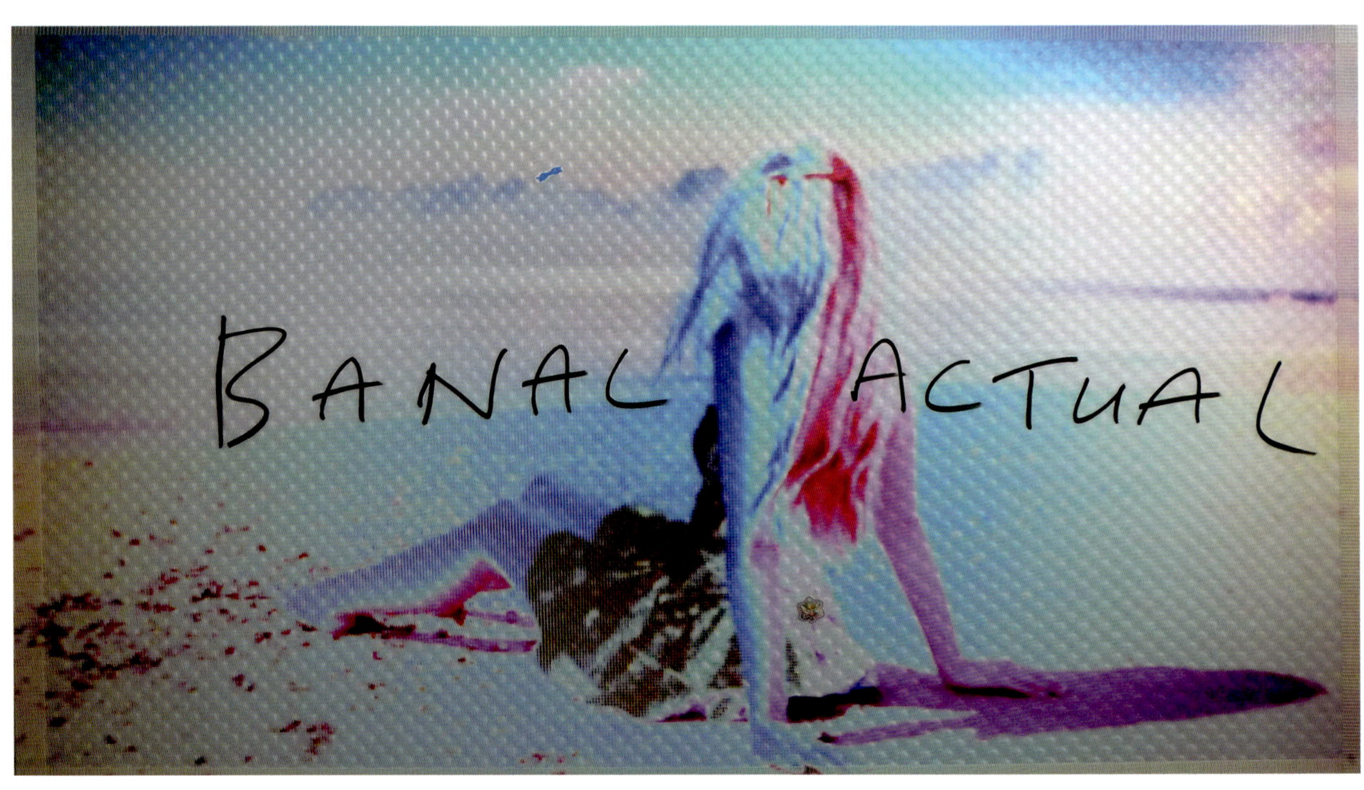


    Clunie Reid, *Banal Actual*, 2011. Digital print, mixed media

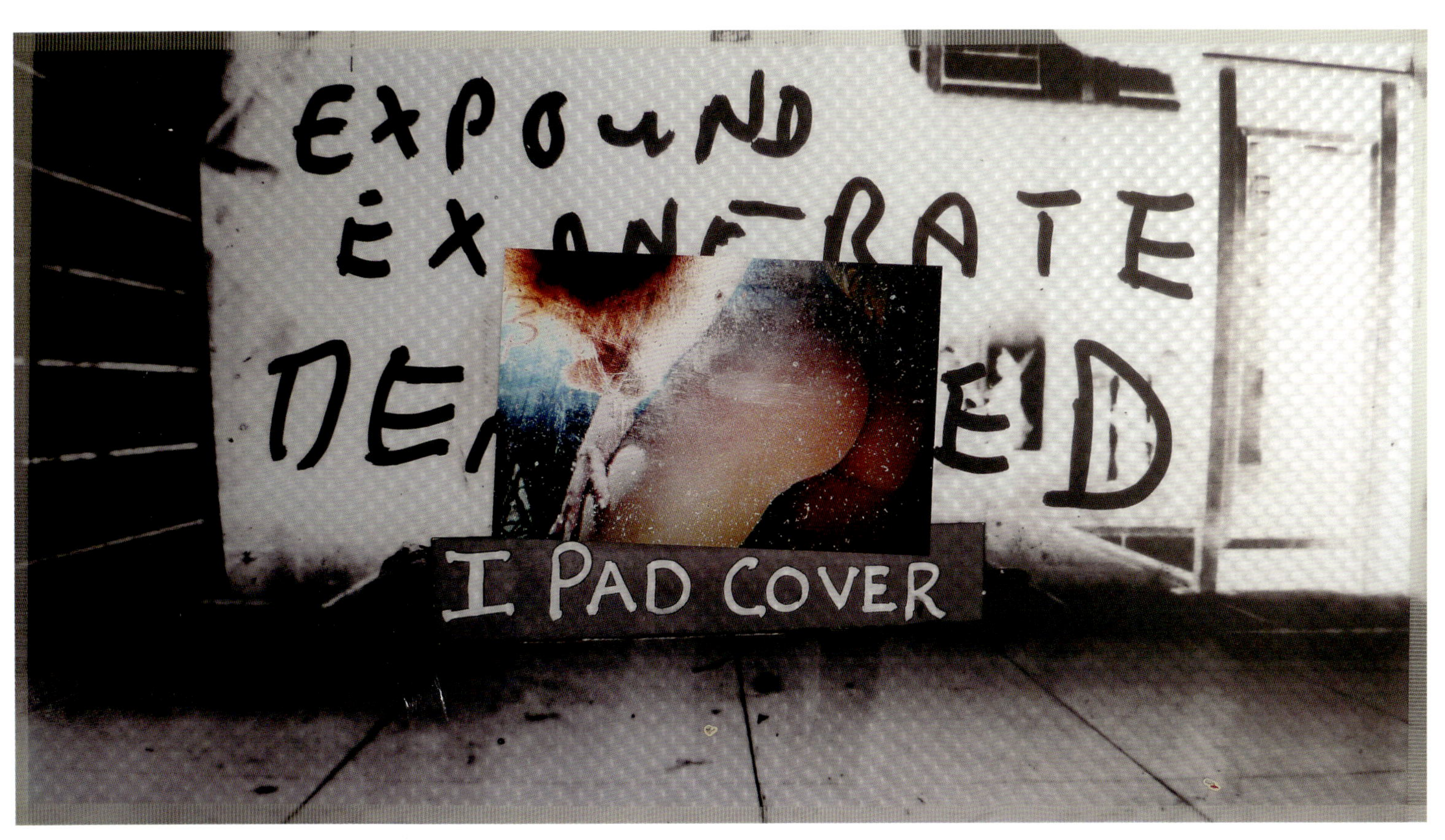


    Clunie Reid, *Cos What's Inside Him Never Dies* (detail), 2011. Digital print, mixed media

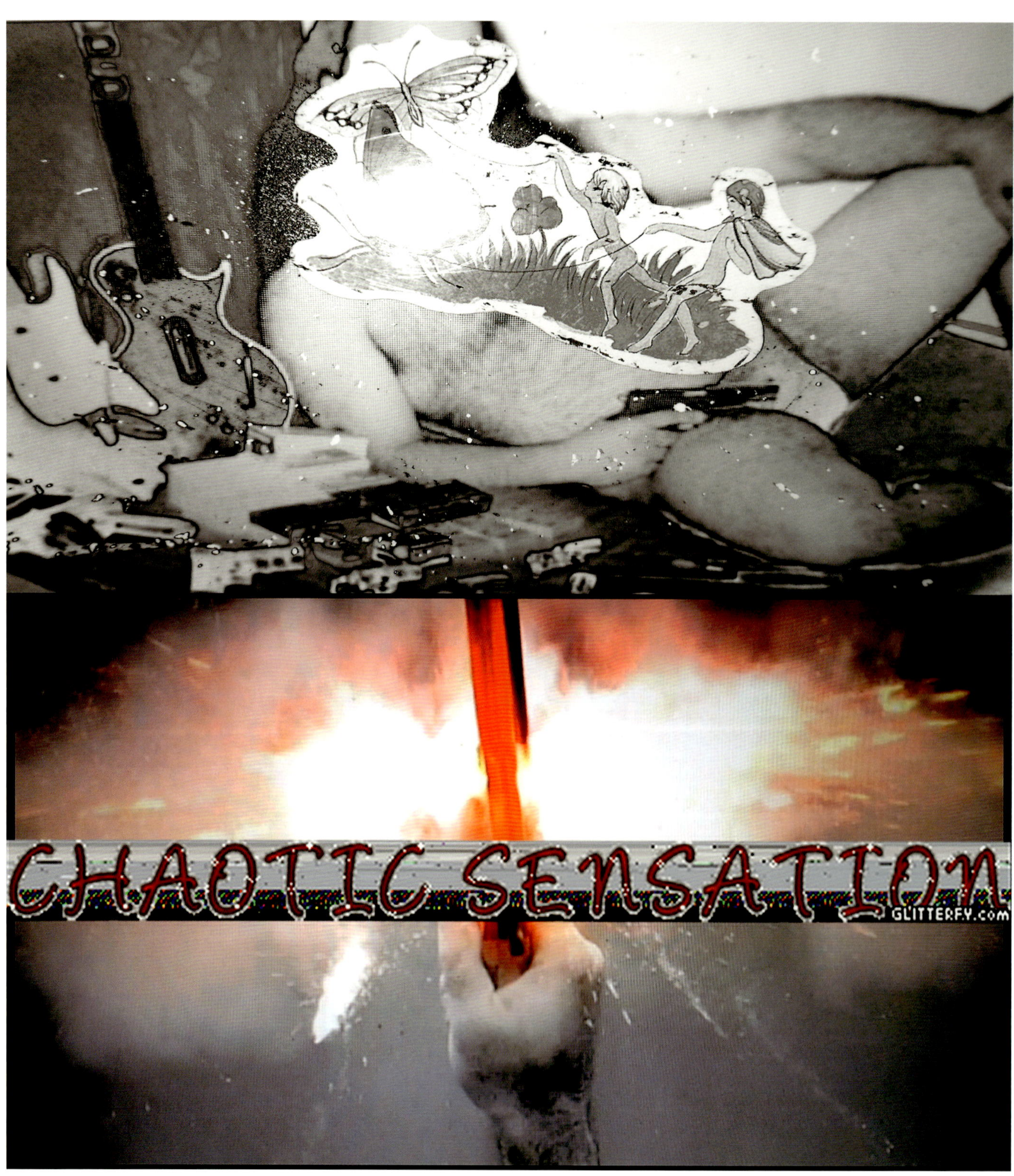


254    Clunie Reid, *Chaotic Sensation*, 2013. Digital image

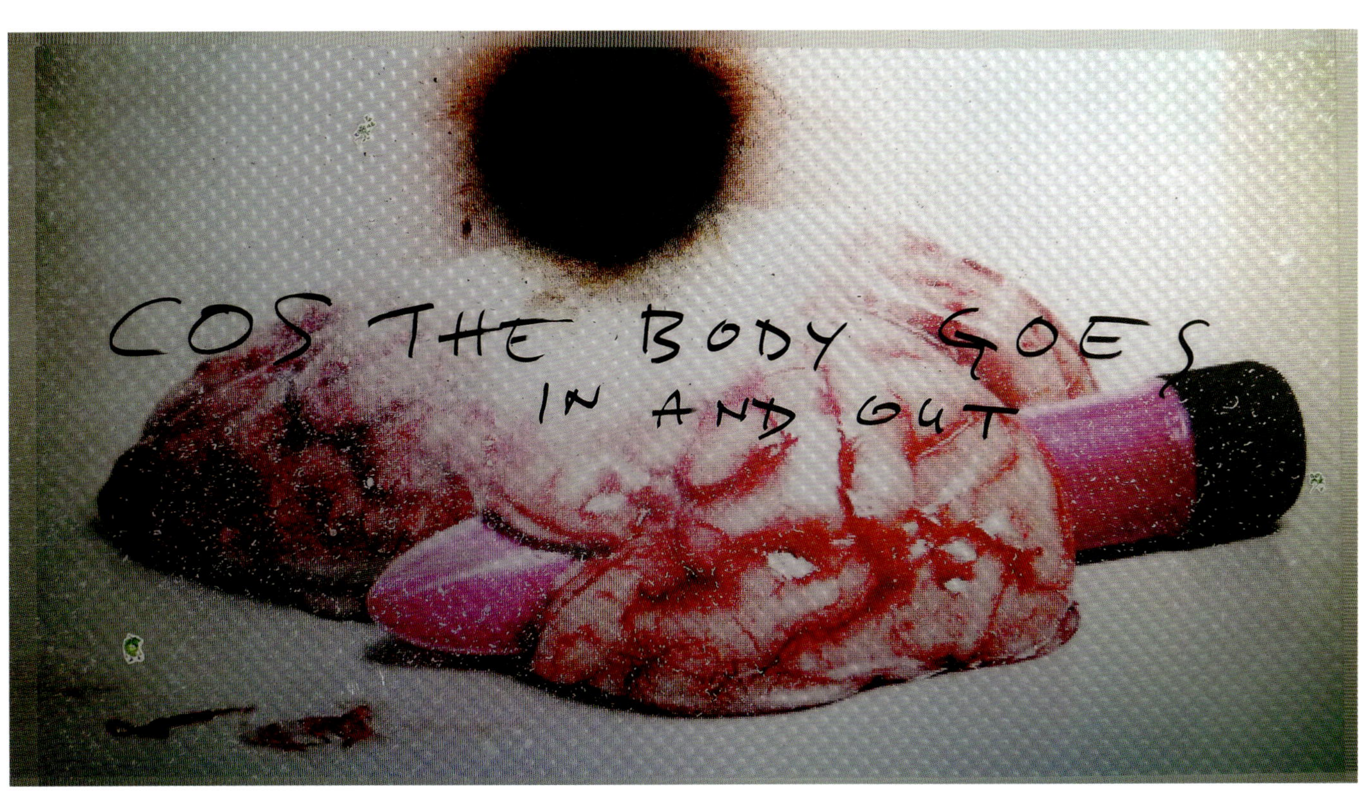



255    Clunie Reid, *Cos the Body Goes In and Out*, 2011. Digital print, mixed media

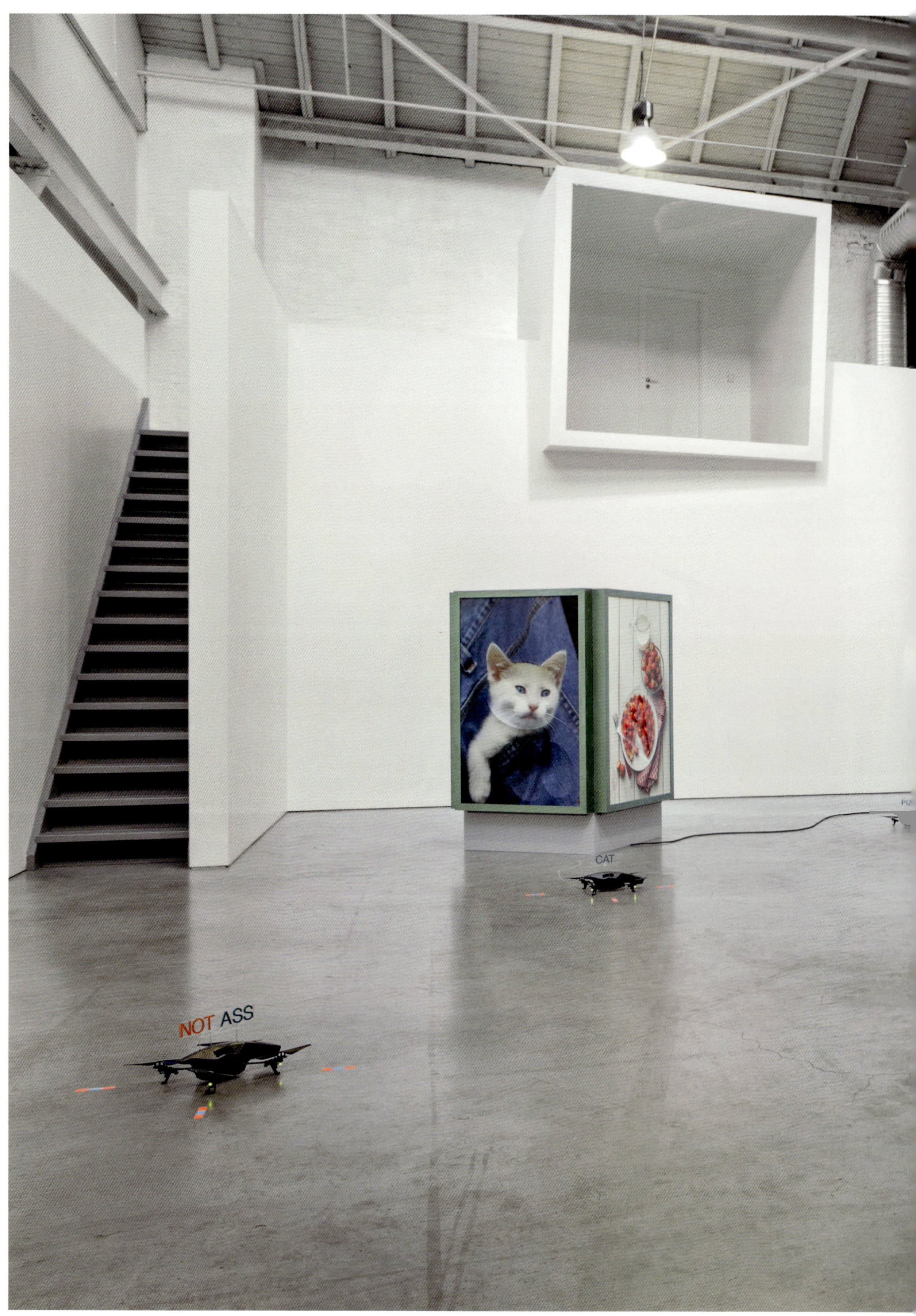


256    Antoine Catala, *Image Families*, 2013. Drones, acrylic letters, digitally printed latex, aluminum, wood (installation view)

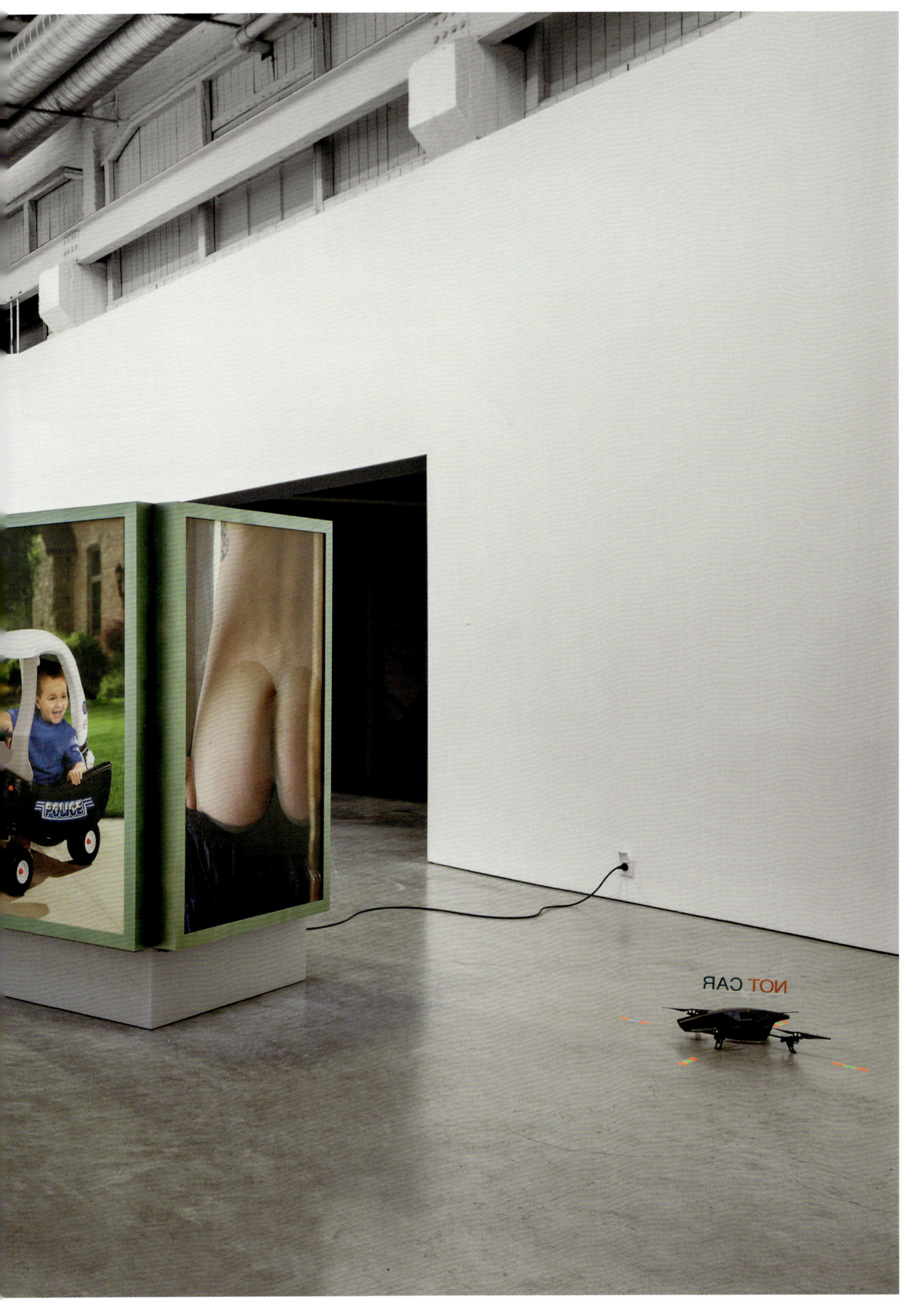
POLICE
NOT CAR

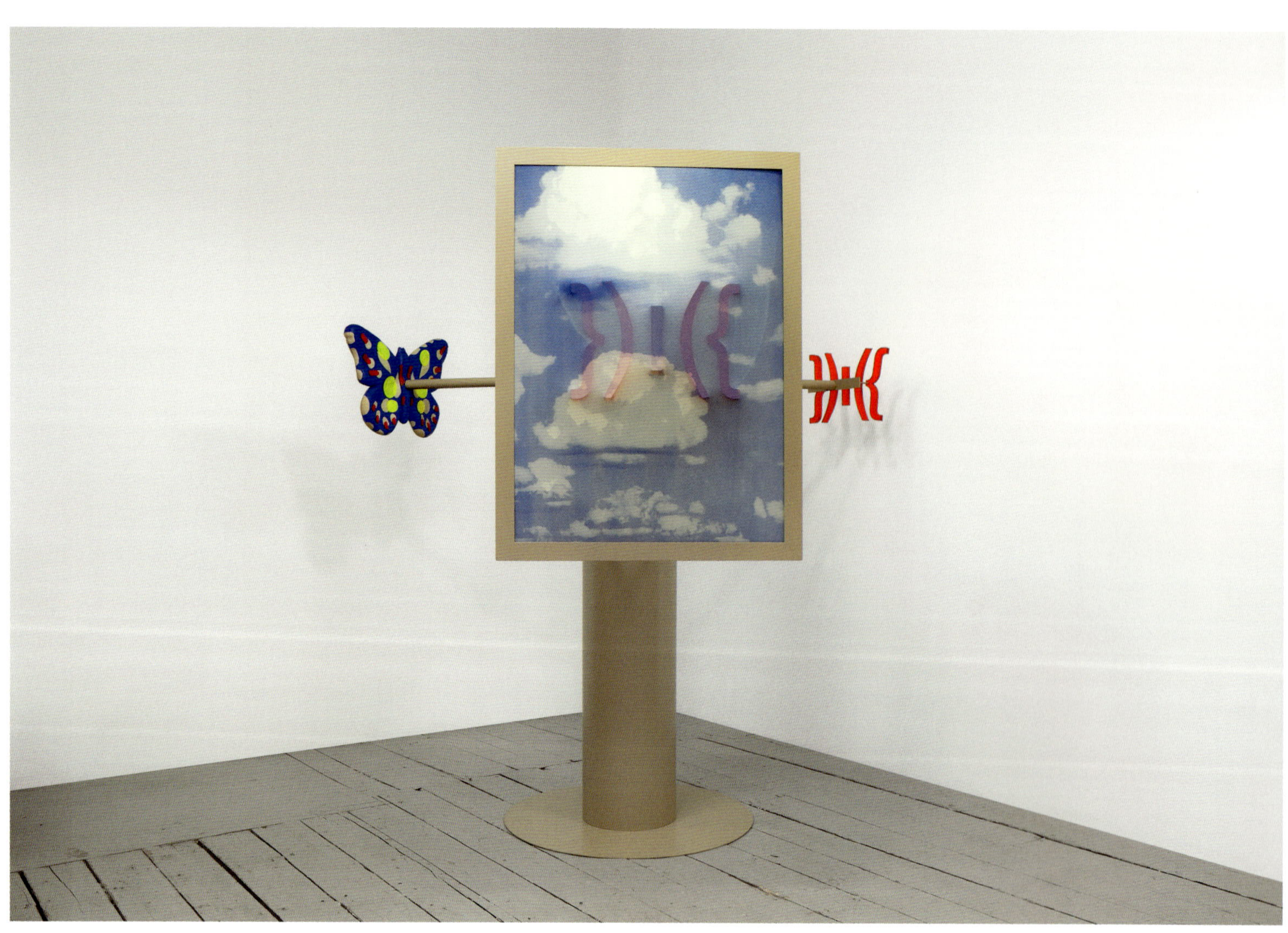

258    Antoine Catala, *Future Together Planet Earth*, 2013. Wood, pump, plastic tubing, powder-coated aluminum, digitally painted latex

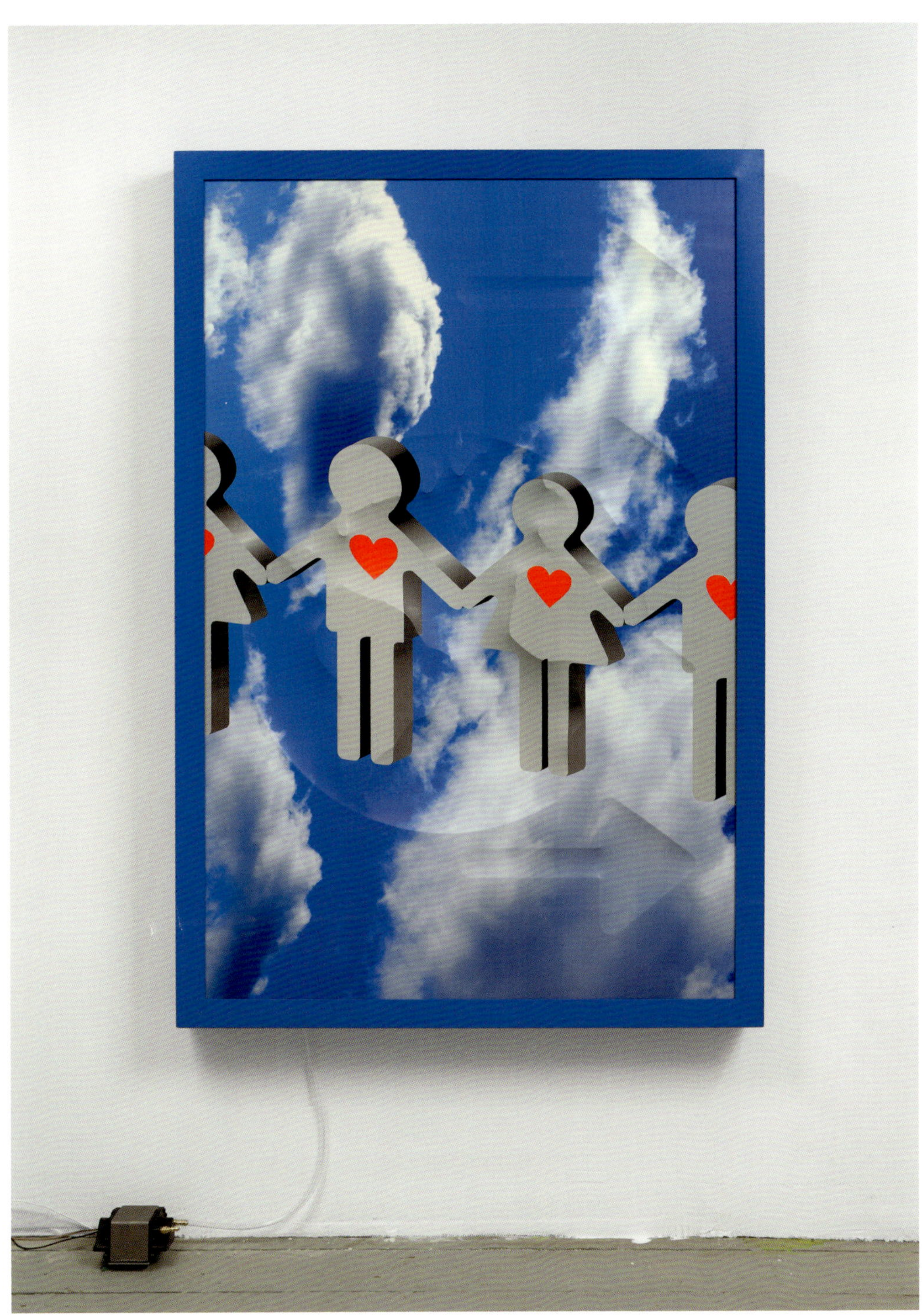

259    Antoine Catala, *ABRACADABRA*, 2013. Aluminum, latex, silicone rubber, electronics, mechanized arm

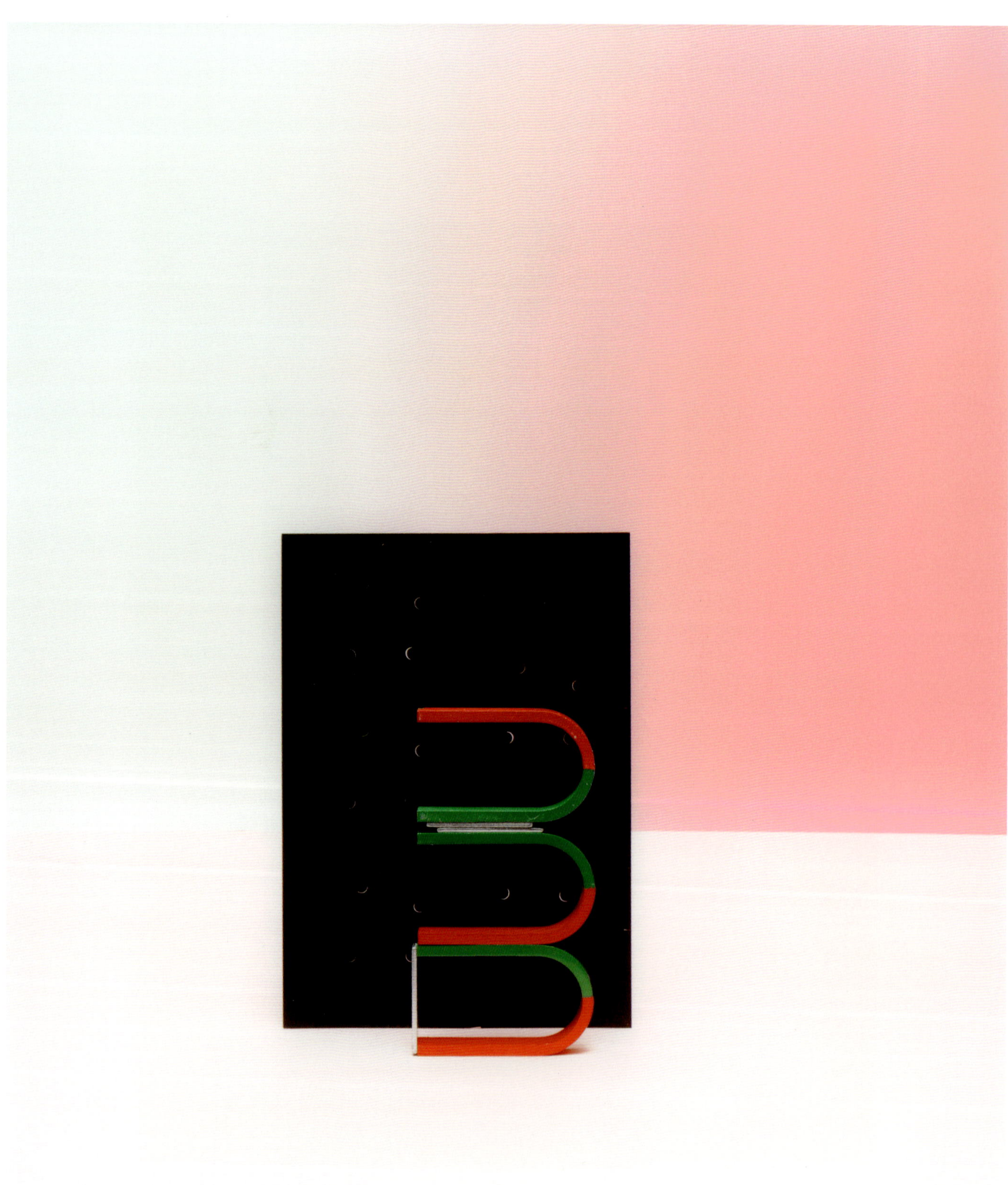

260    Annette Kelm, *Untitled*, 2012. C-print

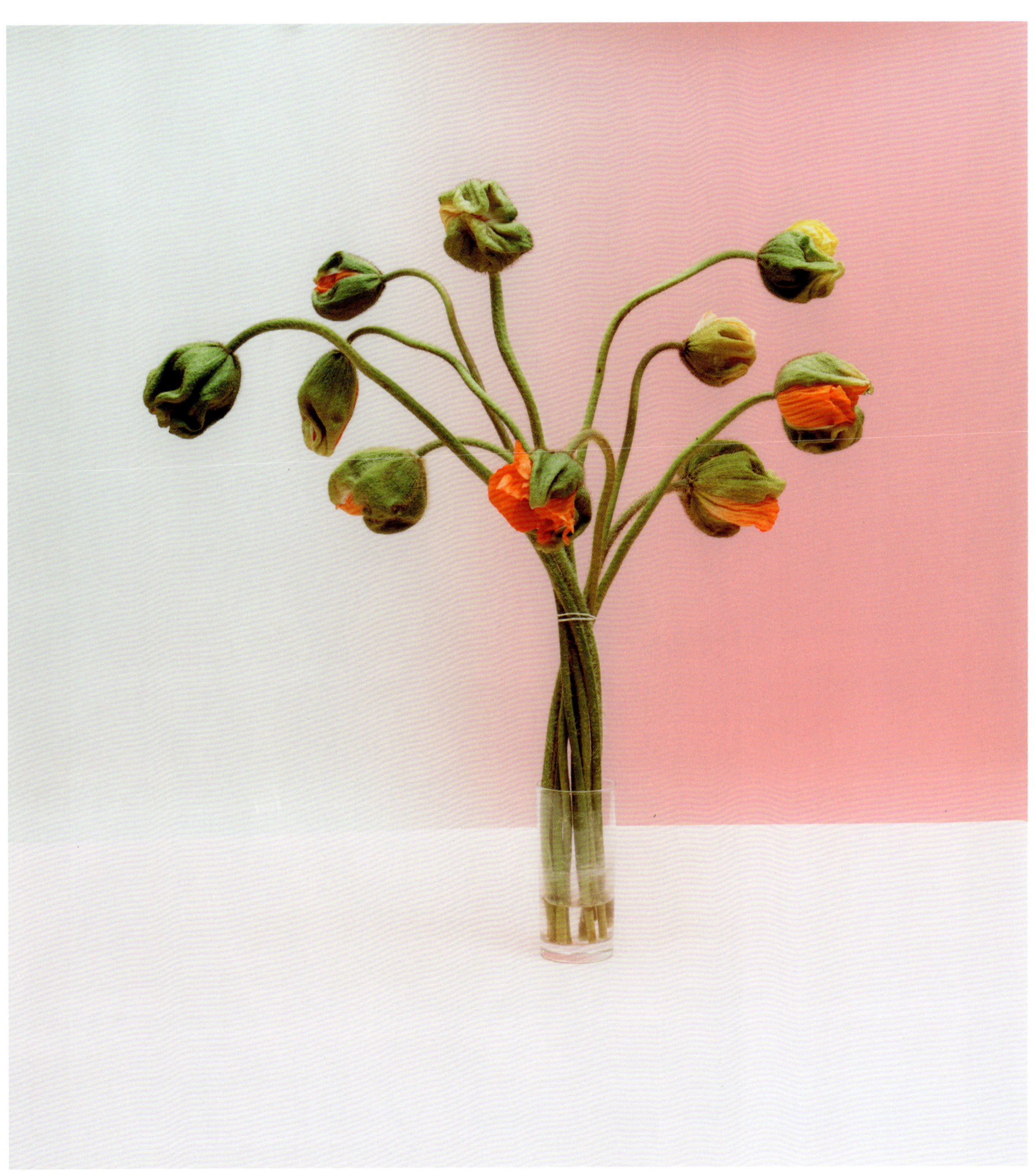

 Annette Kelm, *Untitled*, 2012. C-print

262    Annette Kelm, *Untitled*, 2010. C-print

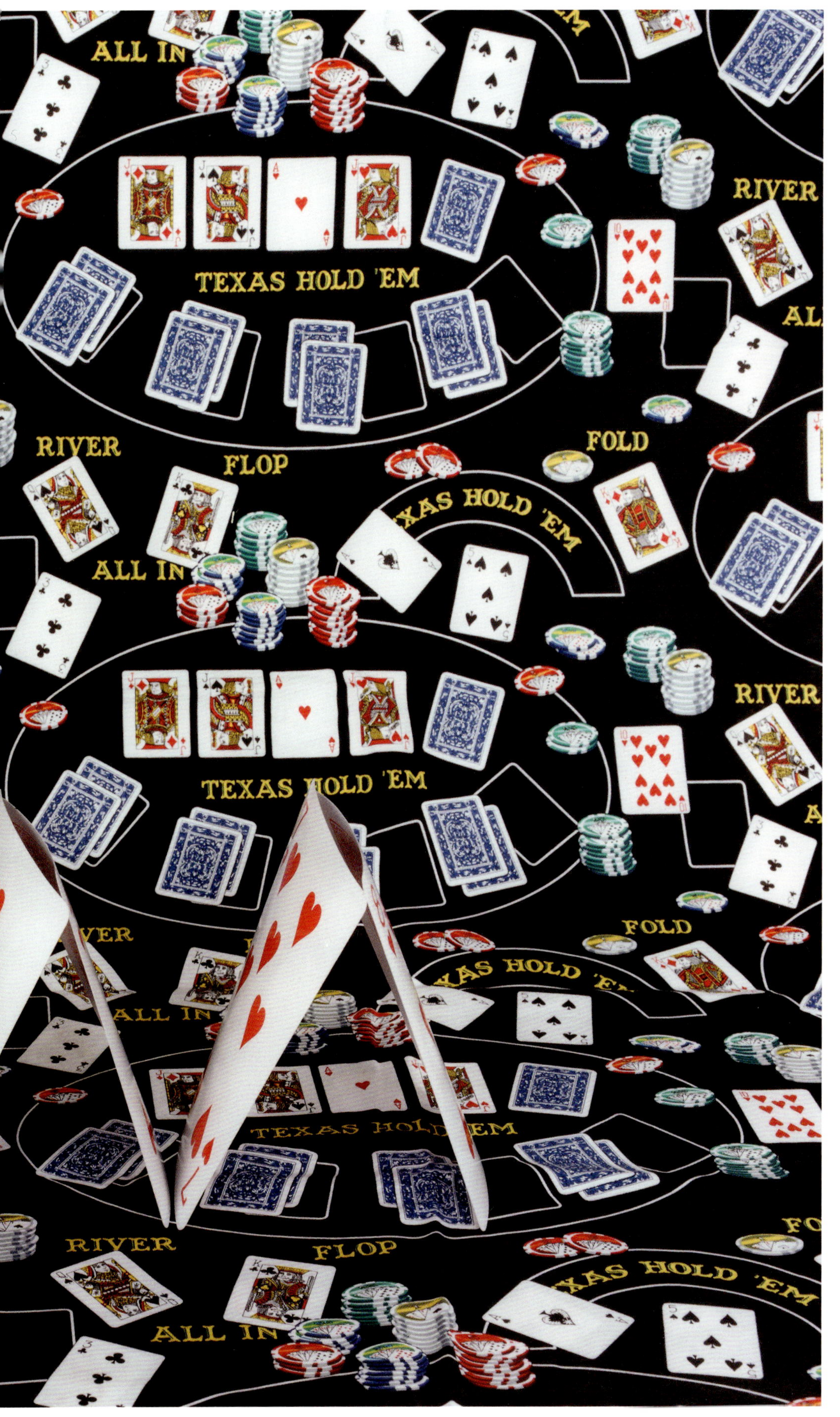

ALL IN
TEXAS HOLD 'EM
RIVER
FOLD
RIVER
FLOP
ALL IN
TEXAS HOLD 'EM
TEXAS HOLD 'EM
RIVER
FOLD
TEXAS HOLD 'EM
ALL IN
TEXAS HOLD 'EM
RIVER
FLOP
TEXAS HOLD 'EM
ALL IN

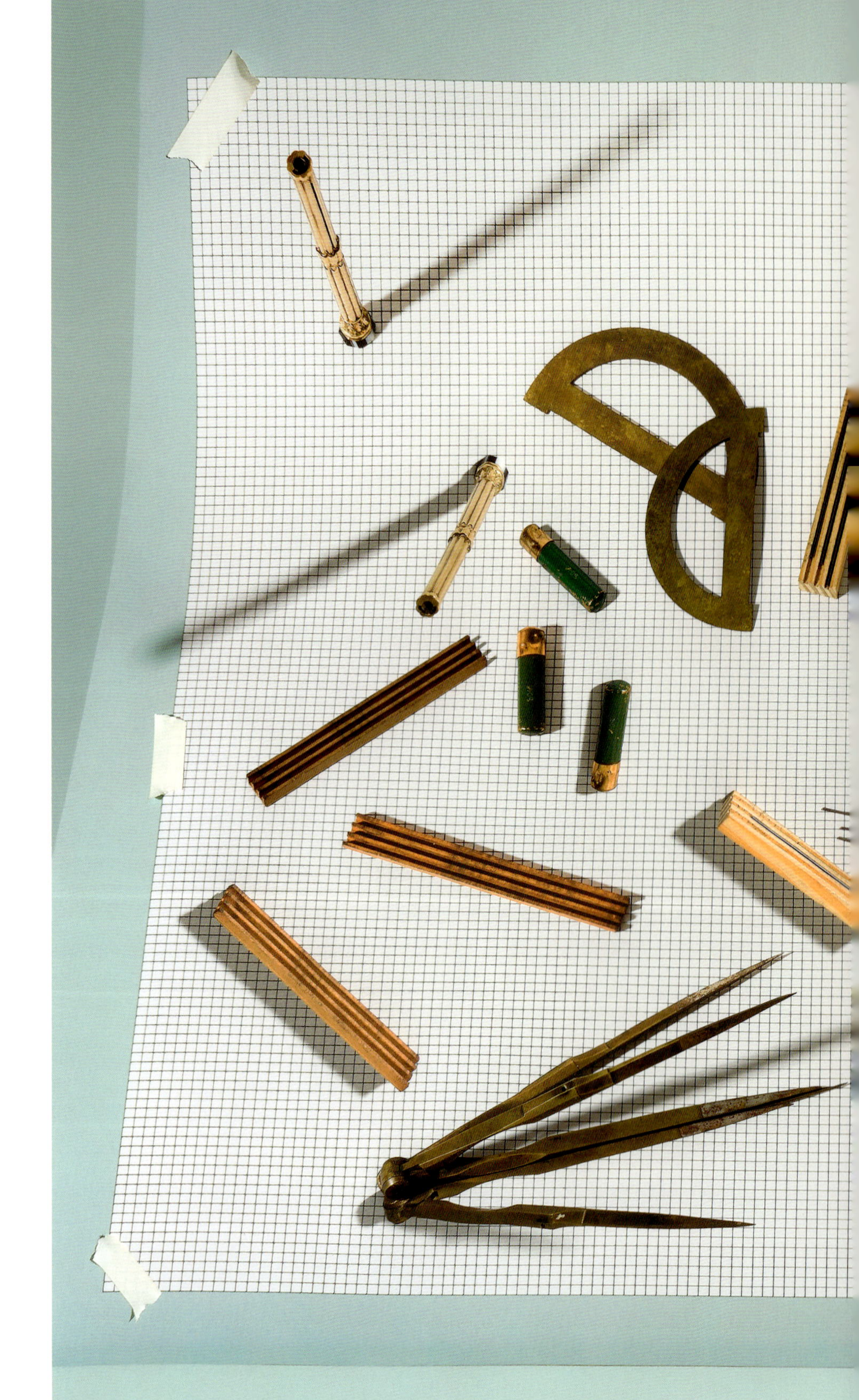

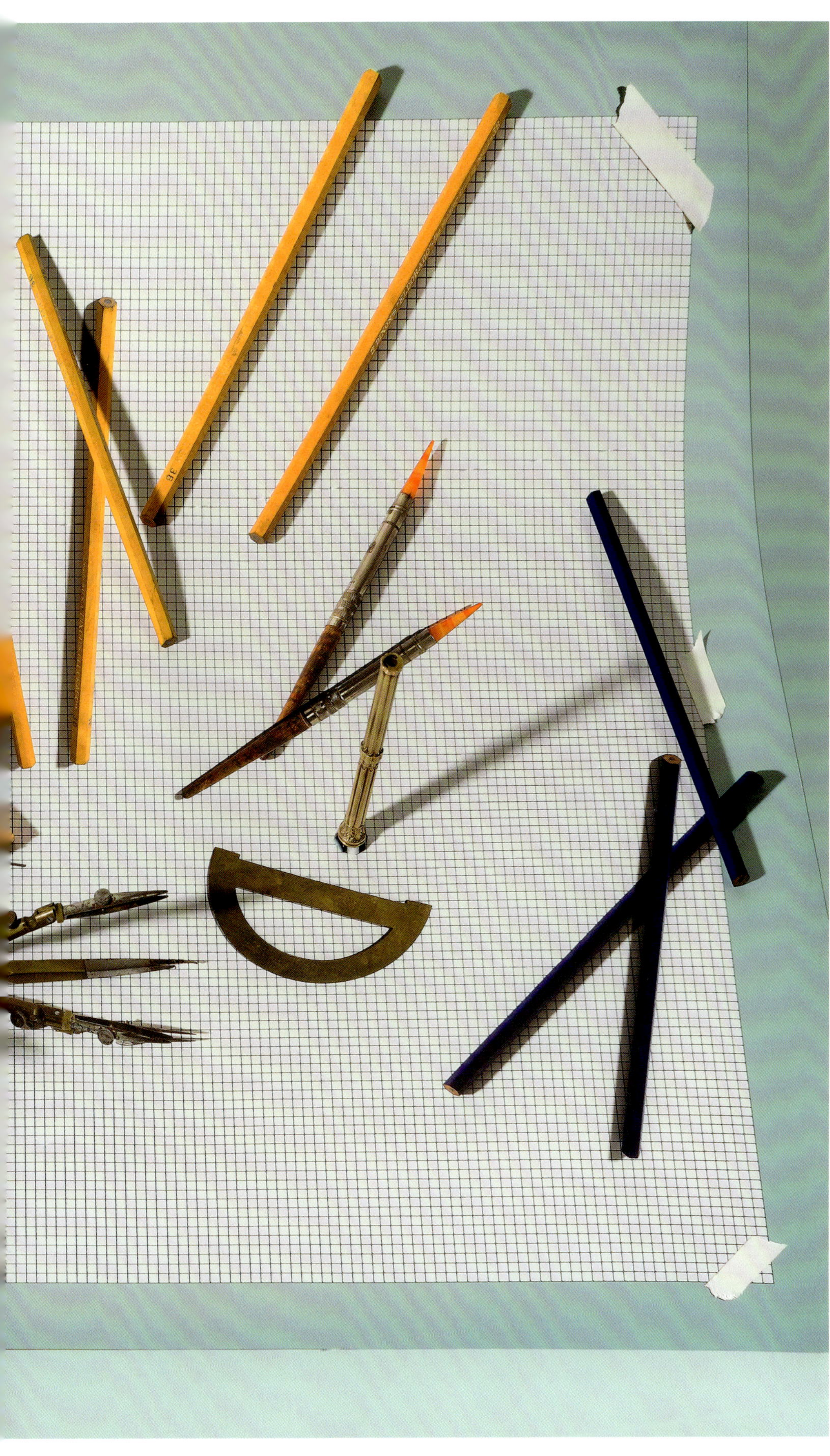

265    John Houck, *Peg and John*, from the series *A History of Graph Paper*, 2013. Archival pigment print

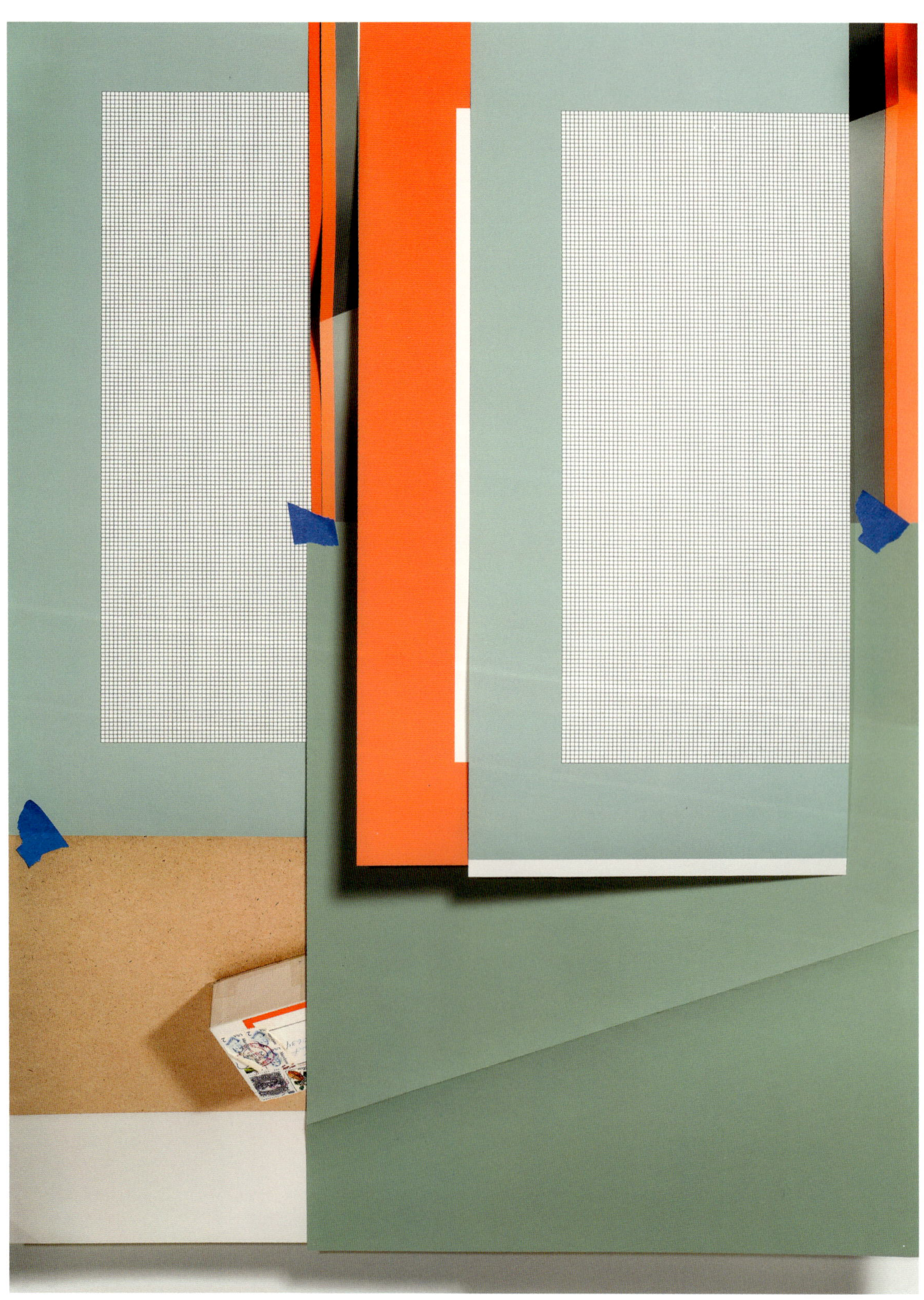

266    John Houck, *Pointing Device*, from the series *A History of Graph Paper*, 2013. Archival pigment print

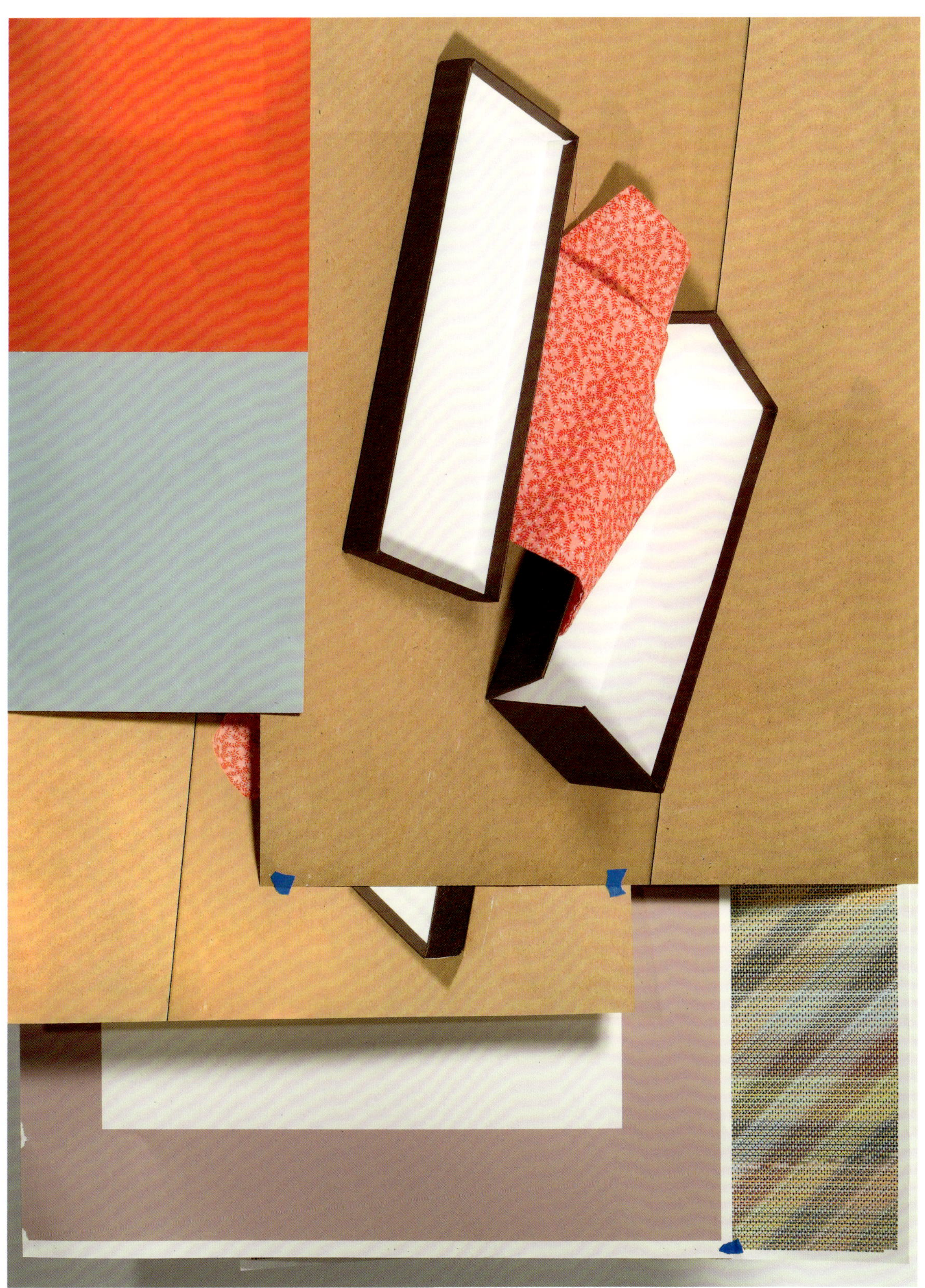

267    John Houck, *A Science of Mountains*, from the series *A History of Graph Paper*, 2013. Archival pigment print

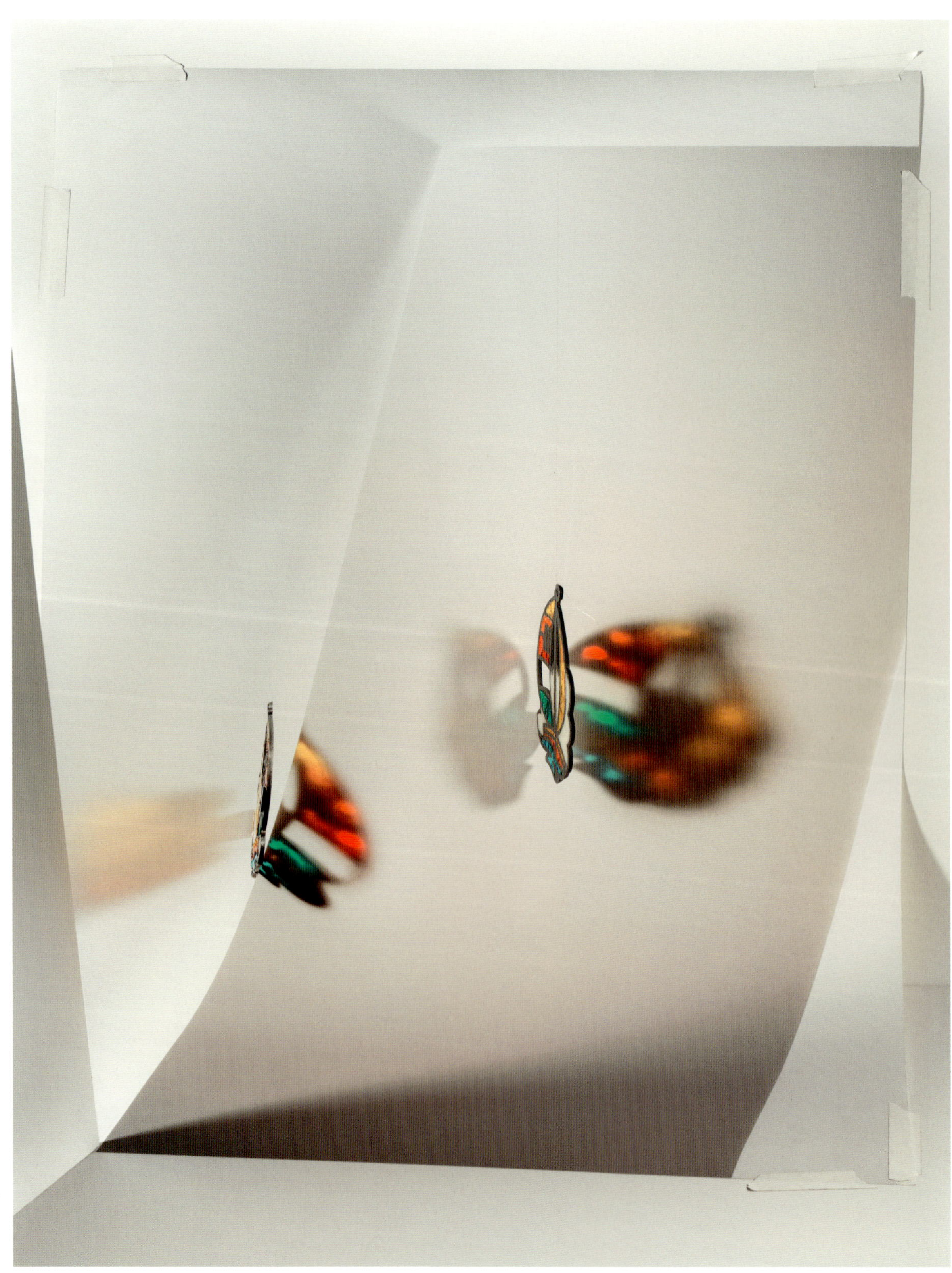

268    John Houck, *Sunups*, from the series *A History of Graph Paper*, 2013. Archival pigment print

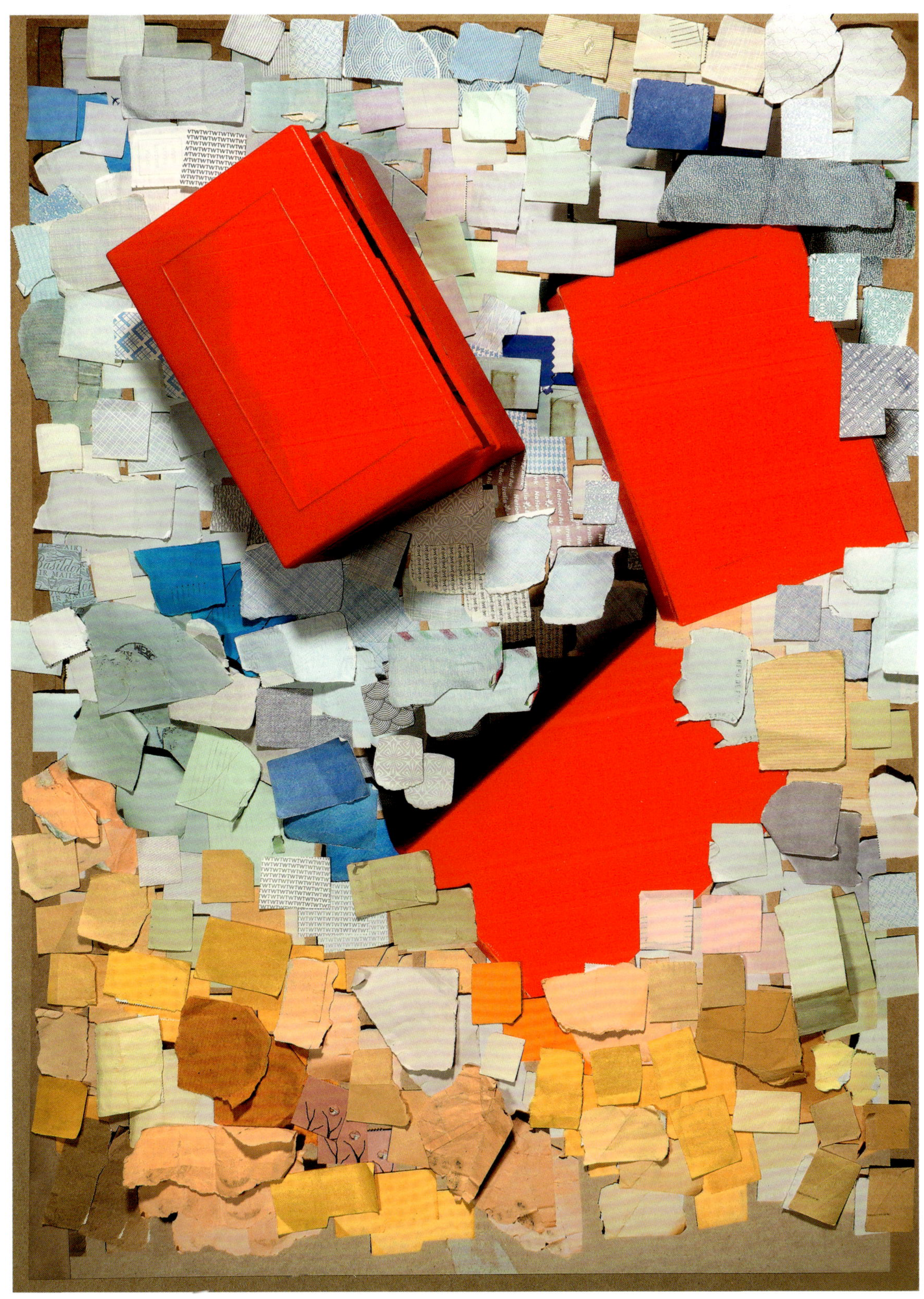

269    John Houck, *Stamp-X, Stamp-Y*, from the series *A History of Graph Paper*, 2013. Archival pigment print

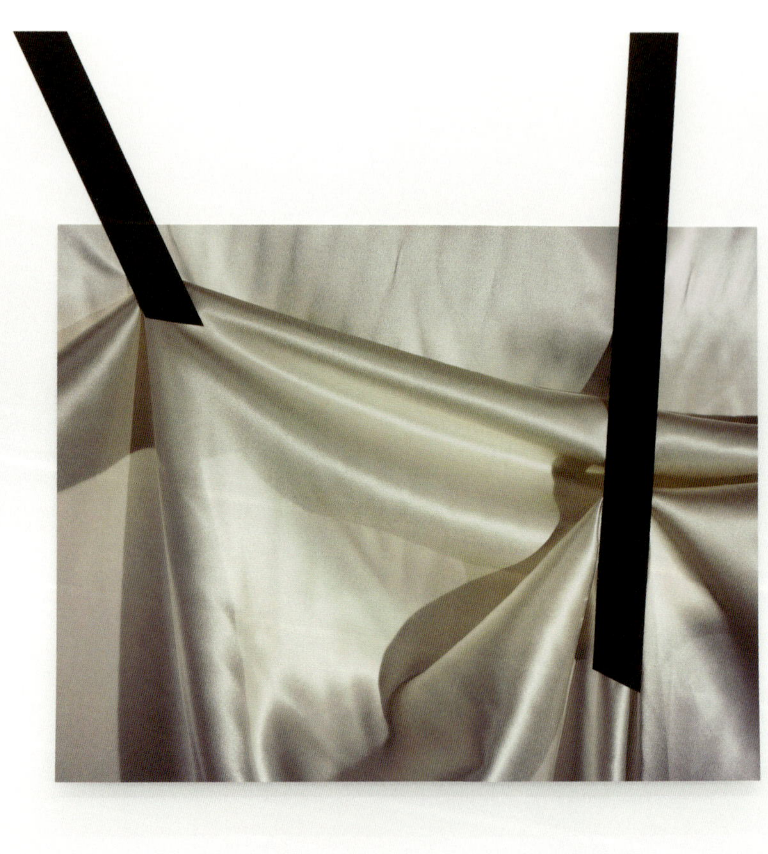

270    Elisa Sighicelli, *Untitled (silk)*, 2014. Gaffer tape and pigment print on archival paper with UV seal

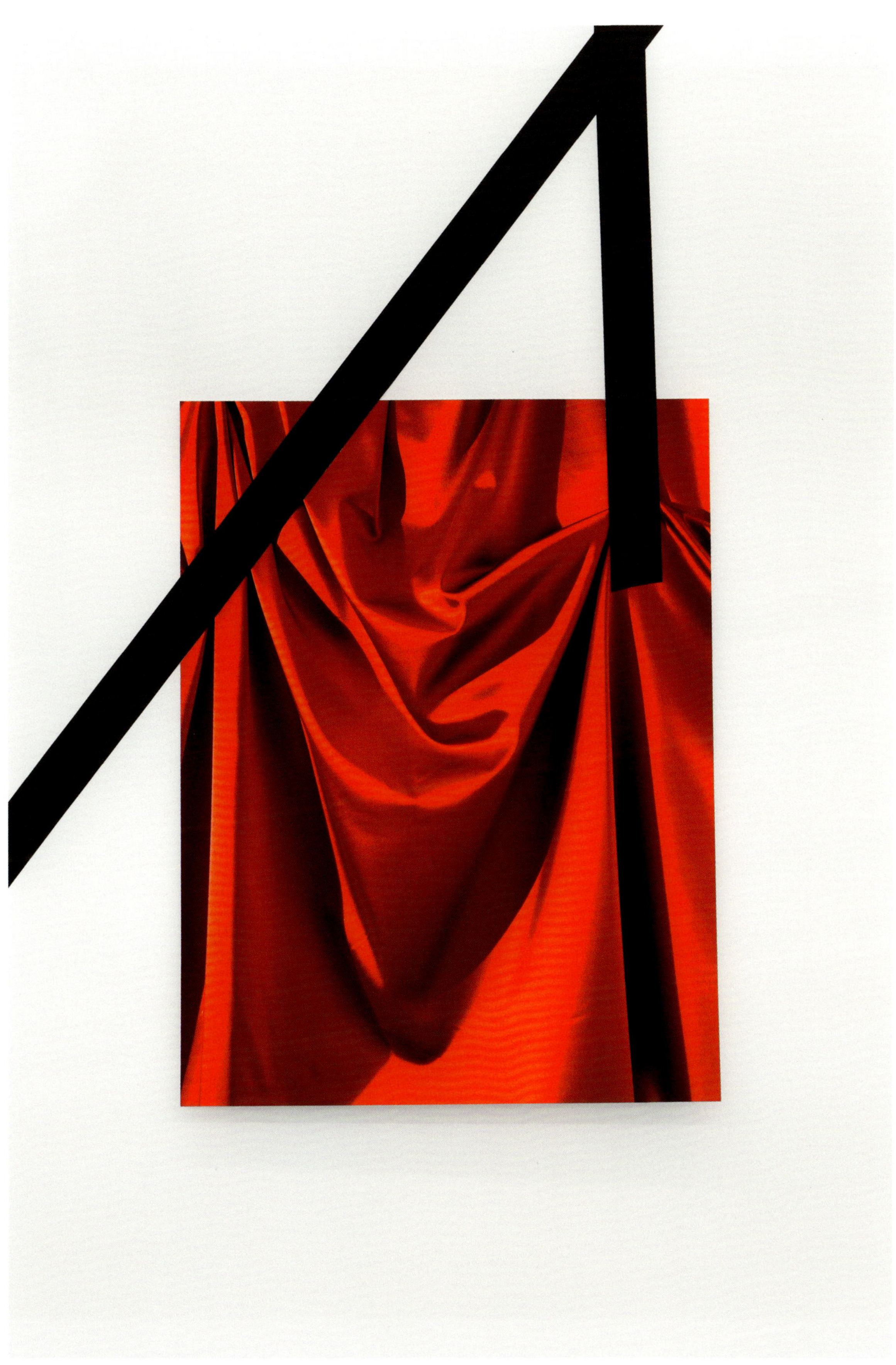

271    Elisa Sighicelli, *Untitled (1577)*, 2014. Gaffer tape and pigment print on archival paper with UV seal

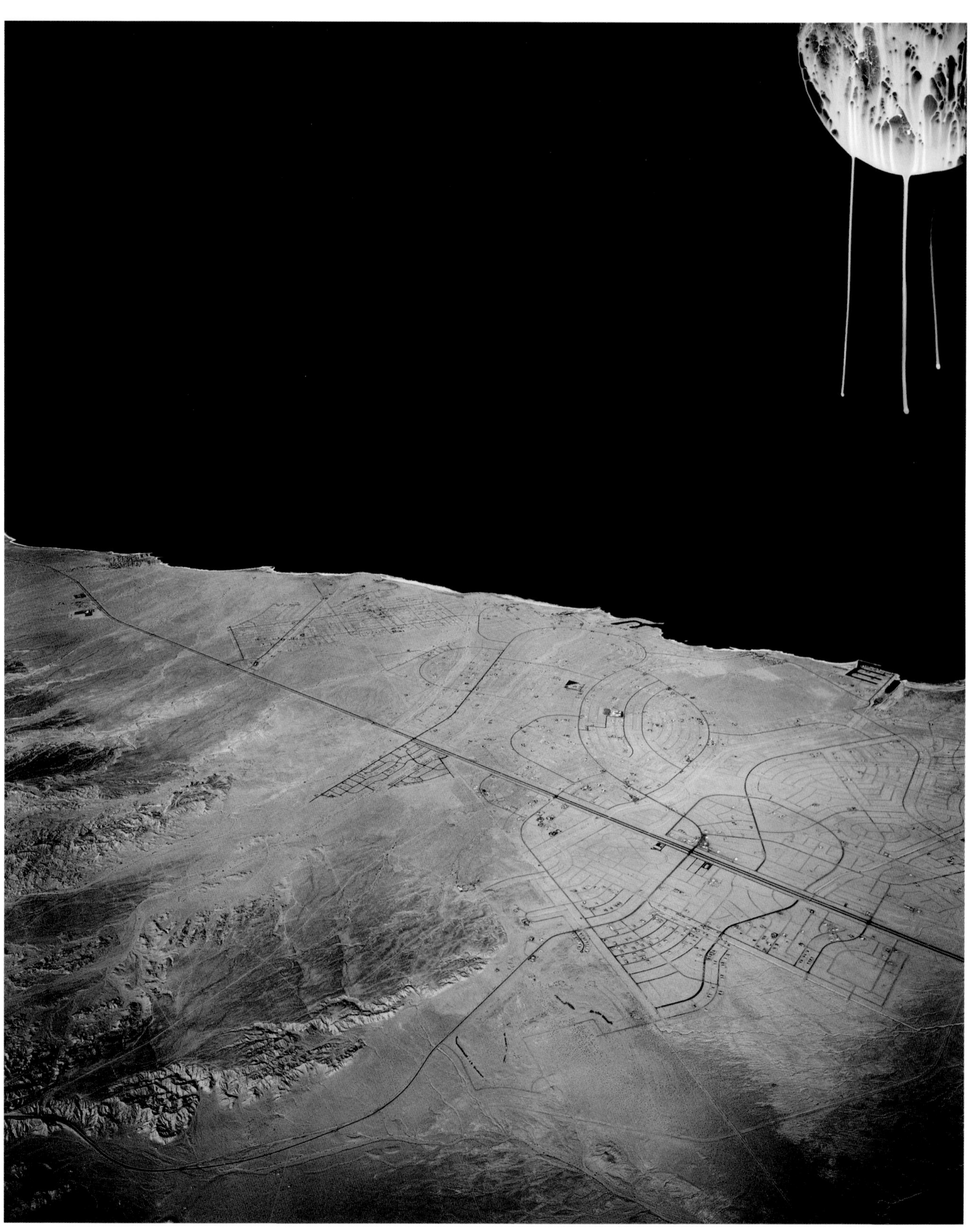

272    Florian Maier-Aichen, *Halbes Bild* (Half picture), 2014. Gelatin-silver print

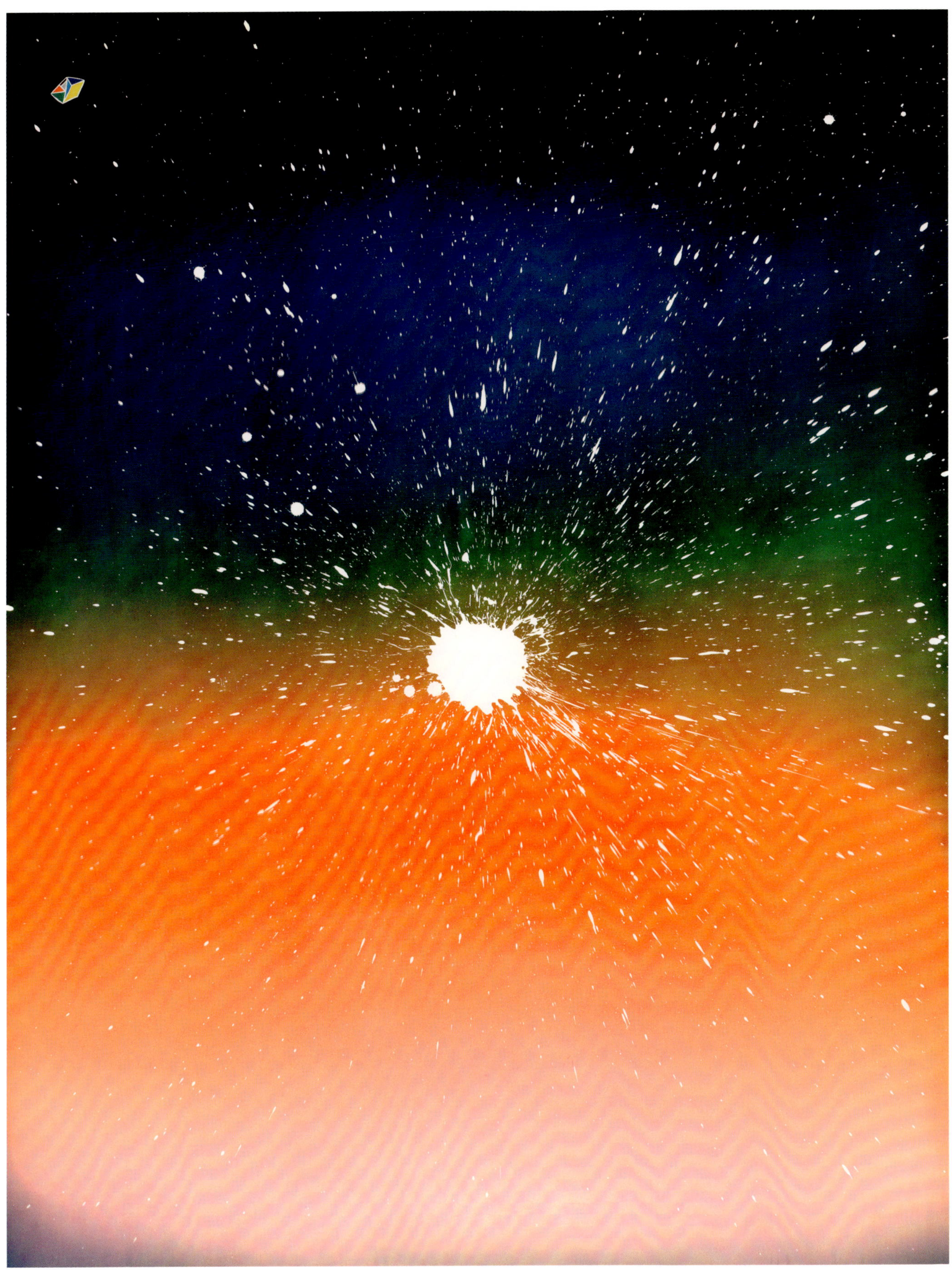

273    Florian Maier-Aichen, *Untitled*, 2013. C-print

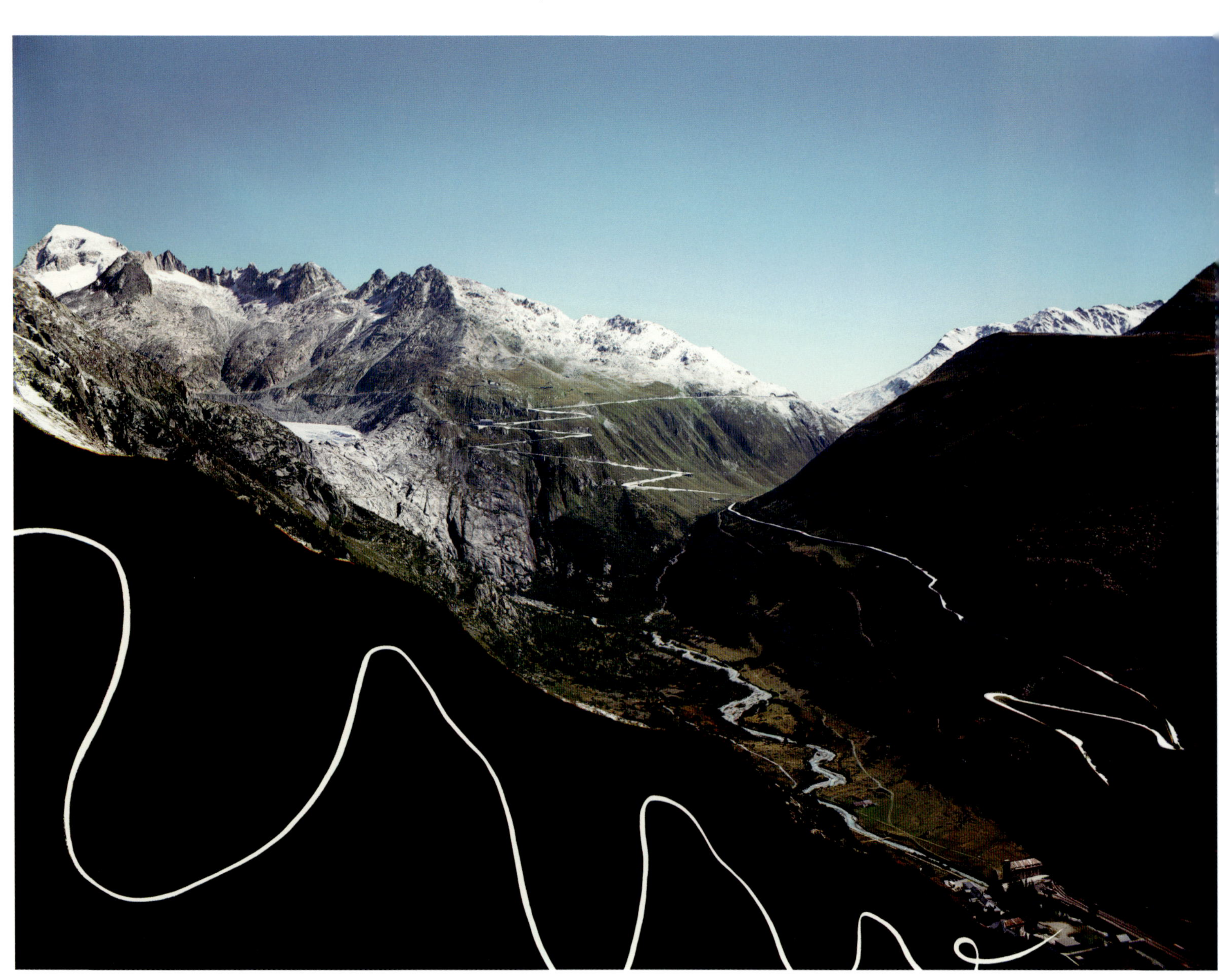

274 Florian Maier-Aichen, *Untitled*, 2013. C-print

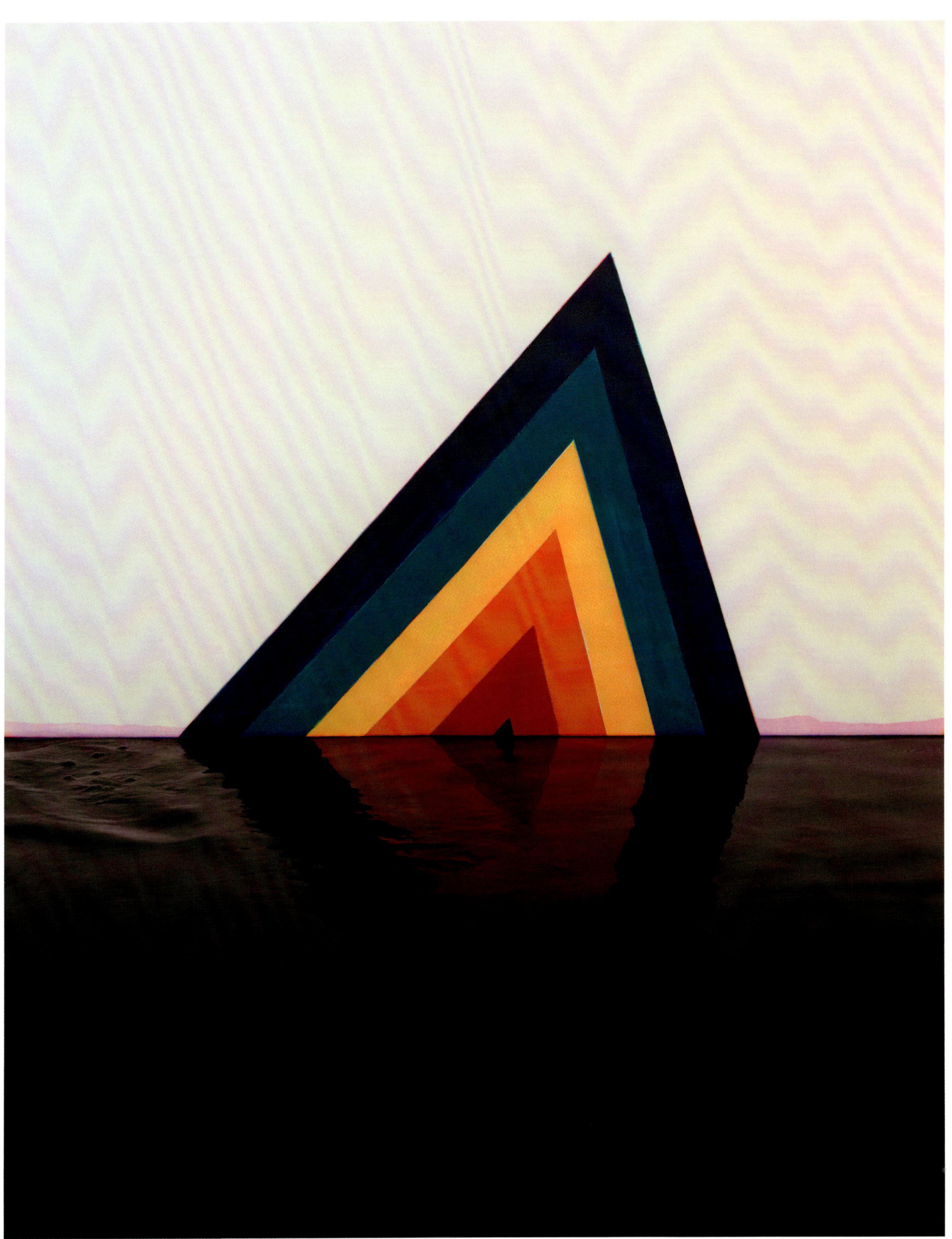

275   Florian Maier-Aichen, *Östersjön I* (Sea I), 2011. C-print

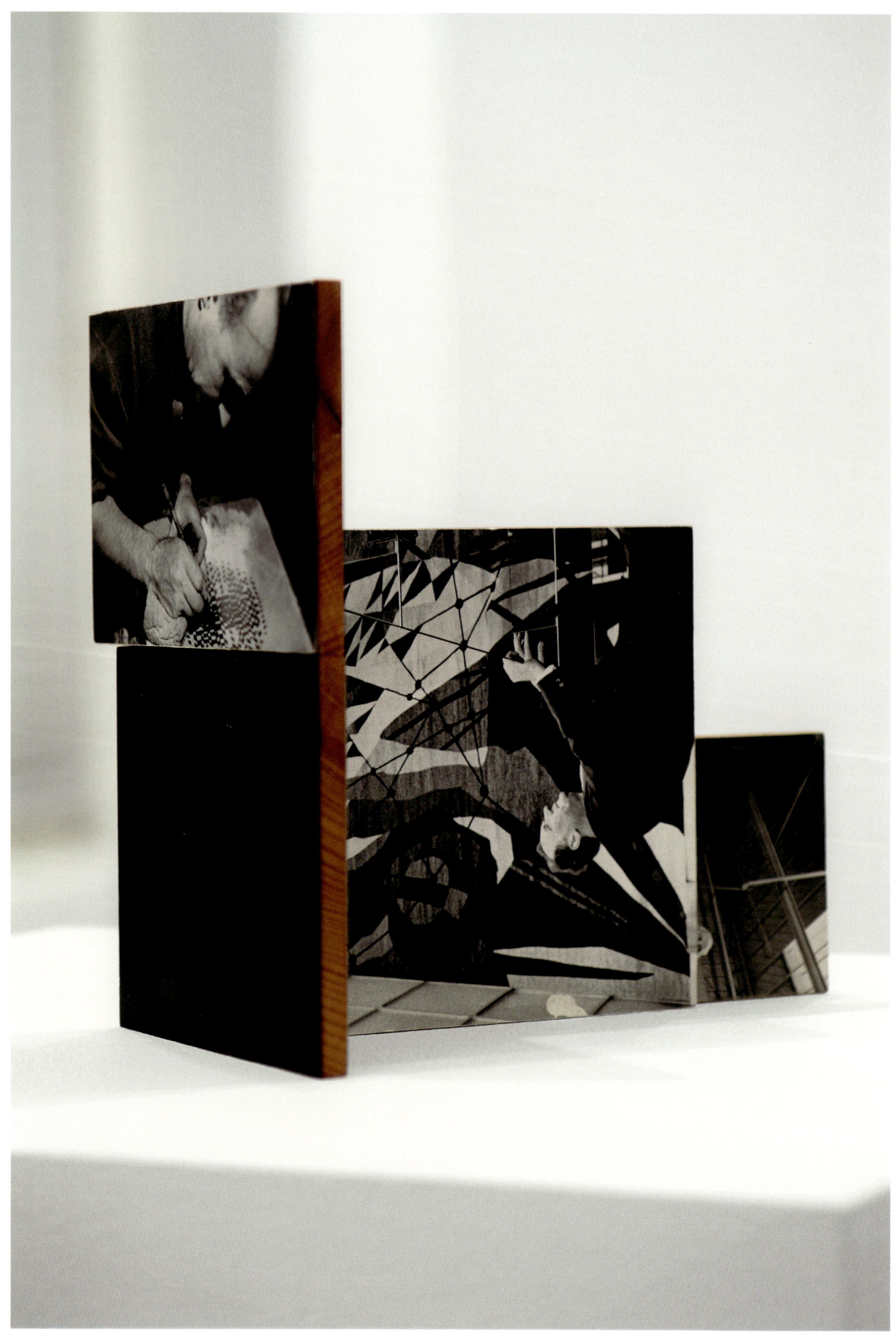

276    Will Rogan, *Mediums 4*, 2010. Paper, wood, beeswax

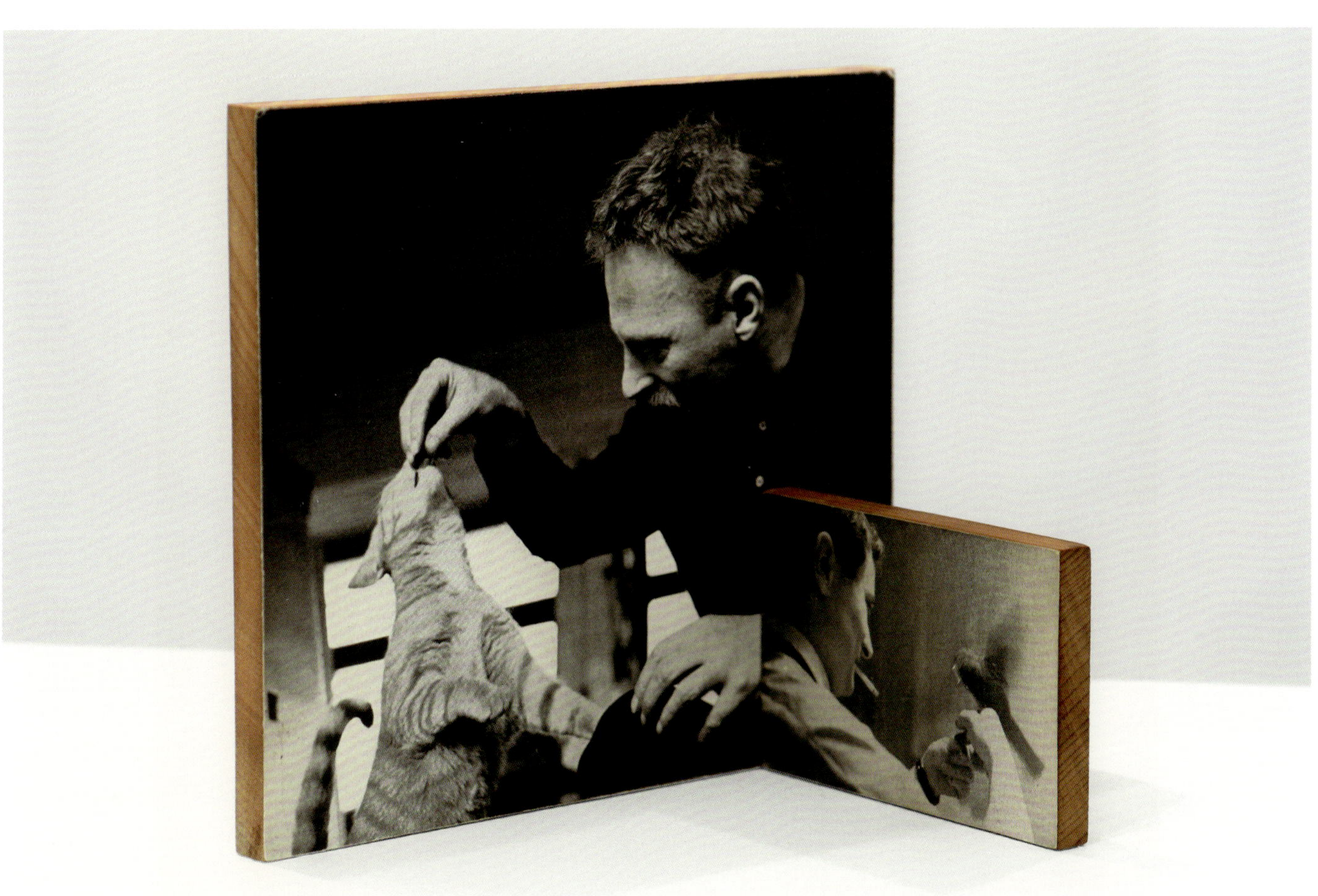

277     Will Rogan, *Mediums 2*, 2010. Paper, wood, beeswax

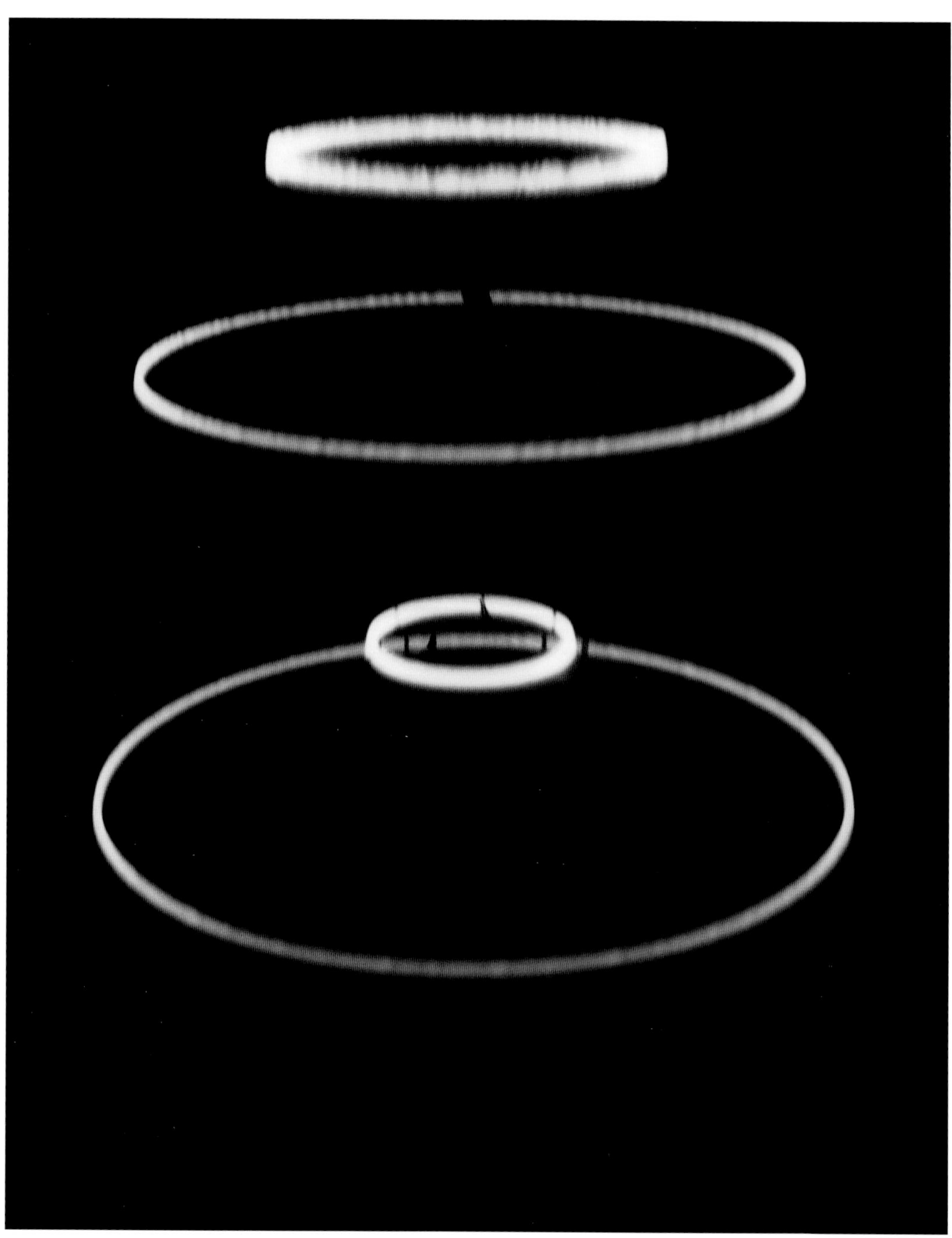

278    Taiyo Onorato and Nico Krebs, *Edition Variation*, from the project *Light of Other Days*, 2009. Direct positive gelatin-silver print

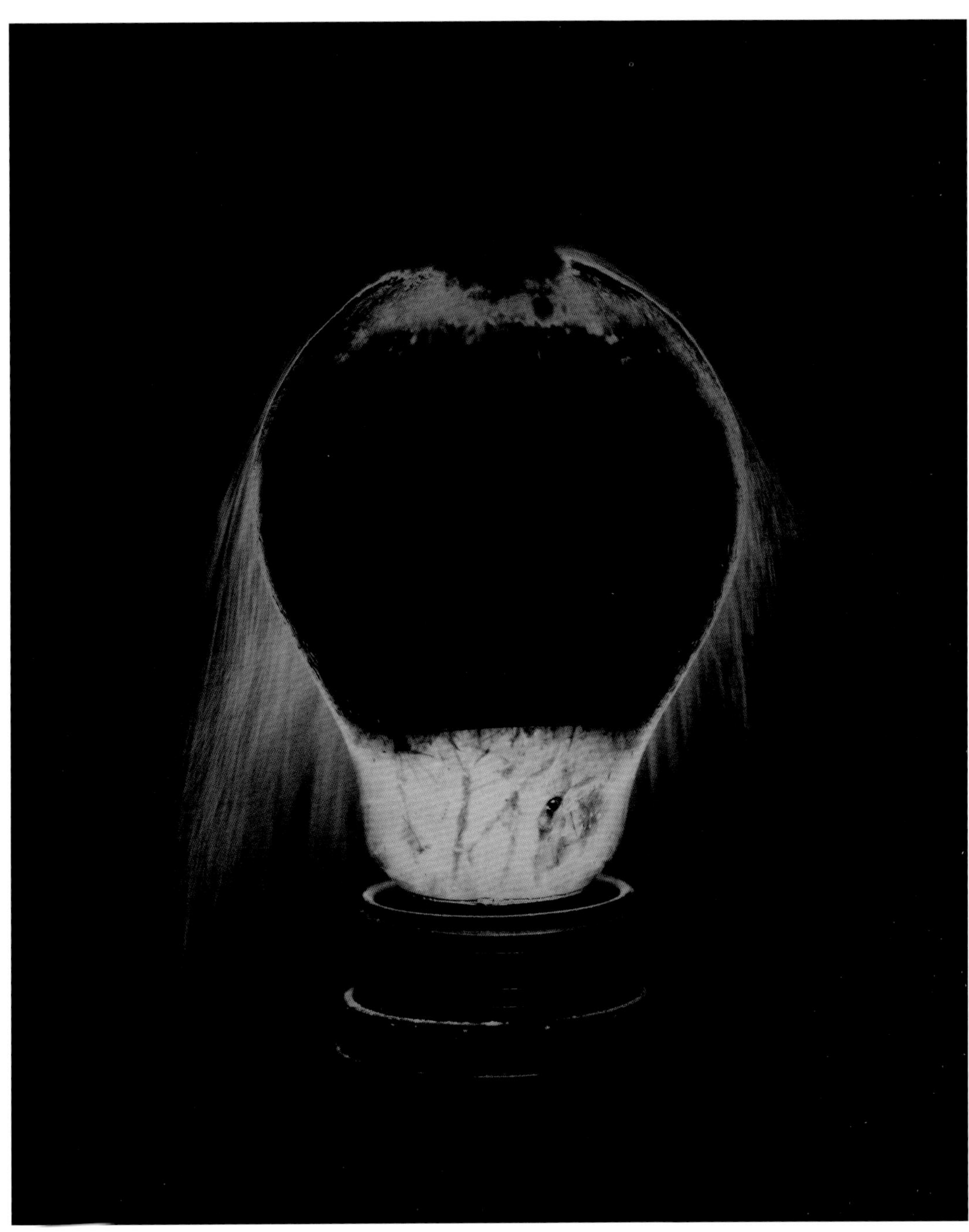

279    Taiyo Onorato and Nico Krebs, *Black Bulb 3*, from the project *Light of Other Days*, 2009. Direct positive gelatin-silver print

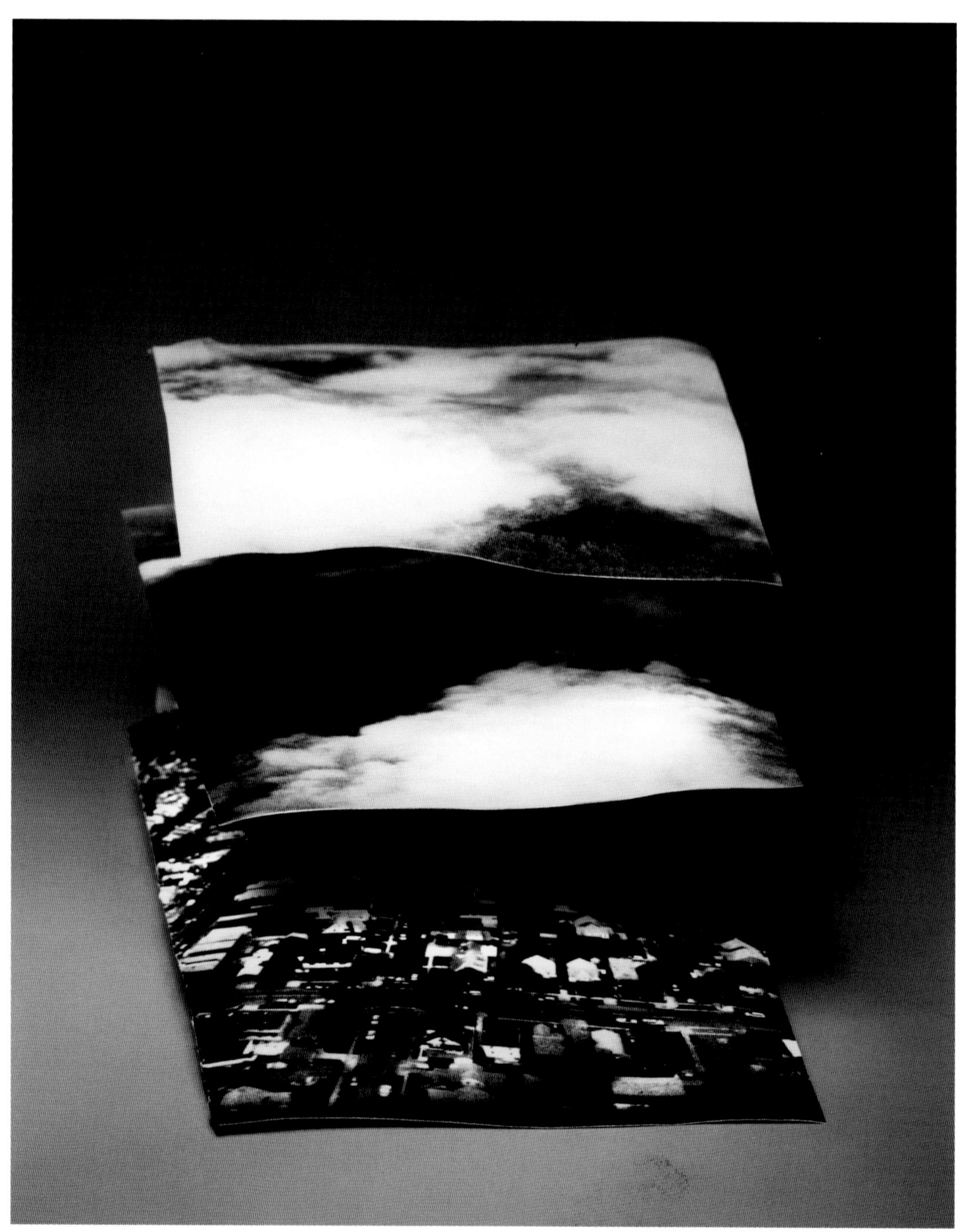

280    Taiyo Onorato and Nico Krebs, *Paper Landscape 4*, 2011. Direct positive gelatin-silver print

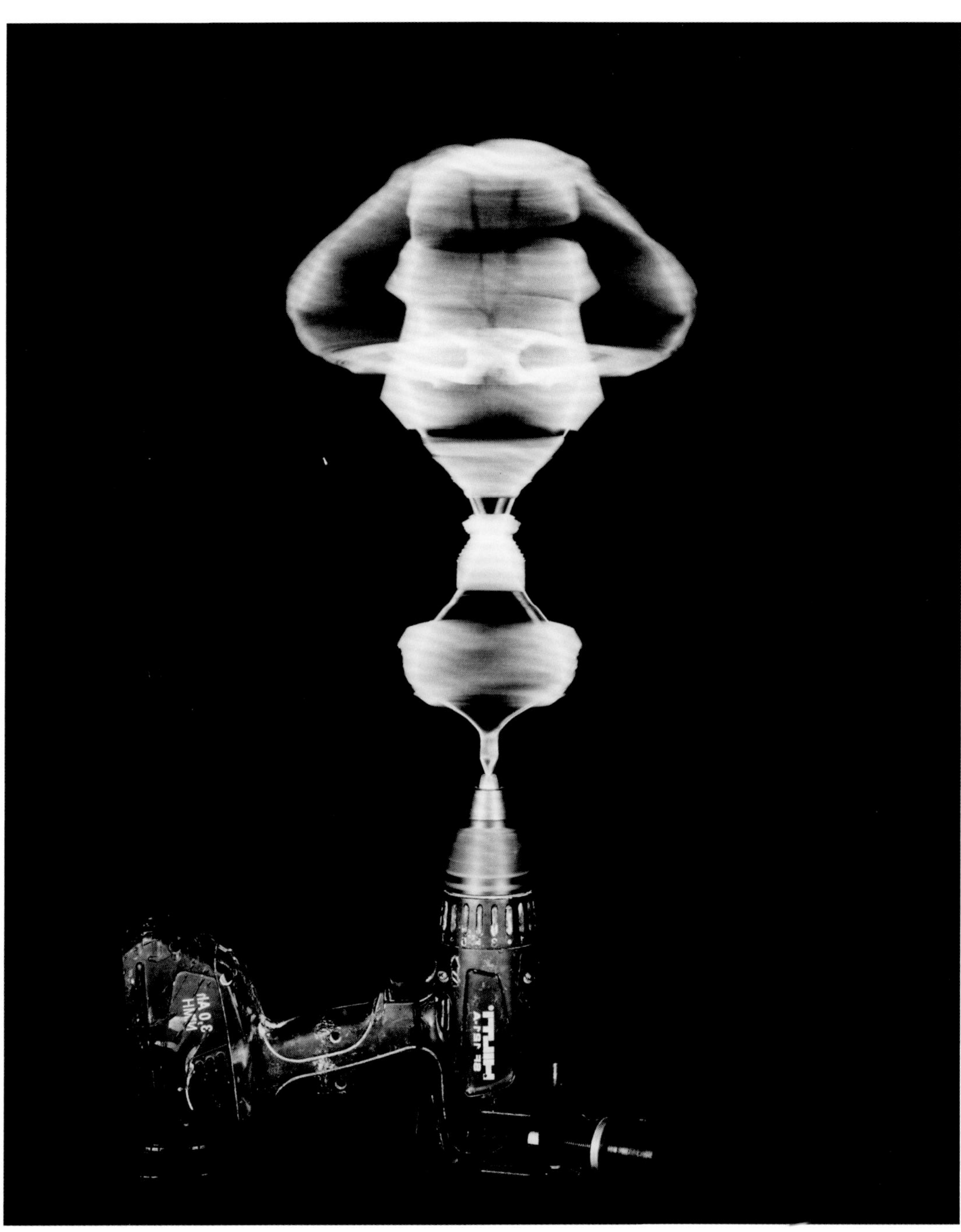



281    Taiyo Onorato and Nico Krebs, *Hilti 1*, from the project *Light of Other Days*, 2009. Direct positive gelatin-silver print

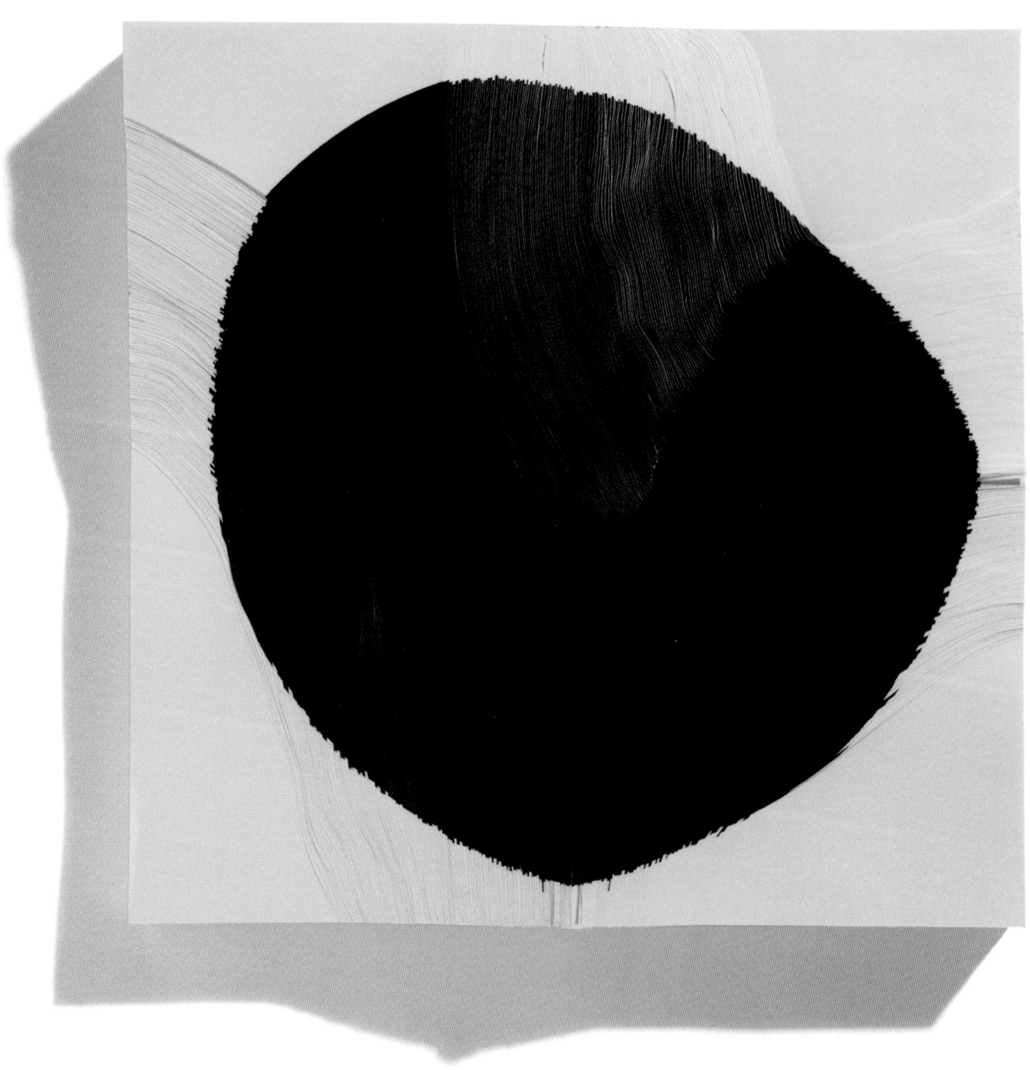

282    Nerhol (Ryuta Iida and Yoshihisa Tanaka), *Circle No. 008*, 2011. Two hundred pages

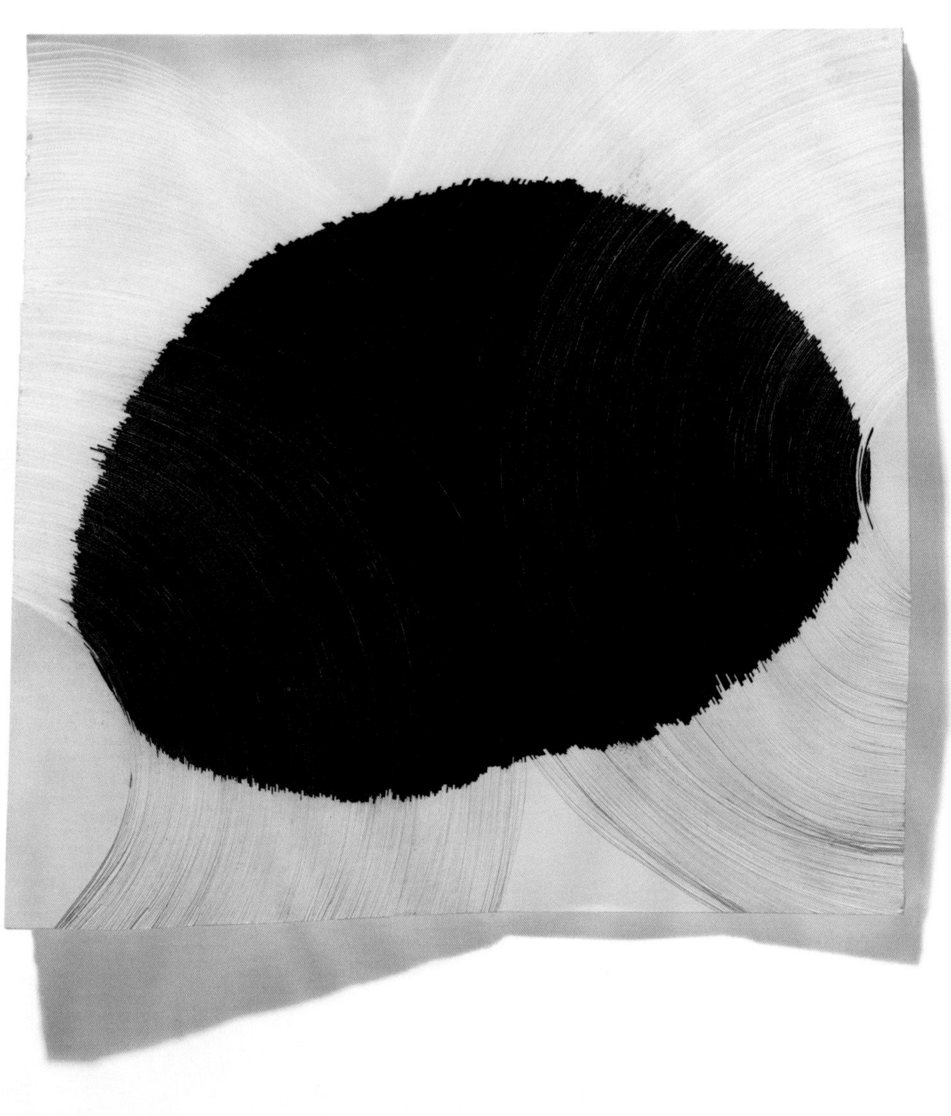

283    Nerhol (Ryuta Iida and Yoshihisa Tanaka), *Circle No. 013*, 2011. Two hundred pages

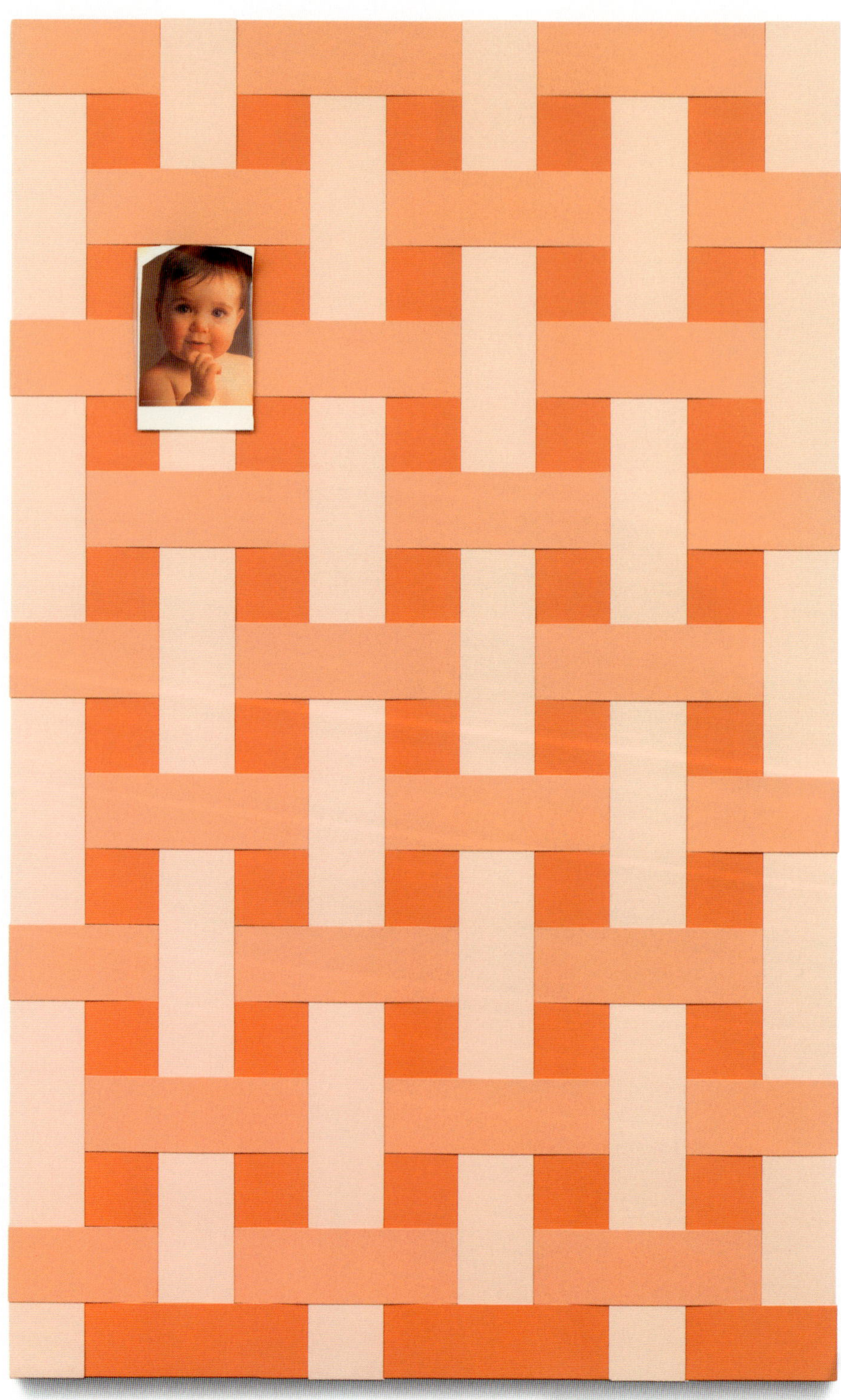

284     Matt Keegan, *Baby*, 2014. Steel, spray-finish, flashcard, magnet

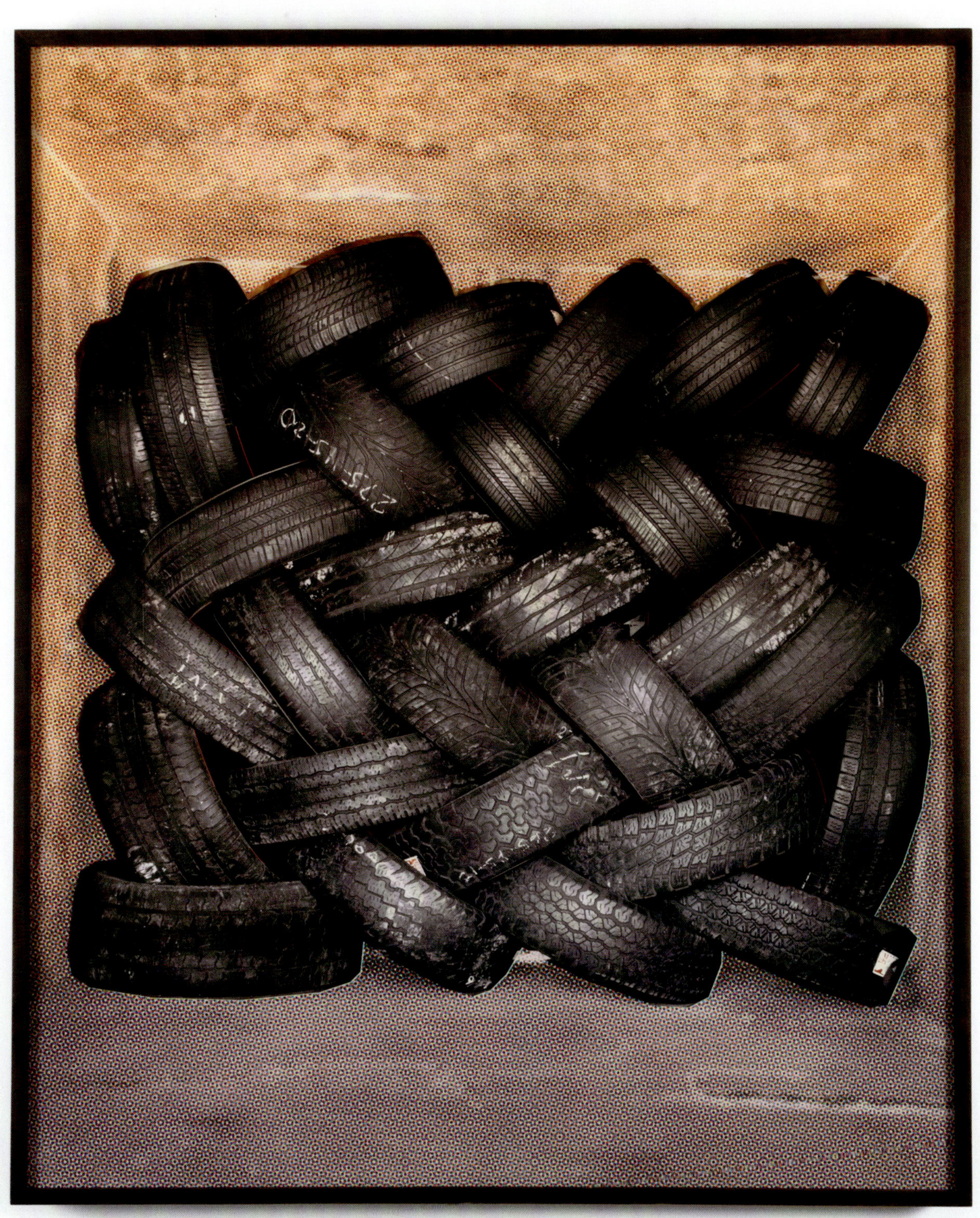

285    Matt Keegan, *Tires*, 2014. Cut and mounted C-print with screen-print on UV Plexiglas

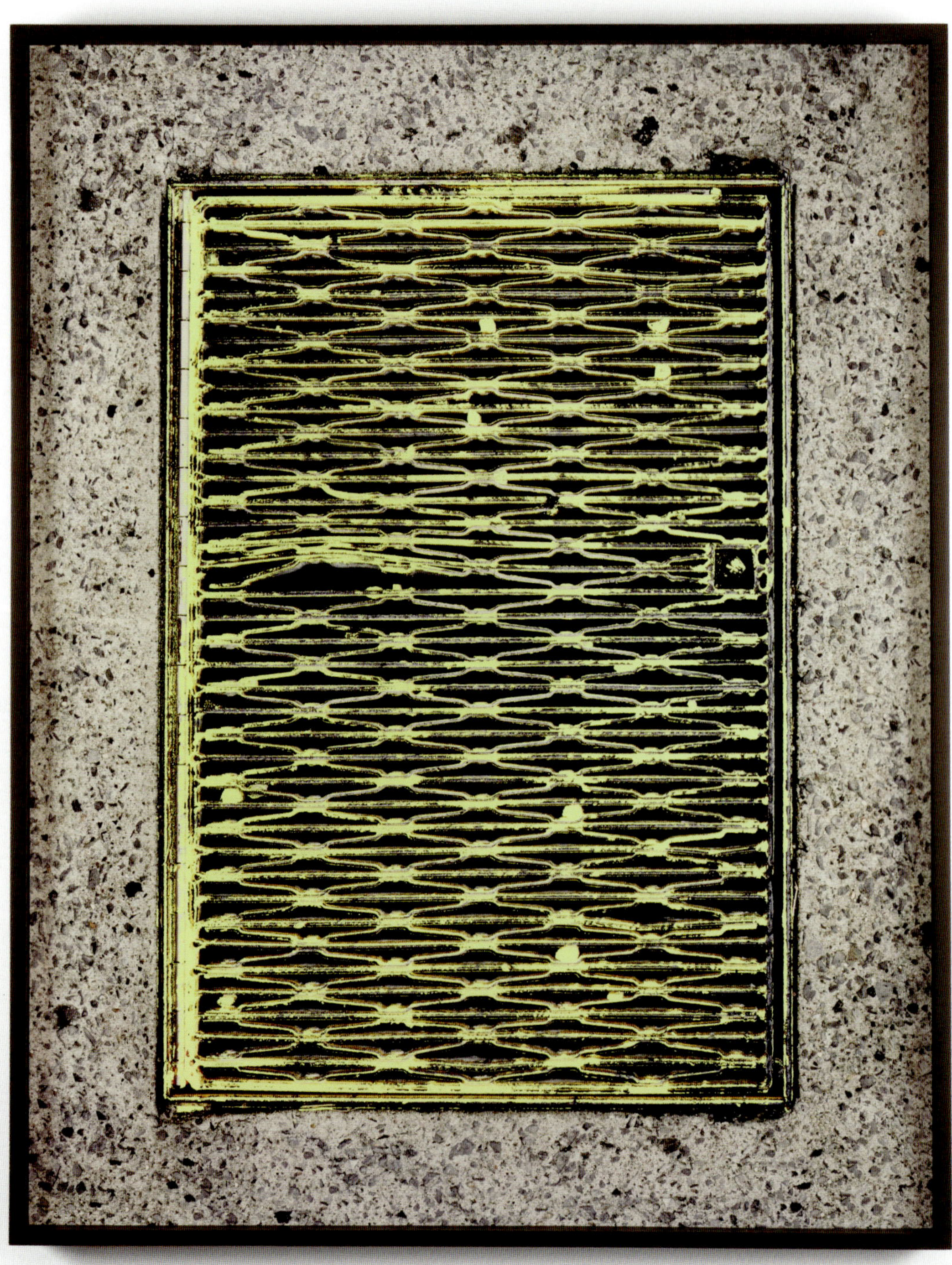

286    Matt Keegan, *Yellow Grate*, 2014. C-print with screen-print on UV Plexiglas

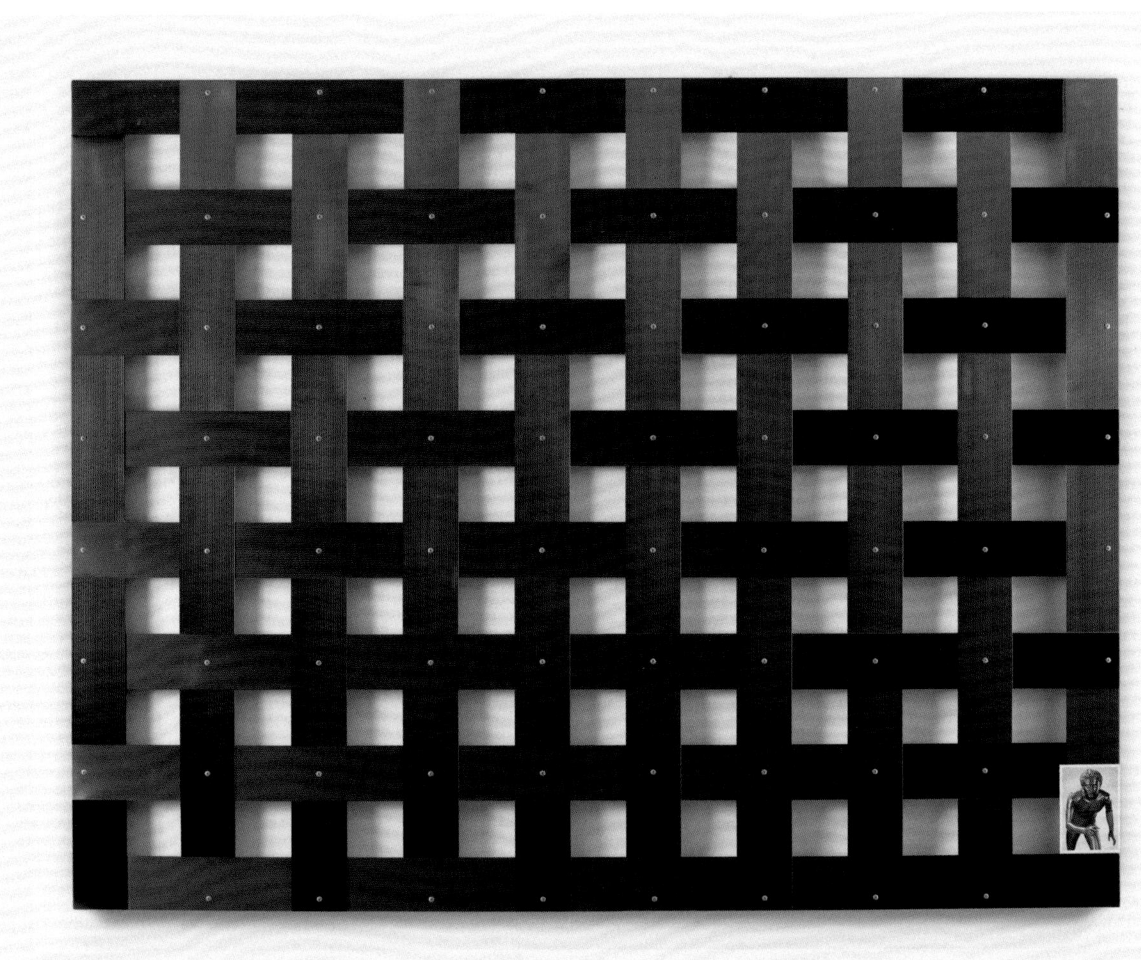

    Matt Keegan, *Untitled*, 2013. Enamel paint, steel, aluminum rivets, postcard, magnet

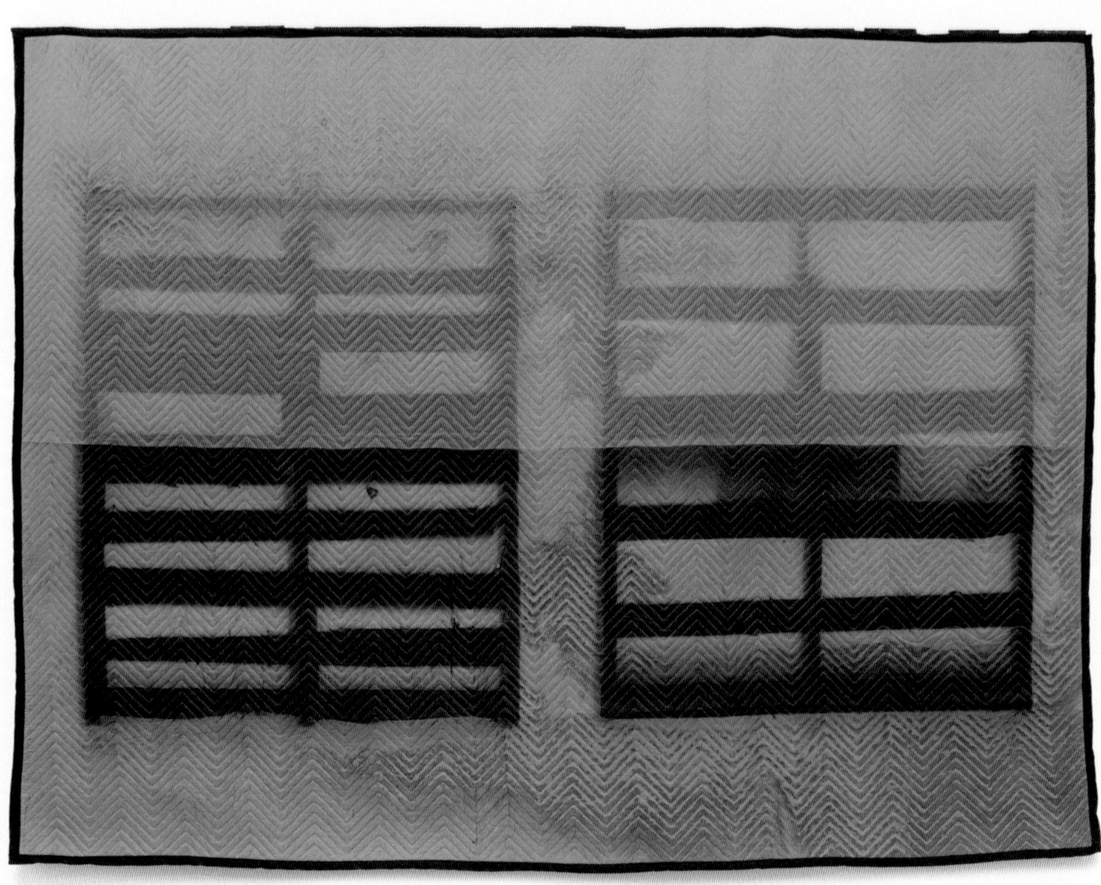

288    Sam Falls, *Untitled (Pomona, CA, Pallet 6)*, 2013. Moving blanket

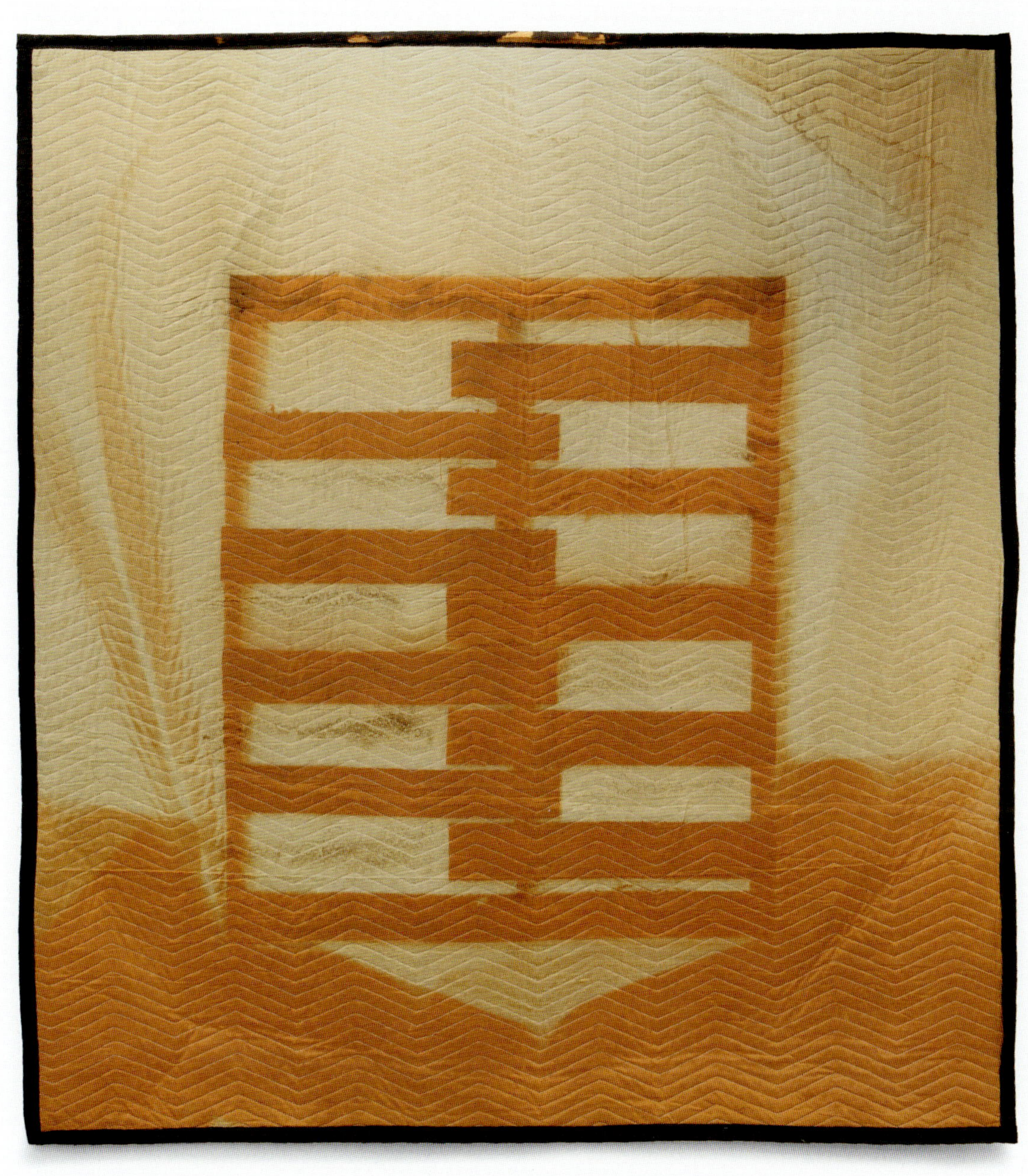

289    Sam Falls, *Untitled (Pomona, CA, Pallet 1)*, 2013. Moving blanket

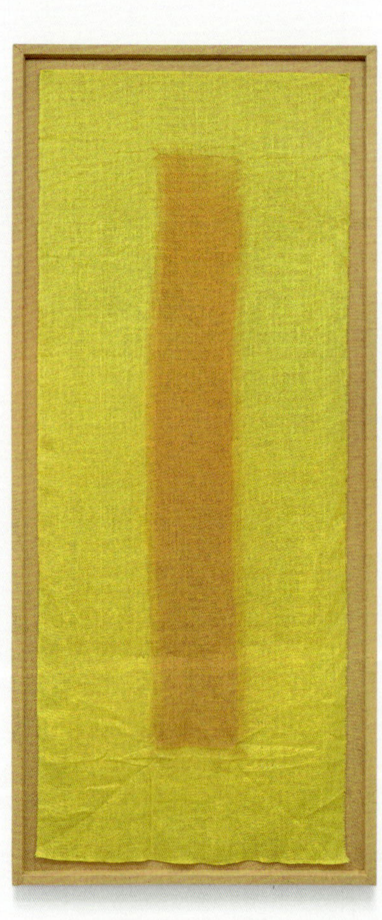

290    Sam Falls, *Untitled (Venice, CA, Bookshelf 4)*, 2013. Pre-dyed burlap

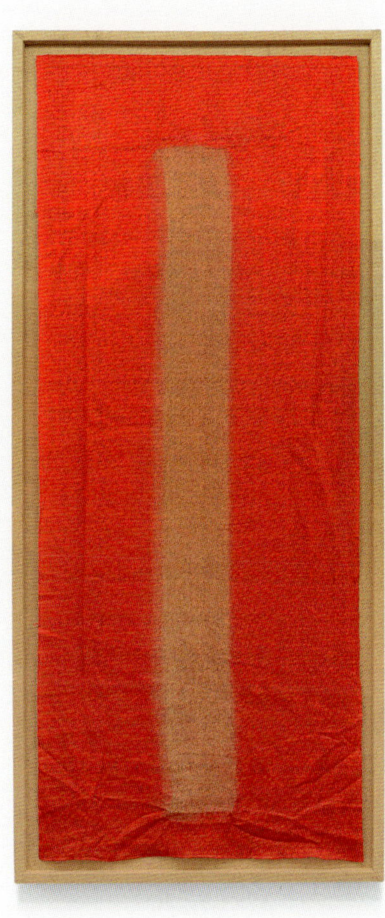

291    Sam Falls, *Untitled (Venice, CA, Bookshelf 2)*, 2013. Pre-dyed burlap

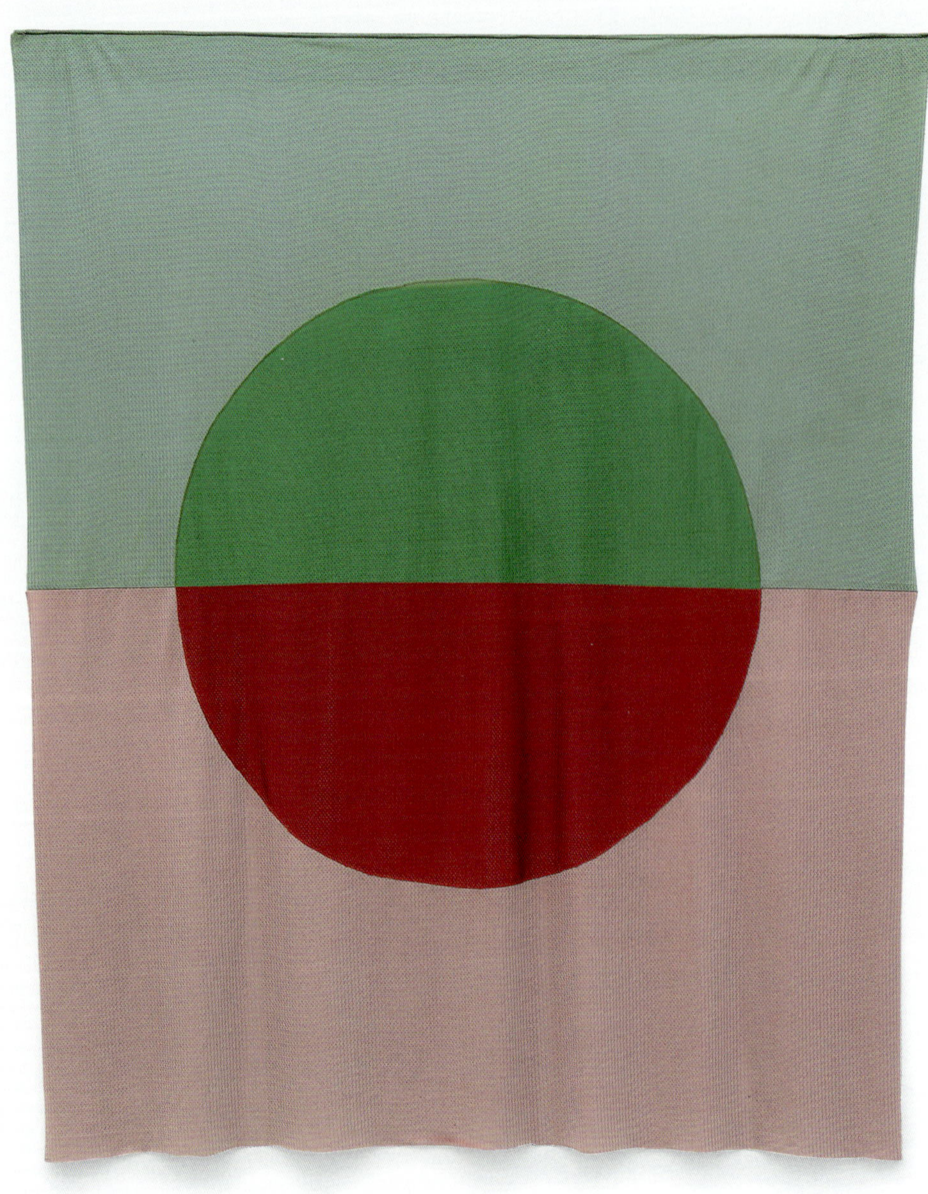

292    Sam Falls, *Untitled (Venice, CA, Double-sided 1)*, 2013. Pre-dyed jersey

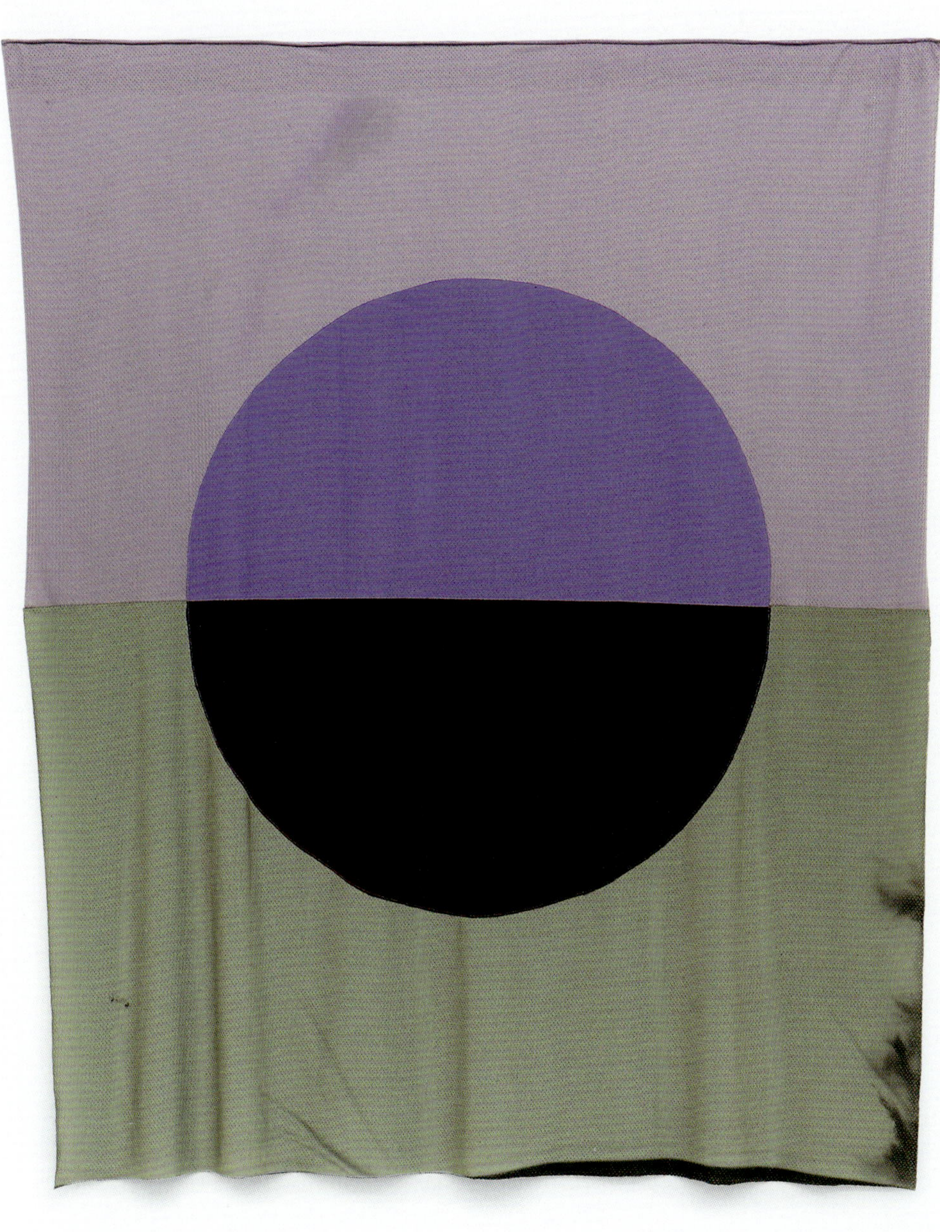

293  Sam Falls, *Untitled (Venice, CA, Double-sided 3)*, 2013. Pre-dyed jersey

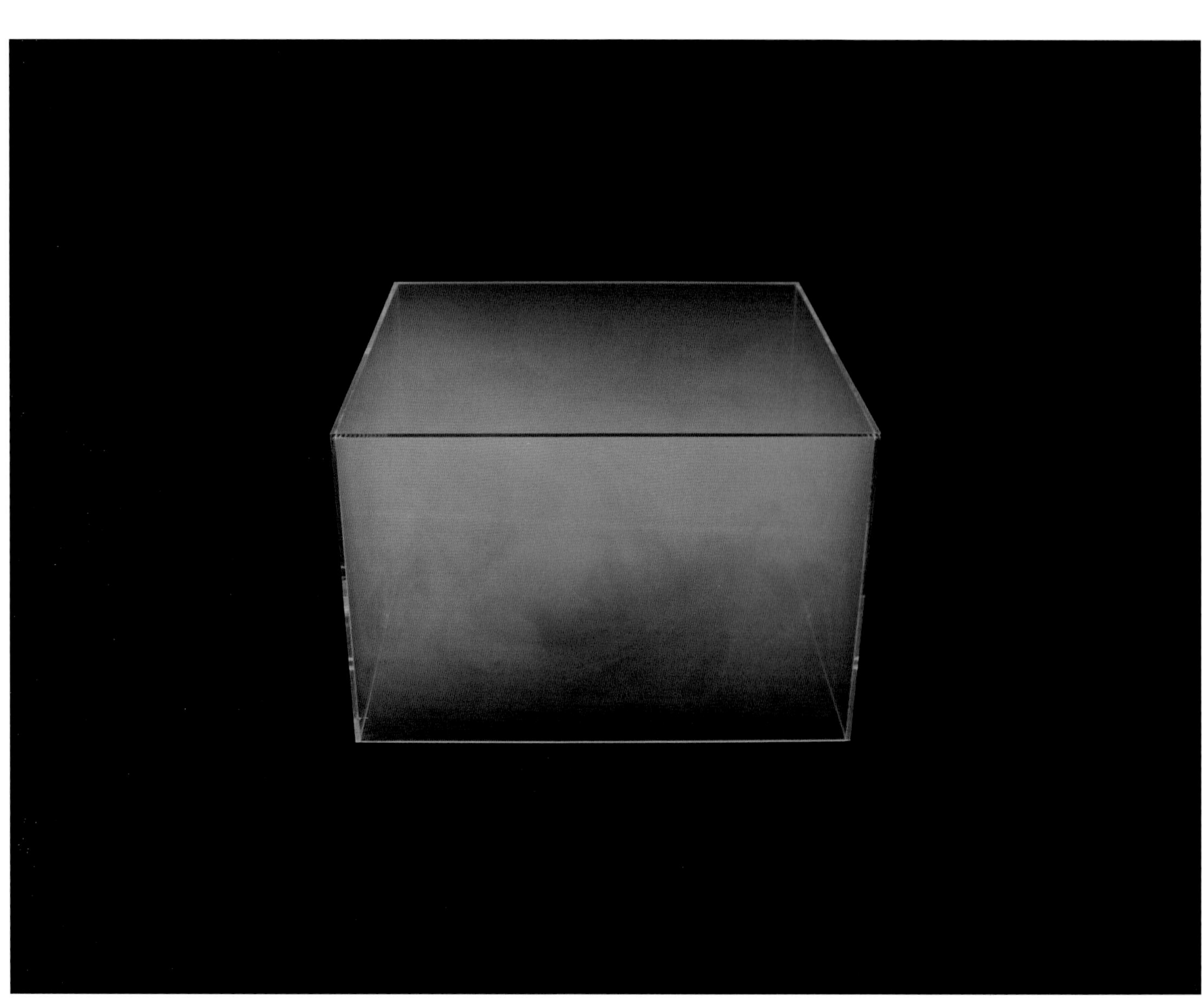

294    Lindsey White, *Fog Box*, 2013. C-print

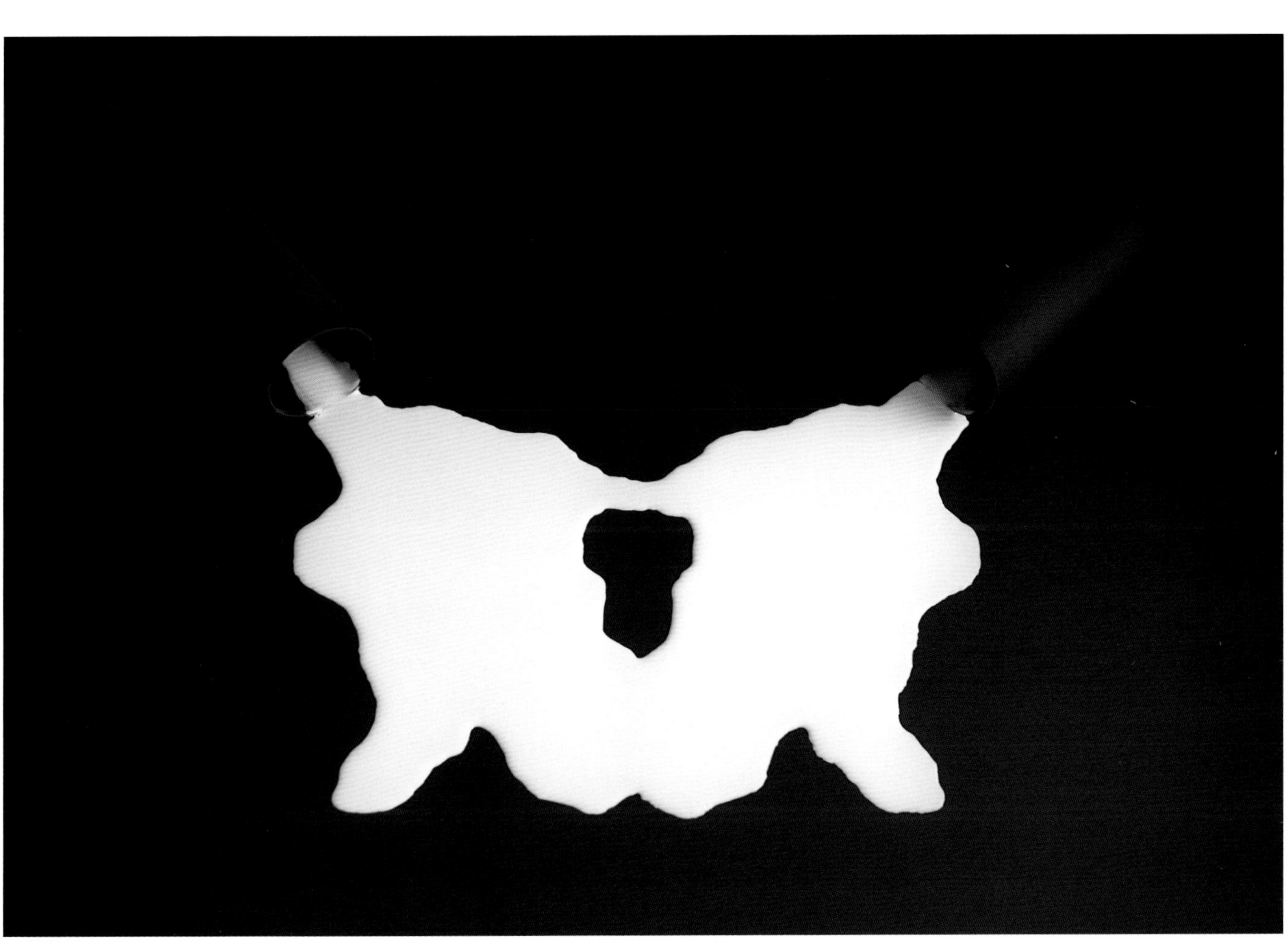

295     Lindsey White, *Spilled Milk*, 2012. C-print

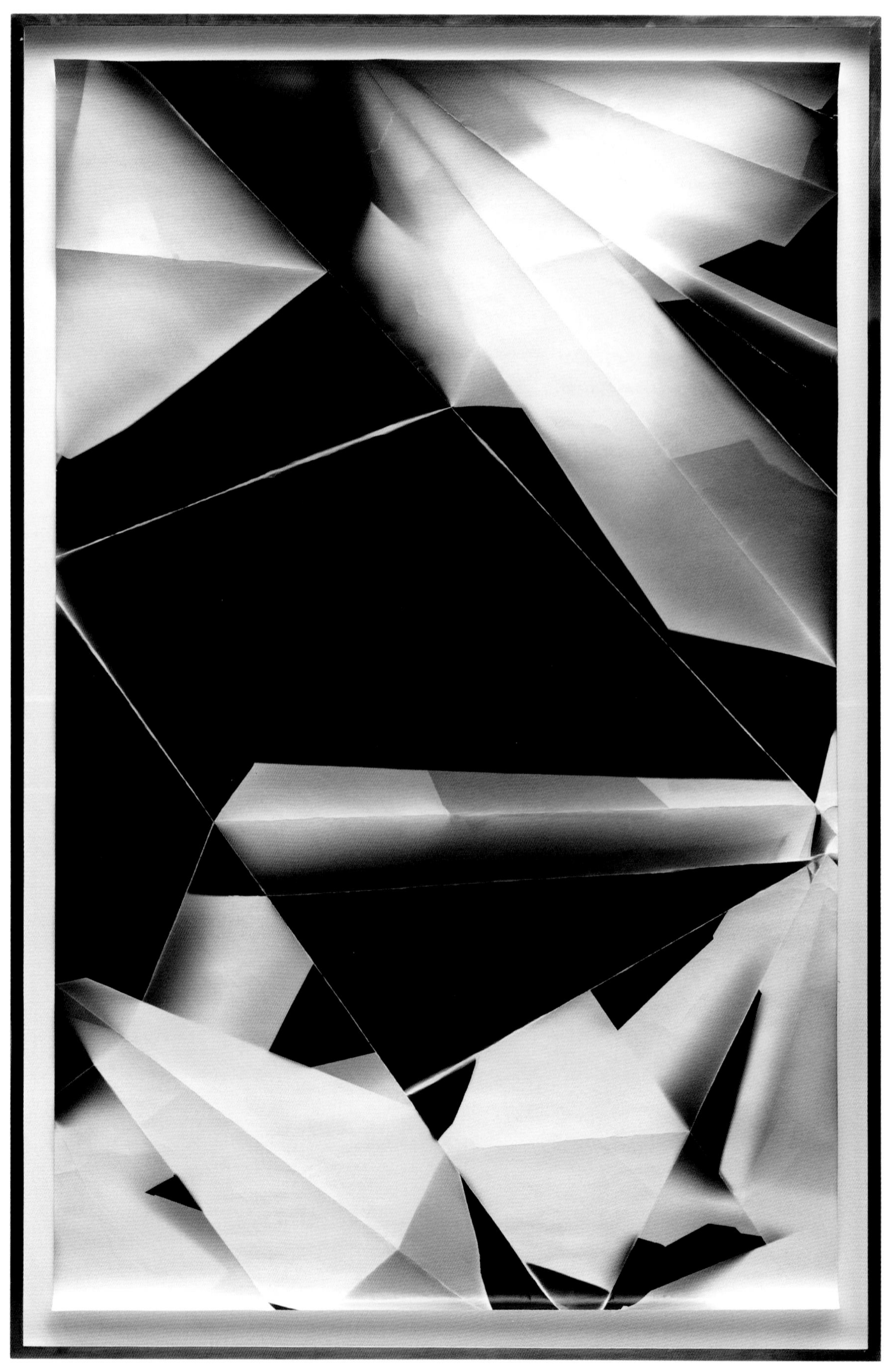

296 Walead Beshty, *Fold (450/1350 directional light sources, June 24, 2008, Annandale-on-Hudson, New York, Foma Multigrade Fiber)*, 2009. Black-and-white fiber-based photographic paper

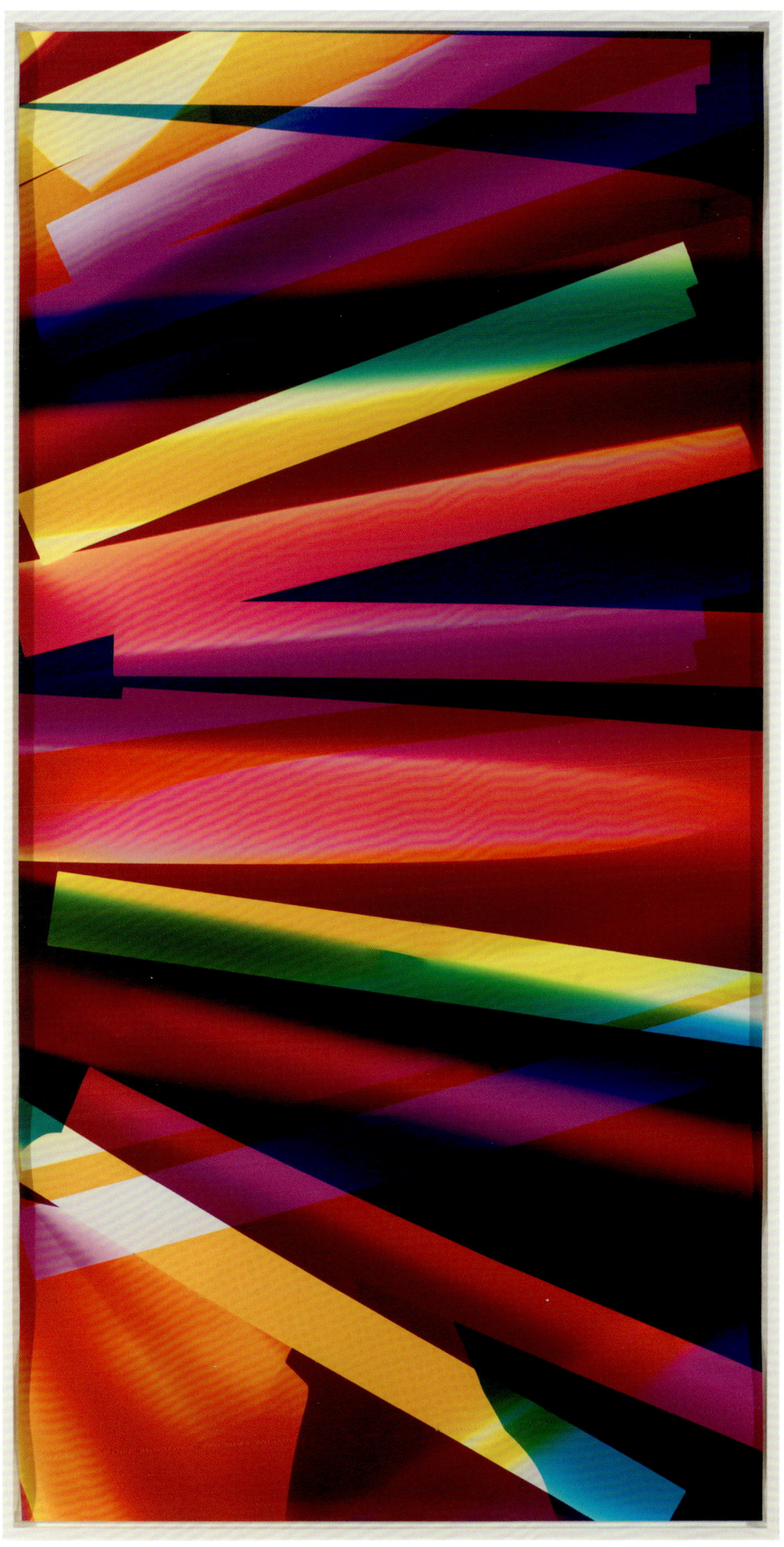

297    Walead Beshty, *Three Color Curl (CMY/Six Magnet: Irvine, California, September 6, 2009, Fuji Crystal Archive Type C)*, 2009. Color photographic paper

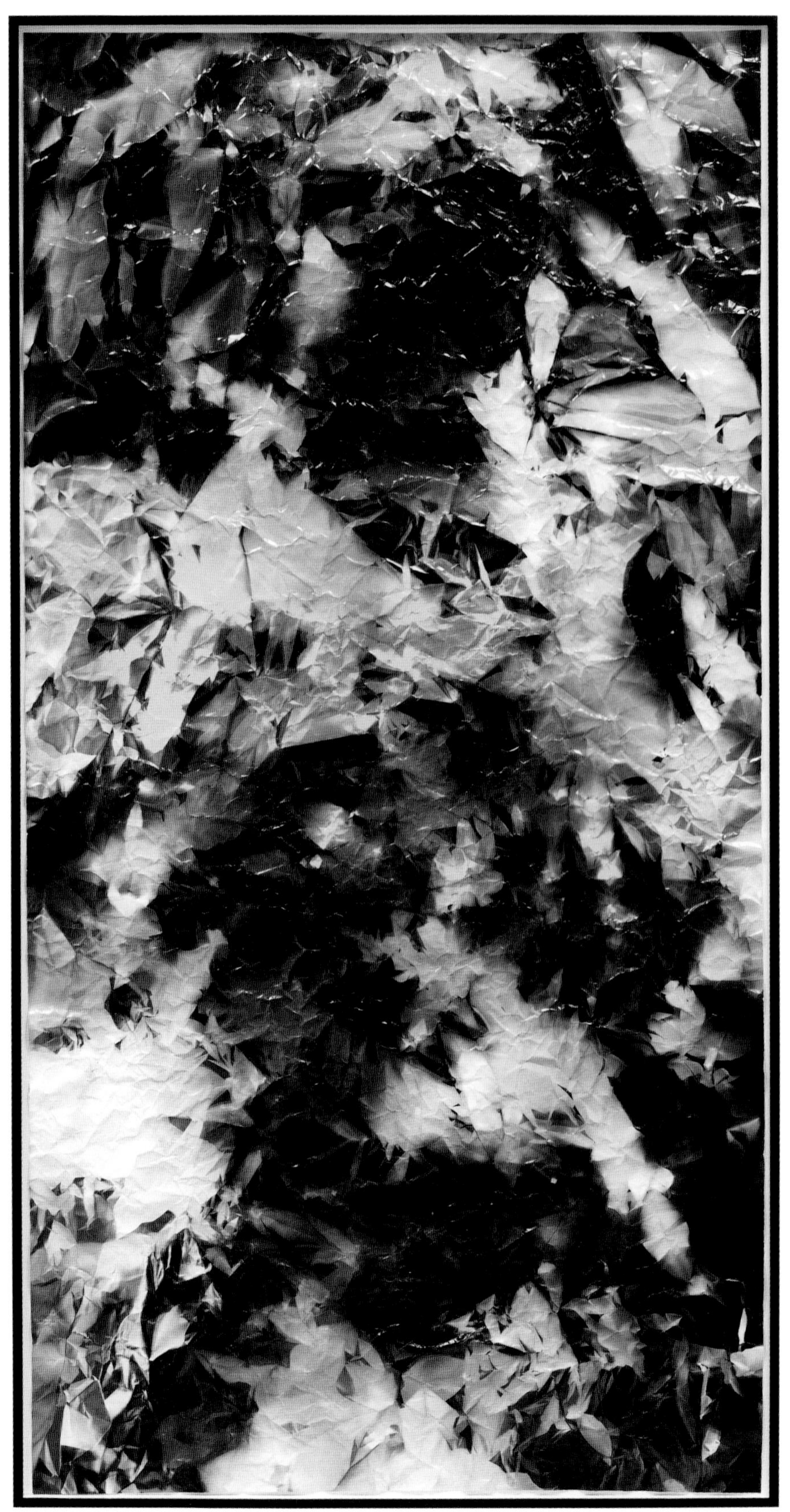

298     Walead Beshty, *Picture Made by My Hand with the Assistance of Light*, 2012.
Black-and-white fiber-based photographic paper

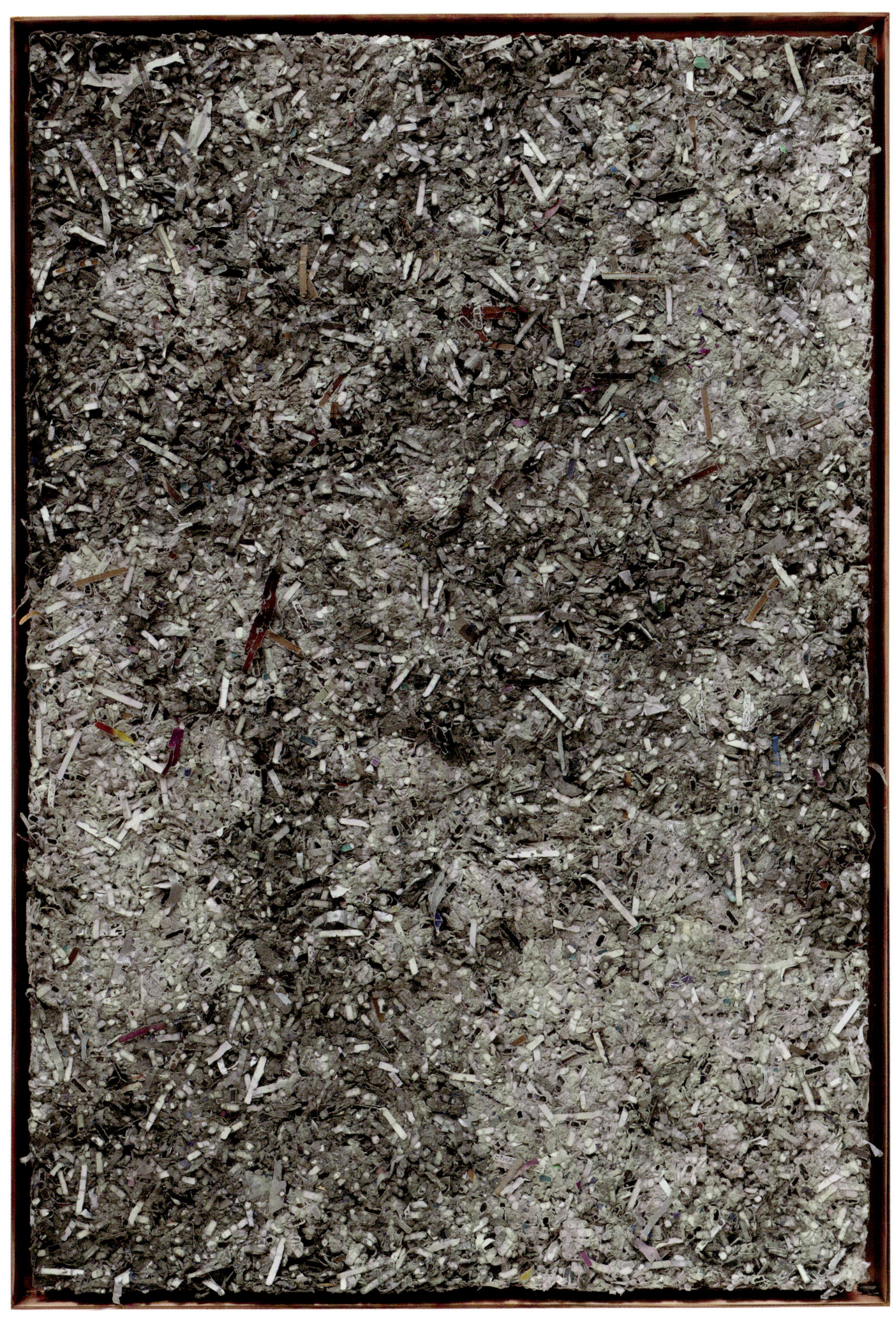

299    Walead Beshty, *Selected Works (2009–2011/November 15, 2010–March 16, 2011)*, 2011. Color photographic paper, black-and-white fiber-based photographic paper, archival inkjet papers

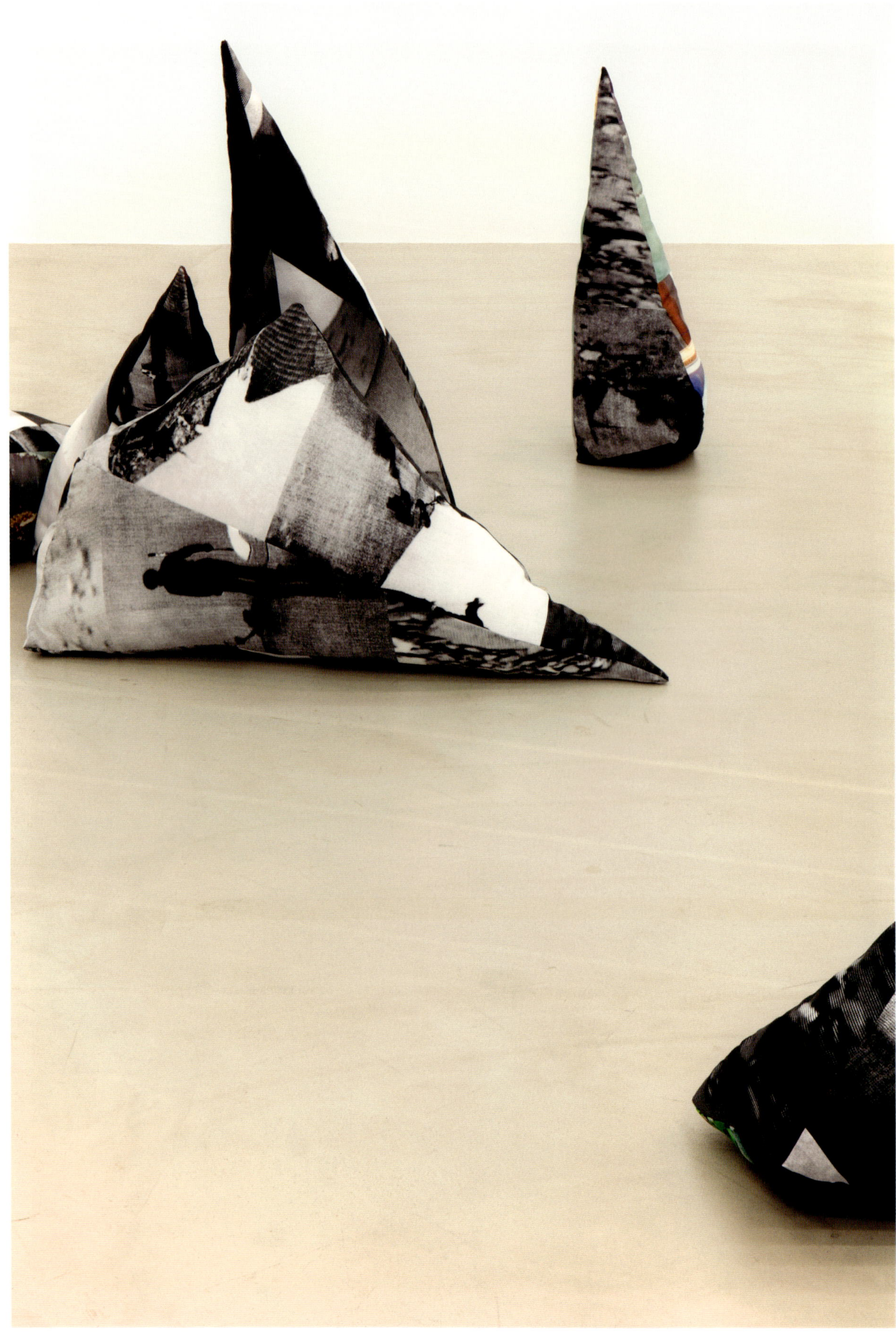

     Takaaki Akaishi, *Cushion (G/P Collection 2 #1)*, 2014. Cushion (installation view)

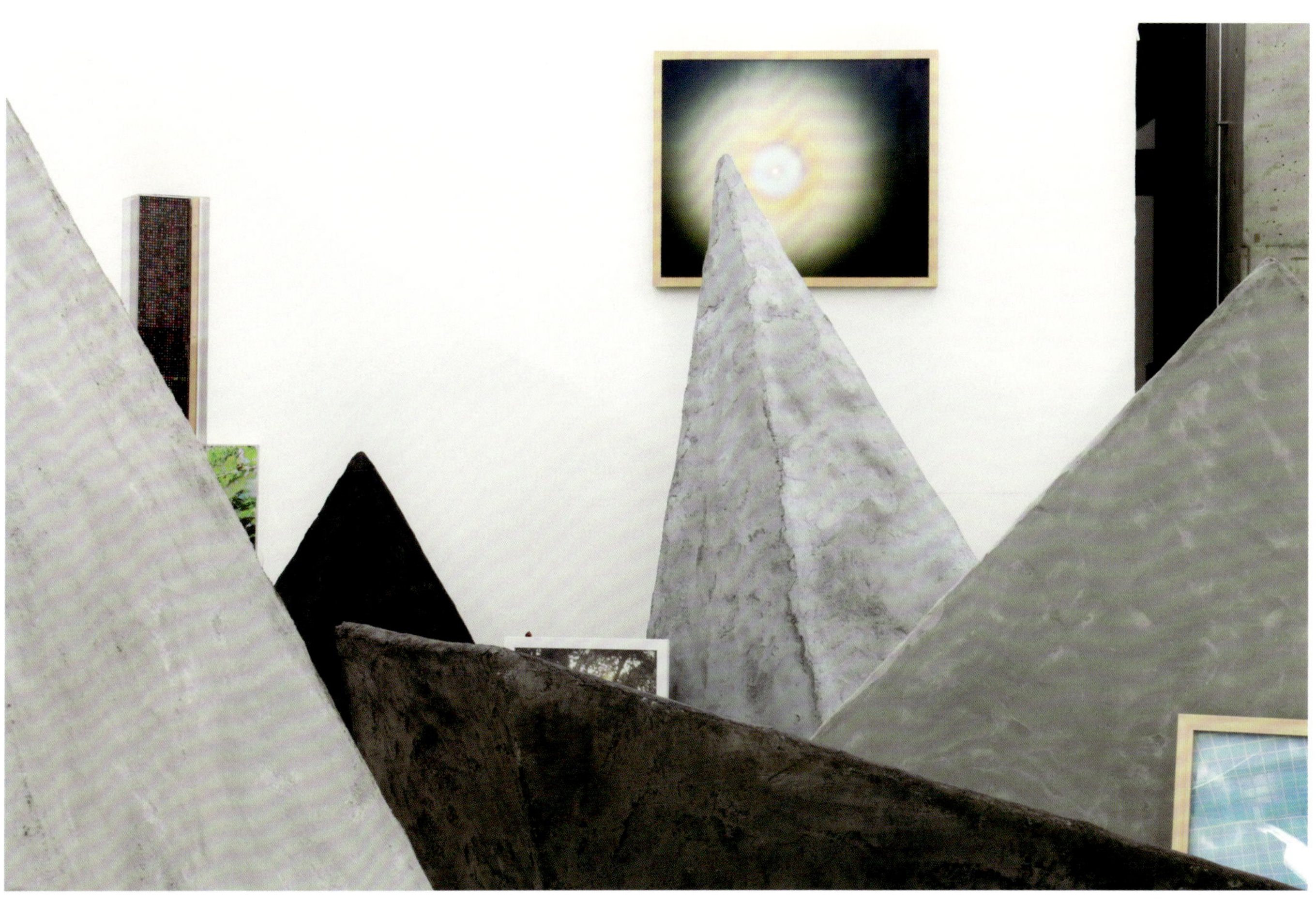

301    Takaaki Akaishi, *Mountain Range*, 2011. Framed photograph, concrete, red stone (installation view)

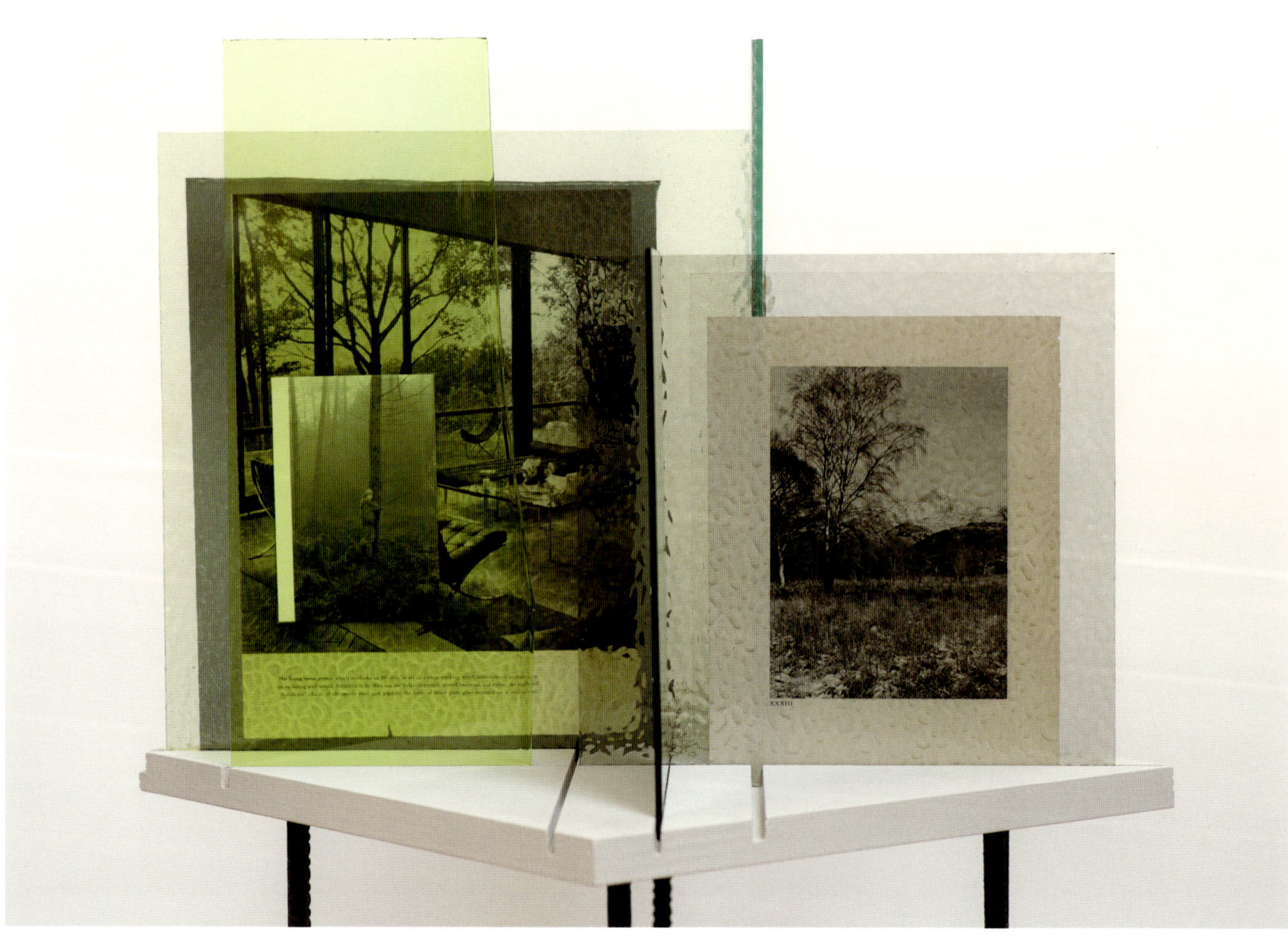

302    Abigail Reynolds, *Begin Afresh*, 2013. Book pages, textured glass

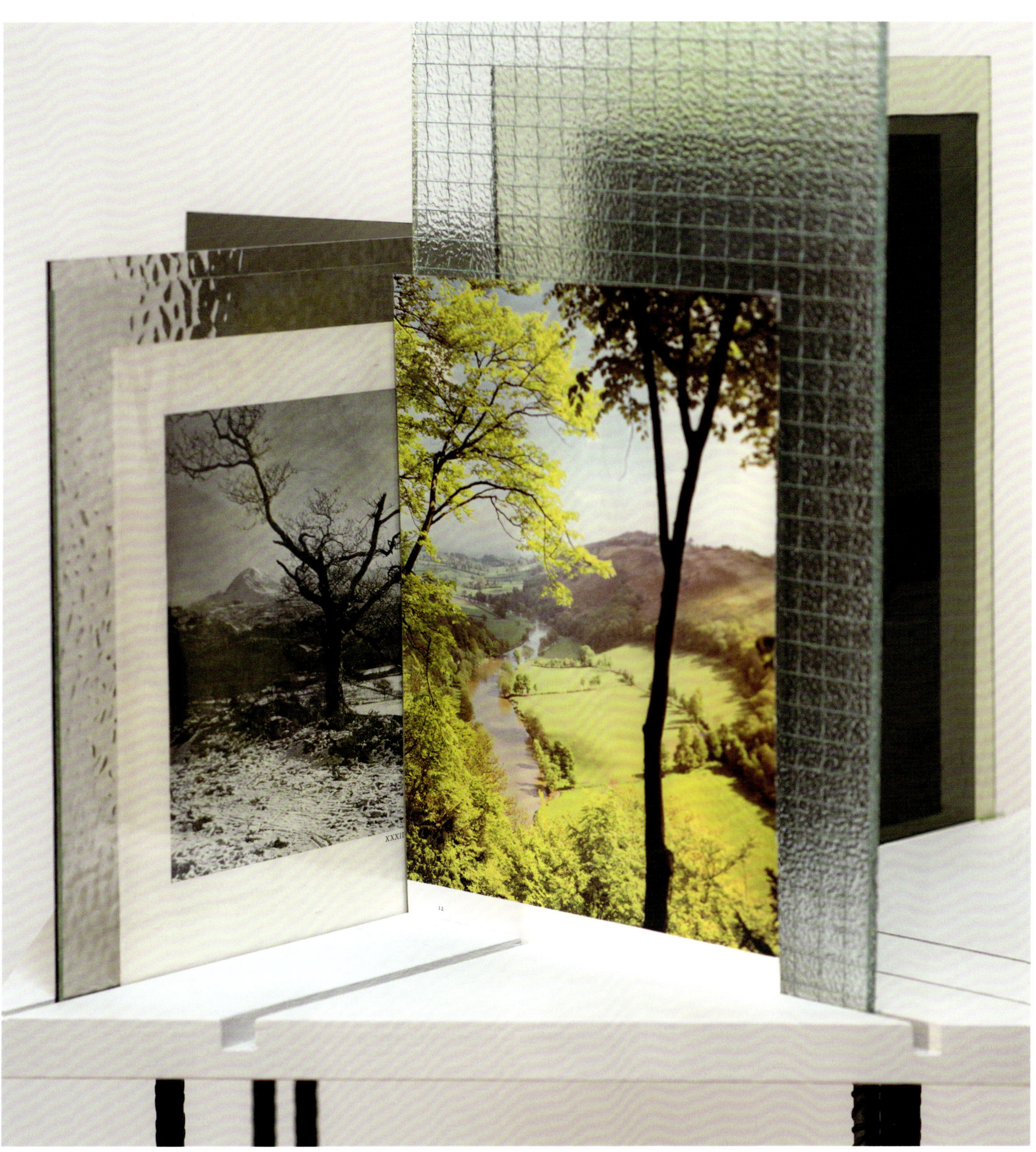

303    Abigail Reynolds, *Begin Afresh*, 2013. Book pages, textured glass

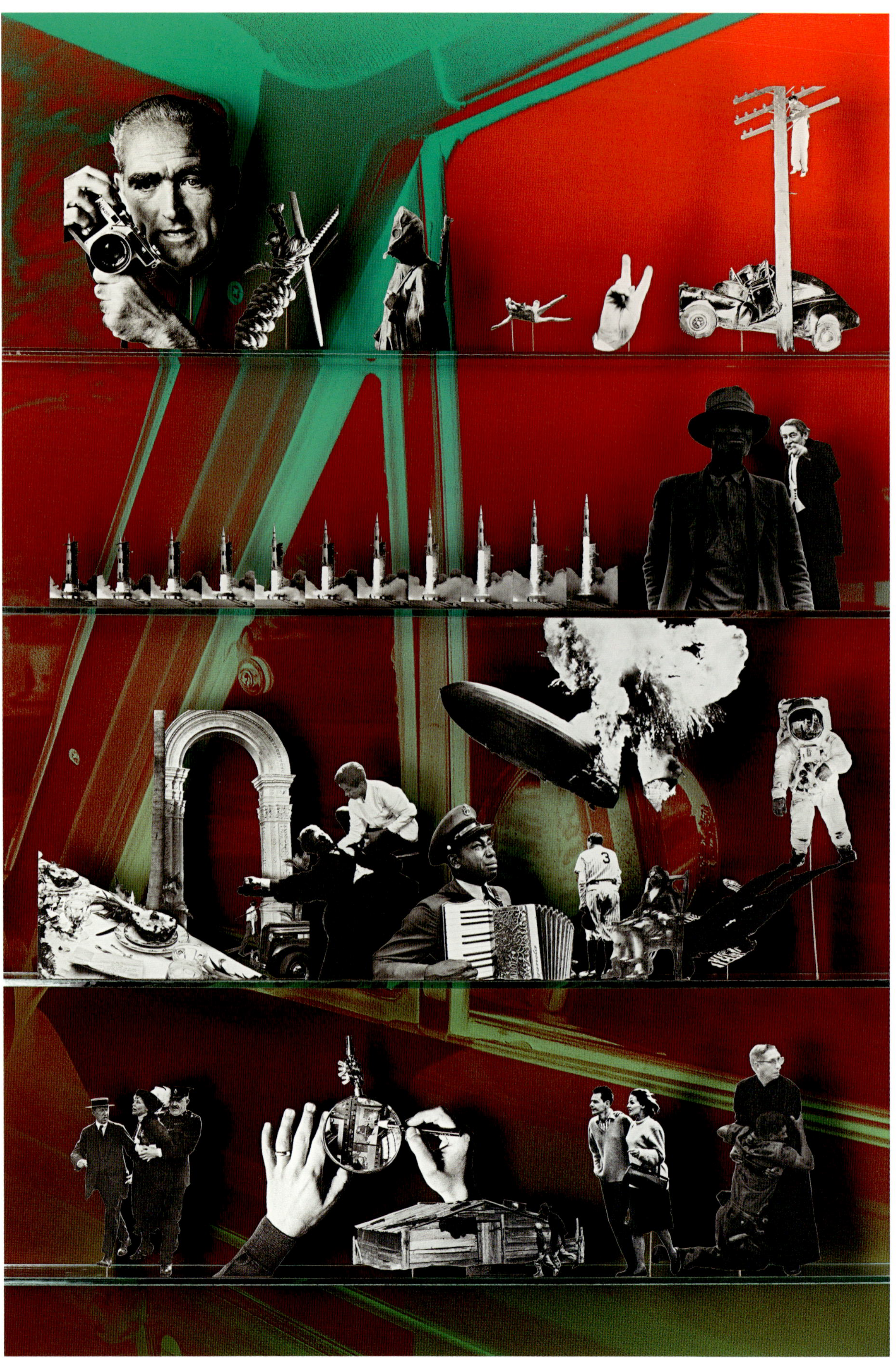

304    Matt Lipps, *Photojournalism*, 2014. C-print

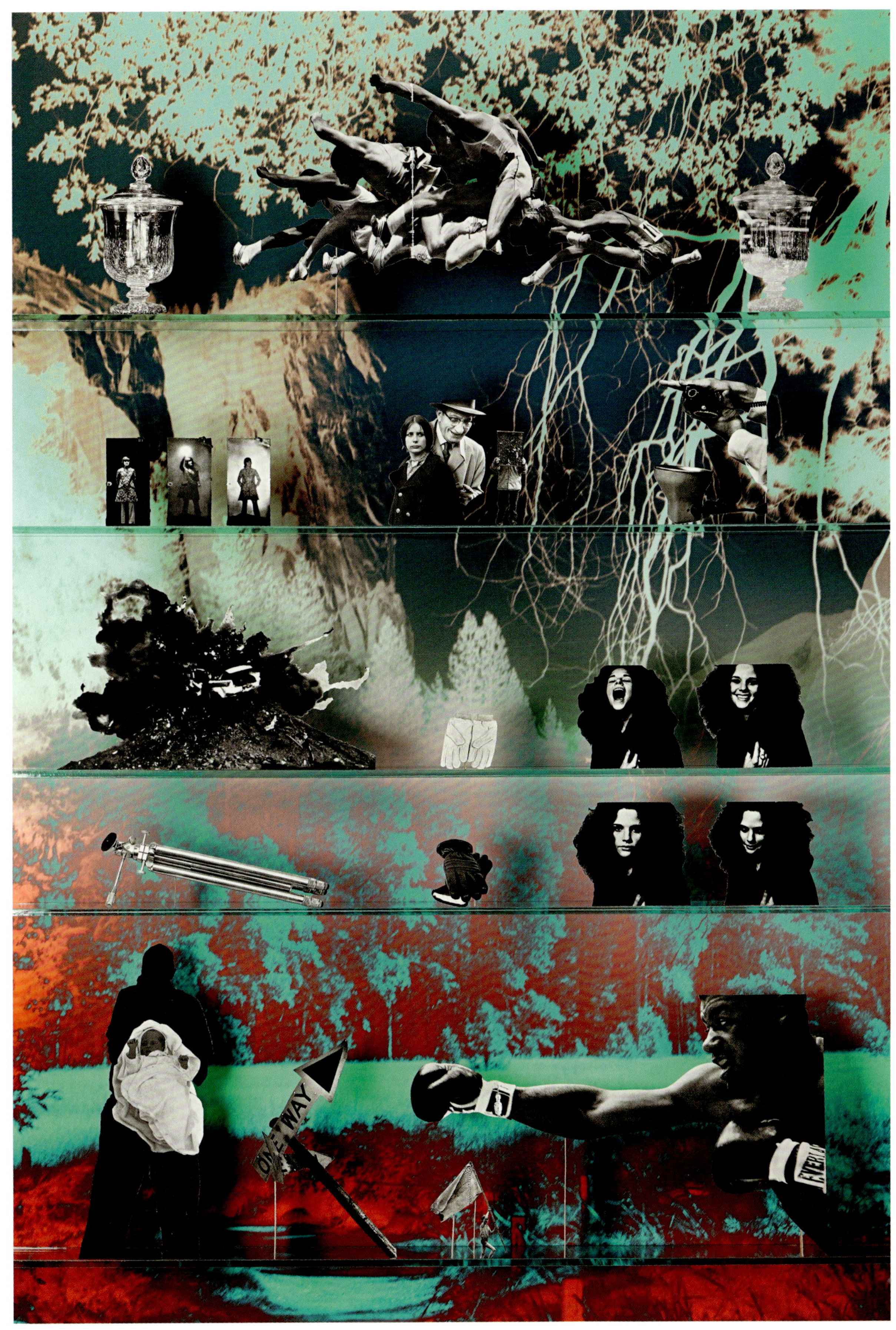

     Matt Lipps, *Special Problems*, 2014. C-print

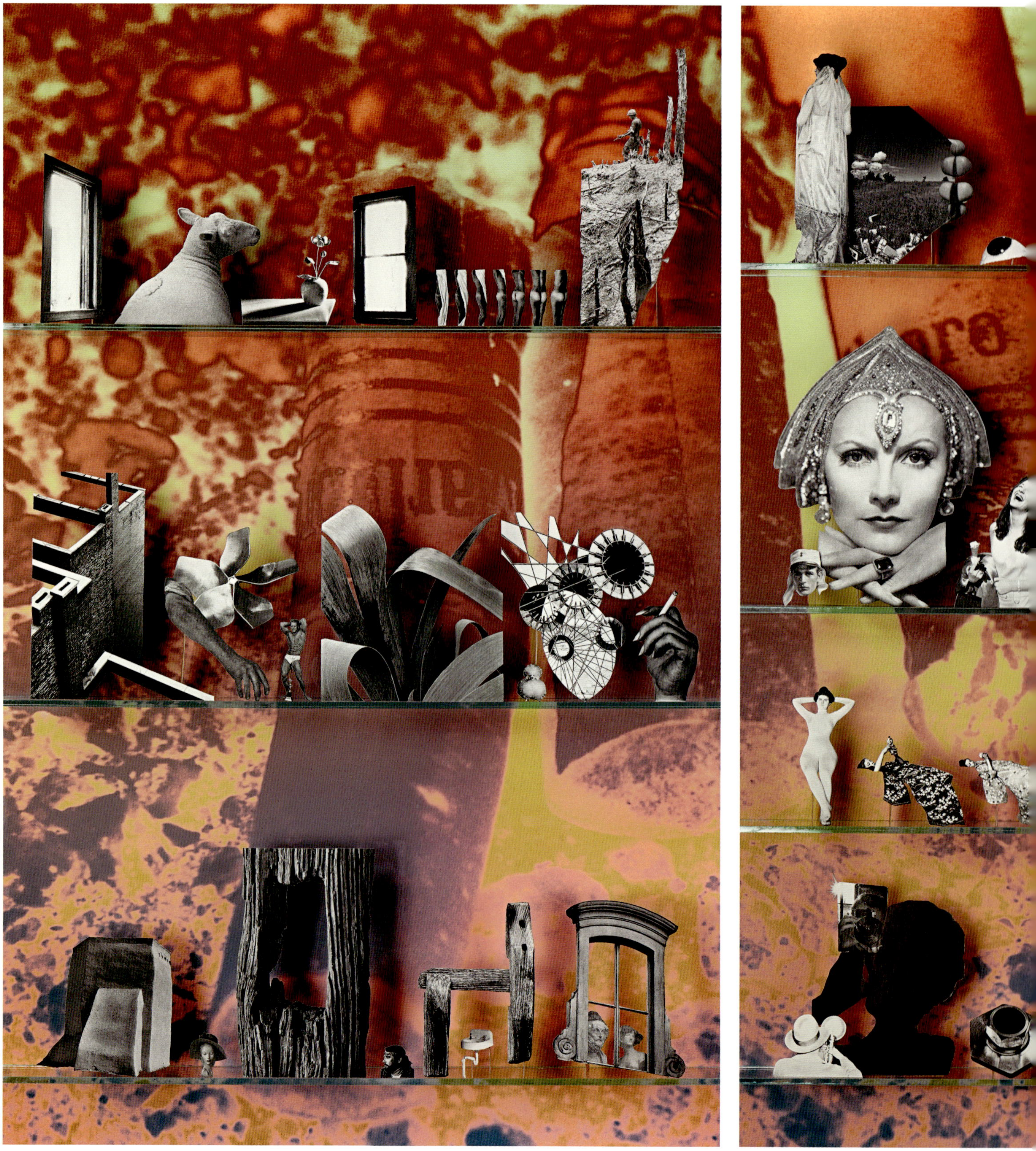

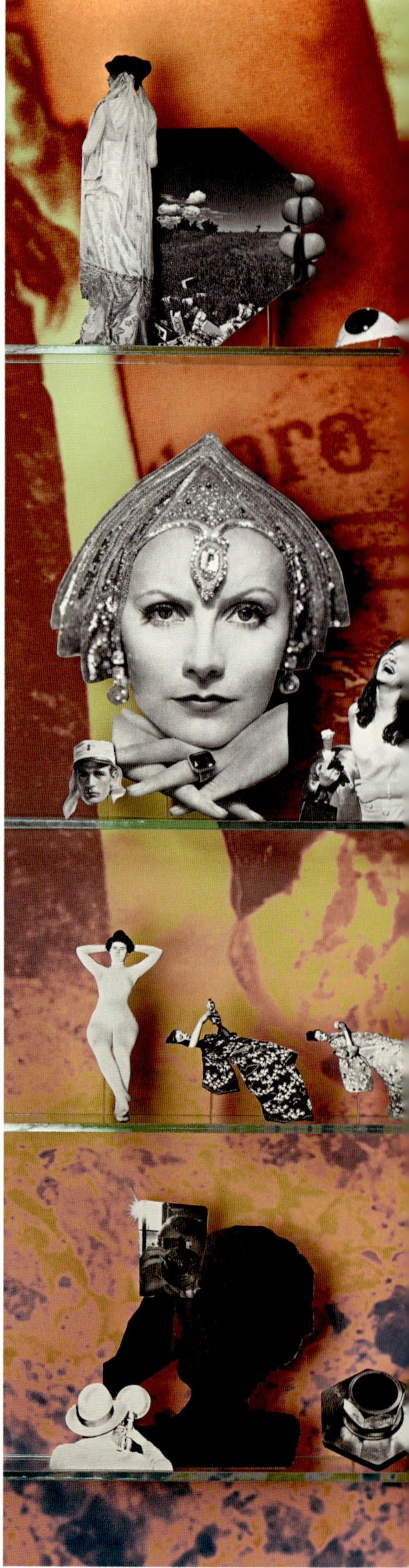

 Matt Lipps, *1973–1975*, 2014. C-print

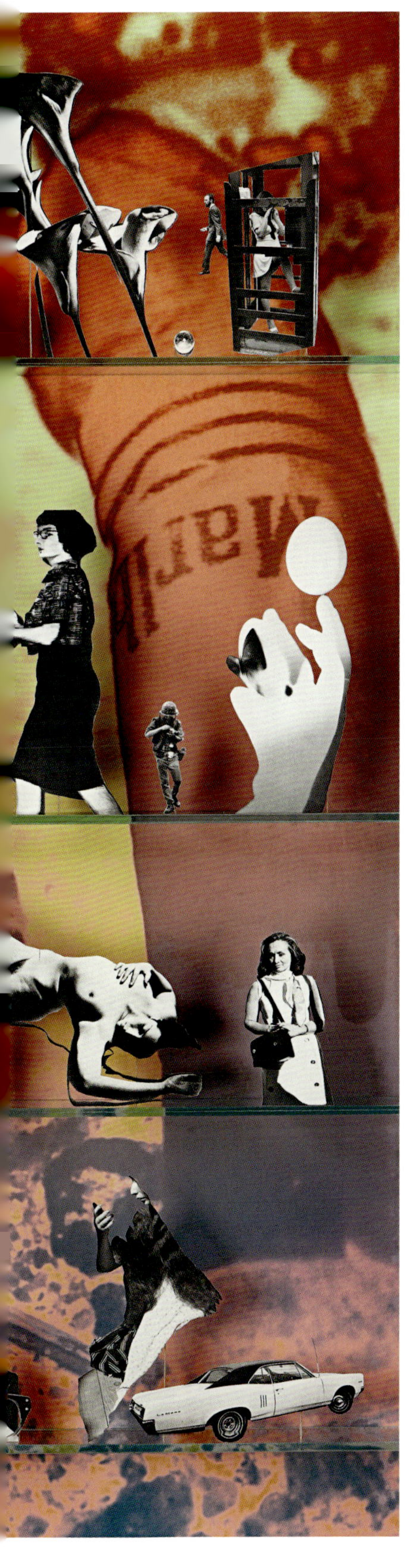

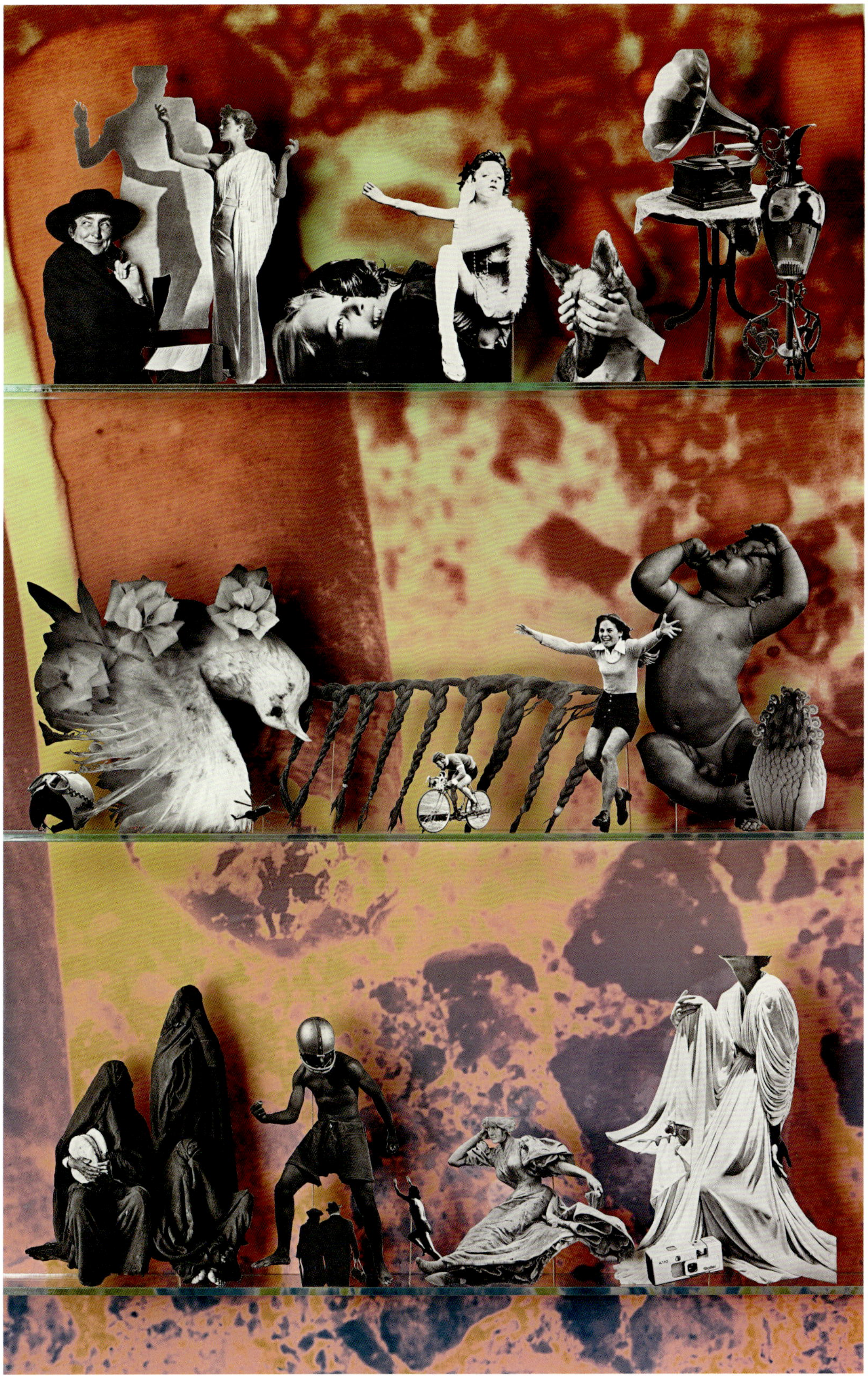

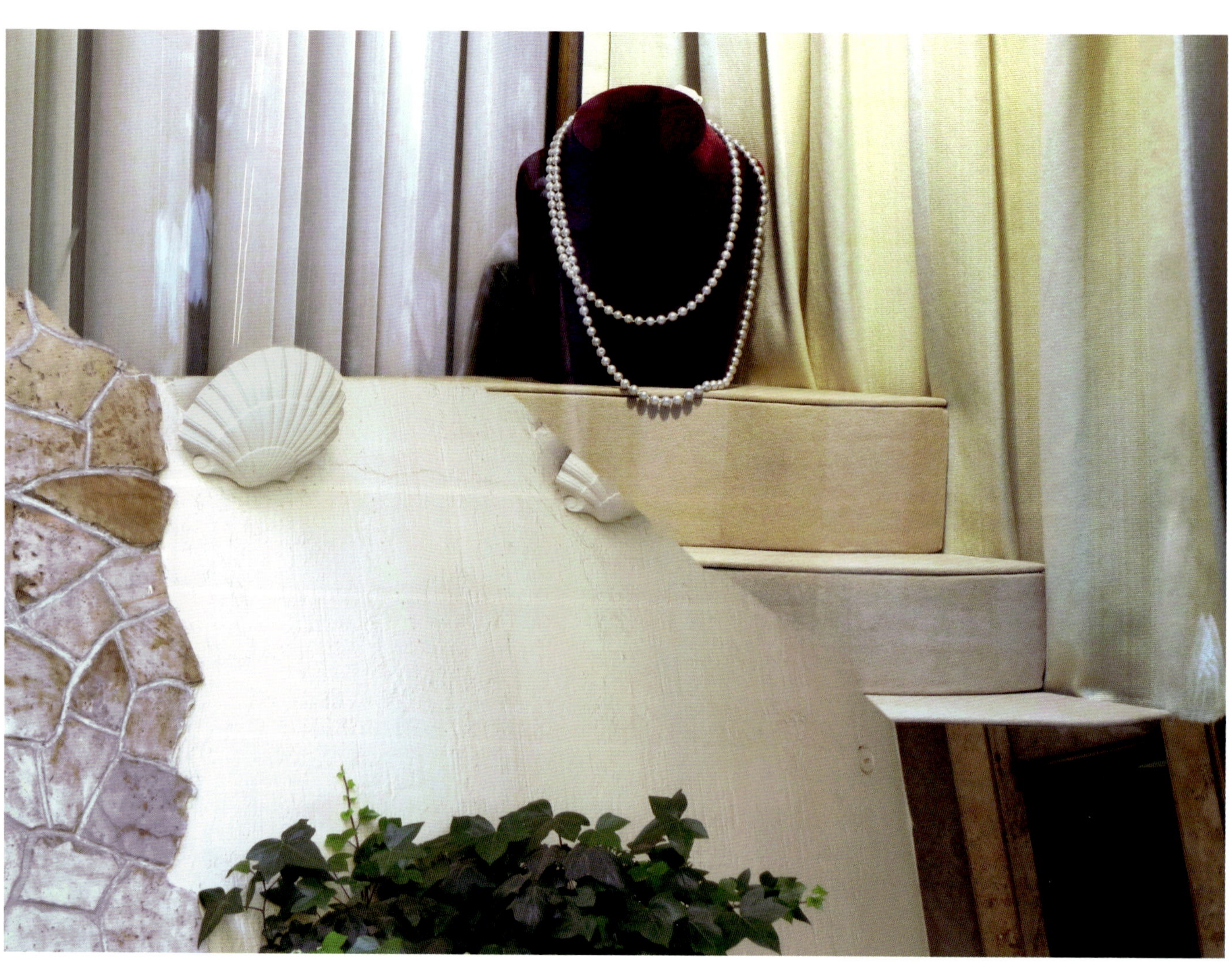

308    Miguel Ángel Tornero, *Untitled*, 2014, from *The Random Series, Madrileño trip*. Digital collage

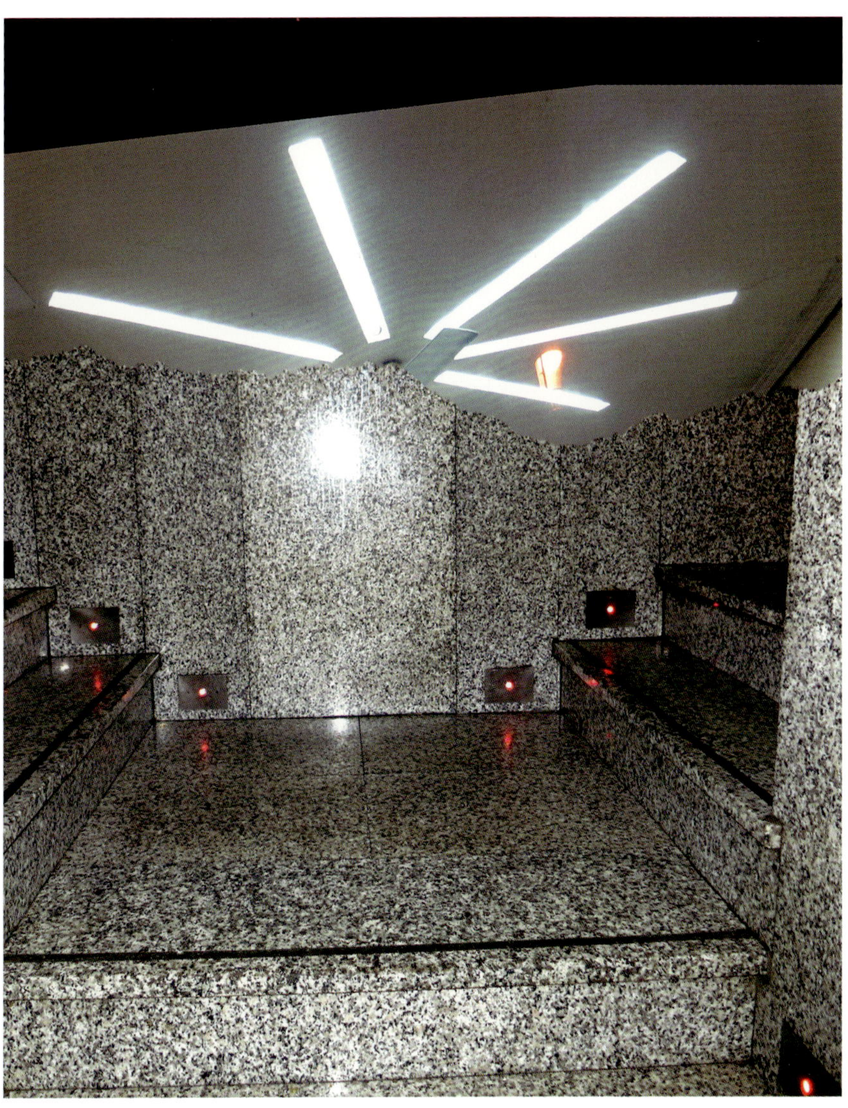

309    Miguel Ángel Tornero, *Untitled*, 2014, from *The Random Series, Madrileño trip*. Digital collage

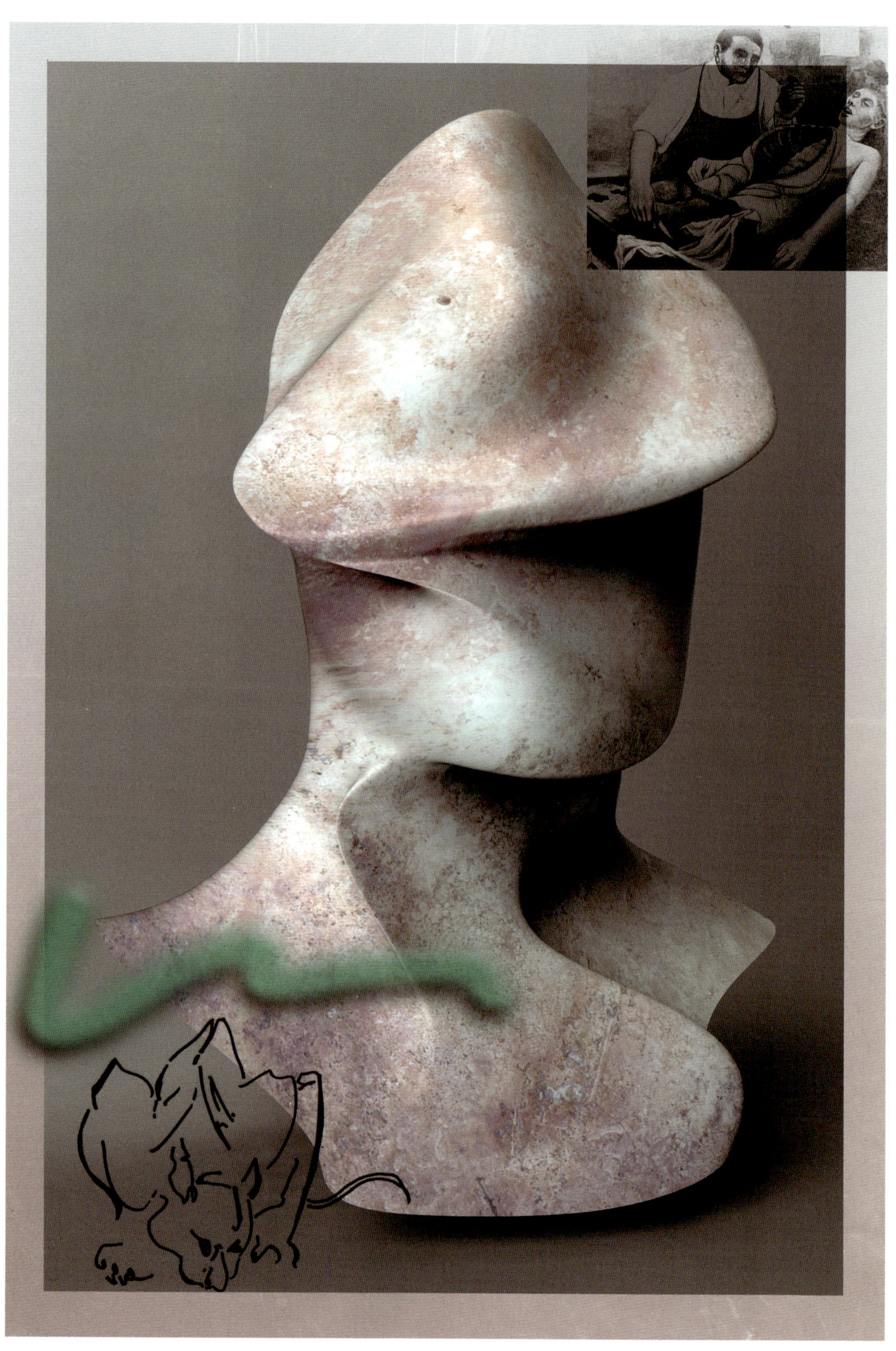

310      Jon Rafman, *New Age Demanded (The heart was a place made fast)*, 2013. Archival pigment print

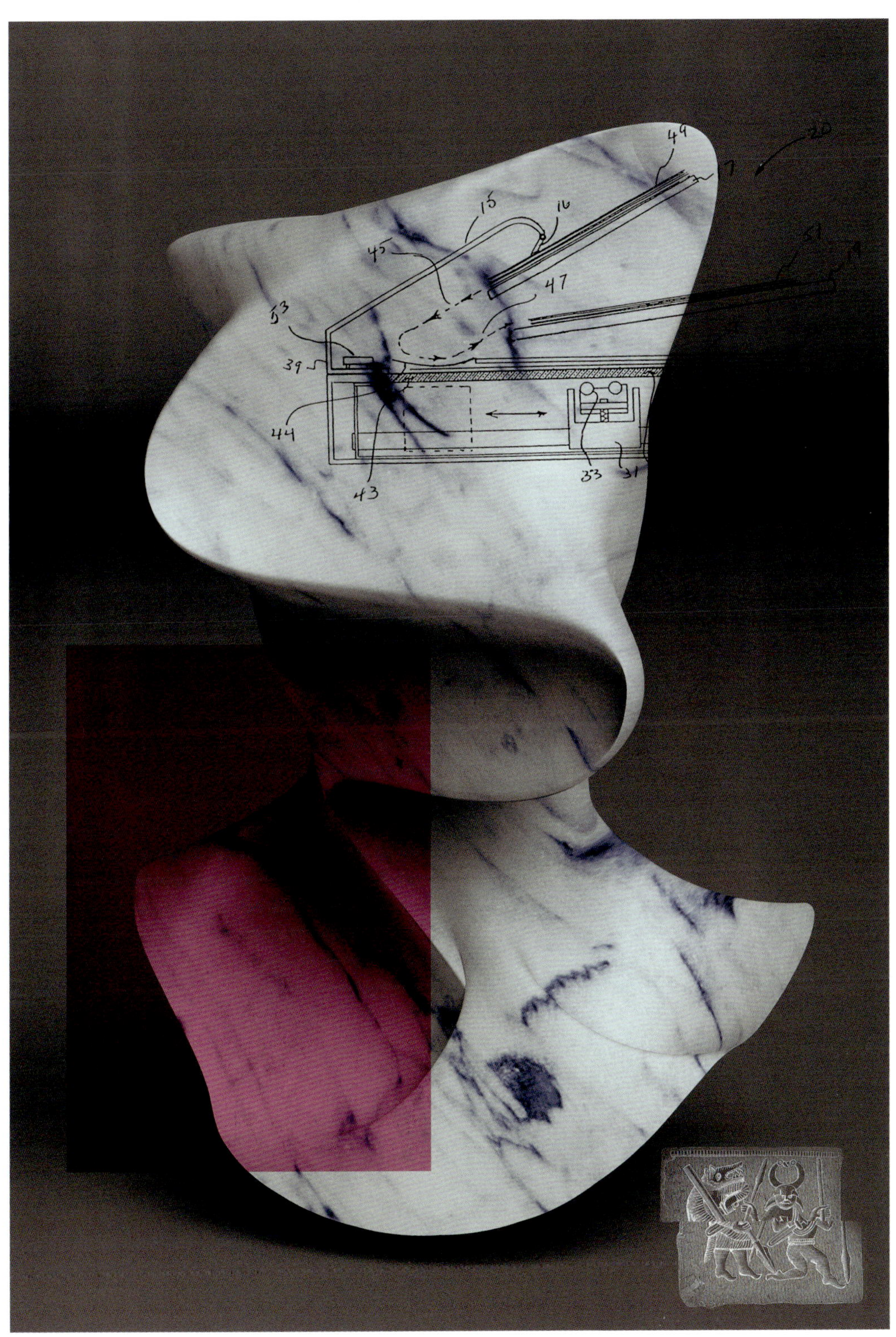

 Jon Rafman, *New Age Demanded (Illegibility of this world)*, 2013. Archival pigment print

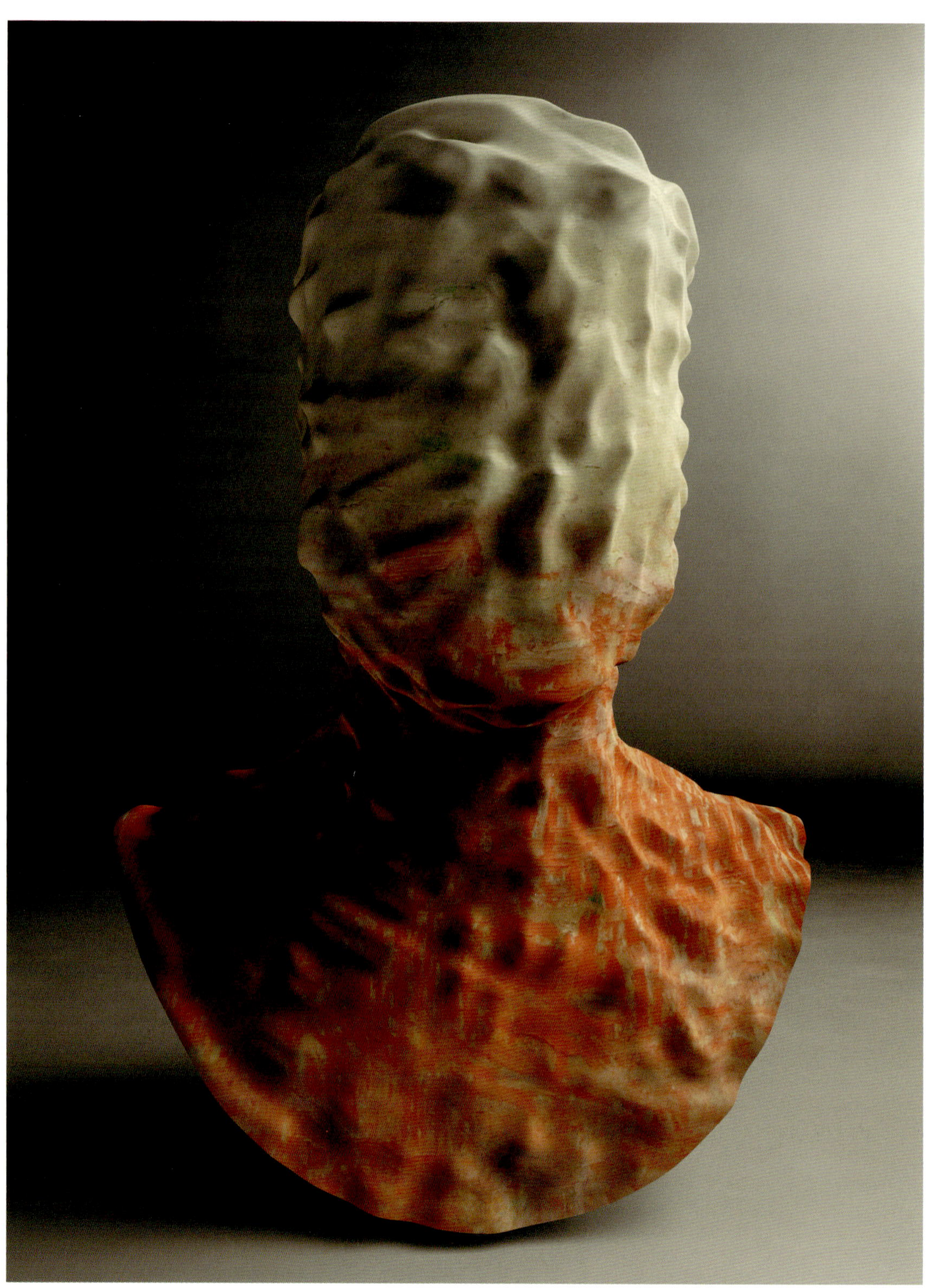

312    Jon Rafman, *New Age Demanded (Craggy Guston)*, 2011. Archival pigment print

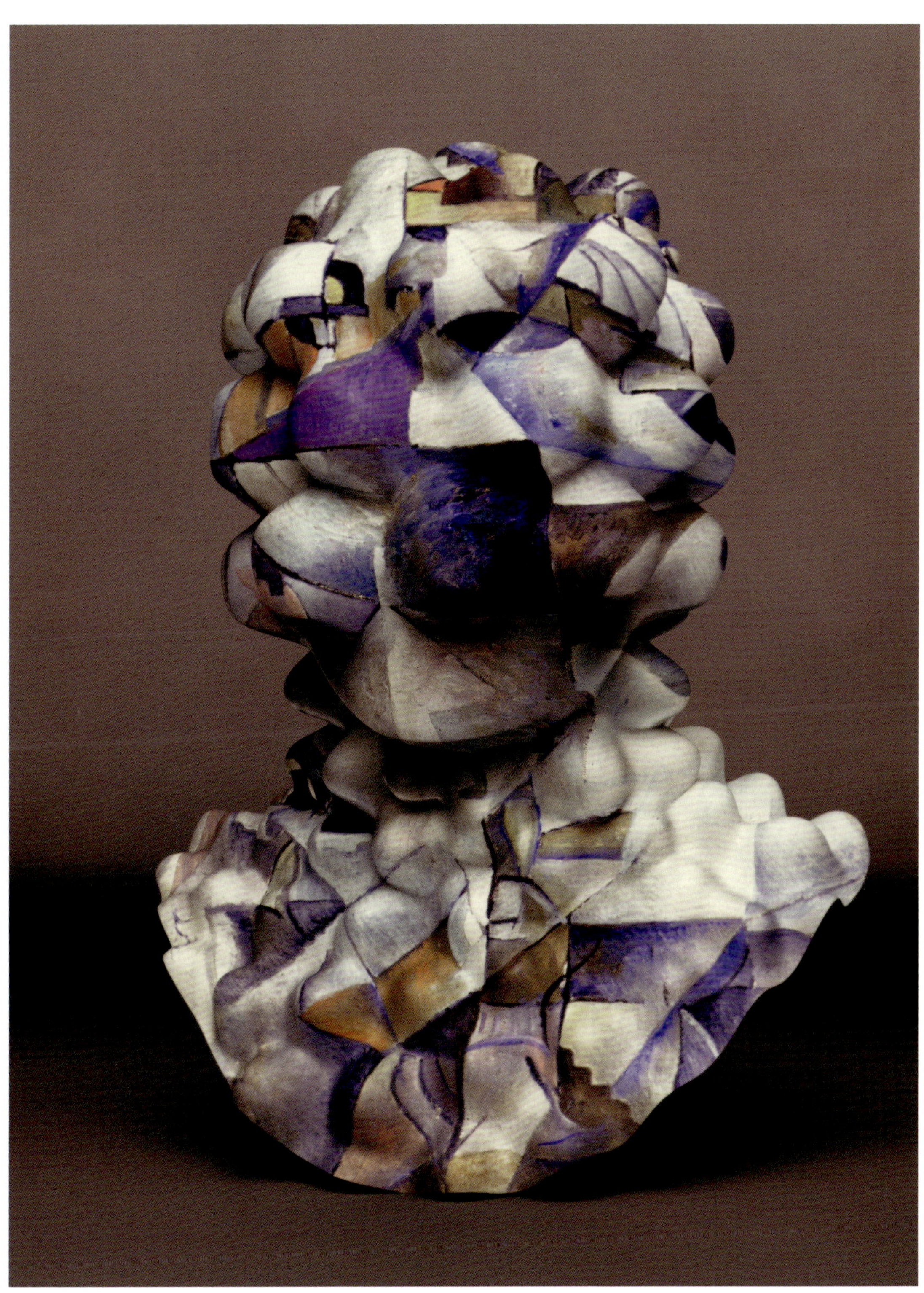

313    Jon Rafman, *New Age Demanded (Bubbly Malevich)*, 2012. Archival pigment print

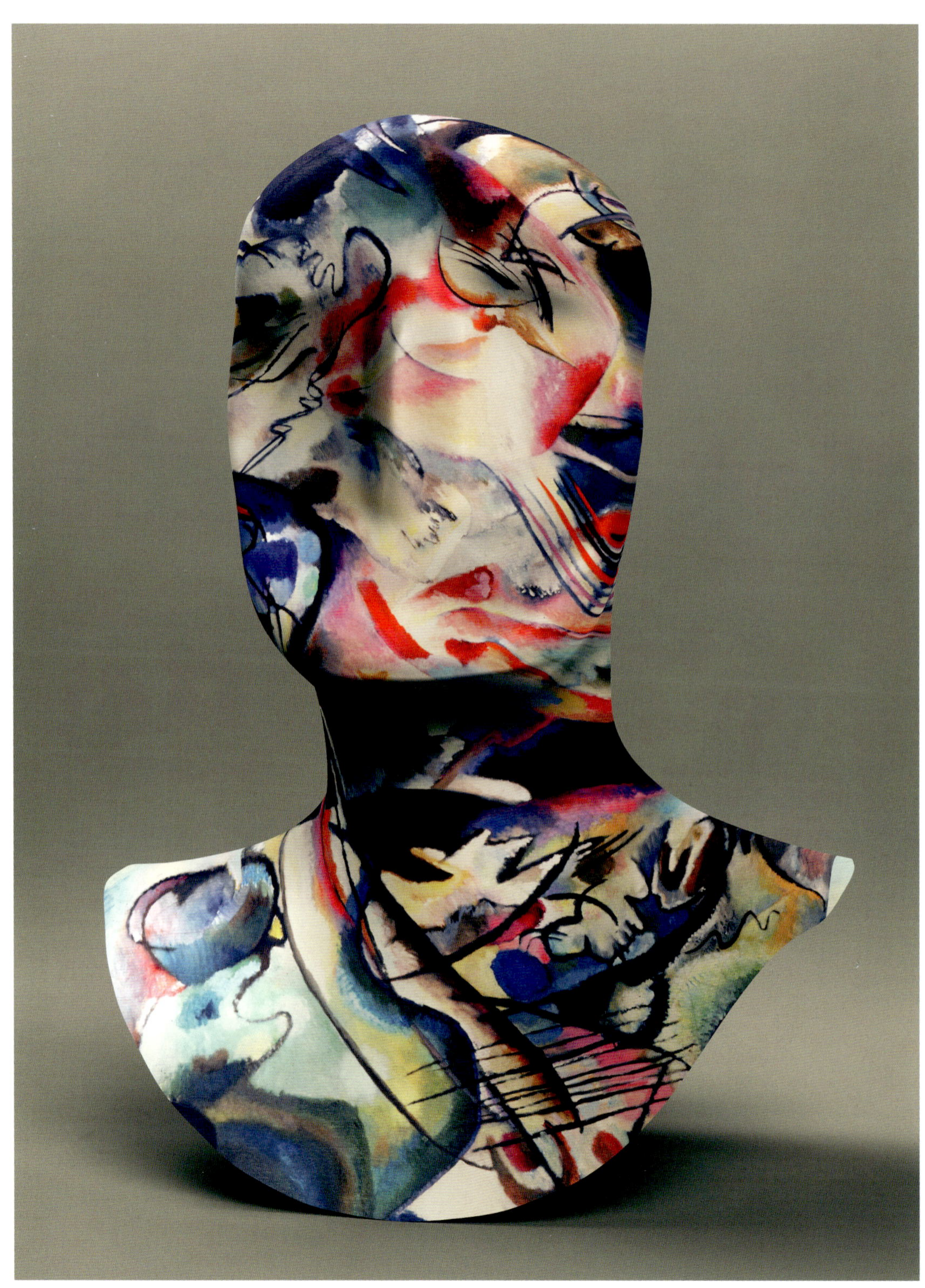

314    Jon Rafman, *New Age Demanded (Subtleface Kandinsky)*, 2011. Archival pigment print

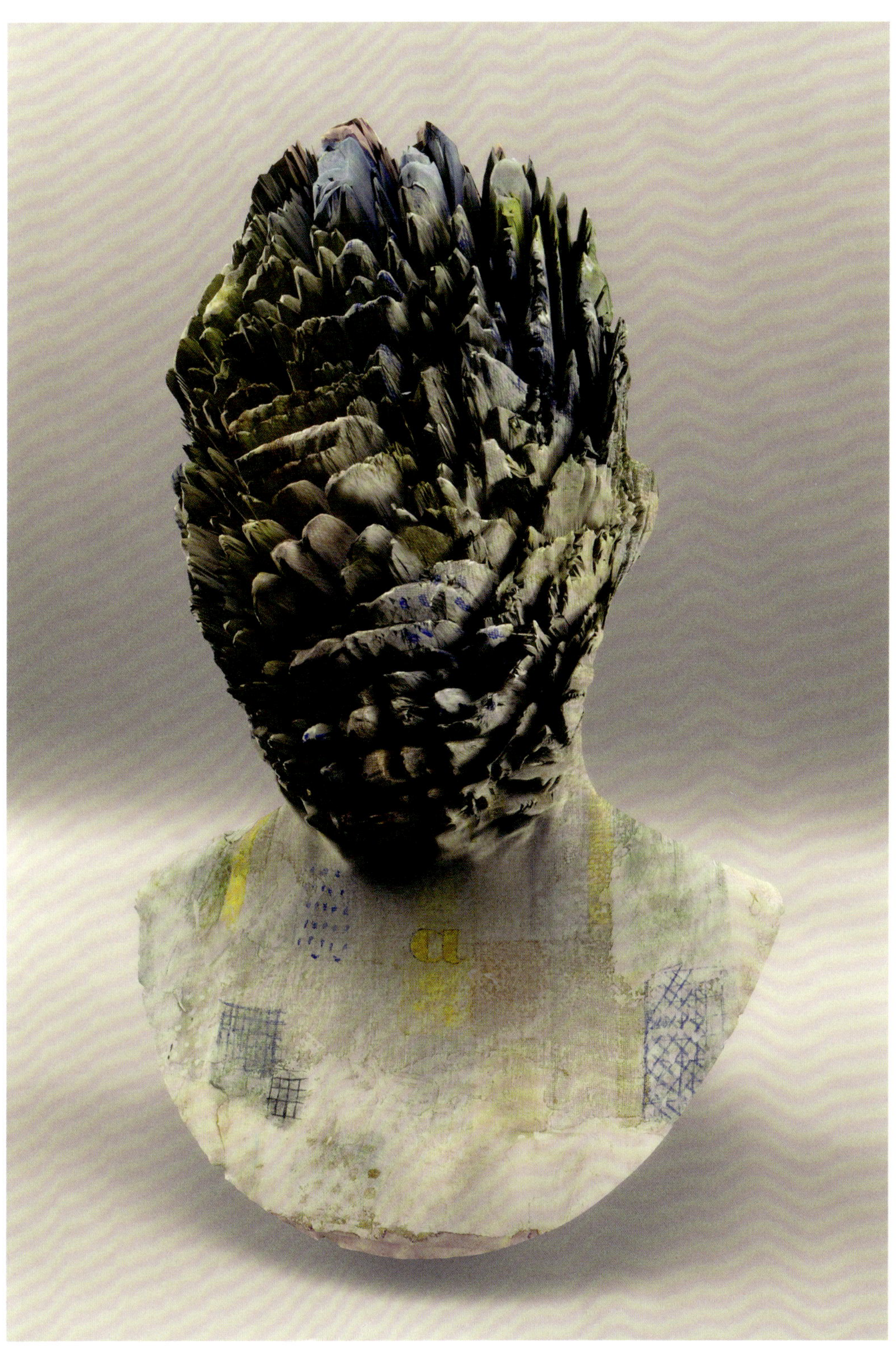

315    Jon Rafman, *New Age Demanded (Celeryface Klee)*, 2012. Archival pigment print

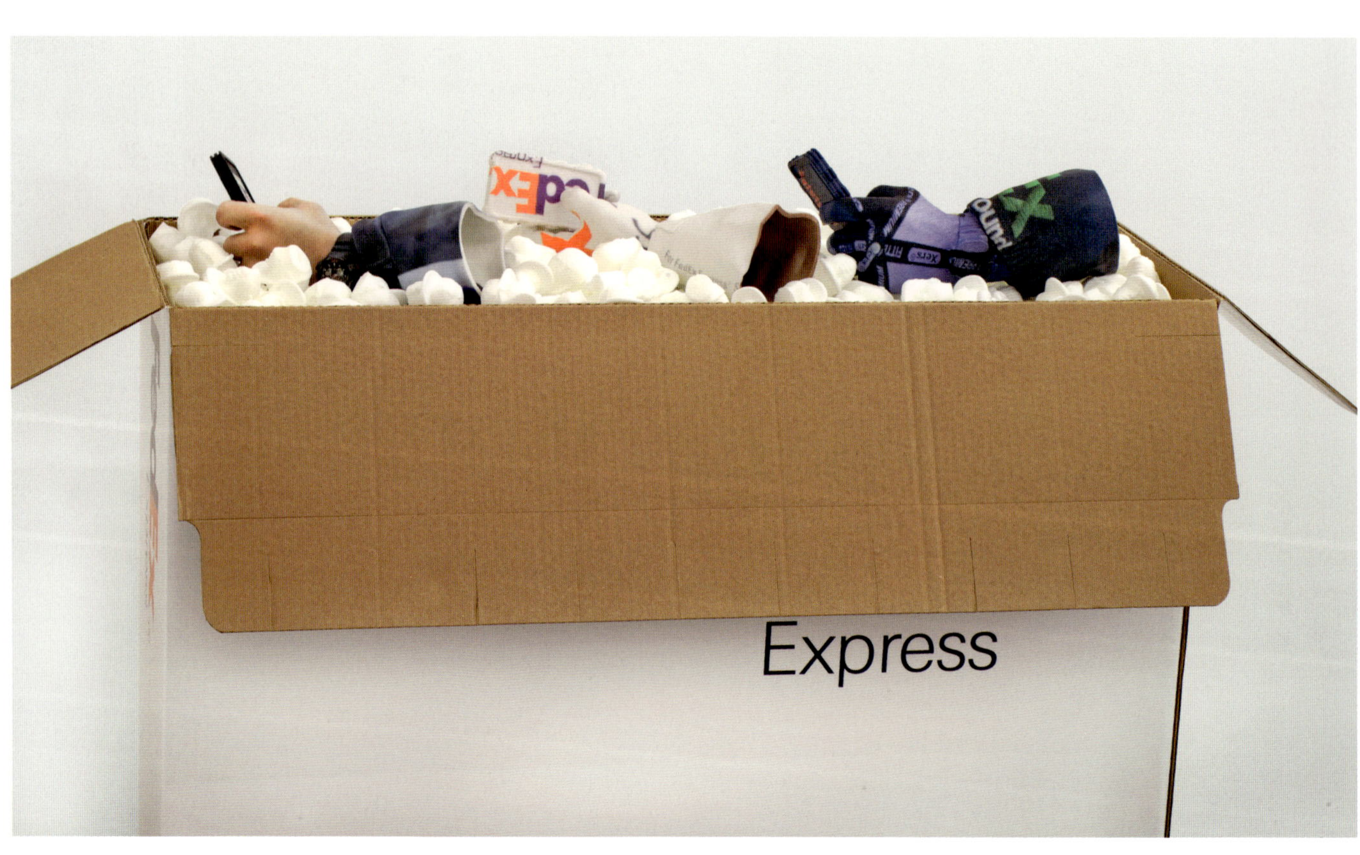

316 Josh Kline, *Unpaid Overtime (FedEx Worker's Hand with iPhone)*, 2014. 3D-printed sculptures in plaster with inkjet ink and cyanoacrylate, cast-urethane foam packing peanuts, vinyl, cardboard

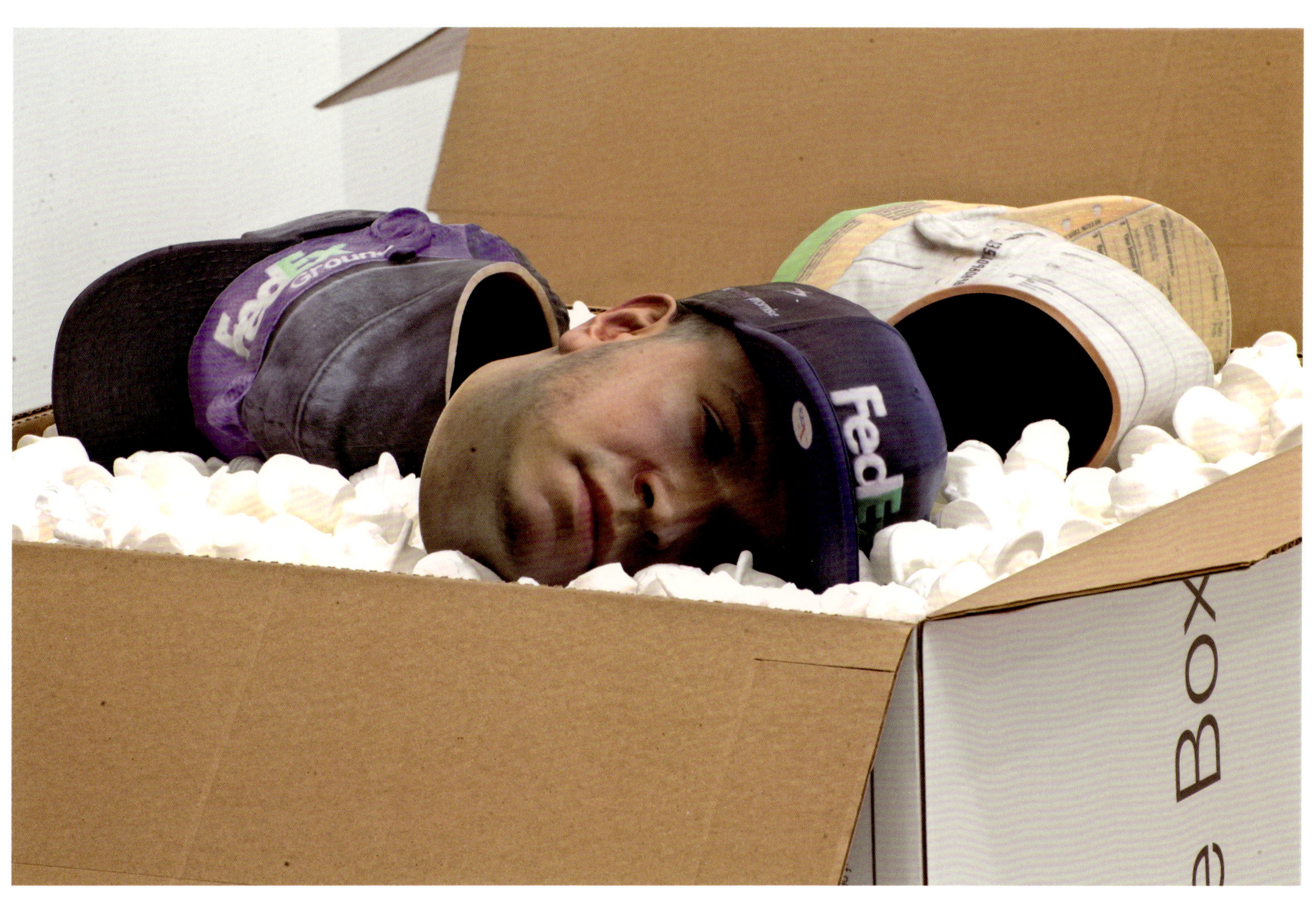

317    Josh Kline, *No Sick Days (FedEx Worker's Head with FedEx Cap)*, 2014. 3D-printed sculptures in plaster with inkjet ink and cyanoacrylate, cast-urethane foam packing peanuts, vinyl, cardboard

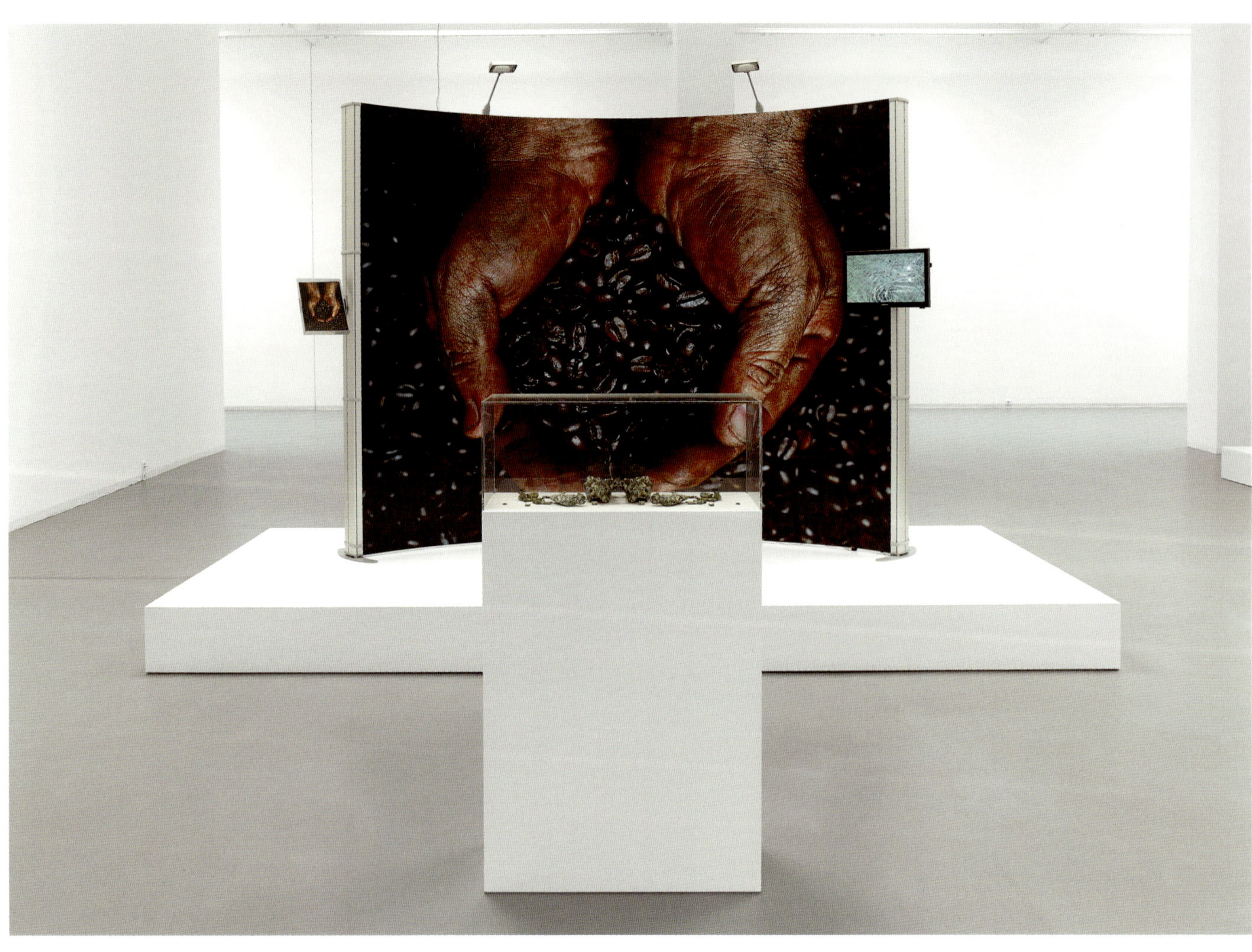

318    Timur Si-Qin, *Selection Display: Octanom Coffeehands*, 2013. Printed-fabric banner display and video

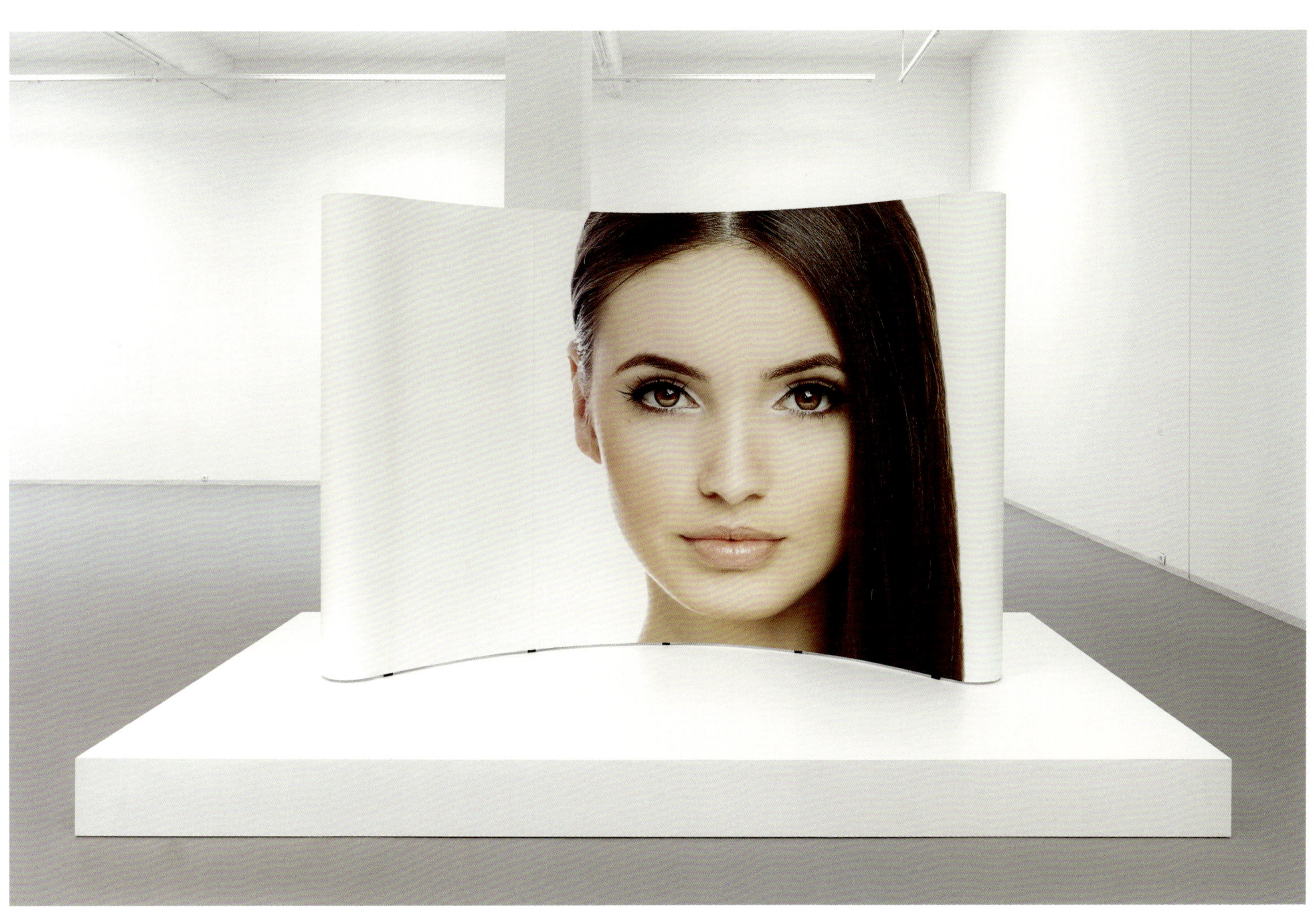

319    Timur Si-Qin, *Selection Display: Gender Dimorphic*, 2013. Printed-fabric banner display

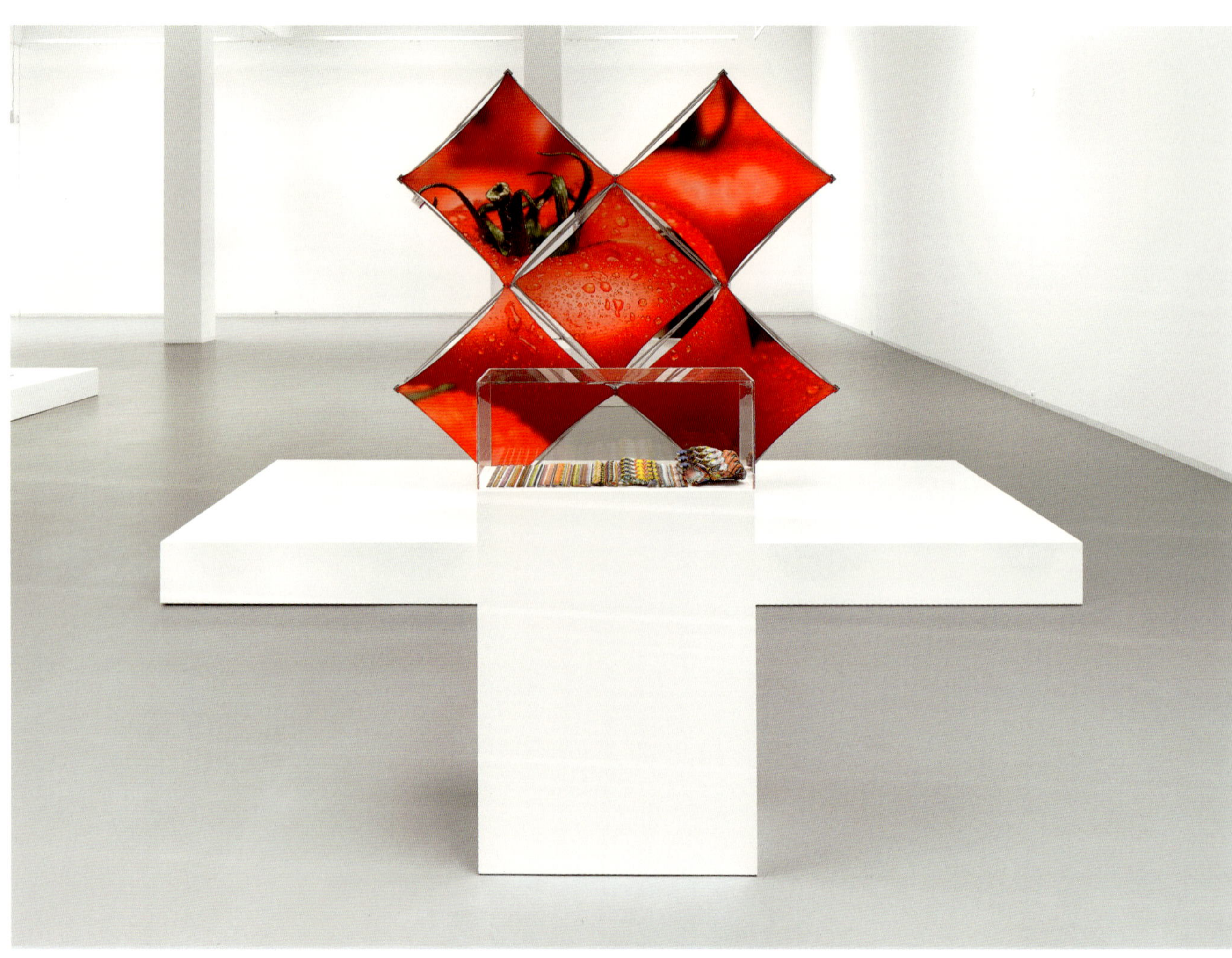

320   Timur Si-Qin, *Selection Display: Tomato Quadra*, 2013. Printed-fabric banner display

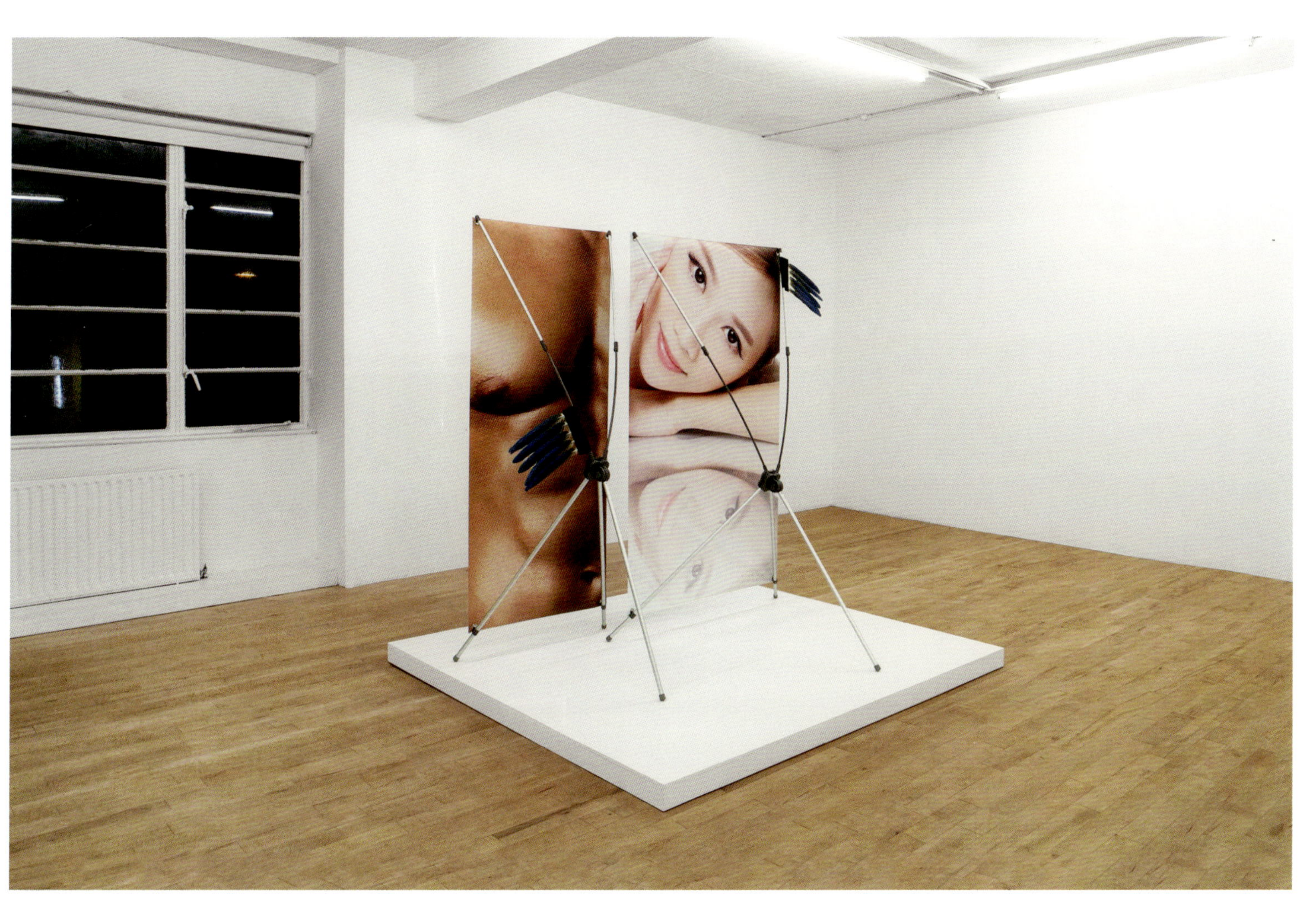

321    Timur Si-Qin, *Deliver Me from Dipolar Spirits*, 2014. Aluminum X-banner stands, PVC block-out banner

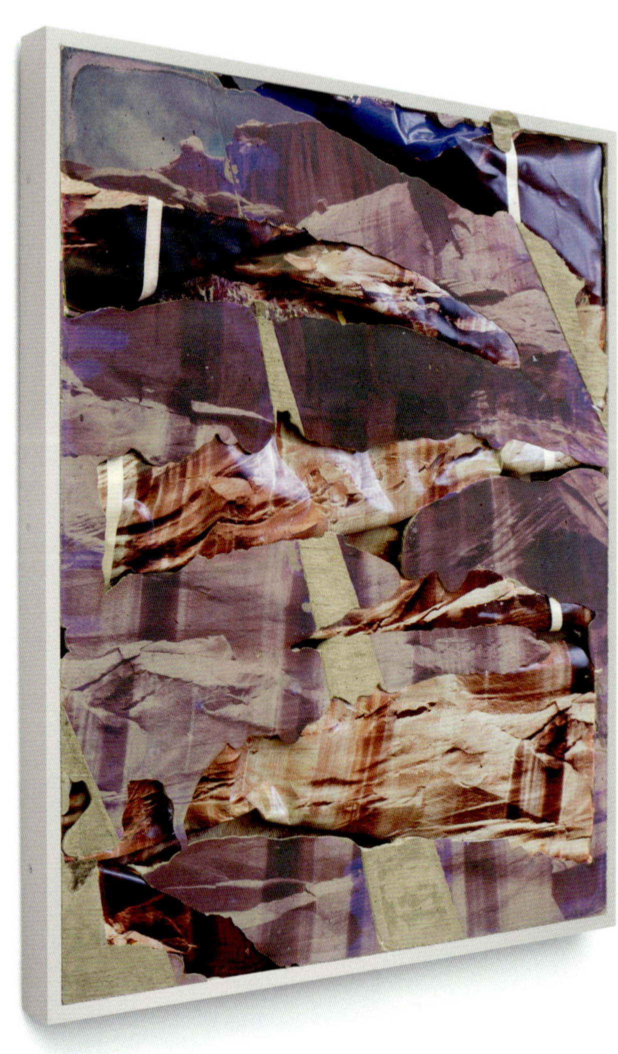

322    Letha Wilson, *Sandstone Canyon Utah (Waterlines)*, 2014. Unique C-print

323    Letha Wilson, *Salt Flats Concrete Fold*, 2013. C-print with UV laminate, concrete

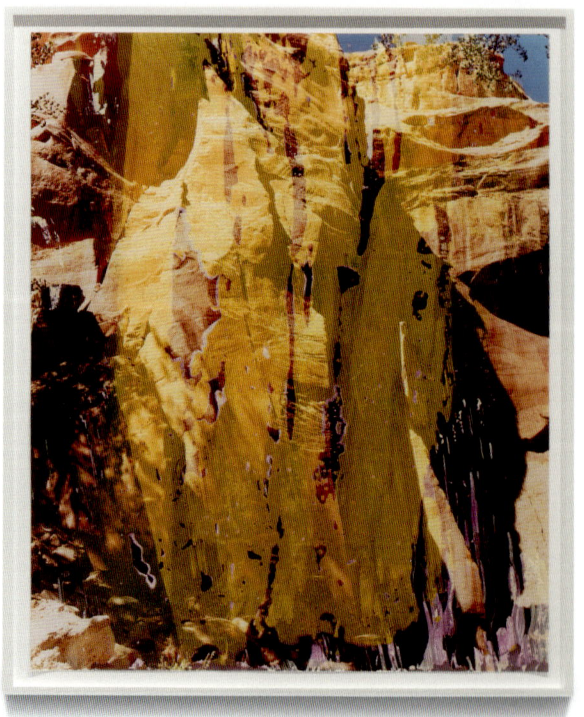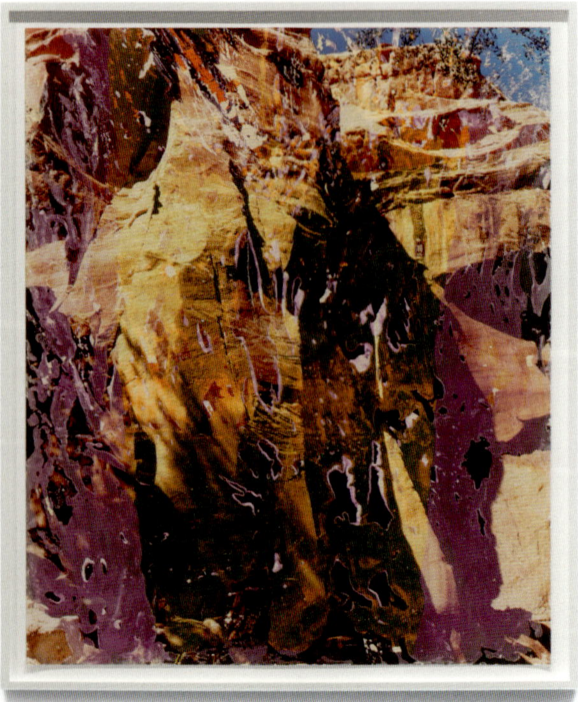

324    Letha Wilson, *Capital Reef Cement Dip (Facedown 2) (Facedown 1)*, 2013. Two C-prints, white Portland cement

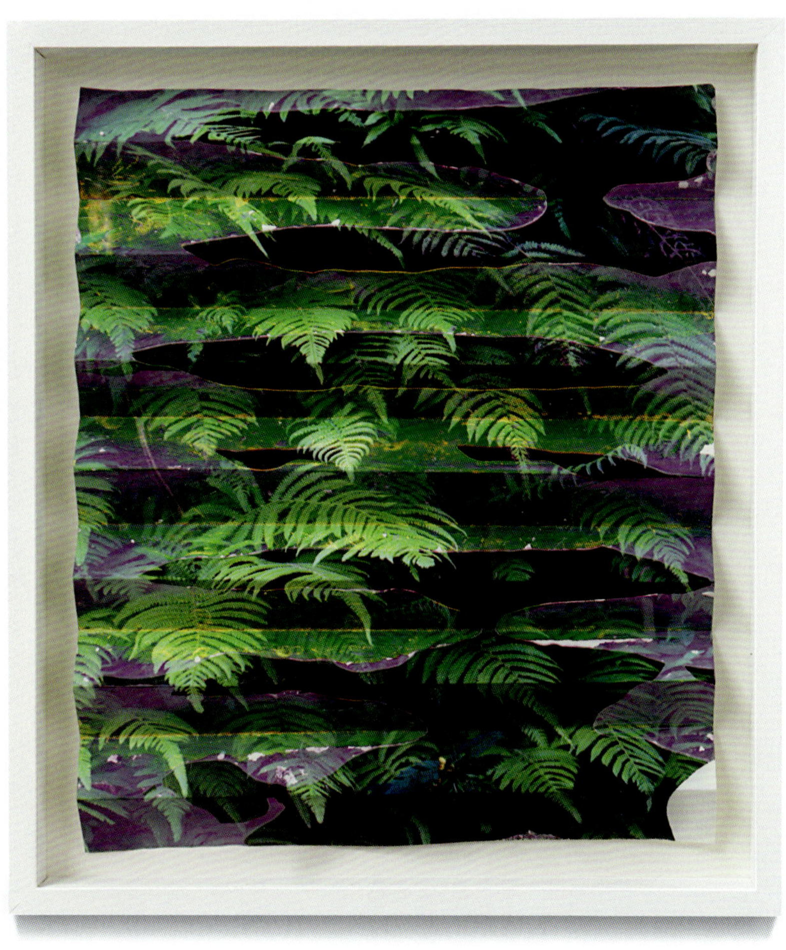

325    Letha Wilson, *Ferns Green Cement Fold*, 2014. Unique C-print, white Portland cement

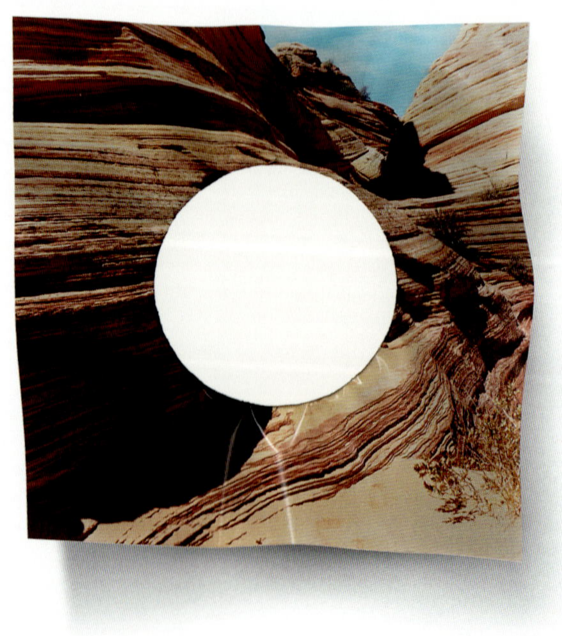

326    Letha Wilson, *Coyote Buttes Wall Punch*, 2015. Unique C-print, drywall

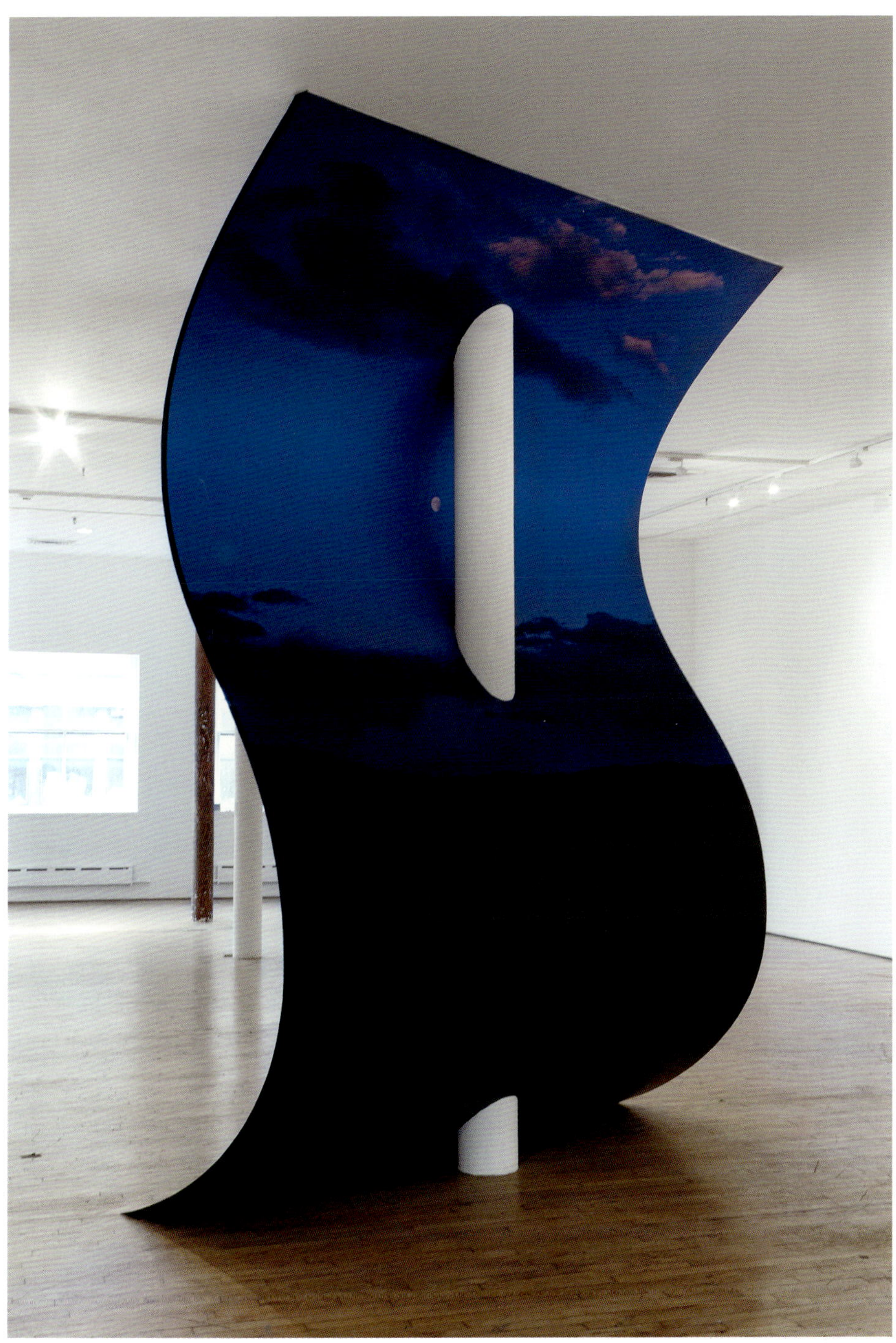

327     Letha Wilson, *Moon Wave*, 2013. Digital print on adhesive vinyl, wood, gallery column

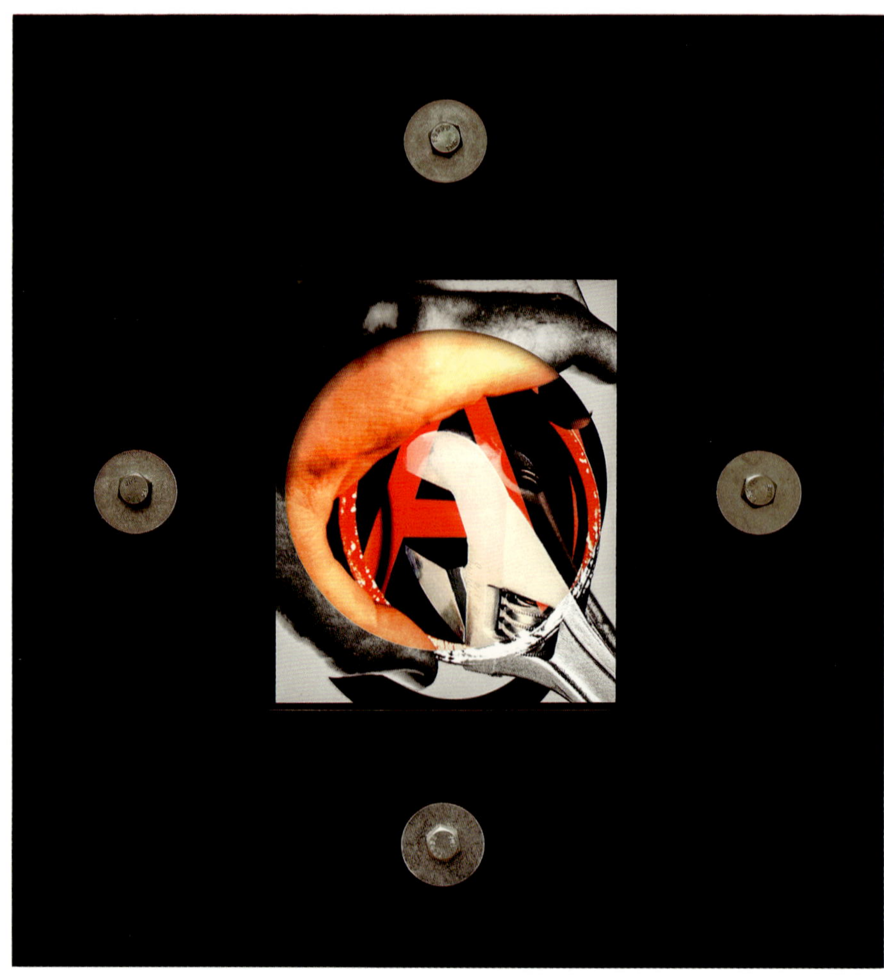

    Joshua Kolbo, *Untitled*, 2013. Archival pigment print on vinyl, C-print in artist's frame

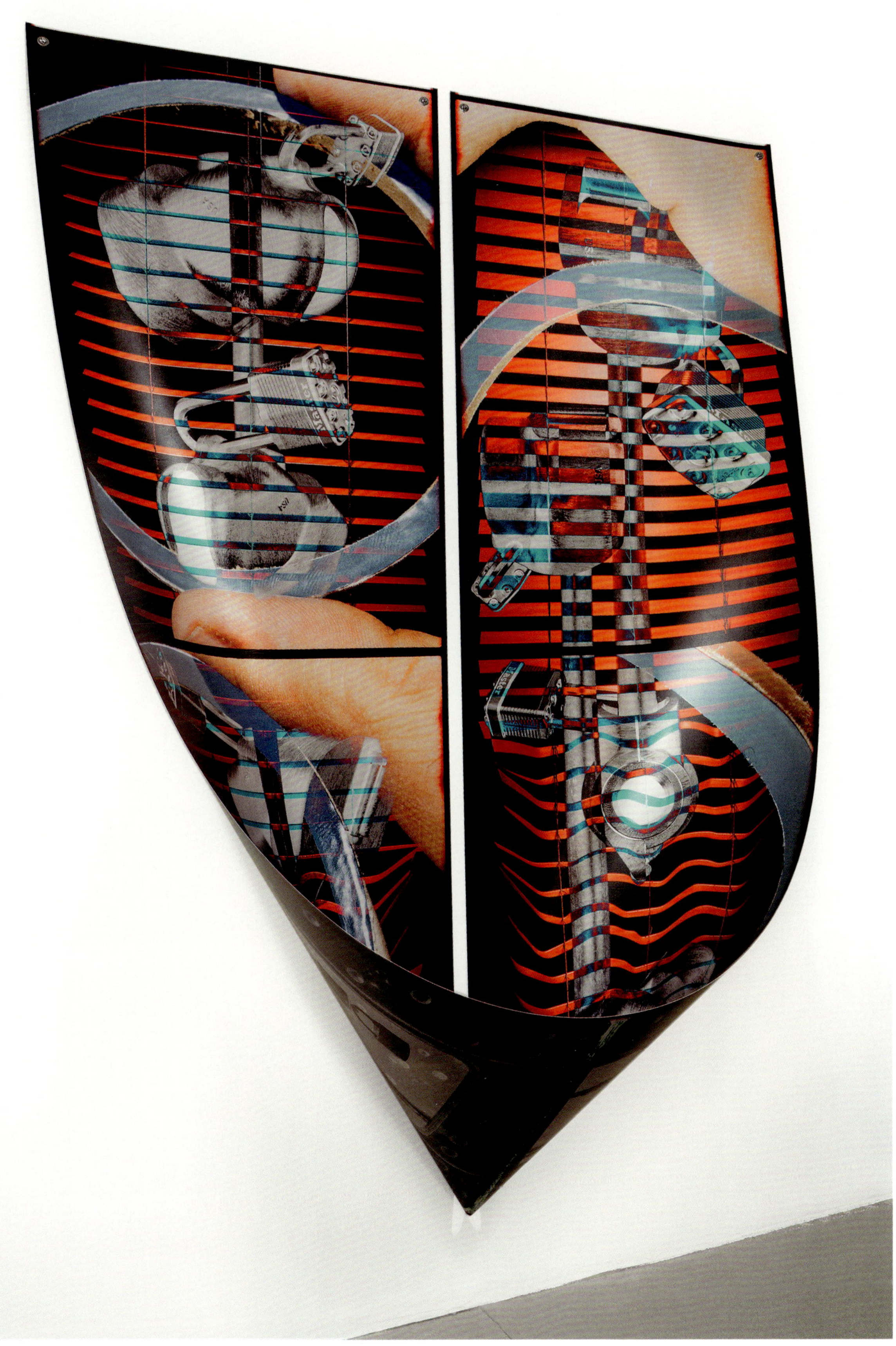

     Joshua Kolbo, *Untitled*, 2014. Two C-prints, UV laminate

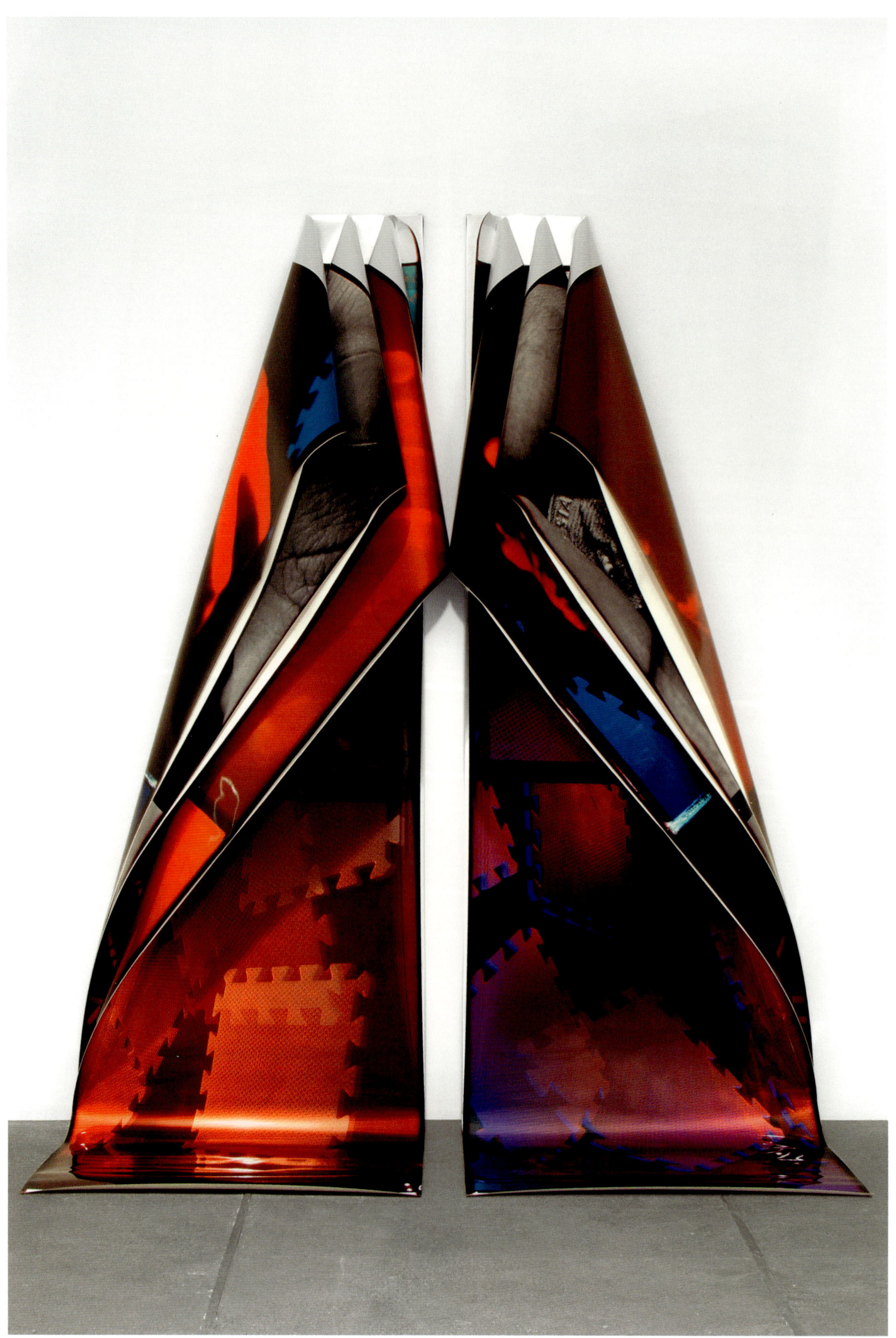

330    Joshua Kolbo, *Untitled*, 2011. Twelve unique C-prints

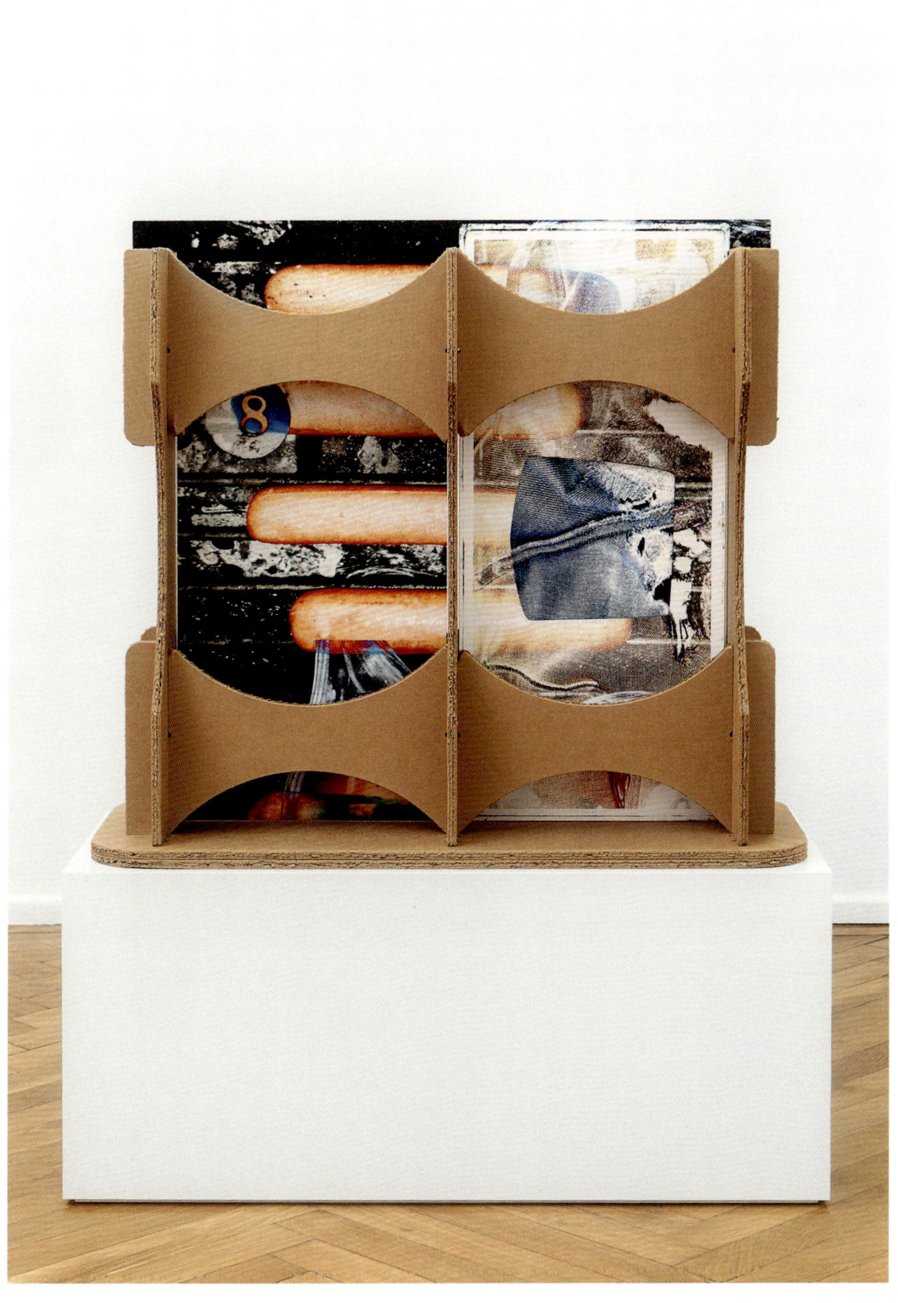

331    Joshua Kolbo, *Untitled*, 2013. CNC-routed cardboard, laser-cut acrylic, archival pigment print on vinyl, digital C-print

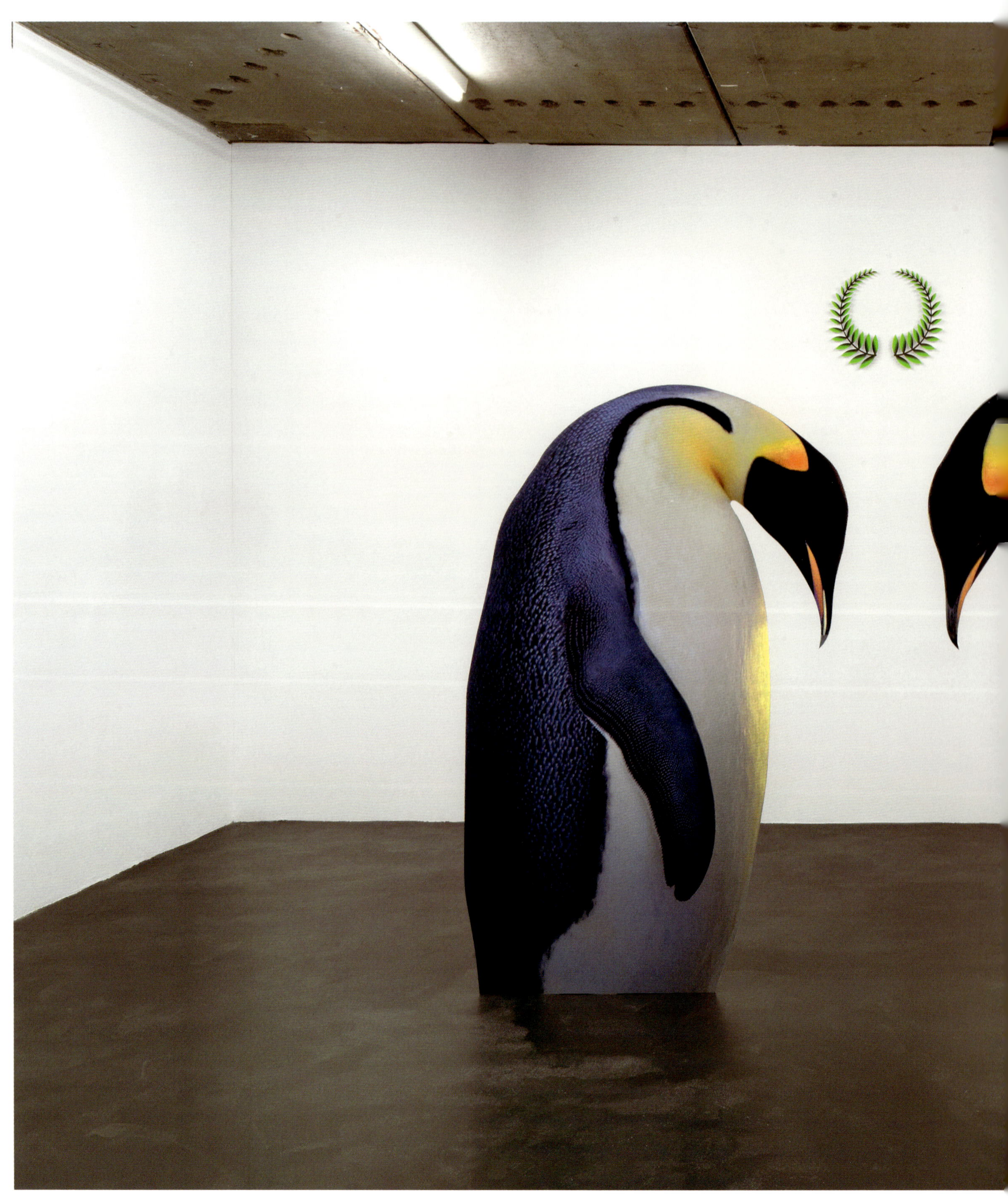

332    Katja Novitskova, *Approximation I*, 2012. Digital print on aluminum Dibond, cut-out display, found image

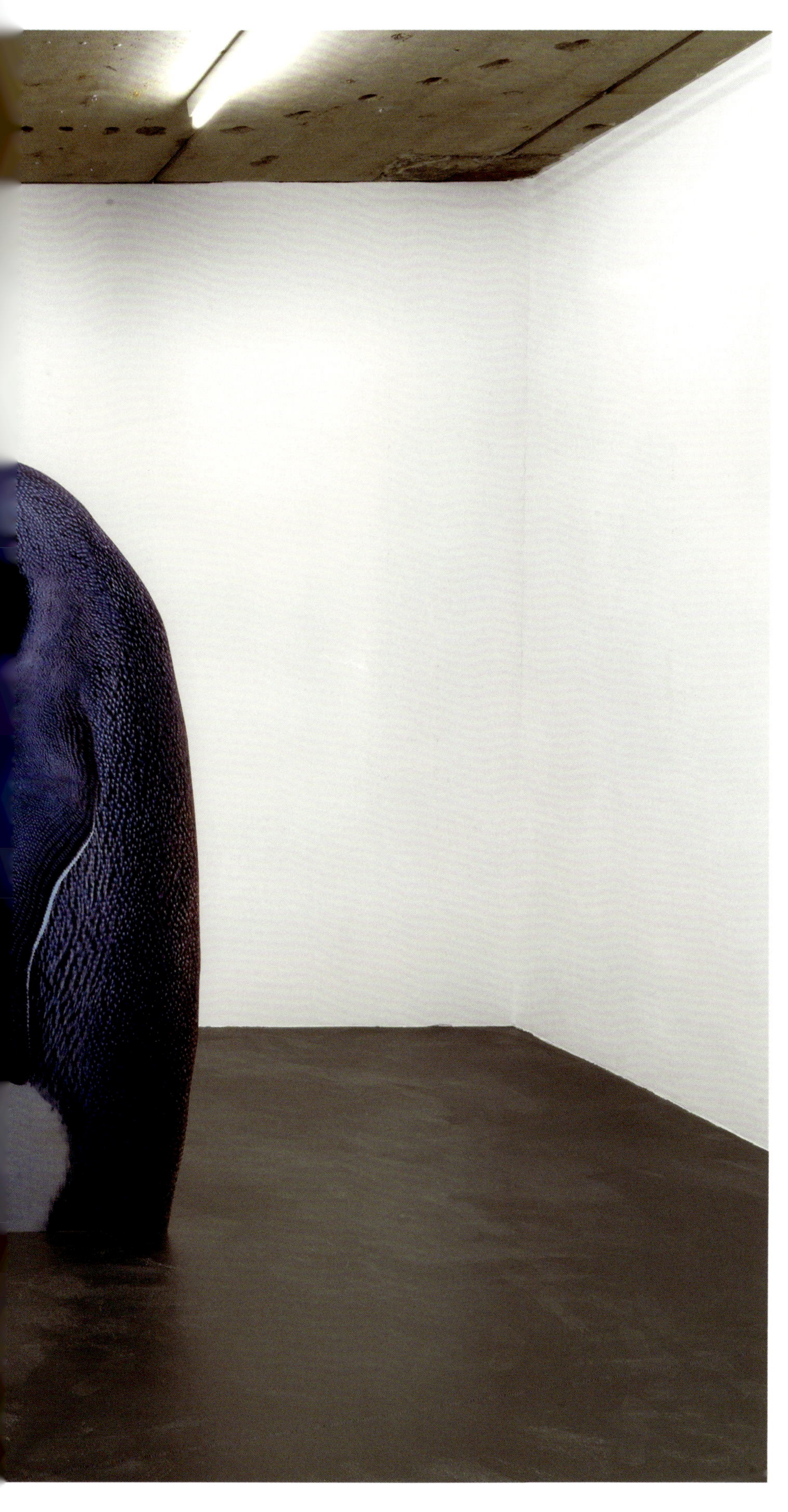

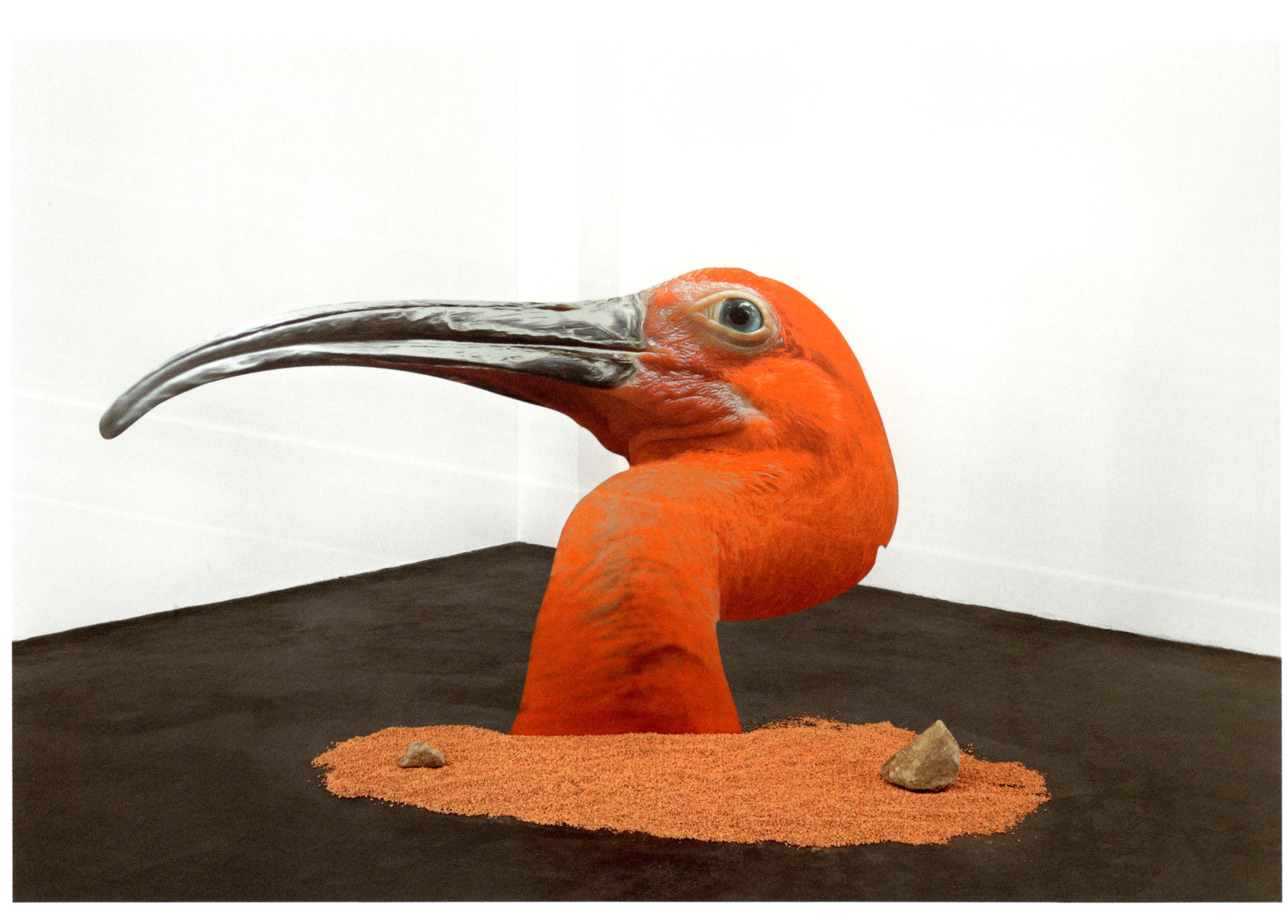

 Katja Novitskova, *Approximation Mars I*, 2012. Digital print on aluminum Dibond, cut-out display, found image

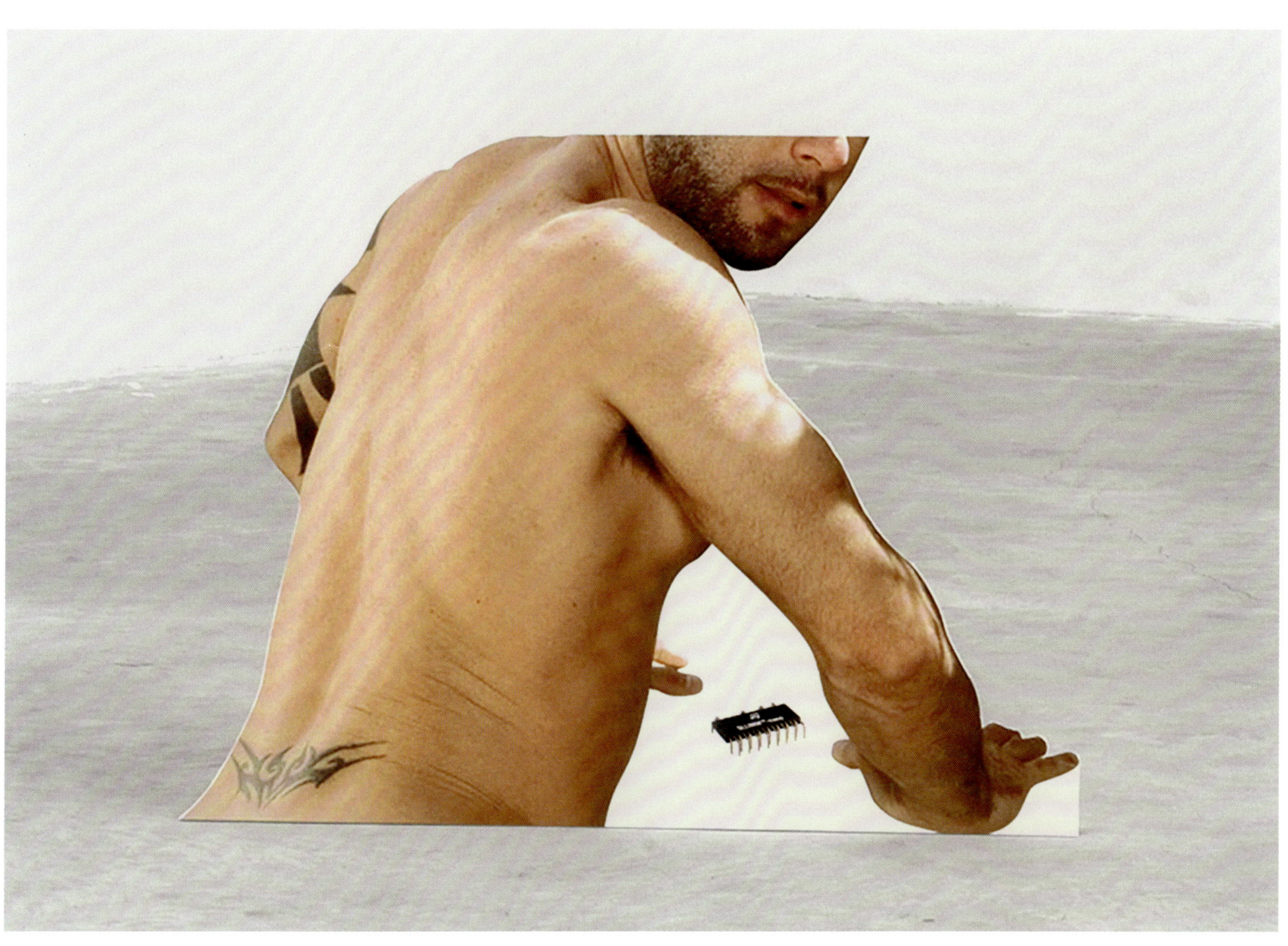

335     Katja Novitskova, *Free Market*, 2012. Digital print on aluminum Dibond, cut-out display, found image of Orlando Toro, found image of a SLLIMM-nano intelligent power module produced at STMicroelectronics factory in Catania, Italy

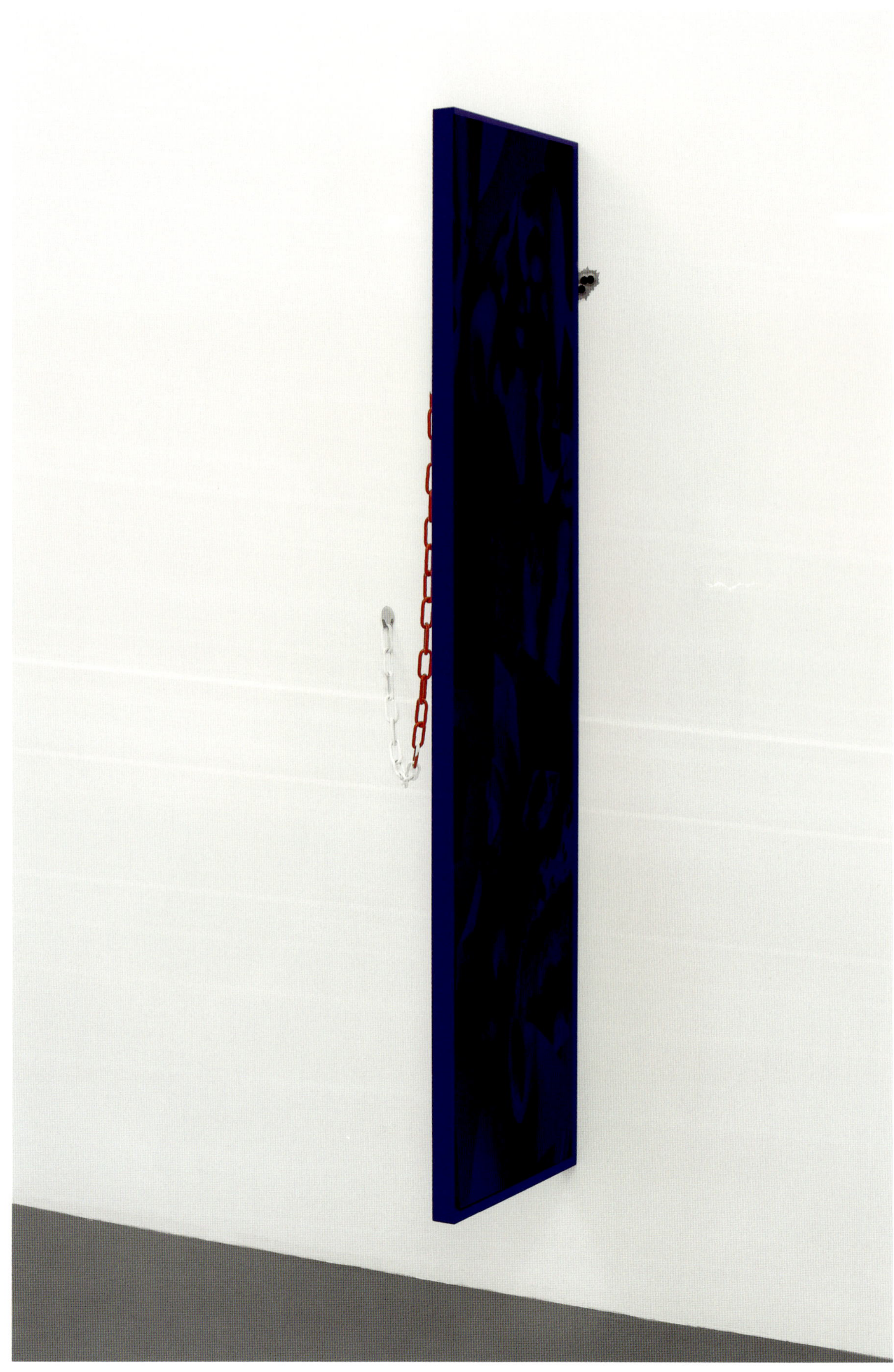

336    Kate Steciw, *Composition 003*, 2014. C-print, Plexiglas, wood, mixed media

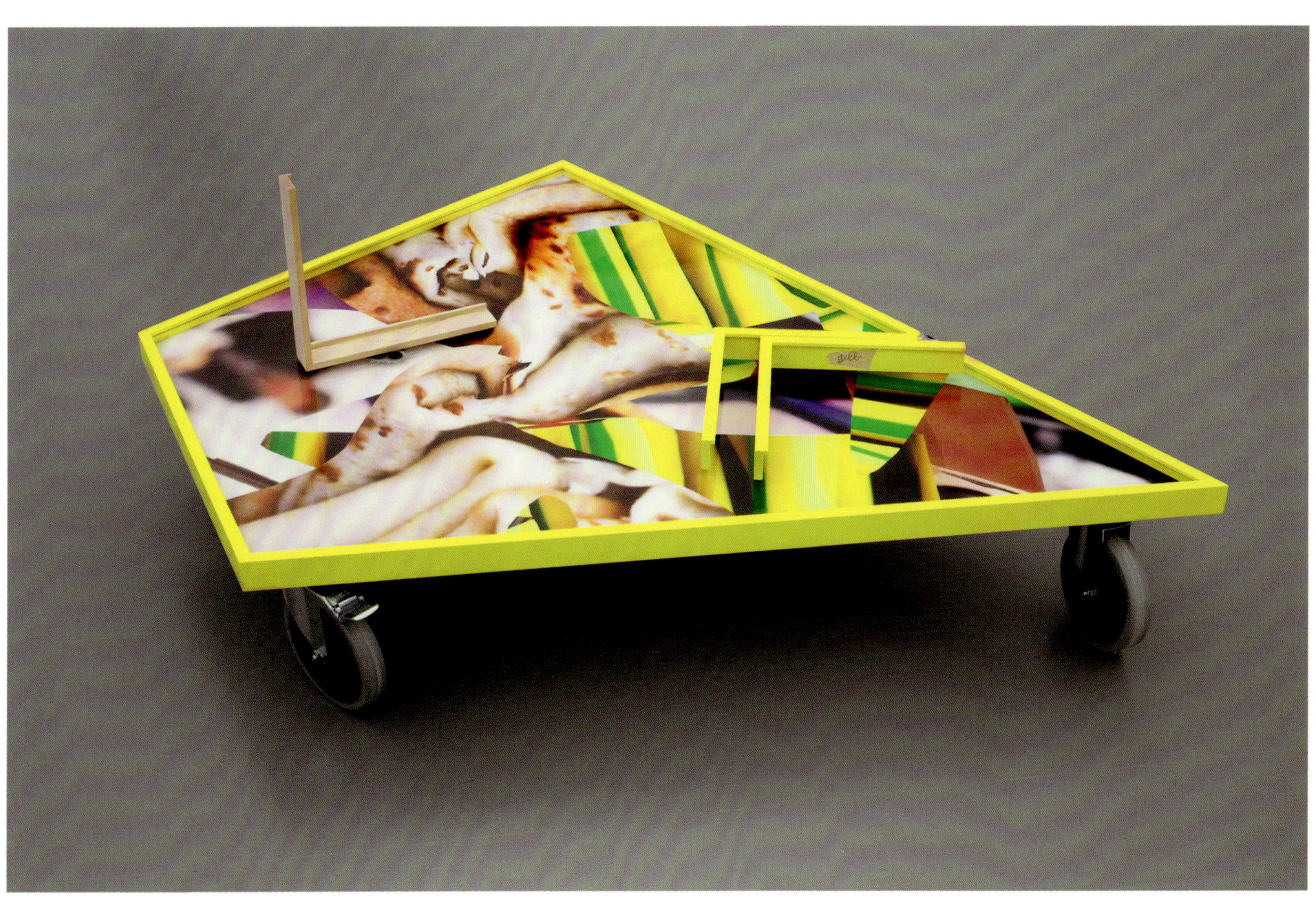

337    Kate Steciw, *Composition 011*, 2014. C-print, Plexiglas, wood, mixed media

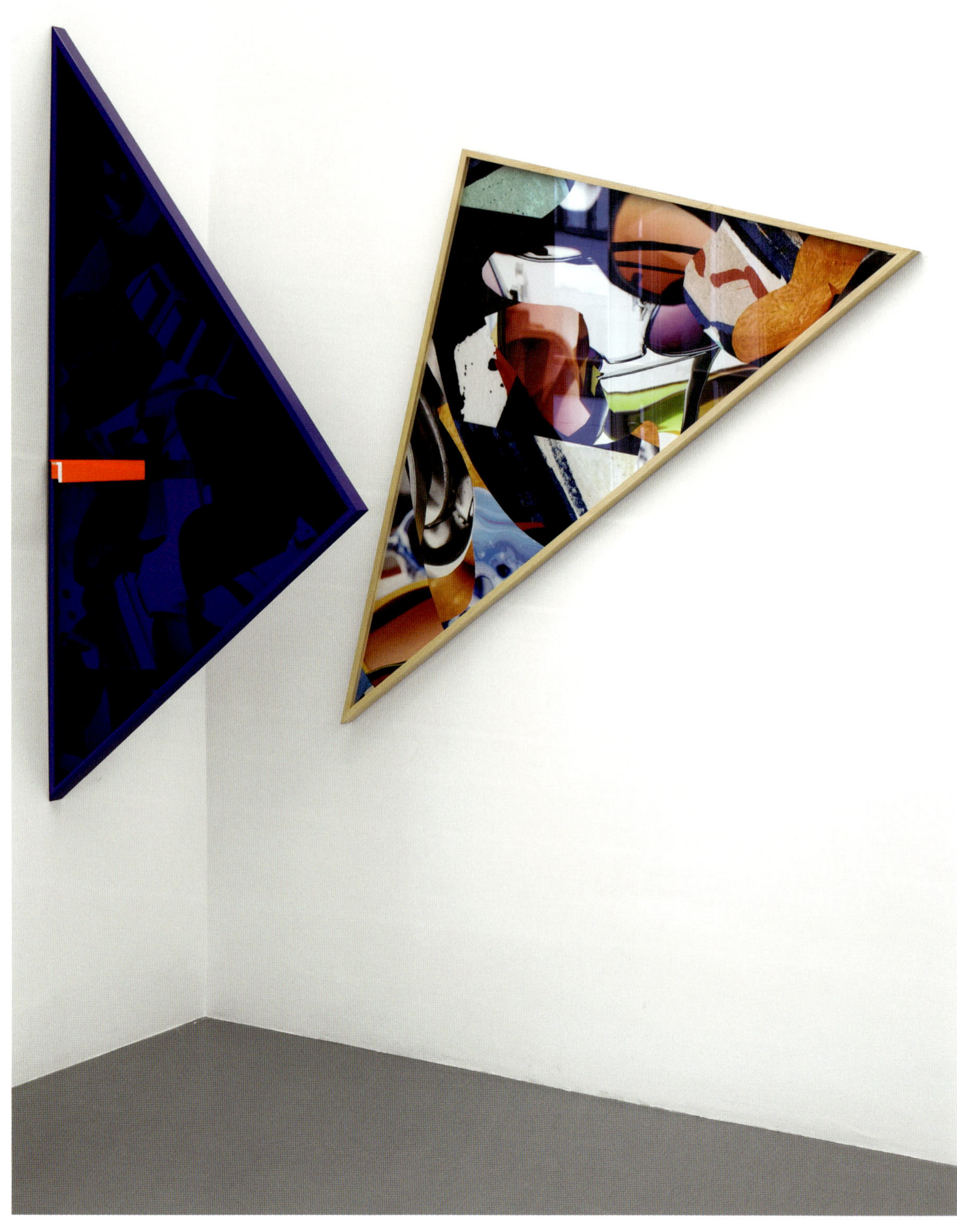

    Kate Steciw, *Compositions 006 and 007*, 2014. C-print, Plexiglas, wood, mixed media

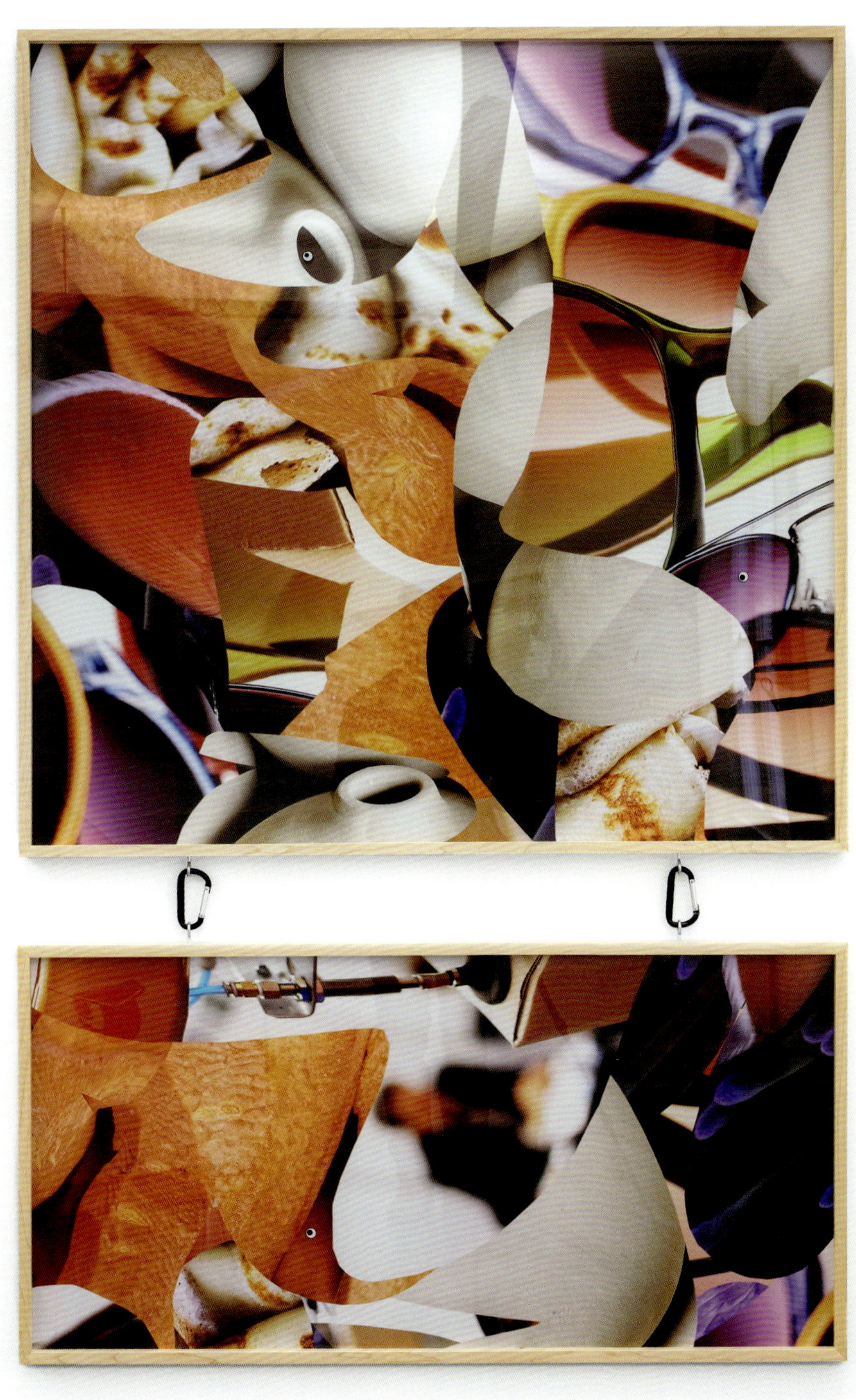

339　Kate Steciw, *Composition 004*, 2014. C-print, Plexiglas, wood, mixed media

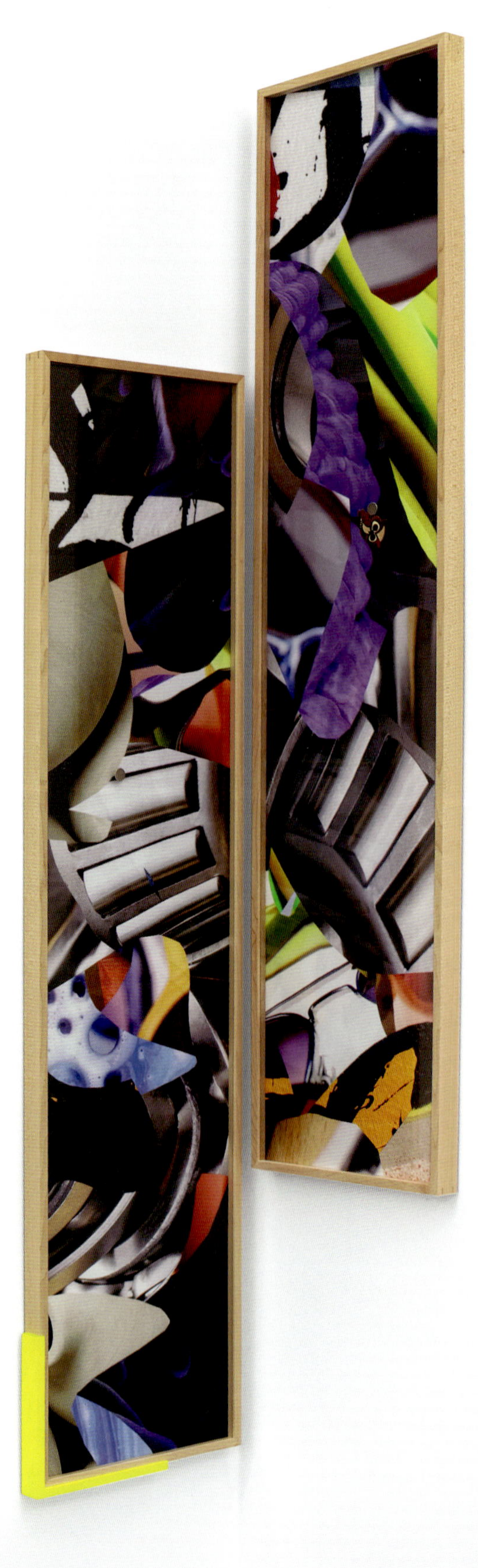

    Kate Steciw, *Composition 001 and 002*, 2014. C-print, Plexiglas, wood, mixed media

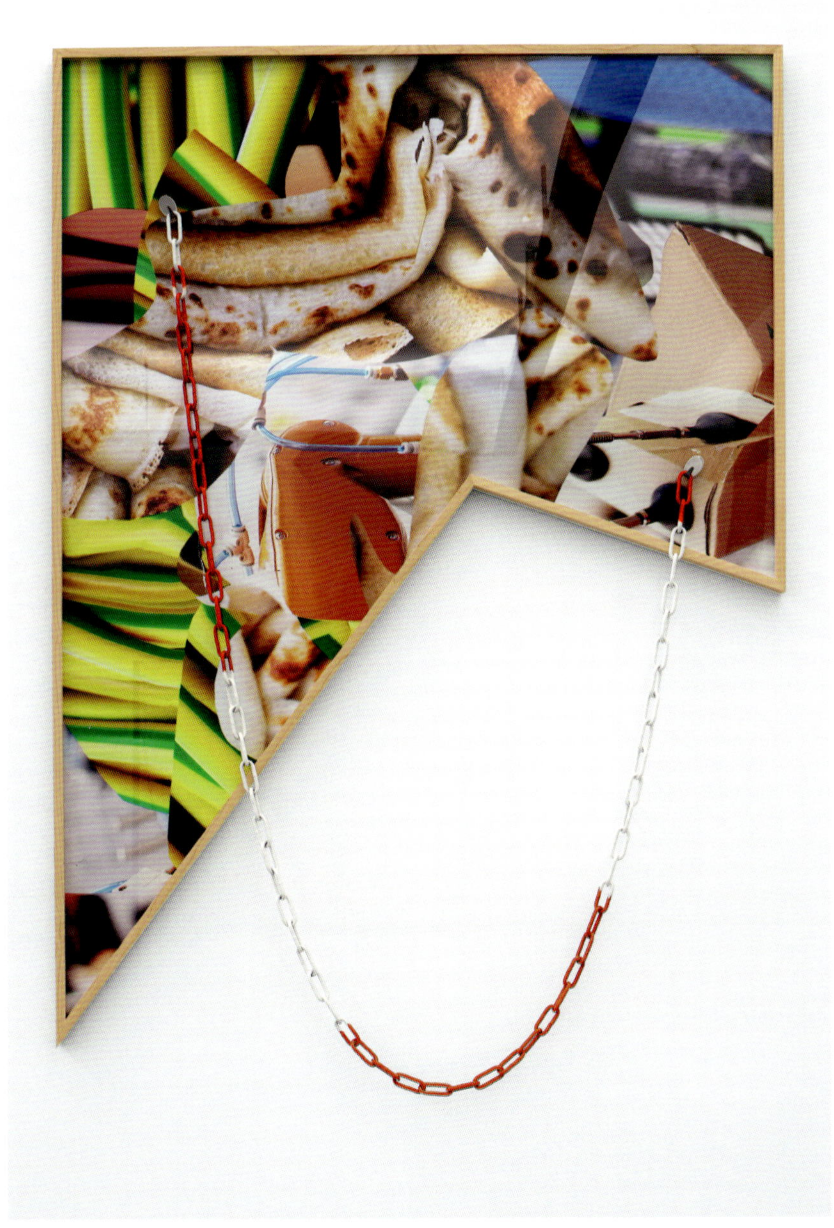

341    Kate Steciw, *Composition 008*, 2014. C-print, Plexiglas, wood, mixed media

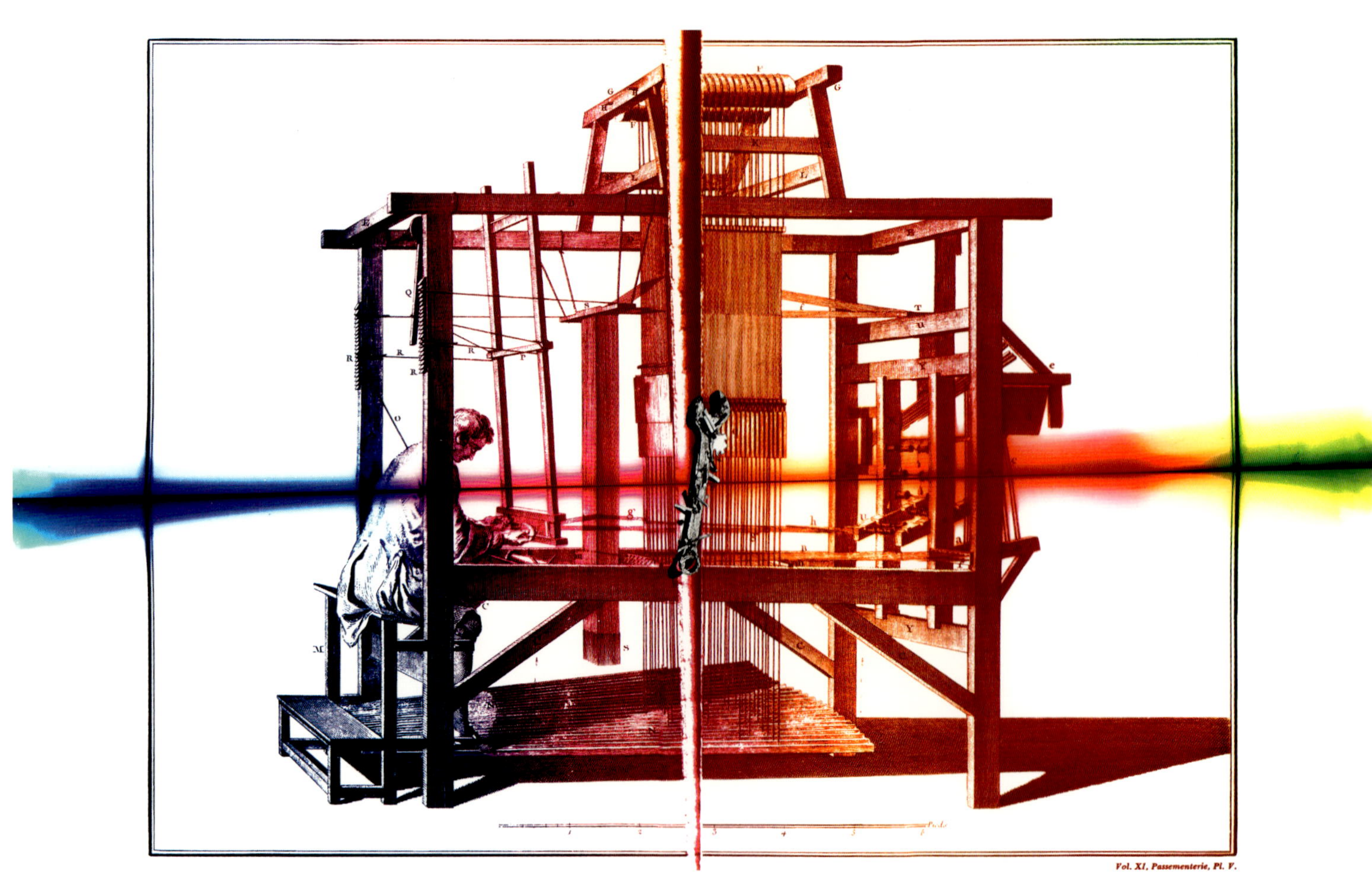



342    Carter Mull, *Typist*, 2011. LightJet C-print on metallic paper

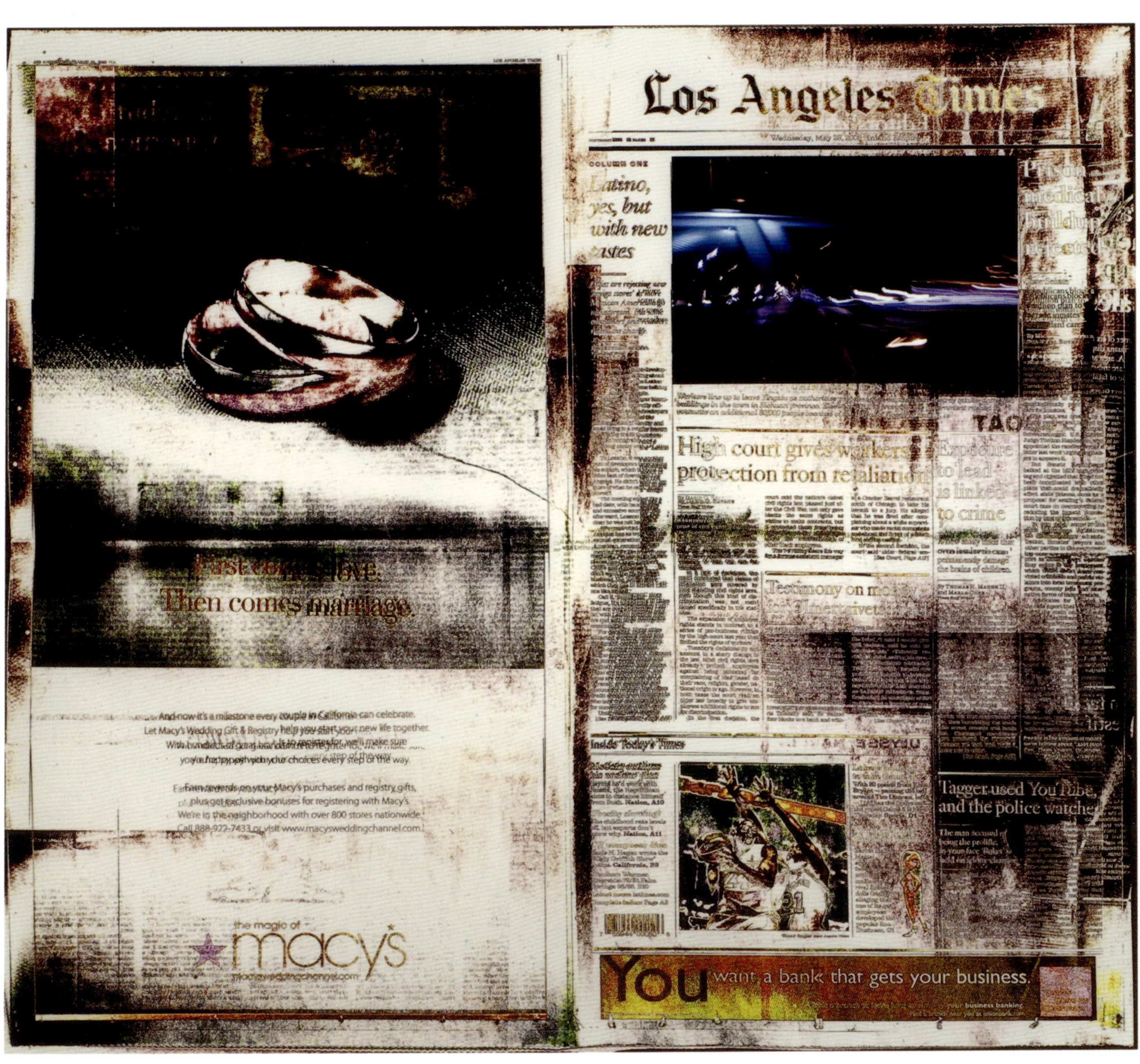

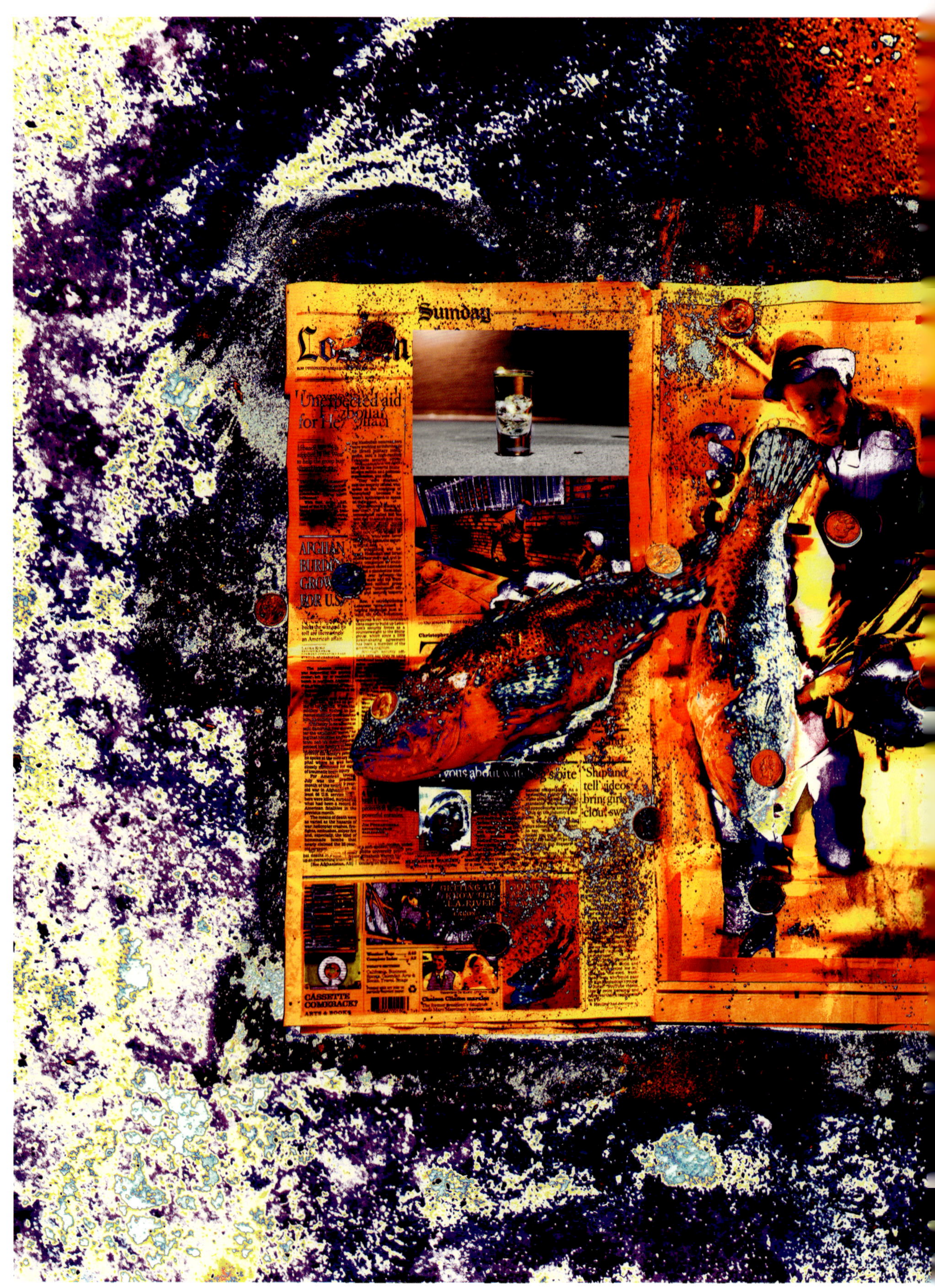

    Carter Mull, *Shot*, 2010. LightJet C-print and pasted print

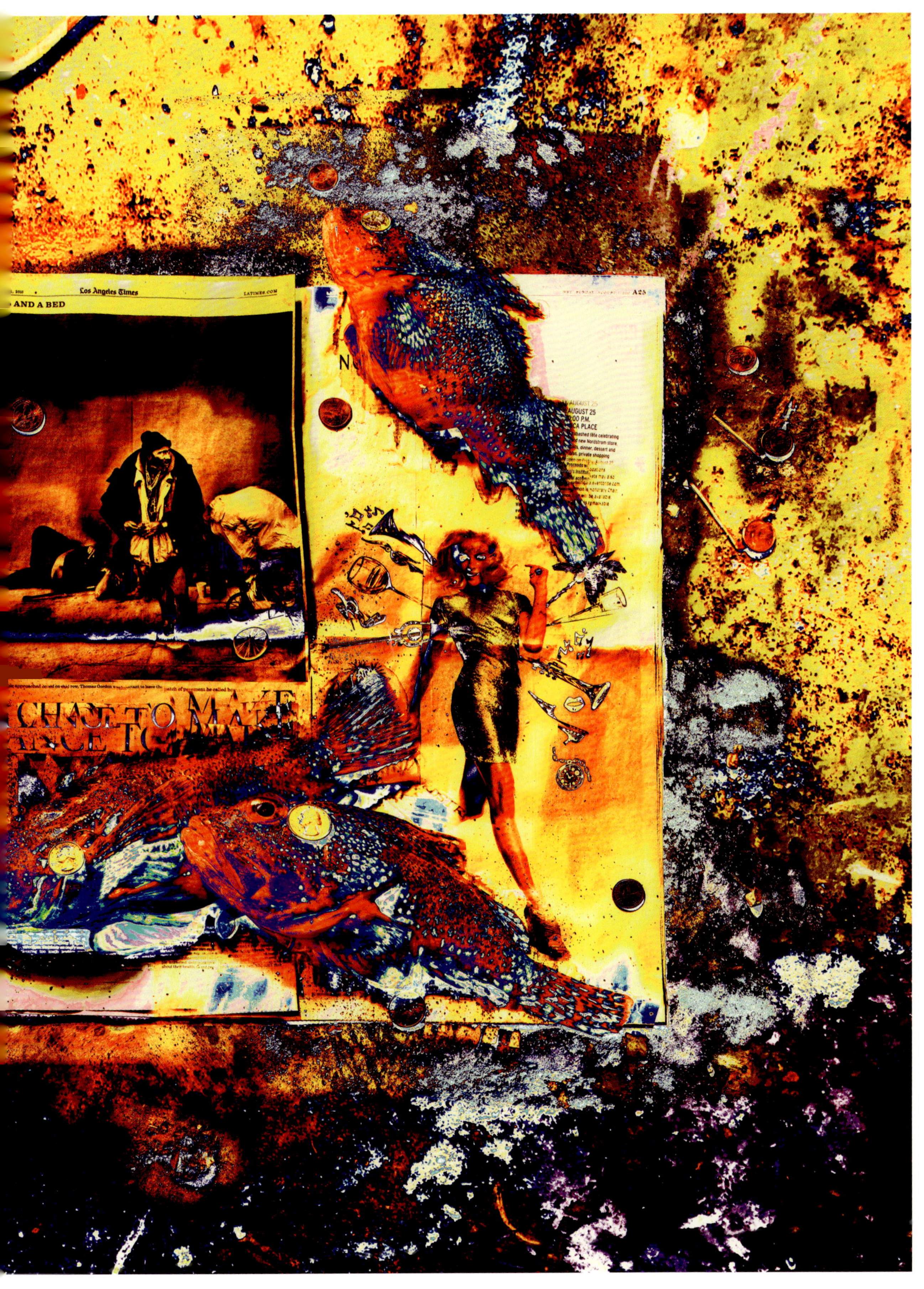

Los Angeles Times
LATIMES.COM
AND A BED
CHANCE TO MAKE

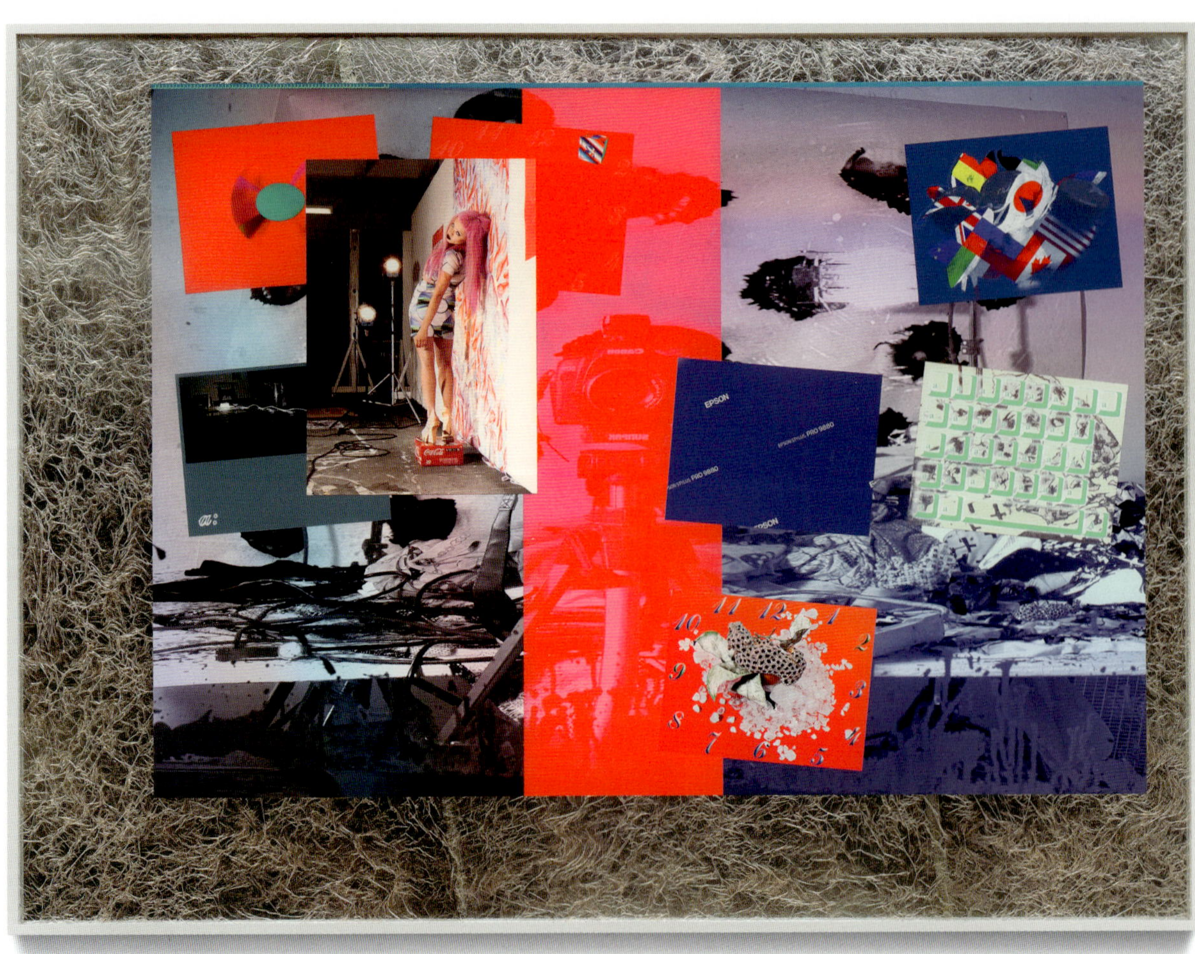

346     Carter Mull, *Gleaning, with the Chanel*, 2013–14. K3 inks on Epson papers, metallic foil, Sintra

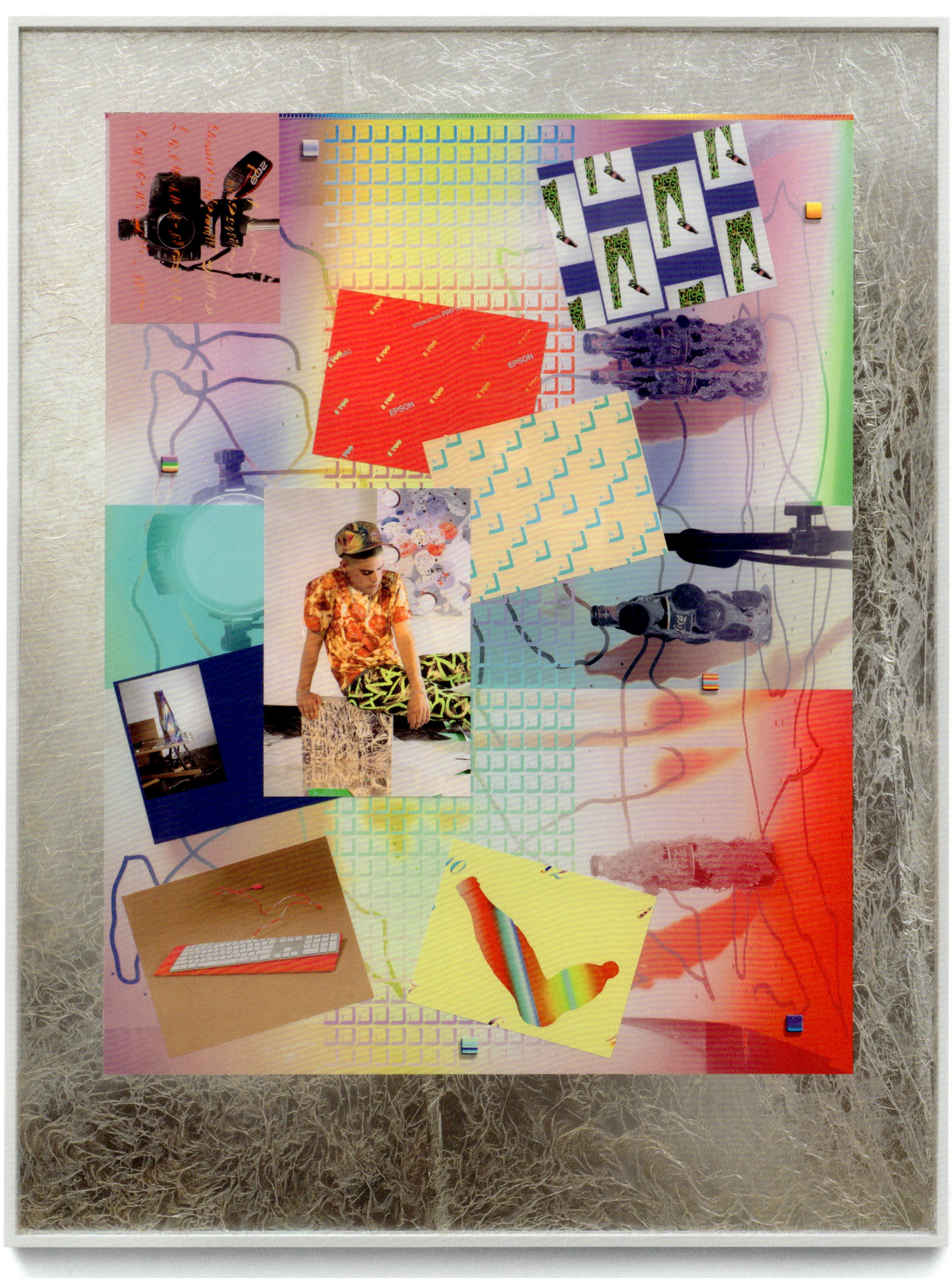

347   Carter Mull, *Nicky, My Neighbor*, 2013–14. K3 inks on Epson papers, metallic foil, Sintra

# Artists' statements

## MICHELE ABELES

My route isn't mapped from the outset, but the process is highly considered and self-reflexive along the way; it maintains certain parameters until, inevitably, I violate them. You take a wrong turn accidentally, you go parallel to the track you're supposed to be on, you go for a shortcut, you take a break to examine the scenery. You redraw the map and start over.

For the series *Re:Re:Re:Re:Re:* (2009–11), the impetus was trying to find a way to approach portraiture but lose the typical psychological baggage and move toward *de-subjectivization*: I was interested in the body not as any sort of vessel of meaning, but as a blank slate. I treated male bodies the same as any other elements in a still life. They became objects. In the series that followed, in 2012, I wanted to find a way to continue addressing physicality and photography, but now leaving the body out.

The way we physically interact with images has changed from object-based images (photographic prints) to screen-based images and an interaction with surfaces, such as touchscreens. These exchanges affect the value and meaning of the images themselves.



## TAKAAKI AKAISHI

When I work, I always try to *make* without thinking too much in advance. When I look back at my practice, the works that I thought very deeply about before their production were not the most successful ones. So for some time, I would settle myself down before clicking the shutter, telling myself: "Think nothing. Think nothing." I tried this way of working for a while…but as time went by, I realized that the process seemed to prioritize *shooting* only. And I was no longer comfortable drifting and wandering.

I thought it might be interesting to create something within an exhibition space, to make something by hand that would be the subject of my photography—in a sense, to reuse my production, to multiply myself so that my work would take place on both sides of the lens. This process, unlike painting, was speedy and offered the capability of repeating things. But it did not last long: bit by bit, this practice became *all* about repetition, and in the end shooting again became the first priority. I was desperate…but from this experience I came to consider the photographic process as an expedient device. When I came up with an idea, I could just make it and then photograph it—and those pictures would become important motivations for the further works. I began to treat photography as a medium that creates connections among my works, a trigger that moves the process forward.



## LOTTA ANTONSSON

Photography is a fast-moving medium: you want the results fast, and you think you know what you see. But in my installations, you can't have that approach—I create context and new meaning for the photographs and photogenic objects that I make, look for, and select. I demand things from the visitor: you need to spend time with my installations. It interests me to ask for this kind of engagement. When you come into the space, you become part of the work.

A medium is defined dialectically by application and technology, each informing and changing the other. Between these poles, some sense of a medium develops. When we use categorical terms, or when we begin with such broad terms, we're aggregating the historically evolving relation between technology and application, generalizing about it, smoothing it out....I don't think there's an ontological dimension to media, and I think it's a waste of time to try to assert one....

I try to think of the detailed applications that are instrumental to the way a particular type of technology has developed at a specific point in time. I'm occupied with, for example, the specifics of color photographic paper, or, in the case of the black-and-white process, with gelatin-silver paper, or even with JPEGs, which I've used in my work as well. I try to see each as containing its own set of qualities and attributes that are contextually determined; otherwise one runs the risk of obscuring the specifics of a particular material or context with vague generalities.



When I started making the work that led to what is featured in this book, in 2006, I was channeling a then-newfound interest in the nineteenth century, photography's role in it, and figures from Courbet to P. T. Barnum. The Metropolitan Museum of Art had just done a survey of Spiritualist photography titled *The Perfect Medium*, which had an important impact on me. The conjuring of the trope of confidence— and its alternate, humbug—was a beginning for me, and a mirror for "the digital." As my work took shape, it ended up being a performance of magic: its staging, its relationship to spectacle and commodity, became central. I came to think about the studio as a theater space and discovered in the ideas of Bertolt Brecht a way to put pressure on this and to picture it. I started to consider how much labor was hidden in the making of a photograph and began making the evidence of these things part of my picture making. In the way I was working, this was not only the physical/optical apparatus of the studio but also the computer's tools.

In the past few years, with increasing intensity, I have come full circle to thinking about picture making as a way around the narrow, spectacular magic of the commodity, and as having a much deeper relationship to genuine possibility.



I use photography as a territory for investigation and marking. I am interested in colors and shapes, clashes between digital and physical, vector and raster. My images are studies of spatial designs and surfaces within a field of photography that has been digitally interfered by layers of materials, patterns, and computer-generated objects.



There are a few formal prerequisites that an image must meet before I'll use it. There's usually (I hope) a synergy between the image I am working on and the images I'm appropriating. Often my images play off the form, color, tone, etc., of the original image, but—if they meet the formal requirements—they still need to untether themselves enough from their original source. I see a need for the images I use to be led around by the image they are collaged onto, and not the other way around. Then there's the content of each individual piece of paper. Sometimes that plays a central role, other times not, but I do pay attention to what's going on and whether I let accidents precede my intentions.

224–27

BIANCA BRUNNER

My practice is about photography and the image itself, always retaining the possibility of an indexical relationship between an image and its subject. The particular works shown in this book, from 2014, explore the correspondence between photography and drawing, and how the fleeting and fragmentary nature of drawing can be communicated through the deliberate and "complete" medium of photography. The brightly colored Harlequin forms develop from sketches and are then constructed from fabric and suspended in my studio, where they are photographed. My intention is to create images in which the subjects are poised between three-dimensionality and flat "drawn" forms.

130–33

STEFAN BURGER

Three Polaroid photographs (3 ¼ by 4 ¼ inches) in a wood press under the pressure of three tons per square meter for a span of two months. Taking a macro photograph of a radish seedling with one hand while turning over a sausage on a barbecue with the other. Two similar C-prints installed on a metal display stand for special offers, which yield under the pressure of the wind. An inkjet print (122 by 78 inches), pasted on a wooden board, leaning on a wall in a museum opposite an open window. Two archers ordered to shoot three arrows from the outside through the window onto the image.

Mounting a photograph on a pole and sticking it into the ground of a brackish Venice canal, watching it drift very slowly away in the current.

Asking the team of museum technicians to build a wall and to cut out a piece of it in the size of a double bed. After the wall is complete, installing a photograph on it. A C-print mounted on aluminum, framed, jammed with two wooden poles under the ceiling. Saving the carpet that was about to be thrown away, which had been installed behind the reception desk of an Austrian photography gallery. Finding a collection of anonymous photographs and taking this as an important document of Austrian photo history.

256–59

ANTOINE CATALA

I guess I have a structuralist perspective: I am interested in the structure of the medium I deal with. I find the structuralist tactics visceral: they deal with embodiment of the medium. Filmmaker Ernie Gehr said: "A moving picture is a real thing and as a real thing it is not imitation. It does not reflect on life, it embodies the life of the mind." I bring in even more physicality to an image— moving or not—to exaggerate the underlying affective relationship we have with it.

## PHIL CHANG 66–71

My work utilizes photographic depiction while also extending from it by relying on modes of duration, materiality, and process with photography. This occurs because I believe that photography is excellent at describing and reflecting the world in the images that it produces of the world. However, I believe that something beyond photographic representation can reflect the world in a more accurate way. This is in how we produce, circulate, and consume photographs. In other words, our social relations around photography are more reflective of the world than mere depictions of it. This belief has informed my decision to rely on photographic depiction and also extends from it. My recent work represents an answer to the question: What strategies must be applied to my photographic work so that it can function only in the context of contemporary art?

## TALIA CHETRIT 54–55

In the black-and-white series *Hands on Body* (2012), I make use of the male anatomy, specifically the hands. Each frame depicts a male hand gripping, pushing into, and engaging with a swath of black velvet fabric. A female form beneath the fabric is revealed by the hands shifting placement and the black negative space. These images start as a portrait of a hand and progress to an encounter between a man and woman.

## JOSHUA CITARELLA 62–65

The contemporary means of image production lend themselves to the trans-mutation of signs in a way that is unprecedented. RGB pixels are implicated as a new *prima materia*, delivering objects from the dim confines of materiality into omnipresent electronic radiance. A global network of images has transfigured all bodies and materials into exchanges of energy. The world is now transcribed through photography in order to be reconfigured with graphics-editing software and transformed into its ideal state. While this universal translation space now allows for an alchemical magnum opus, it has consequently democratized all materials, transmuting lead into gold and vice versa. We lose sight of the interface and are carried away in the fervor of a transcendent promise fulfilled.

## SARA CWYNAR 122–23

I am interested in the way images morph, accumulate, endure, and change in meaning and value over time, and in the effect this has on a collective worldview. My process begins in the compulsive ordering of source images from my own picture taking, and from encyclopedias, the New York Public Library Picture Collection, magazines, flea markets, and people I know. I focus particularly on images from recent history, questioning the mid-to-late-twentieth-century modernist idealism visualized in magazines and advertisements, and in personal and stock photographs. I remove these pictures from circulation and reintroduce them as new images, through the agency of contemporary materials and processes. In doing so, I aim to put forth questions related to the power and influence of images, while situating an individual approach within the visual codes and references of popular photography.

## BRYAN DOOLEY

The panels with which I work are populated with images—at once iconic and banal—and offer the viewer a ground of reference that is in constant flux. The screen-printing of symbols and imagery offers an even further reduced, formal impression of an image, yet still reveals enough for viewers to excavate and produce their own reading. I exploit the viewers' collective understanding of where the image ends and the object begins.



## JESSICA EATON

I am building up information through the camera; film is a relatively fixed variable that can reflect back to me the accumulation of that action. I correct for the print, but it is important to me to see the most direct possible interpretation of what the camera has been told. The "look" of the final image is never my impetus for making a picture. I think a lot of my pictures come from underneath or within. I haven't taken to pushing around the picture plane after exposing the film. I have enough to work with as it is; I haven't hit the limit of the space in which I am working. If I were building the pictures in the *visible*—in any of the number of ways that could be done—I would be both obliterating the contingent aspects and (even more importantly) operating in a way that puts cognitive beliefs of aesthetics or perfection into the foreground. I am much more interested in manifesting the work than in dictating it.



## SHANNON EBNER

Even when I am going to great lengths to communicate, it can take time for viewers to work through the idea that writing and shifting the temporal register of a work of art can be acts of resistance.

For my project *The Electric Comma* (2011–13), I used portable changeable message signs—the LED signs on roadways that alert us to an emergency or delay or collision ahead—which communicate with an implied urgency. For the photographic part of my project, I drain the safety-orange color from the letters and program the computer with my own writing, so it addresses the "dear reader" directly...but these messages are too long to be urgent, so the language functions more as a kind of public surface pattern. I am, in a sense, calling out to the reader, but the message falls apart.



## MARTEN ELDER

Color film was designed to replicate images as humans see them, as accurately as possible. The method was fairly convincing, but never perfect. Over time we became accustomed to the specific way color film rendered the world and accepted it as accurate representation. Film has since been superseded by the image sensor used in a digital camera. Images produced using a digital camera undergo a default processing that is meant to approximate the look of film. But this processing discards other, real information about the world that the new image sensor is able to record. That information can be extracted and mapped to the entire spectrum of tones that the computer display or printer can reproduce. The color information may seem synthetic at first, but those colors exist naturally in the world in the same relative relationship to one another. With conscious attention to visual perception, one can become sensitized to these color relationships.

JASON EVANS

48–53

The two bodies of work represented in this book were made simultaneously and, despite there being no obvious connection between them, they share a preoccupation with looking and how that turns into AN IMAGE. Both projects were intuitively constructed; they both celebrate photographic processes; and they comment on broader issues in visual culture.

*NYLPT* (2005–12) takes as its departure point mediated cityscapes, and a sense of nostalgia for places I had seen only on pages and through others' eyes. Rather than trying to establish an "innovative" approach to street photography, I went with the flow and randomly layered film exposures in the camera. I sequenced eighty of the resulting images into an informal paperback book with a tight sequence; alongside them on the pages is a gradient, showing tones of ink on paper. A further six hundred images appear in an app that generates its own image sequences, accompanied by ever-changing drone music created by an audio synthesizer. The drone functions similarly to the gradient in the printed version of the project: it creates a simultaneous sensory experience to go with the visual experience. Although they share a title, the two outputs have different content drawn from the same body of work, exploring the possibilities of digital-analog "equivalents."

*Pictures for Looking At* (2007–12) started as a response to a popular pseudo-academic idea that all photographic experience must be intellectually contextualized—an idea that has created a biased meritocracy that seems to prioritize the ability to expound in writing over the ability to photograph. These pictures are intended to be looked at and enjoyed. They are produced as posters, which are given away in a gesture that sees the exhibition space as a point of departure.

SAM FALLS

288–93

I have a persistent interest in merging the respective art histories of representation and abstraction by bridging the gaps between photography, painting, and sculpture. By employing the conceptual elements of analog photography (namely time, exposure, and indexicality) and more universal elements (such as sun and rain) with vernacular subject matter, I hope to escape the alienating professionalism of contemporary photography to yield a more direct relationship with the viewer.

For example, the recycled pallet pieces (2013) were made at a Pomona, California, parking lot that is surrounded by shipping companies. They were made on shipping blankets, since the subject matter in all my work dictates the respective substrate. The burlap pieces (2013) were made in my backyard in Venice, California, from a dismantled bookshelf I made at my prior residence, made in the minimalist style

of Donald Judd's work. I wanted to transfer a kind of "domestic minimalism"
back to a work of art, so each shelf became the support and subject of these works.
The burlap was wrapped around the wooden shelves to create a positive image
instead of a negative; inside the frame it is almost as though you are looking
through the work to the burlap frame as the sun faded away all the color.

BRENDAN FOWLER

152–57

The *New Camera* pictures (2010–14) are made with an industrial embroidery
machine, the kind that stitches logos onto jackets and hats and jerseys.
The embroidery machine itself is a modern, industrialized grandchild
of folk-craft techniques; I'm taking those methods back a few steps toward
craft and repurposing them. The source imagery comes from photographs
and continues my long-running engagement with photography as a way to
process and present personal narrative. There are many overlaps between
the procedures by which these images come to be and those of the "straight"
photographs that I produce as standard inkjet prints and then incorporate into
sculptures. The embroidery machine's various errors manifest physically and are
treated as purposeful gestures and choices—like the choices one makes when
using paint, or when considering a printing device's possibilities and limitations.
Because they are made on canvas that has been primed with thinned-out acrylic
paint and stretched on aluminum stretchers, these images can be understood
as paintings (which they probably are, technically) as much as they can be seen
as weavings or embroideries.

My regular camera broke and I replaced it around the same time I sourced my
first embroidery machine; so I equated my camera's replacement with the arrival
of the machine, which itself really signaled the arrival of this new process for me.
The joke goes: "I got a new camera…and…*it's an industrial embroidery machine.*"

VICTORIA FU

82–85

The obliteration of the image—blankets of clotted film grains like enlarged cells
or bacteria, light spilling and making forms we cannot fully control—can offer a
sense of deep, visceral abjection. The destruction of the analog image occurs
by way of a violent erasure of *light*—the originary substance of all photographs.

The human hand coupled with analog film is an accident waiting to happen.
And that controlled damage is why I love working with film. Invisible layers of
post-production, slick image surfaces, software updates, making room for the
top of the image feed—perhaps the very idea of "obsolescence" here is a capitalist
construct. Maybe things are not as interesting if they are whole, virtuosic, fully
realized. There is something radical about glitches, moth holes, in a seemingly
massive and impenetrable system.

I make my pictures alone in my studio, but I view my work as a peculiar collaboration between myself and what I've chosen as my material: images found on the Internet that I print and construct into a three-dimensional tableau, which is ultimately photographed. This process presents limitations as well as unexpected directions, and it is in this way that I don't anticipate a picture's meaning or formal qualities before I begin to make it. Instead, I let the criteria of the process guide the subject matter, discovering what the work is about as it comes to life. So...I'd say that even if the imagery I'm attempting to depict is taken directly from my life experience, the process of making allows for a kind of improvisation that often takes the construction to a fictional place. As far as narrative is concerned, I'm more interested in creating a mood or playing with a particular theme than I am in creating a story. I've been thinking a lot lately about how meaning can be made not only in each particular image, but in the space between them—I think that's where the strongest indication of a narrative is in my work.



The idea created in the image is subject to interpretation—it is no different from the interpretation we bring to all matter, by filtering it into language and consequently meaning. Both original idea and interpretation become perspectives on what exists—means of relating, presenting, ordering, and understanding our experience and engagement with the world. It is not that one is true and the other false; the sign offers a means to engage with the signified; the reference allows recourse to the referent. Photography visually translates all things to surface in the same way we translate all things to language.



A photograph—at least an analog photograph—is always about the past. I am fascinated with the ways in which we mark time through culture. The modes associated with marking time shifted rapidly in the late twentieth century, making ours an era of a new paradigm. Artists born in the later twentieth century may in some sense be prepared to focus on this shift in relation to the human impulse to record existence moving away from the haptic to the virtual.

I have always found the photographic experience intriguing, and important in terms of how we perceive time. My work is related to the notion of collage or montage, the piecing-together of seemingly unrelated material to bring forth a complete and "new" form. Ideally, the resulting form is more expansive than the original components—juxtaposition and perspective are now in play—and addresses several concepts at once. This play with form allows me to explore the limits of a single photograph, a single perspective.

## NANCY DE HOLL

My practice is invested in a process of declassifying images. This is formalized through the depiction of indeterminate subjects that can be liberated from their referential relationship to the world, and by engaging the human impulse to index and order experience. My aim is for the images to sink below their cultural specifics and enter into the collective imaginary through a sequence of formal negations. Ideally, the subtotal of these negations—before the experience of viewing—is a foreign or autonomous image.

In both painting and photography there is the convention of the rectilinear "window" space, which serves as a transitional plane between reality and imagination, external and internal. In relation to this boundary, each of these media offers an experience of the image that the other does not. This alternation or oscillation of the media produces a friction that is useful in my ongoing attempts to find a suspension between these two registers of inner and outer depiction.



## JOHN HOUCK

For the past five years, I have made ostensibly "straight" photographs that paradoxically speak the language of digital manipulation—although my work isn't digitally altered. I approach the prevalence of the digital askance; I prefer the material and "relational"—that is, I make photos of photos of photos. I usually start with something personal, like my experience as a software engineer or my interest in psychoanalysis, and in the feedback loop of photographing and printing I interrupt the technical repetitiveness of my practice in various ways: folding, creasing, arranging, lighting, and allowing the contingencies of the material world to unfold.



## GO ITAMI

I want to keep the possibilities of photography as broad as possible. I don't want to take photographs and just end it there. I believe in photography's multiple forms, regardless of which way it is created. I believe that photography will meet its end if I close myself off and become satisfied with what I have achieved.



## RACHEL DE JOODE

My newer works contain elements that evolve around the art-making process and "me-the-artist" (often my skin, my body) making artwork. Here, I mean work that is presented in a contemporary gallery and then eventually ends up as a JPEG circulating on the Internet. The recurring elements are: the actors involved in the art-making process and the (reduced) signifiers of artwork/sculpture and gallery, such as: wet clay, marble, or pedestals. I play with volume and flatness; the *in-real-life-ness* of the "white cube" (the gallery space) and its web-based installation-documentation. A thread through my art is that I work a lot with issues like two-dimensionality versus three-dimensionality, with proportions and the performativity of the artwork-in-itself, and with surfaces.

The photograms featured here, from 2009, show a tracing of a fragment of the
Berlin Wall. People and time leave marks, and these marks accumulate especially
at times of trauma—political, personal, or meteorological. Here, the graffiti was
an intentional mark, and the age and shape of the fragment an unintentional one.
I didn't want to document the existing fragment; instead, I wanted to get involved
with it, and allow the photogram, as an object, to convey that engagement as
much as the potency of the original event. I always work in intimate relay with my
subjects and my medium; they change me and I change them. I make sculptural
"negatives"; my prints are unique, and I sometimes install them in response
to architecture. My abstract experiments in photography serve the representational
goals of my subjects, whose individual experiences I trust more than I trust
the myth of photographic objectivity.

Matt Keegan                                                                          284–87

For my first solo show, in 2007, I exhibited photographs of broken-up sidewalk
and carefully arranged discarded shoes. Over the years since then, photographs
have become central features of my exhibitions, providing a clear correspondence
with my sculpture. Always shot with natural light, the material I record has a kind
of clarity, and I think of photographs as offering a legibility—or requesting to be
read—just as we read familiar shapes or patterns. Additionally, my photographs
are presented to underscore their direct relationship to the body of the viewer.
Horizontal and vertical planes flip, spaces torque, all to reinforce the connection
between eyes and feet.
    Recently, I have begun screen-printing the Plexiglas used to frame the photo-
graphs—creating a doubling, or "stutter," that vibrates, turning the familiar frame
into an activated space that highlights the sculptural properties of the images.

Annette Kelm                                                                          260–63

I need a place from which to start: it can be a text I am reading, a movie,
a newspaper article, a picture in an advertising brochure, or a tired fly that sits on a
lamp. I usually begin photographing with a strict concept in mind and then I open
it up—due to (and in favor of) playfulness. I am very passionate about photography.
It's fun for me to be part of the discussion about photography in art.

Soo Kim                                                                          100–101

I am interested in the decipherability and indecipherability of the photographic
image. In my work I perform transformative operations that relate to, or mimic,
certain parts of what is pictured, and abstract other areas of the picture. In my
recent *Backlight* series, creases are made along straight lines informed by
a visual cue in the photograph—it might be the side of a building, a power line,
a lamppost. The print is then unfolded and flattened and further creases are made
in response to existing folds, until the entire print is marked with a complex web
of connections. The back of the print is painted a neon-bright color, and geometric

spaces—delineated by the fold lines—are cut out of the print to allow the neon color to reflect back through the voids. This draws attention to the materiality of the photographic image, and also to photography's relationship with light: creating an image that is "light-sensitive." Its glow and appearance shift depending on time of day or lighting conditions. The intangible elements that are the voids between light and shadow intermingle with the concrete photographic image of the city. This creates a new and magical cityscape, one that is perplexing yet peaceful, chaotic yet contemplative, governed by a new set of experiential rules.

188–89

## Yuki Kimura

I've always been concerned with exposing and disrupting the illusion presented by the photograph, and experimenting with the relationship between one photograph and another. The viewer is a necessary intermediary for something to be expressed within those relations. I'm also interested in how one experiences multiple images in the space of the gallery. By placing works so as to create a narrative framework, I usually rely on the structure of the space itself....Basically, because it is not real, the two-dimensional space of the photograph is always incomplete. The more you work with it, the stranger it becomes. In that sense, using photographs in the construction of a physical space creates an experience of that incompleteness.

## Josh Kline

316–17

Much of my recent work deals with technology's impact on human life— what technology means and will mean, socially, economically, creatively. I'm a fan of complexity and informational density in art (and in other media as well). Technology—and, to a lesser extent, the Internet in particular—is in the constellation of topics I'm working with, but so are labor, debt, public relations, advertising, food, economics, aging, design, architecture, the entertainment industry, life extension, digitization, human trafficking, creative work, competitive blood-doping in sports, "posthuman productivity enhancement" at the office, etc. Communication technologies are changing so rapidly. We're in the process of shrugging off a lot of postmodernist thinking, and coming to terms with the fact that technological progress isn't going away. It's obvious to everyone now—people who are involved in art and people who aren't—that we're living in the middle, or maybe at the beginning, of a series of escalating technological revolutions.

200–203

## Lucas Knipscher

Start with a set of photographic assumptions. Assume we are indexically literate. Assume we are materially literate. Assume we are technologically and process-literate. If these assumptions prove false, assume that this literacy is achievable; that this falls within the knowable. It's nice to be in the know, to be intelligent, and to be affirmed.

But photographs are also knowing, intelligent, and affirming. I get the feeling that they are watching me, following me, teaching me. I once used photographs, but now photographs use me. The photographs have become *images*, with a sly

intelligence behind their innocent photographic skins, waiting to be brought inside
the walls, then slipping out, networking and programming behind my vision.
I have a relationship to the image as producer, and also as one being produced.
I must maintain critical acuity as producer and produced.

   We can already see. We have already been programmed to see. We have already
seen. It is a question linked to the artistic program: the artist-as-program. But not
all of the program is visible: something unknown moves beneath the surface.
The camera has been reduced to a symbol of *photographing* and *being photographed*,
which is further reduced to a signifier of the program's regard for us. We are
perceived by the program. But programs don't love, don't care, don't nurture;
they grow by providing us a constrained "self." Is "self" an opportunity?
An opportunity to be the unknowable? Being unknowable introduces vulnerability
into the program: a way to *think images* instead of being *thought by* them. Without
image thinking, we remain in an artificial visual paradise. And what can be said
about paradise, except that we know it when we see it; and the unknowable,
the vulnerable, lie outside the confines of its walls.


JOSHUA KOLBO                                          328–31

To look at an image is to look at an ideology; its manifestation is at once physical,
social, and political. Looking at an image unwinding may not reveal as much
as looking at it as a hyperlinked site of triggers of association. Perhaps more can
be construed from a series of cascading images than from a finite view of a single
image. The logical space left for articulation is the slippery in-between: a space
in which to dissolve boundaries and expand definitions into loose, tangential,
sometimes political philosophies and a heuristic eco/political glossolalia,
which portend an imminent culture of crisis.


TAISUKE KOYAMA                                        96–99

*Seventh Depth* (2014) was created with the Hasselblad H5D-200MS extreme high-
resolution digital camera's multishot system. I photographed the rainbow-colored
inkjet prints from a previous body of work called *Rainbow Form* (2009), moving the
prints while the camera automatically releases the shutter six times, resulting in an
image made up of multiple exposures. The photographs cannot be seen until they
are generated as TIFF or JPEG image formats because this method produces
an "error" in the developing software. By purposefully using a problematic method,
I am able to experiment with multiple exposures that are produced automatically
by the digital device. *Seventh Depth* is a part of an ongoing project called *Rainbow
Variations*, which was begun in 2009.


OWEN KYDD                                            108–13

I have always wondered about the differences between cinematic moments
with photographic qualities versus more static-like images with time added—like
a tableau vivant, or more currently GIFs and screen savers. The idea of duration
as "incomplete time" seems like a way of categorizing a flow of pictures without

relying on models drawn from cinematic discourse. I started making durational photographs in 2006, when still cameras began to include HD video options. In addition to hybrid cameras, flat screens had been developed with resolutions that made video look photographic. Before this, I'd relied on projectors, which meant a darkened room, and, even in the gallery space, that was too cinematic. Video and flat-screen technologies also allowed duration to be a constant variable, and I hoped that my project would then retroactively define other conditions of still photographs. In a sense, I was attempting to reverse the absolute time of the photograph even though I knew it wasn't completely possible.

ELAD LASSRY

72–77

For the pictures featured in this book, I worked exclusively with sourced negatives, mostly acquired via auctions. I was interested in applying my investigation to material I have little control over. Part of this quest rolled over to the handling of these negatives once they arrived at the studio. It was clear to me that they had to go through a set of obstacles before becoming a work. I engaged in a series of absurdly analog techniques to reengage with the prints I made from the negatives. Some negatives were partly overexposed, some were punched with holes. Others were printed without interference, but later partially covered by a tailored casing and blankets.

Digital photography has become a miserable victim of old scholars. The core questions around the picture have little to do with the rapid technological changes that take place. These have always existed, in different forms and levels. For this work, I avoided using any recent technology precisely for these reasons. I really wanted to arrive at my examinations from the back door.

BRANDON LATTU

140–43

Photography has relied on a failed mimicry of human vision for far too long. The chosen direction and bounded rectangle are, like other aspects of representation, political tools that fulfill the desires of some while controlling others and surveying all. The works shown here, from 2007 and 2010, try to get beyond the camera's dependence on a vector from the photographer, through the device to the subject, by recording omnidirectionally instead.

Magic is a mystifying reordering of the expectations of a system of representation; and photography was once perceived as magical in this way. What is needed now is to go beyond magic—to overthrow, supplant, skew, to shift the relationship of representational systems to power. Vision and representation are remarkably seductive and surprisingly malleable; if we are not so fixed on our preformed model of vision, we can make a new model that is relevant to how life is lived now!

JOHN LEHR

44–47

The photographs in the series *Low Relief* (2012–14) are created through a process that embraces both indexicality and invention. The work describes the skin of the city: surfaces and façades that have been transformed by human interaction

and reimagined through subjective perception. Over the past years, my practice
has evolved to include direct observation, onsite intervention, and studio
fabrication. Regardless of how my subjects are found, they are always rendered
at full scale. The prints maintain an uncanny verisimilitude even as they highlight
the difference between a photograph and its referent. The gestures embedded in the
works are records of physicality that hover between the tactile and the intangible.
Scrawls, tears, and splatters are tempered by the presence of scrims and reflections.
If the photographs document anything, it is the transition from a physical society
to a virtual one.

ANTHONY LEPORE124–25

Ten years before I ever picked up a camera, I was a preteen magician. With the
help of my grandfather, I converted a trunk into a portable stage and began
working a circuit of local senior centers. Perfecting tricks like the levitating glass
and the hand guillotine, in rooms full of half-conscious old folks, I specialized
in small illusions and temporary distractions from the mundane. Something
from those early performances continues to materialize in my photographs.

   Recently I built a studio in my father's bikini factory. I spent many of my
childhood Saturdays there, in what felt like a cave studded with neon Lycra
and rivers of bikini strap. Echoes of my early magic tricks resonate in these new
photographs, in mannequin torsos displayed like sections of sawed-in-half ladies
before their sequined restoration. I am creating my own analog illusions and
constructions, built for the camera with the materials of the factory.

ALEXANDRA LEYKAUF78–81

The way I look at images is structural and emotional: that is, I look at things from
within. It is an experience of simultaneous distance and immersion. I try to engage
the viewer in a physical as well as an imaginary relation with my work, allowing
for different points of view and thereby revealing the *hors champs*—the "beyond-
the-scope"—that any kind of image-making engenders. Where am I and who am I
in relation to the image are questions equally relevant whether one is in front of a
Renaissance painting or in a movie theater. I am mostly attracted to photography
and its reproducibility because of its promise and its hopeless failure to provide an
immediate view onto a different reality that is in any way concrete.

MATT LIPPS304–7

My practice begins with the construction of three-dimensional tableaux of imagery
appropriated from popular and high culture, alongside vernacular photographs and
my personal collection of negatives. Using collage strategies, I cut out fragments
from this idiosyncratic archive and make freestanding paper dolls, which are
displayed according to sculptural tropes and theater staging, as well as intuitive
organization. These redeployed elements act as visual prompts playing on viewers'
visual literacy; they point to various moments from our history with the past 170
years of the disseminated image. The resulting constructions are rephotographed

and printed at a much larger size than the originals, thereby creating scale shifts that inspire reflection about the operation of the photographic object on the embodied subject.

At the heart of my practice is a genuine longing to be with photographs, and an acknowledgment of the reciprocal effects of encountering each image in a tactile and sympathetic manner. In this way, I cultivate a promiscuity of vision without undermining the intimacy of the experience of seeing as mediated by the camera.

230–33

## ANNIE MacDONELL

My *Flatness, Light, Black & White* series of photographs (2013) is an attempt to chart the formal properties of the image in the digital age: the image's mutability and propensity for multiple perspectives, its capacity for compression, flatness, and transparency, its ability to generate surface as far as the eye can see. The images were shot documentary-style, in a barbershop, over the course of an afternoon. But despite their documentary allusions, their modest size and traditional black-and-white tonality, the photographs are not photographs at all. What you see are temporary configurations at best, rendered in paper and ink for the sake of publication. But even as we continue to present images in this quaintly familiar form, we acknowledge that they are no longer credible as finite things. If images can be conceived as anything at all, it is as clusters of binary information, expressed as shifting reflections in the glossy black surface of the screen. Their permanence here is no more than an aesthetic affectation, as suspect as algorithmically generated dust and scratches on a JPEG.

272–75

## FLORIAN MAIER-AICHEN

People never like terms such as *painter-photographer* or *draftsman-photographer* because they are hybrids. They want things to be either in *this* category or *that*. What I do is turn the finished photograph almost back into a scribble. Usually a photograph is very finished, precise, and rigorous. It's an end product. But I like to use the end product and turn it into an unfinished state again. Most people think photography and painting should be strictly separate, even though for a long time photography mimicked painting because of a kind of inferiority complex (photography wasn't considered artistic enough). The first photographers tried to use painterly devices until so-called straight photography came into fashion; at that point, all the modern photographers got rid of the painterly baggage. But I think today that photography has become so technical that people have tried to investigate the medium again by researching processes or photography's historical importance. I don't want to be a dogmatist: I think it's fine to combine photography and drawing, or to alter photographs and bring in fictional elements, or just not to be satisfied with photography as a superrealistic medium.

363

PHIL MAISEL                                                                         214–17

I seek specific materials that have a sort of blankness, a banality, or an already-known-
ness about them. I arrange these materials into precarious compositions, which I then
photograph in a sequence. Each photograph I end up making feels like an iteration,
or a step, or a decision, or maybe a question. I shoot digitally and the immediacy
of seeing that two-dimensional representation informs the decisions I make with
the sculptural arrangements. In the work I exhibit, I like to confuse the space of
the image further. I am introducing strategically cut pieces of paper and glassine—
elements utilized in the production of the image itself—back into the image, literally
wedging these forms between the print and the glass of the frame. It feels like a
gesture toward collage, and a way to acknowledge the photograph itself as an object.


EMMELINE DE MOOIJ                                                                    88–91

My current work consists of several large installations that invite physical
interaction: they can function as a set or arena for a series of performances I will
carry out. Or viewers can "wear" different elements of the work. The pieces contain
objects arranged into clusters: photographs, costumes, or objects from the domestic
sphere. Fluidity is an important characteristic in my art, and to achieve this, I use
elements made of textiles: aprons, large gowns, towels, and pieces of fabric draped
around objects and paintings. Round shapes and soothing colors, often yellow and
pink, flow into one another. A piece of fabric with stains is placed on an abstract
photographic image of a box of medication positioned between soft, draped veils.


CARTER MULL                                                                         342–47

I have no formal training with cameras, and only came to consider something
called "photographic seeing" after my time studying at CalArts (California Institute
of the Arts). The lens, like the computer, is an apparatus, albeit with different
structural properties. Over the years, I've tended to deal with digital output
more than with ground glass, as the lens-centric image always seemed problematic:
the monocularity of the camera feels like a constraint, even if what is in front
of the lens compels me. The shroud of unspoken politics surrounds us; similarly,
monocular vision imposes invisible, hegemonic ideologies that have always
been hard for me to accept.


NERHOL (RYUTA IIDA AND YOSHIHISA TANAKA)                                             282–83

We try to capture the figure of things that tend to disappear. You go to drink the
water flowing right in front of you, to quench your severe thirst—but as you scoop
this water up, it runs through your fingers and drifts away down a drain, toward
a place far away from you. When you sit in front of us and the flash repeats, we
can see something—but with these flashes, you start to slip away. Gradually, but
certainly, the real you disappears. Finally, in today's world of business based on
capitalism, many things are fading away at a surprising speed; this is a reality.
Over the course of several minutes, we take around two hundred photographs
of a subject. Then, after printing out all these images and stacking the prints on

top of one another, we sculpt them by cutting away each layer one by one. Over the course of a long time, a single image appears. In front of this phenomenon, it could be thought that, paradoxically, the image is formed through a series of disappearances. This makes the image seem far away. What we cannot help but call "far away" are the various ways in which our distorted, metamorphosed subjects could have spent their time in the past. Still, we think it is valid to believe in this distance. In this way, we find a way toward a metaphor for agitating the constantly disappearing present.

KATJA NOVITSKOVA

Human attention is a material thing; it takes calories and time. Like almost anything to do with our bodies, it has an evolutionary origin: for generations—stemming back even to before our current biological state—we have paid the most attention to things in the environment that are crucial to our survival. Our ancestors were exploring and selecting visual forms, patterns, and narratives that were effective at grabbing their attention and that triggered something within them. Today, attention is a scarce resource for which everyone is competing; it fuels the Internet and the economic structures it has created. In this world, images (both still and moving) are material carriers of attention-grabbing visual intensities that are shared and utilized empathetically. Driven by a personal sense of aesthetics and in response to rapid cultural shifts, global events, and "likes," millions of digital images are created daily; thousands become viral and some end up as iconic. This sheer volume points to an ecological scale of image-making and visual storytelling—it is a human behavioral trait that transforms our planet within wider networks of things.

TAIYO ONORATO AND NICO KREBS

Photography is the medium that once was seen as equal to truth. First, the ultimate collective truth; later, a rather personal, subjective truth; and finally—in the era of perfect manipulation through digital technologies—truth that derives from the intention of the creator. A truth for everyone.

Our truth arises from the belief in the photographic moment. The camera lens is the unmistakable eye. The light traces on negative film deliver proof. This belief is opening the door to a new and exciting little world of wonders. It allows us to be explorers beyond the ordinary. To have fun while transforming weird ideas mingled with childhood dreams, TV commercials, daily newspapers, and art-history lessons into visual sensations that become part of our jigsaw-puzzle reality.

ARTHUR OU

My untitled 2013 series stemmed from my interest in finding a middle ground between painting and photography—to see what the possibilities are by instilling the sensibility of photography into techniques and materials of painting, and, conversely, instilling notions of painting into methods of photographic production. In particular, I was reconsidering Morris Louis's *Unfurled* series of paintings

(1960–61), made with thinned synthetic-polymer paint poured directly from
the edges of the canvas and allowed to drip across the surface. The compositions
resulted both from the application of material and from the pull of gravity.
I wanted to consciously draw out this dual quality in trying to recreate these
paintings photographically. My studio setups consist of painted strips of canvas,
with colors borrowed from Louis. They are hung on a c-stand with the view
camera tilted, so that the composition emulates that of one of the paintings.
A base image exposure of pressed-wood material provides a ground; then the color
strips are additionally exposed onto that ground. The additive layering of exposures
is another play with the process of painting, though the results are inherently
optical, showing the translucency of the layers.

MARINA PINSKY42–43

I made the picture shown here in 2013, at the window of my studio in Los Angeles,
which looks out onto Olympic Boulevard. I was driven by the desire to see past my
fragmentary daily life, to find out the ways for that to be possible. How did my
internal activity accord with the activity going on outside? What qualities of time
could be brought out? I tried to fold together the experience of close looking
and the feeling of seeing far out into space within one plane.

MATTHEW PORTER118–19

The photographs shown in this book, from 2013–14, were made using analog
materials, such as a view camera and film, but then were digitally scanned and
retouched. Film allows for the accumulation of multiple discrete exposures on a
single sheet. The film plays many roles here: it is the record of the event, the visual
reference of the subject, the template by which one composes, and the agent of
the process. Within the frame, objects stack on top of one another, blend where
they overlap, and flatten pictorial space. This process allows photography—a visual
language of boxed, still images—to collage multiple topics into single frames, and to
negate the single focal plane that has long been inherent in lens-based photography.

EILEEN QUINLAN194–99

At the beginning of my photographic work, I was asking big and general questions
about photography: What can it do? What are its limits? How does it circulate and
manifest? What are the conventions of photography? How can I play with them
and subvert them? At the moment, my work is more personal, with all those other
questions about photography operating in the background. I am thinking about
my own life—friendships, family, dreams, but also about my midlife in general and
about vitality, fecundity, the ability to craft things, ideas. I think about how bodies,
memories, and materials are transformed by time, by pressure, by experience,
by violence, by hardship, by chance, and sometimes by design.

JON RAFMAN

I think the single most important demand of the artist is to reflect. Art should provoke recognition. I believe that art objects have the power to *do* things, and to promote social change in the world, but only indirectly. Art can incite reflection, critique, and investigation of social reality, but has no active role. In this way, art is a discursive space through which it is possible to read social change. The concept of art as an autonomous domain is a hallmark of our freedom. For me the romantic desire to dissolve the distinctions and critical relationships between theory and practice, art and politics, is a sign of regression. I believe that the separation of theory and practice, a rift that took place during the era of modernism, was progress, and that it's important to maintain that separation between art, a nonconceptual form of knowledge, and politics and critical theory, which are informed by conceptual knowledge.



SEAN RASPET

Increasingly, images must have the ability to refer to multiple and alternate images, all in densely layered proximity. Images are selected and reproduced in my work for their interchangeability, mutability, and modularity—their ability to sit side by side with strangers without disagreement. Color schemes, lighting conditions, and so on must be compatible across multiple platforms of dispersal. Images are increasingly interlinked, moving toward an automatic consensus (or averaging) that defines the neutral terrain through which subsequent images are refracted. A critique of contemporary art is that, in order to be recognized and function successfully, it must *look like* contemporary art. Paradoxically, a primary criterion for the success of an image is that it must resemble an image.



CLUNIE REID
BANG THE DRUM TO ANOTHER BEAT
BANG BANG/BEAT BEAT!
IT'S ALL GOING OFF BEHIND HER
BANG BANG THE DRUM TO ANOTHER BEAT
IT'S A WHOLE NEW LEVEL OF VIOLATION!
GAS GOES UP/WATER RUNS DOWN
UP/DOWN
IN/OUT
SHE'S READY TO GO OFF
AND THERE'LL BE WATER EVERYWHERE
HE'S READY TO EXPLODE
AND THEN THERE'LL BE BLOOD
BEAT BEAT/BANG BANG!
LIFE IS BUT A DREAM FOR THE DEAD
(Encore, encore, meme, mème, same again, encore)
(Not with a bang but a cliché)
(Repeat with emphasis)

I treat reportage photography as a texture or material that can be folded into open-ended narratives. These narratives spring from the original concerns of the photographs I use, but I redeploy them, rather like refocusing a shot to have a wider depth of field. I work associatively and instinctively. I mesh variant ideologies, technologies, and histories, and though I put the primary reading of a photograph under tension by associating it with other photographs, each image retains its original identity, balancing rather than dominating another. My work invites a very close reading of the original images. I spatialize and mobilize the narratives that most engage me, working with scale and placement. I often use textured and colored glass to hold apart or push together groups of images. When I plan an exhibition, I create a rhythm for the viewer across the space of the gallery.



I feel that working with traditional photography is in part about holding on to something while it passes. This harmonizes well with an aspect of photography that I like, namely that every photograph is of something that has passed. The moment is gone as soon as we hear the shutter click. This aspect of photography appeals to me because it feels familiar and relates to what happens to us as human beings. We, too, are passing and recording simultaneously. Photography is not only about mortality; it is also as complicated a subject and object as I have encountered. It is a record of something and a thing itself. It can be brutally revealing and completely abstract, sometimes at the same time. It is a time and space tool that works in light and silver. It is a radical form.



I am interested in the lifespan of images. I am interested in how an image comes into being, what kind of work it does, how it ages, and when it stops being useful. I think of certain kinds of commercial 3D models as underemployed. The kinds of models that on first blush make sense, but after further scrutiny are *off* in one way or another. These images have made their way into the pictures, stickers, and videos I have been making, sometimes being put to sensible use, and sometimes floating in an indeterminate space, hoping that someday they might have something better to do.



My practice examines the image, its currency, and the idea of authorship through various economic metaphors. In addition to reflecting on authorship and economic systems, my work explores the complex dynamics between the materiality of old-school images and the "spectral," digital way that images circulate today. Often looking to the politics of circulating images as a base referent, each body of work ultimately acknowledges its material legacy, its production situation, its modes of distribution and consumption. My photographs and sculptures seek to locate the artist in relationship to technology and the material world.

SHIRANA SHAHBAZI

When I put abstract images in relation to nonabstract images, the images question
and influence each other....You can go both ways, back and forth, see something
real, lose your path, get back, see a deeper space in the abstract images, see
a flatter image in a landscape, put them into relation. It's about looking
at pictures, and asking yourself questions.

210–11

DANIEL SHEA

I am an artist working in photography and sculpture. My work explores mythology,
fiction, and history set against a backdrop of postindustrial ruins and detritus. My
practice begins with research and involves travel to sites of interest to photograph
and collect (physical artifacts and documents from existing archives), as well as a
focus on the self-contained contexts created in the studio. Recently my practice
has involved making books, fabricating large installations, and exhibiting these
installations with photographic works extracted from the books. The staging
of the installations explores the character and mechanics of postindustrial
mythology. With the sculptural works, I am interested in an imagined provenance,
an ambiguous site of origin, and simultaneously I see them as staging devices.
The photographic component performs in this mythological arena, allowing
the work to exist in the lush fiction of the circumstances that create this myth.

60–61

ERIN SHIRREFF

I think of myself as a sculptor because things, and our relationship to them,
are so primary to my work. For the last few years I have been thinking about
the differences between the physical experience of an object versus a mediated
encounter with something depicted in an image or video. It's a very basic
difference, of course, but I think the nuances and implications of it are endlessly
interesting: the complicated process of looking and recognition, the quality
of attention in an encounter, and the ways that mediation can create an emotional
effect. But maybe I also think of myself as a sculptor because it's a discipline that
can be so open and unformed. A very conventional understanding of sculpture
brings to mind a process of discovery through exploring material, or creating
something by additive or subtractive means. I relate to these processes in a
more metaphorical way, meaning that my studio habits are intuitive: I move
in a direction, but try to allow myself be carried by a lot of improvisation
and not-knowing. It's a process of making, and finding what I'm making,
and then making some more.

318–21

TIMUR SI-QIN

The real advantage of thinking of image conventions as solutions in a dynamic
system is gaining a new perspective and insight into the patterns of image culture.
A perspective that can explain why artists including myself are often inspired by
image conventions. It is not to wage war on reified generalities like "capitalism"
or other forms of authority, but rather because image conventions are evidence

of deeper, primordial processes common to humanity and larger than the individual. The way things seem on the surface in the here-and-now is often generated by the long-in-the-making. Image conventions are naturally occurring formations in the geology of images—formations that, if inspected more closely, reveal the deep history of our past and the real lives lived through it.

### Elisa Sighicelli 270–71

My work is a constant questioning of the medium of photography, of its two-dimensionality, its display apparatuses, and its subject matter. I'm interested in exploring the relationship between representation and reality. By working with the materiality of the photograph I'm looking for ways to extend the space of representation into the real space of the viewer and vice versa, in a play between the two- and the three-dimensional. In my fabric works, the *representation* of the object and the *actual* object photographed seem to coincide. This is due to how the photograph is displayed—with gaffer tape or a nail through the photograph, which appears to be holding up the fabric drapery but is in fact holding the photograph up against the wall. This highlights the inherent tension between the photograph as an object and the image of the photographed object.

### Brea Souders 120–21

Much of my work deals in some way with the idea that nothing is fully knowable… In the context of my images, unknowability isn't just a steering principle; it's a physically manifest factor. There are things left out not because they don't belong, but because the harmony of the piece calls for their absence. I find that honoring absence creates a dynamic that mirrors how I think things really are.

Having control over an entire world, as I do with an image, I might tend to create the thing as I'd ideally like it to be. Complete. Or "complete." But my preference is to have it—even when surreal in appearance—mirror the rules of the real world. Even if it means I'm left grasping in darkness in a metaphorical room of my own construction. Where there isn't a light switch. Or there is, but it doesn't work. Or it only works intermittently. Or it used to work but we don't know if it will again. Illumination isn't guaranteed.

### Kate Steciw 336–41

In a social system in which so much culturally relevant information is transmitted via images, it is in the form of images that we most often encounter the objects of our desire. The image is representational of both the desire and the desired, and if/when the object does materialize it is often represented and disseminated again as an image (documentation). Not only that, but due to the object's origins in mechanical reproduction it too behaves as an image…an image both of its representational intention (a mold-injected decorative sconce as an image of a hand-hewn wooden sconce) and its ideological function (a chair acts as an image of or stand-in for romantic love, casual whimsy, or intellectual integrity). Images and objects function as delivery systems for commerce-driven ideologies.

That said, such systems are entirely reliant on context and composition and are fatally disrupted by even minor interventions.

BATIA SUTER



The underlying motivation in my work is an interest in the iconizing of images and what I call their "immunogenicity"—that is, their capacity to elicit a response—and the circumstances in which they become charged with new associative values. I situate old images in new contexts to provoke surprising reactions and meanings. By this method, and with a sensitivity to hidden harmonies and expressive accidents, I try to generate "hypnagogic" spaces in which pictures can communicate with their own logic, in a force field of imaginative metamorphosis. It is a kind of personal research into the nature of images themselves—those "universal" images that trigger emotions or obsessions in us. What are the hidden rules of recognition and identification that have become entrenched in the histories of culture and evolution? And how are images affected by today's practices of clustering, collating, and collecting? This is, after all, the contemporary condition of pictures: drawn together by similarities, freed from any original purpose and released into their vast, indefinite, and vertiginous diversity.

YOSUKE TAKEDA



A photograph is an image, but an image cannot stand alone; an image is produced through its combination with and transformation into a material form.

MIGUEL ÁNGEL TORNERO



*The Random Series* (2010–14) is an open project in which a photographic exercise is repeated in different cities. The selection shown in this volume was created in Madrid; it proposes a strange encounter with photography, the city, and oneself. For this work, I intensely and instinctively photograph my own day-to-day activities, compiling a series of pictures that will serve as the raw material for the final digital collages. My attitude toward photography—and in this case toward Madrid—is one in which I place priority on curiosity and instinct, combining the features of the flâneur, the Japanese tourist obsessed with documenting everything, and (perhaps most interestingly) the chaotic gaze of the newborn baby, still governed by his or her unconscious life. The snapshots often capture nothing more than subjective sensations; the city is simply the excuse and the setting in which to let myself be receptive to the stimulus of each context. In the process of creating these image collages, I take advantage of the automated capacity of software to "sew" the images together, whether or not they have any real relationship. The parameters of cut-and-paste are unclear, and therefore the unexpected becomes the protagonist and sets the pace of the series. The final result is, to a large extent, left to chance.

A historian has described the ancient Chorrera artisans' approach to their
ceramic objects as a combination of stylization and direct observation.
I relate to that description because I am constantly striving for my images
to rest somewhere in between the actual and the imagined. Many of the formal
decisions I make during their capture and their eventual finalizing through
digital and chromogenic printing processes are attempts to reach a dynamic
balance of observation and abstraction. My hope is that the images give
the sense that they are of something that can be recognized as belonging
to the real world, but also perhaps to the world of dreams, of memory,
and of the imagination.



Even if an image or object is able to be traced back to a source, the substance
(in the sense of both its materiality and its importance) of the source object can
no longer be regarded as inherently greater than any of its copies. When I take
a moving image and represent it through an object (video rendered sculpturally
in Styrofoam, for example), I am positing an alternative method of representation
without ever supplying a way to view the source. A source video exists. The idea
of a source video exists. But the way the object is instantiated denies both the
necessity of an original and adherence to the representational norms that follow
the creation of "video" as both technical device and terminology.



Humans, like many other species, react very strongly to eyes; indeed, it is part
of our evolutionary condition that eyes grasp our immediate attention, virtually
from the moment we are born into this world. In social media, of course, direct
eye contact is not possible. At the same time, social media is allowing our social
behavior to expand and reach ever further. Although what can be mediated seems
limitless, it encourages us to question whether perception itself is fixed to a single
vantage point. Do computers and other techno-materials count as media receivers?
Are all such materials mediating themselves, while also, ultimately, being beyond
us and something more than we can grasp?



My works are shot on 4-by-5 film through hand-cut paper screens. I use film in order
to limit the field of possibilities. You can think of film as allowing for an infinite set
of possibilities, and of digital processes as allowing for an even larger infinity
of possibilities. I find limitations to be generative, so I prefer the smaller field.



The photograph has changed again, radically, and not just from a material
thing to an immaterial non-thing—a transformation that now seems long past
and wholly inevitable. This new change is sociological: while the photograph

was once a way in which some people communicated, it is now the way in which almost *everyone* communicates. This shift is not as simple as saying "Everyone is now a photographer." A more nuanced truth is that now even fewer people are photographers; now that the language of image making has become ubiquitous, its form as art is all the more in question. But perhaps photography as we have known it since the mid-twentieth century should end in this way, not because it has nowhere to go, but because it must be forced to go outside this ever-widening mainstream production and consumption.



LINDSEY WHITE

Through video, photography, and sculpture, I work with the language of magic and comedy in the arena of the "sight gag." Like a good joke, the results tend to pit cartoonish occurrence against the mundane physicality of everyday life. My newest series, *Matter of Fact* (2012), is populated by perfectly broken windows, flawless spills, Hollywood props, dance strobes, and levitating fastballs that allow for an approachable entry point while masking the work's underlying complexity. Both intimate and laughable, my work exists in a world where life and art are clearly in slapstick harmony with one another.



CHRIS WILEY

Over recent years I have been making pictures in Los Angeles, a city whose architectural environs and metaphoric resonances have become my principal subjects. I call these works *Dingbats* (2013–14), borrowing a term that was coined to describe a kind of low-end faux-modernist architecture that proliferated in Southern California and the U.S. Southwest in the 1950s and '60s; it is also the name of a pictographic font that is often used as a placeholder. As this title might imply, the works in the series are concerned, at least in part, with the concept of the *ersatz*—a descriptor pinned on things that strive to be something other and better than they are, whose existence is defined by *being like* rather than simply *being*. The Dingbat building is *like* International Style modernism, but is not International Style modernism. The Dingbat font is like language, but is not language. Los Angeles is like a metropolis, but is not a metropolis. Photography is like the real, but is not the real.



LETHA WILSON

What I know about photography I've learned from trying to make photographs. The proof for me is in the print: something I can see and touch, and more. What I'm looking for in my print isn't perfection, but just an image, an incredible image. It is a wonderful fact that this small black box—gears and parts, metal and glass— can capture an amazing place that I take into the darkroom, from which (with more machines and darkness) photographs emerge. When I see the image it seems familiar and yet as if I'm seeing this place for the first time, even though I was already there. "Wow," I often say to myself, in reference to that image, that place. "Isn't this magic?" For me, some of the magic in photography is in the unknown.

I choose not to learn too much: the gap between knowledge and understanding is fertile ground. I have a similar approach to working with materials in my studio, specifically concrete and cement. The chemical reactions involved in these materials—reactions that suddenly turn rocks and powders into other solid forms— are for me another type of magic. And these two magics combine into new forms and reactions, each time surprising me with variations and possibilities.

Amir Zaki

240–43

For my project *Eleven Minus One* (2010), I carefully reconstructed and reinterpreted, in virtual 3D space, several photographs from the series *Équilibres*, made in the mid-1980s by Swiss artist duo Peter Fischli and David Weiss. The body of work includes a series of short, photorealistic animation loops and a foldout book based on the eleven different ways that a cube can be unfolded. Working with this methodology allowed me to further interrogate the conventions and limitations of photography by exploring depictions of "real" space, but without the restraints of actual physics or forces such as gravity. The book is an interactive object, and can be folded and unfolded in multiple ways, creating grids, cubes, and unfolded boxes, each creating a unique experience and juxtaposition of images. It is important to recognize the book in terms of a limited edition or a multiple. It is also more of an object with sculptural qualities and a tactile nature than a "book" in the traditional sense.

# Acknowledgments

The inspiration for *Photography Is Magic* is grounded in the extraordinary practices of the contributing artists. My thanks go to all of you for your immense generosity of time, and for your work and thoughts, which now constitute the magical substance of this publication.

Thank you to all the kind people in the artists' studios and representing galleries who expedited the process of gathering images, statements, and information.

Thank you to Chris Boot and Lesley Martin for being so enthusiastic from the outset about my proposal for *Photography Is Magic*, and of course for making this book a reality. Amelia Lang has been the best managing editor that I could have wished for. I'm grateful also to Matthew Harvey (production manager) and Lauren Graycar (designer, working with Harsh Patel). Our text editor, Diana Stoll, worked her magic especially upon my essay; I am, as always, deeply grateful for her guidance and expertise. Together, they provided the keenest scrutiny to ensure that this book embodies its concept. Thank you to everyone at Aperture for making meetings fun and productive, and for orchestrating the publication and ongoing life of this book.

I would like to thank a number of people who played important roles in the conception of *Photography Is Magic*. I am eternally indebted to my friend Mary Fagot for taking me to the Magic Castle in Los Angeles for the first time in 2007, and—along with Jesus de Francisco, Mark Allen, and Emily Joyce—for sharing in my wonder and delight at close-up magic. Mark Allen and Machine Project in Los Angeles, and Jason Evans in the United Kingdom, gave me the physical and intellectual space to write and visualize this book over the past three years—you have been crucial supporters of the way I think, and true, creative friends. I also want to thank Lucas Blalock, Graham Callan, Elizabeth Cotton, Shannon Ebner, Sawako Fukai, Marc Lee, Carter Mull, Kate Steciw, Sara VanDerBeek, and Artie Vierkant for countless enlightening conversations— many of the ideas that were raised in them have affected my thinking, and have found their way into this project.

Finally, I want to acknowledge here my sincerest gratitude to this book's designer, Harsh Patel. You agreed to collaborate with me without hesitation and understood—and crafted—*Photography Is Magic* into a creative endeavor that is deeper and wider than I could have hoped. I see equal measures of the ways in which you and I think in this book; we share its authorship.

This book is dedicated to the magic of Tony Picasso and the memory of Hank. CHARLOTTE COTTON

*PHOTOGRAPHY IS MAGIC*
CHARLOTTE COTTON

DESIGNER Harsh Patel
TEXT EDITOR Diana C. Stoll
PRODUCTION Matthew Harvey
MANAGING EDITOR Amelia Lang
PROOFREADER Madeline Coleman
WORK SCHOLARS Victor Peterson II, Lauren Zallo
ADDITIONAL STAFF, APERTURE BOOK PROGRAM
    Chris Boot *Executive Director*
    Sarah McNear *Deputy Director*
    Lesley A. Martin *Publisher*
    Kellie McLaughlin *Director of Sales and Marketing*
    Susan Ciccotti *Senior Text Editor*
COVER ARTWORK Kate Steciw
TYPESET IN PORTRAIT BY BERTON HASEBE

All artists' statements in this volume were gathered by the author.
All are original texts, with the exception of the statements of the
following artists, which were drawn from other sources and have
been amended slightly for this book: Walead Beshty, Antoine Catala,
Daniel Gordon, Leslie Hewitt, Rachel de Joode, Yuki Kimura,
Josh Kline, Elad Lassry, Jon Rafman, Sean Raspet, Shirana Shahbazi,
Timur Si-Qin, Brea Souders, and Kate Steciw.





FIRST EDITION, 2015
PRINTED IN CHINA BY ARTRON
10 9 8 7 6 5 4 3 2

LIBRARY OF CONGRESS CONTROL NUMBER 2015904219
ISBN 978-1-59711-331-1

TO ORDER APERTURE BOOKS, CONTACT:
+ 1.212.946.7154
orders@aperture.org

For more information about Aperture trade distribution worldwide,
visit: www.aperture.org/distribution

**aperture**

APERTURE FOUNDATION
547 WEST 27TH STREET, 4TH FLOOR
NEW YORK, N.Y. 10001
WWW.APERTURE.ORG

Aperture, a not-for-profit foundation, connects the photo community
and its audiences with the most inspiring work, the sharpest ideas,
and with each other—in print, in person, and online.